ASSASSINATION
SCIENCE

D1452552

Also by James H. Fetzer

Author

Scientific Knowledge: Causation, Explanation, and Corroboration
Artificial Intelligence: Its Scope and Limits
Philosophy and Cognitive Science
Philosophy of Science
Minds and Machines *

Co-Author

Glossary of Epistemology/Philosophy of Science
Glossary of Cognitive Science

Editor

Foundations of Philosophy of Science: Recent Developments
Science, Explanation, and Rationality *
Principles of Philosophical Reasoning
The Philosophy of Carl G. Hempel *
Sociobiology and Epistemology
Aspects of Artificial Intelligence
Epistemology and Cognition
Probability and Causality

Co-Editor

Program Verification: Fundamental Issues in Computer Science
Philosophy, Language, and Artificial Intelligence
Philosophy, Mind, and Cognitive Inquiry
The New Theory of Reference *
Definitions and Definability   * *forthcoming*

ASSASSINATION
SCIENCE

Experts Speak Out on the Death of JFK

Edited by James H. Fetzer, Ph.D.

CATFEET
P
PRESS

Chicago

This book and others from CATFEET PRESS™ and Open Court
may be ordered by calling 1-800-815-2280.

*CATFEET PRESS™ and the above logo are trademarks of
Carus Publishing Company.*

Cover photograph used by permission of *The Dallas Morning News.*
Back cover photograph of the editor by permission of Sarah M. Fetzer.

First printing 1998
Second printing 1998

Printed and bound in the United States of America

Library of Congress Cataloging-in-Publication Data
Assassination science : experts speak out on the death of JFK / James
   H. Fetzer, editor.
     p.   cm.
   Includes index.
   ISBN 0-8126-9365-5 (alk. paper). -- ISBN 0-8126-9366-3 (pbk.:
alk. paper)
   1. Kennedy, John F. (John Fitzgerald), 1917–1963--Assassination.
I. Fetzer, James H., 1940–
E842.9.A78 1998
364.15'24'092--dc21

                                                            97-36502
                                                            CIP

John Fitzgerald Kennedy
in memoriam

If a nation expects to be ignorant and free,
in a state of civilization,
it expects what never was and never will be.
— Thomas Jefferson

CONTENTS

Preface   xi

Prologue

The Death of JFK
James H. Fetzer, Ph.D.   1

Part I: Who Are the "Assassination Experts"?   23

A Piece of My Mind: Lundberg, JFK, and *JAMA*
James H. Fetzer, Ph.D.   27

Let's Set the Record Straight: Dr. Charles Crenshaw Replies
Charles Crenshaw, M.D.   37

On the Trail of the Character Assassins
Bradley Kizzia, J.D.   61

Thinking Critically About JFK's Assassination
James H. Fetzer, Ph.D.   85

The JFK Assassination: Cause for Doubt
David W. Mantik, M.D., Ph.D.   93

Postscript
The President John F. Kennedy Skull X-rays: Regarding
the Magical Appearance of the Largest "Metal" Fragment
David W. Mantik, M.D., Ph.D.   120

Part II: The Press Conference that Never Was   141

Statement of 18 November 1993 (#1)
James H. Fetzer, Ph.D.   145

Statement of 18 November 1993 (#2)
James H. Fetzer, Ph.D.   149

Optical Density Measurements of the JFK Autopsy X-rays
and a New Observation Based on the Chest X-ray
David W. Mantik, M.D., Ph.D.   153

Statement of 18 November 1993
Robert B. Livingston, M.D.   161

Supporting Documents

"Commentary of an Eyewitness", *The New Republic*
Richard Dudman   167

Letter to David Lifton of 2 May 1992
Robert B. Livingston, M.D.   168

Fax to Maynard Parker of 10 September 1993
Robert B. Livingston, M.D.   172

Clarification of 16 July 1997
Robert B. Livingston, M.D.   175

Correspondence with *The New York Times*

Letter to Howell Raines of 13 September 1993
James H. Fetzer, Ph.D.   176

Letter to Lawrence K. Altman, M.D. of 1 December 1993
James H. Fetzer, Ph.D.   178

Letter to Arthur Ochs Sulzberger, Jr., of 6 December 1994
James H. Fetzer, Ph.D.   180

Part III: The Pursuit of Justice in a Bureaucracy   183

Letter to The Honorable Janet Reno of 17 September 1993
James H. Fetzer, Ph.D.   187

Letter to Professor James H. Fetzer of 7 December 1993
Mary C. Spearing   193

Letter to Mary C. Spearing of 18 December 1993
James H. Fetzer, Ph.D.   195

Letter to Professor James H. Fetzer of 25 January 1994
Mary C. Spearing   198

Letter to Mary C. Spearing of 30 January 1994
James H. Fetzer, Ph.D.   200

Correspondence with Distinguished Americans

Letter to Professor James H. Fetzer of 4 October 1993
The Honorable Elliot Richardson   201

Letter to Professor James H. Fetzer of 15 November 1993
The Honorable Robert McNamara   202

Letter to Professor James H. Fetzer of 21 November 1994
The Honorable President Bill Clinton   203

Correspondence with the Assassination Records Review Board

Letter to The Honorable John R. Tunheim of 24 October 1994
James H. Fetzer, Ph.D.   204

Letter to Professor James H. Fetzer of 14 February 1995
The Honorable John R. Tunheim   205

Part IV: The Zapruder Film: Seeing but Not Believing   207

Evidence . . . or Not? The Zapruder Film: Can it be Trusted?
Jack White   211

The Case for Zapruder Film Tampering: The Blink Pattern
Mike Pincher, J.D., and Roy Schaeffer   221

The Wounding of Governor John Connally
Ron Hepler   239

The JFK Assassination Reenactment: Questioning the
Warren Commision's Evidence
Chuck Marler   249

Special Effects in the Zapruder Film: How the Film of the
Century was Edited
David W. Mantik, M.D., Ph.D.   263

Epilogue   345

Assassination Science and the Language of Proof
James H. Fetzer, Ph.D.   349

Postscript   373

Apologists and Critics of the Lone Gunman Theory:
Assassination Science and Experts in Post-Modern America
Ronald F. White, Ph.D.   377

x

Appendices

Appendices 413

(A) Observations of JFK Wounds in Trauma Room 1 by
Charles Crenshaw, M.D. 414

(B) FBI Report with Summary of Treatment at Parkland by
Kemp Clark, M.D. 416

(C) Transcript of Parkland Press Conference, 3:16 P.M.,
22 November 1963 419

(D) Signed State of Texas Certificate of Death for John
Fitzgerald Kennedy 428

(E) Unsigned State of Texas Certificate of Death for John
Fitzgerald Kennedy 429

(F) Bethesda Naval Hospital Report of Autopsy on John
Fitzgerald Kennedy 430

(G) Supplementary Report of Autopsy on John
Fitzgerald Kennedy 436

(H) Warren Commission Diagrams of JFK Wounds 438

(I) Certificate of Death for JFK prepared by Admiral
George G. Burkley 439

(J) Partial Transcript of Warren Commission Testimony of
Malcolm Perry, M.D. 440

(K) House Select Committee on Assassinations JFK Autopsy
Drawings 441

(L) JFK Autopsy Photographs Corresponding to HSCA JFK
Autopsy Drawings 443

(M) CIA Dispatch, "Countering Criticism of the Warren
Report", 1 April 1967 444

(N) CIA Advertisement for Photographers 447

Index 450

Acknowledgments 460

Contributors 462

Preface

The scientific evidence [Humes and Boswell] documented during their autopsy provides irrefutable proof that President Kennedy was struck by only two bullets that came from above and behind from a high-velocity weapon that caused the fatal wounds

— *Journal of the American Medical Association*

On 22 November 1963, John Fitzgerald Kennedy, the 35th President of the United States, was assassinated in Dallas, Texas, while his motorcade passed through Dealey Plaza. On 29 November 1963, Lyndon Baines Johnson, 36th President of the United States, appointed a panel of inquiry—chaired by the Chief Justice of the Supreme Court, Earl Warren—to investigate the death of his predecessor. A summary of its conclusions—technically only an advisory report to the President—was published on 27 September 1964. Twenty-six volumes of related testimony and exhibits were published on 23 November 1964. These are among the very few undisputed facts about the death of JFK.

According to the 888-page summary of its findings, the Warren Commission determined that President Kennedy had been assassinated by a lone, demented gunman, Lee Harvey Oswald, who had fired three shots from the sixth floor of the Texas School Book Depository Building and scored two hits, one of which passed through the President's neck and exited his throat, the other of which entered the back of his head and killed him. While denying that it was crucial to their conclusions, the panel inferred that the same bullet that passed through the President's neck had wounded Texas Governor John Connally.

President's Commission on the Assassination of President Kennedy

Chief Justice Earl Warren, Chairman
Senator Richard B. Russell
Senator John Sherman Cooper
Representative Hale Boggs
Representative Gerald R. Ford
Mr Allen W. Dulles
Mr John J. McCloy

J. Lee Rankin, General Counsel

Established by President Lyndon B. Johnson
29 November 1963

JFK had removed Allen Dulles as Director of the CIA. An interesting event occurred between the publication of The Warren Report *and that of the 26 volumes of supporting documents, namely: the Presidential election of 1964.*

This bullet is alleged to have entered Connally's back and shattered a rib before exiting his chest, hitting his right wrist and being deflected into his left thigh, an account that is known as "the single bullet theory". Because the bullet that is supposed to have performed these feats displays only slight distortion, it is known as "the magic bullet". When the House Select Committee on Assassinations re-investigated the case in 1977-78, its report supported these findings, but with the concession that a fourth bullet that missed had apparently been fired from "the grassy knoll" to the front and right of the limousine. This led the HSCA to the conclusion that JFK had been killed as the result of a "probable" conspiracy.

When the Oliver Stone motion picture, *JFK*, was released in 1991, it generated enormous interest in the possibility that elements of the federal government and the military-industrial complex, including especially the CIA, might have been behind the assassination, perhaps with financing from wealthy oil men and the collusion of the Mob. The film was attacked by a large number of critics and columnists, many of whom published their critiques before production was even complete or the movie had been distributed. The controversy has continued to simmer: while most Americans reject the government's conclusions, they are uncertain what to accept with regard to the assassination itself

Perhaps the most telling argument for the official view has been the failure to turn up "hard evidence" of conspiracy in this case, which makes the critics' position appear to be an article of faith rather than a product of reason. The evidence most basic to the official position has always been the medical evidence, including the autopsy report, X-rays, and photographs, on the one hand, and photographic evidence, including especially a film of the assassination taken by Abraham Zapruder, on the other. If crucial evidence of this kind could be proven to have been fabricated, manufactured, or otherwise reprocessed, that would provide hard evidence critics claim has been lacking. The studies published here settle this matter— decisively!

The volume you are about to read presents some of the most important findings about the medical and photographic evidence in the murder of John F. Kennedy yet to be discovered. A specialist in radiation oncology has examined the autopsy X-rays and has discovered that *some have been altered to conceal a massive blow-out to the back of the President's head, while others have been changed by the imposition of a 6.5 mm metal object.* A world authority on the human brain has concluded that *diagrams in the National Archives purporting to be of JFK's brain must be of someone other than John Fitzgerald Kennedy.* A group of experts on various aspects of photographic evidence has now found that *the Zapruder film of the assassination has been extensively edited using highly sophisticated techniques.*

These findings not only completely undermine the official reports of the American government in relation to the assassination but also support the indictment of the Editor-in-Chief and Board of Trustees of a leading medical journal in the United States and of the nation's press for failing to fulfill its obligations and responsibilities to the American people. If we are entitled to the truth about the assassination of John F. Kennedy, then this journal has published material that should not have been published and has not published material that should have been published. And if the nation's press has a duty to report new findings and to expose fabrications and misrepresentations in a case of this kind, then it bears a heavy responsibility for failing to inform the American public, even after repeated and forceful attempts to bring these matters to its attention.

The contributors to *Assassination Science* are among the most highly qualified persons ever to investigate the assassination. They include a distinguished scholar who was Scientific Director of both the National Institute for Mental Health and the National Institute for Neurological Diseases and Blindness in both the Eisenhower and the Kennedy administrations. They include an M.D. specializing in X-ray therapy who also has a Ph.D. in physics, a philosopher of science who is an expert on critical thinking, an attorney who successfully sued the *Journal of the American Medical Association* for defamation, a physician who attended both JFK and Lee Harvey Oswald at Parkland Hospital, and other serious students of this crime.

They were brought together as an unintended effect of the publication of (what turned out to be) a series of articles in the *Journal of the American Medical Association* (*JAMA*) purporting to discuss and evaluate the medical evidence in this case. These were widely promoted as providing definitive scientific evidence supporting Warren Commission conclusions, but actually appear to conceal, to distort, or to misrepresent some of the most important aspects of that evidence. The material published here may therefore be viewed as an attempt to set the record straight, one which suggests that *JAMA* has been grossly abused for apparently political purposes.

It may be difficult to imagine that *JAMA* could conceal, distort, or misrepresent some of the most important aspects of the medical evidence in a case of this kind. It is, after all, one of the leading medical journals in the United States today, and its Editor-in-Chief is a widely respected journalist. Ordinarily, authors of articles published in this journal would be authorities in their fields. That, however, is not true regarding the assassination of JFK, even relative to its medical aspects, about which *JAMA*'s author is no expert, its editor is no authority, and *JAMA* possesses no expertise. What *JAMA* did was to present artfully-written opinion pieces as though they were science.

These opinion pieces are allegedly based upon interviews, initially with James J. Humes and J. Thornton Boswell, two medical officers of the United States Navy, who conducted the autopsy of John F. Kennedy the night of 22–23 November 1963, and subsequently with Pierre Finck, a medical officer of the United States Army, who assisted them. Interviews with physicians are not science, making it difficult to understand why the journal promoted them as though they were. If *JAMA*'s articles are accurate, these physicians even contradict prior testimony they gave to the Warren Commission and later to the House Select Committee on Assassinations (HSCA).

Assassination Science presents studies by physicians, scientists, and other experts that are intended to place the investigation of the assassination of JFK on an objective and scientific foundation. The research they provide exposes fundamental inadequacies in the government's position, especially concerning the authenticity of the most basic "evidence" in this case. The Prologue supplies a general introduction to the book and a global overview of the importance of the findings presented here. Part I reflects reactions to *JAMA*'s publications on this subject, including several contemporary submissions and other efforts to correct *JAMA*'s dissemination of misinformation. Part II records a press conference held in New York City on 18 November 1993, where important discoveries undermining Warren Commission, HSCA, and *JAMA* accounts were presented to reporters, findings which profoundly affect our knowledge of this case but which their papers have yet to print.

Part III demonstrates the virtually complete lack of interest in these matters displayed by the Department of Justice, which appears to possess neither the talent nor the inclination to understand these discoveries or to undertake any appropriate response. Part IV presents the latest studies of the Zapruder film, which traditionally has been regarded as a "clock" by which the sequence of events constituting the assassination has to be measured. The Epilogue has been devoted to the language of "proof" within this context and to whether the existence of a conspiracy and of a cover-up has been proven, which suggests that, given the available relevant evidence, the matter appears to have been settled. The Postscript affords a philosophical framework—which many may wish to read before considering the rest of the book—for understanding the complexities encountered in the investigation of the assassination, many rooted in uncertainties over the authenticity of the evidence.

While almost anyone taking a serious interest in the assassinations of John F. Kennedy, Robert Kennedy, or Martin Luther King, Jr., might be characterized as "an assassination buff", the contributors to this volume cannot be casually dismissed by means of stereotypes. Robert B. Livingston, M.D., David Mantik, M.D., Ph.D., and Bradley Kizzia, J.D., for example, are persons of accomplishment and, in the case of Livingston, especially, of great distinction. They have professions at which they excel apart from research they have undertaken to understand what happened to JFK. They share the belief that the American people are entitled to know the truth about our nation's history.

Moreover, while *JAMA*'s publications brought us into contact with one another—some of us more frequently than others—each of us has continued to pursue his own independent research. We have not been working toward any predetermined conclusions about the assassination, and the fact that the results of our discoveries have proven to be mutually reinforcing is striking and significant. Taken collectively, our findings afford a highly consistent and strongly supported reconstruction of crucial elements of the assassination of JFK. For any analysis of the events of 22 November 1963 to be taken seriously, it must not only provide a logically coherent account of what happened but also explain why investigating this case has been so fraught with problems. The studies in this volume satisfy these conditions.

James H. Fetzer, Ph.D., and David W. Mantik, M.D., Ph.D.,
in Rancho Mirage, California, on 11 June 1997

The documents, articles, and reports presented here are intended to convey at least three lessons. First, that even journals as prestigious as *JAMA* are not immune from political abuse, indications of which abound with respect to its coverage of medical aspects of this case. Second, that new discoveries, including scientific findings of fundamental importance, continue to be made, supporting the possibility that truth is not beyond our grasp. Third, that journals, newspapers, and agencies upon which we all tend to depend do not always serve the people's interests. The pursuit of truth, the protection of justice, and the preservation of democratic instituitions require eternal vigilance. As long as we are ignorant, we are not free.

—James H. Fetzer, Ph.D.

Prologue
The Death of JFK

There are some frauds so well conducted that it would
be stupidity not to be deceived by them.
—Charles Caleb Colton

There was a time when Americans could take for granted that their government told the truth. The very idea that the government would lie to us was virtually unthinkable during the 1940s and the 1950s. During the 1960s, however, things began to change. Lies and deceit over Vietnam, Watergate, and the Iran-Contra Affair disillusioned most of us to the point where we could no longer trust our government. While distrusting government used to be a symptom of paranoia (of the left or of the right), that no longer remains the case. During the 1990s, anyone who takes for granted what the government tells them is regarded as naive. Our problem has thus become that of exercising our rationality to avoid naiveté without becoming paranoid.

There are many who think that the steady erosion of our faith in our government has roots that can be traced to events in Dallas, Texas, on 22 November 1963. Indeed, there appear to be several reasons why we need to understand what happened at that specific time and place. The consequences of that tragedy continue to influence the course of our history. If we knew more about it, we might be better positioned to appraise and cope with those effects. Moreover, we are surely entitled to the truth about our nation's history. Knowing the truth might even contribute to restoring our trust in government. And, if the government *was* involved, then knowing might at least help us to take steps to ensure that it does not happen again.

1

Intermittent polling over several decades has repeatedly confirmed that somewhere between 70% and 80% of the American people do not believe that John F. Kennedy was assassinated by a lone, demented gunman named Lee Harvey Oswald, who is alleged to have fired three shots from the Texas School Book Depository at the President's motorcade, scoring two hits, one of which both injured the President and wounded John Connally, the Governor of Texas, the other hitting JFK in the head, killing him. The vast majority of Americans thus do not believe *The Warren Report*, a far larger percentage of the population than have ever read it.

What may be more surprising is that, although the *The Warren Report* (technically the *Report of the Warren Commission on the Assassination of President Kennedy*, issued in 1964) acknowledged that another shot was fired that missed the President entirely—hitting a distant curb and fragmenting, inflicting a minor injury on the cheek of a bystander, James Tague —it did not conclude whether it was the first, the second, or the third fired. Few Americans realize that the FBI and the Secret Service maintained yet another story according to which all three shots hit, where the first hit the President, the second the Governor, and the third killed the President.

Even more surprising than the existence of multiple versions of the official Warren Report assassination scenario is that the government no longer regards that work as final or complete. When the assassination of JFK was reinvestigated by the Select Committee on Assassinations of the House of Representatives (HSCA), its report of 1979 drew the conclusion that the President "probably" had been assassinated by a conspiracy that involved at least one more assassin, who apparently had been firing from the grassy knoll, as many witnesses who were in Dealey Plaza at the time had maintained. This is now the American government's official position.

Some commentators suggest that the inference to conspiracy does not necessarily follow, since it may have been the case that this second assassin was simply another "lone, demented gunman" acting independently of the other. The hypothesis that two different and unrelated persons might happen to choose precisely the same location and precisely the same time —indeed, exactly *the same moments* of time—to attempt to assassinate the President, however, must surely have a vanishing probability. For someone to take it seriously rather than merely advancing it to obfuscate, confuse, or confound the American people is exceptionally difficult to imagine.

President's death. Ruby was transferred the following day to the county jail without notice to the press or to police officers not directly involved in the transfer. Indicted for the murder of Oswald by the State of Texas on November 26, 1963, Ruby was found guilty on March 14, 1964, and sentenced to death. As of September 1964, his case was pending on appeal.

CONCLUSIONS

This Commission was created to ascertain the facts relating to the preceding summary of events and to consider the important questions which they raised. The Commission has addressed itself to this task and has reached certain conclusions based on all the available evidence. No limitations have been placed on the Commission's inquiry; it has conducted its own investigation, and all Government agencies have fully discharged their responsibility to cooperate with the Commission in its investigation. These conclusions represent the reasoned judgment of all members of the Commission and are presented after an investigation which has satisfied the Commission that it has ascertained the truth concerning the assassination of President Kennedy to the extent that a prolonged and thorough search makes this possible.

1. The shots which killed President Kennedy and wounded Governor Connally were fired from the sixth floor window at the southeast corner of the Texas School Book Depository. This determination is based upon the following:

(a) Witnesses at the scene of the assassination saw a rifle being fired from the sixth floor window of the Depository Building, and some witnesses saw a rifle in the window immediately after the shots were fired.

(b) The nearly whole bullet found on Governor Connally's stretcher at Parkland Memorial Hospital and the two bullet fragments found in the front seat of the Presidential limousine were fired from the 6.5-millimeter Mannlicher-Carcano rifle found on the sixth floor of the Depository Building to the exclusion of all other weapons.

(c) The three used cartridge cases found near the window on the sixth floor at the southeast corner of the building were fired from the same rifle which fired the above-described bullet and fragments, to the exclusion of all other weapons.

(d) The windshield in the Presidential limousine was struck by a bullet fragment on the inside surface of the glass, but was not penetrated.

(e) The nature of the bullet wounds suffered by President Kennedy and Governor Connally and the location of the car at the time of the shots establish that the bullets were fired from above and behind the Presidential limousine, striking the President and the Governor as follows:

(1) President Kennedy was first struck by a bullet which entered at the back of his neck and exited through the lower front portion of his neck, causing a wound which would not necessarily have been lethal. The President was struck a second time by a bullet which entered the right-rear portion of his head, causing a massive and fatal wound.

(2) Governor Connally was struck by a bullet which entered on the right side of his back and traveled downward through the right side of his chest, exiting below his right nipple. This bullet then passed through his right wrist and entered his left thigh where it caused a superficial wound.

(f) There is no credible evidence that the shots were fired from the Triple Underpass, ahead of the motorcade, or from any other location.

2. The weight of the evidence indicates that there were three shots fired.

3. Although it is not necessary to any essential findings of the Commission to determine just which shot hit Governor Connally, there is very persuasive evidence from the experts to indicate that the same bullet which pierced the President's throat also caused Governor Connally's wounds. However, Governor Connally's testimony and certain other factors have given rise to some difference of opinion as to this probability but there is no question in the mind of any member of the Commission that all the shots which caused the President's and Governor Connally's wounds were fired from the sixth floor window of the Texas School Book Depository.

4. The shots which killed President Kennedy and wounded Governor Connally were fired by Lee Harvey Oswald. This conclusion is based upon the following:

(a) The Mannlicher-Carcano 6.5-millimeter Italian rifle from which the shots were fired was owned by and in the possession of Oswald.

(b) Oswald carried this rifle into the Depository Building on the morning of November 22, 1963.

(c) Oswald, at the time of the assassination, was present at the window from which the shots were fired.

(d) Shortly after the assassination, the Mannlicher-Carcano rifle belonging to Oswald was found partially hidden between some cartons on the sixth floor and the improvised paper bag in which Oswald brought the rifle to the Depository was found close by the window from which the shots were fired.

(e) Based on testimony of the experts and their analysis of films of the assassination, the Commission has concluded that a rifleman of Lee Harvey Oswald's capabilities could have fired the shots from the rifle used in the assassination within the elapsed time of the shooting. The Commission has concluded further that Oswald possessed the capability with a rifle which enabled him to commit the assassination.

The Warren Commission's principal conclusions

This fantastic "two demented gunmen" scenario had the effect of high-lighting one of the glaring weaknesses of *The Warren Report*, however, which was its utter failure to establish a rational motive for Lee Harvey Oswald to have wanted to kill John F. Kennedy. This is the genius of the description of the gunman as "demented". Since an insane person may act from irrational motives, the actions of an insane person cannot be expected to be rational. While the Warren Commission never actually maintained that Lee Harvey Oswald was "insane", its report strongly suggested that he was "unstable", citing various aspects of his personal history. But was Oswald really demented?

There have been intermittent indications that he was not. According to Commission member Gerald Ford, *Portrait of an Assassin* (1965), for example, Waggoner Carr, the Attorney General of Texas, reported to the Commission that he had discovered evidence that Lee Harvey Oswald was an undercover agent for the FBI; that he had been assigned number 179; and that he had been on the payroll at $200 per month since 1962, right up to the day of the assassination. The Commission relied on Leon Jaworski, who would become prominent during the Watergate affair, to explore this issue, but his ties to the CIA as a trustee of the M. D. Anderson Foundation have cast doubt upon the diligence of his investigation, which yielded the finding that these were no more than "false rumors".

Jaworski's inquiry, which appears to have been perfunctory, was far from exhaustive concerning possible connections Oswald might have had with the United States. Oswald's military service, defection to the Soviet Union, marriage to a Russian woman, and seemingly insignificant work history would support an alternative (non-demented) interpretation if, for example, he had been covertly working for government intelligence, as he may have been. It is one thing for a single "demented" gunman to have attempted to assassinate the President in Dealey Plaza in Dallas at 12:30 P.M. on Friday, 22 November 1963, however, and quite another for two or more "demented" gunmen to have done the same. If there was more than one assassin, as the HSCA Report implied, then they must have had their reasons. The second government report on the assassination of President Kennedy thus exposed a major defect with the first, one it left unresolved.

Many books about the assassination have appeared since 1963, such as Mark Lane's *Rush to Judgment* (1966), Josiah Thompson's *Six Seconds in Dallas* (1967), Gary Shaw's *The Cover-Up* (1976), David Lifton's *Best Evidence* (1980), Jim Marrs' *Crossfire* (1989), and Robert Groden and Harrison Livingstone's *High Treason* (1989), to name a few of the best. Some of these authors, especially Lifton, have focused on the medical evidence, suggesting that it might hold the key to understanding what took place in Dealey Plaza. The autopsy report, X-rays, and photographs, for example, are usually taken to be the "best evidence" in a murder case.

The assassination of JFK, however, is not a usual case, and the authenticity of the autopsy X-rays and photographs has been challenged not only by Lifton but by others, including Harrison Livingstone in *High Treason 2* (1992). The problems in this case are remarkable, because the autopsy X-rays and photographs do not appear to be consistent with the autopsy report or even with each other. The medical evidence also appears to be inconsistent with reports of numerous eyewitnesses, including physicians and non-physicians, who observed the President's body at Parkland and at Bethesda. The problem thus arises of which if any of our sources qualifies as the "best evidence".

The inconsistency between the eyewitness reports and the other evidence was dispatched in the case of the House Committee by accepting the autopsy X-rays and photographs as authentic, which permitted the members of the Committee to disregard, discount, or discard the eyewitnesses, especially those who reported a massive wound to the back of JFK's head. The situation thus remained in an uncomfortable state of semi-resolution when Oliver Stone's film, *JFK*, was released in 1991, creating a national sensation that enormously stimulated interest in the assassination. While the public might not have read *The Warren Report* or the HSCA inquiry, it was still eager and willing to watch what was shown on the big screen, even a film that implied a conspiracy involving the federal government.

When Charles Crenshaw, M.D., one of the physicians who attended JFK at Parkland, published a book, *JFK: Conspiracy of Silence* (1992), in which he disputed the autopsy photographs, the problem was further compounded. Crenshaw not only assisted in treating President Kennedy on the 22nd but also assisted in treating Lee Harvey Oswald, his alleged assassin, on the 24th, after he was shot down by Jack Ruby in the basement of the Dallas Police Department. Crenshaw described a small wound to JFK's throat and a massive wound to the back of his head, neither of which could have been caused by bullets fired from a position above and behind. [*Editor's note*: See Appendix A.]

The surge of public interest in these events motivated Congress to reconsider the secrecy surrounding most of the official records in this case, the majority of which had been sealed away in the National Archives for 75 years. It would eventually lead to the establishment of the Assassination Records Review Board, charged with the responsibility to supervise the release of major portions of the records. This development occurred in spite of resistance by President George Bush, a former Director of the CIA, who was widely reported to have opposed measures promoting release of these documents and then refused to appoint any members to the board.

Within this context, an extraordinary press conference occurred in New York City on Tuesday, 19 May 1992. A press conference in New York, even in May, might not sound so out-of-the-ordinary, but this one was different. George Lundberg, M.D., the Editor-in-Chief of the *Journal of the American Medical Association* (*JAMA*), announced that *JAMA* was publishing interviews with James J. Humes and J. Thornton Boswell, the pathologists who performed the autopsy on John F. Kennedy at Bethesda Naval Hospital the night of 22–23 November 1963, and with other physicians who had assisted in the President's care at Parkland Hospital in Dallas earlier in the day.

The results of these interviews, Dr. Lundberg reported, provided scientific evidence that President Kennedy was killed by two shots fired from above and behind with a high velocity weapon, thereby confirming the findings of the Warren Commission established by President Lyndon B. Johnson. The autopsy physicians, in particular, were said to have resolved questions that have continued to linger in the aftermath of the assassination, many of which have revolved about the medical evidence in this case, including the crucial question of the nature of the wounds inflicted on President Kennedy and the direction and location from which the bullets may have been fired.

Dr. Lundberg's presentation, which was conducted behind a lectern bearing the logo of the American Medical Assocation, received exceptional attention from the American press, including front page coverage from *The New York Times* (20 May 1992), with an editorial portraying it as "proof against paranoia". Similar reactions occurred across the country. The forceful way in which Lundberg presented his position no doubt contributed to the swift acceptance and rapid dissemination of what he had reported by newspapers and television, including an appearance on *Good Morning America* the following day. He seemed to be an authority on the subject he was addressing.

The articles themselves were actually written by a staff writer named Dennis L. Breo, whose qualifications for this assignment (to the best of my knowledge) have never been explained. Partially based upon interviews with Humes and Boswell, the first of them, entitled "JFK's Death— the Plain Truth from the MDs who did the Autopsy" (*JAMA*, 27 May 1992, pp. 2794–2803), provided ten pages of discussion punctuated with numerous quotes. Unlike ordinary scientific studies, the discourse ranged over a wide range of subjects, including the Garrison inquiry ("a fishing expedition") and the film *JFK* ("rivaling the Nazi propaganda films of Leni Riefenstahl"), with opinions from George Will and Anthony Stone, who possess no discernible expertise regarding the assassination, and photographs of the physicians in lieu of relevant evidence.

George Lundberg, M.D. presents JAMA's *findings to the nation's press on 19 May 1992*

The language Breo employed, moreover, was unlike ordinary scientific language, which typically qualifies findings as "tentative" and subject to further investigation (ideally, experimental replication). Humes and Boswell were said to have conclusively established:

> irrefutable proof that President Kennedy was struck by only two bullets that came from above and behind from a high-velocity weapon that caused the fatal wounds. This autopsy proof, combined with the bullet and rifle evidence found at the scene of the crime, and the subsequent detailed documentation of a six-month investigation involving the enormous resources of the local, state, and federal law enforcement agencies, proves the 1964 Warren Commission conclusion that Kennedy was killed by a lone assassin, Lee Harvey Oswald. (*JAMA*, 27 May 1992, pp. 27–94)

The "six-month investigation" to which Breo referred, moreover, was the Warren Commission's own inquiry, which might be expected to "prove" its own "conclusion", but hardly qualifies as independent evidence, especially when the scope and quality of that investigation itself has been called into question. Indeed, as Sylvia Meagher has shown in *Accessories*

After the Fact (1967), the principal "conclusions" drawn in the 888-page *Warren Report* are contradicted by "evidence" that is found in its 26 supporting volumes.

Breo's sweeping claims were especially unlikely to impress those who suspect that local, state, and federal law-enforcement agencies may have had a hand in the assassination, if not before the fact in its planning and execution, then afterward in covering it up. But the article appeared to have the intended effect. Even the *Duluth News-Tribune* (24 May 1992) rhetorically inquired, "Who are you going to believe, Oliver Stone's movie or the doctors who performed the autopsy on President John F. Kennedy after he was assassinated in Dallas?" The answer may have seemed obvious, especially to those with no special knowledge of the assassination of JFK.

A second article, "JFK's Death, Part II: Dallas MDs Recall their Memories" (*JAMA* 27 May 1992, pp. 2804–2808), in which several of the other physicians who had been present discussed events at Parkland Hospital, appeared with the first. This piece seemed intended to discredit Crenshaw—who had been emphatic in his denunciation of "official" medical findings—implying that he had not even been present at the time and (therefore) could not have made *any* observations of the wounds. This was untrue, as *JAMA* could have determined, since Crenshaw's presence is cited numerous times in the Warren Commission's supporting volumes. But Crenshaw was not consulted in the preparation of these articles, and careful scholarship seems not to have been an important desideratum for *JAMA*.

The publication of these articles and the publicity that they received may have generated other, unintended consequences. Having had a long-standing interest in the assassination, I was stunned by Lundberg's appearance on *Good Morning America* because, from what I knew about the case, he was presenting a highly distorted and very misleading impression of the evidence. As the editor of one journal (*Minds and Machines*) and co-editor of another (*Synthese*), I was also taken aback that the editor of a journal such as *JAMA* would compromise its integrity for what appeared to me to be the dissemination of false information for political purposes.

As a result, I decided to look into this matter in order to determine if my initial impressions were well-founded. I contacted Ronald Franks, M.D., Dean of the Medical School at the University of Minnesota, Duluth, where I am a professor of philosophy, to ask if I might borrow the latest issue of *JAMA*. Much to my surprise, it had not yet appeared and would not reach Duluth for another two weeks. In the meanwhile, following

Franks' advice, I contacted William Jacott, M.D., a faculty member on the Twin Cities campus of the University of Minnesota, who happened to be a member of the Board of Trustees of the AMA and even served as its Secretary-Treasurer.

Jacott was somewhat perplexed by my concerns, especially since that issue of the journal had yet to appear. He therefore asked me to get back to him when I had had the chance to review it. I wrote to him to explain why I was so upset by Lundberg's conduct, which led him to arrange for Lundberg to call me to discuss the matter. The call came as I was sitting down for dinner with my family. When I told him that you could not possibly tell how many shots had been fired or who had fired them from the number that happened to hit, he responded by explaining he (Lundberg) only cared about the shots that had hit the President and no others.

I found this fairly astonishing, since the number of shooters and their locations were obviously crucial to the possible existence of a conspiracy to kill JFK. The more we talked, the more apparent it became to me that this man, who was the editor of one of the most prestigious medical journals in the world, had made up his mind and did not want to be bothered with inconvenient facts. I drew the inference that he had his own agenda, which would be confirmed the following year during the Second Annual Midwest Symposium on Assassination Politics held in Chicago 1–4 April 1993, when he spontaneously volunteered that he was not an expert on the assassination and that his only interest in this case was in his role "as a journalist".

Our phone conversation convinced me that Lundberg was employing improper and unwarranted methods of investigation that led to unjustifiable conclusions. In particular, he appeared to be utilizing the technique of *selection and elimination*, selecting evidence that agreed with a predetermined conclusion and eliminating the rest. This technique is the defense attorney's dream: using it you can prove that every number is even (that every person is female, and so on). It violates a basic principle of scientific reasoning known as *the requirement of total evidence*, which demands that scientific conclusions must be based upon all of the relevant available evidence.

Indications that his motives were at least partly personal have subsequently emerged in the form of a letter from Lundberg to Humes, who is a close personal friend and, like Lundberg, a former military pathologist. As Bradley Kizzia, J.D., has explained in his contribution to this volume and as Gary Aguilar, M.D., has elsewhere observed, Lundberg wrote to Humes on AMA stationery on 26 December 1991 inquiring if

"Jim" had seen the film *JFK*, which he described as, "Three hours and 15 minutes of truth mixed with nontruth mixed with alleged truth." He continued, "For the younger person, not knowledgeable about 1963—very difficult to tell the difference". As the editor of *JAMA*, he asked for an interview to rectify the record "at least about the autopsy".

Lundberg's personal friendship with Humes, whose involvement in medical aspects of this case had been severely criticized, implied he had a serious conflict of interest in covering this matter, which a conscientious editor would studiously avoid. In Chicago on 3 April 1993, he went even further, asserting that, in his view, the film *JFK* was "very skillfully filmed fiction" which he considered to be "a grave insult to the military physicians involved as well as pathologists in general, maybe medicine and a whole lot of innocent people as well". One wonders how Lundberg would have reacted if an outspoken critic of the Warren Report, such as Oliver Stone, had made *JFK* but later admitted that he was "no expert" on the subject of his film.

In the naive belief that those who were ultimately responsible for the publication of the journal and the conduct of its editor would want to know if it was being subjected to abuse, I wrote not only to Jacott but also to the other members of the AMA Board of Trustees—not once, but several times. I received responses from two of them, one of whom (the Immediate Past President of the AMA), John J. Ring, M.D., wanted to know with what degree of certainty anything about the assassination could be known. I responded by sending him ten "proofs" of the existence of a conspiracy or a cover-up in this case, each of which was a valid or proper argument from premises that, although not infallible, were at least not seriously contested by either side.

At the suggestion of another member of the Board, I submitted a summary of my concerns, which was entitled, "A Piece of My Mind: Lundberg, JFK, and *JAMA*", to a special forum of the journal. The forum editor declined to publish on various grounds, suggesting I submit a Letter to the Editor instead. These letters were limited to 500 words, which hardly provided an opportunity to say what I had to say, but I played along, in part because Lundberg had previously invited me to submit such a letter during our phone conversation. It was also rejected, of course, and I have discovered that others were being given exactly the same treatment by *JAMA*.

Charles Crenshaw, for example, was making herculean efforts to have *JAMA* amend its slanderous impressions of his book, which Lundberg referred to as "a sad fabrication", by requesting the publication of a piece he had written with Gary Shaw, an acknowledged expert on the assassination with whom he had collaborated on the book. *JAMA* was unwilling to print it, however, and encouraged him to submit a 500-word letter to the editor, which *JAMA* also declined to publish. Indeed, it would take a civil suit and confrontation with trial before *JAMA* would finally agree to publish a modest reply by Crenshaw as a part of a substantial settlement.

JAMA remained undaunted, however, and published more articles on the assassination. Another "At Large with Dennis L. Breo" appeared with the title, "JFK's Death, Part III—Dr. Finck Speaks Out: 'Two Bullets, From the Rear'" (*JAMA*, 7 October 1992, pp. 1748–1754), prefaced by a piece by none other than George Lundberg, M.D., "Closing the Case in *JAMA* on the John F. Kennedy Autopsy" (*JAMA*, 7 October 1992, pp. 1736–1738). This was identified as an "editorial" in small print at the bottom of each page. I had to admire the chutzpah of an admitted non-expert on the assassination of JFK who could assert—emphatically and without knowledge—that *JAMA*'s articles "had withstood an onslaught of criticism from numerous conspiracy theorists".

More important than the publication of more articles in which participants in the autopsy whose views were already a matter of record reiterated their positions for *JAMA*, however, was the appearance of a handful of Letters to the Editor from members of the AMA who took exception to *JAMA*'s activities. One, in particular, caught my eye, a piece from a fellow named David Mantik, M.D., Ph.D., which resonated with views that were in harmony with my own. As a consequence, I wrote to Dr. Mantik and proposed that we collaborate on a long article or perhaps even a book dealing with the assassination, especially its medical aspects, to which he agreed.

No sooner had I heard from Mantik than I received a phone call from Gary Aguilar, M.D., who was calling from Dallas, where he was attending the 1992 meeting of the Assassination Symposium on JFK, which was becoming an annual affair. Aguilar had heard that Mantik and I were going to collaborate and asked if he might join us. We discussed the matter and I thought it was an excellent idea. He also recommended that a woman by the name of Kathleen Cunningham, well-known to serious students of the assassination for her considerable knowledge of the medical evidence and for her success in obtaining records under the Freedom of Information Act, should join us, with which I agreed. Thus was this research group formed.

I soon discovered that Mantik had submitted a substantial piece on the medical evidence to *JAMA* intended as a corrective to their (in our view) hopelessly inadequate opinions masquerading as science. Not one of us was surprised when *JAMA* declined its publication. It was apparent that Lundberg was firmly in control and that he was unwilling to countenance contrary conclusions, no matter how well-founded. Indeed, the pieces by Crenshaw and by Mantik are among the finest short studies of aspects of the assassination I have ever read, as readers of this volume may judge for themselves. These submissions now finally appear as chapters in Part I.

Meanwhile, Aguilar mentioned the existence of a witness in the case of whom I had previously never heard, a physician by the name of Robert B. Livingston, M.D., who had called Humes the day of the assassination to explain the importance of careful dissection of a small wound to the throat that had been reported over radio and television—a conversation that took place before the body had even arrived at Andrews Air Force Base. This was remarkable in itself, since the autopsy physicians had testified before the Warren Commission and the House Committee that they had not known of a wound to the throat until the autopsy had been completed and the body had been removed for the elaborate state funeral that would take place on 24 and 25 November 1963. They maintained the tracheostomy had obliterated the neck wound.

The tracheostomy had been performed at Parkland Hospital by Malcolm Perry, M.D., a very skilled surgeon, who was attempting to save the dying President. Many witnesses, including Crenshaw, have reported that it was a very clean incision across a small hole just to the right of the trachea. [*Editor's note:* See Appendix A.] This testimony has become especially important in relation to photographs which have become available since the HSCA investigation, because these photographs, which purport to be genuine autopsy photographs, display a large and jagged wound. [*Editor's note:* See Appendix L.] If the wound had looked like this at Parkland, it is extremely difficult to imagine a tracheostomy would have been required. Instead, it would have been critical to staunch the flow of blood into his lungs.

Livingston's report therefore contradicted the sworn testimony of the autopsy physicians. The point was extremely important, because it was their purported lack of knowledge of the existence of this wound that led them to draw the conclusion—as a matter of inference in the absence of a dissection, given the body had already been removed—that the wound to JFK's back for which they had been unable to track any exit "must have" exited through the President's throat. This bullet was then supposed to have impacted the Governor's back, broken a rib, exited his chest, shattered his wrist, and lodged in his thigh in order to account for all the wounds on the basis of only two hits, a feat attributed to a veritable "magic bullet."

If Livingston's report was remarkable, the man himself was exemplary. At the time of his call to Humes, he was the Scientific Director of both the National Institute for Mental Health and the National Institute for Neurological Diseases and Blindness, both of which were located at the NIH Building across the street from Bethesda Naval Hospital. He held these positions in both the Eisenhower and the Kennedy administrations. During a distinguished career, he taught at Harvard, Yale, Stanford, and UCLA, and also founded the first Department of Neurosciences in the world at the University of California in San Diego. Livingston was already a world authority on the human brain.

Moreover, he had extensive experience treating gunshot and shrapnel wounds on Okinawa during the Second World War, where he had supervised a hospital for prisoners of war and injured Okinawans. When he heard the report of a small wound to the throat, therefore, he had recognized the description of a wound of entry. He therefore advised Humes that he had to dissect this wound very carefully and that, *if there was evidence of any shots from the rear*, then there must have been at least two assassins. At about that point in his call, however, Humes told him the FBI insisted they discontinue their conversation.

I was ecstatic that someone with so much expert knowledge and experience relevant to the assassination had surfaced and anticipated he would prove to be an invaluable collaborator in our inquiry. I was not mistaken. Indeed, I now believed that I had come into association with two of the most highly qualified individuals ever to study the assassination. Mantik was not only an M.D. from the University of Michigan but a Ph.D. in physics from the University of Wisconsin and board certified in radiation oncology. He was now corresponding with Burke Marshall of the Yale Law School for permission to enter the National Archives to study the autopsy X-rays and photographs.

Marshall represents the Kennedy family in these matters, and no one may have access to these materials without his permission. We were all enormously relieved, therefore, when permission was formally granted. Mantik would travel to Washington, D.C., and visit the National Archives four times in October 1993. An important aspect of his research would be to subject the autopsy X-rays to optical densitometry studies, an ingenious application of a relatively simple technology, which would enable him to calculate the relative density of the objects whose exposure to radiation had created the images on the X-rays. His discoveries would prove to be sensational.

A major conference was scheduled for the 30th observance of the assassination in Dallas, which we all planned to attend. Livingston had now determined that the brain diagrammed in documents stored at the National Archives must be the brain of someone other than JFK, even though it was identified as JFK's brain. (The actual brain can no longer be found, and photos of it are classified.) Competent witnesses at the time, including Kemp Clark, M.D., the Chief of Neurosurgery at Parkland, had observed two kinds of brain tissue—cerebral and cerebellar—extruding from a massive wound at the back of the President's cranium, whereas the brain shown in the diagrams at the National Archives displays a wholly intact cerebellum. [*Editor's note:* See Appendix B.]

When Mantik returned from the National Archives, his results were, if anything, even more astonishing. His studies had revealed that certain X-rays had been fabricated to conceal a massive exit wound to the back of the skull, one that appeared to correspond to the reports of numerous eyewitnesses at the time that had been dismissed by the HSCA, which had taken the X-rays to be the "best evidence". Now that the inconsistency had been resolved based upon the results of objective, repeatable scientific experiments, it was no longer reasonable—if it ever truly had been—to disregard those eyewitnesses' testimony. A piece of the puzzle had been found.

Given this evidence of a shot to the head from in front, if JFK had been shot in the head from behind, he had been shot at least twice in the head! Moreover, Mantik had also studied the chest X-ray and had discovered that the HSCA account of the path of the "magic bullet" was anatomically impossible. By plotting the location specified for the entrance wound on the President's back and tracking the path that a missile would have had to take in order to exit from his throat at the presumed location, he discovered that it would have had to pass through cervical vertebra. In other words, no bullet could have made such a transit, especially not one that remained in as nearly pristine condition as the one that was supposed to have hit JFK and Connally.

The arithmetic of the assassination began to make more sense. There had always been a great deal of evidence to support the conclusion that the shot to the back had entered at around the third thoracic vertebra at a downward angle, which made it virtually impossible for that missile to have exited higher from his throat. Mantik had confirmed that no bullet could take the path prescribed by the HSCA report. If the bullet that entered his back had not exited his throat, then the throat wound had been a wound of entry for another bullet, as Livingston thought, for which there was considerable independent evidence, including contemporary radio and television reports and articles in *The New York Times*.

{ Daily
d at New York. N. Y.   THE NEW YORK TIMES, SATU

Sniper as He Rides in (

that Mr. Johnson, who had not yet been sworn
in, was safe in the protective custody of the
Secret Service at an unannounced place, presumably the airplane at Love Field.

Mr. Kilduff indicated that the President
had been shot once. Later medical reports
raised the possibility that there had been two
wounds. But the death was caused, as far as
could be learned, by a massive wound in the
brain.

Later in the afternoon, Dr. Malcolm Perry,
an attending surgeon, and Dr. Kemp Clark, chief
of neurosurgery at Parkland Hospital, gave
more details.

Mr. Kennedy was hit by a bullet in the
throat, just below the Adam's apple, they said.
This wound had the appearance of a bullet's
entry.

Mr. Kennedy also had a massive, gaping
wound in the back and cne on the right side of
the head. However, the doctors said it was impossible to determine immediately whether the
wounds had been caused by on bullet or two.

Resuscitation Attempted

Dr. Perry, the first physician to treat the
President, said a number of resuscitative measures had been attempted, including oxygen,
anesthesia, an indotracheal tube, a tracheotomy,
blood and fluids. An electrocardiogram monitor
was attached to measure Mr. Kennedy's heart
beats.

Dr. Clark was summoned and arrived in a
minute or two. By then, Dr. Perry said, Mr. Kennedy was "critically ill and moribund," or near
death.

Dr. Clark said that on his first sight of the
President, he had concluded immediately that
Mr. Kennedy could not live.

According to The New York Times *(23 November 1963), p. 2,
the President was hit in the throat from in front and had
a massive gaping wound to the back of his head.*

If the injury to the throat had not been caused by an exiting missile, however, then that meant that the injuries sustained by Governor Connally had to have been caused by separate shots. (Indeed, some physicians had conjectured that the multiple injuries he had sustained had to have been caused by two separate bullets and not merely one.) Thus, if there were two wounds to the head—one from in front and one from behind, as Mantik's new findings implied, more or less in harmony with Josiah Thompson's *Six Seconds in Dallas* (1967)—then there had to have been at least six shots: one to the back (from behind), one to the throat (from in front), two to the head (one from behind, one from in front), one to Connally and one to Tague.

These were minimums, of course, because there had always been further evidence of other shots that missed, which Gary Shaw's *Cover-Up* (1976), had documented with photographs. And if Connally had indeed been hit by two shots, then the number would creep upward. The evidence that the wound to the back had not exited through the throat, moreover, was substantial, indeed, including Boswell's autopsy diagram, the shirt and jacket the President was wearing at the time, a death certificate executed by Admiral George G. Burkley, who was the President's personal physician, and an FBI report of 9 December 1963, all of which indicate that the bullet had entered below his shoulder to the right of his spinal column around the third thoracic vertebra. [*Editor's note:* See Appendix I.]

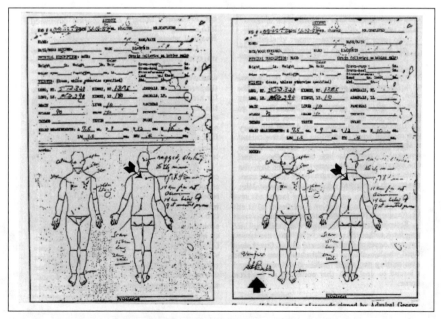

Verified (right) and unverified (left) copies of Boswell's diagram.

The existence of fabricated autopsy X-rays in the assassination of John F. Kennedy should be a cause of profound concern for every American. These materials, after all, were created by and under the control of officers of the United States Navy and Secret Service personnel, including especially SSA Roy Kellerman and Admiral Burkley, as the autopsy report prepared by Humes, Boswell and Finck [*Editor's note:* See Appendix F] and the supplemental autopsy report prepared by Humes [*Editor's note:* See Appendix G] clearly state. They were far removed from the influence of the Mob, pro- or anti-Castro Cubans, KGB, or Lee Harvey Oswald, none of whom could have created them.

About this time Aguilar, Mantik, and Livingston were contacted by Harrison Livingstone, who had heard of these discoveries and wanted to invite them to participate in a press conference in New York City around 22 November 1993. Aguilar and Mantik were somewhat uneasy about this idea, because Livingstone had had volatile relations with the press in the past. They therefore asked me if I would serve as the moderator for this event, which I agreed to do. Livingstone was not happy about this development, but he grudgingly agreed to it. Livingstone's publisher, Carroll & Graf, perhaps the leading publisher of work on the assassination in the world, decided to sponsor the press conference and send invitations to the press.

The press conference was held at 10 A.M. on 18 November 1993 at Loew's New York Hotel. If it was not a total failure, it was not a complete success. Only a handful of reporters showed up, none of us—apart from Robert B. Livingston—followed the script, our talks took far too long, and very little was accomplished. Even though we distributed copies of each of our presentations accompanied by a packet of supporting documents, the only domestic coverage we received was two sentences on CNN the following morning. Livingstone later faxed the message that an AP reporter who had been present had written what he considered to be the best story on the assassination of the last thirty years, but it was apparently killed at the national desk. Much of what we wanted to tell you now appears in Part II.

After the press conference, we traveled to Dallas for the Symposium on the Assassination of JFK, where Mantik, Livingston, and Aguilar gave public presentations reporting the results of their research. Their talks received ovations from those who were present, but coverage of their extremely important work by the national press was nil. I tried again and again to interest the networks, especially ABC, by contacting their *World News Tonight* and *Nightline* programs, but I never got further than a producer for *Nightline*, to whom I sent a 26-page fax to which he did not respond. At this point, therefore, serious students of the assassination knew about these discoveries, but not the American people. I felt profoundly depressed.

Even before the press conference, it had occurred to me that discoveries of this magnitude might interest the Department of Justice. Without any doubt, I thought, they *should* interest the Department of Justice. Between 17 November 1993 and 30 January 1994, therefore, I sent a series of letters to the Department of Justice, initially addressed to Janet Reno, Attorney General, but subsequently addressed to Mary Spearing, Chief, General Litigation and Legal Advice Section, who answered them. In spite of my best efforts, I was unable to convice them that what we had discovered required a reinterpretation of the evidence.

The stance of the Department of Justice was that the issues I wanted them to consider had already been reviewed by the HSCA investigation. In her letter of 25 January 1994, for example, Ms. Spearing advised me, "while the report of the House Select Committee on Assassinations was prepared prior to your allegations, as you noted, it does in fact address many of the issues which you have recently raised." Since the findings I was reporting concerned testimony and conclusions (by Livingston) that had never before been heard and results of experiments (by Mantik) that completely undermined the HSCA report, I considered such a response to be scientifically illiterate and logically absurd. My correspondence with the Department of Justice can be found in Part III.

Given Lundberg's editorial "Closing the Case" on the autopsy of JFK, we were all mildly surprised to discover that he was publishing a third set of articles in *JAMA*, including one by Robert Artwohl, M.D., "JFK's Assassination: Conspiracy, Forensic Science, and Common Sense" (*JAMA*, 24/31 March 1993, pp. 1540–1543) and another by John K. Lattimer, M.D., "Additional Data on the Shooting of President Kennedy" (*JAMA*, 24/31 March 1993, pp. 1544–1547). These pieces appeared in a section entitled, "Special Communications", which I suspect leaves them somewhere between opinion pieces and research articles. I discuss the quality of Artwohl's presentation, which exemplifies many common fallacies of reasoning, in Part I, while Ronald White considers aspects of Lattimer's work in the Postscript.

Lattimer is a urologist who has long championed the government's official account of the assassination (in one or another of its guises). I have sometimes speculated that President Kennedy would be amused that a urologist would be a student of his assassination. But then Gary Aguilar, M.D., a leading critic of the government's handling of the medical evidence, is an opthalmologist. I imagine a conversation in which I explain that "our side has Dr. Aguilar, an opthalmologist, who helps us to see straight, and their side has Dr. Lattimer, a urologist, who helps them to pee straight!" I like to think that Jack would have appreciated the difference.

As luck would have it, I was invited by George Michael Evica, who edits a journal entitled *The Assassination Chronicles*, to organize a symposium on possible tampering with the Zapruder film for a conference that would be held in Dallas during November 1996 by JFK Lancer Productions. I called David Mantik, who thought it was an excellent idea, and we put together a list of prospective participants. It was extremely fortunate that this opportunity brought together some excellent students of the photographic evidence. On 21 November we held a ten-and-a-half hour workshop to critique each other's research, and on 22 November we presented our findings, many of which are found in Part IV.

It seems altogether fitting that one of the chapters of this volume be authored by Bradley Kizzia, J.D., who brought suit against *JAMA* for libel and defamation on behalf of Charles Crenshaw. Many of us hoped that this suit would finally bring major aspects of the assassination into a courtroom for the first time since the ill-fated Garrison investigation. According to a piece published in *JAMA*, *JAMA* settled out of court for $213,000, plus publication of a 500-word commentary by Crenshaw in *JAMA*, which may be the most expensive Letter to the Editor of all time, running $426 per word. The settlement was paid by *JAMA's* insurance, which apparently has been cancelled (*JAMA*, 24/31 May 1995, p. 1633).

Crenshaw's piece, "Commentary on JFK Autopsy Articles" (*JAMA*, 24/ 31 May 1995, p. 1632), literally includes a large section of the Letter to the Editor that *JAMA* rejected in 1993. In an earlier version, he referred to this volume by its tentative title as the place where his original 6,800-word article could be found. *JAMA* refused to publish it in that form, no doubt not wanting to print a line that read, "The AMA Cover-Up in the Assassination of JFK". In an apparent effort to distract attention from Crenshaw's piece entirely, it was listed on the contents page in tiny type under the heading in bold type "**Obituary Listing**".

In "Dennis Breo's Reply" (*JAMA*, 24/31 May 1995, p. 1633), the author reiterates the claim that the Crenshaw book is "a sad fabrication." He also maintains that "Everything learned during 14 months of pretrial deposition supports this belief." But there is an interesting indication that *JAMA* may not really believe what it says. The articles that *JAMA* has previously published are now described as ones in which "The autopsy pathologists reaffirmed their 1963 finding that JFK was killed by two bullets fired from behind", thereby supporting the Warren Commission's conclusions.

Notice the difference, however. In his original article, Dennis L. Breo emphatically proclaimed that they had conclusively established "irrefutable proof that President Kennedy was struck by only two bullets that came from above and behind from a high-velocity weapon that caused the fatal wounds". This most recent sentence appears to be much more qualified and now claims only that the shots were fired from *behind* rather than from *above and behind*. Moreover, it no longer maintains that he was killed by bullets fired from a *high-velocity* weapon, changes that imply *JAMA* may have learned something during 14 months of pretrial depositions.

Both changes are significant. If *JAMA* had done its own homework or if Breo's articles had actually been subjected to "peer review", the Editor-in-Chief might have known that the three autopsy physicians, in sworn testimony before the Warren Commission and the HSCA inquiry, had not only *disavowed* depictions of the shots as having been fired from "above and behind" in favor of affirming they had been fired from "behind" but that they had also expressed considerable *skepticism* about the "magic bullet" theory. Finck, in fact, had dismissed it outright as "impossible" on the ground that there were more grains of metal left in the Governor's wrist than were missing from the bullet. *And these were* JAMA's *witnesses!*

The situation with respect to the character of the weapon that is said to have fired the fatal shots is at least equally significant. As Harold Weisberg in *Whitewash* (1965), Peter Model and Robert Groden in *JFK: The Case for Conspiracy* (1976), and Robert Groden and Harrison Livingstone in *High Treason* (1989), have all previously observed, the Mannlicher-Carcano that is alleged to have belonged to Oswald is not a high-velocity weapon. It follows that either the wounds have been misdescribed as having been caused by high-velocity bullets in the autopsy report, *The Warren Report*, and *JAMA*, or else Oswald has been wrongly accused of killing JFK. And if the wounds have been misdescribed, then neither the autopsy report nor any of the studies based upon it can be trusted.

The ultimate tenability of the government's position depends upon its capacity to successfully explain (or to "explain away") why so much of its own evidence appears to be inauthentic, fabricated, or falsified. There are many—entirely too many—disturbing indications that our government may have been involved in the assassination of JFK, not least of which is considerable evidence that Lee Harvey Oswald was framed, including David Mantik's most recent discovery—namely, that a 6.5 mm metal object was added to certain other autopsy X-rays [*Editor's note*: See the "Postscript" to his contribution to Part I]—and this crucial early memorandum:

November 25, 1963

MEMORANDUM FOR MR. MOYERS

It is important that all the facts surrounding President Kennedy's assassination be made public in a way which will satisfy people in the United States and abroad that all the facts have been told and that a statement to this effect be made now.

1. The public must be satisfied that Oswald was the assassin; that he did not have confederates who are still at large; and that the evidence was such that he would have been convicted at trial.

2. Speculation about Oswald's motivation ought to be cut off, and we should have some basis for rebutting [the] thought that this was a Communist conspiracy or (as the Iron Curtain press is saying) a right-wing conspiracy to blame it on the communists. Unfortunately, the facts on Oswald seem too pat—too obvious (Marxist, Cuba, Russian wife, etc.). The Dallas police have put out statements on the Communist conspiracy theory, and it was they who were in charge when he was shot and thus silenced.

3. The matter has been handled thus far with neither dignity nor conviction. Facts have been mixed with rumor and speculation. We can scarcely let the world see us totally in the image of the Dallas police when our President is murdered.

I think this objective may be satisfied by making public as soon as possible a complete and thorough FBI report on Oswald and the assassination. This may run into the difficulty of pointing to inconsistencies between this report and statements by Dallas police officials. But the reputation of the Bureau is such that it may do the whole job.

Nicholas deB. Katzenbach
Deputy Attorney General

This memorandum was sent to Bill Moyers, LBJ's Press Secretary, by Deputy Attorney General Nicholas deBelleview Katzenbach on Monday, 25 November 1963, the very day that Jackie, Bobby, and Teddy were in the process of burying the dead President and obviously distracted from the investigation of the assassination.

Ask yourself how the Deputy Attorney General, or anyone else on the face of this Earth, could possibly have known within 72 hours of the event whether or not Lee Harvey Oswald might have had an accomplice—someone he might have met in Dallas, in New Orleans, in Russia, or in the Marine Corps. Ask yourself how Nicholas deBelleview Katzenbach, or anyone else, could possibly have known that it was *not* a right-wing conspiracy to blame it on the communists. Ask yourself how he could possibly have known, at this point in time, that Oswald was *not* the patsy he proclaimed himself to be. Ask yourself why speculation about his motivation should be cut off. And ask yourself whether this memorandum was meant to reveal truth or to conceal it.

In the final analysis, has the AMA participated in a cover-up in the assassination of JFK? The evidence that Lundberg abused the journal is clear. To cite an illuminating indication, he publicly proclaimed this "research" was being welcomed into the "peer-reviewed" literature. But it had not been reviewed by experts, and he knew that at the time. He therefore made false representations intended to deceive the public. The Trustees of the AMA, moreover, were told what was going on at the time, yet did nothing about it. The result is that George Lundberg, M.D., with the complicity of the Board of Trustees of the AMA, has now permanently associated the AMA with a cover-up in the assassination of JFK.

The significance of our findings, however, far transcends the discovery of dereliction of duty by the Editor-in-Chief of a prominent journal. What we have discovered here falls into an all-too-familiar pattern of deceit and deception by our government and by the Fourth Estate. If John F. Kennedy was hit by four bullets; if autopsy X-rays have been fabricated to conceal a massive exit wound caused by a shot from in front; if diagrams of his brain have been created to complement that deception; if an absolute minimum of six shots were fired in Dealey Plaza that day; if the Zapruder film has been extensively edited using highly sophisticated techniques; if Lee Harvey Oswald was framed using manufactured evidence; and if the Warren Commission inquiry was merely a political charade—with a phoney bullet, phoney limo, and phoney wounds—then what became of America on 22 November 1963?

— *James H. Fetzer, Ph.D.*

Part I

Who Are the "Assassination Experts"?

In response to the massive publicity that accompanied the first round of articles on the assassination published by *JAMA* (27 May 1992), including the appearance by George Lundberg, M.D., on *Good Morning America*, as the Prologue explains, I contacted William Jacott, M.D., who was a member of the Board of Trustees of the AMA, to convey my distress about the apparent abuse of the journal by its Editor-in-Chief. Jacott arranged for Lundberg to call me, a conversation that convinced me that Lundberg was employing improper procedures of methodology. Because I believed that its journal was running the risk of associating the AMA with a cover-up in this case, I sent a letter to each member of the AMA's Board of Trustees.

I subsequently learned that my timing had been appropriate, insofar as a meeting of the Board of Trustees of the AMA was held in Chicago not long thereafter. Even though my letter was specifically intended as a request for the review of George Lundberg, a member of the Board subsequently advised me that, while it generated considerable informal discussion among the Trustees, it was never brought before the board as a matter of business. If it was discussed further by the Executive Committee, that is something that I have not learned. But even before the Board met in Chicago, I had heard from two of its members in response to their receipt of my correspondence.

The first to contact me was John J. Ring, M.D., who was the Immediate Past President of the AMA. Dr. Ring wanted to know with what degree of "metaphysical certitude" these things could be known. He was a fan of *The McLaughlin Group* hosted by John McLaughlin, a former Jesuit priest, who frequently uses that phrase in raising questions about the certainty of the kinds of knowledge that can be secured about different subjects. So I wrote a letter to Ring on 22 August 1992 advancing five arguments intended to prove the existence of a conspiracy or a cover-up in this case, and then a second on 27 August 1992, advancing another five arguments with the same objective. My arguments for Ring are now incorporated into the Epilogue.

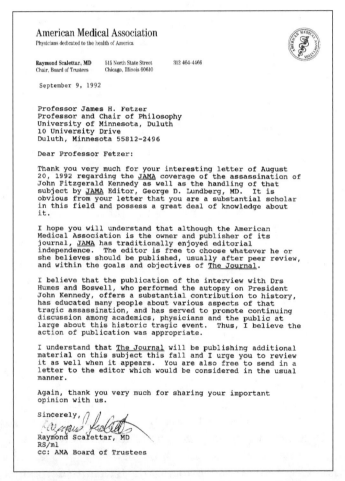

American Medical Association
Physicians dedicated to the health of America

Raymond Scalettar, MD　　515 North State Street　　312 464-4466
Chair, Board of Trustees　　Chicago, Illinois 60610

September 9, 1992

Professor James H. Fetzer
Professor and Chair of Philosophy
University of Minnesota, Duluth
10 University Drive
Duluth, Minnesota 55812-2496

Dear Professor Fetzer:

Thank you very much for your interesting letter of August 20, 1992 regarding the JAMA coverage of the assassination of John Fitzgerald Kennedy as well as the handling of that subject by JAMA Editor, George D. Lundberg, MD. It is obvious from your letter that you are a substantial scholar in this field and possess a great deal of knowledge about it.

I hope you will understand that although the American Medical Association is the owner and publisher of its journal, JAMA has traditionally enjoyed editorial independence. The editor is free to choose whatever he or she believes should be published, usually after peer review, and within the goals and objectives of The Journal.

I believe that the publication of the interview with Drs Humes and Boswell, who performed the autopsy on President John Kennedy, offers a substantial contribution to history, has educated many people about various aspects of that tragic assassination, and has served to promote continuing discussion among academics, physicians and the public at large about this historic tragic event. Thus, I believe the action of publication was appropriate.

I understand that The Journal will be publishing additional material on this subject this fall and I urge you to review it as well when it appears. You are also free to send in a letter to the editor which would be considered in the usual manner.

Again, thank you very much for sharing your important opinion with us.

Sincerely,

Raymond Scalettar, MD
RS/ml
cc: AMA Board of Trustees

An official response from the Chairman of the AMA Board of Trustees

An official response from the AMA came in the form of a letter from the Chairman of the Board of Trustees, Raymond Scalettar, M.D., who thanked me for my "interesting letter" and stated not only that the journal traditionally enjoys "editorial independence" but also that he personally believed the publication of the interview with Humes and Boswell "offers a substantial contribution to history", has educated many people, has stimulated discussion among academicians, physicians, and the general public and was appropriate for publication. He suggested I submit a letter to *JAMA*.

I could not believe that the Chairman of the Board of Trustees of the AMA could be so utterly unresponsive to the issues raised by my correspondence and, in a letter of 15 September 1992, I told him so in no uncertain terms. About this time, I sent copies of my correspondence with Ring and other material related to *JAMA*'s activities to the Board of Trustees. Lundberg, of course, was completely undeterred, and proceeded to publish another set of articles on this subject in *JAMA* (7 October 1992), including an editorial in which he "closed the case" on JFK's autopsy as far as *JAMA* was concerned. This announcement proved to be premature, when, in *JAMA* (24/31 March 1993), he would publish several additional articles.

Although I did not know then, others were having similar experiences. About the same time, Charles Crenshaw, M.D., was making an effort to respond to *JAMA*'s assault upon his character and credibility, with the submission of a lengthy but elegant piece entitled, "Let's Set the Record Straight: Dr. Charles Crenshaw Replies", which was rejected by *JAMA* in a letter from Richard Glass, M.D., Deputy Editor, dated 21 April 1993. Glass suggested that Crenshaw submit a Letter to the Editor. Crenshaw submitted a Letter to the Editor on 12 May 1993, which *JAMA* promptly rejected.

Similarly, on 29 April 1993, David Mantik, M.D., Ph.D., submitted a long study of the medical evidence, entitled, "The JFK Assassination: Cause for Doubt", which was rejected by Lundberg personally "based on our in-house evaluation" rather than on a traditional peer-review. For publication in this volume, Mantik has prepared a new "Postscript" concerning the appearance of a 6.5 mm metal object on the autopsy X-rays of the President's cranium, which provides a model of scientific investigation and a devastating demonstration that this phantom object has been added to the X-rays—a striking illustration of the fabrication of evidence in this case.

Apart from a handful of Letters to the Editor published in *JAMA* (7 October 1992) and a single letter from Cyril Wecht, M.D., J.D., a world-famous forensic pathologist, which *JAMA* could hardly decline (24/31 March 1993), *JAMA*'s approach was apparent: reject longer pieces and encourage letters to the editor, which could then be rejected as well. While Lundberg would subsequently claim Breo's work had "withstood an onslaught of criticism from numerous conspiracy theorists" (7 October 1992), the vast majority of responses and replies were simply rejected, discarded, or ignored.

JAMA's treatment of Charles Crenshaw, M.D., is a case study in the abuse of position displayed by the Editor-in-Chief of *JAMA*. None of us was surprised when a suit for defamation was finally brought against *JAMA* by Bradley Kizzia, J.D., which he discusses in his contribution. *JAMA* went so far as to suggest that Crenshaw was untrustworthy because he had not even been present in Trauma Room 1 at the time and therefore could not have made the observations that he described. Neither George Lundberg nor Dennis Breo made any attempt to interview Crenshaw in an effort to determine his side of the story, which would almost certainly have led to information contradicting what they were to print.

[*Editor's note*: Having watched an interview with Charles Crenshaw that was broadcast over television during a segment of *Geraldo*, I was impressed by his apparent candor and sincerity. During an early conversation, I asked whether, in the many years since the assassination, he had ever been asked to diagram what he had observed in Trauma Room 1. To my astonishment, he told me that he had not, but that it had been an unforgettable experience. On 6 October 1993, he sent the enclosed diagrams to me, which are published here for the first time. See Appendix A.]

The most striking feature of the articles published in *JAMA*, however, is that they are not carelessly composed; on the contrary, as Kizzia has observed, they "were masterfully conceived, slickly written and cleverly worded to give the superficial impression of being based on scientific research". What to this day continues to bother me is the extent to which *JAMA*'s behavior harmonizes with instructions disseminated by the CIA for coping with critics of *The Warren Report* [*Editor's note:* See Appendix M]. It is a formal fallacy known as *affirming the consequent* to infer that, merely because some specific consequence has occurred, any hypothesis that implies it has to be true. But arguments that are deductively invalid are not therefore inductively improper.

Something that looks like a duck, walks like a duck, and quacks like a duck might not be a duck. But the available evidence would suggest that it is and, absent a reasonable alternative explanation, such an inference is warranted. I do not assert absolutely that this was a CIA-style propaganda effort to discredit the government's critics, but it certainly looks like, reads like, and sounds like one. The available evidence suggests that it was and, absent a resonable alternative explanation, such an inference is also warranted. And I assert absolutely that, as an attempt to manipulate public opinion and subvert freedom of speech, it was a disservice to the American people and a most disgraceful episode in the history of American journalism.

— *James H. Fetzer, Ph.D.*

A Piece of My Mind:

Lundberg, JFK, and *JAMA*

James H. Fetzer, Ph.D.

As a professor of philosophy with an extensive background in the study of scientific reasoning, as the editor of one journal (*Minds and Machines*) and the co-editor of another (*Synthese*), and as a citizen who has been disturbed by the dissemination of incomplete and inaccurate information regarding the death of John Fitzgerald Kennedy, I was extremely disillusioned to read the articles on this subject that have been published in *JAMA*, including interviews with Humes and Boswell (27 May 1992) and subsequently with Finck (7 October 1992). In my opinion, these pieces should never have been published, especially in a journal as prestigious as *JAMA*, because they display the application of improper and unwarranted methods of investigation and procedures of inquiry that lead to unjustifiable conclusions and create the impression that the AMA has engaged in a cover-up in JFK's assassination.

I previously conveyed my concerns in this matter to a member of the Board of Trustees, William Jacott, on 24 May 1992, before the appearance of the first of these two issues of *JAMA* but after it had received extensive coverage in local and national news sources on the basis of a press release and other forms of publicity by Lundberg (including an interview on *Good Morning, America* that week). I subsequently wrote to him to elaborate my concerns with reference to articles and editorials that had already appeared in a local newspaper, the *Duluth News-Tribune* (20 May 1992, pp. 6A and 7A), and in *The New York Times* (20 May 1992, pp. A1 and A13). On 10 June

1992, I reiterated my distress after studying that issue of the journal to reaffirm my objections to the conduct of the editor in this case.

Dr. Jacott and I subsequently discussed this matter on 8 August 1992. His response was to propose that he arrange a telephone conversation between me and Lundberg in order for me to explain my position directly to Lundberg. On 12 August 1992, Lundberg contacted me and we discussed the differences in our viewpoints. The substance of our conversation convinced me that I was correct in thinking that the articles were based upon improper methods of research and inquiry, which had led to faulty conclusions presented as facts in a biased and unjustifiable presentation in *JAMA*. Because the issues involved here are so important and because the editor's behavior is so blatant, I wrote a series of letters to the members of the Board of Trustees of the AMA, which outlined these concerns.

The most important problems with the preparation and presentation of these articles I raised during our discussion were the following. When I emphasized to Lundberg that the number and the source of bullets that have been fired at a target cannot be determined on the basis of the number that happen to hit the target, he explained that he had restricted his focus to the two wounds he claims the body had sustained and the question of whether JFK was killed by two bullets which had been fired from above and behind. (Even if JFK had been killed by two bullets which had been fired from above and behind, however, that would hardly establish how many shots had been fired or the identity of whoever fired them.)

When I protested that there was considerable evidence—including the testimony of Malcolm Perry—that the throat wound was a wound of entry, he insisted that it could easily have been an exit wound, as though the conclusion that JFK had been shot twice did not hang in the balance. When I alluded to the autopsy photographs and X-rays and photographs of a bullet impacted on the limousine, of another bullet being picked up from a grassy area behind the vehicle's location, and of the curbing that was hit by a shot that missed (as even the Warren Commission conceded), he was very dismissive, suggesting that photographs and X-rays can be faked and that there is no legal chain of custody to support them.

This attitude bothers me more than any other aspect of our conversation. The problem we confront in attempting to figure out what happened in Dealey Plaza on 22 November 1963, after all, is an historical problem, not a legal one. Moreover, anyone with a serious interest in the assassination should have known that the Warren Commission was never able to establish that Oswald had the motive, the means, or the opportunity to assassinate the President. As various authors have reported, Oswald was observed on the second floor of the Texas School Book Depository by a motorcycle officer and by a supervisor within 90 seconds of the shooting (as Lifton, *Best Evidence* 1980, pp. 350–352, among others, has explained). But if Oswald was on the second floor having a Coke, then he could not have also been on the sixth floor shooting at JFK.

The more we talked the more apparent it became to me that he was operating on the basis of (what might be called) *the principle of selection and elimination*, selecting the evidence that agreed with a predetermined conclusion and eliminating the rest. This approach violates a basic principle of scientific reasoning, which is known as *the requirement of total evidence*. According to the total evidence requirement, scientific conclusions must be based upon all of the relevant evidence that is available, where evidence is relevant when its truth or falsity makes a difference to the truth or falsity of the conclusion. In the case of JFK's assassination, any evidence about the number of shots fired obviously qualifies as relevant.

Violations of the requirement of total evidence are commonly committed by politicians, advertisers, and lawyers, who are typically called upon to present a biased case in support of a predetermined point of view. (We do not expect a used car dealer, for example, to tell us what is wrong with a vehicle, even though some states require "full disclosure".) In courts of law, the requirement is satisfied by having the prosecution and the defense present their cases for the guilt or for the innocence of the accused, where the jury must sort out how the evidence presented fits together in arriving at a conclusion. The interests of both sides are reflected in various ways, including the right to cross-examine the testimony of witnesses.

Insofar as the articles in *JAMA* were based upon unsworn testimony from persons such as Humes and Boswell, whose reputations could irredeemably suffer from any admissions of evidence at variance with their previous testimony and who were not subject to cross-examination, I was struck by Lundberg's reliance upon a double standard. Evidence that upheld the Warren Commission's findings was included (even in cases where it could properly qualify as no more than "hearsay"), while evidence that undermined those findings was excluded (even in cases where it properly qualified as relevant photographic evidence that has gone unchallenged).

Indeed, it is striking how blatantly these articles are biased in favor of the recollections of Humes and Boswell, as though there were no other or more reliable evidence available. Photographs and X-rays might provide more accurate and dependable information than fallible and limited memories, especially nearly thirty years after the event. Yet none of the autopsy photographs or X-rays appear here, much less any photographs or diagrams of Dealey Plaza. No mention is made of the "missile" Humes turned over to FBI agents at the autopsy (see Groden and Livingstone's *High Trea-*

son 1989, for example) nor of the wounds sustained by John Connally, even
though they make it difficult to believe only three shots were fired.

One of the *JAMA* articles, of course, was devoted to interviews with
Parkland physicians who had attended JFK in Dallas. Like its companion
piece, no citations or references were given in support of any quotations or
assertions, as though they should be taken for granted at face value. Much
of this piece was devoted to discrediting the published testimony of Charles
Crenshaw, who has maintained that JFK's fatal wound hit him just above
the right temple (from the right front rather than above and behind). His
views have been elaborated in his book, *JFK: Conspiracy of Silence* (1992),
and indeed he was interviewed following Lundberg's interview on *Good
Morning, America*, during the very same television broadcast.

Malcolm Kilduff reports the President's death

One need not believe every claim that Crenshaw has made concerning
this case to be struck by certain facts. On the page following page 586 of
Lifton's *Best Evidence* (1980), for example, a photograph identified as "Photo
28" shows then White House Press Secretary Malcolm Kilduff pointing to
his right temple in answering a question at Parkland Hospital as to where
the bullet that struck JFK hit his head. And several autopsy photographs in
Livingstone's *High Treason 2* (1992)—found between pages 432 and 433—
show a peculiar "bat wing" configuration that conceals the President's cranium at the same location Crenshaw reports having observed a wound of

entrance. These facts suggest that his testimony should not be so readily dismissed.

The tone in which these articles are written, moreover, ought to give pause to anyone who imagines that they are objective reports of the testimony of these physicians. From first sentence to last, these stories are clearly intended to present the case in support of the predetermined conclusion that the Warren Commission's "findings" were correct. Indeed, the language in which they are written seems to be altogether antithetical to a scientific or medical journal. Instead of qualified characterizations of the evidence and the conclusions that it might render "probable" or perhaps make "likely", many definitive declarations are advanced in a case where it should be painfully apparent that conclusive findings are not available.

Thus, consider the second paragraph found on page 2794 of *JAMA*:

> The *scientific evidence* they documented during their autopsy provides *irrefutable proof* that President Kennedy was struck by only two bullets that came from above and behind from a high-velocity weapon that caused the fatal wounds. This *autopsy proof*, combined with the bullet and rifle evidence found at the scene of the crime, and the subsequent detailed documentation of a six-month investigation involving the enormous resources of the local, state, and federal law enforcement agencies, *proves* the 1964 Warren Commission conclusion that Kennedy was killed by a lone assassin, Lee Harvey Oswald. (Italics have been added here for emphasis.)

This passage, which reads like a promotion for the Warren Commission, not only grossly exaggerates the kind of evidential support that is possible here but ignores the controversial character of the Commission's most important conjectures, including, for example, the single-bullet theory. [*Editor's note*: See the Postscript.]

This emphasis upon "scientific evidence", "irrefutable proof", and so forth ought to be taken as a sign that what is being presented here consists of opinions masquerading as facts. If we know anything about this case at all, it is that "irrefutable proofs" are out of the question. I cannot imagine, moreover, how anyone could take seriously the suggestion that the Warren Commission had "proven" that Oswald killed Kennedy, given everything that is known about the case today. Lundberg's own bias is evident when he extends his personal endorsement on page 2803. His attitude, like those that Humes and Dennis Breo express in the last few paragraphs on this page, is that any other evidence simply does not matter.

———

Since *JAMA* is supposed to be a "peer review" journal, I asked myself what the referees of the articles that appeared in the 27 May 1992 issue should have noted. I would expect comments such as these in any competent referee report, which strongly hints that they were never subjected to review:

p. 2794, left-hand column: the middle paragraph provides an unsupported summary of the Warren Commission's disputed findings as though they had not been repeatedly challenged; moreover, it asserts conclusions regarding the shooter, etc., which go far beyond the medical evidence.

p. 2796, center column: how can a "blatantly obvious" wound create so much controversy? Where is appropriate supporting photographic evidence? If the head was not thoroughly examined, how could he be sure there were no other wounds? What do *photographs of the physicians* prove?

p. 2797, left-hand column: surely Crenshaw never made the absurd suggestion attributed to him here. More important, if the wound really was a large exit wound of the kind the autopsy photographs display, why would a tracheostomy be performed in the first place? Would it be necessary? Would it not be vital to staunch the flow of blood into the throat, etc.?

p. 2799, right-hand column: how could tracking the neck wound have been "criminal"? How could a proper autopsy be completed in its absence?

p. 2800, center column: to conduct a proper autopsy, the clothes were necessary, so how could a proper autopsy be conducted without them?

p. 2800, right-hand column: if the wounds could not be adequately described in words, why were the photographs not provided? Drawings, like memories, can be distorted; there might be many sets of photographs.

p. 2800, right-hand column: repeatedly this author begs the question by asserting that views at variance with those of the Warren Commission are "crazy conspiracy theories coming out of the woodwork". Begging the question in this blatant fashion does nothing to establish the truth.

p. 2801, right-hand column to p. 2803, left-hand column: are these medical personnel experts on the Garrison investigation and on the movie *JFK*? Here and elsewhere, recollections are used to "establish" facts going far beyond what the doctors could be reasonably be assumed to know; yet in other cases, what the doctors could reasonably be assumed to know (such as an Army Lt. Colonel knowing the difference between generals and staff, in the case of Finck, on p. 2802) is forcefully brushed aside. Why are the opinions of Jack Valenti, George Will, Anthony Stone, and Paul Galloway quoted in this piece in *JAMA*? Are they witnesses too?

p. 2804, right-hand column: why not simply show the photos themselves? Here and throughout, why is so much opinion masquerading as fact?

p. 2805, middle column: what did his throat look like *before the incision?*

Summary: there is a disproportionate percentage of opinion and quotation provided in lieu of evidence. The complete absence of documentation undermines the purpose that these "reports" were allegedly intended to fulfill. It reads more like tabloid journalism than scholarly research.

A less partisan and more objective article on the same subject can be found in a recent issue of *U.S. News and World Report* (17 August 1992, pp. 28–42). It should come as no surprise that a piece of this kind, which focuses on the fashion in which the Warren Commission staff conducted its analysis (by interviewing Gerald Ford and numerous members of the staff) would also support their previous "findings". More interesting to consider are its reports that Warren viewed the task of the commission to be establishing that JFK was killed by Lee Harvey Oswald, that the staff itself was composed almost entirely of lawyers rather than of investigators, and that its members were chosen by reliance upon the standard "old boy network".

These considerations provide a partial explanation for how it could be the case that the staff itself tended to function less in an investigative role (which was left almost exclusively to the FBI) and more in a prosecutorial role. As those of us familiar with the television series, *Law and Order*, are no doubt aware, lawyers in the role of prosecuting attorneys seldom conduct investigations of their own but instead are trained to present evidence that tends to establish the guilt of the accused, where that "guilt" itself is a matter about which they have predetermined conclusions. Thus, the staff was well-positioned to "build a case" against Oswald, which was in effect the task they had been assigned by Warren and by LBJ.

Even more instructive than these aspects of the operation of the staff are the accompanying photographs. On page 31, for example, is a familiar photograph alleged to be Oswald wearing a holstered revolver and holding his rife and a communist newspaper, which was used to convict him in the eyes of ordinary citizens. The accompanying discussion conveniently omits the evidence that this picture was one of several that appear to have been faked. (See, for example, the discussion and accompanying copies of three different photos of this type in Groden and Livingstone's *High Treason* 1989.) Even more important than this widely-disputed photograph are those of the staff reconstructing the scene of the crime that appear on pages 38–39.

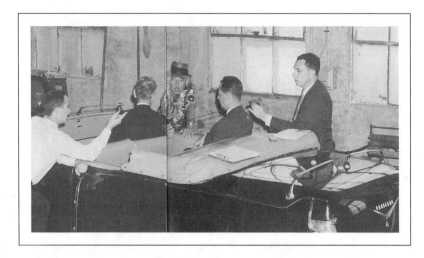

Arlen Specter demonstrating the single-bullet theory

In this case, of course, what we find are three photographs of a vehicle, one of which is described as showing the young Arlen Specter "demonstrating the single-bullet theory". There are several fascinating features of these photographs. One is that this demonstration shows the back wound below Specter's hand by about six inches, thereby illustrating how extremely implausible it is to suppose that a bullet which entered there could possibly have exited through JFK's throat. Indeed, in view of the exact alignment of Specter's hand in relation to the pointer in his hand, which is intended to display the path that a single-bullet would have been required to take if the single-bullet theory were true, this photograph refutes that theory.

Even more striking is the use of a Cadillac for the purpose of reconstruction. JFK, of course, was riding in a Lincoln Continental when he was killed. You do not have to be an expert to recognize the difference between these cars, which include the relative locations of the seats and distance between them. Thus, the single-bullet theory, which is the crucial element that ties together the assassination scenario advanced by the Warren Commission, was not only not based on a reconstruction that used the actual vehicle in which JFK was riding when he was killed but was instead actually based on analysis with a vehicle of an entirely different make. This invalidates any conclusions that were drawn by means of the "reconstruction" which these photographs record. They cannot establish the single-bullet theory.

The precise location of the wound in JFK's back, of course, has proven difficult to identify. On page 37, for example, two diagrams that were used by the Warren Commission are presented, which characterize it as a neck wound. This appears to be indispensable to the single-bullet theory, since otherwise it seems inexplicable how a bullet fired in a downward direction should have exited from the center of his throat at just the level of his tie. The photograph on pages 38–39, however, identifies its location by means of a circular mark (which is evident in this photograph) as a *back* wound, although the single-bullet theory requires that it has to have hit his neck.

The autopsy photographs that appear in Livingstone's *High Treason 2* (1992)—between pages 432 and 433—display two possible wounds, one of which is considerably higher than the other, but both of which are clearly back wounds and not neck wounds. The higher of the two, which Livingstone reports witnesses have said was merely a blood clot, appears to provide such factual basis as there may be for the single-bullet theory. At least, the circular mark locating the back wound in the photo in *U.S. News and World Report* corresponds to this position and not the much lower location of the second wound. Neither location fits the single-bullet theory, however, and there is no other evidence of any other wound to the neck.

The use of the wrong kind of vehicle to reconstruct "the crime of the century" appears to defy credulity, yet the evidence is categorical. The misdescription of the back wound as a neck wound likewise seems to be beyond belief, yet the diagrams leave no doubt. There can be different kinds of "smoking guns", and these appear to be "smoking guns" that discredit the Warren Commission's findings. Other kinds of "smoking guns" can be found in the testimony of persons who claim to have participated in the assassination, such as Chauncey Holt, whose interview with *Newsweek* (23 December 1991, pp. 52–54)—during which he claimed to have brought forged Secret Service credentials to Dealey Plaza—invites further investigation. Yet if the Warren Commission's findings are in doubt, so are the articles in *JAMA*.

Were this matter of any lesser importance, I would not impose upon you to consider these issues further. Before closing, moreover, I ought to express my appreciation to William Jacott for hearing me out and to George Lundberg for talking with me. Lundberg, I might add, expressed his agreement that many aspects of the autopsy had gone wrong, from moving the body from Dallas to the choice of autopsy surgeons. He even invited me to submit a Letter to the Editor for consideration for publication in *JAMA*. My choice of this alternative approach instead reflects my dissatisfaction not just with the contents of the articles that were published in this journal but with his dereliction of duty in allowing their appearance.

For reasons such as these and others conveyed in my correspondence with the AMA Trustees, I believe that the editor of *JAMA* has abused his position by the publication and promotion of these articles on the assassination of JFK. I believe that his conduct has been unprofessional and improper. I therefore suggest that his behavior in this case be subjected to a formal review. In my view, the AMA could make an important contribution by clarifying the attitude of the association about the conduct of its journal editor. Whether or not all of the facts in this case will ever be brought to light, it would be unfortunate for the AMA to be even remotely associated with a cover-up in the assassination of President John Fitzgerald Kennedy.

PHOTOGRAPH BY AP PHOTOGRAPHER

PHOTOGRAPH FROM RE-ENACTMENT

Commission Exhibit No. 900

CE–900 juxtaposing the Altgens photograph of the Lincoln limousine with the Secret Service Cadillac used in the re-enactment

Let's Set the Record Straight:

Dr. Charles Crenshaw Replies

Charles Crenshaw, M.D.

The 27 May 1992 issue of *JAMA* included two articles dealing with medical aspects of the assassination of President John F. Kennedy. Both were written by Dennis L. Breo. The first of these two articles drew on interviews with two of the autopsy pathologists, Dr. James J. Humes and Dr. J. Thornton Boswell. The second article, "Dallas MDs Recall Their Memories," is said to be based on interviews with Dallas doctors who participated in the treatment of President Kennedy at Parkland Hospital just minutes after he was shot. Both *JAMA* articles contained attacks on me and my book, *JFK: Conspiracy of Silence*.

In that book, published in early 1992, I stated:

1. that I participated in the treatment of President Kennedy at Parkland Hospital;

2. that I observed both his head wound and throat wound and that my medical judgment was that both wounds resulted from shots which struck him from the front;

3. that autopsy photographs which I have been shown, said to depict the two wounds, are incompatible with the nature and location of the wounds I saw in the emergency room;

4 that many of my Dallas colleagues reported the wounds to be of the same nature that I had observed;

5. that I participated in the treatment of Lee Harvey Oswald on Sunday, November 24, when he was brought to Parkland;

6. that while Oswald was being treated, I was called to a telephone in the operating room, where I talked with President Lyndon Johnson, who told me that there was a person present in the operating room to take a death-bed confession from Oswald.

I was both hurt and angered by the attacks on my credibility in the *JAMA* articles. I consider them to be distortions of the facts and to be mean-spirited in their tone. I will not engage in requital, nor will I resort to the inflammatory and damaging rhetoric used against me. Instead, I will refute, point-by-point, the allegations made against me and my book.

The reader will notice another fundamental difference between this article and Breo's articles attacking me. *I will cite and document every statement.* The previous *JAMA* article contained no endnotes or citations. *If author Breo had turned to the previous statements of the Dallas doctors he interviewed, he would have found that those statements contradicted what they were telling him, and that, in fact, their previous statements, contemporaneous and under oath, support my description of the President's wounds.* The official record devastates the points Breo attempted to make.

Friday Afternoon: Parkland Hospital

Just after 12:40 P.M. on Friday, 22 November, I entered Trauma Room 1 at Parkland Hospital with Dr. Bob McClelland.[1] Several other Parkland doctors were already there. President Kennedy lay, mortally wounded, on a stretcher. For the next several minutes, I helped administrate emergency treatment to the President and I observed both his throat wound and the wound at the right rear of his head.

I helped to remove President Kennedy's trousers and Dr. Ken Salyer and I performed a cutdown and inserted an IV catheter which fed Ringer's solution into Kennedy's right leg.[2] At the same time, other Parkland doctors were performing a tracheostomy, inserting chest tubes, and doing a similar cutdown on the left leg.[3]

Two wounds were visible. There was a small, round opening in the front of the midline of the throat.[4] This became the site of Dr. Malcolm Perry's tracheostomy incision. In the occipito-parietal region at the right rear of the head, there was an avulsive wound nearly as large as a fist. Bone, scalp, and hair were missing in the region, and brain tissue, including much of the cerebellum, was hanging from the opening.[5] *I considered the throat wound to be an entrance wound and the large head wound to be an exit wound. Along with many of my Parkland colleagues, I believed at the time that President Kennedy had been hit twice from the front. I still believe this today.* [*Editor's note*: See Appendix A.]

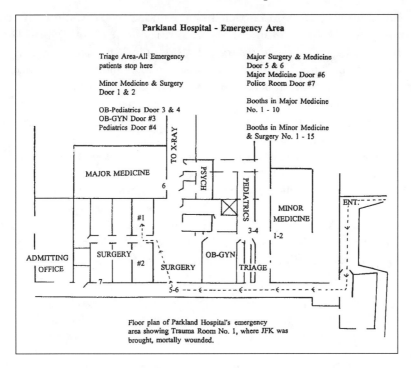

*Diagram of Parkland Hospital indicating the route through which
President Kennedy was taken into Trauma Room #1*

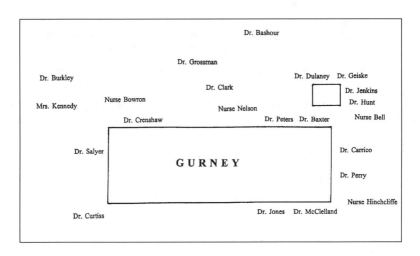

*Diagram of relative positions of individuals in Trauma Room #1
at the time of treatment of President Kennedy*

The author of the *JAMA* article had the audacity to question whether or not I was even present in Trauma Room 1. At one point, Dennis Breo wrote, "Crenshaw, who was a surgical resident in 1963, is not mentioned in the Warren Commission's 888-page summary report . . ."[6] At another point, he wrote, "Since it is hard to prove a negative, no one can say with certainty what some suspect—that Crenshaw was not even in the trauma room. None of the four [Parkland doctors interviewed by Breo] recalls ever seeing him at the scene."[7]

In actual fact, my presence in Trauma Room 1 was noted in sworn testimony before the Warren Commission eight times by five different doctors and nurses who saw me there.[8] *Dr. Charles Baxter, who apparently told Breo he could not recall seeing me there, states in his Warren Commission testimony that I was there*! So does Dr. Robert McClelland, who entered the room with me. Dr. Don Curtis and nurse Margaret Hinchcliffe also testified that I was present. Dr. Ken Salyer, who worked with me on the President's IV, told the Commission the following:

> SPECTER. To what extent did Dr. Crenshaw participate?
>
> SALYER. Dr. Crenshaw participated about the extent that I did. We were occupied in making sure an IV was going and hanging up a bottle of blood.
>
> SPECTER. Is the—is Dr. Crenshaw a resident?
>
> SALYER. Yes, he is a third-year resident. That's the reason I remember him specifically because we were sort of working together there on that.

The record makes it amply clear that I was in Trauma Room 1 doing precisely what I wrote in *Conspiracy of Silence*. Why, then, did Breo make his innuendos? I believe a major purpose for the May 1992 articles was to discredit Charles Crenshaw, and that their author and editor either did not bother to check the official record or chose to ignore what they found there.

Sunday: The White House Telephone Calls

In my book, I told of being on duty at Parkland when Lee Harvey Oswald was brought there and of assisting with his treatment. While I was in the room I observed a large man in a scrub suit, with a gun visible in his pocket. I did not doubt that he was some sort of government agent, and I handed him a sterile mask. At one point, a nurse tapped me on the shoulder and asked me to take a telephone call. In an adjoining office, I talked with President Lyndon Johnson, who told me that we should try to get a confession from Oswald and that a person was present for the purpose of taking that confession.

In an attempt to refute this, *JAMA* quotes Dr. Baxter: "Did that happen? Heavens no . . . imagine that, the President of the United States personally calls for Charles Crenshaw."

It did happen and there is ample proof. It should first be noted that I have never claimed that President Johnson called personally *for* me. I was simply tapped on the shoulder by a nurse to take the call. But the call did occur.

1. Dr. Philip E. Williams, Dallas neurosurgeon, told *The New York Times*: "I vividly remember someone said . . . the White House is calling and President Johnson wants to know what the status of Oswald is. I heard the statement in the operating room, and it was not Dr. Crenshaw's book or anyone else who revived my thoughts about this because I have said this for years."

2. Ms. Phyllis Bartlett was the chief telephone operator at Parkland Hospital that day. She definitely remembers taking the call from a man who identified himself as President Johnson, then transferring the call to the operating room. It was Ms. Bartlett who disconnected the line while I was talking to Johnson. She was attempting to transfer the President to the public relations office. Ms. Bartlett wrote to *The Dallas Morning News* on 15 July 1992: "There very definitely was a phone call from a man with a loud voice, who identified himself as Lyndon Johnson, and he was connected to the operating room phone during Oswald's surgery."

3. The presence of federal agents in the operating room is also well documented. Alex Rosen of the FBI was ordered by Director Hoover to get a man to Parkland to get a statement from the accused assassin. Rosen stated that he has contacted Forrest Sorrels of the Dallas Secret Service office. Sorrels says an agent is already there. The time is 12:18 in Dallas. *The Dallas Times Herald* of Sunday, 22 December 1963, carried a story that an agent wearing hospital clothing and a face mask had waited in vain for a confession from Oswald. In response to this, Dallas SAIC Gordon Shanklin sent an AIRTEL to Hoover which stated in part: "SA Charles T. Brown and SA Wallace R. Heitman made arrangements . . . to be available in the event Oswald regained consciousness. In order to save time and be immediately available, these agents did don operating clothing and took positions outside the operating room." But the agents did enter the room. Dr. Paul Peters, who was present and attending Oswald, said: "There were Secret

Service men intermingled with the operating room personnel . . . some were dressed in green clothes as the surgeons . . . two or three shouted in his ear, 'Did you do it? Did you do it?'"

4. In the *20-20* story which ABC did on my book, the network reported on an examination of the Johnson log for the time period while Oswald was being attended. Quoting historian William Manchester, ABC reported that Johnson had just told Bobby Kennedy, "We've got to get involved, we've got to do something," or words to that effect.

Once again the JAMA articles are incorrect. There is clear and convincing evidence of both the White House telephone call and the presence of federal agents in the operating room—as I stated.

The President's Wounds

There is no doubt in my mind that the attacks on me by a professional journal last summer were occasioned by my assertion that President Kennedy's wounds indicated to a doctor present on the scene that he had been shot from the front, which meant, of course, a conspiracy. The wound I saw in President Kennedy's throat was clearly a smooth and rounded entry wound. The wound in the right rear of the head, both in its location and its nature, must have been inflicted from the front. As I have stated, my conclusion in Trauma Room 1 was that these wounds were made by two shots striking President Kennedy from the front. That is still my firm conclusion today. And the official record—ignored by Breo and *JAMA*—will show that I was not alone in those conclusions.

Dennis Breo talked with several of the Parkland doctors about their experiences and my book. Jim Carrico, Marion T. "Pepper" Jenkins, Charles Baxter and Malcolm Perry were interviewed. In spite of the fact that Breo visited in Dallas, he made no effort to contact me or to get my side of the story. All four of my former colleagues are quoted as having condemned my conclusions about shots from the front and asserted that what they saw in the Trauma Room 1 was completely compatible with the autopsy photographs, as well as the autopsy findings which concluded that Kennedy was shot twice *from the rear, not the front.*

As *JAMA* presented it, this was a case of four Dallas doctors standing firmly against Dr. Charles Crenshaw, sensationalist. These doctors, if quoted correctly, seemed to question everything from motive to sanity. Dr. Baxter is said to have stated that the only motive he could find for me was "a desire for personal recognition and monetary gain"; Dr. Perry, according to the article, said I was on TV "saying this bogus stuff to reach out for his day in the sun;" Dr. Carrico apparently decided I had dreams of grandeur; while Dr. Jenkins, according to the article, said, "Crenshaw's conclusions are dead wrong."

Was I out-numbered? No, not at all. My strongest ally went unmentioned by *JAMA*. My strongest ally is *the record*—the official record—the statements made by Drs. Perry, Baxter, Carrico, and Jenkins long before they ever talked to Dennis Breo and *JAMA*. The strongest "witnesses" against *JAMA* and the four Dallas doctors are the doctors themselves!

Dr. Carrico (upper left), Dr. McClelland (upper right), Dr. Jenkins (bottom left), and Dr. Crenshaw (bottom right) indicate where each recalls the large opening in the back of the President's head. (From KRON-TV, NOVA, and ABC's Nightline.)

The previous official statements of these four doctors, which we will now examine, come from three sources:

1. CE–392. This Warren Commission Exhibit consists of statements written by many Parkland doctors within 2-3 hours of having attended President Kennedy. The statements in CE–392, many of them handwritten, are of immense significance. Not only are they the

first accounts of President Kennedy's wounds based on observation by trained medical personnel, they are also "pure" medical data. That is, when Drs. Perry, Baxter, Jenkins, Carrico, and others wrote their CE–392 statements on Friday afternoon, they had no knowledge of "single-bullet theory," Oswald, "Grassy Knoll," School Book Depository, or other evidentiary factors to affect opinions. They also stand as the only recorded medical opinions about Kennedy's wounds before the body was illegally taken from Dallas by the Secret Service. *CE–392 is found in the Warren Report, pp. 516–537, and should be read by any person who is genuinely interested in knowing where President Kennedy was shot.* It is a shame that Dennis Breo didn't read CE–392 before he went to Dallas.

2. Warren Commission (WC) testimony. All four doctors testified under oath before the Warren Commission in March of 1964.
3. Depositions given to the House Select Committee on Assassinations (HSCA) in 1977. Carrico, Jenkins, and Perry were deposed during 1977, again under oath.

When we examine the four doctor's previous statements, we find that, instead of *refuting* my observations, they actually *support* them.

Dr. Malcolm Perry:
Perry and Kennedy's Head Wound

Within hours of seeing President Kennedy's body, Malcolm Perry described the head wound as "a large wound of the right posterior cranium."[9] Four months later, in testimony before the Warren Commission, Perry would call it "a large avulsive wound of the right occipitoparietal area"[10] and noted that "both scalp and portions of the skull were absent."[11] In 1977, in a deposition for the HSCA, Perry stated that "the parietal occipital head wound was largely avulsive."[12]

These three references to the head wound are clearly consistent with each other. But, as can be clearly seen, they are also clearly consistent with my own description of the head wound. The three times Malcolm Perry has described John F. Kennedy's head wound to an official government body, he has agreed with my description, both in its location and its appearance.

Perry and the Cerebellum

When Malcolm Perry gave his HSCA deposition, he stated: "There was visible brain tissue in the macard and some cerebellum was seen."[13]

Perry and the Throat Wound

Malcolm Perry was in a unique position to observe the wound in the midline of the throat. He made the tracheostomy incision through that throat wound and inserted a tracheostomy tube. Within a few hours of President Kennedy's death, Malcolm Perry was in a classroom at Parkland Hospital, describing Kennedy's wounds to newsmen. A transcript of the press conference exists. In his statements, Malcolm Perry three times identifies the throat wound he has just seen as an entrance wound.

> Q. Where was the entrance wound?
> PERRY. There was an *entrance* wound in the neck. (Emphasis added.)
> Q. Which way was the bullet coming on the neck wound? At him?
> PERRY. It appeared to be coming at him.[14]

> (Later in conference)
> Q. Doctor, describe the entrance wound. You think from the front of the throat?
> PERRY. The wound appeared to be an *entrance* wound in the front of the throat; yes, that is correct.[15] (Emphasis added.)

Dr. Malcolm Perry (right) during press conference at Parkland Hospital. Time is 3:16 P.M., little more than two hours after Perry did a tracheostomy. Three times during this press conference, Dr. Perry referred to the President's throat wound as an entrance wound. [Editor's note: See Appendix C.]

By the following day, evidence suggesting that the shots which struck
Kennedy had come from the Texas School Book Depository above and
behind him had surfaced. Nonetheless, Perry spoke to *Boston Globe* reporter Herbert Black and continued to hold that a bullet had entered
the front of the throat. "It may have been that the President was looking
up or sideways with his head thrown back when the bullet or bullets
struck him."[16] It is clear that on the weekend of the assassination,
Malcolm Perry apparently felt the wound in the President's throat was
an entrance wound—and said so.

At the time Perry testified before the Warren Commission in March,
his early statements about the entrance wound in the throat had become a considerable problem for the Commission. Counsel Arlen Specter undertook some damage control:

> SPECTER. Well, what questions were asked of you and what responses
> did you give at that press conference?
>
> PERRY. Well, there were numerous questions asked, all the questions
> I cannot remember, of course. Specifically, the thing that seemed
> to be of the most interest at that point was actually trying to get
> me to speculate as to *direction of the bullets*, the number of bullets,
> and the exact cause of death. (Emphasis added.)
>
> The first two questions I could not answer, and my reply to them
> was that I did not know, if there were one or two bullets, and I
> could *not categorically state about the nature of the neck wound,
> whether it was an entrance or an exit wound, not having examined
> the President further* ···[17] (Emphasis added.)

The transcript of the press conference does reveal that both Perry
and Dr. Kemp Clark said they were unsure whether one or two bullets
had struck the President, but Perry *did* make a definite statement about
the throat wound, and nowhere in the transcript is found any refusal or
hesitancy in characterizing that wound as one of entrance.

Allen Dulles, of the Warren Commission, joined in the damage control effort, suggesting that Perry take each newspaper clipping which
contained information about his press conferences and correct all "incorrect" quotes attributed to them.[18] Commission records give no indication of whether or not Perry ever did this.

As can be seen, the record shows that on the weekend of the assassination, Dr. Malcolm Perry described the throat wound as an entrance
wound—just as I have. And how did Dennis Breo and *JAMA* deal with
Perry's news conference statement? "Perry appeared at the riotous press
conference on the day of the assassination and said the fatal shot 'might

have come from the front.'"[19] As has been shown, Perry also said three times that the throat wound had been inflicted from the front. Did Breo check the record? (Note: See my Addendum at the conclusion of this article for more on Arlen Specter and the throat wound.)

Dr. Marion T. "Pepper" Jenkins:
Jenkins and Kennedy's Head Wound

In his CE–392, dated 4:30 P.M., three and one-half hours after seeing the President's wounds, Dr. Jenkins described a "great laceration of the right side of the head (temporal and occipital)."[20] Fourteen years later, he told the HSCA: "One segment of bone was blown out—this was a segment of occipital or temporal bone."[21]

Dr. Jenkins saw the same wound I saw—and described it in the same way.

Jenkins and the Cerebellum

Jenkins' CE–392 describes "herniation and laceration of great areas of the brain, even to the extent that the cerebellum had protruded from the wound."[22] In March, four months later, he testified under oath, "Part of the brain was herniated; I really think part of the cerebellum . . . was hanging out of the wound."[23] Jenkins has since stated that he "mis-spoke" when he called the tissue cerebellar tissue.

Dr. Jenkins apparently was still "mis-speaking" fourteen years after the assassination when he was deposed by the HSCA. A summary of his deposition states, "He [Jenkins] noted that a portion of the cerebellum was hanging out from a hole in the right-rear of the head."[24]

And what is *JAMA*'s comment about Jenkins and the cerebellum? "Dr. Jenkins wrote in a 1963 report that Kennedy's 'cerebellum' had been blown out when he meant 'cerebrum.'"[25] A study of the record shows that Jenkins *wrote it* on the day of the assassination, *swore to it* before the Warren Commission four months later, then *swore to it again* 14 years later to the HSCA!

Dr. James Carrico:
Carrico and Kennedy's Head Wound

Dr. Carrico was the first Parkland doctor to enter Trauma Room 1. A few hours later he wrote a description of the head wound he saw. Carrico recorded, "The other wound had avulsed the calvarium and shredded brain tissue present and profuse oozing."[26] In his Warren Commission testimony, he located the wound more specifically: "I saw a large gaping wound located in the right occipitoparietal area,"[27] and he told HSCA there was a "fairly large wound in the right side of the head, in the parietal, occipital area . . . That would be above and posterior to the ear."[28]

Carrico and the Cerebellum

In his Warren Commission testimony, Carrico said, ". . . the skull was fragmented and bleeding cerebral and cerebellar tissue."[29] At another point in his questioning, he said, "I believe there was shredded macerated cerebral and cerebellar tissue both in the wounds and on the fragments of skull attached to the dura."[30] In his 1977 HSCA deposition, Carrico stated, "One could see blood and brains, both cerebrum and cerebellum fragments in that wound."[31]

Carrico and the Throat Wound

In his CE–392 statement on Friday afternoon, Carrico did not specifically call the throat wound an entrance wound, but used another similar word: "Two external wounds were noted. One small *penetrating* wound of mid-neck in lower 1/3."[32] Before the Warren Commission, he gave the width of the throat wound before Perry's tracheostomy as 5–8 millimeters and said it was "fairly round, had no jagged edges, no evidence of powder burns and so forth."[33]

Dr. Charles Baxter:
Baxter and Kennedy's Head Wound

On the afternoon of the assassination, Dr. Baxter wrote, ". . . the rt [sic] temporal and occipital bones were missing, the brain was lying on the table."[34] Baxter then proceeded to read from his CE–392. When he got to the part dealing with bones being missing and the brain lying on the table (see above), Baxter is recorded as having read, "the temporal and *parietal* bones were missing and the brain was lying on the table."[35] The text Baxter was supposed to be reading said "occipital," but Baxter, apparently reading his own handwriting, read the term as "parietal," a location further removed from the rear of the head. The reason for this "misread" is not known.

Baxter and the Cerebellum

Dr. Baxter testified that "the cerebellum was present—a large quantity of the brain was present on the cart."[36]

Baxter and the Throat Wound

When he testified before the Warren Commission, Baxter conceded that the throat wound could have been either an entrance wound or an exit wound.[37] But his other statements about the wound are enlightening: "this wound was, in my estimation, 4 to 5 mm in widest diameter and was a spherical wound . . . so that it was very small."[38] "Judging from the caliber of the rifle that we later found or became acquainted with, this would more resemble a wound of entry."[39] As late as spring of 1992, Dr. Baxter, on ABC-TV's *20-20*, stated that the wound he saw could have been either an entrance wound or an exit wound."[40]

These are the statements, nearly all of them official, of the four Dallas doctors, formerly colleagues, who ridiculed me and my claims in *JAMA*. Let's total the scorecard:

1. I saw a wound in the back of the head—occipital and parietal. So did Jenkins, Carrico, Baxter and Perry. Some say occipital and parietal, others say occipital and temporal. The occipital bone in the rear of the head is mentioned by all of us. The size and nature of the wound is very similar in all our descriptions.

2. I saw cerebellar tissue hanging out of the large head wound. So did Jenkins, Carrico, Baxter, and Perry.

3. I saw a small entrance wound in the front of the throat. Perry called it an entrance wound; Carrico called it a "penetrating wound." Baxter still says it could have been an entrance wound.

Other Dallas Doctors

Many other Parkland doctors were present in Trauma Room 1 and they, too, wrote CE–392's and testified before the Warren Commission. Their statements further bolster my claims:

Head Wound

Dr. Kemp Clark

* CE–392—"two external wounds . . . the other in the occipital area of the skull . . . a large wound of the occipitoparietal area." [*Editor's note*: See Appendix B.]
* WC testimony—"I examined the wound in the back of the President's head." He noted the "presence of the much larger wound in the right occipital region."[41]

Dr. Paul Peters

* WC testimony—"I noted that there was a large defect in the occiput."

Dr. Ronald Jones

* WC testimony—"There was a large defect in the back of the head."

Dr. Gene Akin

* WC testimony—". . . in the back of the right occipitoparietal part of the skull was shattered."

Dr. Robert McClelland

* WC testimony—"I noted that the right posterior portion of the skull had been extremely blasted . . . some of the occipital bone was fractured in its lateral half."

Cerebellar Tissue

Dr. Kemp Clark

* CE–392—"Both cerebral and cerebellar tissue were extruding from the wound." [*Editor's note*: See Appendix B.]
* WC testimony—". . . cerebral and cerebellar tissue being damaged and exposed."; ". . . the loss of cerebellar tissue . . ."[42]

Throat Wound

Dr. Paul Peters

* WC testimony—"We saw the wound of entry in the throat and noted the large occipital wound."

Dr. Ronald Jones

* ". . . a small hole in the midline of the neck thought to be a bullet entrance wound."

Again with these doctors, we see the consistent "Dallas pattern"—small round wound in the front of the throat, large hole opening backward in the right rear of the head, and cerebral and cerebellar tissue hanging from the skull. It was clear to me that bullets had struck President Kennedy from the front.

The Autopsy Photographs

What I saw in the emergency room at Parkland Hospital forces me to disagree with the Bethesda autopsy report which concluded that the President was hit by two bullets "fired from a point behind and somewhat above the level of the deceased."[43] The four doctors interviewed by *JAMA* say they saw nothing which contradicts that finding.[44]

At this point, it must be noted that when the terms "autopsy" and "autopsy findings" are used, one must distinguish between the *autopsy reports* and the *autopsy photographs and X-rays*. Even a casual examination reveals that the two do not match. Among the major differences:

1. The autopsy report locates a small entry wound in the back of the head just to the right of the occipital protuberance.[45] The HSCA medical panel, examining photographs and X-rays, placed this wound 4 inches higher, in the cowlick area, in a different bone, the parietal.[46] Those of us who treated Kennedy in Dallas saw no such small entry wound any place in the head.

2. The autopsy report failed to pinpoint precisely where the bullet exited the head, but stated that the large defect measured 13 cm across and involved the occipital, parietal, and temporal bones of the skull.[47] The HSCA medical panel, relying on the photos and X-rays, decided a bullet exited along the coronal suture, *in front of the ear*. The HSCA found the defect involved the parietal, temporal, and *frontal* bones, but not the occipital.[48] This placed the large skull defect further forward than the autopsy report located it, and considerably further forward than the wound we saw in Parkland. In addition, the wound described in both accounts at Bethesda is much larger than the wound I saw at the back of President Kennedy's head.

3. The autopsy report stated that the tissue taken from the right cerebellar cortex revealed "extensive disruption of brain tissue with associated hemorrhage."[49]

Photographs of the brain examined by the HSCA are said to show no damage to the cerebellum, and the committee so reported in 1978.[50] Several of us saw the cerebellum hanging from the massive head wound and have so reported, some under oath. (There has been heated debate about the nature and location of an alleged wound in the President's neck/back. However, since I never saw this wound, I have chosen not to discuss this controversy.)

The four doctors who commented to Dennis Breo and to *JAMA* are reported to have found no problem with these photographs, in spite of the fact that they obviously show a head wound of a different size in a totally different location than the one they saw and reported on November 22. I find great problems with any photograph which shows a completely intact skull at a point where I saw a hole nearly the size of the fist. I find great problems with any photograph which does not show cerebellar tissue shredded and hanging from that hole. I find great problems with any photograph which shows a large opening *in front of the ear* with a flap of skull hanging open there, where none of us observed any defect on November 22. *There is no way that I can reconcile the autopsy photographs I have seen with the wounds I saw on John F. Kennedy's body in Trauma Room 1 at Parkland on November 22.* That *JAMA* reports that my former colleagues say they can do so amazes me. [*Editor's note:* See Appendix A.]

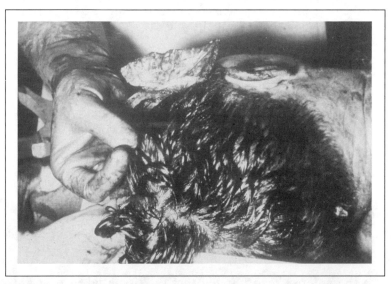

This autopsy photograph shows the back of Kennedy's head completely intact. Compare this with first photograph of the four physicians indicating the location of the wound. All of the Parkland doctors described a large defect at the rear of the head, with bone sprung open and brain protruding.

Evidence has surfaced to indicate that, since the publication of the *JAMA* article, some of the Parkland doctors apparently have tried to stake a kind of compromise position which would allow them to stand by their previous statements about the head wound and still endorse the autopsy photographs as being legitimate. Within weeks of the publication of the *JAMA* article, a forum about the assassination was held in Dallas. Dr. John K. Lattimer was the principal speaker. Also in attendance, and forming a panel, were several Parkland doctors, including Carrico, Baxter, and Jenkins. I asked to be allowed equal time to speak, but this was denied. So was my second request, to be permitted just ten minutes in which to show a videotape presenting my view on the medical evidence. At this forum, several of the Dallas doctors said they would reconsider their sworn testimony about cerebellar tissue being damaged and visible in Dallas.[51] This in spite of the fact that some of them had sworn to its presence as late as 14 years after the fact.[52] It was in trying to explain the obvious discrepancies between autopsy photographs of the back of Kennedy's head (where no damage is seen at all), and their Warren Commission and HSCA descriptions of a large wound and missing bone, scalp and hair, that Drs. Carrico and Jenkins came up with a new "reconciliation": they apparently believe that the head wound they saw is really there in the photographs after all—it is simply under the hair. In their current explanation, the scalp has been reflected by the pathologists and is being held in place. Thus, underneath the hair, shielded from the camera's lens, is actually the occipitoparietal wound we all saw!

In my opinion, this is a completely untenable theory. The reasons for such an opinion are several:

1. The photographs which depict the back of the head are said to have been taken *before* dissection began. No incisions are visible on the head, no flaps are seen anywhere, and no Y-incision is seen.

2. A second set of photographs showing the back of the head intact, have no hands holding the head, so that it would be an impossibility that reflected flaps of scalp are being held in place.

3. X-rays, said to show the skull, show no massive wound in the back of the head underneath the scalp and hair.

4. The photographs show a large defect with a flap of scalp hanging from the skull in front of the right ear. I did not see this, and by their own admission, the other doctors did not see it.

5. Finally, what legitimate reason would the pathologists have for moving the reflected scalp and shielding such a crucial piece of evidence as an exit hole in the back of the head, especially since there are *no* pictures which show this defect?

Photographs of the Throat Wound

Several autopsy photographs show what is alleged to be the tracheotomy incision which Malcolm Perry made through a bullet hole in Kennedy's neck. When I first saw these photos, I was shocked at the size and character of the defect there. According to the autopsy report, the incision measures 6.5 cm in length.[53] When Dr. Humes testified before the Warren Commission, he placed the length of the defect at 7–8 cm.[54] The wound which I saw after Dr. Perry completed his work looked nothing like what I saw in the photographs taken at Bethesda. Dr. Perry had made a small and very neat transverse incision. I took it to be about 1 to 1 1/2 inches in length. It was certainly not of the length I saw in the autopsy photos. The gaping nature of the wound was also inconsistent with what I saw. When the body left Parkland there was no gaping, bloody defect in the front of the throat, just the small bullet hole and the thin line of Perry's incision.

According to the *JAMA* article, the four Dallas doctors have no problem in reconciling the autopsy photos with the tracheostomy incision they observed. "I was right there and the tracheostomy I observed and the autopsy photos look the same—very compatible," Dr. Baxter is quoted as having said.[55] Dr. Carrico said, "I've seen the autopsy photos and they are very compatible to the actual tracheostomy."[56] "They are the same," is the comment attributed to Dr. Jenkins."[57] Dr. Perry qualified his response: "Of course, tissues sag and stretch after death, but any suggestion that this wound was intentionally enlarged is wrong."[58]

Once again, there is a previous record, however. In 1966, three of these doctors estimated the length of the incision Perry made in Kennedy's throat. Their responses were recorded by a researcher. Dr. Carrico said it was "between two and three centimeters—which is close to an inch."[59] Dr. Perry, who made the incision, estimated it at "2–3 centimeters," while Dr. Baxter remembered it as "roughly an inch and a half."[60]

Now, in 1992, these men are said to believe that there is no contradiction between what they saw and the 6.5 to 8 cm gash shown in the au-

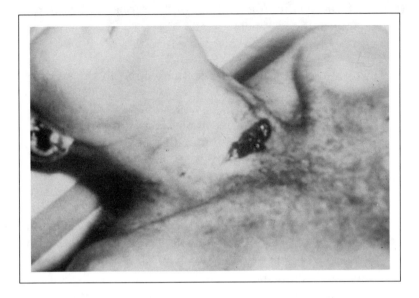

Kennedy's throat as seen in autopsy photograph. The autopsy report says this defect is 6.5 cm in length. In his Warren Commission testimony, Dr. Humes stated the length as 7–8 cm. Dr. Perry estimated the length of the incision he made at 2–3 cm. The incision Dr. Crenshaw saw at Parkland Hospital was straight and neat, nothing like what this photograph shows.

topsy photographs. It seems to me that the reader will have to decide which is the accurate response—an interview recorded in 1966 or an interview done twenty-six years later.

I saw that incision. I also saw the occipitoparietal head wound. When I am shown alleged autopsy photographs which depict wounds that differ so markedly from those I saw at Parkland, I have no choice but to conclude that someone had gone to a great deal of trouble to present a different story than we had seen at Parkland. The result of those wound differences caused the body of President Kennedy to appear more like it had been shot from the rear and less as if it had been shot from the front. [*Editor's note:* See Appendix A.]

Observing the Head Wound

The *JAMA* article seeks to minimize the significance of what we saw in Dallas by implying that the doctors were occupied with life-saving measures and did not have an opportunity to look at the head wound carefully: "In fact, Dr. Jenkins doubts if any of the Parkland physicians even had a good look at the President's head . . ."[61]

Once again, though, there's that pesky record:

- Dr. Kemp Clark—"I examined the wound in the back of the President's head."

- Dr. Robert McClelland—"As I took the position at the head of the table, I was in such a position that I could very closely examine the head wound."

- Dr. Jenkins was interviewed for an article in the *American Medical News* in 1978. In that article, Dr. Jenkins said, "It may be that I and Malcolm Perry MD) [sic] were the first ones aware of the head injury. We were standing at the patient's head and with that thick shock of hair, when he was lying supine on the stretcher, it really didn't show that he had part of his head blown away and part of his cerebellum was hanging out." This, once again, pinpoints the location of the wound at the rear of the head. Note also that in 1978, Dr. Jenkins still recalled the cerebellum—supposedly undamaged—as being blown out of the wound.

- At the Dallas forum last May, one of Jenkins' colleagues related an incident which further emphasizes that the head wound was seen and examined in Dallas. According to the account given there, the Parkland team considered opening President Kennedy's chest and massaging the heart in that manner. Dr. Jenkins then said, "Before you open that chest, you'd better step up and take a look at this head wound." The chest was not opened.[62]

There is ample evidence that we did see the head wound. *It is a simple fact that nearly every Dallas doctor, while under oath, was asked by the Warren Commission where the head wound was located. Each doctor placed the wound in the back of Kennedy's head. Not one of them said he did not know, could not remember, or did not have an opportunity to observe.*

Summary

Without ever having talked with me, *JAMA* Editor Dr. George Lundberg called my book, *JFK: Conspiracy of Silence*, "a sad fabrication based on unsubstantiated allegations."[63] In contrast, he proclaimed the *JAMA* article to be information which "is scientifically sound,"[64] furnishes "the definitive history of what happened,"[65] and "provides irrefutable proof that President Kennedy was killed by two bullets that struck him from above and behind."[66] The record, however, indicates otherwise.

1.   Drs. Perry, Carrico, Jenkins, and Baxter apparently chose to participate in an article in this magazine which distorted the facts of this case.

2.   These doctors had already created a record concerning the wounds of President Kennedy—a record that began just after they saw the body, a record sworn to under oath.

3.   Their record describes a large wound at the rear of President Kennedy's head, the same wound which I wrote about in *Conspiracy of Silence*.

4.   Their record describes a small wound in the front of the throat, just as I saw and described. One of the doctors (Perry) called this an entrance wound within two hours of seeing it, and another (Baxter) admitted in 1992 that it could have been an entrance wound.

5.   Their record describes cerebellar tissue extruding from the head wound, just as I described it in my book.

6.   Photographs of the back of President Kennedy's head show no wound where they (and I) saw a large wound. They say these photos are compatible with their observations. I say the autopsy photographs cannot be reconciled with what I saw at Parkland.

7.   Photographs of President Kennedy's throat show a defect more than twice as long as the tracheostomy incision I remember and more than twice the length these doctors had earlier estimated. They say the photograph is "very compatible" with what they saw at Parkland on November 22.

The record, standing in stark contrast to the statements the four doctors are quoted as having made in the May 1992 *JAMA* article, will not go away. It's a pity that Dennis Breo and *JAMA* chose to ignore that record.

Addendum: Arlen Specter and History's Most Hypothetical Question

When the various Parkland doctors appeared before the Warren Commission, their testimonies were taken by staff counsel Arlen Specter, now a United States Senator from Pennsylvania. The commission had a great problem concerning the throat wound, which all these doctors had seen and many had desribed as being very small, smooth-edged, and rounded—characteristics of an entrance wound. In fact, several of the doctors had called the wound an entrance wound by the time their statements were taken under oath in March of 1964. Instead of simply asking the doctors, "Was this an entrance wound or an exit wound?" or "What did this wound look like to you?", Specter concocted what must be the most convoluted and hypothetical question in history. This question with minor variations was put to each of the Dallas doctors who saw Kennedy's body.

> Specter: "Assuming some factors in addition to those which you personally observed, Dr. Baxter, what would your opinion be if these additional facts were present: First, the President had a bullet wound of entry on the right posterior thorax just above the upper border of the scapula with the wound measuring 7 by 7 mm in oval shape, being 14 cm from the tip of the right acromion process and 14 cm below the tip of the right mastoid process—assume this is the set of facts that the wound just described was caused by a 6.5 mm bullet shot from approximately 160 to 250 feet away from the President, from a weapon having a muzzle velocity of approximately 2,000 feet per second, assuming as a third factor that the bullet passed through the President's body, going in between the strap muscles of the shoulder without violating the pleura space and exited at a point in the midline of the neck, would the hole which you saw on the President's throat be consistent with an exit wound, assuming the factors which I have just given to you?"[67]

In this amazing, 180-word hypothetical question, Specter has asked the doctors, "If the bullet *exited* from the front of Kennedy's throat, could the wound in the front of Kennedy's throat have been an *exit* wound?" [*Editor's note:* See Chuck Marler, Part IV.]

Notes

1. *JFK: Conspiracy of Silence*, p. 77
2. *Ibid.*, pp. 84–85
3. *Ibid.*, pp. 82–86
4. *Ibid.*, p. 79
5. *Ibid.*, pp. 78–79; 86
6. *Journal of the American Medical Association* (hereafter cited as *JAMA*), 27 May 1992, p. 2794
7. *JAMA*, p. 2804
8. Citations are at various places through Volume 6 of *Warren Commission Hearings and Exhibits*.
9. *Warren Report*, p. 521
10. 6 H 11
11. 3 H 372
12. *House Select Committee on Assassinations* (hereafter cited as *HSCA*), Volume 7, p. 302.
13. *Ibid.*
14. White House 1327-C, 22 November 1963, (3:16 P.M.), p. 5
15. *Ibid.*, p. 6
16. *Boston Globe*, 24 November 1963, p. 9
17. 6 H 12
18. 3 H 377–378
19. *JAMA*, p. 2807
20. *Warren Report*, p. 530
21. *HSCA*, 7 H 287
22. *Warren Report*, p. 530
23. Jenkins has since stated that he "misspoke" when he called the tissue cerebellar tissue. Dr. Jenkins apparently was still "mis-speaking" fourteen years after the assassination when he was deposed by the HSCA. A summary of his deposition states, "He [Jenkins] noted that a portion of the cerebellum was hanging out from a hole in the right-rear of the head." And what is *JAMA*'s comment about Jenkins and the cerebellum? "Dr. Jenkins wrote in a 1963 report that Kennedy's 'cerebellum' had been blown out when he meant 'cerebrum.'"
24. *HSCA*, 7 H 287
25. *JAMA*, p. 2807
26. *Warren Report*, p. 519
27. 6 H 6
28. *HSCA*, 7 H 278
29. 6 H 3
30. 6 H 6
31. *HSCA*, 7 H 268
32. 3 H 361–362
33. 3 H 362
34. 6 H 44
35. *Ibid.*
36. 6 H 42
37. *Ibid.*
38. *Ibid.*
39. *Ibid.*
40. *20-20*, ABC-TV, 3 May 1992
41. *Warren Report*, p. 517
42. 6 H 20
43. 6 H 29
44. 6 H 71
45. 6 H 53
46. 6 H 65
47. 6 H 33
48. *Warren Report*, p. 525
49. 6 H 20
50. 6 H 26
51. 6 H 71
52. 20 H 333
53. CE–387, *Warren Report*, p. 543
54. *JAMA*, p. 2805
55. CE–387, *Warren Report*, p. 541
56. *HSCA*, 7 H 107
57. CE–387, *Warren Report*, p. 540
58. *HSCA*, 7 H 125-127
59. CE–391, *Warren Report*, pp. 544–545
60. *HSCA*, 7 H 129
61. Forum in Dallas, Texas, June 4, 1992. Video and audio recordings were made of these proceedings and copies were promised. As of this writing, I have not been able to obtain them, but various persons who attended made notes and also made personal audio recordings of the events.
62. See this article, "Dr. Malcolm Perry"; "Dr. Marion Jenkins"; and, "Dr. James Carrico."

[63] CE–387, *Warren Report*, p. 540

[64] 2 H 361

[65] *JAMA*, p. 2805

[66] *Ibid.*

[67] *Ibid.*

[68] *Ibid.*

[69] Recorded interview, 11 November 1966.

[70] Recorded interview, 11 November 1966.

[71] *JAMA*, p. 2805

[72] 6 H 20

[73] 6 H 33

[74] "At Parkland Hospital tragic memories remain", *American Medical News*, November 24, 1978, p. 14.

[75] Dallas Forum, 4 June 1993. (See #83 above.)

[76] *New York Times*, 20 May 1992, p. B7

[77] *JAMA*, p. 2803

[78] *Larry King Live*, CNN-TV, 21 May 1992

[79] *JAMA*, p. 2803

[80] 6 H 42

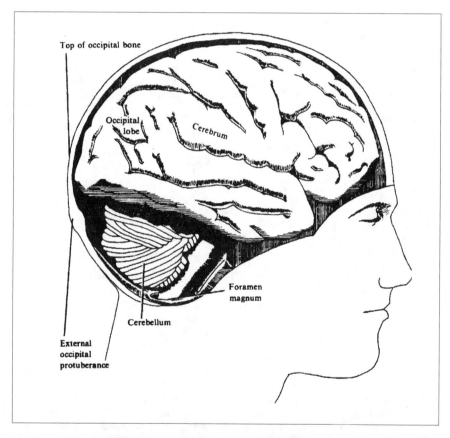

Relationship of cerebellum and cerebrum within the cranium.
[Editor's note: See David Lifton, Best Evidence *(1980),*
Chapter 13, especially page 323.]

On the Trail of the Character Assassins[1]

D. Bradley Kizzia, J.D.

On 22 November 1963, Charles Crenshaw, M.D., was a resident surgeon at Parkland Hospital in Dallas, Texas. As fate would have it, he became an involuntary eyewitness to history when President Kennedy was assassinated that day and brought to Parkland for emergency treatment. Dr. Crenshaw was a member of the trauma team that heroically attempted to save President Kennedy's life by administering the medical techniques for which they were trained. Dr. Crenshaw arrived in Trauma Room 1 with Dr. Robert McClelland and saw the small wound in President Kennedy's throat immediately before Dr. Malcolm Perry used a scalpel to perform a tracheostomy, and during the course of the emergency medical measures and thereafter, Dr. Crenshaw observed the large wound in the back of President Kennedy's head that was described in the contemporaneous medical reports of several of the other physicians on the Parkland trauma team, including Dr. Kemp Clark, the neurosurgeon who pronounced President Kennedy dead. It was Dr. Crenshaw's impression at the time (as well as the express impression of some of the other doctors in Trauma Room One at the time) that the small wound in President Kennedy's throat was a wound of entrance, and the large wound in the back of President Kennedy's head was a wound of exit. Indeed, later on the afternoon of November 22nd, Dr. Perry and Dr. Clark attended a press conference at which time Dr. Perry clearly indicated that he thought the throat wound was a wound of entrance. (Dr. Perry reiterated that opin-

ion in interviews given in the subsequent days following the assassination.) [*Editor's note:* See Appendix C.]

Two days later, on Sunday, 24 November 1963, Dr. Crenshaw happened to be on duty and therefore participated on the trauma team that
tried to save Lee Harvey Oswald's life, after he was brought there following his assassination by Jack Ruby. While involved in the treatment of
Oswald, Dr. Crenshaw accepted a telephone call to the operating room
from a man who identified himself as President Lyndon Johnson. Dr.
Crenshaw was told to relay the message to the other physicians who
were treating Oswald that FBI agents would be available in the operating room to obtain a death-bed confession from Oswald.

Dr. Crenshaw was, therefore, in a unique position with eyewitness
knowledge of some of the most incredible events in United States history. Still, he did not seek the spotlight at that time mainly for reasons
related to his ambition and career-mindedness. Indeed, all of the Parkland
trauma physicians had been specifically warned in clear terms not to try
to exploit their involvement in those historic events at Parkland in November 1963. Dr. Crenshaw thereafter went on to have a distinguished
career as the head of surgery at John Peter Smith Hospital in Fort Worth,
Texas, where he established the Trauma Unit. Twenty-five years later,
however, Dr. Crenshaw suffered two minor strokes that affected his surgical proficiency, thereby leading to his retirement. At that time, he was
approached by a writer who was an acquaintance, Jens Hansen, about
publishing his eyewitness account of the historical events at Parkland
Hospital on that fateful weekend in November 1963. Dr. Crenshaw was
initially reluctant, but ultimately agreed and collaborated with J. Gary
Shaw, a widely recognized expert researcher on the JFK assassination,
to write the book, *JFK: Conspiracy of Silence.*[2] In the book, Dr. Crenshaw
provided his personal account, as an eyewitness to history, about what
happened at Parkland Hospital, and Gary Shaw contributed the setting
and surrounding events related to the assassination and its subsequent
investigation. The book, *JFK: Conspiracy of Silence*, was published in
April 1992, and benefited from the publicity and renewed public interest
in the subject of President Kennedy's assassination that had been generated in preceding months by the release of Oliver Stone's movie, *JFK*.
The book was quickly a success and rose to the top of *The New York
Times* Bestseller List for paperbacks. (Because of the importance of Dr.
Crenshaw's observations that were contained in the book—the first publication by one of the treating physicians that emphatically disagreed
with the Warren Commission's conclusion that President Kennedy was
shot by one gunman from behind—the book's authors thought that the

book would have more widespread dissemination in the less expensive paperback form, as opposed to a hardback version that could have been sold for more money.) Of course, there were some longstanding supporters of the Warren Commission and its lone-gunman theory, including some members of the established media, who questioned Dr. Crenshaw's motives for publishing his observations nearly thirty years after the assassination, but the usual less than enthusiastic treatment by some of the media and Warren Commission apologists was to be expected. The events of May, 1992, and particularly the involvement of the *Journal of the American Medical Association*, however, was not anticipated.

On 19 May 1992, the American Medical Association hosted a press conference in New York City to promote two related articles in *JAMA*'s May 27th edition concerning the assassination of President Kennedy. At the press conference, Dr. Lundberg alleged that Dr. Crenshaw's book was a "sad fabrication based upon unsubstantiated allegations." Mr. Dennis Breo, a *JAMA* writer, was identified as the author of the articles, which erroneously suggested that Dr. Crenshaw's observations, as contained in his book, should not be relied upon because Dr. Crenshaw may not have even been in Parkland Hospital's Trauma Room 1 at the time that emergency treatment was provided to President Kennedy. The press conference received massive media attention, and the *JAMA* articles were widely disseminated. References to the press conference and the *JAMA* articles were even made on the network news and on the front pages of major newspapers across the country.

On May 20, 1992, the day after the *JAMA* press conference, *The New York Times* published an article written by Lawrence Altman, M.D., describing *JAMA*'s "research [as] less than thorough," and pointing out that testimony to the Warren Commission clearly indicated that Dr. Crenshaw had been in Trauma Room 1 and participated in the efforts to save President Kennedy. Dr. Crenshaw thereafter requested *JAMA* to publish a retraction and apology. This request was denied, but Dr. Crenshaw was encouraged to submit his own piece for publication in *JAMA*, which he did. Dr. Crenshaw's rebuttal piece, entitled "Let's Set the Record Straight: Dr. Charles Crenshaw Replies," [3] was refused publication by *JAMA* as allegedly being too long (even though it was barely one half the length of Mr. Breo's articles in the 27 May 1992 issue of *JAMA*); but Dr. Crenshaw was then encouraged by *JAMA* to submit a 500-word letter to the editor. Although believing that a mere 500-word letter would be insufficient to rectify the damage done to his reputation, Dr. Crenshaw nevertheless did submit a 500-word letter to the editor of *JAMA*; but again, *JAMA* did not publish it.[4] In April, 1993, almost a year after the publication of the

JAMA articles that attacked Dr. Crenshaw and the book, *JFK: Conspiracy of Silence*, after no apology, retraction, or even correction or clarification having been published by *JAMA*, litigation was instituted.

The Suit

Gary Shaw, being a co-author of the book that had been called a "sad fabrication" by Dr. Lundberg, *JAMA*'s editor, was joined as a Plaintiff in the case. Mr. Shaw was a resident of Cleburne, Johnson County, Texas. Because the court dockets in Johnson County are not as congested as those in Tarrant County, where Dr. Crenshaw resides, the lawsuit was filed in Johnson County. The suit was filed against the American Medical Association, d/b/a *Journal of the American Medical Association*, George Lundberg, M.D., Dennis Breo, and others, in the 18th District Court of Cleburne, Johnson County, Texas, in Cause No. 73–93. The pleadings filed on behalf of Dr. Crenshaw and Mr. Shaw made the following factual allegations:

> This is a case about the abuse of media power, the violation of journalistic ethics, and the harm perpetrated against individuals in an effort to silence them.

> Good name in man and woman, dear my lord,
> Is the immediate jewel of their souls;
> Who steals my purse steals trash; 'tis something, nothing;
> Twas mine, 'tis his, and has been slave to thousands;
> But he that filches from me my good name
> Robs me of that which not enriches him,
> And makes me poor indeed.
> — Othello (1602–4) act 3, sc. 3, 1.155

Following the release of the movie *JFK* in the late fall of 1991, Warren Commission apologists like David Belin (the self-proclaimed most knowledgeable person in the world about the JFK assassination) embarked upon a crusade, which included a nationwide campaign to attack the movie *JFK* and those allegedly associated with the movie, including critics of the Warren Report like Dr. Crenshaw and Mr. Shaw. Such campaign made frequent use of the media, including appearances on television and publication of written pieces in the print media across the country. Despite the fact (and perhaps due to the fact) that polls unanimously indicated that the overwhelming majority of Americans disagree with the Warren Report, the usual tactic of such Warren Commission supporters has been to personally attack such Warren Report critics, besmirching their reputations and integrity and calling them liars and profiteers. The *Dallas Morning News* was one of the media outlets that provided a welcome forum for such attacks.

Contemporaneously with the campaign to attack those associated with the movie *JFK* and other Warren Report critics, George Lundberg, who is and was editor-in-chief of *JAMA*, embarked upon an effort to utilize the pages of *JAMA* to respond to the movie *JFK* and, in his words, "to set the record straight," under the guise of "objective," "scientific," "peer-reviewed," medical research. (In truth, the resulting defamatory *JAMA* articles were none of these things.) Indeed, Lundberg himself certainly was not objective or detached, since he was a personal friend of some of his interviewees and had a personal agenda. (Lundberg was even pictured and praised in the same *JAMA* articles.) It was the intent of Lundberg, *JAMA*, and Breo (their writer) to utilize the seemingly credible and legitimate forum of *JAMA*, as well as the media and public relations apparatus of the AMA, to try to win back public opinion, silence the critics of the Warren Report, and terminate further discussion of the JFK assassination conspiracy controversy.

Dr. Crenshaw was a surgical resident who participated on the trauma team at Parkland Hospital and in the efforts to save the life of President Kennedy on 22 November 1963. Two days later, on 24 November 1963, Dr. Crenshaw was also on the trauma team at Parkland that tried to save the life of Lee Harvey Oswald. Later, Dr. Crenshaw became and served as Chief of Surgery for John Peter Smith Hospital in Fort Worth, Texas. More recently Dr. Crenshaw stepped down as the active head of surgery at John Peter Smith Hospital, and, along with Mr. Shaw, co-authored the book *JFK: Conspiracy of Silence*, published in the spring of 1992. Because bringing this important information to the public was their paramount concern, the book was printed in paperback only and sold inexpensively.

The book *JFK: Conspiracy of Silence* contains a rendition of Dr. Crenshaw's observations, as an eyewitness to history, regarding events that occurred at Parkland Hospital on that fateful weekend in November, 1963. In the book, Dr. Crenshaw reported that he, along with other medical personnel at Parkland Hospital, observed a small wound of entrance in President Kennedy's throat and a large wound of exit in the rear of President Kennedy's head. These observations by Dr. Crenshaw regarding the nature and location of President Kennedy's wounds were consistent with the reports and testimony provided by other medical personnel who were also present in the Parkland emergency room on 22 November 1963. Dr. Crenshaw also expressed the opinion in his book that such observations regarding the nature and location of President Kennedy's wounds were consistent with shots having been fired from the front of President Kennedy's limousine, an opinion that is inconsistent with conclusions stated in the Warren Report. Thus, Dr. Crenshaw and Mr. Shaw became, along with those associated with the movie *JFK*, additional targets of the campaign of the Warren Commission apologists to refute points made in *JFK* and to discredit critics of the Warren Report. Indeed, because of the timing of the release and initially favorable public reaction to their book, the *Journal of the American Medical Association*, Lundberg, and Breo expanded the scope of their scheme to include attacks upon Dr. Crenshaw and Mr. Shaw.

In April 1992, Mr. Belin traveled to Dallas, Texas, to make one of his many speeches attacking critics of the Warren Report. Apparently on the same trip, he met with representatives of *The Dallas Morning News*. During that meeting, Belin wrongfully attacked critics of the Warren Report as persons "who tell lies about the assassination," "assassination sensationalists," and he accused persons, like Dr. Crenshaw and Mr. Shaw, of "assassination profiteering." Belin even falsely claimed that Dr. Crenshaw "typifies the disinformation." At or around the same time of Belin's meeting with *The Dallas Morning News*, Lundberg and Breo were working on their defamatory articles to be published in *JAMA* on 27 May 1992. On 17 May 1992, *The Dallas Morning News* published excerpts from the "interview" with Belin, including some of Belin's defamatory remarks. However, the lengthy interview was substantially reduced and questions were fabricated or altered by *The News* to focus the published excerpts on Belin's attacks on Dr. Crenshaw and his book.

On 18 May 1992, Lundberg and Breo traveled to New York City to finalize plans and prepare for a large media event conceived by Lundberg. At Lundberg's request, a press conference was to be held in New York City concerning the defamatory *JAMA* articles, because it was believed that more media publicity would be generated in New York. On that same date, other representatives of the AMA, working for Lundberg and *JAMA*, made numerous contacts with members of the media to build up the press conference scheduled for the next day.

On 19 May 1992, *JAMA*, Lundberg, and Breo, conducted and/or participated in a well-planned, well-orchestrated, major press conference for the media in New York City, which was attended by many representatives of the print and television media, including the major television networks and representatives of the national print media. The purpose of the press conference was to generate as much media attention as possible in order to publicize and promote the defamatory *JAMA* articles and the attacks on Dr. Crenshaw and the book. Said plan was successful, in that the press conference was well attended and covered by the media, and news reports concerning the press conference and the defamatory *JAMA* articles were publicized across the nation. *Lundberg even stood behind a podium or lectern that contained the official AMA seal, logo, or emblem, so that photographs and videos taken of Lundberg during the press conference would show the AMA seal, logo, or emblem. The result was to give the false impression that Lundberg's statements were made on behalf of the AMA or at least with the endorsement of the AMA, when in truth, none of what Lundberg, Breo, or JAMA said or published at the press conference or in the defamatory JAMA articles were the official position of the AMA, nor were such statements endorsed by the AMA.* As part of this well-orchestrated media blitz, Lundberg gave an interview with a reporter for *The Dallas Morning News* on 19 May 1992, and on 20 May 1992, *The Dallas Morning News* published a front page article concerning the press conference and the defamatory *JAMA* articles and the attacks on Dr. Crenshaw and the book, erroneously referring to Mr. Breo's articles as "the AMA report."

During the press conference on 19 May 1992, Lundberg, in writing and orally, falsely described the book as a "sad fabrication based upon unsubstantiated allegations." Lundberg further claimed that the motivations for those millions of Americans, like Plaintiffs, who believe that there was a conspiracy behind the assassination of President Kennedy, "are paranoia, desire for personal recognition and public visibility, and profit," and he suggested that the press conference and defamatory *JAMA* articles might silence "the honest conspiracy theorists who have simply not had access to the [alleged] facts." Lundberg further stated the "hope" that by virtue of the press conference and defamatory *JAMA* articles, "the entire current generation that has been fed docufiction on this matter as if it were truth will cease to be misled."

Breo, at the 19 May 1992 press conference and in the articles that he wrote for the 27 May 1992 edition of *JAMA*, sought to discredit the book by wrongfully attacking the integrity of its authors, including the false suggestions that Dr. Crenshaw was not even present when the emergency treatment was provided to President Kennedy at Parkland Hospital on 22 November 1963, that Dr. Crenshaw was supposedly not mentioned in the testimony to the Warren Commission, that Dr. Crenshaw's descriptions of the nature and locations of President Kennedy's wounds were inconsistent with the descriptions given by all of the other medical personnel who saw the wounds, and that no telephone call was received at Parkland Hospital from someone claiming to be President Lyndon Johnson when Lee Harvey Oswald was given emergency treatment there on 24 November 1963. Breo also accused Dr. Crenshaw and Mr. Shaw of being "defamers of the truth" in the defamatory articles published by *JAMA* on 27 May 1992. All of these accusations were and are false. In truth, at least five different witnesses specifically testified to the Warren Commission about Dr. Crenshaw's presence and participation in the efforts to save President Kennedy on 22 November 1963, facts readily available to Lundberg and Breo since the testimony appeared in one of the Warren Commission Report volumes, which also included an index that listed Dr. Crenshaw and the seven references to him in the testimony. Also, numerous witnesses who observed President Kennedy's wounds on 22 November 1963, have described them in a way consistent with the observations of Dr. Crenshaw. Many of these descriptions were also clearly revealed in the testimony to the Warren Commission, some of which appears in the same volume that refers to Dr. Crenshaw, and in reports by Parkland physicians that were in the summary volume that Breo claims that he read. Additionally, other witnesses who were present at Parkland Hospital on 24 November 1963, recall the telephone call from someone claiming to be President Johnson.

The defamatory *JAMA* articles that were authored by Breo, edited by Lundberg, and published in *JAMA* on 27 May 1992, were masterfully conceived, slickly written, and cleverly worded to give the superficial impression of being based on scientific research. In truth, the articles were deceptive and in fact, were not objective or well researched; they were not even scientific or subjected to outside peer review. Lundberg was clearly not objective, and Breo was obviously not knowledgeable about the evidence related to the JFK assassination (probably by design). Indeed, no expert on the JFK assassination at all reviewed the defamatory *JAMA* articles before publication. The articles did, however, successfully accomplish the purpose of creating false impressions regarding Dr. Crenshaw and his book.

The false accusations made by *JAMA*, Lundberg, and Breo concerning Dr. Crenshaw and the book were also all made without any attempt by them to even interview or talk with either Dr. Crenshaw or Mr. Shaw, which resulted in the one-sided, biased, and inaccurate stories that occurred. (Of course, if they had bothered to interview Dr. Crenshaw and Mr. Shaw, they would also have been referred to the Warren Commission testimony regarding Dr. Crenshaw's presence in Trauma Room 1 and of the witnesses with knowledge about the LBJ phone call, which would have deprived them of their ability to later claim lack of knowledge of such information, i.e., plausible deniability.) The fact that they had failed even to try to interview Dr. Crenshaw was pointed out in an article written by Dr. Lawrence K. Altman, published in *The New York Times* on Wednesday, 20 May 1992, the day after the *JAMA* press conference. Dr. Altman's article also pointed out additional errors in the statements concerning Dr. Crenshaw. Dr. Altman wrote:

> But the full [Warren] report makes several references to Dr. Crenshaw. In two, Dr. Charles R. Baxter and Dr. Robert McClelland, two of the Dallas doctors interviewed by Mr. Breo, told the Warren Commission that Dr. Crenshaw was in the emergency room.

(Indeed, Dr. McClelland had told Breo the same thing, yet Breo and *JAMA* failed to mention that, but instead published the false statements to the contrary.) On 26 May 1992, *The New York Times* published a second article by Dr. Altman, in which he pointed out additional errors in *JAMA*'s accusations concerning Dr. Crenshaw. Dr. Altman wrote:

> The merit of the book aside, it turns out that the journal's research was less than thorough. It did not try to interview Dr. Crenshaw. Although the Dallas doctors [allegedly] told the journal they never saw Dr. Crenshaw in the Kennedy trauma room, two actually had told the Warren Commission that he was a member of the team. ...Dr. Crenshaw was also on the team that tried to resuscitate Lee Harvey Oswald after the assassin was shot, and one of Dr. Crenshaw's most astonishing assertions is that he answered a call from the new President Lyndon B. Johnson, who asked about Oswald's condition. ...In the journal interviews, Dr. Charles Baxter, the emergency room chief, denied that such a call was received by any doctor. But the denial came from a surgeon who could not have known about the call because he was not present during Oswald's surgery, Dr. Crenshaw said. Indeed, another doctor has confirmed such a call, although the details and who made it are not clear. The doctor... said he had long remembered reports of two White House telephone calls to the operating room.

Both of Dr. Altman's articles that were published in *The New York Times* were made available and/or received by *JAMA*, Lundberg, and Breo *before* the 27 May 1992 official publication date of the *JAMA* edition that contained the defamatory articles written by Breo. Breo, on Lundberg's orders, even researched the criticisms leveled by Dr. Altman and confirmed that they were justified, yet no effort whatsoever was made by *JAMA* to retract or correct the errors before or after publication. Additionally, *JAMA* received complaints via telephone calls and letters from

members of the American Medical Association and other knowledgeable
readers again citing the false and defamatory statements made about
Dr. Crenshaw in the *JAMA* articles, yet the false statements were never
retracted or corrected by *JAMA*. Instead, Mark Stuart (the director of
AMA's media/public relations office in New York City) responded to one
such complaint by calling the book "a pack of lies." Furthermore, in reply to a letter to *JAMA* that criticized *JAMA* and Breo for falsely suggesting that Dr. Crenshaw was not even present in Parkland's Trauma Room 1
when President Kennedy was treated, Breo quoted from the defamatory
remarks that he had made at the 19 May 1992 press conference:

> For years the American public has been hearing from *people who were not in
> Trauma Room 1 in Dallas* and were not in the autopsy room at Bethesda
> [Maryland], and yet, who have claimed to know what must have happened
> during the medical care of President Kennedy. What we *now* have are the
> reports of the physicians *who were on the scene* ... We *now* have the facts
> about these critical events in the words of *the only people who know these
> facts*—the very facts that the conspiracy theorists have chosen to ignore. (Em-
> phasis added.)

These defamatory remarks were republished by *JAMA* on 7 October 1992,
long after Lundberg, its editor, and Breo, its writer, were fully aware of
the evidence that Dr. Crenshaw was indeed on the scene and in Trauma
Room 1 when President Kennedy was taken to Parkland on 22 November 1963.

Subsequently, the defamatory *JAMA* articles were even reprinted and
redistributed by *JAMA* long after *JAMA* knew them to contain false statements concerning Dr. Crenshaw and his book. One such reprint was sent,
along with a "News Release," to ABC's *Good Morning America* program
in an apparent attempt to sabotage Dr. Crenshaw's appearance there.
JAMA, Lundberg, and Breo have not been able to identify a single other
article published in *JAMA* where any other physician was attacked and
treated in a manner similar to that perpetrated against Dr. Crenshaw in
the defamatory articles in question.

Consistent with *The Dallas Morning News'* biased and unfair coverage of news concerning the JFK assassination (which coverage has fa-
vored Warren Report supporters like Belin, Lundberg, and Breo, and
disfavored witnesses and researchers who have been critical of the Warren Report), *The Dallas Morning News* published an editorial on 24 May
1992 (prior to the official 27 May 1992, publication date of the defamatory
JAMA articles), that praised and commended the *JAMA* articles and those
who were supposedly quoted therein in a way that allegedly confirmed

the conclusions of the Warren Commission. In contrast, the editorial criticized "those who have profited by writing Kennedy assassination books heavy on paranoia and light on facts," and who espouse "hysterical conspiracy claims" and who "irresponsibly seeks to distort the record," all language coincidentally similar to the remarks made by Lundberg at the *JAMA* press conference in New York City a few days earlier.

The Dallas Morning News obtained copies of the *JAMA* articles in advance of publication and provided same to its writer, Lawrence Sutherland, for purposes of writing another article attacking Dr. Crenshaw and his book. This article was published by *The Dallas Morning News* on 28 June 1992. In that article, Sutherland relied heavily upon the defamatory *JAMA* articles and falsely described the book as "peddling lies" and wrongfully attacked Dr. Crenshaw's credibility, even though he never interviewed Dr. Crenshaw or co-author Shaw, in contrast to written policy of *The Dallas Morning News*. Sutherland accused Dr. Crenshaw of lying when he described a large wound that he observed in the back of President Kennedy's head, even though Sutherland knew that other physicians at Parkland had described the wound similarly. Without bothering to interview any other witnesses either, Sutherland and *The Dallas Morning News* republished some of the other false allegations contained in the defamatory *JAMA* articles (see above), that is, that Dr. Crenshaw and Mr. Shaw supposedly made up Dr. Crenshaw's important observations for alleged personal gain and that the phone call to Parkland Hospital on 24 November 1992, by someone claiming to be LBJ supposedly never happened. In July 1992, shortly after publication of the defamatory Sutherland article, a letter was written to *The Dallas Morning News* by the former chief telephone operator at Parkland Hospital, who confirmed Dr. Crenshaw's recollection concerning the telephone call to Parkland on 24 November 1963 by someone claiming to be LBJ; yet *The Dallas Morning News* refused publication of the letter, and Sutherland and *The Dallas Morning News* failed and refused to retract the false statements in the article concerning that point.

The defamatory *JAMA* articles referred to above were published and distributed to hundreds of thousands of Dr. Crenshaw's peers in the AMA, and through the media and otherwise, to millions of readers, listeners, and viewers. The defamatory publications in *The Dallas Morning News* were published and distributed to hundreds of thousands, if not millions, of subscribers and readers of *The News*, it being the only major daily newspaper published in Dallas. The defamatory Belin interview, editorial, and Sutherland article were each published in Sunday editions of *The News*, which had the paper's largest daily circulation—in excess of 800,000.

Dr. Crenshaw attempted to respond to the defamatory attacks upon him by holding a press conference in June 1992, in Washington, D.C., but the press conference was not well attended by the media and received little or no coverage. Neither *JAMA* nor *The News* published anything about Dr. Crenshaw's response.

None of the attackers bothered to even try to interview Dr. Crenshaw or Mr. Shaw before making their false and defamatory accusations. Furthermore, Dr. Crenshaw and Mr. Shaw sought retractions from *JAMA* and *The News* before instituting litigation, but were refused. Moreover, they submitted a rebuttal article to Defendant *JAMA*, which was denied publication. Instead, it was suggested by *JAMA* that a letter to the editor be submitted (with a 500-word limitation). Dr. Crenshaw complied with this request, but publication of the letter to the editor of *JAMA* was then also refused by *JAMA*.

On or about 9 February 1992, *The Dallas Morning News* did agree to publish Dr. Crenshaw and Mr. Shaw's rebuttal article, but after it was prepared and sent to *The Dallas Morning News*, *The News* reneged on the agreement and refused to publish the rebuttal article. However, on Sunday, 18 April 1993, *The Dallas Morning News* did publish in the "Corrections, Clarifications" portion of the paper the following: "it was not the intent of *The News* to suggest that the book authors misstated the facts of Dr. Crenshaw's involvement as a physician at Parkland Memorial Hospital attending President Kennedy on 22 November 1963, and Lee Harvey Oswald on 24 November 1963, or that they had done so out of a motive for profit or any improper purpose." Such correction or clarification was contained among other self-serving language that tended to offset its mitigating effect. Such publication was also too little too late.

Furthermore, *The Dallas Morning News* later indicated that an edited rebuttal article would be published only if Dr. Crenshaw and Mr. Shaw released their claims for damages caused by Sutherland and *The News*. Even later, *JAMA* indicated that it might publish a retraction only if Dr. Crenshaw and Mr. Shaw dismissed their suit to recover for the damages already caused to them. The reality is that Dr. Crenshaw and Mr. Shaw have suffered damages resulting from the foregoing defamations, which subjected them to public hatred, scorn, and ridicule, with resulting embarrassment and humiliation, and loss of book sales (Dr. Crenshaw's book was knocked from the bestsellers' list), damages for which *JAMA*, *The News*, Lundberg and Breo have refused to make amends.

The Discovery

During the course of the litigation, depositions were taken of Mr. Breo, his immediate editor, Dr. Richard Glass, Dr. Lundberg, Dr. Drummond Rennie, who was in charge of *JAMA*'s letters to the editor, and three public relations employees for the AMA, Mark Stuart, Jeff Moulter, and Paul Torini. These depositions, as well as documents that *JAMA* was obligated to produce in connection with those depositions, provided significant evidence to support the suit against the *JAMA* Defendants. The deposition testimony and documents also revealed troubling information about *JAMA*'s coverage of the JFK assassination topic.

Dr. Lundberg, *JAMA*'s editor, has acknowledged that he is no expert on the JFK assassination. He has stated:

> I wasn't in Dallas or Bethesda those days. I am really not much of an expert on this at all. My role in this is that of a journalist along with Mr. Dennis Breo of my *JAMA* staff. I have essentially no primary source of information, nor do I plan any.

Thus, when Dr. Lundberg decided to use the pages of *JAMA* to respond to the movie *JFK*, he called upon his friend, Dr. James Humes, one of the autopsists at Bethesda Naval Hospital on the evening of 22 November 1963. On 26 December 1991, Dr. Lundberg wrote:

> Dear Jim, Have you seen the movie *JFK*? Three hours and fifteen minutes of truth mixed with non-truth mixed with alleged truth. For the younger person, not knowledgeable about 1963—very difficult to tell the difference. *Please* either write the truth now for *JAMA* or let Dennis Breo (and me?) interview you (and Bosworth [sic]) soon to set the record straight—at least about the autopsy. O.k.? Best wishes, George.

Thus, Dr. Lundberg's own letter indicates that there was an agenda prior to publication of the *JAMA* articles in May 1992—"To Set the Record Straight." (Lundberg apparently misspelled Dr. Boswell's name as "Bosworth.")

In a news release publicizing Breo's JFK articles, the AMA publicity department claimed that Humes and Boswell agreed to talk to *JAMA* "their first-ever public discussion of the case—because the interview was to appear in a peer-reviewed, scientific journal." This declaration was, at best, misleading. First of all, both Humes and Boswell had previously testified to the Warren Commission and before the House Select Committee on Assassinations (the latter investigation resulted in a report very critical of Humes and Boswell's autopsy and reached the conclusion that

President Kennedy was probably assassinated through a conspiracy). Also, the "interview" with Drs. Humes and Boswell was not published in *JAMA*, nor released at the May 19th press conference in New York City as claimed in the press release. Rather, Mr. Breo's articles based in part upon such interviews were published in *JAMA*, copies of which were disseminated at the press conference.

Furthermore, the press release suggested that the articles were "peer-reviewed" and "scientific." This was not the case. First, according to *JAMA*, the articles were written by Dennis Breo, who is not a medical doctor, nor a scientist by any means. In his sworn deposition testimony, Mr. Breo claimed that the articles that he wrote on the JFK assassination "were a work of journalism," not scientific articles, and therefore were not submitted for outside peer review. Indeed, Mr. Breo described himself as "illiterate about the peer review process," and stated that there is a different process for articles submitted by *JAMA* writers like himself.

> Well, the journalists, the staff journalists on *JAMA*, just write articles that are reviewed by their editors and that's—there is no outside review.

> Q. No peer review?
> A. No.

Curiously, Mr. Breo, like Dr. Lundberg, was no expert on the subject of the JFK assassination. He testified under oath as follows:

> By Mr. Kizzia:
> Q. Well, let me ask you this. Can you say for sure that prior to 1992 you had read any books pertaining to the JFK assassination?
> A. I can't say for sure. I mean, it was not a burning interest of mine.

Indeed, Mr. Breo apparently did not even know much about Dr. Crenshaw or his book before writing the articles that attacked both. Excerpts from Mr. Breo's sworn deposition testimony include the following:

> Q. Is it true, Mr. Breo, that you believe that face-to-face interviews are preferable because they're more effective?
> A. Normally, yes, I found that to be the case.
> Q. And you normally do face-to-face interviews; is that right?
> A. Yes.
> Q. Isn't it true, Mr. Breo, that prior to writing that article you had not sat down and talked to Dr. Crenshaw?
> A. That's correct.
> Q. You did not interview him; is that right?
> A. I did not.

Q. Just yes or no, sir. Did you read the 26 volumes of testimony to see if Dr. Crenshaw was mentioned in there prior to writing the articles?

A. No.

Q. Do you know whether any of the other AMA employees or representatives who were involved in the press conference had read Dr. Crenshaw's book prior to the press conference?

A. Those involved in the press conference?

Q. Yes, sir.

A. I don't know. My belief [is] they had not.

The editor of *JAMA*, Dr. Lundberg, was also apparently lacking in knowledge about Dr. Crenshaw and his book before making his derogatory statements at the May 19, 1992, press conference. The following are excerpts from Dr. Lundberg's sworn deposition testimony:

Q. Did you try to find out anything about Dr. Crenshaw before you made your remarks at the press conference in New York City on May 19th, 1992?

A. I did not.

Q. Did you know that Mr. Breo had not—not only had not interviewed Dr. Crenshaw, had not even tried to interview Dr. Crenshaw before you—before he wrote his articles that were published in *JAMA* on May 27th, 1992?

A. Yes. I knew that.

Q. Can you state here today under oath that you know for a fact that you had received the copy of the book [*JFK: Conspiracy of Silence*] . . . before the press conference on May 19th, 1992?

A. I've testified that I do not remember what date I received it, so I cannot testify for a fact as to when I received it since I don't recall.

Q. As far as you know, had any employee or representative of the AMA or *JAMA* done any research to find out about Dr. Crenshaw and his background, credentials, and accomplishments?

A. I don't know.

Q. When did you first learn that Mr. Breo did not intend to or had not tried to interview Dr. Crenshaw?

A. I suppose in April—My best recollection is April, 1992.

Q. How was it brought to your attention that he did not try to interview Dr. Crenshaw or that he did not intend to try to interview Dr. Crenshaw?

A. I believe he told me.

Q. What did he tell you?

A. That he was not going to interview Dr. Crenshaw.

Q. Do you know whether or not Mr. Breo did any research into Dr. Crenshaw's involvement on the Parkland trauma team on November 22nd, 1963?

> A. I do not know.
> Q. Did you yourself do any research?
> A. I did not.

In view of the lack of expertise and scholarly research within *JAMA* concerning the JFK assassination in general, and Dr. Crenshaw and his book in particular, one wonders why the Breo articles were not submitted to outside experts for review before publication, particularly publication in a journal that was described as "peer reviewed" and "scientific." However, when asked about this, Mr. Breo's immediate editor, Richard M. Glass, M.D., stated in his sworn deposition as follows:

> Q. Was there any consideration given to submitting Mr. Breo's articles to some outside review?
> A. No. That just wouldn't have been the process for journalism articles.

Perhaps the truth was just not that important to *JAMA*. The following are additional excerpts from the sworn deposition testimony of Dr. Lundberg:

> Q. Was there an intent on your part, or as editor of *JAMA* on *JAMA's* part, to create the impression through the second article that Dr. Crenshaw was not on the trauma team that tried to save President Kennedy's life?
> A. No.
> Q. Was it important to you as editor of *JAMA* to try to avoid creating that impression?
> A. No.
> Q. Did you do anything to try to verify whether or not what Dr. Altman said about the testimony of physicians to the Warren Commission concerning Dr. Crenshaw's involvement on the trauma team?
> A. Yes.
> Q. What did you do to verify that?
> A. I asked Mr. Breo to check into whether somewhere in one of those volumes of the Warren Commission whether that was there.
> Q. You didn't do it yourself?
> A. I did not.
> Q. Did Mr. Breo report back to you?
> A. He did.
> Q. And what did he tell you?
> A. He said that there were some mentions of Crenshaw's name in some of the volumes at the Warren Commission.
> Q. Did you give any consideration to publishing a clarification on that point?
> A. No.

Q. Why not?

A. We don't publish clarifications.

Q. Did you give any consideration to publishing a correction on that point?

A. Yes.

Q. Was that around the time of your having read Dr. Altman's article in May 1992?

A. Yes.

Q. Why did you ask Mr. Breo to go check to see if Dr. Crenshaw was mentioned in testimony before the Warren Commission?

A. To see if he was.

Q. Why did you want to know?

A. To see whether there had been such testimony and whether Dr. Altman's statement was correct.

Q. It turned out that there had been that testimony?

A. According to what Mr. Breo told me.

Q. Which in your mind verified what Dr. Altman had said?

A. Yes.

Q. So what, if anything, did you do with this information you received from Mr. Breo to verify that point made by Dr. Altman?

A. I reviewed what Mr. Breo had written in his article and determined that it was factually correct as stated and did not warrant a correction or a retraction.

Although Mr. Breo stated in the second part of the JFK articles that "some suspect that Crenshaw was not even in the trauma room," when asked about that under oath, Mr. Breo could not identify any individuals who told him that they suspected that.

Q. Who were you referring to as supposedly suspecting that Dr. Crenshaw was not in the trauma room?

A. That's just a literary reference. Nobody in particular.

But Mr. Breo *did* knowingly omit from the article mention of information that demonstrated Dr. Crenshaw's involvement.

Q. You did not mention the fact that Dr. McClelland told you that he and Dr. Crenshaw had walked into Parkland's emergency room together in your article, did you?

The Witness: I did not.

Of course, what Dr. McClelland told Mr. Breo was consistent with his testimony to the Warren Commission:

> Dr. McClelland: Immediately upon hearing that, I accompanied the Resident, Dr. Crenshaw, who brought this news to me, to the emergency room, and down to the Trauma Room 1 where President Kennedy had been taken immediately upon arrival.
>
> Mr. Specter: And approximately what time did you arrive in Emergency Room 1?
>
> Dr. McClelland: This is a mere approximation, but I would approximate or estimate, rather, about 12:40.
>
> Mr. Specter: And who was present, if anyone, at the time of your arrival?
>
> Dr. McClelland: At the time I arrived, Dr. Perry—would you like the full names of all these?
>
> Mr. Specter: That would be fine, I would appreciate that.
>
> Dr. McClelland: Dr. Malcolm Perry, Dr. Charles Baxter, Dr. Charles Crenshaw, Dr. James Carrico, Dr. Paul Peters.

Dr. Charles Baxter, another physician interviewed by Mr. Breo, had testified similarly to the Warren Commission verifying Dr. Crenshaw's presence:

> Mr. Specter: Can you identify any other doctors who were there at that time?
>
> Dr. Baxter: Oh, let's see—I'm not sure whether the others came before or after I did. There was Crenshaw, Peters, and Kemp Clark. Dr. Bashour finally came. I believe Jackie Hunt—yes—she was, I believe she was the anesthesiologist who came.

Although Mr. Breo wrote in his articles that he interviewed these doctors "in the wake of a new book written by one of their former Parkland Hospital colleagues, Charles Crenshaw, M.D.," he denied under oath during his deposition testimony that one of the purposes in writing the *JAMA* articles was to respond to Dr. Crenshaw's book.

> By Mr. Kizzia:
>
> Q.   Was one of the purposes of the publication of the articles that you wrote for *JAMA* to respond to Dr. Crenshaw's book?
>
> A.   No.

Mr. Breo's editor, Dr. Glass, however, acknowledged the opposite during his deposition:

> Q.   Was one of the intents or purposes of part two of the articles that were published in *JAMA* on May 27th, 1992, that was written by Dennis Breo to respond to Dr. Crenshaw's book?
>
> A.   One of the intentions was to have the Dallas physicians who were there respond to the book.

Although during the 19 May 1992, press conference in New York City, Dr. Lundberg stood behind a lectern upon which a large American Medical Association seal or emblem had been placed, so that it would be displayed in videotaping and photographs of the press conference, Dr. Lundberg acknowledged in his sworn deposition testimony that his statements and those of Mr. Breo's, at the press conference and in the *JAMA* articles, were *not* the official position of, nor endorsed by, the AMA.

> Q. Were the statements contained in the two articles that Mr. Breo wrote which were published in *JAMA* on May 27th, 1992, statements of the official position of the AMA?
> A. No.
> Q. Were the statements that Mr. Breo made at the May 19th, 1992, press conference statements of the official position of the AMA?
> A. No.
> Q. Were the statements that you made at the May 19th, 1992, press conference statements of the official position of the AMA?
> A. No.

The Settlement

By the fall of 1994, the litigation had been on going for a year and a half. Many pretrial battles had been fought, including time-consuming procedural and discovery disputes. Dr. Crenshaw and Mr. Shaw had each undergone multiple days of deposition questioning. Due to his poor physical health, Dr. Crenshaw, in particular, had been worn down by the process. In October of 1994, the parties to the litigation attended a court-ordered mediation. Mediation in the Texas state court practice is an informal, non-binding gathering of the parties, their attorneys, and a court-appointed mediator with the intended purpose of trying to reach an amicable settlement. In this case, the mediation lasted a full day, but the *JAMA* Defendants ultimately agreed to pay Dr. Crenshaw and Gary Shaw $200,000.00, reimburse a substantial portion of their court costs, and publish a rebuttal article (to be written by Dr. Crenshaw and Mr. Shaw) in *JAMA*. While the amount of the settlement money would not come close to full compensation for the damage caused to their reputations, both Dr. Crenshaw and Mr. Shaw placed considerable value on the publication of the rebuttal article, a remedy that no court or jury had the power to order.

At the time of mediation, the *JAMA* Defendants insisted that as part of the settlement, the amount of money to be paid was to be kept confidential. Several weeks later, after apparently having received some criticism about *JAMA*'s handling of the case and the settlement, the *JAMA* Defendants claimed that the entire agreement was supposedly to be kept confidential. Of course, this was a curious claim, not only due to its belatedness, but also due to the fact that part of the settlement provided for publication of a rebuttal article, which would inherently seem to belie confidentiality. Nevertheless, Dr. Crenshaw and Mr. Shaw reluctantly acquiesced to the demand by the *JAMA* Defendants to keep the settlement confidential from that point forward, but later the *JAMA* Defendants once again changed their mind and decided that no confidentiality provision whatsoever (not even as to the amount of money paid to Dr. Crenshaw and Mr. Shaw) should be required as part of the agreement.

Ultimately, approximately $213,000.00 was paid to Dr. Crenshaw and Gary Shaw, on behalf of the *JAMA* Defendants, to partially compensate them for the damages to their reputations and reimbursement for a portion of their court costs. Additionally, in the 24/31 May 1995 issue of *JAMA*, a limited and edited version of Dr. Crenshaw's rebuttal article was finally published. Of course, this was more than three years after the original articles were published that led to the defamation suit; and *JAMA* refused to publish the well-documented rebuttal article originally submitted by Dr. Crenshaw. Instead, *JAMA* insisted upon severely limiting the length and censoring the content of the piece. Also, no apology or retraction was published. Rather, *JAMA* aggravated the situation and emphasized its irresponsibility by publishing a new smear piece about Dr. Crenshaw, Mr. Shaw, their book, and the case. The following is one of many letters that was sent in an attempt to dissuade *JAMA* from stooping to this new low.

April 21, 1995

George D. Lundberg, M.D.
Journal of the American Medical
Association
515 North State Street
Chicago, Illinois 60610

Re: Charles Crenshaw, M.D. and Gary Shaw v. Lawrence Sutherland, et al. Cause No. 73-93; In the 18th Judicial District Court of Johnson County, Texas

Dear Dr. Lundberg:

Although the above-referenced case has been settled, I am writing to you (with Mr. Babcock's permission) to make another plea on Dr. Crenshaw's behalf that *JAMA's* proposed "commentary" not be published.

I have enclosed a copy of the rebuttal article that was published by *The Dallas Morning News* on Sunday, December 19, 1995, pursuant to the settlement agreement reached in the above-referenced case. This rebuttal article was published without any response or further attacks upon Dr. Crenshaw or his book by *The News*. As you may know, *The Dallas Morning News* had previously published a correction/clarification in the "Corrections, Clarifications" section of the newspaper (a copy of which I have also enclosed). Of course, *The Journal of the American Medical Association* has to date not published a correction or clarification concerning any false impressions created by the misleading and inaccurate statements and publications by *JAMA* and its representatives to the erroneous effect that Dr. Crenshaw was not even in Parkland Hospital's Trauma Room 1 on November 22, 1963, when President Kennedy was treated there. This failure on *JAMA's* part to correct and/or at least clarify the misimpressions that it created is obviously unfortunate. What is even more regrettable is that *JAMA* apparently intends to publish a new smear piece about Dr. Crenshaw at the same time that it belatedly publishes Dr. Crenshaw's brief rebuttal article, which was edited and severely limited by *JAMA*.

Just in case you did not receive copies of my prior correspondence to your attorney objecting to the commentary proposed by *JAMA*, I have enclosed additional copies of letters dated December 27, 1994, February 20, 1995, February 27, 1995, and March 6, 1995. The "commentary" is inaccurate and grossly misleading and unfair. For example, the proposed piece knowingly and intentionally continues to foster the false impression that Dr. Crenshaw was not involved in the emergency care given to President Kennedy at Parkland Hospital on November 22, 1963. Certainly, you now know that several witnesses, including Drs. McClelland and Baxter, testified under oath to the Warren Commission that Dr. Crenshaw was there. Dr. McClelland testified then and told Dennis Breo in 1992 that he and Dr. Crenshaw entered the Parkland Emergency Room at the same time (W.C. Vol. VI, pp 31–32). Dr. Crenshaw was the first doctor named by Dr. Baxter when asked during his Warren Commission testimony about doctors on the Parkland trauma team that worked on President Kennedy (W.C. Vol. VI, p. 40). Dr. Baxter's later expression of uncertainty was in response to a question about "other doctors" in addition to those he had already identified (W.C. Vol. VI, p. 41). For *JAMA* to falsely suggest otherwise is outrageous considering the harm already caused. The proposed "commentary" also tries to perpetuate the false allegation that Dr. Crenshaw's descriptions of JFK's wounds have been inconsistent with the descriptions of the wounds given by many other witnesses, including the Parkland doctors, at the time of the assassination. As you know, the reports and testimony provided to the Warren Commission by numerous witnesses contained descriptions of the nature and location of President Kennedy's wounds that were virtually identical to Dr. Crenshaw's descriptions. There are other inaccuracies in the proposed "commentary" that can be specifically pointed out to you if you are interested.

I urge you as Editor of *JAMA*, to reconsider publishing the additional "commentary" that further attacks Dr. Crenshaw. Professionalism, indeed decency, and certainly fairness would seem to dictate that *JAMA* refrain from doing so, particularly since so much damage has already been caused to Dr. Crenshaw. The principles of fair and objective journalism should not be abandoned in favor of pride and the emotional urge to have the last say. As I have emphasized before, there is no adequate means for an individual, like Dr. Crenshaw, to even respond, much less rectify the harm caused by publication of misinformation to hundreds of thousands of his peers. The power of mass communication should not be exercised so irresponsibly. I would also point out and/or remind you that the release language in the settlement agreement in this case applies only to one publication in *JAMA*, not to other publications such as oral statements or other written statements, or even to republications or reprints.

Very truly yours,
D. Bradley Kizzia

Unfortunately, nothing could convince *JAMA* that it should not publish the new "commentary," not even the knowledge that it contained misleading and false statements, was contrary to journalistic ethics, and was harmful. *JAMA*'s commentary even included the preposterous claim that all of the information developed during discovery supports its position in the litigation! The sampling of deposition excerpts from *JAMA*'s own witnesses, as shown above, obviously prove otherwise. The medical oath of "do no harm" simply does not apply to *JAMA*'s brand of medical journalism.

It seems incredible that the awesome power of the media, including *JAMA* and those that reported on the New York City press conference, can be employed so irresponsibly to damage individuals in the eyes and minds of millions of people, which damage can never be undone. Private individuals obviously do not have the power or resources to adequately respond to attacks in the mass media. The legal system provides only a partial remedy. Because of the freedom provided to the media by the First Amendment to the United States Constitution, no court can legally order publication of a correction or apology; but consider the chilling effect on an individual's exercise of free speech on a controversial subject that vilification (or fear of same) in the mass media can have. As philosopher Joseph Hall once said: "A reputation once broken may possibly be repaired, but the world will always keep their eyes on the spot where the crack was."

One wonders whether *JAMA*, its editor, and Mr. Breo really believe that their handling of this matter has served to dignify an allegedly prestigious, scientific medical journal. Do they really think that trying to destroy the reputation of a distinguished and honorable medical professional who merely offered his opinions on a controversial subject was appreciated by its readers? The potentially devastating power of the free press requires that it be responsibly exercised, a notion that *JAMA* apparently has either failed to learn or merely has decided to ignore and abandon in the case of the assassination of John Fitzgerald Kennedy.

Notes

1 This chapter is excerpted from *Conspiracy to Silence: JFK Doctor's Legal Triumph over the AMA and the Media as an Eyewitness to History,* a manuscript in progress concerning the litigation filed by Charles Crenshaw, M.D. and Gary Shaw, authors of *JFK: Conspiracy of Silence,* against publishers of allegedly defamatory attacks against Dr. Crenshaw and/or the book following the book's publication.

2 Charles A. Crenshaw, Jens Hansen, and J. Gary Shaw. *JFK: Conspiracy of Silence* (New York: Signet, 1992).

3 See David Mantik, Part IV.

4 Dr. Crenshaw's 500-word letter to the Editor of *JAMA* was finally published two years later as part of the settlement with *JAMA*. See *JAMA* (May 24/31, 1995), p. 1632.

The most familiar Oswald backyard photograph, which was used to convict him in the mind of the American public. For an excellent discussion of reasons for thinking it was faked, see Robert Groden, The Search for Lee Harvey Oswald *(1995). [Editor's note: See Part IV.]*

Thinking Critically about JFK's Assassination

James H. Fetzer, Ph.D.

Students who wonder whether the study of critical thinking has benefits in coping with problems in the world may want to consider the following critique of an article by Robert Artwohl, M.D., "Conspiracy, Forensic Science, and Common Sense", that recently appeared in *The Journal of the American Medical Association* (24/31 March 1993), pp. 1540–1543. It affords a nice illustration of uncritical thinking on an important subject that affects everyone. It also illustrates the fallacy of supposing that articles that appear in reputable sources, such as *JAMA*, are therefore credible. This article is surely not.

Fallacy #1: first paragraph, left hand column, p. 1540:

ARTWOHL: "correspondence to the *Journal* indicates many physicians are still sympathetic to a key proconspiracy tenet regarding the Kennedy assassination: that the autopsy physicians conspired with the military, the Central Intelligence Agency (CIA), the Federal Bureau of Investigation (FBI), the Secret Service, and other agencies of government to disguise and suppress medical evidence that would show President Kennedy was publicly executed in Dealey Plaza on November 22, 1963, by multiple gunmen."

This is an example of *the straw man* fallacy, which creates an artificially inflated version of a position in order to destroy it and thereby claim to have discredited readily available but more defensible versions thereof. Notice, for example, that JFK could have been killed by multiple gunmen without a conspiracy involving the autopsy physicians; that the autopsy physicians could have been unwitting pawns; that the entire military and CIA and FBI or whatever need not have been involved for there to have been a conspiracy, and so forth. A conspiracy does not require mass meetings, pep rallies in Washington Stadium, or anything of the like to exist and succeed.

Consider a parallel argument concerning the Iran-Contra affair: Reagan would have had to consult with his cabinet, the White House, the Central Intelligence Agency (CIA), the State Department and numerous ambassadors, and so on. Everyone in Washington would have had to know. So the Iran-Contra affair could never have taken place. Or that legal segregation, for example, should be opposed because it means blacks will be moving into your neighborhood, they will be living next door, dating your daughter, fathering your grandchildren. Or that gay rights means that gays are going to be able to rent rooms in your home, seduce your sons, embarrass your wives and your friends, throw naked parties in the backyard, on and on.

Fallacy #2: second paragraph, left hand column, p. 1543:

ARTWOHL: "To simulate the neck wound, they fired through 14-cm-thick gelatin blocks or animal muscle."

This is a case of *misdescribing—or even fabricating—evidence*. What *neck* wound? We know of an injury to the throat, which Malcolm Perry originally described as a small wound of entrance. We know of one or more possible back wounds, which do not align properly to have been the entry wound for an exit wound at the location of the throat wound. So what wound is Artwohl discussing?

This can also be described as a case of *begging the question* by taking for granted something that is disputed and not in evidence. In the form of a question, this is known as the *leading question*, which attorneys are permitted to use in questioning hostile witnesses in courts of law. When the issue is whether O.J. murdered Ron and Nicole, the prosecutor might ask a hostile witness, "Mr. Simpson, what made you think your plan would work?" Of course, there are *drawings* of a neck wound that were used during the Warren inquiry, but the existence of a corresponding neck wound is another thing entirely.

Fallacy #3: third paragraph, left hand column, p. 1543:

ARTWOHL: "To investigate the head wound, his group fired at gelatin-filled skulls from a distance of 270 feet, approximately the distance from the Texas School Book Depository to President Kennedy's head at the time of the fatal shot . . . Olivier, a scientist, used his realm of expertise and he formed a reasonable conclusion: Oswald's rifle and ammunition were capable of inflicting both of President Kennedy's wounds."

Several fallacies are going on here at once. Notice the presumption that JFK was hit by only two bullets ("both of [his] wounds"), which obviously *begs the question*, since there is conflicting evidence of a back wound, a throat wound, and possibly two head wounds, not to mention evidence of other missiles that appear to have been fired at the President. Moreover, no indication is given of whether the rifle used (described as "Lee Harvey Oswald's gun") was in the same condition in which it was originally said to have been found (with a misaligned sight, etc.). Nor is there mention of any other experiments conducted by firing from other locations, such as the grassy knoll, the Dal-Tex Building, or the Criminal Courts Building. This is another case of *special pleading* by considering only evidence favorable to your own pre-determined point of view and ignoring the rest.

Notice especially that the only question addressed is whether or not it is *possible* to inflict such wounds with a rifle of that kind. Even if it were possible, that hardly shows that it *happened* or even that its occurrence is *probable*. If Oswald was on the second floor having a Coke, for example, then he could not have been on the sixth floor firing at Kennedy. If the foliage on a Texas oak would have obscured the vision of anyone who fired at the motorcade at the time of the first shot, it is silly to suppose it was fired from that location. Nancy Sinatra *could* have inflicted the damage described *if* she had been there shooting at JFK. The question is not whether a reworked Mannlicher-Carcano could possibly have done the damage— incidentally, precisely which wounds are being accounted for here: the imaginary neck wound? some specific head wound?—but the actual cause of the actual wounds that the President sustained.

Fallacy #4: fourth paragraph, left hand column, p. 1543:

ARTWOHL: "One must also remember that what might seem unusual or even impossible to the inexperienced may be quite common to the expert. The relatively small amount of deformation of the so-called pristine bullet is a rally cry for the conspirati. However, forensic pathologists with extensive gunshot wound experience do not find this unusual."

This is a nice example of the *appeal to authority*. There are two kinds of appeals to authority, however, only one of which is fallacious. The fallacious appeal occurs when someone who is an authority in one area is cited as an authority in another. The non-fallacious appeal occurs if someone who is an authority in an area is cited in relation to that area. Citing Einstein on religion, for example, might be fallacious, but citing Einstein on physics is not. In this case, the author is identified with a "Department of Emergency Medicine", but is not otherwise described. Moreover, "forensic pathologists with extensive gunshot experience" who do not find this [lack of deformation] "unusual" are uncited except for an "oral communication" from a V. G. M. DiMaio. But the case of JFK and the magic bullet is hardly a normal case, and no evidence is cited that establishes that the slightly-deformed bullet under consideration could reasonably have been supposed to have caused all the damage it has to have caused if the magic bullet theory is true. The question once again is not merely one of possibility but of probability or of actual fact. Observe that the evidence cited is essentially anecdotal ("story telling") instead of comparative studies under controlled experimental conditions.

Since this concluding section of his paper is entitled, "Forensic Science and Common Sense", it is intriguing that here he is appealing to expert opinion to *correct* common sense, which might indeed find the idea that so much damage could be done with so little deformation improbable or impossible. If common sense and expert opinion conflict, then one might as well cite whichever "evidence" strengthens your cause. This appears to be a methodological inconsistency that functions as a case of *special pleading*. (Calling those who hold views contrary to your own by odd names, such as "conspirati," coincidentally, does not automatically make their opinions false or your's true. Instead it suggests that arguments for your position may be few and far between.)

It may be appropriate to observe that Lattimer commits a different kind of fallacy in describing the same bullet as "deformed" and "decidedly not pristine" in Figure 4 on p. 1546, for example. What is going on here is a tacit shift in the *comparison class* that determines the meaning of the description of the bullet as "pristine". The bullet shown in Figure 4 may be "deformed" in relation to bullets in mint condition, but it is surely "pristine" in relation to the deformed slugs that typically result from inflicting the kind of damage this one is supposed to have inflicted. Using language that is ambiguous in this fashion is to commit the fallacy of *equivocation*.

Fallacy #5: first paragraph, middle column, p. 1543:

ARTWOHL: "The autopsy findings and all photographic and available assassination films support the fact that there were two shots from the rear."

Blatant *question begging*. This claim is highly disputed on many grounds and cannot be a "fact" if it is untrue. There appear to have been at least two shots from the front and multiple shots from the rear.

Fallacy #6: first paragraph, middle column, p. 1543:

ARTWOHL: "Although the preponderance of nonmedical evidence indicates that Lee Harvey Oswald acted alone as a maladjusted individual killing President Kennedy with a Mannlicher-Carcano rifle, it cannot totally disprove his acting with (or being duped by) a small private group of conspirators in a plot to assassinate President Kennedy."

Question begging in the first instance, but curiously concessionary and disingenuous in the second. The "nonmedical evidence" to which he refers is no doubt *The Warren Report*, which was never able to establish that Oswald had either the motive, the means, or the opportunity to assassinate the President. So this part is clearly begging the question. To admit that Oswald might have "acted with . . . a small private group of conspirators in a plot to assassinate President Kennedy", however, is remarkable in several ways. Why would the group have to be *small*? Moreover, how small is "small"? If we add one more member to a small group, is it still small? Why couldn't it be *fairly large*? And why does it have to be *private*—to imply that it is not "public"? Do assassins normally conspire in public? A small group plotting together would still be a *conspiracy*. So what he is apparently trying to subtly convey is that "public officials" (of the government) could not possibly have been involved. But how could he *possibly* know? This is more purely gratuitous begging the question.

Fallacy #7: second paragraph, middle column, p. 1543:

ARTWOHL: " there are large problems with logic and common sense with the government-led or government-involved conspiracy theories."

Straw man. No one suggests that the govenment as such was involved, which would invite the question, "If so, which branch?" Individuals who happened to be government officials may have been involved in a conspiracy without it being either government led or government involved. Logic and common sense require that all of the evidence be considered.

Fallacy #8: second paragraph, middle column, p. 1543:

ARTWOHL: "If the Secret Service, the FBI, the CIA, and other agencies with close access to the President wanted to dispose of him, they could have availed themselves of a number of covert means of dispatch. It is difficult to believe a government-led team of President's assassins came up with the following complex plan. First, take several years setting up Lee Harvey Oswald. Then, get him a job in the Texas School Book Depository so he could be in position to kill the President and meticulously plant evidence with which to frame him. For the central piece of evidence, obtain a cheap mail-order rifle with an inexpensive sight. (Apparently no one thought to spend a few more dollars and get a more credible rifle.) Arrange to have the President fired upon from several different directions using at least three teams of marksmen. (Why would it take several teams of marksmen, not one, not two, but, by conspirati count, three to six volleys of gunfire to hit a slow-moving target at close range with the fatal head shot?) After the President is hit with multiple bullets from multiple directions, the military and numerous government agencies, beginning right at Parkland Hospital, move quickly to conceal multiple bullet holes from civilian physicians (or coerce them all into silence), whisk away bullets, alter the President's body, forge roentgenograms and photographs, and alter every home movie and photograph of the assassination to conceal the true nature of the injuries and the number of accomplices involved."

Absolutely vintage *straw man*. Notice, for example, that conspiracy scenarios do not require involvement by "the military" or "government agencies", numerous or not, but only by enough people in the right places at the right times. Depending on who wanted JFK dead—there are quite a few candidates, from LBJ and J. Edgar Hoover to Charles Cabell and other associates of the CIA, including anti-Castro Cubans and the Mob— it may have been more fitting to assassinate him in public, especially by having a plausible patsy to throw off public suspicion, than to remove him by covert means, which would inevitably create questions and motivate inquiries that might have been inconvenient. Moreover, a public execution sends signals of many kinds about who really controls power in the USA. Artwohl betrays a remarkable lack of imagination about the possibilities of conspiracies of different kinds, where there could have been a number of alternative assassination scenarios, with other "patsies" waiting in the wings if the Dealey Plaza scenario had not played itself out.

Moreover, it would have been essential to have the means to make sure the President was killed. Triangulated fire provides a standard method of ambush, especially in the case of a moving target, which can be difficult to hit under the best of conditions. (Is Artwohl familiar with the problems involved in hitting relatively small moving targets from 100 yards or so? Here I think his lack of knowledge betrays him. Having several teams would be virtually indispensable to guaranteeing the success of the kill.) Moreover, the problem with the rifle may well have been that easy access to quality weapons that could be bought on any corner store in Dallas would not leave a paper trail to implicate Oswald. Not all the photographic evidence needed to be dealt with—only the most important. Some photographs were not picked up at the scene of the crime, which is one of a number of reasons the case has remained alive. And if Artwohl really wants to understand the behavior of the physicians at Parkland, for example, he ought to pick up a copy of Charles Crenshaw's *Conspiracy of Silence* (1992). This exaggerated caricature of assassination theories may look impressive on the surface, but resorting to such arguments betrays the superficiality of his position.

Fallacy #9: third paragraph, middle column, p. 1543:

> ARTWOHL: "The most astonishing feature of this plan is that the plotters would have to have been confident in advance they would be able to recover every bullet, find every witness, control the movements of hundreds of witnesses, and destroy every photograph and home movie that had incriminating evidence and leave behind those that did not."

Another *straw man*. It is not the case that every bullet had to be found, every witness intimidated or killed, or every photograph or home movie recording incriminating evidence be distorted or destroyed. But the more the better. It would certainly be advantageous if you could control the course of any legal investigation by local, state, or federal authorities, perhaps by taking matters out of their hands, if that were something that could possibly be arranged. The key is having a story that diverts attention from the actual motives of those who were behind the assassination onto a patsy, preferably one far removed (even apparently of the opposite political persuasion) from those of the conspirators. Artwohl appears to be ignorant of the vast literature on this subject, from *Six Seconds in Dallas* (1967) to *Farewell America* (1968) to *Best Evidence* (1980) to *The Fish is Red* (1987) to *High Treason* (1989) to *Act of Treason* (1991) to *High Treason 2* (1992) and many other works that provide substantial evidence of conspiracy and cover-up in the assassination of John Kennedy. He mentions a few works, including *Conspiracy* and *Crossfire*, but merely to lampoon them. His understanding of this case appears to be shallow.

Fallacy #10: fourth paragraph to end, middle and last column, p. 1543:

ARTWOHL: "In the illogical world of the Kennedy assassination conspiracy and its associated booming entertainment industry, any fact or finding that contradicts the popular Rube Goldberg scenario is dismissed as disinformation. Any contrary document or photograph is judged to be a government forgery. Any person or group who questions the conspirati's erroneous or unsubstantiated claims is denounced as a coconspirator or dupe. . . . Even *JAMA*, its editor, and the American Medical Association have been added to the proconspiracy list of accessories after the fact. As the years pass, one thing becomes abundantly clear: for the conspirati, it is conspiracy above all else, including forensic science, and common sense."

Ad hominem (abusing the man). Saving the best for last, Artwohl goes out in a blaze of criticism, which impugns the motives of everyone who ever doubted the account found in *The Warren Report*. The inadequacies of this position are enormous, since a scientific analysis of any phenomenon must be based upon serious consideration of all of the available evidence. If *JAMA*, its editor, and the American Medical Association are now candidates for being accessories after the fact, it may be because the editor of *JAMA* appears to have abused his position by repeatedly publishing articles that display the application of improper and unwarranted methods of investigation and procedures of inquiry that lead to false or unjustified conclusions and create the indelible impression that the AMA has engaged in a cover-up in the assassination of JFK.

The JFK Assassination:
Cause for Doubt

David W. Mantik, M.D., Ph.D.

Ignorance is preferable to error; and he is less remote from the truth who believes nothing, than he who believes what is wrong.
—Thomas Jefferson

Recent articles in the *Journal of the American Medical Association* (*JAMA*) have concluded that only two shots, both from the rear, struck JFK. This position is loyal to the Warren Commission (for simplicity, its supporters are described here as *loyalists*). The opposition (here described as *critics*) argue for more than one gunman, i.e. a conspiracy of one stripe or another. A recent *JAMA* editorial[1] implied that dissent among well informed persons (especially physicians, *JAMA*'s intended audience) ought now to cease. The present discussion, however, departs radically from this view. It is argued here that much of the JFK data is still subject to serious dispute. The critics believe that the evidence in this case is like a soap bubble: it changes hues depending on the viewer's position —and sometimes vanishes entirely.[2,3,4,5] Primary emphasis here is placed on the medical evidence: first, because it is so critical to this case and, second, because *JAMA* has recently aroused more interest in it. Central to this discussion will be evidence for two successful shots from the front in addition to what were probably two successful shots from the rear.

The Autopsy: The Skull Wound

The senior autopsy pathologist, James J. Humes, recently stated to *JAMA*[6] that both the entrance and exit wounds were readily evident on the skull. This is, at the least, misleading. What the pathologists saw initially was a very large skull defect (hole). There was no obvious exit site and only a suggestion of an entrance site. This was confirmed by Humes in his testimony[7] to the Warren Commission; he reported that until very late in the autopsy, "A careful examination of the margins of the large bone defect at that point . . . failed to disclose a portion of the skull bearing . . . a wound of—a point of impact on the skull . . ." The absence of an exit site was also confirmed by the third pathologist, Pierre A. Finck, in a long letter subsequently sent to his superior, Brigadier General J. M. Blumberg, at the Armed Forces Institute of Pathology. His description of an absent exit wound on the skull was quoted by the House Select Committee on Assassinations (HSCA): "No exit wound is identifiable at this time . . ."[8]

There was a suggestion of an entrance site but this evidence was, at best, incomplete. Regarding this 15 x 6 mm proposed entrance wound in the occipital scalp, Finck[8] added that there was only a *portion* of a crater present on the underlying skull. Of this same proposed entry site, Boswell[9] stated, ". . . there was a hole here, only *half* (emphasis added) of which was present in the bone that was intact." It seems apparent, therefore, that the skull itself, other than containing a large defect, offered only minimal clues to a transiting bullet.

Humes described the autopsy as concluded by 11 P.M.,[10] but then added[4] that at some later time, ". . . I would have guessed it was midnight or 1 o'clock in the morning . . . ," three bone fragments (Humes, apparently in error, recalls only two in *JAMA*[11]) were received in the morgue by Dr. John H. Ebersole, the radiologist. Radiographs,[12] but apparently no photographs, were taken of these. Their exact discovery site has never been certain, but many critics accept their authenticity. The pathologists placed the largest bone fragment (10 x 6.5 cm and triangular[13]) into the right anterior parietal area, near the vertex. According to the autopsy protocol,[14] minute metal particles were seen at one corner on the radiographs, where there was ". . . a portion of the perimeter of a roughly circular wound presumably of exit which exhibits beveling of the outer aspect of the bone and is estimated to measure approximately 2.5 to 3.0 cm in diameter." These metal particles suggested to the pathologists that a bullet had passed nearby. Though the pathologists stated that the direction of the bullet was apparent from the beveling on this largest bone fragment, what they completely failed to describe, is how they determined the orientation of this fragment. It was solely this orientation, based on the exit site, that determined the direction of the bullet. If this orientation had changed by x degrees, so also would the trajectory have changed by x degrees. Despite the centrality of this concept, the pathologists remained strangely silent regarding this essential step.

The difficulty faced by the pathologists was described vividly by Humes:[15] " It was not so easy to accurately locate the wound of exit because of the great disruption of the fragments and loss of tissue and bone in that area, so that we placed it a little behind or a little below or a little wherever [sic] in relation to what now we may collectively decide . . ."

Humes[13] provided further insight into their difficulties at the autopsy: "To state what the problem was, the basic problem was [sic], as we reflected the scalp, various fragments of bone, some fell into the cranial cavity, some came to the table, some adhered to the dura and so forth . . ." When asked by Allen W. Dulles whether the point of exit in the skull could be clearly determined, Humes[16] responded, "No sir, it was not, other than through this large defect . . ." Then several minutes later he[17] added, "The fragments were so difficult to replace in their precise anatomic location." On another occasion, when commenting on the skull radiograph, he[18] said, ". . . this bullet was so disrupt[ive], those fragments I think could virtually be any place." In 1977 the HSCA tried to fit in yet one more piece of skull. This was the Harper fragment,[19] discovered after the autopsy, trapezoidal shaped and 7 x 5.5 cm. Of this attempt Dr. Charles S. Petty[20] admitted: "Well, it's [referring to the skull] terribly fragmented, and we can't really reconstruct it."

In spite of this understandable confusion, the pathologists have now claimed in JAMA[6] to have "irrefutably" completed just such a reconstruction of entrance and exit wounds. This achievement would have occurred at a stage when there was one less bone fragment than was available to Petty, an experienced forensic pathologist. After reviewing the evidence, he found further reconstruction impossible. The critics also note that there is no surviving photograph or radiograph to confirm these reconstructions. Reliance must therefore be placed on the integrity and accuracy of the pathologists. If, for example, this large fragment were placed somewhat more posteriorly (or especially if it were rotated by 180 degrees), the pathologists might well have concluded just the opposite: that a shot came from the front. Subsequent reviewers were therefore unable independently to verify either of these reconstructions. The fragments themselves were probably buried with the body.

Moreover, even if the anterior placement and orientation were correct, as some critics concur, the skull beveling seen might well have resulted instead from an oblique shot from the right front. This is, in fact, exactly

the type of trajectory described by Dr. Kemp Clark,[21] the Parkland Hospital
(Dallas) neurosurgeon: it was "tangential" and caused by a bullet which hit
"the right side of his head." Whether the beveling and metal fragments
seen on the 10 cm bone fragment could have been caused by a tangential
shot from the front has never been addressed by wound ballistics experts:
no experiments were performed and no literature references were cited to
rule this out. The critics conclude, therefore, that the "irrefutable evidence"
cited by the pathologists for the skull entry and exit sites is considerably
less than certain.

The proposed entry site on the posterior skull presented yet another set
of difficulties. According to testimony twice repeated by the second pathologist, J. Thornton Boswell,[9,22] with Humes at his side, the right posterior entry wound of the skull was also reconstructed late that night. It is
striking that such an absolutely essential step in the autopsy (possibly the
most important of the evening) was not even mentioned in the FBI autopsy
report[23,24,25] prepared by James W. Sibert and Francis X. O'Neill, who were
both eyewitnesses to the autopsy. David Lifton[26] has suggested that both
men had left the morgue before 1:00 A.M., at which time the autopsy had
seemed complete. The three bone fragments most likely arrived after this
time. At this early morning hour, then, based primarily on these bone fragments, the pathologists[11] placed the entry site at 2.5 cm to the right of the
external occipital protuberance (EOP) and slightly above it. The smallest
of the three late arriving bone fragments fit right into this site according to
Boswell.[9,22] It is extraordinary that Humes[22] has admitted to having no recollection of this most critical step; in the absence of such a reconstruction
the evidence for this entry site would be greatly weakened. Despite this
state of knowledge, the pathologists concluded that a shot from the low
right posterior occiput had exited near the top front of the head, to the
right of midline (Note A). In view of the extensive damage to the skull and
the literal movement of skull fragments during the autopsy, critics question whether such a reconstruction could be reliable. What is clear is that
the essential conclusion about the head trauma—a single shot from the
rear—was based primarily, not on evidence found on the skull itself, but
rather on these bone fragments, whose origin and ancestry have remained
uncertain.

Despite Humes' admitted ignorance of this entry wound reconstruction
and its absence from the FBI autopsy report, many critics still accept this
reconstruction, but will argue—based on the pattern of brain trauma,[28] the
eyewitness testimony, and the photographic evidence—it still cannot rule
out that a second shot struck from the right front a short time later.[29,30,31]
Evidence on the skull for such a second shot might well be absent since all

of the missing bone fragments were never found. In fact, without the late arriving bone fragments, the pathologists' lack of knowledge of the exit wound would have been equally great. In addition, such a frontal shot may have entered through a large gap in the skull which was blown out just an instant before by the exiting posterior shot. Dr. John Lattimer's experiments,[32] for example, show skull missing in exactly this area after a single posterior shot. The trauma from the first shot could easily destroy post-mortem photographic and radiographic evidence of such a frontal shot. However, there is one major empirical support for such a frontal shot which could persist: this would be a large right occipital skull defect. This issue is central to this case and shall be addressed in detail later; suffice it to say that the eyewitness testimony seemed unanimous that a large right occipital defect did exist. The pathologists did not directly contradict this; instead, they avoided a clear description of this area. The radiographs may also yield more information on this point.[33] From these considerations and others to be developed below, the critics ultimately conclude that a single posterior head shot is, at best, misleading and possibly not a complete explanation.

The maximum length of the skull defect was described as 17 cm on Boswell's face sheet[34] but only as 13 cm by Humes in the autopsy protocol. Why would Humes exclude Boswell's opinion from the written protocol? The critics answer that since the 17 cm measurement would place the posterior border of the skull defect near the EOP and therefore imply a large hole in the right occiput, Humes deliberately understated this number to make it appear as though the large defect were more anterior. However, the author[33] and, independently, several of his colleagues, have measured and photographed this 13 cm distance on several skulls (measured from near the coronal suture). Even this 13 cm distance extends well into the upper portion of the occipital bone.

In addition, if Boswell's recollection of the EOP is correct, there must have been a visible hole (assuming it to be a separate hole) near the EOP until very near the end of the autopsy. The area of the small bone fragment that was said to fit into this hole near the EOP was 3–4 square cm.[12] The total diameter of this entry wound, therefore, must have been at least several centimeters, yet no other observer at Parkland or Bethesda ever saw such a separate hole, which surely should have been easily visible. That the wounds were easy to see is confirmed in *JAMA* by Humes:[35] "The wounds were so obvious that there was no need to shave the hair before photographs were taken." Yet this supposedly obvious entry wound cannot be seen anywhere on the posterior head photograph,[36] which was presumably taken at the beginning of the autopsy, before any reconstruction. Its conspicuous absence has naturally led critics to question the authenticity of the photograph.

The pathologists themselves never clarified whether there was just one large defect or two separate defects, one large and one small. When this question was put to Ebersole, this author was told that the distance between the EOP entry wound and the posterior border of the large defect was only 2 to 2.5 cm.[37] This description clearly places the large defect well into the occiput, perhaps even into the low occiput. (Pertinent to this, it is also useful to recall the diagram[38] of the large skull defect agreed upon by the Warren Commission after interviewing the pathologists; the large defect shown there also extended either into or very close to the occipital bone.) Furthermore, since the width of the reconstituted bone fragment was also about 2 to 2.5 cm,[12] there may well have been only one large defect before reconstruction. In other words, the only bone between the small hole and the large hole was probably just this small fragment. This large defect then would have encompassed the proposed entry wound.

Such a conclusion is entirely consistent with other eyewitness testimony, especially since no one saw a separate entrance hole. This single, large defect would have encompassed much of the right posterior skull. Since the entry hole was low in the occipit, near the EOP, this large defect would also then have had to be low in the occiput. This suggests to critics a shot from the front. It is most pertinent that the experiments of both Lattimer[32] and the government experts at the Edgewood Arsenal[39] consistently produced primarily anterior skull defects when 6.5 mm Mannlicher-Carcano bullets were fired into the rear of these skulls. Most loyalists, aware of the significance of absent right occiput, are therefore forced to argue that the right occiput must have been intact, especially in light of these ballistics experiments. The condition of the right posterior skull has, not surprisingly, assumed a central role in this entire debate.

The loyalists also note that no bullet fragments were found in the left brain on the radiographs and they suggest that this rules out a shot from the right front. But critics respond that this may be overly simplistic: the frontal trajectory may well have been tangential, entering near the right temple and exiting through the right posterior skull. The remaining right lateral skull, easily seen on the anterior-posterior (AP) radiograph,[40] is consistent with this interpretation.

The Autopsy: The Back and Throat Wounds

At the conclusion of the autopsy only a shallow right back wound had been identified. The FBI autopsy report[23] stated that it entered ". . . a short distance . . . the end of the opening could be felt with the finger." At the 1969 Clay Shaw trial, Finck[8] testified that its depth was "the first fraction of an inch." In correspondence to Brig. Gen. J. M. Blumberg (1 February 1965), Finck[8] stated, "This wound cannot be probed with the soft probe available." Finck[8] also testified on 24 February 1969, when explicitly asked if he had attempted to probe the wound, "I did." Humes[41] concurs that the neck wound was not dissected: "Dissecting the neck was totally unnecessary and would have been criminal [sic]." None of the autopsy findings therefore suggest a penetrating wound to the back.

In the autopsy report, the back wound was located 14 cm inferior to the mastoid tip and 14 cm from the acromion. No distance from midline or from scapula was stated, though Humes described it as being just above the scapula.[42] The pathologists claimed to have known nothing of a throat wound until the next morning, when Humes spoke to Dr. Malcolm Perry in Dallas.[41] [Editor's note: See Appendices F and J.] Humes has consistently claimed that the wound was obscured by the tracheostomy. This state of ignorance has been contradicted by Ebersole,[43] however, who more than once has stated his awareness of the throat wound that night. The present author[37] was also advised by Ebersole that he was aware of the throat wound at the autopsy, based on a telephone call by someone to Dallas after 10:30 P.M. that evening.

Admiral G. G. Burkley was the only physician who was present at both Parkland and Bethesda. He arrived in time to suggest that JFK be given Solu-Cortef.[44,45] At Bethesda, he apparently acted as liaison to the Kennedy family. Though Burkley apparently missed the Parkland press conference, it still seems inconceivable that none of the Parkland physicians and none of his own associates mentioned the throat wound to him. There would have been time to talk on the flight back that afternoon. (Curiously, the throat wound was not mentioned by Burkley in the death certificate prepared by him. [Editor's note: See Appendix I.] Unfortunately, Burkley's reason for this omission has never been elicited; he was never asked to testify.) In the ordinary course of events, Burkley, more than anyone else, should have been aware of the throat wound. Is it conceivable that, if he knew, he would have kept this information from the pathologists? Though this question cannot be answered with certainty, there is more than one source which strongly suggests knowledge, at the autopsy, of the throat wound, despite statements to the contrary by the pathologists.

On 27 January 1964, the Warren Commission met in Executive Session. This top secret transcript was released only some years later after a Freedom of Information Act litigation was filed. During this session, J. Lee Rankin,[46] General Counsel for the Warren Commission, quoted from an autopsy report (possibly the FBI version) which described a fragment (not a whole bullet) exiting the throat as the cause of the throat wound. To place this event in context, it should be recalled that the pathologists submitted their final autopsy protocol on Sunday, 24 November 1963. After Humes' reputed Saturday morning (23 November) conversation with Dr. Malcolm Perry of Parkland, he speculated that the back wound and the throat wound were caused by a transiting shot from the rear. This bullet, in his view, exited undeflected and intact through the throat.

Since the pathologists did not explain the throat wound by an exiting *fragment* after their talk with Perry, the conjectured fragment quoted by Rankin must necessarily have been discussed *before* this call to Dallas. This discussion could not have occurred between the autopsy and the Dallas telephone call (only several hours had passed and Humes had been at a religious commitment[47]), so the pertinent discussion could have transpired only at the autopsy itself. This quote, therefore, suggests knowledge *during the autopsy* of the throat wound. It does not, however, make clear *who* was aware of the throat wound. Humes' surprisingly nonchalant state at the end of the autopsy, despite apparently failing to find the neck bullet, is illustrated by his comment to *JAMA*:[41] "We knew we would find the explanation sooner or later." How did he know this? And, if not at the autopsy, then when? Is he implying that they had agreed to ignore the throat wound until after they phoned Dallas the next morning?

Lt. Richard A. Lipsey,[48] an aide to Major General Wehle, told the HSCA that, while at the autopsy, the pathologists described three [*sic*] shots striking JFK from the rear, with one bullet entering the rear of the head and exiting the throat. The HSCA agreed that, even though Lipsey had based his conclusions on observations at the autopsy, there could be no throat exit from the head bullet because the pathologists believed that the throat wound was an exit from the upper back wound. But the HSCA overlooked the critical issue. The issue was not whether Lipsey was right or wrong in his explanation of the throat wound (the pathologists, after all, supposedly reached their final conclusions only *after* their telephone call to Dallas), but whether he correctly recalled any discussion at the autopsy about the throat wound. How could the throat wound have been *debated* at the autopsy if no one had known about it? And if there had been no discussion of a throat wound at the autopsy, why would Lipsey *invent* such a conversation? The HSCA seemed insensible to the doors that were opened with these comments.

Surprisingly enough, this same scenario was also reported by *JAMA*[49] on 4 January 1964, in referring to the autopsy findings: "The third bullet hit Kennedy in the back of the right side of the head. A small fragment of this bullet also angled down and passed out through Kennedy's throat . . ." Lipsey apparently was not the only one who had heard a discussion of the throat wound at the autopsy.

At a news conference that afternoon at Parkland Hospital, Dr Malcolm Perry[50] three times described the throat wound as one of entrance. [*Editor's note*: See Appendix C.] This interview was carried by the major television networks, radio, and reported by UPI. It seems most likely that some of the several dozen persons at the autopsy would have heard this media report of a frontal throat shot. In fact, Dennis David, who was Chief of the Day for the Bethesda Navy Medical School, reported that he went into the office of the Master at Arms and listened to the radio with none other than Dr. Boswell late that afternoon.[51] Finck has informed *JAMA*[52] that he was spending a quiet evening at home with his wife when he was called at 7:30 P.M. by Humes. He may therefore also have listened to media reports; he has not, however, commented publicly upon this. Even the HSCA[53] concluded, "It is conspicuously *unclear* (emphasis added) from the autopsy report alone that during the autopsy, the pathologists were unaware and failed to recognize that there was a missile perforation in the anterior neck."

Based on these considerations, as well as several eyewitness reports (Ebersole is one, but there are others not cited here), some critics conclude that the pathologists were aware of the throat wound that night. Feigning ignorance would have excused them from dissecting a possibly nonexistent transit wound. Other critics, less willing to blame the pathologists, suggest that their superiors may have deliberately withheld this information from them, possibly to protect their innocence, but also possibly to ensure that dissection of the hypothetical bullet track would not be done. What seems clear to most observers, in any case, is that no one at Parkland or Bethesda saw both the back and throat wounds on the same occasion and that no one ever dissected the hypothetical track between them. This transit trajectory is therefore pure speculation, according to the critics.

The autopsy protocol also contradicts the initial comments of the Parkland physicians,[54] both those who observed the throat wound themselves and also those who heard it described. It was said to be a small round wound (pencil-sized) entirely consistent with an entry bullet; initially, no one described it as an exit wound. Only later, after a long paragraph of hypothetical preconditions listed by Arlen Specter during the official inquiry, did they concede that it could have been an exit wound.[55] [*Editor's note:* See Charles Crenshaw, Part I.] However, none of them has ever said, based on appearance alone, that an entry wound was unlikely. The critics wonder what additional data could have changed their minds. They never saw the body again, nor did they ever see the throat wound again. The critics suspect that their testimony—or the impression conveyed by their testimony during Specter's questioning—was modified for reasons unrelated to their personal observations.

In the autopsy protocol, the back and throat wounds are described as "presumably" of entrance and "presumably" of exit, respectively. [*Editor's note*: See Appendix F.] The recent reports of the pathologists to *JAMA*[6] have elevated their degree of confidence to a much higher level than presumption. Yet, amazingly enough, the pathologists have never offered any clues to support their quantum leap toward certainty. Critics naturally wonder what additional evidence the pathologists could possibly have seen since the autopsy to have so increased their degree of confidence. If there is such evidence, after all, why have they failed to share it?

On the photograph of the back,[56] the wound lies slightly above the right scapular spine. Visibly this appears to be at the level of the upper thoracic spine rather than at the level of the lower cervical spine. The thoracic location was confirmed by the HSCA,[57] which placed it precisely 1.1 cm *inferior* to the first thoracic vertebra, T1. Since the lung typically extends close to the *superior* border of T1, a transit trajectory at this level would almost certainly have resulted in a pneumothorax.[55,33] Since none was seen, however, this proposed transit trajectory is immediately called into question. An alternate, more superior, trajectory is suggested by the chest radiograph which shows minor trauma to the right T1 transverse process.[58] The corresponding cephalad-caudad level on the chest radiograph is the disc at C7-T1. In the autopsy protocol, the pathologists described an apical pulmonary contusion which is quite consistent with the same vertical level. This evidence then suggests a trajectory through a cross sectional level near the C7-T1 disc, or possibly slightly above this. According to the HSCA[59] the bullet entered 5 cm to the right of the midline. Because the lateral edge of the C7 transverse process is also nearly 5 cm from the midline, the bullet necessarily would have had to pass directly through the C7 transverse process, or possibly even the body itself.[33] The corresponding cervical fracture, which should have been severe from such a direct hit, is not seen. It is also useful to recall that the cervical transverse processes present a very tight barrier in the vertical direction, so that this argument is independent of the vertical level in the cervical spine. The proposed transit trajectory therefore seems purely imaginary—at both the cervical and upper thoracic levels. Humes was admittedly ignorant[60] of the cross sectional anatomy which is pertinent to this proposed trajectory. (This ignorance should not be surprising since CT scans of the body did not come into widespread use until the late 1970s.)

In most adult males, the distance (Note B) from midline to acromion is 21 to 24 cm; since the back wound was 14 cm from the acromion, the calculated distance from midline to the wound should then be 7 to 10 cm. Entry this far lateral yields a horizontal trajectory angle much too large (30 degrees) to fit with the sixth floor sniper's nest in the Texas School Book Depository. This is true even if JFK's torso were slightly rotated—the HSCA[61] suggested a 5 degree rotation at most. The angle from the limousine to the Depository can be easily measured from overhead photographs or accurate maps of Dealey Plaza; it is about 10 degrees. The large discrepancy between 10 and 30 degrees has never been explained. Most critics conclude therefore that the back wound resulted from a nonpenetrating wound, for example, shrapnel, a defective or nonpristine bullet, or possibly even a postmortem injury, intentional or unintentional.

Though the official version is that no bullets or large bullet fragments were found at the autopsy there are, surprisingly, several distinct hints to the contrary. On 4 January 1964, *JAMA*[49] reported that "The first bullet . . . hit JFK in the upper part of the right back shoulder. The bullet did not go through his body and *was recovered during the autopsy* (emphasis added)." *The Washington Post*[62] of 18 December 1963, confirmed that a bullet was removed from deep in the shoulder. The *Post*[62] reaffirmed this several years later on 29 May 1966, reporting that the information had initially been confirmed with the FBI before publication. As late as 26 January 1964, *The New York Times*[63] reported that a bullet had lodged in JFK's right shoulder. In an interview with David Lifton, Admiral David Osborne[64] (then Captain and Chief of Surgery at Bethesda) insisted that he saw an intact bullet that night. He stated that he knew this ". . . because I had that bullet in my hand, and looked at it."

And again:[64] "Well, the bullet existed, I'm sure of that." Dennis David[65] has also told David Lifton that he typed a receipt for four large lead fragments that night; the total amount of metal was more than one bullet. Jerrol F. Custer,[66] the Bethesda radiology technologist, has reported seeing a bullet (or large fragment) fall out of the back when JFK was first elevated off the table in order to insert a radiographic plate. There is also in evidence an FBI receipt for a missile.[67] It is incredible that this receipt was not given to the Warren Commission; it became public[67] for the first time in 1966. The discovery in JFK's body of another bullet, or even large fragments comprising more than one bullet, would imply a fourth shot and strongly suggest a conspiracy—because of the time constraints for one gunman.

There is, in addition, a readily visible 3 x 5 cm discoloration on the right upper back, just below the lower neck fold. The HSCA[68] described this as a contusion or post-mortem lividity. It is unfortunate that no microscopic slides were prepared from this site to provide further clues to etiology. But it is most peculiar that this is well *above* the visible back wound. Why this particular site, of all possible sites on the back, should show discoloration is strange. The critics naturally wonder whether this discoloration was a contusion produced by a nontransiting frontal bullet or fragment that stopped near this site. Even the entire twelve volumes of the HSCA offer no explanation for this obvious discoloration. (The Warren Commission, of course, could not comment on this because they studied no photographs.)

The Autopsy: The Pathologists' Performance

The reliability of the autopsy protocol has been challenged for several reasons: logical inconsistencies, inappropriate ignorance, and obvious departures from standard practice. The central conclusion of only two shots, both from the rear, depends crucially on *trust* in the pathologists' abilities (for example, on their reconstructions of both entry and exit wounds). In view of this required trust, any reasonable observer would like to have *evidence* of their reliability. What is found, however, is just the opposite. A list of these pathological aberrations follows.

1. The posterior skull entry site was later raised by pathological and radiological reviewers[69] by the astonishing distance of 10 cm (four inches)! If the pathologists' entry wound were wrong by 10 cm, how then can anyone be certain that their exit wound site was any more accurate? Such a large error in placement of the exit wound could reverse the trajectory!

2. The largest radiopaque object on the skull radiographs is in the cowlick[70] area; this is several centimeters above the junction of the two lambdoidal sutures and the coronal suture. It is 6.5 mm in diameter (the same size as the Mannlicher-Carcano bullet), is nearly round, and is the most obvious object on the extant radiographs (even to a five year old, as the author can verify). Yet it was not mentioned by the pathologists, even though they described and physically removed two clearly smaller fragments. In addition, all three signed a statement that contained this sentence:[71] "However, careful examination at the autopsy, and the photographs and x-rays taken during the autopsy, revealed no evidence of a bullet or of a *major portion* of a bullet in the body of the President . . ." Ebersole also confirmed to this author that no large bullet fragments were seen on the radiographs the night of the autopsy.[37] It is inescapable, therefore, that serious controversy exists about the authenticity of the obvious 6.5 mm object now seen on the AP radiograph. It would have been possible, even in 1963, to add such an object to a radiograph.[33] [*Editor's note:* See Mantik's Postscript.]

3. A trail of dustlike metal fragments was described in the autopsy protocol and in Humes' testimony[72] as beginning near the EOP and ending above the right frontal sinus. The largest fragment recovered (7 x 2 mm) was located just above this sinus.[73] Humes has now confirmed this trail to *JAMA*.[11] Ebersole's description[37] to this author also concurred with this

trail. During the HSCA interviews, even Dr Joseph Davis,[60] a pathologist on the Forensic Pathology Panel, reported that he saw tiny metal fragments along this same trajectory. Amazingly, however, this is *not* what the extant radiographs show. On the lateral radiograph, small radiopaque objects begin near the cowlick area, more than 10 cm above Humes' trail. This apparent trail then extends forward on a nearly horizontal plane. (This description could just as well be reversed in space—there is no directionality.) Why would Humes describe the trail in this location to *JAMA*, when it is in such obvious conflict with the radiographs? And why was he not questioned about this by *JAMA*?

4. All three pathologists, including Finck, who was said to be skilled in wound ballistics, reported that they could not see the throat wound despite inspecting the entire perimeter of the tracheostomy.[55] Subsequent pathologists, however—looking at only photographs—easily saw the inferior portion of this wound at the edge of the tracheostomy.[74] It is particularly odd that this wound was not seen by the three pathologists insofar as their self-admitted task was to find the missing bullets.

5. Humes[75] before the Warren Commission (7 to 8 cm) and Boswell on his autopsy diagram (6.5 cm) did not even agree on the size of the tracheostomy. To *JAMA*,[11] Humes altered his reported size by nearly a factor of two to fit more closely with standard sizes; he decreased it to 3 to 4 cm, only half of what he had stated to the Warren Commission.

6. Humes (13 cm), in the autopsy protocol, and Boswell (17 cm), on his diagram,[76] disagreed by a surprisingly large amount with each other on the size of the skull defect. It is difficult to understand how a ruler could be read so differently by two professionals standing at the same table and examining the same body. If Humes' measurement were done after reconstruction of the posterior entry wound it would, of course, be the smaller of the two measurements. But it is Humes, not Boswell, who failed to recall this step. In any event, the reconstituted fragment is too small to explain this 4 cm difference between the two pathologists.[12]

7. The pathologists reported the back wound as 7 x 4 mm, with the long axis vertical.[42] Subsequent pathologists measured this as 9 x 9 mm, a rather large discrepancy in size, to say nothing of shape.

8. Later review panels[59] described the lateral distance of the back wound from midline as 5 cm; the pathologists' measurements, as noted above, imply at least 7 to 10 cm.

9. To *JAMA*, for the first time in the history of this case, Humes[11] has admitted that he had prepared a diagram at the autopsy. For the critics, especially, this news was a major confession. This is in striking agreement with what Boswell[77] told Josiah Thompson: "Yes, I'm sure there was another sheet, which had that measurement on it, and which had height, weight, and some other information. I'm sure of it." Humes has also stated to *JAMA*[41] and to the HSCA[78] that he faithfully copied *everything* that he had burned in his fireplace; if so, where is the diagram that he now admits to having prepared? The critics, and some loyalists, too, have often wondered at the paucity of information on Boswell's diagram and the great difficulty of interpreting it. In view of the above revelation, is it possible

that Humes' mysterious lost diagram was intended to be the primary one, but later had to be destroyed because it was not consistent with the official version of two bullets from the rear?

10. One of the most amazing and serious oversights was the pathologists' failure to coronally section the brain. The brain was examined nearly two weeks later, thus giving Humes ample time to review standard protocols for this. With this much time to prepare, ignorance can hardly be the explanation. Is it conceivable that Humes would have undertaken such a momentous task without reviewing in detail standard protocols, especially since, by his own admission, he was not experienced in gunshot autopsies?

11. No abrasion collar was reported for the back wound. For Finck especially, a presumed expert in such matters, to overlook such a critical (and often central) item in forensic pathology is truly extraordinary. Later reviewers[79] immediately noted this essential feature. It seems difficult to explain this omission as mere incompetence.

12. Humes has assured *JAMA*,[80] regarding their Warren Commission presentations: "These drawings are very accurate . . ." However, when the vertical level of the back wound shown in Humes' drawing was reviewed by the HSCA, Dr. Michael Baden[81] reported: "We place the entrance perforation a bit [*sic*] lower, almost 2 inches lower than depicted in the Warren Commission exhibit." After this announcement, the critics were not sure whether they should have been more astounded at the supposed error made by Humes or, rather, the surprising deprecation by Baden of a large 5 cm discrepancy. After the HSCA's attempts to minimize the 10 cm skull entry wound discrepancy, and now this additional 5 cm discrepancy, the critics naturally wonder what outer limits the loyalists would accept as tolerable in an autopsy.

13. On one occasion Humes stated that the shot to the head came from above[82] and on another[83] he claimed that the anatomic data could not answer this question. The critics naturally wonder how the evidence could possibly have changed during this interval, or if Humes' memory were defective, how it could fail him on such a major question.

14. In the Supplementary Autopsy Report[14], the mass of the brain is 1,500 gm, at the upper limit of normal. Yet Humes stated to *JAMA*[11] that the upper two-thirds of the right cerebrum was missing. These two statements are mutually exclusive. Also, quite astonishingly, no fresh brain mass was stated, yet masses were listed for other less critical organs.

15. To *JAMA*, Humes[80] stated, "I believe in the single bullet theory that it struck Governor Connally immediately after exiting the President's throat." However, when queried by the Warren Commission on exactly the same point he said,[84] "I think that is extremely unlikely." Actually he stated this twice in quick succession to the Warren Commission[85] so there can be no possibility of misunderstanding him (Note C). Then, after all this testimony, Boswell[87] and Finck,[88] who were listening to it, offered their unqualified support for it. These totally opposite statements by Humes are absolutely irreconcilable. Even more astonishing, he seems (*JAMA*, too, for that mat-

ter) to be oblivious to this. No questions have been asked and no explanations have been offered by him for this astounding behavior.

16. In addition to the above major concerns, the HSCA[89] faulted the pathologists on yet other serious issues that are not detailed here. Forensic pathologists such as Milton Helpern[90] and Charles Wilber[91] have seriously criticized their performance. And finally, Dr. Michael Baden,[92] who chaired the HSCA Forensic Pathology Panel, described the autopsy as "woefully inadequate" and noted that neither Humes nor Finck had ever done an autopsy involving a gunshot before! Although Finck was the designated expert, he had only sat in an office and reviewed records of US military personnel[92] who had died of gunshot wounds. In view of the judgment required to reconstruct the reported two skull wounds, the pathologists' lack of actual experience with gunshot wounds seems germane.

In the face of all of these concerns, critics, perhaps not so unreasonably, are somewhat chary of relying exclusively on statements from the pathologists, especially when they are described as "irrefutable proof." The critics would like some independent confirmation of these conclusions which, they believe, is at best difficult and frequently impossible to find.

If not the reliability, at least the forthrightness of the pathologists has recently been proven questionable. Both Humes[93] and Finck,[94] in response to *JAMA*, have persistently refused to comment on JFK's chronic Addison's disease. Now, however, *JAMA* (Note D) has confirmed this diagnosis,[95] based on autopsy findings. (This was not the first attempt by *JAMA*. On 10 November 1964, *JAMA* sent an inquiry to Admiral E. C. Kenney, which was forwarded to Admiral G. G. Burkley. After three months no response was received by *JAMA*[99] from Burkley.) The pathologists, for over 29 years now, by their dogmatic silence on this point, have covered up a major medical fact. If the pathologists have hidden this fact, merely by their selective silence, what else may yet lie hidden in their collective silence regarding the remainder of the autopsy? Gary L. Aguilar, M.D.,[100] and physician colleagues recently submitted to *JAMA* for publication a list of 20 critical questions still unanswered by the pathologists. This was eventually, of necessity, published elsewhere. Pertinent to this, when Humes was interviewed after his HSCA appearance by Paul Hoch,[101] he replied, "I wish they'd asked some more questions . . . I was surprised at the Committee members . . . They sort of had a golden opportunity, you know. I was there, but they didn't choose to—and it didn't bother me one way or the other. Whatever pleased them, pleased me." The critics naturally wonder what Humes was thinking about; were any of these 20 questions in his thoughts?

The pathologists have only raised further suspicion by hiding from the media, to say nothing of hiding from their own colleagues. To date, they have never appeared in an adversarial setting in which they were required to respond to critical questions. Even Dr. Cyril H. Wecht, a member of the Forensic Pathology Panel for the HSCA and a long-time critic of the Warren Commission, was prevented from directly questioning his own colleagues in pathology. This was accomplished by the simple expedient of excluding him merely because he had already viewed the autopsy materials.[102]

[*Editor's note:* The author has deleted a section discussing the Zapruder film, which has now been superceded by his contribution to Part IV.]

The Autopsy: The Photographs

There is one reason that subsequent pathologists concurred with a head shot from the rear. It is the presence of an apparent entry wound near the cowlick area on the photograph.[36] In fact, if this were authentic, identification of this wound would hardly require any special expertise. The much more difficult question is one of authenticity. The main witness for alteration is, surprisingly enough, the chief pathologist, Humes himself. When queried about this visible wound, he said,[112] "No, no, that's no wound." He affirmed this again:[113] ". . . I can assure you . . . there was no defect corresponding to this [upper location] in the skull at any point. I don't know what that is. It could be to me clotted blood. I don't, I just don't know what it is, but it certainly was not any wound of entrance." Some loyalists may propose that the scalp was simply being lifted up for this photograph. However, Humes[114] was explicitly questioned about this and he said, "That is not the case." His very next words were, again commenting on the posterior head photograph,[114] "Because I submit to you that, despite the fact that this upper point that has been the source of some discussion here this afternoon is excessively obvious in the color photograph, I almost defy you to find it in that magnification in the black and white." Finck[115] had the same opinion as Humes when he testified several years earlier at the Clay Shaw trial: ". . . I don't endorse the 100 mm . . . I saw the wound of entry in the back of the head . . . slightly above the EOP, and it was definitely not 4 inches or 100 mm above it." These dramatic testimonies by Humes and Finck have not deterred numerous subsequent pathologists, simply by viewing the photographs (none of them examined the body), from claiming that the upper cowlick wound was the entry site.

To *JAMA*, Humes[35] stated that the true wound near the EOP was so obvious that shaving the hair was not required; it is this supposedly genuine wound that Humes (and everyone else for that matter) cannot see on this same photograph. According to the HSCA,[116] "Drs. Ebersole, Finck, and Boswell offered no explanation for the upper [visible] wound . . ." Shortly afterward the HSCA[116] stated, "Dr. Finck believed strongly that the observations of the autopsy pathologists were more valid than those of individuals who might subsequently examine photographs." And, eventually, the HSCA[116] summarized its own plight: " The panel continued to be concerned about the persistent disparity between its findings and those of the autopsy pathologists and the rigid tenacity with which the prosectors maintained that the entrance wound was at or near the EOP." Despite this astonishing state of affairs, the authenticity of the photograph has never been properly addressed and the defiant testimony of the pathologists themselves has been totally ignored (Note F). The critics naturally wonder what additional evidence the loyalists could possibly require before entertaining serious doubts of their own.

To virtually every eyewitness, these photographs are perplexing. They show a completely intact right posterior skull, which is in absolute conflict with the medical records of numerous Parkland physicians.[118] Even on a widely broadcast *Nova* television program on PBS in 1988 involving four Parkland physicians, the placement of their hands well behind the right ear to locate the large skull defect is in gross conflict with the posterior head photographs. This conflict persists in the memories of ancillary personnel at Bethesda,[119] and even with the measurements and descriptions of the pathologists themselves. The autopsy protocol specifically describes the skull defect as extending into the "occiput." The photographs, however, show the defect far above the occipital bone. The pathologists were never asked if these photographs were accurate. In fact, on the one question they were asked based on the photographs (regarding the posterior entry wound), they disagreed by four inches!

To the critics this situation is prima facie evidence of either alteration or else an unimaginable and simultaneous incompetence by three supposedly qualified pathologists. In his HSCA testimony,[120] Humes clearly agreed with the cowlick entry site while pointing at the lateral radiograph (best seen on videotape), but in *JAMA*[11] he reverted to the EOP site (Note G). Also, he and his colleagues had previously drawn the entry site on an actual skull for the HSCA. A photograph of this identification was printed by the HSCA;[121] it undeniably shows the *lower* EOP site. This skull photograph stands in astonishing conflict with Humes' radiographic testimony. He was never asked about this incredible discrepancy.

Since the photographs were reported as taken *before* the autopsy, the posterior head photograph should at least show the defect which Boswell reconstructed with a late arriving bone fragment. The scalp entry wound described by the pathologists was 15 x 6 mm; before insertion of the bone fragment it should have been larger[12] by about 2 cm, yielding a total diameter close to 3.5 cm, certainly large enough to be seen easily on the photograph, just as Humes claimed. Such a defect is nowhere in evidence.

Loyalists respond that distinguished experts have verified that the multiple skin and facial features on the photographs are indeed JFK's. Many critics accept this conclusion for the skin and facial landmarks, but protest that the scalp hair was not (and intrinsically could not be) authenticated. For the critics, therefore, the central issue of scalp authenticity remains unresolved.

At least six Parkland physicians saw cerebellum, usually reported as injured, through the skull defect; their reports appear for all to read in the widely available Warren Report.[118] To make the point even clearer, Dr. Kemp Clark, the neurosurgeon, in a handwritten note[118] described seeing both *cerebral* and *cerebellar* tissue. The intact posterior skull, as seen on the posterior head photographs, however, clearly prohibits viewing a structure as inferior as the cerebellum.

The photographs contain no identifiable overhead (vertex) view of the skull defect or even a useful view from the right lateral. Either of these could have resolved some of the current conflicts. Critics regard the absence of such views as highly suspicious, particularly since Humes recently advised *JAMA*[35] that no significant aspect was left unphotographed. Finck also stated to *JAMA*[122] that he had helped to photograph the posterior skull entry wound, which is the same wound near the EOP that cannot be seen by anyone.

Perry[123] first described the tracheostomy wound to Lifton as 2-3 cm wide, but he later altered his public statements and took responsibility for the much larger incision seen in the photographs. Critics note that tracheostomy incisions are rarely more than 3 or 4 cm wide. Even Perry's colleagues at Parkland do not recognize his work in this photograph.[124] Ebersole has expressed his own surprise to this author at the appearance and especially the size of this incision.[37] Some critics, though certainly not all, have suggested that the throat wound was enlarged before the autopsy in order to look for a bullet.

Multiple sources have described the back wound as distinctly lower than seen in the photographs:

a. Burkley's death certificate:[125,126] stated as T3.
b. Boswell's diagram (approved by Burkley):[34] the wound appears to be at about T3.
c. Ebersole[37] to Mantik: T4.
d. JFK shirt and coat: size, location, and orientation of holes.[127]
e. J. Lee Rankin:[46] while viewing a photograph, he stated that the bullet entered *below* the shoulder blade.

    f.   FBI agents Sibert and O'Neill.[23]

    g.   Secret Servicemen Clint Hill[128] and Glen Bennett.[129]

Critics wonder whether the back wound may have been raised on the photograph so that an (imaginary) exit through the throat might seem more feasible. Humes' measurements imply that the back wound was at least 7 to 10 cm lateral to midline, in distinct disagreement with the HSCA pathology panel, which placed it only 5 cm from midline. The 7 to 10 cm location would scarcely permit an anterior midline exit, as already noted above. A pneumothorax—which was not seen—would have resulted from either (a) the more lateral location of 7 to 10 cm or (b) the T-3 level. Neither of these anatomic descriptions therefore seem consistent with a transit trajectory through the upper chest.

The Autopsy: The Radiographs

The number of skull radiographs in the official record is three; of these, only two are printed in the public record. Jerroll F. Custer, the radiology technologist at the autopsy, has reported taking at least five skull radiographs,[130,131] including one oblique/ tangential view of the large posterior defect. Ebersole[37] also informed this author that a total of five or six views of the skull were obtained. In addition, one of the HSCA radiologists, Dr. David O. Davis, referred to other skull views that he had seen;[132] this is a particularly odd comment, especially since nothing else has ever been said about these other views. The critics naturally wonder if views showing the large posterior defect were culled out some time after the autopsy.

The radiologists who consulted for the HSCA concluded that there was no suggestion of a shot from the front. It is strange, however, that the evidence for this conclusion was based almost exclusively on the lateral skull radiograph. The condition of the right posterior skull, based on the AP radiograph, was largely ignored. There appear to be surprising findings on the AP view that warrant further investigation.[33] Were the radiologists deliberately avoiding the condition of the right occiput on the AP view? Quantitative scans of the original AP radiograph could still be done to ascertain just how much bone remains in the right occiput.[33] So far, however, access to this material has been remarkably limited and the proper studies have never been done.

Some radiologists described an entry wound near the cowlick area, 10 cm above the EOP. However, radiologist William B. Seaman[133] observed, regarding the proposed cowlick entry on the lateral skull radiograph, that this upper point "... suggests entry but is not conclusive." He also said that he could *not* denote beveling of the skull at that point.[133] Despite this equivocation, Dr. Michael Baden,[134] Chairman of the HSCA Forensic Pathology Panel, altered the meaning of plain English to conclude that ". . . all of the radiologist consultants with whom the panel spoke with [*sic*] and met with [*sic*], all concluded that without question there is an entrance bullet hole on the upper portion of the skull . . ." Dr Seaman was not invited to comment on this statement.

The critics wonder where these experts would have placed this entry wound on the AP view. Based on HSCA data,[135] the entry was 1 cm above the 6.5 mm radiopaque object. At this site on the AP radiograph there is no apparent entry hole. There is instead a small transverse defect clearly narrower than the 6.5 mm object seen here. The bone fragment in this vicinity is otherwise intact. A corollary question is whether this bone fragment lies on the posterior or anterior surface of the skull. If this bone fragment lies on the anterior skull surface, then the posterior skull surface is nowhere evident, an intolerable situation for the loyalist. If the fragment is on the posterior surface, there is no evident ingress. The loyalists must therefore choose between (a) absent right occiput or (b) no visible entry site on the AP radiograph.

Radiologists described fracture lines as radiating outward from the proposed cowlick entry site. On the AP view, however, these lines do not actually extend to the proposed entry site; they stop short of it. Dr. David O. Davis[132] was careful to choose his words: ". . . the linear fractures seem to more or less [*sic*] emanate from the embedded metallic fragment." Unless they unequivocally extend to this 6.5 mm object they cannot represent fracture lines caused by a posterior skull bullet.

The apparently linear, nearly horizontal "trail" of radiopaque densities seen near the vertex on the lateral skull radiograph lies well above the proposed cowlick entry site. A spinning bullet would be expected to eject small pieces of metal at a wide range of angles and not solely in the small solid angle that is seen. In addition, the trail would be expected to be cone shaped, narrower at the beginning and wider toward the end; instead, it shows no such effect at all. Moreover, the "trail" is obviously too high to fit with the proposed entry site. And, on the AP view, the "trail" simply vanishes; there is no "trail" at all. The apparent trail on the lateral view is merely an optical illusion; the particles are, in fact, widely scattered in space. The AP and lateral views are so different, in fact, that some observers have wondered whether they are even spatially compatible. Dr. David O. Davis[132] stated his own impression as follows: "It is not possible to totally explain the metallic fragment pattern that is present from some of the metallic fragments located superiorly in the region of the parietal bone, or at least projecting on the parietal bone are [*sic*] actually in the scalp. The frontal view does not give much help in this regard and it is impossible to work this out completely." Surely, if one of the HSCA's foremost experts had difficulty with the locations of these radiopaque objects, they deserve more attention.

Authenticity Issues

It is not within the customary province of pathologists or radiologists to address authenticity issues. These specialists sometimes even seem embarrassed or awkward when asked about possible alterations. Though some steps were taken by the HSCA to rule out modifications, other steps either were not or could not be taken. Some loyalists will not even discuss this question. As authenticity is often at the forefront of the critic's mind, conversations with loyalists often stop suddenly and uncomfortably at this point. Some critics, however, will never rest easy until more attention is paid to these issues.

The loyalist naturally responds to authenticity issues by reciting the studies of the HSCA.[137] Several serious, still unresolved questions regarding the photographs and radiographs have already been listed above. The loyalist also emphasizes that the Bethesda personnel gave their seal of approval to these items after reviewing them at the National Archives.[138] The critics reply, however, that apparently none of them, not even the radiologist Ebersole, noticed the obvious, nearly circular 6.5 mm object on the AP radiograph or, if they did, they failed to describe it. It is astounding that Humes, after spending the better part of a day at the Archives while reviewing this material, has admitted[139] that he failed to see the presumed skull entry wound near the cowlick area on the posterior photograph. This is the same photograph that is now the subject of so much dissension. Is it remotely possible that he was not shown this photograph at the Archives? Finally, if one of these individuals had suspected that something was different, would he have said so publicly? What consequences would have followed such a statement? Might it not have been easier quietly to assume that his memory had failed him? By analogy, it is useful to recall that even now some of the Parkland physicians seem more persuaded by the photographs than their own previously well documented initial recollections.

The critics' list of candidates for alteration may seem long. It should be noted, however, that scarcely any critic insists that all of these have been modified. In fact, a modest but critical alteration to one or a small number might be quite sufficient. A good illustration of such a minimal requirement is the entry wound seen on the posterior head photograph, which even Humes could not accept. Such a change, all by itself, could totally alter the complexion of this case. The candidates are listed here.

1. *The autopsy protocol.* The first draft was certified by Humes as burned by him in his home fireplace.[140,141] No questions were asked and no explanations were offered for this behavior. (Humes did explain why he burned his autopsy room notes,[142] but was never asked why he burned his *first draft.*) The complete disappearance of Humes' autopsy diagram has already been noted. He was never asked, in view of his statement that he had faithfully copied everything, why this absolutely critical item never showed up anywhere. Finally, the wording of the final draft seems deliberately vague, imprecise and unprofessional.

2. *The Zapruder film.* On frame 313, the authenticity of red cloud of presumed blood and tissue and the two linear streaks (purported to be bone fragments by Lattimer) have both been challenged, on photographic[143] and scientific (physics) grounds.[33] Further studies may yet provide more insight into these issues.[33] [*Editor's note:* See Part IV and especially David Mantik, Part IV.]

3. *Photographs.* The location and appearance of both the skull and back wounds have been questioned. There are also numerous identical poses[144] which suggest to the critic that crucial incriminating photographs have been removed only to be replaced by simple duplicates (so that the total number would not change). Humes' disagreement with the posterior skull wound on the photograph raises very serious authenticity concerns. It may be the central issue in this entire case. Even the photographer himself, Floyd Riebe,[131] has denied the authenticity of this photograph, particularly with respect to the supposedly intact posterior skull. What additional evidence, the critics wonder, is required before loyalists would be willing to consider this issue seriously?

4. *Radiographs.* The 6.5 mm object embedded in the posterior skull near the cowlick area was described neither by the pathologists nor by the radiologist Ebersole at the autopsy, even though they all viewed the radiographs in the morgue and they were all looking for bullet fragments. Was it added later to implicate the Mannlicher-Carcano bullet? This 6.5 mm object is presumably the cross section of a bullet. Amazingly, however, both the nose and tail (Warren Commission Exhibit Numbers 567 and 569) of this same bullet (Note H) were said to have been found in the front of the limousine.[146,147] How is it possible for a nearly complete cross section

from somewhere *inside* the bullet to embed itself on the *outside* of the skull? Experts[148] have never seen even a nose fragment from a fully jacketed bullet embed itself in this manner, 1 cm *below* the entry site, to say nothing of an *internal* cross section performing such an astounding feat. In addition, the "trail" of small radiopaque objects (presumably bullet fragments) has changed location in space by 10 cm, and these radiopaque objects may also have increased in size. There appears to be a trail on the lateral skull view but not on the AP; are these spatially compatible? Were subtle changes made in the posterior portion of the lateral skull radiograph in order to cover a large defect there? It is noteworthy that, despite the claims of authenticity by the HSCA, this critical posterior area was never examined for authenticity. And, finally, why were findings on the AP radiograph either ignored or misinterpreted?

5. *Neutron activation analysis.* The bullet fragments examined by the HSCA in 1978 should have been identical to those examined in 1964 by the FBI. They had exhibit numbers which implied identity. The technique itself would not have altered the masses. Yet, amazingly enough, as clearly shown in tables compiled by Wallace Milam[149] from the original HSCA data[150] and the FBI bench notes, all the masses (except for one tiny fragment) had grown within the space of 14 years! In addition, the size and shape of the original larger skull fragment (7 x 2 mm) had changed in a *spatially impossible manner* when it later appeared in a photograph by the HSCA.[151] Have substitutions been made?

Logical Issues[152]

Even if two shots struck JFK from the rear, as *JAMA* maintains, that says nothing about the total number of shots fired. Even the HSCA agreed that two shots hit from the rear. Yet because it concluded that another shot was fired from the front (but missed, in their view), the HSCA endorsed a probable conspiracy. *JAMA*'s conclusions by themselves, therefore, cannot rule out a conspiracy. Though *JAMA*'s editor[153] has clearly stated that he does not disagree with this logical conclusion, this same editor nevertheless permitted his designated writer, Dennis Breo, to violate this same consideration in the same issue of *JAMA*! Breo[154] stated, "How Lee Harvey Oswald, a political fanatic and the *lone* (emphasis added) gunman bought by mail order a surplus World War II Italian rifle . . ." Without any prelude, Breo thus claims that a conspiracy has been ruled out. How this conclusion logically follows from the interview with Dr. Finck (who is the purported subject of this article) or, for that matter, from any of the other medical evidence discussed by *JAMA*, is never clarified by Breo. On the contrary, he appears to introduce issues which lie far beyond the medical evidence. To address the *nonmedical* issues in the debate of lone gunman versus conspiracy would require at least an entire monograph. Is it possible that Breo's (or even *JAMA*'s) biases are showing here?

To the critics, the requirement of total evidence (taking into account all of the available evidence) is seriously violated by the loyalists. They seem to select whatever data fits their view and ignore whatever does not. They may, of course, respond that the critics dismiss evidence in a similar fashion by invoking alterations as an excuse whenever they dislike the data. To this, however, the critics at least answer that modifications can usually be subject to testing, while the overt suppression of data can never be subject to testing. Moreover, because of the obvious inconsistency of at least some of this data, as extensively outlined above, participants in this debate, no matter which side is selected, must make some difficult choices: for example, for the posterior skull entry wound (contrary to the equivocations of Dr. Petty), they must choose between either the lower EOP site or the 10 cm higher cowlick entry site—both cannot be correct. Neither Humes nor subsequent reviewers ever suggested that there were two posterior skull entry wounds. (Because of the time constraints for a lone gunman, two wounds would immediately suggest a conspiracy.) Other dilemmas have been noted above. If alteration is not invoked as an explanation for these inconsistencies, then some other reason (or reasons) must be advanced.

The Historical Milieu

From the earliest days after the assassination, authors assembled long lists of JFK's enemies. As intricate interlocking webs emerged among these groups, the possibility of conspiracy loomed ever larger in the minds of the critics. To the critics, the loyalists seemed to inhabit a world in which government employees were incapable of gross evil. Critics stand aghast at the thought processes displayed by G. Robert Blakey, Chief Counsel to the HSCA, when he was interviewed on *Crossfire* about Oliver Stone's movie. He said[155] that if ". . . the shot came from the front, there was a cover-up, therefore the military-industrial complex did it, therefore my nation is corrupt, and that's just obscene." If current (or even past) government employees are excluded *a priori* from the list of suspects, how can any investigation follow evidence which might possibly point in that direction? And if the same investigation is led by Blakey, which it was, what questions might automatically be ruled out by subordinates who are expected to follow orders, no matter whether explicitly or implicitly stated?

Some critics suggest that the loyalists' view of human nature derives from outmoded and sanguine philosophies antedating the two World Wars—or at least antedating Watergate. They wonder if loyalists have truly noted the astonishingly wide range of behavior seen in the human species, particularly when careers, reputations, or fortunes are at stake. The American government itself has by no means always been exemplary: witness the Gulf of Tonkin "incident," the My Lai massacre cover-up, Watergate, Iran-Contra, Iraqgate, and many others. Is the JFK assassination (at least in its post-mortem aspects) merely one more example of similar behavior? Conversations tend to founder when these issues are encountered.

Though critics accept generic government incompetence as an explanation for some strange features of this case, nevertheless, the ongoing inaccessibility of much of this data (such as photographs and radiographs) seems to some critics yet one more sign of an ongoing government cover-up of the assassination. The Assassination Disclosure Materials Act of 1992 could help allay some cynicism, depending on how it is implemented. Certainly many more specialists should be given access to these materials. A greater sense of openness and accessibility could even lessen widespread suspicion of government institutions. If indeed there is nothing to hide, why should the government wish to promote the appearance of impropriety? In March 1993, Dr. Robert Artwohl, a loyalist, was admitted to the National Archives to view the JFK artifacts. Though the timing of this visit, which occurred shortly before Artwohl appeared at the side of *JAMA*'s editor during a public debate, seems an odd coincidence, this development by itself is encouraging. More experts should be given access. Critics believe their own experts should be given equal time.

Summary

This discussion has reviewed some of the contradictory medical and scientific evidence in the JFK assassination. The confused nature of these data make it impossible to exclude shots from the front. There is, moreover, strong evidence for at least two shots from the front. Evidence for a frontal throat shot includes the original testimony of the Parkland physicians, the anatomy of the upper chest/lower neck, the nonpenetrating back wound, and the statements of Bethesda personnel and the national media who reported a bullet (or at least large fragments) found in the shoulder/neck area. Evidence for a frontal head shot includes the double motion on the Zapruder film, the deficient explanations of the loyalists for the posterior head snap, the descriptions of the Parkland physicians, the pattern of brain trauma, the eyewitness testimony of nonphysicians (Dealey Plaza, Parkland, Bethesda) and, most especially, the absent right occiput.

Critics claim that foreigners (Europeans are often cited[156]) are much more on their side in this debate. It is said that foreigners regard Americans on such issues as oddly innocent or even naive, unable or unwilling to recognize pertinent historical parallels. They point out that in these foreign conspiracies it is often a powerful political opponent who has benefited most. Why should America be different? Are Americans a species different from the rest of the human race? It is here perhaps more than anywhere else that loyalists and critics part company. It is notable that this has nothing at all to do with the basic facts of the case.

The renowned Cambridge don, C. S. Lewis, who also died on November 22, 1963, once met someone who claimed to have seen a ghost, yet for the rest of his life, refused to believe in ghosts.[157] For him, seeing was not believing. For the loyalist, too, believing in political evil may be a prerequisite to seeing. In addition, a measure of courage may be required to face the ominous consequences of such a belief: the comfortable foundations of American civilization, and especially its political norms, are quickly called into serious question. Embarking on such a journey cannot be lightly undertaken; even for Americans who are famous and educated, it is much less painful to look away.

Even full disclosure of the JFK data might leave some persons in these two camps still separated, so wide is the chasm that divides them. When facts alone are insufficient to settle disputes, our human prejudices stand exposed. Eventually, if we wish truly to understand this case, we must all recognize in ourselves the color of our own preconceptions.

Notes

Acknowledgments. Through its recent attention to the JFK assassination, *JAMA* has dramatically increased the motivation for this discussion. My sincere appreciation goes to the following individuals for their encouragement, critical data, and indispensable critiques:

Gary L. Aguilar, M.D.	Leslie Keough
Joseph N. Riley, Ph.D.	Douglas E. DeSalles, M.D.
William G. Keough, Ph.D.	John Szabo, M.D.
James H. Fetzer, Ph.D.	David Lifton
Sherry Szabo	Patricia L. James, M.D.
Wallace Milam	Cyril H. Wecht, M.D., J.D.

[*Editor's note:* The original version of this paper was composed in April and revised in May of 1993. It has undergone minor revisions during July of 1997 for its publication in this volume.]

A. As the autopsy began, the pathologists were told that three shots had been heard and that JFK had fallen forward, bleeding from the head. They were also told that a rifle barrel had disappeared into an upper floor of the Texas School Book Depository.[14] It is now well known that JFK fell *backward*. [*Editor's note*: This issue is explored further and reassessed in Part IV.] The other two statements have also been vigorously debated. The critics naturally wonder what conclusions the pathologists would have reached if they had been correctly told that JFK had fallen backward, and also that there were four shots and that at least one shot had come from the front—all positions with some support, according to the critics. Even the HSCA was in complete agreement with each of these positions. The pathologists were also told that the (note the singular article) assassin had been apprehended. Since Oswald was shot *before*[27] they completed their final draft, it is perhaps not so surprising that they reached the conclusions they did.

B. Since the tip of the acromion is readily palpated, this distance is easily measured on adult males. There is an alternate approach, which is well known to radiation oncologists from irradiation of the mantle area in Hodgkin's Disease. It is rarely possible to see both acromia on a 17-inch-wide radiographic film; two separate overlapping films are usually required to encompass the mantle area. If both acromia could fit onto a 17-inch film, the distance from midline to either acromion would be 17 x 2.54 / 2 = 21.6 cm.

C. Between these two statements, Humes had told the HSCA[86] yet a third version, exactly midway between these two extremes—the agnostic's view: "From our point of view . . . the peripheral things as to whence cometh the missile and where it went and various other things and [the] so-called single bullet theory has been, in part, attributed to us, and that's not our doing . . . Those kinds of things are peripheral, but we've been sort of involved, or our names have been involved, with those kinds of conjectures that we really can't make any definite opinion about or scientific opinion about [*sic*]."

D. Addison's disease was clinically confirmed in 1977 by Joan and Clay Blair,[96] after interviewing one of JFK's physicians, and published in their book, *The Search for JFK*. Prior to that, in 1967, Dr John Nichols had published his own very convincing observations in *JAMA*.[97] J. A. Nicholas[98] had previously described three patients with adrenal insufficiency who had successfully undergone surgery. One of these was an otherwise unidentified 37-year-old male who had had lower back surgery at Cornell University Medical College in New York City on 21 October 1954. Nichols noticed that *The New York Times*, of 22 October 1954, had announced on page 17 that Senator Kennedy had had surgery on 21 October 1954. Removal of a metal plate four months later was also coincident in the medical journal and in *The Times*, thereby providing yet one more confirmation of JFK's identity.

E.   This estimate of 400 gm is very conservative. It assumes that nearly all of the bone fragments went straight forward. If instead these bone fragments had a significant component of transverse linear momentum (i.e. up, down—or even backward), the required mass of the ejected brain tissue would be correspondingly larger, perhaps even much larger. It should also be noted that Alvarez's choice of 10% for the ejected mass is a realistic illustration but is not essential. It is possible both to calculate and measure speeds of the ejecta from data in the Alvarez paper; the ejecta speeds are 40–50 ft/sec. The distance traveled by the bone fragments in Lattimer's[104] experiments can be shown to be consistent with these speeds. With this information, it is then easy to calculate the ejected masses required to produce the JFK head recoil speed[106] of 1.6 ft/sec. These masses are indeed significant.[33]

F.   Recently in *JAMA*[117] Dr. Charles S. Petty endorsed Humes' placement of the skull entry wound: "There were no bullet defects other than those described by Humes in his report." What Petty does not say is that when he served on the HSCA Forensic Pathology Panel he officially disagreed with Humes by 10 cm (four inches). He voted for the photographic cowlick entry site instead of the pathologists' EOP site. He now seems disingenuously to want to have it both ways! Or if his opinion has changed, he has not informed his readers of that change of mind, nor has he stated his reasons for such a turnabout.

G.   Humes (and Boswell, too) gave yet a third location for the posterior skull entry wound. When questioned by Petty before the HSCA[9] Humes replied, "[It's] *below* (emphasis added) the EOP." When this question was repeated with some apparent incredulity by Petty, Humes assured him, "Right." And then Boswell chimed in: "It's to the right and *inferior* (emphasis added) to the EOP."

H.   Since more than three bullets would likely mean a conspiracy (because of the timing problems), the loyalists insist on only three bullets. In the loyalists' view, one bullet ("the magic bullet") traveled intact through both Kennedy and Connally. Another bullet missed. Unless large fragments of this latter bullet ended up in the front of the limousine, only the bullet that traversed Kennedy's head could have both (a) left two large fragments in the limousine and also (b) embedded a 6.5 mm fragment in the cowlick area of the skull. The Warren Commission[145] did conclude that these two large fragments came from the bullet that passed through JFK's head.

Postscript

The President John F. Kennedy Skull X-rays:

Regarding the Magical Appearance of

the Largest "Metal" Fragment

About four years ago I sat down to breakfast with my 7 year-old son and my 5 year-old daughter. I had just decided that it was time to try a simple experiment. Over the preceding months my attention had been drawn to the JFK autopsy X-ray films

(Figures 1 and 2). Since my schedule at that time permitted almost no free moments, I had chosen that brief interlude at the breakfast table to stare again at the puzzling prints of these films in David Lifton's *Best Evidence* (a best seller first published in 1980). In particular, the mysteries of the 6.5 mm object seen there had puzzled me. It was supposedly the largest piece of metal on the skull films, but the pathologists could not recall it—nor did they remove it! Defenders of the pathologists had offered one absurd explanation after another in their defense. These excuses had ranged from a proposal that they had actually removed it—even though they never described it—from the back of the skull (where it was obviously located). In fact, the pathologists persisted in saying only that they had removed the much smaller fragment above the right frontal sinus. Another defense was the inevitable psychological one—they were so harassed that they couldn't see straight! Or perhaps it had simply fallen off before they could retrieve it!

This object seemed ridiculously plain to see, but I wondered just how easy this could be. So I decided to try Christopher, our seven year old. "Christopher," I said, "Could you come here and find the bullet?" In a second, he was at my side and, without hesitation, he pointed straight at it. Now I wondered how far I could carry this, so I turned to our five year old, who was seated across the table and hadn't seen Christopher point. "Meredith," I said, "Do you think you could find the bullet?" So she marched around the table and looked at the print, momentarily puzzled. "Well, what's it supposed to look like?" she asked. When told that it was white, there was only a fleeting hesitation before she pointed at the correct area and said, "Is that it?" Unfortunately, I could not also fairly ask my wife since she was the medical director of our local emergency room!

In the official version then, we are supposed to believe that what could not be seen at the autopsy—by three experienced pathologists, one radiologist, numerous ancillary medical personnel, and all too many onlookers—could be spotted almost instantly (and independently) by five year-old and seven year-old children. The point of this essay is to resolve this riddle. Before we arrive at that point, however, some history is in order.

A Brief History

The X-ray film in question was taken from the front, with JFK lying on his back at the Bethesda Naval Medical Center. The X-ray film was placed directly behind his head and the X-rays entered from the front. This is an anterior-posterior view, usually abbreviated simply as "AP". This film (Figure 1) shows a nearly round, 6.5 mm, very white object within the upper part of the right orbit. At the 4 to 6 o'clock quadrant, however, a section is missing, so that it is not perfectly round.

On the lateral film (Figure 2), a small fragment is scarcely visible (on prints) at the rear of the skull, near the cowlick area. This was much easier to see, though, on the X-ray films at the National Archives. On this lateral view it is about the same height as on the AP—about 6 mm high, but it is only 3 to 4 mm wide (i.e., from front to back).

On the AP view, this object is overwhelmingly the most impressive metal-like object. That was confirmed all too quickly by my children. (They would have had more trouble on the lateral view.) On this AP view, there is another small piece of metal—7 x 2 mm. It lies directly above the right frontal sinus. The pathologists always refer to this one when asked about the largest fragment—and they did remove it. It was later subjected to several scientific tests. Reference to this fragment is also found in the FBI report prepared by Sibert and O'Neill (Warren Commission Document CD–7), who were present at the autopsy that night.

This same 7 x 2 mm piece of metal can also be seen on the lateral view (Figure 2), where it does indeed lie just above the right frontal sinus—exactly where the pathologists described it. The FBI report also refers to a second, somewhat smaller, fragment: "The largest section of this missile as portrayed by the X-ray appeared to be behind [*it should have said above*] the right frontal sinus. The next largest fragment appeared to be at the rear of the skull at the juncture of the skull bone [*probably the lambdoid suture*]." My own comments appear in italics here.

Roy Kellerman of the Secret Service (who sat in the right front seat of the limousine during the shooting), was interviewed by Jim Kelly and Andy Purdy at the Holiday Inn North, St. Petersburg, Florida (24 and 25 August 1977, p. 3) for the House Select Committee on Assassinations (HSCA). He said that the skull X-ray film showed a ". . . whole mass of stars, *the only large piece* (emphasis added) being behind the eye which was given to the FBI agents when it was removed." Since it was the 7 x 2 mm fragment that was removed, the implication is clear —Kellerman, like *everyone* else, knew nothing about the much larger 6.5 mm object that is so obvious on the AP view. It is surely odd that none of the government panels ever asked the four autopsy physicians whether they had seen this 6.5 mm object *during* the autopsy.

When the HSCA asked chief pathologist James J. Humes about the largest metal fragment, for example, he unhesitatingly referred to the fragment above the right frontal sinus (7 HSCA 251). He never did discuss this 6.5 mm object on the AP that is unequivocally at the *back* of the skull (as determined from the lateral view). When Gary Aguilar, M.D., recently asked assistant pathologist J. Thornton Boswell about this fragment, Boswell also only described the fragment above the right frontal sinus. And he clearly added that all the other metal fragments were very small, distinctly smaller than the 7 x 2 mm fragment above the right frontal sinus. And he made no mention at all of the most obvious fragment on the AP film.

Shortly before his death several years ago, I was able to ask the radiologist, John H. Ebersole, M.D., this same question (telephone conversations of 2 November and of 2 December 1992). At the moment of that question, the entire interview came to an abrupt halt—the question remains forever unanswered. My tape recording of that interview has now been donated to the Assassination Records and Review Board (ARRB) as part of their collection. Anyone can play it for themselves. It has some other interesting moments, too.

After reviewing the X-ray films on 1 November 1966, at the National Archives, the autopsy pathologists, the radiologist, and the photographer stated, "However, careful examination at the autopsy, and the photographs and X-rays taken during the autopsy, revealed no evidence of a bullet or of *a major portion of a bullet* (emphasis added) in the body of the President . . ." This statement is remarkable for what these reviewers do not say: they fail to comment on what they actually saw on the films *during this review* on 1 November 1966!

The eyewitness testimony, therefore, is unanimous—this 6.5 mm object was not seen at the autopsy. It first appeared in the historical record after the Clark panel review in 1968. Its magical appearance at that time is what has prompted the title of this essay. (One member of the Clark Panel was Russell Fisher, M.D., Mary-

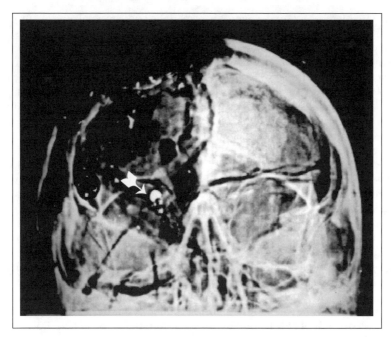

Figure 1. The official AP (anterior-posterior) X-ray of JFK's cranium.

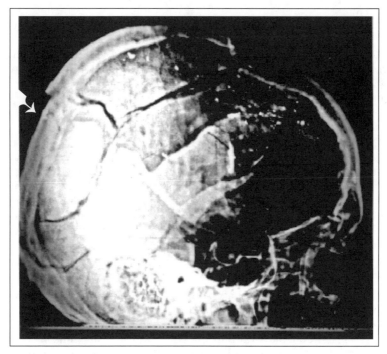

Figure 2. The official right lateral X-ray of JFK's cranium.

land State Medical Examiner, who performed the controversial autopsy in 1978 of John Paisley, a probable CIA operative; see William R. Corson, et al., *Widows*, 1989, Chapter 8).

There are additional puzzles about this object. According to the Warren Commission (Exhibit Numbers 567 and 569), both the nose and tail of this same bullet were found in the front of the presidential limousine (see Lifton, 1992, Chapter 4 and Warren Commission Hearings, 1964, Vol. 17, p. 257). But how is it possible for a nearly complete cross section from somewhere inside the bullet to embed itself on the *outside* of the skull? Experts have never seen even a nose fragment from a full metal jacketed bullet embed itself in this manner, let alone a cross section from inside a bullet. (*See* Bonar Menninger, *Mortal Error*, 1992, p. 68). In addition, the fragment is *not* at the bullet entry site selected by the HSCA—it lies one cm *inferior* to their chosen entry site! How does such a metal fragment migrate one cm below its supposed entry site and then *embed* itself into the skull after such a migration? It sounded to me as if someone had invented smart bullets before the smart bombs of the Gulf War. Needless to say, no one has ever explained this queer migration— but that is the official story!

Logically, it made more sense to me that this 6.5 mm object had been superimposed onto the X-ray film. There is a very good reason why someone might want to do that. The rifle attributed to Lee Harvey Oswald was a 6.5 mm Mannlicher-Carcano—exactly the same rather unusual caliber as this object! Furthermore, Lee had supposedly shot JFK from the sniper's nest in the Texas School Book Depository, which was *behind* Kennedy. Therefore, since this bullet fragment was the right size and it was located on the back of the skull, we were supposed to believe that Lee did it.

But how could someone change an X-ray film without using razor blades and tape? Of course, no government investigation could take such an unconventional proposal seriously, so it was never explored. The HSCA did compare X-ray films taken of JFK before his death and after, from which they confirmed that the autopsy X-ray films were really JFK's. Although I also have done that—and concur with the conclusion—that was not really germane to the issues surrounding this 6.5 mm object.

I thought it might be interesting to look at the autopsy X-ray films. So I wrote a letter to Burke Marshall, the Kennedy family attorney. He controls access to all of the autopsy material, even though they are actually stored at the National Archives. About a year (!) later, I received formal permission to see them. In fact, over the years I have reviewed them on seven different days. (I also got to examine the autopsy photographs, JFK's clothing, the 7 x 2 mm fragment, and the "magic bullet.") On my first visit, I obtained some really strange measurements on this object. Shortly afterwards, I thought of how to do the whole experiment right. Before I get to that point, though, I must introduce the subject of optical density.

About Optical Density

X-rays are created by exposing objects to radiation and capturing their images on film. Where X-ray films are very black, many X-rays have hit the film. For example, the air around the skull in these autopsy films is very black. Where the bone is very thick, however, the X-ray film looks quite transparent (white in books). The area around the ear (the petrous bone) is especially clear because it is the densest bone in the body. Simply by looking at a film, a radiologist (or anyone else who wants to learn) can tell a lot about the tissues that the X-rays encountered in their path to the film. It is easy for him (or her) to spot a bone—or an air cavity—because they are so distinctive. So the more tissue in the path of the X-rays, the whiter the image; the less tissue, the darker the image. It is rather like trying to read a sign in a dense fog. The harder it is to see the sign, the more fog is in the way—just like trying to read a metal sign in the X-ray beam through a lot of bone. And vice versa; where there is little fog, the sign is easy to see, just like a metal sign would be easy to see on an X-ray film taken in air.

If you wanted to know how much tissue (relatively speaking) the image represented at any point on the X-ray film, you could measure how black or white the image was at that point (by measuring how much light gets through at that site). The optical density at any point is directly related to light transmission. Such measurements are very simple to make. After calibrating a small device (the densitometer), the film is placed on the surface which is a light box. At one point on the surface there is a second (small) light source that shines through a tiny hole (usually one millimeter in diameter, although this can be varied, as I did in these experiments). The point on the X-ray film that you want to measure is placed directly over this small hole and the arm above the table is brought down to make a tight contact with the film at that point, so that no outside light can interfere. Inside the arm is the detector that measures how much light actually gets through the film. The machine reads this in optical density units.

Optical density is technically defined as

$$OD = \log_{10}(I_o/I),$$

where Io is the incident light intensity and I is the transmitted intensity. This definition has the advantage of making optical density proportional to the amount of silver halide reduced to black metallic silver. For example, if two films of OD equal to one (10% of the light gets through) are overlaid, the combined OD will be two (1% of the light gets through), which makes good sense from the point of view of physics. An OD of zero represents 100% transmission—all the light gets through. If you took an X-ray film of a really thick piece of lead, that's about what you would see. An OD of 1.00 represents a transmission of 1/10 or 10%; an OD of 2.00 represents a transmission of 1%; an OD of three yields 0.1%; an OD of four, 0.01%, and so on.

In daily radiological practice, ODs of most X-ray films are centered around 1.0. This choice is automatically made by the human eye for convenience in discrimination among commonly viewed human tissues as seen on an X-ray film. The usual working range is from about 0.5 to 2.0. It is unusual for the OD of observed tissues to exceed 3.0 except as a byproduct of exposure requirements at other sites on the film. An OD of 2.0 will appear quite dark, while an OD of 0.5 will appear nearly transparent.

A Thought Experiment

If this 6.5 mm object was a fake, it should not yield measurements consistent with real metal. For example, there might be especially bizarre results when comparing the ODs from the lateral to the ODs on the AP—because one view has real metal and the other does not. Let's use fog again to illustrate this principle. Suppose you are in a dense fog trying to read a sign. Also imagine that your twin is standing in the sunshine well outside of the fog. He can see how thick the fog is between you and the sign, because he can see where it starts and where it ends (for example, you might think the fog goes all the way to the sign—but you might be wrong!) Meanwhile, though, you can also tell where the fog is thickest—that's where the sign will be hardest to read. You could even develop a kind of scale for measuring just how much fog there was between you and any part of the sign. And your twin, on the other hand, would be like someone looking at the AP view—on that view anyone can see with his own eyes how thick the metal is from left to right. But if you look at the lateral X-ray film and you measure the ODs (that's like looking through the fog) you also would be able to tell (relatively speaking) how thick the metal was.

So what would happen if the image on the AP had been faked? Suppose someone had simply made the image more transparent *at just this site* so that it would look like a cross section of a bullet. What would that do to the ODs? On the AP view, the ODs would be very low (0.5 or a little more—which is what they are). And this would tell us that the metal here was very, very thick. It might even make us think of lead, because X-rays have a hard time getting through lead. But if you next looked at the lateral view (I'm assuming that this X-ray is authentic—as we will see later), you would see for yourself (just using your eyes—no ODs) that the metal was only a thin sliver (from front to back). So you would then have a paradox: you could see with your own eyes that it's quite thin on the lateral view (from front to back), but the ODs (taken on the AP) would tell you that it's very thick! So obviously something would have to be wrong.

That was the experiment I proposed to do. I wanted lots and lots of OD measurements along lines in many directions. But first I had to do something creative. I borrowed a very precise gear mechanism from our X-ray measuring tank (we use this to measure how intense the X-rays are at any specific depth). Next I built a sturdy little plastic jig and secured the gear mechanism to it. Then I screwed the entire apparatus to the densitometer. More importantly, though, I could now manually scan the films in a systematic manner and get 100 measurements every centimeter! Using a razor blade edge, I also reduced the size of the small transmission hole to nearly 60 microns—that was quite small, much less than the usual one millimeter. That would allow me to measure very narrow areas on the film, which I needed to do since I was taking 100 data points every centimeter. Now I was ready. Best of all, when I tested it, the whole thing worked and was small and easy to carry. So I took it with me to the National Archives.

Back at the Archives

At the Archives, I first focused on the lateral X-ray film. I scanned the 6.5 mm object from top to bottom, at 0.1 mm increments (Figure 3 and Table 1). What was quite surprising to me was how little the ODs changed from just outside this object (where there was bone) to inside the object—that meant that it must be quite thin (from left to right inside the skull). This was a very promising start, because it should have looked quite thick—after all, on the AP view, I could see that it was 6.5 mm thick (from left to right). So I had discovered a serious inconsistency right away. And there were more to come. On this lateral film, I actually scanned this

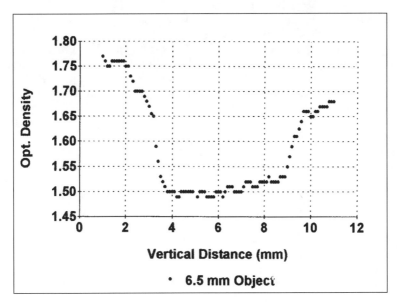

Figure 3. JFK lateral skull X-ray: 6.5 mm object.
Vertical scan: superior to inferior.

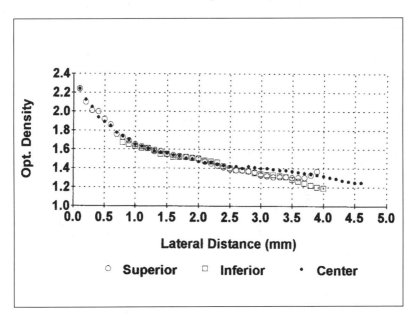

Figure 4. JFK lateral skull X-ray: 6.5 mm object.
Horizontal scans: posterior to anterior.

object from top to bottom in several parallel lines, but these were all quite similar, so only one of them is shown in Figure 3.

I continued with the lateral X-ray film, but next I scanned it from back to front instead of from top to bottom. This would be really interesting. I could see on the AP that the object had been chewed out at the 4 to 6 o'clock quadrant. That meant that there was a lot less metal at the bottom. So on the scan near the bottom, the ODs should show a lot less metal (i.e., the image should look darker and the ODs should be higher). In Figure 4, three scans are shown, going from back to front. One scan (S) was taken near (but still inside) the superior border, another (C) was taken near the center, and a third (I) was taken near the inferior border (but still inside). The data from these three scans were nearly identical to each other, except near the front surface of the 6.5 mm object—here the ODs were lowest on the inferior scan. That meant there was *more* metal at the bottom than at the center or at the top (on going from left to right within the skull). But that was exactly the *opposite* of what was obvious to the eye on the AP view! On the AP view, anyone can see that the width is much less than 6.5 mm at the bottom—where the section was chewed out. But these ODs tell us just the opposite—that there was *more* metal at the bottom! If anyone had wanted evidence of forgery, this was about as good as it could get, but there was still more to come.

Object	OD	Apparent Width*	Actual Width**
6.5 mm	1.50	thin	2-3 mm
amalgams	1.00	wider	10 mm
7 x 2 mm	1.60	thin	2 mm

*from right to left
**as seen on the AP view

Table 1. ODs on the Lateral Skull X-ray.

I also measured the ODs just outside of this metal fragment at postions corresponding to each hour of the clock; starting at 12 o'clock. These ODs are 1.72, 1.45, 1.33, 1.25, 1.11, 1.24, 1.41, 1.59, 3.30, 3.24, 3.49, and 3.44. The largest number here were measured in the air behind this fragment. The smallest numbers were found anterior to the fragment, where the ODs inside and outside the fragment were very similar. That similarity implies that the fragment is extremely thin at its anterior edge.

I next turned to the AP view and scanned across the center of this 6.5 mm object, going from right to left (Figure 5 and Table 2.). This scan tells us that there is more metal (quite a lot more) on the right side than on the left side (by "right" and "left" I always refer to the skull's left and right sides). That was a little odd, of course, because the object initially had looked round and uniform. Then I decided to remove my glasses and take a good look at it. (I am extremely near sighted, so with my glasses off I can see small things—like splinters in my children's fingers—

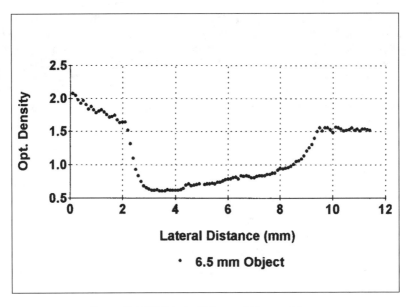

Figure 5. JFK AP skull X-ray: 6.5 mm object.
Horizontal scan: right to left.

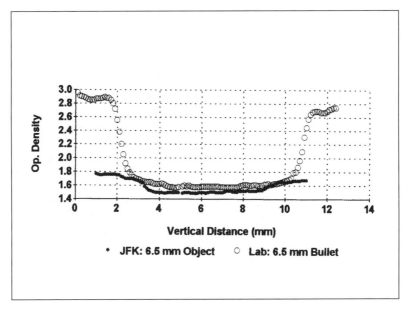

Figure 6. Lateral skull X-rays: JFK vs. lab.
Vertical scans: superior to inferior.

really well.) To my amazement, I could actually see that this object was not one but two! It was a superposition of images! Just inside the right border of this object I could see a crescent shaped metal fragment; its right border was almost perfectly parallel with the right border of the 6.5 mm object. Its (right to left) width was only about 2–3 millimeters across at most places. It was quite irregular and ragged look-ing—like shrapnel often is. Additonal little bits and pieces were splattered around inside the 6.5 mm object and there were even tiny pieces just outside the 6.5 mm object. These latter pieces were so small, however, that I hadn't seen them in prints that appear in books. And at the bottom it was definitely wider—exactly what the ODs had told me! I suddenly understood—I was seeing the original shrapnel *through* the superimposed 6.5 mm object! And what I saw there was completely consistent with *all* the measured ODs! This was the authentic fragment that James Sibert and Francis O'Neill had described [*Editor's note*: in their FBI report about the autopsy].

Object	OD	Apparent Length*	Actual Length**
6.5 mm	0.60	very long	3-4 mm
amalgams	0.74, 0.78	long	30-40 mm
7 x 2 mm	1.44	short	2 mm

*from front to back
**as seen on the lateral view

Table 2. ODs on the AP Skull X-ray.

In a wonderful book, *The Technique of Special Effects Cinematography* (1965/85), p. 177, Raymond Fielding reports that a typical outcome in superposition spe-cial effects is the "phantom" effect, in which background detail can be seen through an actor. If this X-ray image had been produced by a photographic superposition process—I later show that it was and how to do it—then that would explain my ability to see the original metal fragment right through the forged object. As care-fully as I could, I then sketched the real shrapnel—the sketch is still in my notes. But on the AP view, the OD scan through the 6.5 mm object also tells us (Figure 5) how much shrapnel (relatively speaking) there was on the *original* X-ray film. The 6.5 mm object, since it was faked, is most likely uniform in OD (when you see how it was done that will be obvious) so any *changes* in OD across this object (on the AP) are probably due to the original shrapnel. The OD graph shows just what I saw with my glasses off—the original metal is almost completely on the right side of the 6.5 mm object.

When I got home I realized that I had another experiment to do: what would a *real* 6.5 mm metal fragment look like on an X-ray film—and what would the OD scan look like? I already had a 6.5 mm Mannlicher-Carcano bullet—someone had given me one. It was time to sacrifice it. I sawed off about 3 mm of the base—there was obvious lead in the bullet. From previous experiments, I already had several authentic human skulls. So I taped this bullet fragment to the back of the skull, just like in the autopsy X-ray films. I adjusted the skull position under the fluoroscope until it matched the autopsy X-ray films and I took a lateral X-ray film. It really looked very similar to the autopsy film: it was in the right spot and it overlapped the skull bone just right. Then I scanned it (Figure 6). In the same figure, for comparison, is the 6.5 mm object from the lateral autopsy film. Note that the ordinate (the vertical scale) has been greatly changed from Figure 3, in order to show both on the same graph.

This comparison is quite striking. Whereas the OD of the autopsy 6.5 mm object was almost the same as the background bone (it was only about 0.2 OD units more transparent), the OD of the real metal was almost 1.5 OD units more transparent. This is quite a large difference: it meant that the image of the real metal transmitted over 10 times as much light as the area right outside of it—but the autopsy image did not even transmit twice as much light as the area just outside of its borders. That's why it was so hard to see in the prints that I had been looking at. This experiment was telling me the same thing that I had already learned at the Archives. On the lateral view, a real 6.5 mm piece of metal should have looked much whiter (or more transparent) than the object on the lateral autopsy X-ray film. On the autopsy film, it was real enough, all right, but it was thin—much thinner than 6.5 mm—just as Sibert and O'Neill had said, and just as I had seen with my naked (and myopic) eyes on the AP view.

Next I looked at the teeth. The teeth are not seen in the prints in this book—or anywhere else for that matter. But they are very easy to see on the X-ray films. Kennedy had extensive dental repairs; except for the incisors and canines, he had fillings almost everywhere. Most of these amalgams were probably inserted during his pre-adult years and (typically) would have been composed of nearly equal parts of mercury and silver. Both of these elements have high atomic numbers and therefore would naturally appear transparent on an X-ray film. On the AP, these amalgams mostly overlap one another—they are like a long slab of dense mercury and silver that is many centimeters long. The reason these dental amalgams important is that the teeth can serve as a superb measuring stick for how much metal there is in *other objects on the same film* (in a relative sense). In particular, I had found that the OD of the 6.5 mm object on the AP was about 0.6, which suggested that it was very thick (from front to back). So I wondered how this would compare to the amalgams.

As I expected, these amalgams were quite transparent. The ODs on the right side of the AP view were about 0.78; on the left, they were 0.74, on average (see Table 2). These values all imply *less* metal (front to back) than for the 6.5 mm object! How could that be? How could the 6.5 mm object be longer (front to back) than all of those dental amalgams added together? On the lateral film, I could see with my eyes that this 6.5 mm object was only 3-4 mm thick (from front to back)—that was clearly much, much *thinner* than all of those dental fillings all lined up—by almost a factor of 10! But that is what the OD data were telling me—so this made no sense at all. But, of course, if someone had simply overexposed this area to lighten it up (so that it would look like 6.5 mm shrapnel), then that's what should be expected.

Now recall that the pathologists actually removed one metal fragment from the skull. On the AP view, this 7 x 2 mm fragment has an OD of 1.44 (see Table 2), a much higher number than the OD of 0.60 for the 6.5 mm object *on the same film*. These widely differing ODs suggest that the 6.5 mm object is, by far, the thicker of the two (from front to back). But we can see their actual thicknesses (from front to back) on the lateral view—and they are nearly identical! So this makes no sense either. (I had to be sure, of course, that overlapping tissue within the skull—on the AP view—did not confound this conclusion. I was able to assure myself that this was not a problem by obtaining OD data just outside of these objects and also by correlating the lateral and AP views.) On the lateral view, the OD of the 7 x 2 mm fragment was 1.6 (see Table 1). This provided strong evidence that the 7 x 2 mm fragment was real—the ODs on the lateral and AP were consistent with one another. And I also knew that they were consistent with what I saw with my naked eyes. So this real fragment behaved quite differently from the faked 6.5 mm object.

There was one last question: on the *lateral* view, how did the ODs of the teeth compare to ODs of the 6.5 mm object? And here, again, there was nothing remarkable—which, in itself, was strong evidence that this fragment had not been altered on this view. The ODs of the teeth are about 1.00 (see Table 1). From the above graphs, we have already seen that (on the lateral view) the ODs of the 6.5 mm object are about 1.5, so the teeth must contain much more metal (from left to right within the skull) than the 6.5 mm object. From the data already reviewed here, we know that the 6.5 mm object is not really 6.5 mm wide—it is really closer to 2 to 3 mm wide. Since the dental amalgams are significantly wider than this (as seen with the naked eyes on the AP view), the ODs of the amalgams and the (real) 2–3 mm fragment are completely consistent with each other—which could not be true if the object were 6.5 mm wide!

The evidence for alteration from this data is therefore quite overwhelming. All lines of evidence point in the same direction and are consistent with one other. To make this very transparent, I shall summarize all these arguments as follows:

1. On the lateral view, the 6.5 mm object (by the OD data) measures much thinner (left to right) than a comparable slice from a real Mannlicher-Carcano bullet.

2. On the AP view, a superposition of images inside this 6.5 mm object is evident to the naked (myopic) eye: one is the genuine bullet fragment described by Sibert and O'Neill, while the second is a phantom introduced in the darkroom at some later date.

3. On the AP view, the OD scan across this 6.5 mm object is entirely consistent with what the naked eye sees: most of the real metal is on the right side.

4. On the lateral view, there is more metal (by the OD data) at the inferior pole of this 6.5 mm object (left to right) than at the center or at the superior pole. To the naked eye, however, the 6.5 mm object has a bite taken out precisely at this level—so the OD data (on the lateral film) are grossly inconsistent with the (AP) visual image.

5. On the AP view, the ODs of the 6.5 mm object tell us that it is thicker (front to back) than all of the dental amalgams superimposed on one another!

6. On the lateral view, the OD measurements tell us that the 6.5 mm object is much thinner than one dental amalgam! This is, of course, what should be expected, since the lateral view is authentic and the real metal was only 2-3 mm across (right to left).

7. On the lateral view, the ODs of the 6.5 mm object and the 7 x 2 mm fragment (the real one) are similar—as they should be for fragments about 2 mm thick (from right to left). This is consistent with the FBI report, but not with the visible 6.5 mm object on the AP view.

8. On the AP view, the 6.5 mm object is astonishingly thicker (by OD data) than the 7 x 2 mm object (from front to back), even though the unaided eye can see (on the lateral view) that they are actually about the same thickness.

All this evidence is completely self-consistent—and it tells us that the 6.5 mm object was not originally on the AP view. But how could someone add an image of a bullet onto an X-ray film? The X-ray films (and the photographs, too) were treated with a kind of reverence by the government agencies who examined them (the HSCA, especially)—as if they were immutable objects of nature. Their attitude was that witnesses could lie or could be mistaken, but that the autopsy X-rays and photographs would never mislead; thus, if the X-ray films and photographs disagreed with the witnesses, wasn't it obvious that it must be the witnesses who were wrong? Although everyone knows that photographs can be forged—a practice that started even before the Civil War—see Fielding, 1965/85, pp. 73-74, for some fascinating photographs—surely there could be no tampering with a Presidential autopsy! In any case, it was simply taken for granted that X-ray films such as these, once taken, could not be changed.

Unfortunately, what everyone had forgotten was that X-ray films can be duplicated (by a photographic process in the darkroom, using light alone)—so that if photographs can be altered, so can X-ray films! After I discovered how to do this for myself, I began to experiment. I even produced a skull X-ray film with a scissors inside the skull—as if the neurosurgeon had forgotten an entire scissors. It was fun to show this at lectures. But the really remarkable thing was not the location of the scissors—it was the *color* of the scissors! Since surgical scissors are metal, this should have looked transparent (or white). Well, this scissors was black—meaning that it was scissors composed of thin air!

Some unexpected problems

Before we pursue this discovery, however, I must mention some surprises that I had to confront. Modern duplicate X-ray films have an emulsion only on one side, like photographic film. Standard X-ray film, on the other hand, has an emulsion on both sides—and so did these autopsy X-ray films! This surprising observation put me off the scent for a while. I was not familiar with double-sided emulsions being used for making copies. If these films had had images on just one side, I might still have been able to argue that they were copies. But then I noticed that the *image* appeared on both emulsions! I could conclude this because the emulsion had peeled off in several places so that I could see one emulsion at a time. Actually, I used the background grid lines on the film for this purpose, which was just as good. There were about 2.3 lines per millimeter, and with my glasses off I could see these well. I also used a high power microscope to confirm that the image occurred on both sides; because the depth of field was so shallow, I could focus on one side at a time. This observation made me think that the films had to be originals. Furthermore, when I tried to copy an image onto a double emulsion film, the films turned a bizarre greenish color—which was clearly unnatural.

As time passed, however, all of these issues were resolved. One evening, as I was puzzling over these conundrums, I decided to phone a very good friend, a superb diagnostic radiologist at the hospital where I work. He did not have an immediate answer either, but said that he would dig through his library of old medical physics books. A short time later he called back with some astonishing news—in the mid- to late-1960s the film manufacturers began adding a dye to their emulsions so that it was no longer possible to use it for making good duplicates (John B. Cahoon, Jr., *Formulating X-ray Techniques*, 1961/65). My jaw dropped! Now I understood why I had failed to make good copies when using double emulsion films! The next night my wife and I flew to San Francisco and I can still remember my elation over this discovery as we walked down the aisle to take in *The Phantom of the Opera*.

In those days, hardly anybody (perhaps no one) used single emulsion duplicating film like everyone does today. The Kodak catalog from 1963 does not list it, although it does appear in catalogs from a few years later. Instead, everybody made duplicates by using regular double emulsion film—only they had to be clever about it. I slowly discovered all of this in talking to older technicians and radiologists. It was the technicians especially who remembered this, because they were the ones who had to do it! And as I searched the old textbooks I was amazed at what I found. They contained detailed recipes for copying film onto standard double emulsion films—down to the second in exposure time (Cahoon, 1961, pp. 40–43). This was all done with a simple light box—no X-rays were needed. And this same author (a radiologist) even said that this technique was so good that it was hard to tell the original (Figure 15A) from the copy (Figure 15B), and to prove his point, he printed them side by side. At least in the book, I couldn't tell them apart either.

So this mystique about the immutability of X-ray films (at least in that era) was wrong. Neither the Warren Commission (which did not actually review the X-ray films) nor the HSCA (which did review them in the late 1970s) considered the issues that I have presented here. Without a properly recorded chain of custody, of course, X-ray films would have been no more legitimate in a courtroom than photographs. Nowadays, however, it would not be possible to do this with double emulsion film; the dyes added to the emulsion simply won't permit realistic looking X-ray films. As a final note on this matter, last fall Dr. Cyril Wecht recommended that I serve as an expert witness in a case in which a question of forged X-ray films actually arose. My findings (for several reasons) were that the films in that case were authentic. (I was a little disappointed not to be able to use my knowledge in a more exciting manner!)

The final mystery was the presence of an image on both emulsions. From my training in radiation oncology, I had remembered that not too much light crosses over from one emulsion to the other in an X-ray film. Such crossover is considered undesirable because it tends to fuzz out the image. Then one day I phoned the experts at Kodak. Two of them got on the line, including Arthur G. Haus, Director of Medical Physics, and we a had a round table discussion. (I later had the pleasure of meeting Haus at one of my specialty meetings in Los Angeles; he also graciously reviewed this article for me.) In the course of that conversation, they stunned me. They said that for film in the 1960s, a great deal of light could cross over from one side to the other—sometimes even enough to produce a nearly equal image on both sides, even though it was exposed to light from only one side! So there, at last, was the explanation. In the early 1960s, nothing special had to be done to copy a superior image onto a double emulsion film. Furthermore, the image would be nearly equal (and of good quality) on both emulsions, just as I had seen on the autopsy films. That was because the 1960s films were not as good as our present ones—crossover is more limited nowadays. (See Arthur G. Haus, 1995, Characteristics of Screen-Film Combinations for Conventional Medical Radiography, Eastman Kodak Publication No. N-319.)

How it was done

So now, at last, we can explain what happened. Sometime after the autopsy the original X-ray films were taken to the dark room for copying. There is a clue as to when this event occurred. Within one month after the autopsy, John Ebersole, the radiologist, was called to the White House to look at the X-ray films. The strange episode about "Aunt Margaret's skirts" (HSCA Record No. 180-10102-010409, Agency File No. 013617, pp. 5-6) suggests that Ebersole was being tested on his reaction to the altered films. (The official excuse of needing his help for a Kennedy bust makes no sense. If X-ray films were really useful for this purpose, then those taken during life would have been much more appropriate than the badly fragmented skull seen at the autopsy.) Ebersole, however, is either very tongue-in-cheek about all of this or else astonishingly naive. (Also read about the experiences of the technologist Jerrol Custer below.)

A simple piece of cardboard (or whatever you wish to imagine) was cut out in the shape of a 6.5 mm fragment; it is anyone's guess as to why the bite was taken out (most likely, though, a perfect circle would have looked too suspicious to be shrapnel). Then the film was duplicated in the usual fashion, using light in the darkroom. But before the duplicate film was developed it was exposed one more time. This time the cardboard template was placed over the duplicate film so that light could only pass through this 6.5 mm hole. That area on the duplicate film then, when developed, would look very transparent, just like the autopsy 6.5 mm object. In fact, the variety of things that I could do with this approach was limited only by my imagination. One day I took my daughter's tracing template for a pteranodan to the office; when I went home that night I had a skull X-ray film with a pteranodan inside! (I had to use single emulsion film, of course.)

So the pathologists were right, after all. They really hadn't seen that 6.5 mm object at the autopsy. The entrepreneur who did this had to be clever, however. If he had simply placed a counterfeit image onto the AP view willy-nilly, most likely it would not have been spatially consistent on the two views. But, by using something that was already there, Mother Nature solved the problem for him. He did not bother to alter the lateral—there was no need to. All he had to do was add the fake image right over the pre-existing shrapnel that the FBI had reported. Mother Nature had already located this image on both films consistent with reality, so he had no decisions to make. In fact, a small army of expert radiologists have noticed no problems at all with the AP film—which is not a discredit to them. These issues are only accessible through OD measurements. Of course, in retrospect, it would be interesting now to ask the radiologists about the "phantom" image—i.e., being able to see the original shrapnel through the 6.5 mm object. But that might not be fair, because they are not experts in special effects cinematography!

Summary

Now, in view of all of the above, it would be extraordinarily interesting to ask the pathologists some more questions. If we are fortunate, that may actually have occurred within the past 18 months. When the ARRB recently interviewed these men, they had already received from me several questions about this 6.5 mm object—specifically submitted in preparation for the interviews with these men. That report will be made public before the ARRB expires on September 30, 1998. At this time, all I have heard (second hand) is that the pathologists conveyed the impression that they wanted to be somewhere else.

One last comment needs to be made. I had the great pleasure of meeting Jerrol Custer, the X-ray technician from the original autopsy, during our press conference in New York on 18 November 1993. Although he does not specifically recall a 6.5 mm object, he admits that his memory is now fuzzy about this. But he definitely recalls that he took several sets of skull films. The radiologist, Ebersole, told me (on tape) that he took at least five X-ray films of the skull. He also told the same story to the HSCA (HSCA Record No. 180-10102-010409, Agency File No. 013617, p. 19; pp. 45–46, and p. 51), a document was finally released in 1993. The problem is that there are now only three skull films—not nearly enough to match the five or six that both of these men recall. And if anyone would know, they should—and on this point, they agree with each other, even though they have not spoken to one another since the autopsy.

Custer recalls a remarkable occurrence. On the day after the assassination, at the Bethesda Naval Medical Center, he was asked to take X-ray films of skull fragments and bullet fragments taped together. He was directed to do this by someone in his department and also by a plainclothes agent whom he did not know! (See Harrison Livingstone, *High Treason II*, 1992, pp. 216–217.) His story fits all too well with what I have described here; it also suggests that a fabrication team was at the autopsy site as early as the following morning. Probably none of Custer's films were used, however. Sooner or later, this team would have recognized that this goal was much easier to achieve in the darkroom with a simple template, as I have described above. (They might not have known this immediately, however, since there were no recipes for altering X-ray films—especially for Presidential autopsies!)

It is safe to conclude that the current AP skull film in the National Archives cannot be an original, which must have been destroyed. For the success of the fabrication team, it would have been essential not to leave too many films in the file—the more that were left, the more alterations would have been required. Although they are easy enough to make, the real challenge then would have been to complete the alterations consistently from film to film. Custer recalls taking an oblique X-ray film (taken through the large occipital defect), where matching that view precisely to the altered AP view would have posed a colossal challenge. It would have been better to leave as few X-ray films behind as possible. (On the second lateral film, the posterior skull, including the 6.5 mm fragment is cut off; Custer says he did not have enough room in the autopsy suite to get his portable unit in proper position for this. This one could therefore be safely left in the collection.) There are other (measurable) reasons for suspecting that the other two (both lateral) skull films have also been altered. These changes occur in another area, which would not have interfered with identifying them as Kennedy's. In fact, Custer has stated—repeatedly and emphatically—that the current skull X-ray films do not look like the ones that he took. I think I know what he means, but that is a story for another book.

One final conclusion may be drawn. The shallow wound in JFK's back has long been a puzzle [*Editor's note*: This is the wound located at about the level of the third thoracic vertebra.] The pathologists were unable to find any penetrating bullet track there. But now that we know that real shrapnel was located at the original site of the 6.5 mm object and can see that it lies on the *outside* of the skull—and because a tiny piece of metal is visible on the *outside* of the left scalp—it is not unreasonable to propose that shrapnel (probably from this same posterior shot; some witnesses describe such a bullet) also produced the superficial back wound. Since shrapnel typically does not penetrate very deeply, that would explain the tiny scalp fragment perfectly. That finding would have added another shot to the Warren Commission's scenario and would have forced them, on that basis alone, to posit two or more assassins. It should come as no surprise, therefore, that such a possibility was not one that was ever entertained.

References

1. Lundberg, G.D., Closing the case in *JAMA* on the John F. Kennedy autopsy. *JAMA. 1992; 268, 1736.*
2. Wecht, C.H., Smith, R.P., The medical evidence in the assassination of President John F. Kennedy. *Forensic Science*. 1974; 3, 113, 114, 127.
3. HSCA 1978; 7, 244.
4. HSCA 1978; 7, 137.
5. Baden, M.M., *Unnatural Death*. 1989, 9.
6. Breo, D.L., JFK's death—the plain truth from the MDs who did the autopsy. *JAMA*. 1992; 267, 2794.
7. WCH 1964; 2, 353.
8. HSCA 1978; 7, 101, 102, 122.
9. HSCA 1978; 7, 246.
10. WCH 1964; 2, 349.
11. Breo, D.L., *JAMA*. 1992; 267, 2798.
12. HSCA 1978; 7, 121.
13. HSCA 1978; 7, 245.
14. Official autopsy report on President Kennedy. *JAMA*. 1964; 190 (4), ad pp. 98-100.
15. HSCA 1978; 7, 264.
16. WCH 1964; 2, 370.
17. WCH 1964; 2, 371.
18. HSCA 1978; 1, 329.
19. HSCA 1978; 7, 122.
20. HSCA 1978; 7, 250.
21. WCH 1964; 6, 28.
22. HSCA 1978; 7, 260.
23. Warren Commission Documents, 1964; Record Group 272, CD-7, pp. 280–285.
24. Epstein, E.J., *Inquest*, 1966, Special Appendix.
25. Thompson J., *Six Seconds in Dallas;*1967, Appendix G, CD-7.
26. Lifton, D.S., *Best Evidence*; 1992, Chapter 21.
27. WCH 1964; 2, 374.
28. Riley, J.N. The head wounds of John Kennedy, I. One bullet cannot account for the injuries. *The Third Decade*. 1993; 9:1.
29. Thompson J., 1967: 91.
30. Commission on CIA Activities Within the United States, Panel of Consultants Meeting, April 18, 1975. Washington, DC. Gerald R Ford Library, Ann Arbor, Michigan.
31. Lifton, D.S., 1992, Chapter 2.
32. Lattimer, J.K., *Kennedy and Lincoln, Medical and Ballistic Comparisons of their Assassinations.*; 1980, 254.
33. Mantik, D.W. Unpublished work.
34. HSCA 1978; 1, 229.
35. Breo, D.L.,*JAMA*. 1992; 267, 2797.
36. HSCA 1978; 7, 104.
37. Mantik, D.W., Telephone conversations with John H. Ebersole, November 2 and December 2, 1992.
38. Livingstone, H.E., *High Treason*, 1990, 28ff.

39. Olivier, A.G, Dziemian, A.J. Wound Ballistics of 6.5 mm Mannlicher-Carcano Ammunition. US Army Edgewood Arsenal Technical Report CRDLR 3264. March 1965.
40. HSCA 1978; 7, 240, 244.
41. Breo, D.L., *JAMA*. 1992; 267, 2799.
42. WCH 1964; 2, 351.
43. Lifton, D.S., 1992, Chapter 23.
44. Bishop, J., *The Day Kennedy Was Shot*; 1968, 202.
45. Crenshaw, C.A., *JFK, Conspiracy of Silence*; 1992, 82.
46. Weisberg, H., *Whitewash IV*, Frederick, Maryland; Harold Weisberg; 1974, 102.
47. HSCA 1978; 7, 16.
48. HSCA 1978; 7, 20.
49. Lewis, T., Washington News. *JAMA*. 1964; 187, 15.
50. White House transcript 1327-C; Lyndon Johnson Library, Austin, Texas. 22 November 1963.
51. Lifton, D.S., 1964, Chapter 25.
52. Breo. D.L., JFK's death, part III—Dr. Finck speaks out, 'two bullets, from the rear', JAMA 1992, 268, 1749.
53. HSCA 1978; 7:93.
54. WCH 1964; 6:1-82.
55. HSCA 1978; 7, 101.
56. HSCA 1978; 1, 186.
57. HSCA 1978; 6, 55.
58. HSCA 1978; 7, 93, 98.
59. HSCA 1978; 7, 175.
60. HSCA 1978; 7, 254.
61. HSCA 1978; 6, 46.
62. HSCA 1978; 6, 302.
63. *The New York Times*, January 26, 1964, p. 58.
64. Lifton, D.S., 1992, Chapter 29.
65. Lifton, D.S., 1992, Chapter 19.
66. Livingstone, H.E., *High Treason II*; 1992: 209.
67. HSCA 1978; 7, 12.
68. HSCA 1978; 7, 50.
69. HSCA 1978; 1, 301.
70. Carnes, W.H., Fisher, R.S., Morgan, R.H., and Moritz, A. 1968 Panel review of photographs, X-ray films, documents and other evidence pertaining to the fatal wounding of President John F Kennedy on November 22, 1963 in Dallas, Texas. Washington, DC, National Archives; January 16, 1969.
71. HSCA 1978; 7, 136.
72. WCH 1964; 2, 353.
73. WCH 1964; 2, 354.
74. HSCA 1978; 1, 217.
75. WCH 1964; 2, 361.
76. HSCA 1978; 1, 229.
77. Lifton, D.S., 1992, Chapter 18.
78. HSCA 1978; 7, 257.
79. HSCA 1978; 7, 86, 175.
80. Breo, D.L., *JAMA*. 1992; 267, 2800.
81. HSCA 1978; 1, 233.
82. WCH 1964; 2, 358.
83. HSCA 1978; 7, 263.
84. WCH 1964; 2, 374.
85. WCH 1964; 2, 376.
86. HSCA 1978; 7, 263.
87. WCH 1964; 2, 377.
88. WCH 1964; 2, 381.
89. HSCA 1978; 7, 17, 134, 177, 193.
90. Houts, M., *Where Death Delights*; 1967, 62-75.
91. Wilber, C.G., *Medicolegal Investigation of the President John F Kennedy Murder*; 1978.
92. Baden, M.M., 1989, 6-11.
93. Breo, D.L., *JAMA*. 1992; 267, 2803.
94. Breo, D.L., *JAMA*. 1992; 268, 1752.
95. Lundberg, G.L., *JAMA*. 1992; 268, 1737.
96. Blair, J., Blair, C., Jr., *The Search for JFK*; 1976, 17.
97. Nichols, J., President Kennedy's adrenals. *JAMA*. 1967; 201, 115.
98. Nicholas, J.A., Burstein, C.L., Umberger, G.J., Wilson, P.D. Management of adrenocortical insufficiency during surgery. *Arch Surg*. 1955; 71: 737.

99. Official autopsy report on President Kennedy. *JAMA*. 965; 192:63. Letters, editorial comment.
100. Aguilar, G.L., Mantik, D.W., James, P.L., Smith, W.S., White, A., Another letter to *JAMA*. *The Third Decade*. 1993; 9, 28.
101. Lifton, D.S., 1992, Chapter 24.
102. HSCA 1978; 7, 202.
103. Alvarez, L. A physicist examines the Kennedy assassination film. *Am J Phys*. 1976; 44, 813.
104. Lattimer, J.K., Lattimer, J., Lattimer, G. An experimental study of the backward movement of President Kennedy's head. *Surgery, Gynecology, and Obstetrics*; 1976; 142, 246.
105. HSCA 1978; 1, 404.
106. Alvarez, L., 1976; 44, 821.
107. HSCA 1978; 1, 414-417.
108. Shepherd, G.M. *Neurobiology*; 1988, Chapters 17-23.
109. Eyzaguirre, C., Fidone, S.J., *Physiology of the Nervous System*; 1975, 248.
110. HSCA 1978; 7, 174.
111. Walker, A.E., *Cerebral Death*; 1981, 33.
112. HSCA 1978; 7, 251.
113. HSCA 1978; 7, 254.
114. HSCA 1978; 7, 260-261.
115. Lifton, D.S., 1992, Chapter 22.
116. HSCA 1978; 7, 115.
117. Petty, C.S., JFK–An Allonge. *JAMA*. 1993; 269, 1553.
118. *The Warren Commission Report*; 1992, Appendix VIII.
119. Livingstone, H.E., 1992.
120. HSCA 1978; 1, 327.
121. HSCA 1978; 7, 115.
122. Breo, D.L., *JAMA*. 1992; 268, 1750.
123. Lifton, D.S., 1992, Chapter 14.
124. Livingstone, H.E., 1992: 113.
125. Shaw, J.G., Harris, L.R., *Cover-up*; 1992, 162.
126. Warren Commission Documents, 1964; Record Group 272-E-52, CD 371.
127. HSCA 1978; 7, 80-84.
128. WCH 1964; 2, 143.
129. WCH 1964; 18, 760.
130. Livingstone, H.E., 1992: 209.
131. Hatfield, S., RT disputes X-ray photos in JFK case. Ad*vance, For Radiologic Science Professionals*. 1992; 5, 7.
132. HSCA 1978; 7, 200-203.
133. HSCA 1978; 7, 212-214.
134. HSCA 1978; 7, 242.
135. HSCA 1978; 7, 205.
136. Lifton, D.S.,1992, Chapter 31.
137. HSCA 1978; 7, 37,43-53.
138. Humes, J.J., Boswell, J.T., Ebersole, J.H., Stringer, J.T. Report of inspection by naval medical staff on November 1, 1966, at National Archives of X-rays and photographs of autopsy of President John F Kennedy.
139. HSCA 1978; 7, 255.
140. Weisberg, H. *Post Mortem*; 1975, 524.
141. WCH 1964; 2, 373.
142. HSCA 1978; 7, 257-258.
143. Livingstone, H.E.,1992, Chapter 17.
144. HSCA 1978; 7, 47.
145. *The Warren Commission Report*, 1992, 87.
146. Lifton, D.S.,1992, Chapter 4.
147. WCH 1964; 17, 257.
148. Menninger, B., *Mortal Error*; 1992, Chapter 7.
149. Milam, W., Private communication.
150. HSCA 1978; 1, 517, 561-562.
151. HSCA 1978; 7, 392.
152. Fetzer, J.H. Unpublished letters to *JAMA*.
153. Lundberg, G.D., *JAMA*. 1992; 268, 1738.
154. Breo, D.L., *JAMA*. 1992; 268, 1754.
155. DiEugenio, J., *JFK, Cuba, and the Garrison Case*; 1992, 378.
156. Baden, M.M., 1989, 5.
157. Lewis, C.S., *Miracles*, 1947: 7.

A Random House promotion for Case Closed *from* The New York Times
(24 August 1993), p. B4, insinuating that those who are critics of
The Warren Report *are virtual traitors to their country*

Part II

The Press Conference that Never Was

In late October of 1993, David Mantik, M.D., Ph.D., Gary Aguilar, M.D., and Robert B. Livingston, M.D., were invited to participate in a press conference by Harrison Livingstone, co-author with Robert Groden of *High Treason* (1989) and author of *High Treason 2* (1992). He had learned about Mantik's studies of the autopsy X-rays and about Livingston's conclusions regarding the diagrams of the brain stored in the National Archives. He was about to publish a new book, *Killing the Truth* (1993), which printed material from the four of us, including several of our submissions that *JAMA* had rejected.

For reasons explained in the Prologue, Mantik and Aguilar wanted me to serve as moderator. Since we were expecting a substantial turnout from the press, I planned for each of us to make brief presentations that would take in total no more than 30–35 minutes to present. We then expected the floor to be open to discussion, most of which we presumed would focus upon Mantik's discoveries and Livingston's observations. Mantik had not only found that the lateral cranial autopsy X-rays of JFK had been fabricated but also that the trajectory for the "magic bullet" plotted by the HSCA could not be sustained and that there were indications that JFK had taken two bullets to the head. The problem would be to explain how he had discovered this.

The fabricated X-ray serves as an appropriate illustration. X-rays are created by projecting radiation through an object that is suitably situated in relation to a photographic plate. The object will absorb radiation proportional to its density, where denser objects absorb more than do those that are less dense. Consequently, denser objects permit less radiation to impact on the photographic plate, thereby creating a lighter image. Using an extremely sensitive device known as *an optical densitometer*, it is possible to measure the amount of light an X-ray permits to pass through it.

Using this technique, Mantik was able to reconstruct the density of the objects that created the X-ray and detected a striking abnormality. The properties of the lateral images reveal that very dense material (possibly of a kind employed in oncology) was used to "patch" a major defect to the back of the head—not by filling in the cranium at the location where many witnesses reported having seen a gaping wound, apparently, but by superimposing X-rays to create composite fabrications. He has replicated these results many times by repeated measurements and by fabricating X-rays.

Only Livingston actually stuck to our game plan. On the occasion of the assassination, he had called Humes at Bethesda Naval Hospital to discuss the importance of the small wound to the throat he had heard about from radio and television reports. During this conversation, which occurred on Friday afternoon, before the plane carrying the President's casket had landed at Andrews Air Force Base, he had emphasized how important it was to carefully dissect the wound, especially since, if there had been shots fired from the rear, then there would have had to have been more than one assassin. [*Editor's note:* See his Clarification.]

In addition, Livingston, a world authority on the human brain, had come to the conclusion that the diagrams of the brain stored in the National Archives, which displayed an intact cerebellum, must be of the brain of someone other than JFK. He knew from observations made by competent physicians who had attended JFK, including Kemp Clark, M.D., the Director of Neurosugery at Parkland Hospital, that cerebellum had been seen extruding from a massive wound to the back of the President's head. He had concluded that the diagrams and the observations could not have been of the same brain.

These were striking and important developments. But he also explained that a friend of his named Richard Dudman had been present in Dallas as a reporter for *The St. Louis Post Dispatch* at the time of the assassination. He had observed what appeared to be a through-and-through hole in the windshield of the Presidential limousine, which may have been located in the upper left-hand corner. Livingston subsequently learned that the Secret Service had obtained a dozen windshields from the Ford Motor Company, allegedly for "target practice". He speculated that securing that many windshields raised doubt regarding whether the windshield in the National Archives was on the car in Dallas.

Although we were not aware of it then, Roy Schaeffer had noticed something others have overlooked in the Altgens photograph, perhaps the most famous picture taken in Dealey Plaza at the time. (Schaeffer has also found indications a bullet passed through high on the back seat of the limousine in Commission Exhibits CE-346, CE-353 and CE-874.) While it has been published in many places, especially excellent prints can be found accompanying an article by Richard Sprague, "The Assassination of President John F. Kennedy: The Application of Computers to the Photographic Evidence", *Computers and Automation* (May 1970), on pp. 44–45, and in Robert Groden, *The Killing of a President* (1993), which includes a similar two-page print on pp. 30–31. (CE-900 includes a cropped Altgens photograph.)

The windshield in the Altgens photograph

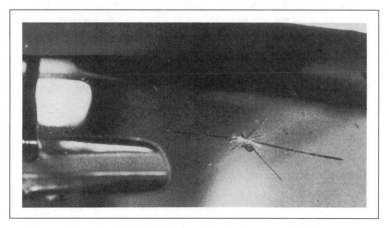

The windshield the Secret Service later produced

What Schaeffer noticed is that, slightly to the right and barely above the upper-right-hand corner of the center-mounted rear-view mirror (looking toward the vehicle as it is displayed in the photograph), there is something that has the appearance of a small spiral nebula at exactly the location the President's left ear would be visible were it not obscured by a white image. The small spiral nebula has a dark spot at the center, strongly suggesting a through-and-through bullet hole. This is quite different from the windshield that the Secret Service produced, which shows a star-like configuration. Groden (1993), p. 36, has published photos of both, side by side.

When all was said and done, the press conference had run about two-and-a-half hours. Aguilar read two new papers of his own—which are not presented here—so I also read something that I had prepared for him. Although Mantik had been successful in explaining his optical densitometry studies to those who were present, the results were nevertheless disappointing. We received exactly two sentences on CNN the following morning and some international coverage, but nothing more appeared in the national press. We flew from New York to Dallas for the Assassination Symposium on JFK, which in this case was being held overlapping the 30th observance of that event, where Mantik and Livingston would present their findings.

At this point in time, therefore, experts on the assassination were familiar with these developments, but not the American people. I was acutely distressed and sought to rectify the situation. For several days, I tried to persuade ABC that it should pursue this story, but *World News Tonight* thought that it was appropriate for *Nightline*, and *Nightline* would not bite. The closest I came to making progress in convincing anyone that it was worth taking seriously was a conversation I had with an associate producer of the program, Mark Nelson, who asked me to send him information. I sent along a 26-page fax, but after that, he refused to take my calls.

Unwilling to admit defeat, I subsequently sent letters to Ellen Goodman of *The Boston Globe* (dated 30 November 1993), to Lawrence K. Altman, M.D., of *The New York Times* (dated 1 December 1993), and to several others. Only a few months before, I had written to Howell Raines in his capacity as Editorial Page Editor to criticize Christopher Lehmann-Haupt's review of Gerald Posner, *Case Closed* (1993), and later I would write to Arthur Ochs Sulzberger in his capacity as Publisher objecting to the obituary of Marion "Pepper" Jenkins, which cited *Case Closed* as though it were a serious work. These publications by *The New York Times* were convincing evidence that, when it came to JFK, even our most distinguished paper had a lot to learn. Its literary style may have been more sophisticated than the Random House ads it ran targeting Warren Commission critics as though they were traitors, but they had a similar effect.

—*James H. Fetzer, Ph.D.*

18 November 1993   **James H. Fetzer, Ph.D.**

Recent articles on the assassination of JFK that have appeared in JAMA and Gerald Posner's new book, Case Closed, purport to reinforce the Warren Commission's familar findings. All three sources agree that JFK was hit by only two bullets that were fired by a high velocity weapon, that they caused his fatal wounds, that they were fired from above and behind by a Mannlicher-Carcano rifle and that Lee Harvey Oswald was the only one who fired them.[1]

The national press warmly embraced these reaffirmations. A lead editorial in The New York Times, titled "Two Shots, From the Rear", swallowed JAMA whole and described its articles as "proof against paranoia".[2] U.S. NEWS published a long report on Case Closed, lauding it as "a brilliant new book [that] finally proves who killed Kennedy".[3] Dick Cavett said that anyone who now continues to reject the single bullet theory "must have a few loose screws".[4]

JAMA has emphatically proclaimed that the autopsy pathologists settled the matter once and for all, asserting, "The scientific evidence they documented during their autopsy provides irrefutable proof that President Kennedy was struck by only two bullets that came from above and behind from a high-velocity weapon that caused the fatal wounds" and that an extensive investigation had demonstrated that the Warren Commission was right.[5] But the evidence we present today demonstrates that their conclusions were wrong.

The "extensive investigation" to which JAMA appeals to justify the Warren Commission's findings turns out to be the Commission's own inquiry, which blatantly begs the question. The principal evidence was an autopsy report that used The Washington Post to imply three shots had been fired from the Texas School Book Depository in its opening "Clinical Summary"! This move enabled the Commission to take for granted what it was intended to prove.

JAMA's articles are similarly scientifically insignificant because they were produced by the selection of evidence in support of a predetermined point of view. I emphasized this idea in a series of letters to the AMA Trustees.[6] Case Closed fares no better. Posner appropriates one side of a study of the assassination that was conducted by Failure Analysis Associates, after it was commissioned by the ABA to prepare both sides for a mock trial, which ended in a hung jury.[7] If Posner told us that he was presenting just one side of the story, that might be acceptable. But he never explains his methodology.

Here is an example. He reports that Oswald qualified twice with scores of of 212 in 1956 and of 191 in 1959. This sounds fine, since 212 makes him

1

a "sharpshooter" and 191 a "marksman".8 But what about 1957 and 1958?
He should have been qualifying once a year.9 Moreover, while this might
make him "an excellent shot" in relation to "the average male", it depends
on how that notion happens to be defined. Do we include young boys who
have never held a rifle and old men too weak to fire one? If he dropped
21 points between 1956 and 1959, why not expect him to drop 21 more
by 1962? Who knows how bad a shot Oswald might have been by 1963?

JFK was allegedly killed by a Mannlicher-Carcano, which is a cheap, unreliable and inaccurate bolt-action weapon. Posner lists anything that makes
a silly choice look plausible and ignores or distorts inconvenient evidence
(Appendix A). He maintains "It(s) low kickback compared to other military
rifles help(s) in rapid bolt-action firing", but neglects to say that the action
on Oswald's rifle was so difficult that it pulled expert marksmen off target.
Even his Marine Corps training was not conducted with a bolt-action rifle!10

Posner tells us that the muzzle velocity of Mannlicher-Carcanos is 2,000 fps.
His appendix on "The Ballistics of Assassination" is based upon this premise.
But he might have also told us that this makes them medium to low velocity
weapons.11 If JFK was killed by bullets from a high velocity weapon, then
Posner has proven that he was not killed by a Mannlicher-Carcano. If we
are permitted to pick and choose our evidence, we can "prove" almost anything. This is the technique employed by your typical used-car salesman.

Studies that draw conclusions that do not take account of all the available
relevant evidence violate a basic requirement of scientific reasoning.12 So
why does the nation's press heap praise upon an obvious piece of fakery?

In one respect, I would commend Posner, however, when he endorses the
principle that conflicts in testimony ordinarily should be resolved in favor
of earlier recollections, when memories are less likely to be contaminated.13
When we follow Posner's advice, our strongest evidence about the nature
of the wound to the throat is the Parkland Press Conference (Appendix B),
where Malcolm Perry described it three times as being a wound of entry,14
and our strongest evidence about the wound to the head is testimony about
his treatment at Parkland, such as Kemp Clark's summary (Appendix C), in
which he described cerebral and cerebellar tissue extruding from the back
of the head.15 This establishes strong evidence for two hits from the front,
and means that, when we follow Posner's principle, we contradict his book.

Like Mr. Cavett, many have been impressed by the application of computer
technology to analyze this crime. To project the three cones that take in the
sixth floor of the Depository as the sniper's location, however, you have to

2

determine the location of the wounds and trajectories of bullets that made them. That requires calculating angles of impact relative to the position of the body order to infer back to their source. Search through the entire 607 pages of this "brilliant new book" and you still will not find them. Of course computers can be programmed to draw cones like these, but they must be told where to draw them. If JFK had an entry wound in his throat, where is the cone for this wound? And if he had an exit wound in the back of his head, where is the cone for that wound? Posner is posing with technology.

NOTES

1. These articles appear in The Journal of the American Medical Association (JAMA) issues of 27 May 1992, 7 October 1993, and (most recently) 24/31 March 1993. The book is Gerald Posner, Case Closed (Random House, 1993).

2. The New York Times (National Edition), 20 May 1992, p. A14.

3. U.S. NEWS (Special Double Issue), 30 August-6 September 1993. See also a book review in The New York Times (National Edition), 9 September 1993.

4. I watched Cavett say this, but I cannot remember the exact (recent) date.

5. The Bethesda autopsy report, for example, describes "two perforating gun-shot wounds inflicted by high velocity projectiles" as the cause of death. See Report of the Warren Commission (The New York Times, 1964), p. 504. It is repeated by JAMA 27 May 1993, p. 2794, and by Posner, Case Closed, p. 303.

6. I contacted Willam Jacott, Secretary-Treasurer of the Board of Trustees of the AMA, about my concerns when I first discovered what was going on. He arranged for a telephone conversation between me and Lundberg. I subse-quently sent a series of letters to the trustees. For a history, see Harrison Edward Livingstone, Killing the Truth (Carroll & Graf, 1993), Appendix H.

7. Patricia Holt, "Assassination Enigma Endures", San Francisco Chronicle Book Review, 5 September 1993, p. 10. Her review of Posner's book, "The JFK Assassination, Revisited", pp. 1 and 10, is an excellent piece of its kind.

8. The term "marksman" requires disambiguation. Ordinarily, a person is a "marksman" if they are highly qualified with a rifle. In miliary termin-ology, however, "marksman" is also the lowest level of qualification with a rifle. So a marksman (in the second sense) is not a marksman (in the

first sense). Moreover, there are three categories of qualification with a rifle, based upon a total possible score of 250 points (50 points possible at each of five distance-position combinations). "Experts" must score at least 220, "sharpshooters" must score between 210 and 219, and "marksmen" between 190 and 209. 170, for example, would be unsatisfactory.

9. I served in the Marine Corps from 1962 to 1966 and was stationed at the Marine Corps Recruit Depot in San Diego from 1964 to 1966. Annual qualification with a rifle was always vigorously enforced for all Marines.

10. Oswald's Marine Corps rifle training did not include using a telescope, firing down from a six-floor building, or firing at a moving target, either.

11. Posner asserts that the muzzle velocity of the Mannlicher-Carcano is 2,000 fps on p. 104, p. 319n, p. 338, and again on p. 474. However, as John Withers, Precision Handloading (Stoeger Publishing, 1993), p. 135, for example, observes of the use of this term, "Today, most contemporary shooters would agree that a high velocity rifle cartridge is one whose bullet is propelled at a muzzle velocity of about 2,500 feet per second or faster." Others who have made the point that Mannlicher-Carcanos are medium or medium-to-low velocity rifles include Peter Model and Robert Grodon, JFK: The Case for Conspiracy (Manor Books, 1976), p. 86, and Robert Grodon and Harrison Edward Livingstone, High Treason (Berkeley Books, 1990), p. 214.

12. This is the total evidence requirement. Evidence is relevant whenever its truth or falsity makes a difference to the truth or falsity of a conclusion.

13. Posner remarks, "Resolving every conflicting account is impossible. However, the statements can be sifted for internal inconsistencies and judged for credibility. Testimony closer to the event must be given greater weight than changes or additions made years later, when the witness's own memory is often muddled or influenced by television programs, films, books, and discussions with others" (p. 235). His own book fares poorly by these criteria.

14. The transcript of the Parkland Press Conference was not given to the Warren Commission on the ground it was part of over 200 hours of television coverage, which the networks had not yet had time to transcribe. It should be apparent, however, that it would have had to have been among the very first presentations covered on 22 November 1963 and could have been easily made available to the members of the Commission without great effort.

15. Clark's summary was published in the Report of the Warren Commission (New York Times, 1964), pp. 483-484, but not as a report to the FBI.

4

18 November 1993   James H. Fetzer, Ph.D.

~~As a member of the AMA~~, I am dismayed with the editor of JAMA. He has grossly abused his position and created the impression—which no doubt will long endure—that the AMA has contributed to (and thereby participated in) a cover up in the assassination of JFK. To be somewhat more precise, he has used the journal to perpetrate "a cover up of the cover up", by reaffirming findings that were <u>never justifiable</u> as though they were <u>always justified</u>.1

Let me explain. The logical structure of the Warren Report, ~~as Dr. Fetzer has clearly implied,~~ is that of one question-begging argument depending upon another for its own validation. The Warren Report takes for granted that the autopsy report is sound. The autopsy report, in turn, takes for granted that its "Clinical Summary" is sound. Its "Clinical Summary", however, reports no more than some rumors and speculations published in <u>The Washington Post</u>!

It may be helpful to recollect the time line of these events. John F. Kennedy was assassinated at approximately 12:30 P.M. on Friday afternoon. He was pronounced dead at 1:00 P.M., a half-hour later. That was on the 22nd. The body was transported to Washington on the Presidential plane and taken to Bethesda. The body arrived around 7:30 P.M. on Friday for an autopsy that would last well into the night and would not conclude until the early hours.

The article in <u>The Washington Post</u> cited in the "Clinical Summary" was published on Saturday the 23rd, after the autopsy was done and the body gone. We therefore confront the curious situation that the offical autopsy report of the death of our president begins by summarizing information published in a newspaper <u>after the autopsy was complete</u>! 2 This conjures up images of Humes, Boswell and Finck rushing to read <u>The Washington Post</u> in order to know what their autopsy report should say. It gets curiouser and curiouser.

In order to appreciate Dr. Mantik's experiments, it should be observed that there has always been substantial evidence that the head wound was in the back of the head. At least forty-one(!) witnesses reported seeing a massive wound there, testimony you can find condensed in Appendix D. Ordinarily, the only reasonable explanation of the convergence of their <u>testimony</u> that there was a gaping wound to the back of the head would be that there <u>was</u> a gaping wound to the back of the head. But this case was not "ordinary".

What inhibited drawing this obvious inference was the existence of contradictory evidence in the form of the autopsy X-rays and photographs, which display an intact scalp. Here is an example, which may be familiar. Walter

1

Cronkite talked about it during a NOVA special. Given autopsy X-rays and photographs that display an intact scalp, the only inference that it appears possible to draw is that the witnesses were simply wrong. Indeed, if they were authentic, that would be the right inference to draw. But they aren't. Dr. Mantik's findings thus enable us to draw an otherwise obvious inference.

The situation with regard to the throat wound is just as curious. Once again, there has always been substantial evidence that the throat wound was one of entry. This testimony is condensed in Appendix E. As Dr. Fetzer earlier observed, Malcolm Perry, who performed the tracheostomy and absolutely had to know, asserted during the Parkland press conference—not once, not twice, but three different times—that this was a small, round wound characteristic of a wound of entrance. This question lingered in doubt only because the Bethesda physicians claimed that they didn't know about it at the time.3

Among the highly suspicious actions that Humes took in relation to the autopsy is that he destroyed the "first draft" of his autopsy report. If he only learned of the existence of the throat wound on Saturday morning, as Arlen Specter has suggested, then this behavior might have been justifiable. Thus, in U.S. NEWS (October 10, 1966, p. 49), Specter implied that Humes altered his findings upon learning for the first time, on Saturday morning, that the tracheostomy performed by Dr. Perry in Dallas had obliterated a bullet wound in the front of the President's throat.4   Indeed, Perry would later maintain that the had been "misquoted" during the press conference and, when questioned by Specter before the Warren Commission, would say that his conversations with Humes were on Saturday, after the autopsy itself was complete.5

There is a growing body of evidence that the pathologists already knew of the existence of a wound to the throat prior to the autopsy. This includes not only the Parkland transcript (Appendix B) and the Clark summary (Appendix C) but testimony by John H. Ebersole, the Bethesda radiologist, who, in documents that have only now become available by an Act of Congress, described conversations between Bethesda and Parkland that occurred during the autopsy at least seven different times.6 And we now have the testimony of Dr. Robert B. Livingston, who was the Scientific Director of the two National Institutes of Health in 1963, who called Humes the afternoon of the assassination to discuss the importance of the wound to the throat, of which he had learned from coverage that day. You will hear about this from him.

If Humes already knew about the throat wound, especially as a wound of entry, prior to the autopsy, he could not have learned for the first time of its existence until after it had been done. By pretending that he did not know about it till the body was no longer available for examination and dissection,

2

Humes could then "infer" it was an "exit" for the back wound, which could be relocated upward where it would penetrate the body on the back of the neck, thereby becoming consistent with the (Dallas) death certificate description of Kennedy's death as due to "multiple gunshot wounds of head and neck"!7

Once we accept this testimony about conversations between Perry, Humes, and Livingston on the 22nd, we have strong evidence for these conclusions:

(1) that Humes, Boswell, and Perry lied under oath, etc.;
(2) that government officials promoted a cover-up; and,
(3) that the single-bullet theory is entirely indefensible.

Even more importantly, an entry wound to the throat also destroys the sole assassin scenario—unless JFK was looking back toward the Book Depository Building when he was struck in the throat, as Perry himself proposed before he was pressured into changing his testimony (which illustrates the strength of his enduring, sincere belief that the throat wound was a wound of entry).

We are told that eternal vigilance is the price of liberty. Without a critical and observant press, our nation cannot remain free. We must never forget!

NOTES

1. Dr. Mantik and +were among those to protest JAMA's conduct by writing [*Dr. Aguilar*] letters to JAMA, some of which were published. They have been reprinted along with a group-written letter that JAMA refused to publish in Harrison Livingstone's Killing the Truth (Carroll & Graf, 1993), Appendices F and G.

2. Report of the Warren Commission (The New York Times, 1964), p. 500.

3. On behalf of my collegues who are present, Dr. Fetzer and Dr. Mantik, I [*Dr. Aguilar*] want to record our profound indebtedness to our colleague who is absent, Kathleen Cunningham, for her generous and unstinting efforts in investigating the assassination at considerable inconvenience and personal expense. She has believed in the "throat wound ignorance theory" for a longer time than any of the rest of us and deserves credit for researching this matter.

4. One of the earliest studies to invite attention to this issue was a piece by David Welsh and David Lifton, "A Counter Theory: The Case for Three Assassins", In the Shadow of Dallas (see especially pp. 68-69), which was published by Ramparts as a summary of research conducted during 1966.

3

5. A partial transcript of his testimony may be found here as Appendix F. A different view comes from a Parkland Hospital emergency room nurse, Audrey Bell, who told Harrison Edward Livington that on the morning of 23 November 1963, "Dr. Perry was up all night. He came into my office the next day and sat down and looked terrible, having not slept. I never saw anybody look so dejected! They called him from Bethesda two or three times in the middle of the night to try to get him to change the entry wound in the throat to an exit wound. They really grilled him about it. They hounded him for a long time." See <u>High Treason 2</u> (Carroll & Graf, 1992), p. 121.

6. This testimony has just been released under the new declassification law. The Clark summary, incidentally, is important for several reasons, not least of all because it hints that the physicians had Parkland medical reports in hand describing a wound to the throat <u>before they wrote their own report!</u>

7. The Certificate of Death, which is signed by Theron Ward, Justice of the Peace, and dated December 6, 1963, describes the death as due to "multiple gunshot wounds of the head and neck". The Bethesda autopsy report states <u>"CAUSE OF DEATH:</u> Gunshot wound, head", but provides further elaboration. <u>Report of the Warren Commission</u> (The New York Times, 1964), pp. 500-504.

[*Editor's note:* See Appendices D, E, F, and J.]

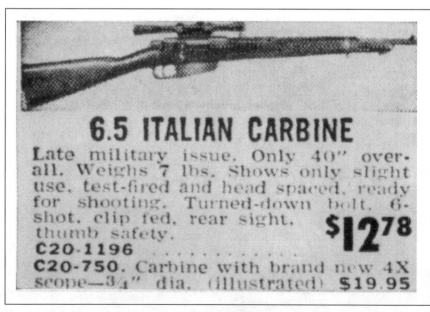

Catalogue ad for the alleged Oswald rifle, a six-shot, clip-fed, Italian carbine, which is not a high-velocity weapon

This version is intended for a public talk to a lay audience.

OPTICAL DENSITY MEASUREMENTS
OF THE JFK AUTOPSY X-RAYS
and
A NEW OBSERVATION BASED
ON THE CHEST X-RAY

David W. Mantik, M.D., Ph.D.

In this talk I will present new evidence that the autopsy X-rays of President John F. Kennedy have been altered, that there were 2 shots which struck the head, and that the magic bullet is anatomically impossible.

Just before Halloween this year, I visited the National Archives on four separate days to examine the autopsy X-rays and photographs. While there I used a technique -- called optical densitometry -- to study the X-rays. This technique has been available for many years but has never been applied to the JFK autopsy X-rays. It measures the transmission of ordinary light through selected points of the X-ray film. If I had measured thousands of points I could have constructed a three dimensional topographic map of the X-rays. The higher points on this map would represent the blackest areas of the X-ray film and would correspond to areas in the body where the most X-rays had passed through to strike the film. In a way, therefore, the information contained in the X-ray film is converted from two dimensions into three dimensions and is that much richer in detail. The range of peaks and valleys on such a topographic map would be expected to fall within a well defined range for a normal human skull. Any values which lie outside of this range -- and especially those which lie unnaturally far outside -- would not be consistent with ordinary skulls and would raise questions of authenticity.

Abnormal Optical Density Measurements

In an X-ray the whiter areas represent denser tissues, such as bone. That is because fewer X-rays strike the film and, during the development process, this area turns relatively lucent. On the other hand, less dense tissues, such as air, permit more X-rays to pass through to the film and these areas then become dark. With that in mind, I shall turn to the JFK autopsy X-rays. On the skull X-rays taken from the side -- they are called lateral X-rays -- in the rear portion there is an obvious large white area that is easy to see on both the left and right skull X-rays. By contrast, in the frontal area the X-ray is unusually dark. When I first saw these two areas I was struck both by how extremely

1

white and how extremely black they looked. Both areas looked very different from what I
was used to seeing in my own patients. I was therefore very anxious to measure these
areas for optical density to see if they were normal or not. What I found was quite
astonishing. The posterior white area transmits almost 1000 times more light than the
dark area! This large difference was seen on both the left and right lateral skull X-rays. I
suspected that this large ratio was nowhere near normal so I measured these same areas
for patients whom I had seen in the clinic. Their X-rays looked entirely unremarkable to
me -- like hundreds of others that I had seen. My measurements showed only small
differences in optical densities between the front and the back. At most, the rear portion
of the skull was slightly whiter and transmitted up to twice as much light as the anterior
portion. I concluded therefore that the measured differences of about 1000 between the
front and back of the JFK skull were too large to be explained by any ordinary
differences as seen in typical patients. In fact, the very lucent area at the rear of the skull
was almost as lucent as the densest bone in the body -- and I actually measured this on
the JFK autopsy X-ray. This bone is the one which surrounds the ear canal. Not only is
this bone around the ear very dense, but it is also very thick -- it extends from one side of
the skull to the other. In order for the white area at the rear of the skull to match the
whiteness of this very dense bone, all of the brain in this posterior area would have to be
replaced by very dense bone -- and the bone would have to extend from one side of the
skull to the other. No human skull is constructed in this fashion.

     I was fortunate to have for comparison an 8 x 10 black and white print, obtained
from the National Archives, of a lateral skull X-ray, taken of JFK during his lifetime.
This extreme range of whiteness to blackness is not seen in this X-ray print, as judged by
the unaided human eye. Unfortunately, these X-rays are kept at the JFK Presidential
Library in Massachusetts and were not made available to me for optical density
measurements.

     Besides the two lateral skull X-rays --one left and one right -- I also examined the
X-ray taken from the front. There is a 6.5 mm nearly round so-called bullet fragment seen
within the right eye socket. On the lower border of this fragment, at about the 5 o'clock
position, a large bite is missing. The left to right width of this object at this lower level is
therefore much less than the width of this object at its center. On the lateral X-ray,
therefore, using the optical density measurements, I would naturally have expected this
object to appear thicker at the center than at the bottom. To my surprise, however, the
optical density measurements showed just the opposite: they implied distinctly more
metal at the bottom! This fragment clearly does not behave like an object which was
physically present on the body during the original X-rays. If, on the other hand, it was

2

added later as a second image to the original frontal X-ray, as in a composite, it could hardly be expected to be consistent with the lateral X-ray. Because no one bothers to take optical density measurements, anyone who prepared such a composite would not have worried about making the two views consistent for optical density.

This disagreement between the frontal X-ray and the lateral X-ray was not found in other objects on the X-rays. For example, there is a 7 x 2 mm metal fragment located well above the right eye. This is seen on both frontal and lateral views. On the lateral view its optical density was quite homogeneous. That is what I would have expected from the way it looks from the front. It therefore appears to be real -- that is, it was located on the body during the original X-rays. In fact, the pathologists described removing it. By contrast, it is most peculiar that the pathologists did not remove the much larger and more obvious 6.5 mm round object which should have been quite accessible at the back of the skull. Considering that the pathologists' main task was to find bullets, or at least large bullet fragments, it is astonishing that they did not even describe this object! My work suggests that they did not see it for a good reason -- perhaps it was not there, at least not in its present appearance. I should also add that when I asked the autopsy radiologist, Dr. John Ebersole, whether he saw this object on the X-ray on the night of the autopsy, he refused to answer my question and he abruptly terminated what had otherwise been a reasonable conversation. JAMA has so far refused to publish my article which contained a summary of my conversation with him. Unfortunately, Dr. Ebersole passed away several months ago. I believe that I was the last to ask him questions about the autopsy.

I noticed several additional odd features in this large white area at the rear of the skull. If this white area really represents a normal bone fragment, it should have about the same shape on both the left and right lateral X-rays, allowing, of course, for small differences in perspective. In fact, however, the superior border has a distinctly different shape on these two lateral views: on the left view, a small, but distinct, peninsula juts upward at one point where no similar feature is seen on the right view. The other, more normal appearing, bone fragments do not show such odd features.

On close inspection, this remarkable white area is distinctly wider on one lateral view than on the other. This implies that it was located closer to the right side of the skull. On the frontal X-ray, such an extremely dense object should have been as visible as a tyrannosaurus rex in downtown Manhattan at noon. However, when I looked at the frontal X-ray, there was no such beast to be seen.

The aberrations seen on these X-rays are so diverse that no explanation can accommodate such an ensemble except for the explanation of composites, i.e., they are composed of superpositions of more than one image. Most likely, the original image was

3

authentic. There are numerous unique features of JFK in these X-rays which were confirmed both in this study and in the prior study of the House Select Committee on Assassinations (HSCA). After the original image was reproduced by an X-ray copying machine, and before development, a second image was most likely superimposed on the first. This technique could have been used to add both the very dense area at the rear on the lateral X-ray and also the 6.5 mm object on the frontal view. Such a technique, of course, had no guarantee of producing consistent optical densities. On the contrary, it almost guarantees inconsistency.

You may well ask why no physician has officially proposed composites before. Well, you must remember that such composite X-rays are simply not seen in clinical practice. If you have never in your life seen a ghost would you recognize one if you saw one? And if you really did see one, would you admit that you believed in ghosts? Harry Livingstone tells me that his radiologist friend, Dr. Donald Siple, had actually suspected for some time that these X-rays were composites, so perhaps I am actually arriving at this conclusion rather late in the game. Quite possibly, there are many more of us out there than anyone has suspected. After today we may find out!

A Search for the Posterior Bullet Entry Site in the Skull

The HSCA concluded that a bullet entered the back of the head slightly above the 6.5 mm object which is seen on the frontal skull X-ray. They reached this opinion based on observations of the lateral views. Oddly enough, they did not comment on the location of this bullet hole as seen on the frontal X-ray. On this frontal X-ray, I carefully scanned the area above the 6.5 mm fragment, looking for their described bullet hole. As judged by optical density measurements, there is no such hole anywhere in this vicinity.

An alternate, but much lower site, was emphatically described by the autopsy pathologists in their official HSCA testimony and was recently confirmed in their interviews with the Journal of the American Medical Association (JAMA). Unfortunately, I could not do satisfactory measurements at this lower site on the frontal skull X-ray because there is dense bone from the front of the skull which overlaps this site. If, however, this lower site is correct -- and it is generally agreed that there are no other candidates for this bullet entry site -- then there is no good explanation for the obvious and numerous metallic fragments near the top of the skull, at least 4 inches higher than the lower entry site. I have always found it odd that these fragments near the top of the head were not described by the pathologists. Even JAMA did not venture to ask the pathologists about these oddly located metal fragments which are so obviously

4

inconsistent with a lower entry site. The pathologists suggested that the bullet which entered from the rear headed toward an area well above the right eye. But these dense metal objects are so far from this path that they are impossible to explain without invoking a second bullet near the top of the skull. This was exactly the dilemma that the HSCA tried to resolve by elevating the entry site on the back of the head by nearly 4 inches. Since I could not find an entry site at this location in my measurements, the HSCA entry site is quite unlikely. The pathologists' much lower site then becomes that much more likely. On this point, my work is in rare agreement with JAMA. The numerous bullet fragments near the top of the skull, however, would then require a second bullet for their explanation. This is clearly not in agreement with JAMA. This obvious conflict has never been addressed by the pathologists -- no one has even asked them about it! JAMA refused to publish a jointly authored letter to the editor when we raised this question. Jerroll Custer, the radiology technologist who took the X-rays, and who is here today, has confirmed to me that this collection of metal debris was indeed present on the original X-rays.

The Chest X-Ray

I also found some surprising results based on the chest X-ray. I made accurate measurements of the width of the spine directly on the X-ray. The front to back thickness of the body at this site (14 cm) as well as the distance of the back wound from the midline (4.5 to 5.0 cm) were supplied by the HSCA. Since this latter distance can be measured independently on photographs of the back, I also did this. The so-called exit site at the front of throat was described by the Parkland doctors as being very near the midline. When I placed these measurements onto a cross section of the body and then connected the bullet entry and exit sites by a straight line, I immediately saw that the "magic" bullet had to go right through the spine. This path would have caused major damage to the spine and would have been very obvious on the chest X-ray. In fact, there is no major trauma like this anywhere in the spine. Because of the impenetrable vertical barrier produced by the transverse processes up and down the entire cervical spine and because of the total width of the cervical spine, there is no place for the bullet to pass through anywhere in the neck and still exit through the midline of the throat. If, instead, the upper chest is considered as a possible bullet trajectory site, then another problem arises. The bullet would have to go right through the lung. But no lung damage of this type was seen by the pathologists and none is seen on the X-rays either. This "magic" bullet simply cannot enter through the back wound and then exit through the throat wound without hitting the spine -- or else causing major lung trauma! It is odd that this rather simple reconstruction with exact measurements has never been done before. Its very simplicity, however, provides direct evidence that the object which entered the back could not have exited at the front of the throat. This throat wound, which looked like an entrance wound to the Parkland physicians when they first described it, may indeed have been an entrance wound.

Summary

This work has demonstrated singular features in the JFK autopsy X-rays. The range and number of these is so great that there can be only one satisfactory explanation -- these images are composites. Even to the unaided eye they appear to be composites. Now optical density measurements have added further confirmation for this view.

In addition, strong evidence is cited to demonstrate that two shots struck the skull. Finally, a simple anatomic reconstruction shows that the "magic" bullet truly had to be magical to pass through the spine without leaving a trace of serious trauma.

Acknowledgments. Generous thanks are due to Mr. Steven Tilley and Mr. David Painter for donating extraordinary amounts of time to attend me while these measurements were made at the National Archives. My thanks also must needs go to Mr. Burke Marshall for granting me permission to view the JFK autopsy materials and to the Kennedy family for permitting this intrusion. Dr. Cyril Wecht graciously accompanied me to the National Archives during one of my visits. I thank him for keeping the critics' questions alive for so many years. David Lifton was a regular source of motivation and information. The Assassination Archives and Research Center (AARC), headed by Mr. Jim Lesar, provided assistance in more than one way. My colleagues, Dr. Gary Aguilar, Dr. James Fetzer, Dr. Gary Keough, Dr. John Szabo, and my wife, Dr. Patricia James, have provided no end of encouragement. On the other hand, my children, Christopher (8) and Meredith (6), have done everything possible to discourage the completion of this study. I should thank them for keeping some balance in my life. Perhaps some day they shall understand why the National Archives took precedence over a fourth consecutive day at Busch Gardens.

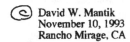 David W. Mantik
November 10, 1993
Rancho Mirage, CA

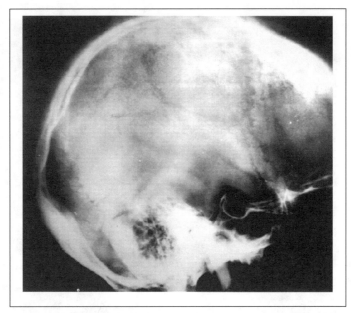

A pre-mortem (while living) X-ray of JFK's cranium (right-side)

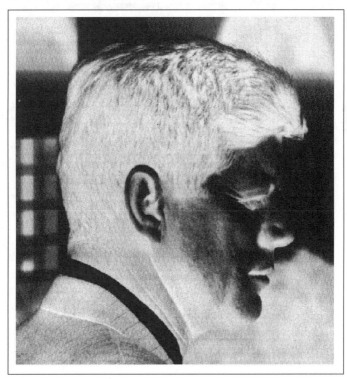

A right profile of President John Fitzgerald Kennedy

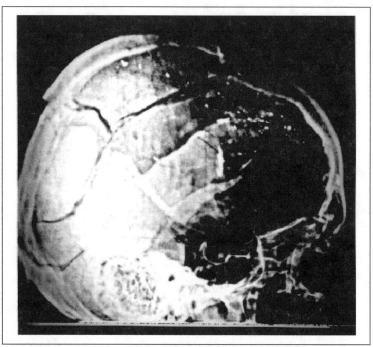

The official post-mortem right lateral X-ray of JFK's cranium

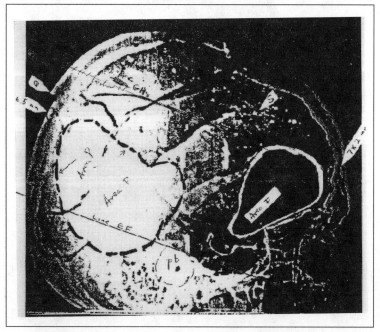

Mantik's analysis of the right lateral X-ray of JFK's cranium

18 November 1993   **Robert B. Livingston, M.D.**

My "revelations" are three: Two are based on highly credible medical testimony. The third is from a trusted friend, an "eyewitness," who published in *The New Republic* that on the 22nd of November 1963, he saw a "hole" in the windshield of the President's limousine.

Medical Evidence:

1. It was reported at the time--and reinforced in subsequent testimony by physicians who attended the dying President at Parkland Hospital in Dallas--that on initial examination, prior to the tracheotomy, they found a small wound in the President's neck near the midline, just to the right and slightly below the trachea. (See Appendices B and E.)

2. Also reported from Parkland Hospital was that large amounts of cerebellar tissue were extruding from the wound in the back of the President's head. (See Appendices C and D.)

A small wound from a high-velocity projectile indicates a wound of entrance. I know this from authoritative studies in medical literature which analyzed ballistic wounds. Characteristically, high velocity bullet or shrapnel wounds show a small, neat wound of entry and a much larger wound of exit. This has been thoroughly analyzed with high-speed photographic and X-ray analyses. As a projectile advances through air, there is a supersonic shock wave that forms a V-shaped shroud that expands alongside and has a turbulent zone which follows behind. When the bullet or shrapnel penetrates living tissues, this shock wave balloons out conspicuously, causing extensive cavitation and an irregular, splitting-tunneling of ruptured tissues which trace the path of the projectile. When the missile leaves the body, tissues are splayed outward, and the skin is split open by force of the compression wave travelling ahead of and trailing alongside the projectile. Such a bullet or shrapnel fragment invariably causes a large wound of exit--with the skin usually split in a cruciate or star-shaped fashion.

My experience in this respect is not simply academic: I personally cared for hundreds of bullet and shrapnel wounds in my service in the Navy Medical Corps during the battle for[1] Okinawa, where I established and directed the only hospital for wounded Okinawans and Japanese prisoners of war throughout the duration of that battle. There were several instances, moreover, when our hospital was strafed by Kamikaze pilots. On two such occasions, physicians operating with me, with our hands in the same wound, were themselves wounded. One lost the use of his left hand and the other, with shrapnel smashing through his right shoulder, had a paralyzed flail arm ever after. He was driven to convert from being an orthopedic surgeon to being a radiologist.

The Parkland Hospital physicians were thoroughly experienced in treating bullet wounds. They could readily recognize wounds of entrance, and clearly distinguish them from exit wounds.

Because of my position as Scientific Director for two of the National Institutes of Health--the National Institute for Mental Health and the National Institute of Neurological Diseases and Blindness--because I had met President Kennedy while serving in the U.S. Public Health Service during the transition from Eisenhower to Kennedy and throughout the Kennedy administration--because I knew several Cabinet members and other principals, and, most importantly--because my scientific responsibilities were directly pertinent to the conduct of the President's autopsy and interpretations of damage to his nervous system, I paid careful attention to the unfolding news. Thereby I learned that: a) there was a small frontal wound in the President's throat, and b) substantial parts of the cerebellum were extruding from the wound in the back of his head.

Because the wound of entry in the front of his neck required that the President had to have been assaulted frontally, this seemed to me to be a matter of utmost importance for the autopsy. I therefore telephoned from my home in Bethesda to the Bethesda Naval Hospital where the autopsy was to be performed. This was prior to arrival of the President's casket from Dallas to Andrews Air Force Base. I was put through to the Officer of the Day who quickly provided telephone access to Commander James Humes who was to head the autopsy team.

Dr. Humes said he had not heard much reporting from Dallas and Parkland Hospital because he had been occupied preparing to conduct the autopsy. I told him about reports describing the small wound in the President's neck. I stressed that, in my experience, that would have to be a wound of entrance. I emphasized the importance of carefully tracing the path of this projectile and of establishing the location of the bullet or any fragments. I said carefully, that if that wound were confirmed as a wound of entrance, that would prove beyond peradventure of doubt that a bullet had been fired from in front of the President--hence that if there were shots from behind, there had to have been more than one gunman. At just that moment, there was an interruption in our conversation. Dr. Humes returned after a pause to say, "Dr. Livingston, I'm sorry, but I can't talk with you any longer. The FBI won't let me." I wished him good luck, and the conversation ended. I wondered aloud to my wife, who had overheard my side of the conversation, why the FBI would want to interfere with a discussion between physicians relating to the important problem of how best to investigate and interpret the President's wounds. Now, with knowledge of the apparently prompt and massive control of information that was imposed in order to fix the responsibility for the assassination of President Kennedy on a single assassin--working alone--I can appreciate that the FBI interruption of our conversation may have been far more meaningful than I presumed at the time.

I conclude, therefore--on the basis of direct, personal experiences--that Dr. Humes did have his attention drawn: (a) to the small neck wound of projectile entry, (b) to its significance for the autopsy as well as (c) for its potential forensic significance. Dr. Humes' testimony to the Warren Commission that he only learned about the neck wound *on the day after completion of the autopsy*, after he had talked with Dr. Perry in Dallas by telephone, means that the autopsy (and Dr. Humes) were already under explicit non-medical control prior to the start of the autopsy. (See Appendices H and I.)

Significance of Cerebellar Extrusion

With respect to the large amount of cerebellum reported protruding from the wound at the back of the President's head, this is also highly significant. Several physicians--I believe all of the physicians attending the President at Parkland Hospital--testified that they saw cerebellum protruding from the wound in the back of the President's head. Among those, Dr. Kemp Clark is known by me as a distinguished neurosurgeon who certainly would not be mistaken about identifying cerebellum--even after it had been forced out of a messy, clot-filled wound. Nor is Dr. Crenshaw likely to be mistaken, either: He described the cerebellum as "hanging outside the wound by a thread of tissue."

The blow-out of the cerebellum, ejected upwards through the tough tentorium, and thrust posteriorly out through the gaping wound in the rear of the skull would have required a violent *sub-tentorial* explosive force that would have had to rupture the tentorium and force large portions of the cerebellum posteriorly, out through the occipital wound.

The cerebellum is attached by three stout bundles of fibers that arise from and deeply penetrate into each side of the brainstem. If these six sturdy attachments were torn loose so as to leave only a thread of tissue attaching the cerebellum, then the *brainstem itself must have been thoroughly disrupted*. This pontine segment of the brainstem is just posterior to those centers that govern arousal and that support consciousness. Such cerebellar uprooting would probably have led to an abrupt eclipse of the President's consciousness, more assuredly even than the massive disruption of the right hemisphere and cutting through the posterior corpus callosum.

It is important to recognize that the cerebellum is anchored tightly to the brain stem and is separated from the main chamber of the skull by a thick, dense, strong sheet of dural tissue, the *tentorium*, which is firmly anchored to the skull four-fifths of the way around the rim of the posterior chamber (fossa) of the skull. Tentorial attachments leave only a small opening between the posterior fossa and the main brain cavity. This opening encircles the midbrain which, in turn, connects the lower brainstem with the rest of the forebrain.

The point of entry of the occipital-parietal bullet, although somewhat variously located in different documents, has never been positioned below the occipital protuberance, which is the landmark for the level of tentorial attachment posteriorly.   Any bullet shock-wave applied from above, therefore, would press *down* on the tentorium and force the brainstem *downward*, not upward and backward.   At the angle of trajectory presumed for this posteriorly entering bullet, it would be very unlikely to disrupt the tentorium, and if it did, it would certainly not force cerebellum to be extruded posteriorly.

Therefore, if cerebellum was extruding posteriorly--and I believe the medical witnesses at Parkland Hospital could not have been mistaken about this--that means there had to be powerful forces exerted from beneath, which developed sufficient shock against the tentorium to rupture it upwards and simultaneously to detach and extrude cerebellar tissue through the wound in the back of the President's head.   This might have been caused by a bullet entering his neck from in front, or perhaps a fragment of such a bullet, passing upward through the floor of the posterior fossa and disrupting the cerebellum and tentorium.

Questions have also been raised concerning the supposed temporal lobe bullet with a postulated entry point somewhat above and directly in front of the President's right ear.   This possible entry point is related to the so-called "bat-wing" configuration that appears in autopsy photographs of the President's head, and to "Photo 28" that appears in David Lifton's *Best Evidence*.   This presumably was caused by a bullet that invaded the President's skull from a frontal angle on the right side.   If a bullet with this entry location did not blow out the back of the President's head, then it might have pointed downward sufficiently to smash into the posterior fossa and disrupt cerebellum and rupture the tentorium, with the observed effects of cerebellar extrusion.

As you have learned from Dr. David Mantik, photographs in the archives identified as pictures of the President's brain plainly show the cerebellum in superior and lateral views as being intact.   This is also true for the drawing, presumably from a photograph of the President's brain: the cerebellum is drawn in as though it had not been disrupted.

It simply cannot be true that the cerebellum could have been seen extruding from the occipito-parietal wound--by several experienced and thoroughly competent physicians--*and for the same brain* to be seen in superior and lateral photographs, and depicted in a drawing (superior view) showing the cerebellum as being apparently intact.   A conclusion is obligatorily forced that the photographs and drawings of the brain in the National Archives are those of some brain other than that of John Fitzgerald Kennedy.

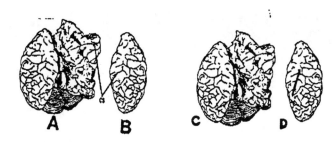

A.   HSCA exhibit F-302.   Drawing made from photograph of brain illustrating subcortical damage.
B.   Mirror image drawing of left hemisphere in Figure A. Distortion due to damage and/or post-fixation artifact is minimal.
C.   HSCA exhibit F-302 (again). Drawing made from photograph of brain to show subcortical damage.
D.   Mirror image drawing of left hemisphere in Figure A. Black line illustrates schematically the direct cortical damage predicted based upon skull X-rays, which Dr. Mantik has now demonstrated to be composites.

These figures are from Joseph N. Riley, Ph.D., "The Head Wounds of John Kennedy: 1. One Bullet cannot Account for the Injuries," in: *The Third Decade* (March, 1993), pp. 1-15. These particular drawings appear on page 5.

The Hole in the Windshield

In the supporting documents (Appendix J), there is a single page from the 21 December 1963 issue of *The New Republic*. It is entitled "Commentary of an Eyewitness." It was written by Richard Dudman, a reporter for the St. Louis Post-Dispatch. Dick Dudman is a classmate of mine from Stanford. He telephoned me about this from Dallas shortly after the assassination; and our families had a dinner discussion on this subject in Washington, D.C. within a week or so of the assassination. Dick Dudman told me about the windshield then, although to the present he does not know whether the hole he saw penetrated the windshield. He was prevented by the Secret Service from testing the hole's presumed patency by probing it with a pen or pencil.

There is evidence that the Ford Motor Company had an order for a dozen windshields for the Lincoln limousine similar to that which bore President Kennedy on the day of his assassination. These were for "target practice," presumably to see how much or how little security the windshield provides. But that "target practice" on a dozen windshields leaves in some doubt *whether the windshield in the National Archives* is the same one that was in the Kennedy limousine at the time of the assassination.

Note Mr. Dudman's unambiguous eyewitness account: "A few of us noticed the hole in the windshield when the limousine was standing at the emergency entrance after the President had been carried inside. I could not approach close enough to see on which side was the cup-shaped spot that indicates a bullet has pierced the glass from the opposite side." [Notice here, also, that the *exit* of a bullet through glass is larger than its *entrance*, according to the same physical principles that obtain when a bullet penetrates flesh, viz., the small entry wound in the President's neck.]

In our personal conversations, Dick Dudman was informative in a further sense: The "hole" in the windshield was high up in the left hand corner of the windshield. In that location a bullet could not have directly nicked or penetrated the windshield if it had been fired from the sixth floor of the Texas Book Depository Building. Therefore, if such a nick or hole was not in the windshield when the limousine turned the corner from Houston Street to Elm Street, it would have had to be caused by a projectile with a quite different direction, casting additional uncertainty on the "single assassin" hypothesis. These implications are weaker that those relating to the wound in the President's neck, but offer further indications that *another gunman* shot at the President at about the same time.

Robert B. Livingston, M.D., with David W. Mantik. M.D., Ph.D.,
in Rancho Mirage, CA, on 12 June 1997

THE NEW REPUBLIC   Dec. 21, 1963   J - 1

Commentary of an Eyewitness

Some of the points raised here bothered me on the scene in Dallas, where I witnessed President Kennedy's assassination and the slaying of the accused assassin two days later. Three circumstances – the entry wound in the throat, the small, round hole in the windshield of the Presidential limousine, and the number of bullets found afterward – suggested that there had been a second sniper firing from a point in front of the automobile.

The throat wound puzzled the surgeons who attended Mr. Kennedy at Parkland Memorial Hospital when they learned how the Dallas police had reconstructed the shooting. Dr. Robert McClelland, one of the three doctors who worked on the throat wound, told me afterward that they still believed it to be an entry wound, even though the shots were said to have been fired from almost directly behind the President. He explained that he and his colleagues at Parkland saw bullet wounds every day, sometimes several a day, and recognized easily the characteristically tiny hole of an entering bullet, in contrast to the larger, tearing hole that an exiting bullet would have left.

A few of us noticed the hole in the windshield when the limousine was standing at the emergency entrance after the President had been carried inside. I could not approach close enough to see on which side was the cup-shaped spot that indicates a bullet has pierced the glass from the opposite side.

As for the number of bullets, although all who heard them agreed there were three shots, authorities repeatedly mentioned four bullets found afterward – one found in the floor of the car, a second found in the President's stretcher, a third removed from Governor Connally's left thigh, and a fourth said to have been removed from President Kennedy's body at the Naval Hospital in Bethesda. On the day the President was shot, I happened to learn of a possible fifth. A group of police officers were examining the area at the side of the street where the President was hit, and a police inspector told me they had just found another bullet in the grass. He said he did not know whether it had anything to do with the assassination.

With these circumstances in mind, I returned to the scene to see where a shot from ahead of the President's car might have originated. From the stretch traveled by the car when the shots were fired, a large sector in front is taken up by a railroad viaduct. It crosses over the triple underpass, through which the motorcade was routed. No buildings are visible beyond the viaduct; it forms the horizon.

Between the tracks and the near side of the viaduct is a broad gravel walkway. Along the side is a three-foot concrete ballustrade, with upright slots two

or three inches wide. At each end is a five-foot wooden fence that screens the approaches to the viaduct.

Normal Secret Service procedure is to have local police stationed on and under any such overpass before a Presidential motorcade approaches. The standing order also is to clear each overpass of all spectators. The Secret Service now declines all comment on the assassination, refusing to answer the specific question as to precautions taken with respect to that particular viaduct. Railroad police seem to have been assigned responsibility there. The area is marked with no-trespassing signs as private railroad property. Railroad police chased away an Associated Press photographer who tried to set up his camera there before the motorcade arrived. But the precautions apparently were not perfect. Early reports of the shooting told of a police pursuit of a man and woman seen running on the viaduct. There was no report that they were caught. Regardless, their presence indicates that unauthorized persons had access to that vantage point.

The south end of the viaduct is four short blocks from the office of the Dallas Morning News, where Jack Ruby was seen before and after the shooting. He had gone to the News office to make up an advertisement for his strip-tease place. An employee remembered the time as 12:10 p.m., because the ad deadline was noon and Ruby often was late. The advertising man Ruby wanted to see had gone out to watch the motorcade; he returned at 12:45, unaware that the President had been shot. No one remembered for sure seeing Ruby between 12:15 and 12:45. The shooting was at 12:30.

If the entry wound in the throat presents any problem to the FBI in analyzing the crime, the agency has not indicated this by its actions. Dr. McClendon said a few days ago (December 9) that no official investigators, from the FBI or anywhere else, had questioned the surgeons at Parkland Hospital about their observation of the throat wound.

Conclusions reached in a post-mortem examination at Bethesda would have questionable validity. The doctors at Dallas had made their incision through the bullet hole in performing a tracheotomy in an effort to restore satisfactory breathing. The hole was slightly below the Adam's apple, at the precise point where a tracheotomy normally is performed. Changes in tissue in the several hours before the body reached Bethesda, moreover, would have increased difficulty of reconstructing the path of the bullet.

RICHARD DUDMAN

RICHARD DUDMAN is a reporter for the St. Louis Post-Dispatch and author of Men of the Far Right.

Richard Dudman's "Commentary of an Eyewitness," which appeared in The New Republic *(21 December 1963) p. 18*

1

Robert B. Livingston, M.D.
7818 Camino Noguera
San Diego, California 92122-2027
Tel: (619) 455-0306; Fax: (619) 455-1874

(310) 445-2301 Fax
(310) 445-2300 Tel

2 May 1992

PAGE ONE OF FOUR PAGES

David Lifton
11500 West Olympic Boulevard
Los Angeles, California 90064

Dear David Lifton:

This is a copy of a letter I have sent by Fax to Harrison Edward Livingstone. I have also printed a copy to send to Peter Dale Scott for his information. I send this to you with the hope that you would be willing to respond by obliging me to do a better job of presenting the experiences herein related, experiences that concern the assassination of President Kennedy, the autopsy and the Lincoln limousine windshield, as per our discussion over the telephone today. I look forward with keenest anticipation to reading *Best Evidence*. Many thanks for the contact and your advice.

Your book, *High Treason 2: The Great Coverup: The Assassination of President John F. Kennedy*, has attracted my personal and professional interest. I write to contribute a couple of specific, although minor, experiences that may add to your avalanche of already compelling evidence that a conspiracy was involved in the assassination of President Kennedy.[1]

I was employed by the U.S. Public Health Service as Scientific Director of the two National Institutes of Health in 1963, when President Kennedy was assassinated. In that office I had witnessed the marvelous transition of government and public engagement from

---

[1] Please permit me to introduce pertinent information about myself by way of this footnote: I am a Professor of Neurosciences Emeritus at the University of California San Diego (UCSD) where I founded the world's first Department of Neurosciences--in 1964. Previously, I taught Pathology at Stanford, Physiology at Yale, Psychiatry at Harvard, Anatomy and Physiology at UCLA, and Neurosciences at UCSD, always trying to learn how the human brain works, structurally and functionally. This is an easy way to make a living--inasmuch as nobody knows how the brain works. In mid-career, I served as Scientific Director, combining direction of Basic Research for two of the National Institutes of Health: the National Institute for Mental Health, and the National Institute of Neurological Diseases and Blindness.

During World War II, I served as a Lieutenant (j.g.) to Lieutenant in the U.S. Navy Medical Corps (Reserve) in the Pacific Theater, including creating and directing the only hospital for wounded Okinawans and Japanese throughout the Battle of Okinawa. Medical and surgical responsibilities required my examination and treatment of a large number of bullet and shrapnel wounds.

At UCSD I produced a film, *"The Human Brain: A Dynamic View of its Structures and Organization,"* which you may have seen on BBC, NOVA, National Geographic Specials or otherwise. The film won numerous national and international documentary film awards. It is considered by practitioners of modern brain imaging, those engaged in Positron Emission Tomography and Magnetic Resonance Imaging, as a "gold standard of normal human gross neuroanatomy."

2

Eisenhower to Kennedy and was keenly interested in Kennedy as a human being, as a hope-inspiring national and global leader; and, abruptly--tragically--as a victim of a terrible human, national, and international tragedy--cut down by a fusillade of gunfire that made him promptly unconscious, catastrophically disabled, and within a few short hours, thoroughly dead. An important consciousness snuffed out before all our astonished eyes. My concern has grown almost to alarm, over the years, that the full information concerning his assassination has been denied public examination.

I heard realtime broadcasts relating to the shots in Dallas while I was in the process of leaving the Massachusetts General Hospital, in Boston, to take an Eastern Shuttle to Washington, D.C., on the afternoon of November 22, 1963. I was thereafter riveted by taxi radio and later radio and television descriptions of the sequences of events following the shooting. I was carefully attentive to information from eye-witness reports: acoustic perceptions of gunfirings, visual perceptions of the physical and human layout and movements throughout the Plaza--to the front, to the sides, to the rear of the President's limousine--and possible sources of the shooting: from the overpass?--from the Grassy Knoll?--from the School Book Depository?

There were immediate arresting descriptions of the crowd's breathtaking, startled dismay, police motorcyclists' and Jackie Kennedy's responses, combined, after a longish latency, with limousine and cyclist accelerations, some protective Secret Service responses--and some prudent ducking and flattening of the crowd, prompted by those unexpected, sharp staccato bangs: --loud exhaust backfires? --firecrackers? --gunfire? --how many?

There were descriptions of President Kennedy leaning forward, reaching up for his throat, "as if to adjust his tie," Jackie Kennedy rising, turning, and climbing over the trunk to try to aid her husband and enlist Secret Service help, the President's head jerking backwards, and his body slowly toppling forward and to his left, while the motorcade accelerated, with his head coming to be cradled in Jackie Kennedy's lap. Eyewitness reporters seemed immediately convinced that President Kennedy had been hit and perhaps seriously wounded, while the parade turned into a flank route flight to the Parkland Hospital. Most of the prompt reporting of where the shots may have come from seemed to focus on the overpass, and less emphatically, the grassy knoll, as the most likely sources of the attack.

Reports from the Parkland Hospital described a massive wound to his head, the President being unconscious and completely paralyzed--physicians and nurses laboring to support his life. Then there was the detail of "a small wound in his neck, just to the right of his trachea." The doctors, while preparing an emergency tracheotomy, tried to establish whether whatever missile had entered the President's neck might have penetrated his lungs. He was, after an agonizing interval, pronounced dead.

The small neck wound, as has been repeatedly emphasized, must be a wound of entry. The President's head was described as having such a large defect of skull, and torn and macerated scalp, over the right side and back of his head [the mostly right, parieto-occipital region]. After reflecting the scalp further and looking into the cranial vault without having to rongeur or gigli-saw any stable bone--in order to open the skull for a preliminary look, someone reported that the brain was sufficiently exposed and torn apart in the right hemisphere that you could see down practically to the level of the thalamus.

I didn't hear anything from Parkland about the cerebellum being exposed or falling out. The cerebellum would likely have been spared direct damage, being protected by

3

the tough, well anchored, overlying tentorium which is not mentioned as having been breached in any of the documentation I have seen. I assumed from the outset that the occipito--parietal wound on the right side must be a blow-out wound of exit, and presumed that the left hemisphere may have remained largely intact.

*   *   *

Also relevant, I learned from a former classmate of mine from Stanford who was then a reporter for the *St. Louis Post-Dispatch,* Richard Dudman, that he was one of the White House press group that accompanied the President to Dallas. Not getting much information from the Parkland Hospital, Dick went out to inspect the Lincoln limousine in which the President and Connolly and their wives had been riding. He thought he saw, for certain, that there was a through-and-through hole in the upper left margin of the windshield. He described the spaling-splintering of glass at the margins as though the missile had entered from in front of the vehicle. When he reached over to pass his pencil or pen through the hole to test its patency, an FBI or Secret Service man roughly drew him away and shooed him off, instructing him that he wasn't allowed to come so close to that vehicle.

If there were a through-and-through windshield penetration, in that location, according to Dick, it had to come from in front. According to him, it would have been impossible to hit the windshield in that location from the overhead angle from the School Book Depository, nor would a through-and-through penetration have been likely to be caused by a ricochetting bullet bouncing up from the rear.

*   *   *

What is *most* relevant from my personal experience is that on that same evening, before the President's body on Air Force One had arrived at Andrews AFB, I telephoned the Bethesda Navy Hospital. I believe that the call was made before the plane arrived because I recollect that it was following that call that I watched Robert S. McNamara (Bob McNamara, is a long-standing, since 1952, mountain-climbing and hiking companion of mine) receive the Kennedy entourage and the casket being lowered on a fork life from the rear of the Air Force One onto the field tarmac.

Inasmuch as I was Scientific Director of two of the institutes at the NIH--and both institutes were pertinent to the matter of the President's assassination and brain injury--the Navy Hospital operator and the Officer on Duty put me through to speak directly with Dr. Humes who was waiting to perform the autopsy. After introductions, we began a pleasant conversation. He told me that he had not heard much about the reporting from Dallas and from the Parkland Hospital. I told him that the reason for my making such an importuning call was to stress that the Parkland Hospital physicians' examination of President Kennedy revealed what they reported to be a small wound in the neck, closely adjacent to and to the right of the trachea. I explained that I had knowledge from the literature on high-velocity wound ballistics research, in addition to considerable personal combat experience examining and repairing bullet and shrapnel wounds. I was confident that a small wound of that sort had to be a wound of entrance and that if it were a wound of exit, it would almost certainly be widely blown out, with cruciate or otherwise wide, tearing outward ruptures of the underlying tissues and skin.

I stressed to Dr. Humes how important it was that the autopsy pathologists carefully examine the President's neck to characterize that particular wound and to distinguish it from the neighboring tracheotomy wound.

4

I went on to presume, further, that the neck wound would probably not have anything to do with the main cause of death--massive, disruptive, brain injury--because of the angle of bullet trajectory and the generally upright position of the President's body, sitting up in the limousine. Yet, I said, carefully, *if that wound were confirmed as a wound of entry*, it would prove beyond peradventure of doubt that that shot had been fired from in front--hence *that if there were shots from behind, there had to have been more than one gunman.*. Just at that moment, there was an interruption in our conversation. Dr. Humes returned after a pause of a few seconds to say that "the FBI will not let me talk any further." I wished him good luck, and the conversation was ended. My wife can be good witness to that conversation because we shared our mutual distress over the terrible events, and she shared with me my considerations weighing the decision to call over to the Bethesda Navy Hospital. The call originated in the kitchen of our home on Burning Tree Road in Bethesda, with her being present throughout. After the telephone call, I exclaimed to her my dismay over the abrupt termination of my conversation with Dr. Humes, through the intervention of the FBI. I wondered aloud why they would want to interfere with a discussion between physicians relative to the problem of how best to investigate and interpret the autopsy. Now, with knowledge of the apparently prompt and massive control of information that was imposed on assignment of responsibility for the assassination of President Kennedy, I can appreciate that the interruption may have been far more pointed than I had presumed at that time.

I conclude, therefore, on the basis of personal experience, that Dr. Humes did have his attention drawn to the specifics and significance of President Kennedy's neck wound prior to his beginning the autopsy. His testimony that he only learned about the neck wound *on the day after* completion of the autopsy, after he had communicated with Doctor Perry In Dallas by telephone, means that he either forgot what I told him [although he appeared to be interested and attentive at the time] or that the autopsy was already under explicit non-medical control.

That event, coupled with Dick Dudman's report to me around the same time, of what appeared to him to be a penetrating hole through the Lincoln windshield, seems to me to add two grains of confirming evidence to the conspiracy interpretation. Incidently, sometime later, I learned that the Secret Service had ordered from the Ford Motor Company a number of identical Lincoln limousine windshields--"for target practice". It seems to me that they might have wanted to learn how much protection could be expected from such a windshield. Alternatively, they might have wanted to produce an inside nick in a windshield, without through-and-through penetration, so that they could substitute that nicked windshield for the other one, if it were needed for corroborative evidence relating to the Warren Commission's investigative interpretation and thesis.

I hope that this information may be helpful in some measure. With every good wish,

Yours sincerely,

Robert B. Livingston, M.D.
Professor of Neurosciences Emeritus, UCSD

FAX

To: Maynard Parker, Editor, *NEWSWEEK*
444 Madison Avenue, New York, NY 10022
Tel: (212) 350-4470; Fax: (212) 350-5146

From: Robert B. Livingston, M.D.
Professor of Neurosciences Emeritus, UCSD
7818 Camino Noguera, San Diego, CA 92122-2027
Tel: (619) 455-0306; Fax: (619) 455-1874

10 September 1993
PAGE ONE OF FOUR PAGES

Dear Maynard:

I wouldn't bother you with this, but since the files on JFK's assassination have recently been opened, new interest is focussing on evidence which casts doubt on the "single assassin" conclusion of the Warren Commission.

I was Scientific Director of the National Institute for Mental Health and (concurrently) of the National Institute of Neurological Diseases and Blindness, at the time of the assassination. These two institutes are obviously relevant to interpretations of brain damage sustained by the president.

On the basis of November 22, 1963, broadcasts from Parkland Hospital, I felt obliged to call Commander James Humes, at the Bethesda Naval Hospital, who was about to perform the autopsy. Our telephone conversation was completed before the body arrived at Andrews AFB. I called to retail media reports from Parkland Hospital that there was a small wound in the front of his neck, just to the right of the trachea.

Humes said he hadn't been paying attention to the news, but was receptive to what I had to tell him. We had a cordial conversation about this. Based on my knowledge of medical and experimental analyses of bullet wounding, and personal experiences caring for numerous bullet and shrapnel wounds throughout the battle of Okinawa, I told him that a small wound, as described, would have to be a wound of entry. When a bullet

1

I - 2

exits from flesh, it violently blows out a lot of tissue, usually making a conspicuous cruciate opening with tissue protruding. A wound of entry, however, just punctures as it penetrates. So I stressed the need for him to probe that wound to trace its course fully and to find the location of the bullet or fragments. I especially emphasized that such a wound had to be an entry wound. And since the president was facing forward the whole time, that meant that there had to be a conspiracy. As we talked about that, he interrupted the conversation momentarily. He came back on the line to say, "I'm sorry, Dr. Livingston, but the FBI won't let me talk any longer." Thus, the conversation ended.

Two important subsequent events are noteworthy: Commander Humes did not dissect that wound, and when asked why not, in the Warren Commission hearings, he said that he didn't know about the small wound in the neck until the following day when he had a conversation with Dr. Perry at Parkland Hospital.

A further issue concerns reports of the appearance of cerebellar tissue in the occipital wound. This was first reported "live" as observations by an orderly, and by a nurse, both of whom were in the surgery where attempts to resuscitate the president were conducted prior to his death. I didn't give any credibility to those stories and dismissed them from my focus at the time, attributing what I thought must be mistaken identification of cerebellum to a likely lack of familiarity with neuroanatomy by two non-medically trained individuals. It would be easy to assume cerebellum in looking at macerated cerebral tissue protruding from a bloody wound. But since then, around six reputable physicians who saw the president at that time have testified that cerebellum was extruding from the wound at the back of his head. That is an important clue, indicating that something must have burst into the posterior fossa with sufficient force to uproot the cerebellum and blow a substantial hole through the heavy, covering, well-anchored, tentorium, which separates cerebellum from the main chamber of the skull.

There is a third clue, relating to a probable hole in the

2

upper left corner of the limousine windshield, which I learned about on that day, or the next, from a reporter for the *St. Louis Post Dispatch*, my friend and Stanford classmate, Dick Dudman-- whom you probably know. According to the spaling of the glass, Dick was convinced that it was a through-and-through penetration, but wasn't permitted to test that by putting his pen through the presumed hole.

Well, I have long been urged to document these experiences: I had correspondence with Peter Dale Scott, a Professor of English at UC Berkeley, David Lifton, author of *Best Evidence,* and, as well, and Harrison Edward Livingstone (no relative) somewhat over a year ago which I can transmit to you if you are interested. More recently, I have had numerous conversations and visits with Gary Aquilar, an ophthalmologist in San Francisco, and conversations with James Fetzer, a Professor of Philosophy at the University of Minnesota, in Duluth. I have made and distributed to family and friends copies of this correspondence, and also a 45-minute video-tape recording that recounts these experiences, including reading some of the correspondence. Such distribution was advised so that if anything untoward happened to me, the documents would speak for themselves.

Today I received a three-page Draft Fax from Jim Fetzer which he was addressing to 60 MINUTES in New York, describing what I have described above. I told him to not send that fax, to which he agreed.

If the matter is to be considered "newsworthy" I would feel a great deal better if you would give me your advice as to how best to proceed. I would much prefer *NEWSWEEK* to handle the matter, with your shepherding, if you will, than a slam-bang program where one guy says he had an important telephone conversation with another guy, and the other guy says he doesn't remember any such conversation: End of dialogue. That kind of treatment seems to me to add more confusion rather than clarity to the situation.

I end this by expressing to you my personal dilemma over what might be best to do, if anything. You can appreciate that I am concerned that the assassination has not been been

3

I - 4

adequately clarified, after 29+ years. And, also, that I have a respectful willingness to contribute this sort of evidence--if you and others consider that to be advisable. Some thoughtful people have implied that if I remain silent my life may be in danger! [which is to me unbelievable], and that the best security is to make the evidence public.

Again, my apologies, Maynard, for dragging you into this: I trust your judgment and will respect your advice. With every good personal wish,

Yours   sincerely,

Bob   Livingston

---

16 July 1997   Robert B. Livingston, M.D.

Careful readers may have noticed, as David Lifton has observed, that there is an inconsistency between my Letter to David Lifton of 2 May 1992, where I report having heard nothing from Parkland about exposed cerebellum, and my Statement of 18 November 1993, where I describe hearing of extruding cerebellum by way of radio and television coverage on 22 November 1963. I am (increasingly) confident that my later statement rather than my letter is correct. I specifically recall hearing information about extruding cerebellum that was attributed (by reporters) to an orderly, to a nurse, and to a doctor (as sources) at the time. I also remember quite clearly that this was one of the issues that I was going to discuss with Humes before the FBI cut us off.

On reports of sources of the shots, speculation about shooters on the grassy knoll or in the vicinity of the Triple Underpass were supported by descriptions of large numbers of persons rushing to those locations immediately after the assassination. The press was widely broadcasting two shots to the President —one to the throat, one to the right temple—that were fired from in front and those appeared to be the most obvious places for their origin. I am grateful to David Lifton for bringing these matters to my attention through Jim Fetzer, because I want the record to be clear and unambiguous about my experiences. I appreciate the opportunity the editor has provided to make this clarification.

A clarification provided by Robert B. Livingston, M.D.,
on 16 July 1997, in response to questions posed by David Lifton

UNIVERSITY OF MINNESOTA

Duluth Campus   *Department of Philosophy*   *10 University Drive*
Duluth, MN 55812,2496

13 September 1993   *218-726-8548*
Fax: 218-726-6386

Mr. Howell Raines
Editorial Page Editor
The New York Times
229 West 43rd Street
New York, NY 10036

Re: Christopher Lehmann-Haupt's Review of Gerald Posner's Case Closed

Dear Editor,

     Gerald Posner has set a new standard for revisionist historians. If evidence does not support your version of events, ignore it, distort it or simply make it up. JFK's back wound was about five inches below his shoulder, not on the back of his neck. The throat wound was a wound of entry, not of exit. His blood and brains were blown out to the left rear, not the right front. The photo Marina is supposed to have taken of Oswald is one of three that Dallas police appear to have faked. He had neither the motive nor the means to kill Kennedy. He admired JFK, he was a mediocre shot, the rifle was unreliable—and he was on the second floor having a Coke when the President was shot.

     There is at least as much evidence for these contentions as there is for Posner's. During a press conference at Parkland Hospital, for example, Malcolm Perry described the throat wound as a wound of entry—not once, but three times! Transcripts are held by CBS and by the LBJ Library, but it was also reported by Tom Wicker in The New York Times (23 November 1963), p. 2. Moreover, on the death certificate signed by Admiral George Burkley, the back wound is described as "in the posterior back at about the level of the third thoracic vertebra", the location depicted on the inside front-cover of the Report of the Warren Commission published by The New York Times.

     Posner treats possibilities as though they were probabilities, no matter how unlikely. His position implies Oswald sprinted about 136 feet across the sixth floor, concealed his rifle, ran down four flights of stairs, darted into the lunchroom and bought himself a Coke between 12:30 and 12:31 PM, which is not only implausible on its face but rather difficult to reconcile with Howard Brennan's account of a lingering assassin, not to mention that several women who were on the stairway reported that he simply wasn't there at the time. Posner combines locations where Oswald was observed by witnesses (about 10%) with hypothetical speculations (about 90%) in constructing his scenario.

1

Mr. Howell Raines   13 September 1993

So far as I am able to discern, that 10% typifies the truth content of Posner's work. None of us should be surprised that books like this are published. What is more distressing is that a reputable newspaper such as The New York Times should endorse an obvious piece of fakery as "brilliant"! It takes no brilliance to distort evidence, trash witnesses and rewrite history to fit a preconceived point of view. If your editors, writers, and reviewers do not know enough to recognize garbage in a matter of this magnitude, what confidence can we have in your reporting on lesser events? And what has become of the critical standards that used to typify American journalism?

Yours truly,

James H. Fetzer
Professor

Ford Made Key Change In Kennedy Death Report

WASHINGTON, July 2 (AP) — Thirty-three years ago, Gerald R. Ford changed — ever so slightly — the Warren Commission's main sentence on the place where a bullet entered President John F. Kennedy's body when he was killed in Dallas.

Mr. Ford's change strengthened the commission's conclusion that a single bullet passed through Kennedy and wounded Gov. John B. Connally, — a crucial element in the commission's finding that Lee Harvey Oswald was the sole gunman.

Mr. Ford, who was a member of the commission, wanted a change to show that the bullet entered Kennedy "at the back of his neck" rather than in his uppermost back, as the commission originally wrote.

Mr. Ford said today that the change was intended to clarify meaning, not alter history.

"My changes had nothing to do with a conspiracy theory," he said in a telephone interview.

According to The New York Times *(3 July 1997), p. A8, Warren Commission member Gerald Ford changed the description of the President's back wound from "his uppermost back" to "the back of his neck", an alteration that greatly enhanced the plausibility of the "magic bullet" theory.*

Even the use of "his uppermost back" appears to be highly misleading, since the wound was between his shoulder blades at the level of the third thoracic vertebra, which would be about six inches below the collar. [Editor's note: See the Prologue and Appendix I.]

UNIVERSITY OF MINNESOTA

Duluth Campus   *Department of Philosophy*   *10 University Drive*
                                                                               Duluth, MN 55812-2496

                                                                               218-726-8548
                                                                               Fax: 218-726-6386

1 December 1993

Lawrence K. Altman, M.D.
The New York Times
229 West 43rd Street
New York, NY 10036

Dear Dr. Altman,

   As it happens, I am a member of a research group that includes Gary
Aguilar, M.D., and David Mantik, M.D., Ph.D., that has been investigating the
medical evidence in the assassination of JFK. We—Dr. Mantik, in particular—
have made significant discoveries about the X-rays in this case, which Dr.
Mantik has now established scientifically to be composite fabrications.

   We presented our findings during a press conference at Loew's Hotel in
New York on November 18th. Unfortunately, because it was being sponsored
by a publisher, Carroll & Graf, at the invitation of an author with whom the
press has had uneasy relations, Harrison Livingstone, no one came. At least,
no one with an appropriate medical and scientific background was present.

   A woman from Reuters struggled to compose a piece (copy enclosed),
which presented a very flimsy version of what we were presenting. Something else went out via the Xinhua Overseas News Service, but what I have
is only a fragment (copy enclosed). These pieces do not appear to be very
successful in conveying the nature and significance of what we have done.

   I would be grateful if you could take a look at what we have found. I
am enclosing a fairly complete compendium of what was presented at that
time. In addition to our presentations, the appendices were also provided.
I hope you agree that our findings are of great importance to this case. If
you would like to contact any of those involved in this inquiry, please reach
me at (218) 726-7269 (office) or at (218) 724-2706 (home).

                                                        Yours truly,

                                                        James H. Fetzer
                                                        Professor

enclosures

M. T. Jenkins, 77, Doctor Who Tried To Revive Kennedy

By WOLFGANG SAXON

Dr. Marion Thomas Jenkins, the Texas anesthesiologist who tried to resuscitate both President John F. Kennedy and his assassin, Lee Harvey Oswald, 31 years ago, died on Monday at his home in Dallas. He was 77.

The cause was stomach cancer, his family said.

Testifying during the Warren Commission's investigation in 1964, Dr. Jenkins related the particulars of the President's wounds and the actions he and his colleagues took on Nov. 22, 1963. His testimony was taken at Parkland Hospital by Arlen Specter, then the assistant counsel of the commission and now a Republican Senator from Pennsylvania.

Dr. Jenkins again was in the emergency room two days later for the treatment of Oswald, who was gunned down by Jack Ruby while in police custody. The doctor's role was described in the best-selling book by Gerald L. Posner, "Case Closed: Lee Harvey Oswald and the Assassination of J.F.K." (Random House, 1993), which sought to refute the various conspiracy theories about the murders.

Dr. Jenkins was born in Hughes Springs, Tex., the son of a country doctor. He was a graduate of the University of Texas at Austin and received his medical degree from its medical branch in Galveston in 1940.

He became the director of the Department of Anesthesiology at Parkland in 1948 and professor and chairman of the Department of Anesthesiology at the Medical School in 1951.

Dr. Jenkins and a colleague devised a procedure that is used every day in operating rooms around the world when they found that by giving an intravenous saline solution to surgical patients with strong blood pressure and pulse, the need for a blood transfusion was reduced.

Dr. Jenkins is survived by two sons, Dr. Gregory L. Jenkins of Los Gatos, Calif., and Dr. Philip N. Jenkins of Dallas; a daughter, Christine L. Jenkins of Los Angeles; a brother, Vance K. Jenkins of Hughes Springs, and two grandsons.

More obituaries appear on preceding page.

23 MV 94

C18

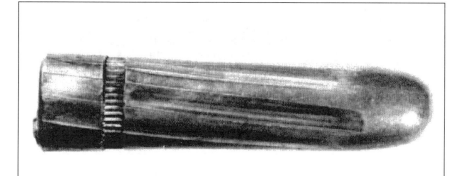

The copper-jacketed, 6.5 mm "magic bullet."

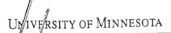

UNIVERSITY OF MINNESOTA

Duluth Campus   *Department of Philosophy*   *10 University Drive*
                                                            Duluth, MN 55812-2496

6 December 1994   *218-726-8548*
                                                            Fax: 218-726-6386

Arthur Ochs Sulzberger
The New York Times
229 West 43rd Street
New York, NY 10036

Dear Mr. Sulzberger,

As an admirer of the paper you publish, I have been dismayed at the irresponsible coverage of recent developments in the assassination of JFK provided by The New York Times. An obituary of Marion "Pepper" Jenkins that appeared on 23 November 1994, for example, included a promotional citation of a recent book by Gerald Posner entitled Case Closed as though it were an authoritative source on the assassination, when that is manifestly not the case, as virtually every serious student of this subject is aware.

In spite of a fatuous review of this book in your own newspaper, the work is known to be a blatant misrepresentation of evidence in this case. Mr. Posner took the prosecution brief prepared for a mock-courtroom trial by Failure Analysis Associates, disregarded the corresponding brief prepared for the defense, and pubished it without proper acknowledgement. If you want confirmation, please contact Roger McCarthy, CEO of FAA, who can easily be reached at (415) 688-7100 (phone) or (415) 688-7366 (fax).

The New York Times is therefore participating in perpetuating a hoax on the American people, first, by a completely irresponsible review of this work, second, by citing it in an obituary (of all places!) as though it were a responsible source. There are many other works of vastly greater merit on this subject, some of which—such as David Lifton's Best Evidence—have also been best-sellers, yet I do not find them cited in your newspaper. I deign to suggest that a paper as distinguished as your own surely can do better.

Indeed, major developments involving the medical evidence are taking place without discernable attention from the fourth estate. I enclose a copy of the student newspaper of this campus, the UMD Statesman (27 January 1994). This issue includes an article based on a lecture in which I summarized some of these developments. It is ironic and painful that a student paper should be more responsible than our newspaper of record.

Yours truly,

James H. Fetzer
Professor

UMD | STATESMAN

Volume 64, Number 15   DULUTH, MINNESOTA   Thursday, January 27, 1994

JFK cover-up exposed by UMD professor

Fabricated evidence links Kennedy assassination with federal government

By Zach Johns
Staff Writer

Startling new evidence has been found about the assassination of John F. Kennedy. The team of researchers who made these discoveries was organized by Dr. James H. Fetzer of UMD's philosophy department, who presented this information last Wednesday evening at a lecture in Kirby Ballroom.

Fetzer and his colleagues have found new medical evidence that conclusively shows JFK was shot from two different directions, therefore making the "lone gunman" theory impossible and a conspiracy definite.

This is underscored by new evidence brought forth by Fetzer's team that JFK's autopsy photos and X-rays had been fabricated. In recent years many conspiracy theo-

---

New Findings in the Assassination of JFK

• Autopsy X-rays and photographs proved fabricated.

• Magic bullet theory proven impossible.

• Kennedy hit at least four times: once in throat (from front), once in back (from rear), twice in head (from front and rear).

• Autopsy drawings and photos of Kennedy's brain concluded to be of a brain other than JFK's.

---

ries have abounded, charging everyone from the Cubans to the mob to the Soviet Union with the crime.

Fetzer says fabrication of the autopsy X-rays can only point to a cover-up from within the United States Government.

One member of Fetzer's group is Dr. David W. Mantik. Mantik is a Ph.D. physicist and M.D. radiologist who trav-

eled to Washington D.C. and examined autopsy X-rays and photographs in the National Archives on four separate occasions.

He says that even when he first looked at the X-rays with his naked eye, there seemed to be too much contrast between the light and dark sections in relation to X-rays he had been used to seeing.

He applied a special tech-

nique known as "optical densitometry" to study the X-rays. That technique had never been used before on JFK's X-rays. Using this technique Mantik discovered that the autopsy X-rays are composites – superpositions of more than one image – and thereby altered.

Mantik's discovery also provides powerful evidence of two bullet wounds to the head, while the Warren Commission states there was only one.

In addition, on the basis of his study of the chest X-ray, Mantik discovered that the "magic-bullet" theory is impossible because, according to his calculations, the bullet would have to have struck Kennedy's spine.

The X-rays show no damage that would have been caused had the wounds been inflicted the way the official

report describes them.

In combination with other evidence, these findings indicate that President Kennedy was hit at least four times: once in the throat (from in front), once in the back (from the rear), and twice in the head (once from the front and once from behind).

The Warren Report and HSCA report, both of which affirm that he was hit only twice, therefore, have been completely discredited by Dr. Mantik's discoveries.

An associate member of Dr. Fetzer's team is Dr. Robert B. Livingston. Dr. Livingston has reported a conversation he had the day of the shooting with Commander James Humes, who headed the autopsy team at Bethesda Naval Hospital.

Livingston, who was the Scientific Director of both the

JFK to 4

UMD STATESMAN

JFK: Cover-up discovered

From 1

National Institute for Mental Health and the National Institute of Neurological Diseases and Blindness in 1963, paid close attention to the news reports coming in.

When he heard that there was a small frontal wound in the President's throat, he considered it a "matter of utmost importance for the autopsy." The reason he felt that information was so important was because a small hole means an entrance wound, which meant Kennedy must have been shot from the front.

In his conversation with Humes, Livingston stressed the importance of tracing the path of the bullet and that, if it were confirmed as a wound of entrance and if there were bullets that were shot from the rear, then there would have to be more than one gunman. At that moment, Livingston says, their conversation was interrupted. After the pause, Humes said, "Dr. Livingston, I'm sorry, but I can't talk with you any longer. The FBI won't let me."

Despite Dr. Livingston drawing Dr. Humes' attention to the throat wound and stressing its importance, Dr. Humes said in his testimony before the Warren Commission that he had only learned about the throat wound the day after the autopsy.

Dr. Livingston believes that this testimony and the FBI's intervention "means that the autopsy [and Dr. Humes] were already under explicit non-medical control prior to the start of the autopsy."

Dr. Livingston, who had extensive experience with bullet and shrapnel wounds serving with the Navy Medical Corps during World War II, is also a world authority on the human brain.

He has noted that several of the physicians attending the President at Parkland Hospital testified that they saw cerebellum protruding from the wound in the back of the President's head. But the autopsy photographs show the cerebellum completely intact.

Based on multiple sources of expert testimony describing cerebellum tissue extruding from the head and comparing that testimony with drawings and photographs of the brain that are available at the National Archives, Livingston has concluded that "the photographs and drawings of the brain in the National Archives are those of some brain other than that of John Fitzgerald Kennedy."

Fetzer's group presented all of this information on Nov. 18, 1993 at a press conference in New York City. Because it was sponsored by an author of a new book and his publisher, only a few reporters turned out. The reporters who were there were mostly book reviewers, not versed in the assassination.

Although a reporter from the Reuters news service wrote a story focusing on the fabrication of the X-rays that received some international attention, a more comprehen-

JFK to 11

JFK: Press shuns story

From 4

sive story written by an Associated Press reporter was apparently killed at the national desk.

Thus far, the most national coverage that has been on the assassination are two sentences on CNN the morning following the press conference.

Fetzer observed that both Mantik and Livingston presented their findings at a conference on the assassination of JFK held in Dallas Nov. 18-22 of last year and received standing ovations.

"This lack of coverage is difficult to understand," said Fetzer. "At this point there has been more international coverage than national coverage!"

Thus, at present, experts brought to these discoveries are aware of these developments, but ordinary citizens are not. Fetzer stressed the importance of these discoveries. "The American people are entitled to know what happened to this country on Nov. 22, 1963, and we are going to do whatever we can to ensure that they find out."

[Editor's note: *A highly accurate story apart from the headline, which gave me too much credit. I was reporting on the discoveries others, such as David Mantik and Robert B. Livingston.*]

Part III

The Pursuit of Justice in a Bureaucracy

Cynical readers may find it difficult to believe that the nation's most sophisticated newspaper, *The New York Times*, could be ignorant about developments in the assassination of JFK, one of the few momentous events of modern American history. And, indeed, the circumstances under which our discoveries have received no significant national exposure lend themselves to more disconcerting interpretations. An article by Carl Bernstein, "The CIA and the Media", *Rolling Stone* (20 October 1977), for example, suggests that our most powerful news organizations have worked hand-in-glove with the CIA in the past. Perhaps that relationship has continued to this day.

Bernstein's analysis of this unhealthy relationship is laced with illustrations, including the conduct of Joseph Alsop, once one of our leading syndicated columnists, who took pride in his work for the CIA, which apparently included suggesting to President Lyndon Johnson that the investigation of the assassination of his predecessor might be well-served by appointing a committee of inquiry, which became the Warren Commission. Even more disturbing to me personally, however, was Bernstein's report that certain news executives had entered into formal secrecy agreements with the CIA, including, to my dismay, Arthur Ochs Sulzberger, Sr., of *The New York Times*.

One of the problems with maintaining rational beliefs in the times in which we live, as explained in the Prologue, is the need to avoid naiveté without becoming paranoid. We can sustain our most cherished beliefs in the face of contrary evidence by pursuing the practice of selection and elimination, but that approach dictates we ignore evidence that is both relevant and available. Without inviting paranoia, there are other indications that coverage of these striking, even sensational, findings in the assassination of JFK may have been suppressed for reasons other than ignorance.

Bernstein reports that, according to CIA officials, their most valuable associations by far have been with The New York Times, CBS, *and* Time, Inc.

We made other attempts to reach out to the press to advise them that major developments were afoot. When Robert B. Livingston, M.D., and I were contemplating our alternatives for disseminating new information about the assassination, I suggested that we send a fax to *60 Minutes*, in which we describe his conversation with Humes on 22 November 1963, which contradicts Humes' sworn testimony to the Warren Commission and to the House Select Committee on Assassinations. Livingston was reluctant to do so, however, because of the confrontational character of the program. Instead of that, he preferred to fax his findings to *Newsweek*.

One of his reasons for taking this approach, moreover, was that Livingston and Maynard Parker, the Editor-in-Chief of *Newsweek*, were both members of the Board of Trustees of Stanford University. Thus, he felt more comfortable proceeding in this fashion because Parker was someone he knew and felt he could trust. The fax was sent out on Friday, 10 September 1993, and by Monday, 13 September 1993, I had received a call from the office of Maynard Parker advising me that the material we had sent was being forwarded to Evan Thomas in Washington, D.C., who was then completing a special issue focused on the assassination of JFK.

The special issue of *Newsweek* appeared on 22 November 1993, but there was not a word reporting what Livingston had to say. Instead, the bottom line was that there had been a cover-up, but it had been benign, simply an attempt by bureaucracies to cover their tails in the aftermath of the assassination, where they had badly blundered by failing to offer the President adequate protection and by neglecting the threat posed by Lee Harvey Oswald. So the critics were right—there had been a cover-up! But everyone could rest easy, because it was nothing to be worried about.

When we then appeared at the press conference on 18 November 1993, copies of each of our statements were given to each member of the press along with a bound set of supporting documents. Included in that set was a copy of the fax that Livingston had sent to Maynard Parker. If anyone noticed that the Editor-in-Chief of *Newsweek* had been given a scoop he declined to pursue, I have not heard about it. In preparing for the press conference, I had a conversation with Kent Carroll of Carroll & Graf, who explained to me that we should spell everything out and that I must not forget reporters are not investigators. That may be part of the problem.

My efforts to interest the Department of Justice in our findings were if anything even more disheartening. I wrote to Janet Reno, Attorney General (with supporting documents), but I heard from Mary Spearing, Chief, General Litigation and Legal Advice Section. She appreciated my efforts, but suggested I study the HSCA report, which had appeared in 1979. I found this hard to believe, since the information that I was conveying, which had not been available in 1979, went far beyond the scope of the HSCA investigation, which was predicated upon the assumption that the autopsy X-rays were authentic and were the "best evidence" in this case.

In her letter to me of 25 January 1994, Spearing explained that every unsolicited letter is reviewed by at least three attorneys who are familiar with the assassination investigation and that, while they would be glad to receive further "new evidence" from me, they regret that "we will be unable to reply to your letters in the future." In my response of 30 January 1994, I observe that, unless these attorneys possess the scientific qualifications to appraise Dr. Mantik's studies, their opinions are completely irrelevant. The concerns I am raising are scientific questions about matters of fact and not legal questions that could be answered by attorneys.

I had incidentally mentioned two of Robert B. Livingston's friends, Robert McNamara and Elliot Richardson, in my letter to Janet Reno of 17 September 1993, which Livingston thought inappropriate. I therefore wrote to them to explain the context in which this had occurred. Their replies are printed here. Moreover, on 4 November 1994, during a recent congressional campaign, President Bill Clinton visited Duluth. I gave a copy of a video I had made about the assassination to an aide I met in the gym, where the President would later speak, but I did not presume it would actually find its way to him. I was grateful to receive his letter of 21 November 1994.

Although the Department of Justice appears to have neither the talent nor the inclination to pursue these new developments, I still believe that there are some promising indications of renewed interest in these matters. On 24 October 1994, for example, I wrote to John R. Tunheim, Chairman of the Assassination Records Review Board, to invite his attention to work by Mantik and Livingston, which had been presented during our ill-fated New York press conference. [*Editor's note:* See Part II.] Very much to my surprise, he responded in his letter of 14 February 1995 by inviting me to meet with him in order to pursue these matters further. We had a very cordial conversation.

A more important indication that the country might finally be moving in the right direction has been the appointment of John Deutch as Director of the CIA. Among his first acts has been to "clean out the upper echelons of agency management", a change even *The New York Times* (22 May 1995, p. A10) has endorsed. I can only hope that his successor, George Tenet, will possess half of his integrity and a quarter of his courage. If cases like the assassination are ever to be legally resolved, however, we need special prosecutors who can convene grand juries, negotiate plea bargains, grant immunity, and issue subpoenas, as Elliot Richardson, "Special Counsels, Petty Cases" (*The New York Times*, 5 June 1995, p. A11), has observed. The pursuit of justice requires no less.

—*James H. Fetzer, Ph.D.*

UNIVERSITY OF MINNESOTA

Duluth Campus   *Department of Philosophy*   *10 University Drive*
Duluth, MN 55812-2496

17 September 1993

218-726-8548
Fax: 218-726-6386

The Honorable Janet Reno
Attorney General of the United States
Department of Justice
Tenth and Constitution Avenues, NW
Room 4400
Washington, D.C. 20530

Re: **New Evidence in the JFK Assassination**

Enclosures:

> (1) Robert Livingston letter to David Lifton of 2 Mary 1992
> (2) Robert Livingston letter to Harrison Livingstone of 5 May 1992
> (3) Partial transcript of Perry's Press Conference of 22 November 1963
> (4) Partial transcript of Perry's Testimony before the Warren Commission
> (5) Short Curriculum Vitae, Robert B. Livingston, 1993
> (6) Brief Curriculum Vitae, 1993, Robert B. Livingston, M.D.

Dear Madam Attorney General,

This letter brings to your attention a witness whose testimony appears
to provide conclusive evidence that James Humes, one of the medical officers
who performed the autopsy on John F. Kennedy at Bethesda Naval Hospital,
had knowledge of the existence of a wound to the throat and of its importance as evidence of a shot fired from the front--and therefore of a second
gunman--on Friday, the 22nd, prior to conducting the autopsy, even though
he has claimed that he only learned of a wound to the throat the following
day, Saturday, the 23rd, after the autopsy was over. In 1963, this witness,

Robert B. Livingston. M.D.,

was the Scientific Director of (both) the National Institute for Mental Health
and the National Institute for Neurological Diseases and Blindness, which are
branches of the National Institutes of Health, a position he held originally in
the Eisenhower Administration and later in the Kennedy Administration. He
was then (and remains) an international authority on the human brain, with
extensive military experience in dealing with bullet and shrapnel wounds.

Dr. Livingston is extremely well-known and highly respected, not only in
his field of expertise but also through his official and unofficial contacts with
government officials, including, for example,

1

Janet Reno, Attorney General of the United States   17 September 1993

Elliott Richardson, former Attorney General; and
Robert McNamara, former Secretary of Defense;

who number among his personal friends. The importance of his experiences
in relation to the assassination are well-understood by those with whom he
has had correspondence, including, for example,

Harrison Livingstone, author of High Treason 2; and
Peter Dale Scott, author of Crime and Cover-Up.

If you would like to know more about the man himself or the importance of
his testimony, I recommend that you contact these persons for verification
of his past positions and ongoing relationships with McNamara and Richardson and of the significance of what he has to say with Scott and Livingstone.

Perhaps I should provide an outline as background to his testimony. As
you will discover from his letters to David Lifton and to Harrison Livingstone
(Enclosures (1) and (2)), Dr. Livingston telephoned Dr. Humes the afternoon
of Friday, 22 November 1993, to advise him of the evidentiary importance
of the wound to the neck that was being widely reported on radio and television, especially as a result of the Parkland Press Conference held earlier in
the afternoon, where Malcolm Perry, the surgeon who performed a tracheostomy on JFK, stated three times that the wound to the throat was (or appeared to be) a wound of entrance (Enclosure (3)).

One of the most suspicious actions taken by Humes in relation to the autopsy is that he destroyed the "first draft" of his autopsy report. If he only
learned of the existence of the throat wound on Saturday morning, as Arlen
Specter has remarked, however, then this behavior might have been justifiable. Thus, "Specter suggests that Dr. Humes altered his findings upon learning for the first time, on Saturday morning, that the tracheotomy performed
by Dr. Perry in Dallas had obliterated a bullet wound in the front of the President's throat" (In the Shadow of Dallas, p. 69, citing 2 WCH 367). (Indeed,
Perry would later maintain that he had been "misquoted" during the press
conference and, when questioned by Specter before the Warren Commission,
would say his conversations with Humes were on Saturday (Enclosure (4)).)

If Humes already knew about the throat wound, especially as a wound of
entry, prior to the autopsy, he could not have learned for the first time of its
existence until after it had been completed. Given that Humes did not know
about it till the body was no longer available for examination and dissection,

2

Janet Reno, Attorney General of the United States   17 September 1993

he could then "infer" that it was an "exit" for the back wound, which could be relocated upward where it would penetrate the body on the back of the neck, thereby becoming consistent with Theron Ward's death certificate description of Kennedy's death as due to "multiple gunshot wounds of head and neck"!

If Dr. Livingston's testimony concerning his conversation with Humes on the 22nd is accurate, then it provides strong evidence for these conclusions:

    (1) that Humes, Boswell, and Perry lied under oath, etc.;
    (2) that government officials promoted a cover-up; and,
    (3) that the single-bullet theory is almost certainly false.

Even more significantly, an entry wound to the neck also destroys the single assassin scenario (unless JFK was looking back toward the Book Depository building when he was struck in the throat, as Perry himself suggested before he was pressured into changing his testimony, which illustrates the strength of his enduring belief that the throat wound was one of entrance).

The "throat wound ignorance theory"--namely, that the doctors feigned ignorance of the throat wound in order to suppress evidence that would undermine the all-too-familiar official version of the assassination--seems to be very difficult to resist in light of Dr. Livingston's testimony. I believe it provides the key to understanding, not the assassination itself, necessarily, but the cover-up. In this sense, it may properly be regarded as a "smoking gun". From the nature of the cover-up, moreover, inferences concerning the assassination itself almost certainly can be more easily drawn.

If you would like to have more evidence in support of the throat wound ignorance theory, I would be glad to put you in contact with researchers who have access to copies of the death certificates, the transcript of the Parkland press conference, and other documents obtained under the Freedom of Information Act related to Enclosures (3) and (4). If you would like for me to do so, I can send you a video-tape of Dr. Livingston's testimony. (I have added enclosures (5) and (6) for your use.) If there is any way in which I may be of assistance in this matter, do not hesitate to contact me.

Yours truly,

James H. Fetzer
Professor

Office: (218) 726-7269
Home: (218) 724-2706

3

For Jim Fetzer 12/Sept '93

1

Brief Curriculum Vitae, 1993   **Robert B. Livingston, M.D.**

Education: Stanford University (AB, 1940); Stanford University School of Medicine (MD, 1944); (Residency, Internal Medicine [under Arthur L. Bloomfield], Stanford University Hospitals, 1943-1945).

Academic Appointments: Stanford University (Instructor of Pathology [under Alvin Cox], 1943-45); Yale University School of Medicine (Instructor to Assistant Professor of Physiology [under John F. Fulton], 1946-52); (concurrently) Harvard Medical School (Assistant Professor of Psychiatry [under Harry Solomon], 1947-48); UCLA School of Medicine (Associate Professor to Professor of   Anatomy and Physiology   [under H. W. Magoun and John Field], 1952-57); Adjunct Professor, Mid-Career Course, U.S. State Department, 1957-1964; Founding Chair, UCSD School of Medicine, Department of Neurosciences (Professor of Neurosciences, 1964-1989 [with Theodore H. Bullock, Robert Galambos, Reginald Bickford, John O'Brien, Marjorie Seybold, Fred Gage, Robert Terry, and Robert Katzman]; Guest Professor of Neurosciences, at *Hirnforschungsinstitut der Universität Zürich* [under Konrad Akert], 1971-72); Science Advisor to His Holiness, the Dalai Lama], 1989--).

[Aim of academic career is to investigate combinations of nervous and mental functions, using a variety of neuroanatomical, neurophysiological, behavioral and clinical techniques and disciplines.]

Advanced Training: Université de Génève (National Research Council Senior Fellow in Neurology, [under Oscar Wyss], 1948-49); Universität Zürich (ditto [under Walter Rudolph Hess], 1949); Collége de France (Wilhelm B. Gruber Fellow in Neurology, [under Alfred Fessard], 1949-50); Oxford University (ditto [under F.S.C. Little and Paul Glees], 1950); Universitet Göteborg (US Public Health Service Senior Fellow in Neurology, [with Bo Gernandt and Holger Hydén], 1956); Massachusetts Institute of Technology (Research Associate, Neurosciences Research Program, [under Francis O. Schmitt], 1961-1973).

National Service: US Navy Medical Corps (Reserve), World War II. Lieutenant (j.g.) to Lieutenant: Established and directed the hospital for wounded Okinawans and Japanese POWs throughout the battle of Okinawa, U.S. Navy Bronze Star, 1945; "Interpreter" for surrender of Japanese Army in North China, [U.S. Marine Corps needed people with even modest Chinese and Japanese language training], 1945; Chief, Medical Battalion Laboratory, 2nd Marine Division, Tiensin and Peking, throughout "Cease-Fire" between Kuomintang and Chinese Communists, 1945-46; *Executive Assistant* to the President, National Academy of Sciences, and Chairman, National Research Council, 1950-52; *Scientific Director*, National Institute for Mental Health, and (concurrently) National Institute of Neurological Diseases and Blindness, 1957-1964; Member, first Life Sciences Committee, NASA, advisory for life support systems, safety, communication, and selection of first Astronauts, 1958-63; first *National Scholar*, National Library of Medicine, 1964.

International Diplomatic Contributions: International Physicians for the Prevention of Nuclear War (IPPNW), winner of 1985 Nobel Prize for Peace, IPPNW Emissary [with Lars Engstedt] to Egypt, Jordan, Syria, Kuwait, Bahrian, and Saudi Arabia,

2

to persuade Arab physicians to contribute internationally to the prevention of nuclear war; IPPNW Ambassador, to Tibetan Government-in-Exile, Dharamsala, India. Contributed to three successive East-West Dialogues 1987, 1989, 1990 on *Mind and Life* [under Tenzin Gyatso, His Holiness, The Dalai Lama, winner of the 1989 Nobel Peace Prize]. Participant, two international diplomatic missions conducted by the Center for the Study of the Person [under Carl Rogers] in Rust, Austria, and, with Gay Swensen [after Rogers' death] in San José, Costa Rica, [under President Arias], to establish a dialogue between the governments of Nicaragua and the United States.

Research Contributions: Neocortical representations of visceral functions in monkey and chimpanzee [with Ernest Sachs, Jr., Sam Brendler, and José Delgado]; Human frontal and cingulate cortical representations of visceral functions [with William P. Chapman, William H. Sweet, and Kenneth E. Livingston]; Plasticity of muscle synergy in humans [with Alfred Fessard, Jean Paillard, and Auguste Tourney]; Eye movements controlled by frontal eye fields and occipital visual fields in monkey; Frontal motor representations in deep sulci of cats [with José Delgado]; Localization of frontal eye fields in cats; Head turning and eye deviation elicited by stimulation of frontal cortex in freely moving cats [under Walter Rudolf Hess, with Donald A. MacDonald]; Explosive decompression at high altitude [with Samuel Gelfan and Leslie Nims]; Use of biological potentials to warn of anoxic anoxia [with Harold S. Burr]; Segregation, origin and destination of first-order sensory dorsal column axons [under Paul Glees]; Central control of ascending sensory pathways [with Raúl Hernández-Peón and Harald Scherrer]; Cortical influences on brain stem conduction systems, and on brain stem arousal mechanisms [with John D. French, Raúl Hernández Peón, W. Ross Adey and José Segundo]; Cerebrospinal fluid equilibria; Somatic functions of the nervous system [with Raúl Hernández-Peón]; Differential seizure susceptibility in monkey cortex [with John D. French]; Prevention of seizures in monkeys by intravenous procaine injections [with John D. French, Bruce Konigsmark, and Ken Richland]; Vestibulo-spinal motor projections [with Bo Gernandt, Sid Gilman, and Magdolna Iranyi]; Brain mechanisms and behavior; Neurophysiology of brain stem reticular formation [with Frederic G. Worden]; Neurophysiological contributions to internal medicine [with Frederic G. Worden]; Longitudinal spinal and brainstem reflex systems relayed through the bulbar reticular formation [with Muneo Shimamura]; Dynamics of acoustic pathways under control of middle-ear muscles [with Arnold Starr and Peter Carmel; What makes the sloth so slothful? [with T.H. Bullock, Donald B. Lindsley, and Robert Galambos]; Central control of receptors and sensory transmission systems; Role of central nervous mechanisms relating to reinforcement; Ultrastructure of myelin glial-axonal junctions, and functional dynamics of synaptic boutons [under Konrad Akert]; Cinemorphology of whole human brain serial surfaces, in registration, exposed at microscopically thin intervals throughout the entire brain in 68 "normal" human brains [with Roy Mills and Thornton Egge]; Three-dimensional reconstruction of one whole human brain, using interactive computer graphics [with Kent Wilson, Bill Atkinson, and Bud Tribble, III]. A film on this subject [produced under Sy Wexler] won sweepstakes awards at all major international documentary film festivals in 1976/7, and has been shown repeatedly on NOVA, National Geographic Society, BBC, OMNIMAX, and many other television programs, worldwide. Undernourishment affecting human brain development in the U.S. [under Doris H. Calloway, with Helen Ross, and Elisabeth Stern]. Expeditions include: Ships' Physician and Chief Diver, Scripps Institution of Oceanography Expedition CAPRICORN [under Roger Revelle and Walter Munk], 1951-1952; Alpha Helix Expedition to the Amazon [with Theodore H. Bullock and Donald B. Lindsley], 1968; Expedition to Panama [with Theodore H. Bullock and Robert Galambos] 1970.

3

Research Publications: Some 200 research publications including a few research monographs. Chapters on Neurophysiology in a textbook for psychologists; Chapters on Neurophysiology in a textbook for psychiatrists--these latter were republished as a separate monograph,   *Sensory Processing, Perception, and Behavior,* 1978; Section on Neurophysiology consisting of a dozen chapters in *Best and Taylor's Physiological Basis of Medical Practice,* 11th Edition, 1985, 12th Edition, 1990.

Lectureships: AAAS Holiday Science Lecturer, for State-wide honor high school students: Florida, 1958, Oregon, 1959; National Sigma Xi Lecturer, 1960 and 1961; Queen Kamehameha Lecturer, University of Hawaii School of Medicine, 1965; AAAS Chautauqua Lectureship [shared with Elisabeth Stern], 1978 and 1979; Sachs Memorial Lecturer, Dartmouth Medical School, 1981.

Extra-Curricular Activities: Co-Incorporator [with John F. Fulton], the *Journal of the History of Medicine* , 1951. Participated closely with Leo Szilard in founding the Council for Abolishing War, which became the *Council for a Livable World* , 1962. Co-Incorporator [with Richard J. Barnet, Marcus Raskin, and Christopher Jencks], of the *Institute for Policy Studies,* 1962. Co-Incorporator [with Fritjof Capra] of the Elmwood Institute, 1979. Active [under Bernard Lown] in   *International Physicians for the Prevention of Nuclear War,* as Emissary and Ambassador; Deputy Council representative for U.S. national   *Physicians for Social Responsibility;* House of Delegates, 1986-88, President, 1992.

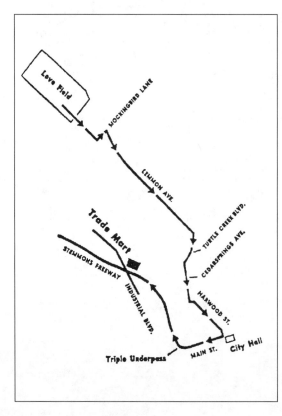

A map of the motorcade route published in The Dallas Morning News *(22 November, 1963), which does not indicate the detour actually taken through Dealey Plaza via Houston and Elm Streets. Continuing through Dealey Plaza on Main Street to Industrial Boulevard would have provided a more direct route to the Trade Mart, where JFK was scheduled to speak. [Editor's note: See Robert Groden,* The Search for Lee Harvey Oswald *(1995), p. 103.]*

U. S. Department of Justice

Criminal Division

Washington, D.C. 20530

DEC   7 1993

Professor James H. Fetzer
Department of Philosophy
Duluth Campus
University of Minnesota
10 University Drive
Duluth, Minnesota   55812-2496

Dear Professor Fetzer:

Your two recent letters to the Attorney General regarding
the assassination of President John F. Kennedy were referred to
the Criminal Division of the Department of Justice for response.
You submitted "new evidence" related to the emergency treatment
and subsequent autopsy of President Kennedy in November 1963.
You expressed particular concern about the frequently debated
topic of the direction of the bullet which caused a wound to
President Kennedy's neck. In addition to providing copies of
correspondence discussing this issue, you endorsed certain
published conspiracy theories.

As you are probably aware, in 1978, the United States House
of Representatives Select Committee on Assassinations issued a
detailed report regarding President Kennedy's assassination.
That report includes evaluations of the findings of the Warren
Commission and of numerous other assassination theories which
emerged after the Warren Commission completed its work. The
Select Committee's final report and accompanying 12-volume set of
hearing reports, the latter consisting of exhibits and evidence
considered by the Committee, were released to the public and are
available in many public libraries. Those Congressional
publications provide a detailed analysis of autopsy findings and
address many of the issues which you have raised regarding the
assassination of President Kennedy.

Since the House Select Committee report, there have been
numerous private evaluations of physical evidence from the
assassination, including autopsy photographs and reports. The
Federal Government has also released virtually all of its records
related to the assassination investigation, which records are
being made available to the public through the National Archives.
We believe that the issues which you have raised have been
thoroughly examined over the years, and that the evidence and

2

analyses now available to the public from government and private
sources address your concerns.

We appreciate your efforts in contacting the Department of
Justice regarding this matter of mutual concern.

Sincerely,

Jo Ann Harris
Assistant Attorney General

Mary C. Spearing, Chief
General Litigation and
Legal Advice Section

*James H. Fetzer, Ph.D., with Robert B. Livingston, M.D.,
in Shelter Island, California, on 13 June 1997.*

UNIVERSITY OF MINNESOTA

Duluth Campus   *Department of Philosophy*   *10 University Drive*
                                                                                Duluth, MN 55812-2496

18 December 1993   *218-726-8548*
                                                           Fax: 218-726-6386

Mary C. Spearing, Chief
General Litigation and
     Legal Advice Section   PERSONAL AND
Criminal Division   CONFIDENTIAL
U.S. Department of Justice
Suite 200, Wash. Ctr. Bldg.
1001 G. Street, N.W.
Washington, D.C. 20530

References:

    (a) Letter from Mary C. Spearing to James H. Fetzer of 7 December 1993
    (b) Letter from James H. Fetzer to Janet Reno of 17 September 1993 with
        enclosures re: **New Evidence in the JFK Assassination**
    (c) Letter from James H. Fetzer to Janet Reno of 27 September 1993 with
        enclosures re: **New Evidence in the JFK Assassination**
    (d) Letter from James H. Fetzer to Janet Reno of 14 December 1993 with
        enclosures re: **Fabricated Evidence in the Assassination of JFK**

Dear Ms. Spearing,

    This letter is written to lodge a complaint about your casual and dismissive response in reference (a) to information that I sent to the Attorney General via references (b) and (c). The first paragraph of reference (a) acknowledges the receipt of "two recent letters to the Attorney General" but does not otherwise identify them with respect to their dates or their contents, which included several specific enclosures in each instance. Your letter indicates no file number or other identifying number, leading me to suspect that it might be impossible to retrieve my correspondence, were it appropriate to do that.

    Let me indicate several reasons why I cannot take your reply seriously as a response to the information provided by references (b) and (c). You say I submitted "new evidence" using quotes around that phrase as an indication that what I submitted is not really <u>new evidence</u>. In your second and third paragraphs, moreover, you refer to the report of the House Special Committee on Assassinations as a rebuttal to my submission. But the testimony to which I invited attention was not presented to the HSCA and therefore was neither accepted nor rejected during that investigation. It therefore surely qualifies as "new evidence" in relation to the HSCA report that you mention.

I

Mary C. Spearing, Chief   18 December 1993

Moreover, the information that I provided in references (b) and (c) actually undermines the conclusions of the HSCA report. The testimony of Dr. Robert B. Livingston, who was the Scientific Director of the two National Institues of Health in the Eisenhower and Kennedy Administrations (making him the highest ranking scientist in both administrations), in particular, provides decisive refutation of the claim—advanced repeatedly—that Bethesda physicians Humes, Boswell and Finck did not know of a bullet wound to the throat until Saturday, the 23rd, after the autopsy had been completed, as I explained in reference (a). (See especially enclosures (1) and (2) thereto.)

You trivialize the importance of this testimony, which comes from an unimpeachable source, in the first paragraph of reference (a), in which you assert that I wrote to "express concern about the frequently debated topic of the direction of the bullet which caused a wound to President Kennedy's neck" and that, in addition to providing copies of certain correspondence, I "endorsed certain published conspiracy theories". This summary of what I did is highly misleading, however, since I was not "expressing concern" but providing evidence, which appears to be conclusive, that Humes et al. have made false statements to the Warren Commission and the House Committee.

If this evidence is accepted—and I cannot imagine why it should be rejected, especially out of hand as you have done, by anyone with a serious interest in this case—then it provides the strongest corroboration of (what reference (b) referred to as) "the throat wound ignorance theory". Thus, I was not merely "endorsing" certain theories about the assassination—the official account being only the most inadequate—but actually submitting some very important evidence, which retains its probative force whether you recognize it or not. Other significant evidence was provided by reference (c), including the Swinford FBI report, describing exposed cerebral and cerebellar tissue.

As I explained in reference (b), the new evidence to which I invited the attention of the Attorney General provides support for several conclusions:

(1) that Humes, Boswell, and Finck lied under oath, etc.;
(2) that government officials promoted a cover-up; and,
(3) that the single-bullet theory is almost certainly false.

It also destroys the Warren Commission's hypothesis of a sole assassin firing from the Texas School Book Depository Building. According to your response in reference (a), however, this amount to no more than my "endorsement" of "certain published conspiracy theories". Such a reply is totally unacceptable.

Mary C. Spearing, Chief   18 December 1993

I have now sent additional evidence to the Attorney General by means of reference (d). The evidence that I have provided there invites attention to several new discoveries made by David Mantik, M.D., Ph.D. Dr. Manik is both a Ph.D. in physics (Wisconsin) and an M.D. (Michigan), who is a board-certified radiologist practicing in California. Dr. Mantik visited the National Archives four times during October and repeatedly examined the X-rays of President Kennedy's skull and body that are preserved there. As you may discern from reading enclosure (3) and Appendix G, he has discovered that the X-rays are fabrications and that the HSCA single-bullet theory is wrong.

Dr. Mantik's findings are of the greatest importance to this case and go far beyond the HSCA inquiry. Indeed, Robert Blakey has acknowledged on several occasions—some of which I have on tape, if you want to view them—that testimony of many witnesses—such as Charles Crenshaw, M.D.—was not taken because the house committee had access to "better evidence", namely, the autopsy X-rays and photographs. I therefore hope that you do not plan to respond to reference (d) by referring again to the HSCA report, which has been discredited by Dr. Mantik's objective and repeatable scientific findings.

I would also observe that other evidence provided by reference (d) deserves serious consideration, including, for example, Dr. Livingston's conclusion that the diagrams and photographs in the National Archives that purport to be of the brain of John F. Kennedy must be of someone else's brain. It does not take a rocket scientist to appreciate that the opinion of a world authority on the human brain in a case of this kind must be taken seriously. I therefore hope that you will not again trivialize the importance of what I am submitting. I am not alone in believing that the Department of Justice has neither the talent nor the inclination to examine this case objectively. I therefore urge the appointment of a special prosecutor to pursue this case.

Yours truly,

James H. Fetzer
Professor

c: Jo Ann Harris, Assistant Attorney General
Louis J. Freeh, Federal Bureau of Investigation
The Honorable Janet Reno, Attorney General
The Honorable Al Gore, U.S. Vice President
The Honorable Bill Clinton, U S President

U. S. Department of Justice

Criminal Division

Washington, D.C. 20530

JAN 2 5 1994

Professor James H. Fetzer
Department of Philosophy
Duluth Campus
University of Minnesota
10 University Drive
Duluth, Minnesota 55812-2496

Dear Professor Fetzer:

Reference is made to your letter of December 18, 1993,
copies of which you indicated were sent to the President,
Vice President, Attorney General, Assistant Attorney General for
the Criminal Division, and Director of the Federal Bureau of
Investigation. You will recall that you objected to the response
which you received from this office to two previous letters to
the Attorney General regarding the assassination of
President Kennedy.

We are troubled by your view that you "cannot take [our]
reply seriously" and we will attempt to address your specific
concerns regarding the response which you received. You
complained about our failure to identify the dates of your two
letters to the Attorney General which led to our response. In
your letter of December 18, 1993, you identified three letters
(dated September 17, 1993, September 27, 1993, and
December 14, 1993) which you sent to the Attorney General; our
letter was a reply to the two letters in that list which you sent
prior to the date of our reply. You also objected to our failure
to recite the contents, including specific enclosures, of those
letters, beyond our brief summary of your theme. While we did
not believe that it was necessary to provide you with an
inventory of the enclosures which you sent to us, we can confirm
that we received all attachments, including correspondence from
Robert Livingston, various transcripts, an FBI report, and your
<u>curriculum</u> <u>vitae</u>.

You also objected to the use of quotation marks in our
reference to your submission of "new evidence." The quotation
marks were intended to reflect that we were quoting your
characterization of your submission. In fact, over the more than
30 years which have passed since the assassination, numerous
conspiracy theorists have debated the same aspects of the
assassination which you recently questioned -- the integrity of
named medical personnel involved in examination and autopsy of

2

the President's body in 1963, the direction of the bullet which struck the President and the resulting impact upon his body, whether additional bullets struck the President, and whether there were additional assassins. These issues have been repeatedly examined by both the government and numerous private interests in response to theories and allegations raised by others. Accordingly, while the report of the House Select Committee on Assassinations was prepared prior to your allegations, as you noted, it does in fact address many of the issues which you have recently raised.

As you may be aware, the Department of Justice has a wide range of criminal justice and other responsibilities. While the Department has devoted substantial investigative, technical, and legal resources to the Kennedy assassination during the past 30 years, other demands upon our personnel necessitate some limits upon our efforts in providing responses to the substantial volume of letters which we receive from frequent correspondents regarding the Kennedy assassination. Every unsolicited submission is reviewed by at least three attorneys familiar with the assassination investigation, and referrals are made to the FBI as appropriate for further inquiry; but, it is not possible to provide detailed written discussions of specific evidentiary issues submitted to the Attorney General. Accordingly, while we would be pleased to continue to review any "new evidence" or opinions which you refer to the Department, we regret that in the interest of conservation of scarce resources we will be unable to reply to your letters in the future.

We appreciate the efforts of private researchers who have continued to evaluate the evidence related to the Kennedy assassination. The ongoing disclosure, through the National Archives, of almost all Executive Branch and Congressional documents related to the assassination should facilitate such efforts. Further, the publication of assassination theories will continue to support a very constructive process of public debate regarding this important event in our history. We appreciate your interest in the assassination and your willingness to advise the Department of Justice of your views.

Sincerely,

Jo Ann Harris
Assistant Attorney General

Mary C. Spearing, Chief
General Litigation and
Legal Advice Section

UNIVERSITY OF MINNESOTA

Duluth Campus   *Department of Philosophy*   *10 University Drive*
                                                                                  Duluth, MN 55812-2496

30 January 1994   *218-726-8548*
                                                                                  Fax: 218-726-6386

Mary C. Spearing, Chief
General Litigation and   **PERSONAL AND**
    Legal Advice Section   **CONFIDENTIAL**
Criminal Division
U.S. Department of Justice
Suite 200, Wash. Ctr. Bldg.
1001 G Street, N.W.
Washington, D.C. 20530

References:

    (a) Letter from Mary C. Spearing to James H. Fetzer of 25 January 1994
    (b) "JFK Cover-Up Exposed", UMD STATESMAN (27 January 1994)

Dear Ms. Spearing,

    In reference (a) you indicate that the "new evidence" I provided by my earlier correspondence had been dealt with by the HSCA inquiry and other investigations. Since I was reporting to you the results of studies of the X-rays conducted in October 1993 employing a scientific technique known as "optical densitometry" which had never before been employed for this purpose, your response is not only logically absurd but scientifically illiterate.

    I understand that you pass my submissions past three attorneys knowledgeable about the assassination, but unless they possess the relevant scientific qualifications to appraise Dr. Mantik's studies—by virtue of possessing a Ph.D. in physics and an M.D. with a specialty in radiology, for example—their opinion is completely irrelevant. This is a scientific question about a matter of fact and not a legal question that could be answered by a set of attorneys.

    I have no interest in embarrassing you personally or the Department of Justice. But I want you to know that this story is gradually making its way into the public domain. (Take ten minutes of your time and read the article in reference (b), which is enclosed. It will be time well-spent.) If you ever involve yourself personally in a case rather than supervise those who deal with them, this is the time. You must come to grips with this development.

Yours truly,

James H. Fetzer
Professor

enclosure

ELLIOT L. RICHARDSON
INTERNATIONAL SQUARE BUILDING
1825 EYE STREET, N.W.
WASHINGTON, D.C. 20006

October 4, 1993

Professor James H. Fetzer
Department of Philosophy
University of Minnesota
10 University Drive
Duluth, Minn   55812

Dear Professor Fetzer:

Thank you for your letter of September 26, 1993 and its enclosures. They raise disturbing questions -- questions that I didn't know my friend Bob Livingston is uniquely able to shed light on.

As to the use of my name, I suppose I would like to have been consulted in advance, but if I had been I would gladly have consented to its use for the purpose in which it appears.

With best wishes,

Sincerely,

Elliot L. Richardson

cc: Dr. Robert B. Livingston

Robert S. McNamara

1455 Pennsylvania Avenue, N.W., Washington, D.C. 20004

November 15, 1993

Dear Professor Fetzer:

Please accept my sincere apologies for the delay in
responding to your September 26 letter re Robert
Livingston's testimony on the assassination of President
Kennedy. Your letter was received during Mr. McNamara's
absence from Washington. Upon his return several weeks
later, he did ask me to write to you. Apparently the
letter became attached to another, and it has just come to
my attention.

In response to your letter, Mr. McNamara asked me to say
that he is not qualified to discuss the matters raised by
Bob Livingston's letter, and that it was his impression at
the time, that the Warren Commission had made a thorough
report.

Again, I apologize for the delay in transmitting Mr.
McNamara's remarks to you.

Sincerely,

Jeanne Moore
Secretary to
Robert S. McNamara

James H. Fetzer
Professor
University of Minnesota
Department of Philosophy
10 University Drive
Duluth, MN 55812-2496

THE WHITE HOUSE

WASHINGTON

November 21, 1994

Mr. James H. Fetzer
Professor of Philosophy
University of Minnesota, Duluth
Duluth, Minnesota 55812

Dear James:

Thank you for the videotape. It
was thoughtful of you to share your work
regarding the assassination of President
Kennedy.

I appreciate your generosity and wish
you the best.

Sincerely,

Bill Clinton

UNIVERSITY OF MINNESOTA

Duluth Campus   *Department of Philosophy*   *10 University Drive*
Duluth, MN 55812-2496

218-726-8548
Fax: 218-726-6386

24 October 1994

The Honorable John R. Tunheim
Chief Deputy Attorney General   CONFIDENTIAL
The State of Minnesota
102 State Capitol
St. Paul, MN 55155-1002

Re: New Evidence in the Assassination of JFK

Dear Mr. Tunheim,

    As it happens, I am a professor of philosophy at the University of
Minnesota, who teaches on the Duluth campus (Enclosure (1)). During 19-
92, I organized a research group to investigate the assassination of JFK
in response to a series of articles that appeared in The Journal of the
AMA (JAMA). Our results have been significant (see, for example, Enclos-
sures (2) and (3) and the summary of our findings provided by the article
in Enclosure (4)).

    Although I have made repeated efforts to convey these findings to
the Department of Justice, the response I have received has been hopelessly inadequate (see Enclosure (5)). It is extremely distressing to
have made what appear to be major discoveries of new evidence in this
case and to have them casually dismissed by the Department of Justice.
I would be grateful for any advice or assistance that you might be in a
position to provide.

    I would be happy to provide you with supporting materials about any
aspect of our discoveries, in person or by mail. I would be glad to travel to Minneapolis to meet with you, if that would be appropriate. I am
certain that I could arrange for you to contact or to meet with Dr. David
Mantik, Dr. Robert Livingston, or other members of this group, if that is
something that you would prefer. I hope you will agree that our findings
are of great importance to this case.

                                        Yours truly,

                                        James H. Fetzer
                                        Professor

Enclosures:

    (1) Curriculum Vitae for James H. Fetzer, Ph.D.
    (2) Statement by David Mantik, M.D., Ph.D.
    (3) Statement by Robert B. Livingston, M.D.
    (4) Copy of UMD STATESMAN (27 January 1994)
    (5) Correspondence with the Department of Justice

Assassination Records Review Board

600 E Street NW ▪ 2nd Floor ▪ Washington, DC 20530

February 14, 1995

James H. Fetzer
Professor, University of Minnesota
10 University Drive
Duluth, MN 55812-2496

Dear Professor Fetzer:

I very much appreciated receiving your letter and accompanying materials regarding the research that you and others have done on the assassination of President Kennedy. I found your materials to be very interesting and I regret that I have been unable to respond until now. The Assassination Records Review Board has been busy organizing its work including hiring staff and securing office facilities. I am very interested in meeting with you to learn more about the research you have done. Perhaps we could meet in St. Paul at a time that would be convenient for you. A meeting involving other members of your research group should perhaps await an opportunity to include Review Board staff in the meeting.

As I am sure you are aware, the focus of the Review Board is to locate and secure all documentary evidence of the assassination for eventual public release. It is certainly not our mission to solve any of the mysteries that remain surrounding the event, but we are certainly interested in any kind of material -- written, photographic or otherwise -- that would shed light on this very important subject.

Please give my office a call and we can set up a time to discuss these issues more fully. Again, I thank you for your interest in the work of the Review Board.

Sincerely,

John R. Tunheim

John R. Tunheim
Chair

Telephone: (202) 724-0088 ▪ Facsimile: (202) 724-0457

ADDRESS FOR REVIEW BOARD CHAIR:
102 State Capitol ▪ St. Paul, MN 55155 ▪ Telephone: (612) 296-2351 ▪ Facsimile: (612) 282-5097

*Using known dimensions of the communist newspapers "Oswald" is holding,
it is possible to prove that this photo is a fake. The subject is too short
to be the person Jack Ruby killed—who was about 5' 10" tall—
or the newspapers are too large to be genuine.*

Part IV

The Zapruder Film: Seeing but Not Believing

For the 1996 JFK Lancer Conference that would be held in Dallas 21–23 November, I was invited by Debra Conway and George Michael Evica to organize a session on the possibility that the Zapruder film might have been edited or otherwise altered to misrepresent events in Dealey Plaza on 22 November 1963. After extensive discussion, we agreed to hold a preliminary workshop on the 21st that would be limited to a small group of investigators for us to have the opportunity to exchange our findings and critique our results prior to their presentation during the public session to be held on the 22nd. The workshop would last ten-and-a-half hours and be followed by a four-and-a-half hour symposium.

The workshop participants included David Mantik, David Lifton, Jack White, Chuck Marler, Noel Twyman, Ron Hepler, Roy Schaeffer, and Robert Morningstar, with contributions by Martin Shackelford, Art Snyder, and Sherry Gutierrez. The public session held on the 22nd involved presentations by Jack White, Chuck Marler, Noel Twyman, David Lifton, David Mantik, and me. In my capacity as chair of this session, I provided a framework for understanding reasoning about the evidence in this case from the perspective of what is known as "inference to the best explanation", which is addressed in the Epilogue. The chapters included here are representative of what we presented in Dallas.

After 20 years of thinking about the authenticity of the Zapruder film, Jack White provides us with a veritable cornucopia of cinematic anoma-

207

lies that establish a *prima facie* case that it has been edited in many different ways. What I mean by this assertion is that, unless these anomalies can be "explained away" on rational grounds, their existence supports drawing the conclusion that tampering has occurred on the basis of an inference to the best explanation. If there are better explanations for the white blob, the pink "spray", Greer's head-turn, the missing car-stop, the missing Connally left-turn, the peculiar change in the visual field and so on, it is not obvious.

Jack White has achieved near-legendary status within the assassination research community for his excellent work on the photographic evidence, including studies of the backyard photographs of Lee Harvey Oswald that establish—conclusively, in my view—that they have been faked. [*Editor's note*: See, for example, *The Third Decade* (September 1991) and *The Third Decade* (May 1992).] Although he mentions in passing the popular sentiment that it is difficult to prove a negative, there is an underlying ambiguity that overlooks the difference between *non-existence claims* (such as that there is no intelligent life elsewhere in the universe) and *negations of generalizations* (such as that it is not the case that every President has been assassinated).

The reason why it may be possible to have conclusive evidence that some of the evidence in this case—the autopsy X-rays or the diagrams of the brain, for example—has been subject to fabrication or alteration is because "proofs" of this kind do not require exhaustive research of every possibility but only the establishment of specific fabrications or alterations. Thus, the attempt to prove that the backyard photographs are genuine and not merely real—no one would dispute that they *are* photographs and "real" in that sense—would require establishing that the subject was indeed Oswald, that he had posed as portrayed at that specific location at some specific time, and so forth, which is far more difficult than finding specific features of photos proving them fakes.

Ron Hepler astutely observes that when the presence of a feature or the absence of the feature renders an hypothesis inconsistent with the evidence, it should be discarded in favor of alternative hypotheses that are consistent with the evidence, as inference to the best explanation requires. In this case, he discovered indications that John Connally was struck twice, once by a bullet that entered his back and shattered a rib before exiting below his right nipple (at about frame 315) and once by a bullet that hit his right wrist and impacted in his left thigh (at about frame 338), a round that appears to have been fired from the Dallas County Records Building. This study by itself supplies enough evidence to refute *The Warren Report*—even on the basis of the *edited* Zapruder film!

As Mike Pincher, J.D., and Roy Schaeffer report, an important study by Philip H. Melanson that appeared in *The Third Decade* (November 1984) substantiates the claims advanced by David Lifton, *Best Evidence* (1980), pp. 555–557, for example, that the film was in the possession of the National Photographic Interpretation Center run by the CIA already Friday night, 22 November 1963. In their reconstruction of this occurrence, they calculate that the film left Dallas about 4 P.M. CST, arrived in Washington, D.C., by 10 P.M. EST, and was reprocessed in time for a new original and three copies to be returned to Dallas by 7 A.M. CST the following morning. Their study offers many indications that the film was subjected to editing by the CIA, the most important of which is the blink pattern observed in the film, which deviates from the pattern to be expected.

Not the least striking feature of Chuck Marler's contribution, which focuses upon the Warren Commission's use of phoney numbers that were changed from those established by the original surveyors of Dealey Plaza, is how beautifully it illustrates the methodology employed by the Commission's staff: if the evidence does not confirm the predetermined conclusion, then ignore it, distort it, or fake it. It may come as no suprise that Arlen Specter played a major role in manufacturing this evidence, analogous to those we have previously discovered with regard to the magic bullet theory and the hypothetical question in Part I, which lend support to Marler's proposal that he be tried for obstruction of justice.

David Mantik, M.D., Ph.D., provides a fascinating and comprehensive study of multiple indications that the film has been subjected to at least two kinds of editing, which might be called *vertical editing* (removing whole frames) and *horizontal editing* (editing within frames). His background magnification analysis provides convincing evidence that, as the limousine passes the Stemmons Freeway sign, features in the immediate foreground are being edited out and background features magnified, with an average magnification effect of 1.6:1. Although it may be initially puzzling why the limousine appears to recede to the very bottom of the visual field up until frame 313, when corrections are made for this effect, the limousine moves back toward the center of the visual field.

Even more importantly, Mantik amasses eyewitness and other photographic evidence in support of a reconstruction of the missing frames, which concludes that the driver, William Greer, actually brought the vehicle to a stop in Dealey Plaza after bullets had begun to be fired. This was such an obvious indication of Secret Service complicity in the assassination that it had to be edited out. In agreement with Josiah Thompson, Mantik finds that JFK was hit at least twice in the head—once from behind and once from in front—but that these hits were temporally separated by as much as a second or more and merged together during the process of reconstituting the film. This may be the most brilliant example of inference to the best explanation in a complex case that we shall ever confront.

An important point of which Americans are generally unaware is that legal procedure permits photographs and motion pictures to be used as evidence in courts of law only when a foundation for their introduction has been established by eyewitness testimony. According to *McCormick on Evidence*, 3rd Edition (1984), Section 214, concerning photographs, movies, and sound recordings, for example:

> The principle upon which photographs are most commonly admitted into evidence is the same as that underlying the admission of illustrative drawings, maps and diagrams. Under this theory, a photograph is viewed merely as a graphic portrayal of oral testimony, and becomes admissible only when a witness has testified that it is a correct and accurate representation of the relevant facts personally observed by the witness.

The practice of the Warren Commission and apologists for its findings appears to be the opposite, where photographs and films—including X-rays—have been used to discount the testimony of eyewitnesses, which is the better legal evidence.

A widely-held belief holds that eyewitness testimony tends to be unreliable. It was one of the more remarkable aspects of Mantik's research, therefore, that he discovered a strikingly high degree of agreement among multiple witnesses about shots that hit the President's head. This led him to a review of the current literature on the reliability of witnesses, including Elizabeth Loftus, *Eyewitness Testimony* (1996). On Table 3.1, he discovered a summary of research with 151 subjects, which reported that, when subjects considered what they were observing to be salient (or significant), they were 98% accurate and 98% complete with respect to their observations—reinforcing their importance as evidence and offering one more indication that popular opinions are not always true.

The problem with photographs and films—including X-rays, we now know— is that they can be subjected to alteration and fabrication. Controversy over the admissibility of photographs of O.J. Simpson wearing Bruno Magli shoes, which his civil counsel maintained had been faked, offers a recent illustration—one that tarnished Robert Groden's reputation, in spite of his excellent work on the assassination of JFK. The Oswald backyard photographs, which have been shown to be fakes (as I have explained above), turn out to support Oswald's contention at the time that his face had been imposed upon someone else's body. What is fascinating about this discovery is that it would have been unnecessary to frame a guilty man, one more striking indication Oswald was the "patsy" he proclaimed himself to be.

— *James H. Fetzer, Ph.D.*

Evidence . . . or Not? The Zapruder Film: Can It Be Trusted?

20 Years of Thoughts About the Authenticity of the Zapruder Film

Jack White

In the mid-1970s when I first was privileged to meet legendary editor, author and JFK researcher Penn Jones, Jr., I had already been studying the assassination for more than ten years. I had developed a slide show called *The Framing of Lee Harvey Oswald* which I would show to anyone willing to listen. In due time, I showed it to Dallas researcher Mary Ferrell, and she said, "Penn must see this."

She invited to her house to see my show, as I recall, Penn, Gary Shaw, the late Larry Ray Harris, and several other researchers. We all sat around well past midnight discussing the case and the slides I had shown. All were highly complimentary, but a comment that Penn made stuck with me.

> "Your show is very good, but it is too general and repeats information mostly already known or published by others. To really do good research, you need to *specialize*! Pick out one or two JFK subjects that really interest you, and *then research the hell out of them*," Penn advised me in his usual colorful manner. I soon refocused my research into two areas which interested me most . . . (1) all the photographs related to the assassination, and (2) the identity of the accused assassin, Lee Harvey Oswald.

The first area was a natural outgrowth of my occupation . . . advertising art director and photographer. I was rather expert with still cameras, had shot thousands of slides, and operated my own darkroom.

The second area interested me for several reasons. Oswald, his mother, and his brother all had resided in Fort Worth, my home town. I already was familiar with his defection and many other things about him. Yet the investigation of him by the Warren Commission seemed very superficial. And the motive ascribed to him seemed absurd. It was obvious that Oswald probably was operating on behalf of some intelligence agency, and was controlled by his handlers to take the fall for the assassination.

Penn invited me to one of his lectures, and I eagerly accepted. The highlight of his talk was the showing of Mark Lane's *Rush to Judgment* film, and a showing of the Zapruder film which was photographed from a movie screen. It was very poor quality and dark. It was spliced onto the end of the Lane film, which was on 16mm, and to get it to 16 mm, Penn had projected a small 8 mm copy on to a screen and rephotographed it with a 16 mm camera. Poor as the image was, it was a shock I will never forget, to see the President's head explode. It made me ill.

Afterward, I learned that Penn had for sale small 8 mm spools of the Z-film. He had been among those who helped "liberate" the film (into the hands of researchers) while a copy of it was in the possession of New Orleans District Attorney Jim Garrison. Garrison let it be known among researchers who were helping him that the subpoenaed Z-reel would be in his office overnight without special security, and well . . . if someone happened to "borrow" it overnight and have it duplicated . . . well, he just would not have any idea how that could have happened.

A word to the wise was sufficient. Copies were made and the film returned to the DA's office without its being missed. Penn and several other early researchers ended up with copies, which they then had further duplicated. The color was poor, the quality was bad, but there it was for anyone to see . . . the Zapruder film of the killing of John Fitzgerald Kennedy.

I gladly paid Penn the $20 cost for the small 8 mm spool, even though I did not have a projector . . . but I quickly remedied that by purchasing one. I guess I was the only person around who owned a projector just to show a single strip of film lasting less than 20 seconds. From then on, I opened each slide presentation by cranking up the little projector and shocking the spectators by showing the Z-film. Without fail, the audience gasped audibly each time as the President's head exploded.

I was both sickened and fascinated as I watched this silent 8 mm film over and over during my JFK lectures. I had no reason then to doubt that it was the most accurate record of what had happened in Dealey Plaza.

Later Penn obtained from Robert Groden a much better 16 mm copy of the film, which had been steadied by Rotoscoping. The color was much superior to the murky 8 mm pirated copy. It had a sound-on-film narration by Penn. I was one of the first to purchase one of these superior copies from Penn for $90. Again, I did not have a 16 mm projector, so had to invest about $600 in a Bell and Howell 16 mm sound projector. Even though all my lectures were free, I felt that this investment would vastly improve the impact of my slide show. I was right; audiences were fascinated by such a graphic depiction of the execution of the President.

Then in 1977 I obtained excellent 35 mm slides of each frame from Groden slide copies. After careful frame-by-frame study, I began to have questions about seeming anomalies I had noticed. As possibly the first researcher to speak publicly on these questions of tampering, I have pointed out many of these things in my lectures for more than 15 years, as Jim Marrs documents in his 1989 book *Crossfire*.

First let me state that my area of photographic expertise is "still" photography, not motion pictures; I have never owned or operated a movie camera. Although many of the principles are the same, I have hesitated to get too involved in researching this important motion picture film, because true expertise is required and hard to establish . . . and it is difficult to defend one's observations without proper qualifications.

However, even without movie expertise, anybody with a good eye and a little common sense can make valid observations when examining a movie one frame at a time, for then it becomes an inspection of a series of still photos, each frozen in time, and not necessarily dependent on movie technology. So in examining the slides of each frame, here are some of the things I have noticed:

1. The white "blob" on JFK's right temple. It is very white, changes size and shape, moves around and seems to show that the President's forehead was missing. The part of JFK's head which remains seems totally inconsistent with the autopsy reports and witness observations.

2. The pink "spray" of brain matter goes only forward and is obvious for only one frame. I believed it should go backward from the exit wound and be seen for several frames.

3. Greer's sudden head turn to look at JFK seems unnaturally abrupt. Other researchers have done intensive studies of the timing of Greer's movement.

4. Numerous witnesses reported that the limousine nearly came to a complete stop, yet I cannot detect a limo stop either in the motion or still frames. The brake lights come on, but the limo speed seems

to remain constant. The blinking lights in front seem to not be uniform. [*Editor's note:* See Mike Pincher and Roy Schaeffer, Part IV.]

5. Connally said he turned to his left to look at the President, then turned to his right. The film does not show this. Other parts of his testimony, as well as that of other limo occupants, do not seem to match what is seen.

6. After Kennedy has been hit, there is no blood on Connally's right cuff from a magic bullet wrist wound, and he continues to grip his Stetson hat. Such massive damage would have caused blood to spurt immediately, and it seems that for the single bullet theory to work, blood would have been seen quickly after JFK is wounded. And, of course, if his major major wrist nerves were severed, he could not have continued to hold the hat.

7. As the limo gets closer to Zapruder, the field of view seems to decrease more than it should, almost as if Zapruder was zooming in on the limousine, yet he testified that the zoom was set on maximum telephoto for the entire film. The cropping of the limousine seems too extreme at the bottom, cropping out the Newmans, who were standing by the curb. I believe the Newmans should have appeared in the foreground at about the time of the head shot. But if frames have been eliminated, leaving the Newmans in the frame would present major problems; therefore I think the fabricators zoomed in and cropped the Newmans out of these crucial frames. Perhaps even the reflections of the Newmans in the shiny side of the car could have been a problem. For instance, examination of Willis 5 slide reveals much detail of the TSBD reflected in the trunk. It seems reasonable that the Z-film should also show reflections.

8. Unnatural jerkiness of movement or change of focus or movement is apparent in certain frame sequences. In two frames, in the foreground of each, the limousine is in sharp focus. But in the background, Jean Hill and Mary Moorman are sharp in one frame and blurred in the adjacent frame. This is repeated in the next two frames. Photographically, this is impossible, I believe.

9. A white spot on the grass behind the limousine seems to move erratically rather than smoothly as it should, and seems to change size and shape. Dr. David Mantik has done a very thorough analysis of this phenomenon.

In subsequent years, I have continued to study the film, plus books and articles about it, and other researchers have suggested to me other possible areas of tampering. The most significant of these are:

Observation 1

Ron Redmon, a school principal in Indiana, has studied the Z-film extensively. Ron discovered that approximately 20 spectators along the north Elm curb east of the Stemmons sign do not appear to move for more than three seconds, while every spectator on the south curb does move. By overlapping images from two slide projectors, I determined that Ron was probably correct. It seems to me that a single image of the 20 spectators had been repeated over and over. It seems improbable that in this period of time not a single person moved an arm or leg, waved, or changed position to any noticeable extent. Ron speculates that when frames were removed in this sequence, spectator movements would have been very jerky, so they had to be stabilized by repeating them. In correspondence with me, Ron also mentioned many other possible signs of tampering, which he summarized in *The Fourth Decade* in March of 1995. These include:

A. In frames 144–153 (one-half second), spectator Hugh Betzner has moved a distance which exceeds human speed capability . . . indicating excised frames.

B. In frames 155–161 (one-third second), spectator Linda Willis has turned 180 degrees and comes in contact with spectator Robert Croft, another instance of superhuman speed . . . again indicating excised frames.

C. In frames 161–180 (approximately one second), Linda Willis takes several steps, and Rosemary Willis takes several steps . . . again much too fast, indicating excised frames.

D. Looking at the Stemmons sign, in frame 161 it is in perfect condition, but by frame 183 there is a significant notch on the top left edge, yet by frame 188, the notch disappears.

E. In frame 255, Ron speculates that a fake shadow has obscured driver William Greer, to his west. Since the sun was overhead and to Greer's left, Ron says this shadow is inconsistent.

F. In frames 312–321, Governor Connally turns 90 degrees in one half-second. Also the white spot on the grass in the background moves more than 10 feet in one half second.

G. In frames 321–336, JFK's head moves from the seat back to leaning forward with his head in contact with Jackie's left arm in less than one second, seemingly too fast.

H. In frames 153–155 (one-ninth of a second), a woman who is the thirteenth person east of the Stemmons sign has shifted her feet significantly . . . more than should be possible.

I. In frames 335–336 (one-eighteenth of a second), Jackie moves her right arm a significant distance. Ron reminds us that laboratory tests show that a human eye blink is one-twenty-fifth of a second, and a flinch or startle response of moving an arm, leg or head takes one-fifth of a second as a basis for his conclusions.

J. Comparing the Willis 5 and Betzner photos, which are almost simultaneous in time, Ron notes that in Willis five adults and a child can be seen framed between the posts of the Stemmons sign, but in the Betzner picture, from a similar angle and a split second earlier, the same persons are not seen. Also, two women appearing in Zapruder in this sequence (188–210) should be seen in Willis and Betzner are not seen.

K. In recent correspondence with me, Ron cites Dan Rather's description of the film and compares it to what is seen. Rather, of course, was one of the first persons to view the Z-film. Early in his commentary, Rather says the film shows . . . "The President's automobile was preceded by one other car . . . [the film does not show this] . . . the President's black Lincoln automobile made a turn, a left turn, off Houston Street onto Elm Street [the film does not show this]. It got about 35 yards from the corner of Elm and Houston . . . at the moment the President put his hand up and lurched forward and it was obvious he had been hit . . ."
The present film begins with the limo already on Elm at frame 133 and the forward lurch is between frames 188–200. "Governor Connally," Rather continued, ". . . in the seat just in front of the President, sensed something was wrong . . . . his coat was unbuttoned . . . and as he turned he extended his right hand toward the President, he exposed his entire shirt front and chest . . . and was wounded with . . . a second shot (as Redmon comments, no existing Zapruder frames show the specific action that Rather describes, with the governor in full turn with hand extended toward the President). Rather continues, ". . . the third shot hit the President, and . . . his head went forward with considerable violence." Was Rather looking at an unaltered different film . . . or is he just a lousy reporter?

L. Ron also documents how several lampposts seen in the Z-film have seemingly changed locations compared to other photos taken that day. He goes into this in detail in an unpublished manuscript. In comparing the Bond slides, the Bronson slide and the Z-film, some of the lamp-posts seem to change position.

M. In frame 213, Ron notes that shadows of several bystanders are at the right border of the frame, disappear in frames 214–216 and reappear in frames 218–19, a seeming improbability.

N. Ron has compared the known Bronson slide with the Z-film, and concludes that either the known slide has been cropped, or else there was a second unknown Bronson slide, because an FBI document describes things not seen in the Bronson slide.

O. In the Altgens photo, motorcycle officer Chaney seems to be directly abreast the limo, looking directly into the face of JFK; no Z-slide can be found which shows this.

P. Also in the Altgens photo, a shadow in the street of a spectator aligns with officer Martin's motorcycle. The Z-frames that show this shadow/bike alignment are 240–242. But the problem with this is that Jackie Kennedy, Greer, and Kellerman are shown in entirely different positions than in the Altgens photo.

Q. Ron also has devoted extensive study to indications that a freeway sign similar to the Stemmons sign, known to exist and seen in other photos, cannot be seen in the Z-film, but should be.

Observation 2

Chuck Marler discussed with me, and also wrote articles regarding his motion study of the limousine, his study of the flashing limousine lights, and the rapid turn of Greer. Along with Noel Twyman, Chuck made extensive motion picture studies of head turns, and found that a head turn of 150 degrees in one-eighteenth of a second is impossible, as Greer is shown doing in frames 302–303. Chuck's test show that such a head turn should have taken at least 5 frames. What happened to the four other frames?

Observation 3

Milicent Cranor discussed with me what she interprets as condensation streaks she thinks are bullet paths, and also her evidence that frames have been removed in several places, particularly relating to Connally movements and JFK movements following the head shot. She did an extensive study of Connally's movements from photos and witness statements, and says the Z-film does not correspond to other evidence. Also Milicent claims to have at one time viewed at a major network studio a version of the Z-film which contained things not seen in the present film. She asked to see the film at a later time to confirm what she had seen earlier; her request was refused.

Observation 4

Richard Bartholomew discussed with me why he thinks numerous frames have been selectively removed. Richard is a relative by marriage of the Zapruder family, and thus has some inside information. He says Mr. Z was troubled by several things he distinctly remembered seeing no longer being in the film, such as certain movements by Kennedy and Connally he could not find. Richard also noted that frame 227 has a motion blur in which Connally's head seems to face in opposite directions.

Observation 5

Dr. David Mantik has discussed with me why he thinks certain frames have been removed and/or resized. He agrees with my impression that the film seems to zoom-in as the limo nears the point of the head shot. He has done a thorough mathematical analysis of the white spot on the grass in the background which seems to change size and shape and moves about erratically. He also thinks the Newmans may have been cropped out of the foreground to disguise the effect of missing frames.

Observation 6

Harry Livingstone, in *Killing Kennedy*, brought many of these valid observations together into a single source, despite numerous technical inadequacies. I will not attempt to summarize Harry's many excellent observations here, as he covers them thoroughly in his book. He repeats many of the observations that I and other researchers have pointed out as being possible areas of tampering.

Observation 7

Daryll Weatherly, in an appendix to Livingstone's book, presents his Vector Analysis blurring study, which is perhaps the most important new scientific evidence of tampering. Again, I will not summarize his findings here, as it is better to read it in Harry's book. Essentially, Weatherly has noticed motion "streaks" in various frames by which he can make determinations using mathematical calculations which he calls Vector Analysis. It is a little over my head, but I highly recommend that it be read by everyone interested in the possibility of tampering. If Weatherly is correct, his analysis alone may prove tampering.

Observation 8

Robert Morningstar, like Mili Cranor, also has discovered condensation lines (or vapor trails) of possible bullet paths in certain frames. He also has showed me a frame from a CD ROM version of the film, which I have as yet been unable to verify, in which Jackie's face is totally blank, without eyes, nose or mouth. And on another frame, he has discovered a mysterious very tiny register mark (+) in the extreme lower right corner of one frame. Morningstar, working in conjunction with earlier research done by Roy Schaeffer, has developed an excellent analysis of the limousine's flashing lights, which in the Z-film do not flash at the expected flash rate. This was first pointed out to me about 1990 by researcher Schaeffer, and a year or so later by Chuck Marler. In 1996 at the JFK Lancer Conference in Dallas, Morningstar learned of the flashing light studies of Schaeffer and Marler, and has taken it several steps further with a highly analytical research paper, which appears to show conclusively that frames have been removed from the film.

Observation 9

Jim Marrs furnished me a copy of a letter by Chester Breneman, Dealey Plaza surveyor, who assisted *Life Magazine* and the Secret Service with motorcade reconstructions. Breneman had been furnished color enlargements of all Z-frames to work from. Breneman wrote, "On 3 frames after a frontal entry shot, *we saw blobs leaving the back of the President's head and disappearing on the fourth frame.*" These blobs cannnot be seen on the existing Z-film. Breneman also said that, "many of the frames used for positioning during reinactments were not included among those published, and that *all the frame numbers had been changed.*"

Observation 10

Researcher Alan Eaglesham, Ph.D., has done a study which shows that, in two frames of the Muchmore film, the position of JFK does not correspond with the President's position at approximately Z-280.

These are all valid reasons to distrust the Zapruder film as evidence. These are questions which must be resolved. I do not know the answers. Because movie photography is beyond my field of expertise, I have no way of knowing the "who and how" of possible tampering. Some researchers and self-proclaimed "experts" deny the possibility of tampering because technically in the 1960s it was "impossible" to tamper with 8 mm film and have it appear to be a camera original. But I know enough about photography in general to say that almost anything is possible in image alteration, even though the general public may be unaware of it. Much further study is needed. But let me close by just saying this: *If even one of these anomalies noticed by researchers is valid . . . then the Zapruder film has indeed been tampered with . . . and thus is a false record of the crime of the century!*

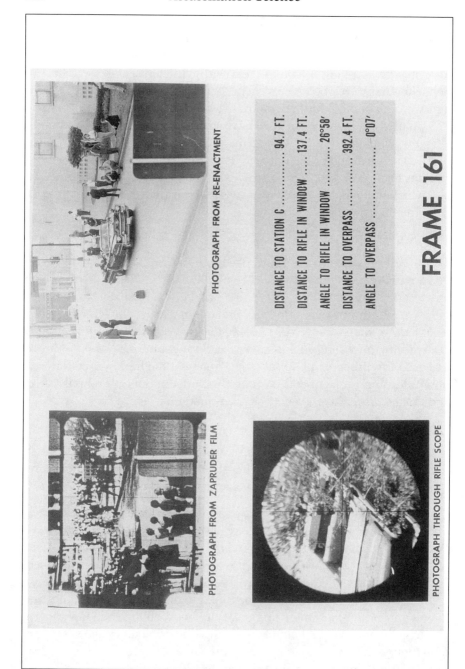

PHOTOGRAPH FROM RE-ENACTMENT

DISTANCE TO STATION C .... 94.7 FT.

DISTANCE TO RIFLE IN WINDOW ..... 137.4 FT.

ANGLE TO RIFLE IN WINDOW .... 26°58'

DISTANCE TO OVERPASS .... 392.4 FT.

ANGLE TO OVERPASS .... 0°07'

FRAME 161

PHOTOGRAPH FROM ZAPRUDER FILM

PHOTOGRAPH THROUGH RIFLE SCOPE

Commission Exhibit No. 888

The Case for Zapruder Film Tampering:
The Blink Pattern

Mike Pincher, J.D., and Roy L. Schaeffer

It has long been presumed that the world-famous Abraham Zapruder film of the 22 November 1963 assassination of President John F. Kennedy in Dallas, Texas, is the single most demonstrative piece of evidence in that crime. It has been used to calculate the number of shots fired that fateful day, when and from where. The Warren Commission placed heavy reliance upon it in incriminating Lee Harvey Oswald, and the Commission's critics have likewise used it to proclaim the impossibility of the "lone gunman" hypothesis.

But regardless of the leanings of the analyst, the film is traditionally perceived on a "what you see is what you get" basis—not on its inconsistencies and incongruities. Its fundamental reliability has rarely been challenged. The purpose of this paper is to show that, after the initial development of the film at the Kodak film processing laboratory in Dallas, crucial editing was performed within an approximate five-hour time period between the assassination itself and the debut of the film to the news media the following morning in Zapruder's "Jennifer Jr., Inc." dress shop on Elm Street directly across from the Texas School Book Depository. Editing of such a wholesale nature leads to the inevitable conclusion that there has been a conscious concealment of compelling evidence establishing a conspiracy to kill the President.

It will also be shown that the conspicuous editing at Z-132–133 (wherein one of the lead police motorcycle escorts proceeding westward down Elm Street in the middle lane vanishes into thin air to be instantly replaced by the Presidential limousine in virtually identical position) was not a harmless deletion of extraneous action but, rather, part of an overall effort to conceal vital information in ascertaining the true assassination scenario.

Specific Instances of Film Editing

The Zapruder film that is most widely shown to the public contains 486 frames,[1] and can be broken into three parts based on their scenery. The *First Scene* was prior to frame labeling and consisted of 16 frames. Therein, Beatrice Hester is sitting down on a park bench, with her husband Charles sitting on concrete steps immediately to her right. Marilyn Sitzman, their friend, is standing facing them about equidistant between them, her back to the viewer. The park bench was only a few yards from the pedestal on the North Pergola where the Zapruder assassination footage was taken. Beatrice is wearing a green dress and looking toward her husband. She is seen holding her purse on her lap with her right hand, with her left hand motionless near her chin. Charles is dressed in a dark suit and is looking toward Marilyn, with both of his hands grasping a brown lunch bag between his two legs as he is leaning slightly forward. Marilyn is wearing a black head scarf and beige dress; she faces the Hesters and appears to be talking to them.

In this brief footage there are basically two principal movements occurring within .9 seconds of film, one visible to the naked eye on close scrutiny and one not. The visible movement is of Marilyn's right forearm swinging upward rapidly to her waist to complete the folding of her arms within six frames, about one-third of a second at 18 fps, an impossible feat. The second movement, invisible to the naked eye, is Charles' head turning 60 degrees in one frame to look at Beatrice, another impossible feat. The viewer would have to see that frame in isolation.

The reader is advised that this overall 16-frame sequence appears on most copies (absent special deletion) and can only be practically observed by using a single-frame counter on most VCRs. This sequence is of paramount importance because this editing reflects the technique utilized throughout the numbered frames in the main body of the film.

From frame Z-001–132, *Scene Two* captures the movement of three lead motorcyclists reaching the intersection of Houston and Elm Streets. Therein, one of the three leaves the formation by proceeding north on Houston Street while the other two complete the turn onto Elm. Zapruder continues to film the progress of the two cyclists approaching him on

Elm Street until frame Z-132. At Z-133, *Scene Three* shows the Presidential limousine replacing the cyclist as aforementioned and proceeding westward down Elm Street about three seconds prior to the first shot (presuming its occurrence at Z-189) and continues until after the assassination is completed and the film ends at Z-486.

Three other specific instances of film deletions appear, first, between Z277–287 [where Charles Brehm's son magically appears clapping his hands next to his father, an impossible movement within an approximately one-half second time interval (further explained later)], second, at Z-312–313 [the head blast] and, third, Z-315–321 [limousine driver and Secret Service agent William R. Greer's head movements from back to beyond perpendicular (front) while front seat passenger Secret Service agent Roy Kellerman remains practically stationary looking to his front]. The Z-312–313 head blast, depicting a full mushroom cloud expulsion of blood and brain tissue within the confines of two frames, confounds all natural laws of physics. This effusion achieves *full vertical height* within one-ninth of a second, defying the normal stimulus and reaction time of one-quarter of a second. In real time, presuming the generally recognized Zapruder film speed of 18.3 frames per second (fps), this apex would require 4.5 frames to occur.[2]

At Z-315–316, Greer begins turning his head from looking back and facing the President to returning to the front at about 15 degrees, an exaggerated movement. At Z-316–317, however, the head turn is an incredible 110 degrees, an impossibility within the confines of a single-frame, one-eighteenth of a second time interval.

Likewise, the two-frame, one-ninth of a second, 125-degree scenario, is also impossible. Although Greer's turning of the remaining 40 degrees at Z-317–321 to fully face the steering wheel is conjectural, his total 165-degree turn in the space of six frames at a one-third of a second time span is beyond human capability. Realistically, Greer's total movement, back to front, would take at least a full second to accomplish.[3]

There is demonstrable physical evidence to help verify this premise. If the reader flashes his hand in front of his face in approximation of one-third of a second, it appears as a blur. The eyes are incapable of staying in full focus in following this action. If Greer's 165-degree movement in one-third of a second truly depicted real time, it would likewise appear as a blur. But blurring of this nature is not seen in the Zapruder film. Also noteworthy is that shortly after frame Z-295, and before the Z-313 head shot, Texas Governor John B. Connally's torso quickly turns and falls toward wife Nellie's lap and they both descend at an unrealistically accelerated pace toward her jump seat, which is directly behind the driver's-side front seat. When the viewer is alerted to these phenomena, they are readily observable. But without such prompting, they are routinely bypassed. Therein lies the rub. Continuity in the film is preserved well enough to elude all but the most probing eye. How is this possible?

The "How" of Film Editing

It is submitted that this deception was accomplished by excising frames in a systematic, frame-by-frame manner throughout the film so that the film speed was reduced to its present 18.3 fps status from an original 48 fps (Zapruder himself reportedly claimed to have used 24 fps but his camera had only two frame settings; see Enclosure 1).[4] This deletion appears to have been done without considering the blink rate. But by doing so, the edited frames appear more in synch with the remaining action than they actually were, creating an illusion of uniformity and consistency.

The evidence substantiating this position is best appreciated by chronologically tracing the film's processing. The assassination itself took place at about 12:30 P.M. CST. Zapruder returned promptly to his dress shop, immediately called the FBI office in Dallas from that location, and then brought his camera to WFAA-TV (which was near the dress shop), where he did a live interview with Jay Watson. During this time, the Kodachrome film was delivered to an Eastman Kodak lab across from Love Field in Dallas. This lab specialized in a developing technique required for Kodachrome film that is most commonly called K-14 processing.[5]

After accompanying Zapruder from the television interview, Zapruder and Forrest V. Sorrels, head of the Secret Service in Dallas, both arrived there at about 2:00 P.M. CST.[6] The development of the original took about an hour-and-three-quarters[7] and, after quickly reviewing the film, Zapruder and Sorrels went to the Jamieson Film Company on Bryan Street in Dallas to have three copies of the original made, which appear to have been contact prints.[8] Shortly before 4:00 P.M. CST, the copies were completed.

Because of the copying techniques employed, at least the original and one copy (a work print) were flown from Love Field to Andrews Air Force Base in Washington, D.C., a 1,307-mile trip, and transported to the National Photographic Interpretation Center (NPIC) in Suitland, Maryland, located about eight miles from Andrews.[9] The approximate timing was a 4:00 P.M. departure plus four and one-half hours flight time plus one hour for the difference in Time Zones from CST to EST. Therefore, the film arrived at Andrews about 9:30 P.M. EST and, according to our best estimate, was in the hands of the NPIC not long after 10:00 P.M. EST, a calculation that coincides with David Lifton's report that the film was in the possession of the CIA already on Friday night, the day of the assassination.[9]

That the film was flown to Washington and in the hands of the Secret Service by 9:55 P.M. EST receives support from a handwritten memo by Max Phillips, Special Agent for the Protective Research Section (PRS) of the Secret Service.[10] An important study by Philip H. Melanson, which appeared in *The Third Decade* (November 1984), explains that the Secret Service was dependent upon the CIA for technical assistance, including the analysis of photographs and films. The most important evidence that he discusses is CIA item #450—nine pages of documents related to analysis of the Zapruder film by the NPIC for the Secret Service—obtained under the Freedom of Information Act by Paul Hoch. Melanson's study substantiates the conclusion that the CIA had the film and reprocessed it that night.[11]

At NPIC, the original was reviewed and a least partially edited. Then, a modified camera having similar characteristics to Zapruder's Bell & Howell camera made a duplicate copy to replace it. In turn, three copies were made of the duplicate using a standard optical printer. The entire process took about five hours and was completed by about 3:00 A.M. EST.[12] (See Enclosure 3, depicting the probable editing and copying methodologies used at NPIC.) Departing from Suitland, Maryland at about 3:15 A.M. EST, the film was returned to Love Field at about 6:45 A.M. CST on 23 November 1963 and delivered to Zapruder's dress shop by the Secret Service at about 7:00 A.M. CST.

It was sold by Zapruder sometime after 8:00 A.M. CST to Richard Stolley, who, as bureau chief of *Life* magazine in Los Angeles, California, had flown to Dallas on 22 November 1963 to cover the assassination. Reportedly around 6:00 P.M. CST, Stolley had learned of the film through *Life* part-time reporter Patsy Swank, who called from the Dallas police headquarters. Looking up Zapruder's phone number in a phone directory, he tried to contact Zapruder at his residence at approximately 15 minute intervals, finally reaching him at about 11:00 P.M. CST.[13]

Zapruder told him that he would meet him at the dress shop at 9:00 A.M. CST the following morning. However, Stolley in fact arrived there an hour earlier and reached an agreement that conveyed to him certain film rights. At about 9:00 A.M. CST on 23 November 1963, the film was shown once by the Secret Service at Zapruder's dress shop to a small press corps that included Dan Rather of CBS, a representative from *The Saturday Evening Post,* and a member of the Associated Press. Immediately thereafter, Stolley snuck out the back door with the duplicate original and one copy and transferred them to Chicago for analysis and production at the R.R. Donnelley Graphics Company *Life* laboratory.[12] Thirty-one Black and White individual frames were thereafter published in *Life*'s 29 November 1963 issue.

Physical Evidence of Film Tampering

The most unique physical evidence of film tampering at NPIC is the presence of a *register mark* at Z-028, appearing as a plus (+) sign just above and to the right of a woman wearing a red blouse with blue vertical and horizontal stripes. (See her location using Robert Groden's book, *The Killing of a President*, at page 22 [Z-188—she is the fourth person to the left of the Stemmons Freeway sign] and at page 25 [excerpted from the Charles Bronson film].)

A register mark may be used as a guide in aligning scenes in a film or film copies to an original, and, in this case, in all likelihood, served as a centering and focusing aid to help keep a duplicate film at a 1:1 ratio. It is not detectible to the naked eye at Z-028 but is observable when the frame is enlarged through a viewer device.[15] Here, it was placed strategically between the second and third road strips from the crosswalk on Elm Street. If one marks that spot, it is seen that after the Presidential limousine pops into view, the register mark corresponds to Kennedy's position at Z-188 or approximately when the first shot occurs.

It also appears that an emulsion removal mark was strategically placed on the film in one frame about the time that Jean Hill and Mary Moorman first appear.[16] The mark was most likely used for co-ordinated editing of such other assassination films as the Marie Muchmore and Orville Nix 8mm films in an effort to avoid any inconsistencies between them.

The "Why"?

We now know the fact of editing and the how. What remains is the "why"? What action has been deemed not fit for public consumption? The explanation cannot concern its graphic nature. We plainly see the dreaded consequences of a head shot, wherein, along with the foregoing expulsion, there is in plain sight the near removal of the President's skullcap. We also see the wounding of Governor Connally and a bewildered Jacqueline Kennedy trying to crawl onto the trunk. The only logical conclusion is that these excisions promote the concealment of the specific activities of specific actors, primarily in the Presidential limousine. It is beyond the scope of this paper to explore these conspiratorial specifics.

An advantageous effect—if not conscious design—of the film speed reduction is that the illusory time in which a single assailant could have accomplished the deed is expanded. If the three-shot scenario at the accepted time frame of 5.6 seconds for the 18.3 fps is considered from Z-210–313, that time reduces down to 4.3 seconds at 24 fps. Based on Government testing, the minimum firing time between shots for the suspected 6.5 mm Mannlicher-Carcano rifle (disregarding the time required for aiming the weapon) is 2.3 seconds,[17] making the Warren Commission three-shot version under the 24 fps Zapruder was reported to have used problematic, at best. [*Editor's note:* See Enclosure 1.]

Even if the 5.6 seconds parameter for 18.3 fps is not accepted, any different reference point is nonetheless correspondingly expanded by the 18.3 fps conversion, thereby superficially enhancing the feasibility of that hypothesis.

The editing at Z-132–133 can now be placed in a more proper perspective. Despite Secret Service regulations prohibiting greater than 90-degree turns in Presidential motorcades, the Kennedy limousine made an extraordinarily wide 120-degree turn from Houston Street to Elm Street, showing the impropriety of the selected motorcade route.[18] Zapruder probably captured this event, as he filmed the limousine's progress on Elm Street in its entirety.[19] At the very least, this omission for many years circumvented raising many appropriate questions.

The Proof is in the Pattern

Are our proofs of editing now exhausted? Hardly. There were discernible (although different) emergency light blinking patterns on the front grills of both the motorcade lead car, a 1964 Ford Falcon driven by Dallas Police Chief Jesse Curry, and the Presidential limousine, a modified 1961 Lincoln Continental convertible. The Z-132–133 editing totally omits the Curry car from view and drastically reduces the viable observation time for the alternate blinking pattern of the emergency lights on the front grill of the limousine. [*Editor's note:* There are no such lights on the rear.] This makes comparisons more difficult and the idea of making comparisons for purposes of detecting editing less apparent.

The emergency light pulse rate was a constant one established at .41 seconds by an electronic flip-flop switch installed into the electrical circuitry. At 18 fps, if unaltered, the Zapruder film would feature the emergency light pulse occupying about seven frames per side. Using the Robert Hughes film, these durations were calculated by observing the limousine as it approached the intersection of Main and Houston streets. The blinking pattern probably escaped alteration there because the assassination itself occurred on Elm.

The Hughes film shows the limousine emergency lights blinking in a constant and consistent pattern except when the vehicle is actually making the right turn onto Houston Street, wherein the signal pattern is changed by an override switch that was operative at all turns. After the turn is completed, the pattern returns to normal.

However, the Zapruder film emergency light blinking pattern lacks this consistency. By examining the blink pattern from Z-133 to Z-181, it is clear that more than seven frames are seen in the pattern, indicating a faster speed than 18 fps. The limousine is hidden from view by the Stemmons sign between Z-182 and Z-211. Once past there, an irregular (and therefore altered) pattern is perceived, but only briefly, as Zapruder's camera angle makes the pattern unobservable after Z-238.

The emergency light blinking pattern is of great evidentiary value in the confirmation of film editing and is only observable when a frame-by-frame reference is made. This must be charted out, as it is not noticeable with the naked eye. (See Enclosure 4-A through 4-C for an illustration of this pattern on a frame-by-frame basis. 4-A explains how the *expected* pattern for the limousine was mathematically determined by using the Hughes film, 4-B is a graphic showing the *actual* pattern on a frame by frame basis, and 4-C is a graphic showing the *expected* pattern in any given 18-frame sequence.)

The Sun Flare that Got Away

Despite great pains taken during the editing process, not all evidence of conspiratorial implication in the Zapruder film was deleted. At Z-330–332 (and verifiable in the Orville Nix film version as well), a flare of light appears emanating from the chrome strip just above the windshield on the right side of the center-positioned rear view mirror holder. This light dispersal is not consistent with a mere reflection from the Sun. It radiates out beyond what would be expected from that source, appears too much as a burst, is peculiarly confined to a small portion of the strip itself and lasts for too brief of a time period. This is the only occasion in the Zapruder film wherein such a flare appears.

There was, however, physical evidence recovered on the night of the assassination which helps explain this phenomenon. Warren Commission bullet fragments 567 (the nose portion, which weighed in at 44.6 grains) and 569 (the tail portion, which weighed in at 21 grains) were found on the front seat of the limousine directly below the chrome strip in question and were purportedly matched to the Mannlicher-Carcano rifle associated with Oswald.[20]

This can be linked to the flare of light where such an effect is consistent with the reflection of sunlight off the debris caused by a bullet striking the chrome strip. [*Editor's note*: A photograph of the damage to the chrome strip may be found in the Epilogue.]

The sun flare appearance at Z-330 and the presence of the chrome strip indentation at that same spot are not coincidental. An assassination photograph taken by Mary Moorman—that corresponds to somewhere between Z-315 and Z-321 on the Zapruder film—shows that the visor rod (attached where no indentation appears) was not separated from the chrome strip at that time. Therefore, the indentation could not have been the result of an earlier shot during the assassination itself or from any previous occurrence.

What is the significance of this finding? Assuming 18 fps, it is compelling evidence that there was a shot at Z-330 which followed a head shot at Z-313 by less than a second afterward (because there are only 17 frames between the two shots). Yet, Neutron Activation Analysis (NAA) tests conducted in 1964 by the Atomic Energy Commission (AEC) on behalf of the FBI found no traces of blood on either fragment.[21]

After further NAA testing was conducted in 1977 by Dr. Vincent Guinn, nuclear chemist at the University of California, Irvine, on behalf of the House Select Committee on Assassinations (HSCA), the inference was drawn that both fragments came from the same bullet.[22] But that implies the Z-313 head shot could not have come from the Oswald rifle. In fact, it could not realistically have come from the same shooter—even if he had used two separate weapons (and there is absolutely no evidence in the case to support that conclusion). It seems inevitable that there had to have been a minimum of two assailants; hence, a conspiracy.

Why was this sun flare appearance not deleted as well? In the space of (what we take to be) roughly five hours of editing, it probably was simply overlooked. Perhaps it might have thrown everything out of delicate synch, but, more than likely, it went unnoticed in the zeal to edit out more obvious infringements.

Was All Editing "Coordinated"?

As to the aforementioned co-ordinated editing efforts at NPIC to synchronize the Zapruder film with other assassination footage, we have already seen that these efforts were not a complete success.

As aforementioned, between Z-277 and Z-287, at Z-277, the Presidential limousine is seen just beginning to pass two persons standing close to the curb near the limo, namely, Charles Brehm and the famous "Babushka lady". She is standing directly behind Brehm, who is clapping his hands as the limo slowly passes in front of him. Unseen at Z-277 is Brehm's son, who is standing behind his father and directly in front of the Babushka lady. Ten frames later, the son is standing next to his father and clapping, a movement impossible in the approximate half-second assigned him. In real time, this would require at least 1.2 seconds.

Among other examples, in frame 42 of the Marie Muchmore film (which corresponds to Z-313), it can be observed that the President's head is angled or sloped downward to a greater degree than at Z-313 itself.

Conclusion

In sum, the evidence suggests that our government assumed control of the Zapruder film as well as a substantial portion of the overall JFK assassination film record and, in so doing, reduced them to historical forgeries. Consequently, it appears to have concealed crucial information from an unsuspecting public. Such *judicious* editing at prominent junctures of the assassination footage strongly hints at a conspiracy, with elements of the government directly involved. Although this conclusion stands on its own merits, a similar finding is supported by the Z-330–332 editing oversight (the sun flare), which by itself seems to destroy the notion of a single shooter.

Notes

1. Harold Weisberg, *Case Open* (New York: Carroll & Graf, 1994), p. 13. The official numbering of each frame of assassination footage was done by FBI Agent Lyndal L. Shaneyfelt, a laboratory agent.
2. This has been determined by co-author Schaeffer from timing experimental video footage taken by Dr. John Lattimer of head shots of human skulls filled with brain matter painted white. The entire explosion lasts slightly less than half a second. The rate of expansion and contraction of this event is practically the same. Because the human skull has an anatomical pressure cavity, the full effusion and vertical expulsion of brain matter could not reach apex within the bare confines of Z-312–313 as depicted in the Zapruder film.
3. In January of 1990, co-author Schaeffer observed Greer's remarkable head movement from back to front within six frames of the Zapruder film at Z-315–321. Using a real person to reenact this movement, he determined that the most realistic time to accomplish this feat would be one full second. Even if reasonable minds were to differ on the precise real time required, one-third of a second is physically impossible under any measure.
4. Harold Weisberg, *Whitewash II* (Hyattstown, MD: Harold Weisberg, 1966), FBI document dated 4 December 1963 by Robert M. Barrett, file no. DL 89-43, Appendix, p. 184.
5. The K-14 process is a complicated, reversal-type procedure created by Eastman Kodak laboratory. The Kodachrome film consists of three separate color layers placed on a support base. After the film is processed, each of the three layers

containing the colors cyan, magenta, and yellow change into a three-in-one color transparency positive film.

6. Harold Weisberg, *Photographic Whitewash* (Frederick, MD: Harold Weisberg, 1967 and 1976), FBI agent Switzer interview with Willis, dictated 19 June 1964, Appendix at pp. 181–183, esp. p. 182.

7. Co-author Schaeffer served a six-year, government-sponsored apprenticeship in film development through the auspices of the International Typographical Union in Colorado Springs, Colorado, from 1963 to 1969. He has ascertained the developing time for the Kodachrome film by extrapolating data provided in *Photo-Lab-Index* (Dobbs Ferry, NY: Morgan & Morgan). It is published yearly and the relevant data is the same in each publication.

8. Weisberg (1966), the FBI document dated 4 December 1963 by Robert M. Barrett in the Appendix at p. 184. It is co-author Schaeffer's opinion that a Bell & Howell model J made contact prints, instead of optical prints. It should be noted that an optical printer omits any photographic scenery in the sprocket hole area. A contact printer does not. [*Editor's note:* Noel Twyman has spoken with Bruce Jamieson, who has told him it was not done with an optical printer. See David Mantik, Part IV.]

9. See Enclosure 3. The editing and copying methodologies described therein show why the original and at least one copy were necessary. David S. Lifton, *Best Evidence* (New York: MacMillan, 1981, Carroll & Graf, 1988), pp. 555–557.

10. Enclosure 2 is a copy of the memo published in Josiah Thompson, *Six Seconds in Dallas* (1967), p. 311. Harold Weisberg, *Photographic Whitewash* (1967), p. 138, prints a copy that indistinctly indicates the date of "11/22".)

11. Philip H. Melanson, "Hidden Exposure: Cover-Up and Intrigue in the CIA's Secret Possession of the Zapruder Film", *The Third Decade* (November 1984), pp. 13–21.

12. Lifton reported that the process of reproducing an original and three prints of the reproduced Zapruder original would be expected to take about seven hours. He did not attempt to co-ordinate the times from known data at various process points as the authors of this article have done, nor did he consider any other sources as the co-authors have in order to arrive at this time frame.

13. Michael Benson, *Who's Who in the JFK Assassination* (New York: Carol Publishing Group, 1993), pp. 431–432. See the entry for Stolley, Richard B..

14. Oliver Stone and Zachary Sklar, *JFK: The Book Of The Film* (New York: Applause Books, 1992), pp. 410–412.

15. Co-author Schaeffer discovered this mark while examining a copy of the Zapruder film through a viewer device in early 1993. Schaeffer believes frames Z-141 and Z-028 were used to help align two scenes (Z-001 to Z-132 and Z-133 to Z-485.

16. At the ASK Symposium on the Assassination of JFK in April of 1993, researcher Robert Morningstar pointed out the emulsion removal mark during a debate with Robert Groden on "Gestalt Editing". Co-author Schaeffer believes it was used to help co-ordinate other films so that they appear to align with the Zapruder film.

17. Robert J. Groden, *The Killing of a President* (New York: Viking Penguin, 1993), p. 125.

18. Benson (1993), p. 426. See the entry for Secret Service Agent Sorrels, Forrest V.

19. Groden (1993), p. 19.
20. *The Warren Commission Report* (New York: McGraw-Hill, 1964), p. 87 and pp. 515–516; *The Warren Commission Report* (New York: St. Martin's Press, n.d.), p. 85 and pp. 557–558.
21. Neutron Activation Analyses were conducted for the Warren Commission and also for the HSCA inquiry. A useful summary may be found in Lifton (1980/88), pp. 556–559.
22. Testimony of Dr. Vincent Guinn, *HSCA* Vol. I, p. 504.

Argumentatively, the conclusion reached by Dr. Guinn as to the identification of these bullet fragments as being from the same bullet is debatable. During its own inquiry, the Warren Commission had found that the fragments could be identified as having been fired by the same rifle but not as fragments of the same bullet; see, for example, *The Warren Commission Report* (New York: St. Martin's Press, n.d.), p. 85 and pp. 557–558.

However, since there were *variations* in composition between the two fragments, the finding ought to have been that they were fragments of *different* bullets, as a number of authors have observed. See, e.g., Peter Model and Robert J. Groden, *JFK: The Case for Conspiracy* (New York: Manor Books, 1976), pp. 69–70 and p. 79.

Similarly, since Dr. Guinn reported observing highly atypical variations in the composition of 6.5 mm bullets manufactured by the Western Cartridge Company, the strongest inference he ought to have been able to reach under those conditions was that *no definite conclusion* could be drawn. Compare Robert J. Groden and Harrison E. Livingstone, *High Treason* (Baltimore, MD: The Conservatory Press, 1989), esp. pp. 200–201.

Gerald Posner, it may be worth noting, speciously concludes that: "This *lack of uniformity* among the Carcano bullets allowed him [Guinn] to match the fragments with a degree of certainty normally not available, even in a sophisticated test like neutron activation" [Gerald Posner, *Case Closed* (New York: Random House, 1993), p. 342]. (Emphasis added). This argument is specious for at least two reasons: firstly, the referenced bullets were 6.5 mm but not specifically *Carcano* bullets; and secondly, the "degree of certainty [that was] normally not available" in this case would have been "total uncertainty" due to the *hetero*geneity of the bullets (i.e., their *lack of uniformity*).

Regardless of the accuracy of the Guinn findings, two salient points are apparent. Firstly, no conclusion as to the heterogeneity or homogeneity of the bullets or fragments therefrom can alter the reality of two separate shots for the head shot and chrome strip shot. This is due to the lack of blood or brain tissue found on either of the two limousine front seat fragments and the clear presence of a sun flare at Z-330–332, a bare 17 frames after the head shot, and the lack of evidence of damage to the chrome strip in the Moorman film after the head shot but prior to the sun flare.

Secondly, regardless of the starting postulates assumed by the "lone gunman" advocates, they once again inexorably lead to contradictory and therefore non-sustainable results, Posner's aforementioned analysis being a primary case in point.

FEDERAL BUREAU OF INVESTIGATION

Date December 4, 1963

ABRAHAM ZAPRUDER, 3909 Marquette Street, Dallas, advised that on November 22, 1963, he was standing in the park area north of Elm Street and just west of the intersection of Elm and Houston Streets. He had taken this position in order to take 8 millimeter movie film of the President and the Presidential motorcade as it passed by him. He stated he had with him a Bell and Howell 8 millimeter zoom-lens camera, which was either a 1962 or 1963 model. He advised he had loaded this camera previously with a 25-foot roll of 16 millimeter film, which in effect affords 50 feet of 8 millimeter film. He had shot the first 25 feet earlier and had reversed the roll and shot a few feet on November 22, 1963, at the park area of some girls who work in his office, prior to the arrival of the Presidential motorcade. He stated his camera was fully wound, was set, (manually, on maximum zoom-lens). The camera was set to take normal speed movie film or 24 frames per second. The control buttons for the zoom-lens were not touched once he started taking photographs of the Presidential motorcade.

ZAPRUDER stated that he first picked up the motorcade as it made the turn on to Elm Street from Houston Street. The motorcade then passed behind a street directional sign and from that point on until it disappeared from sight to his right, or the west, he was taking moving pictures of the President's car. He stated he had started taking pictures prior to the first shot being fired and continued taking pictures until the motorcade disappeared to his right. ZAPRUDER advised he could not recall but having heard only two shots and, also, stated that he knew that from watching through the viewfinder that the President had been hit. He stated he took the exposed film immediately to the Jamieson Film Company on Bryan Street, Dallas, and stayed with the film through its entire processing. He had the original print and three copies made. The film was in color. The original is on 16 millimeter film, and according to Mr. ZAPRUDER is much clearer than those appearing on 8 millimeter film. He subsequently turned over two copies to the United States Secret Service and sold the original and one copy to Life Magazine.

Mr. ZAPRUDER turned over to Special Agent ROBERT M.

2

BARRETT his Bell and Howell 8 millimeter zoom-lens camera described above. He requested that the camera be returned to him after it had served its use to the FBI. He advised this camera had been in the hands of the United States Secret Service Agents on December 3, 1963, as they claimed they wanted to do some checking of it. He, also, stated he had received a call from the Bell and Howell Company who stated they wanted to place the camera in their archives and would replace the camera with a new one.

| on 12/4/63 | at Dallas, Texas | File # DL 89-43 |
| by Special Agent ROBERT M. BARRETT /gmf | | Date dictated 12/4/63 |

This document contains neither recommendations nor conclusions of the FBI. It is the property of the FBI and is loaned to your agency; it and its contents are not to be distributed outside your agency.

Enclosure 1. FBI Interview with Abraham Zapruder

9:55 p.m.

To :   Chief Rowley
From :   Max D. Phillips
Subject: 8mm movie film showing President
            Kennedy being shot

Enclosed is an 8mm movie film
taken by Mr. A. Zapruder, 501 Elm St, Dallas
Texas (RI 8-6771)

Mr Zapruder was photographing
the President at the instant he was shot.

According to M. Zapruder the position
the assassin was behind Mr Zapruder

Note: Disregard personal scenes
shown on Mr. Zapruder's film. Mr. Zapruder
is in custody of the "master" film. Two prints
were given to SAIC Sorrels, this date.
The third print is forwarded.

                             66

                 M. D. Phillips
                 Spec Agent – PRS

CD 87

Enclosure 2. Secret Service Memo of 22 November 1963

It should be made clear at this point that the camera used to
duplicate the Zapruder film was not a standard optical printer,
the camera used had special attachments especially equiped
to handle the duplication of the film. When duplicating the
film special care was taken when deleting the sprocket hole
area where dye marking were located. These marking are normally
placed on the film when made at a Kodak laboratory.

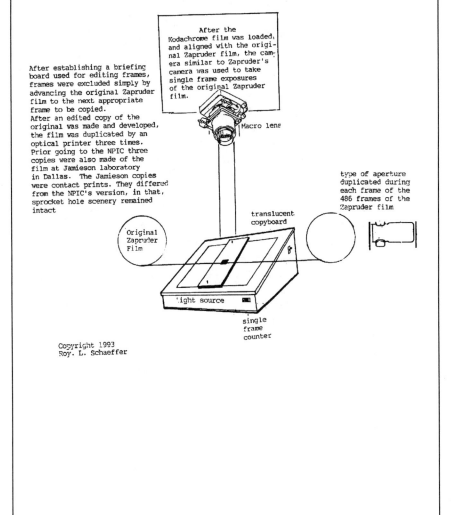

After the
Kodachrome film was loaded,
and aligned with the original Zapruder film, the camera similar to Zapruder's
camera was used to take
single frame exposures
of the original Zapruder
film.

After establishing a briefing
board used for editing frames,
frames were excluded simply by
advancing the original Zapruder
film to the next appropriate
frame to be copied.
After an edited copy of the
original was made and developed,
the film was duplicated by an
optical printer three times.
Prior going to the NPIC three
copies were also made of the
film at Jamieson laboratory
in Dallas. The Jamieson copies
were contact prints. They differed
from the NPIC's version, in that,
sprocket hole scenery remained
intact

Macro lens

type of aperture
duplicated during
each frame of the
486 frames of the
Zapruder film

translucent
copyboard

Original
Zapruder
Film

light source

single
frame
counter

Copyright 1993
Roy. L. Schaeffer

Enclosure 3. The Camera used to Duplicate the Zapruder Film

HOW THE PRESIDENTIAL LIMOUSINE EMERGENCY LIGHT BLINK RATE WAS
DETERMINED

Each emergency light on the Presidential Limousine was
calibrated to illuminate for .41 seconds as determined by measuring
the alternating emergency limousine blinking pattern seen in the
Robert Hughes film.

If the film speed of Zapruder's Bell & Howell camera was 18.3
frames per second, each light would remain on one side for 7.38
frames before transferring to the other side; if the speed of the
camera was about 24 frames per second, each light would remain on
one side for 9.8 frames of film before transferring. The limousine
light pattern was at a constant rate established by an electronic
flip-flop switch installed into the electrical circuitry.

If the film was not edited, each of the emergency lights would
blink at a constant rate and a consistent pattern would be indicated
by examining the appearance and location of the light pulses per
each individual frame.

Because Zapruder's camera only had two settings: 16 and 48 fps., and
the blink rate was more than seven continuous flashes per side, the film
in Zapruder's camera had to run at a faster setting than 18.3 fps.   By
closely examining the blink rate chart from Z-133-238 the altered film
appears to fluctuate between 12 to 24 fps.

Enclosure 4-A. How the Limousine Blink Rate was Determined

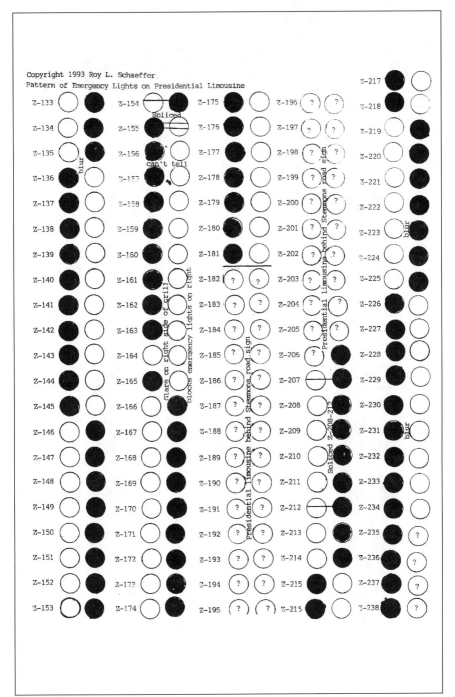

Enclosure 4-B. The Blink Light Pattern Observed on the Z-Film

If no editing was done to the Abraham Zapruder film this would be the actual pattern seen on the two emergency lights embedded on the front fender grill of the Presidential limousine during frames Z-133-Z-238. For eighteen frames the blinking pattern would be constant as seen in this diagram. The lights as seen below would be off for at least two frames, and on for about fourteen frames during a one second period, if the setting on Zapruder's camera was set at 18.3 frames per second. In 1967 the original emergency blinking lights were replaced with new ones. The emergency lights were moved to the front grill of the limousine. The new lighting system had a completely different blinking pattern from that of 1963.

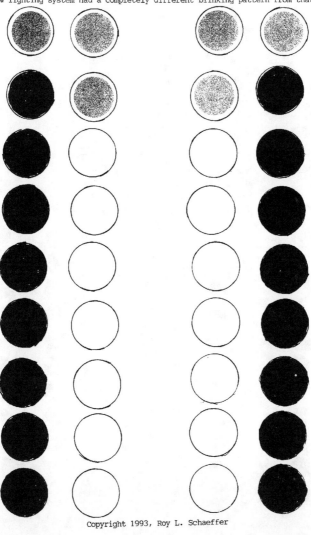

Enclosure 4-C. The Expected (Normal) Blink Rate Pattern

The Wounding of Governor John Connally

Ron Hepler

The Single "Magic" Bullet Theory continues to endure as the official version of the wounding of Governor John Connally. Many highly regarded critics of the Warren Commission, rightly dismiss the idea that one bullet wounded both men, but accept the general time frame of the Governor's wounding. But if the presence of a fact, or the lack of a necessary fact, makes a theory impossible, then that theory must be discarded and a new theory developed which includes all of the known facts. To date what has been occurring is rather to ignore the evidence that doesn't fit the existing theory. I would like to offer a different scenario of the wounding of Governor Connally—one that is observable on the Zapruder film, is backed up by numerous testimony, and is supported by scientific evidence.

When I first began studying this case I was attracted to the wounding of Governor Connally because little attention had been paid to it, yet it is central to the Single Bullet Theory. I had read about the Governor's Lapel Flap, shoulder drop, and puffed cheeks. While I recognized that the time separation between these events logically precluded that they were all the result of a single bullet strike, I had no reason to believe that the Governor had not been wounded during that time frame.

In this commonly accepted view, the Governor was wounded shortly after the throat shot to the President, but long before the fatal headshot. Yet, two thirds of all ear witnesses of three shots, including Secret Ser-

239

vice Agents William Greer and Roy Kellerman seated in the front of the limousine, tell a story diametrically opposed to this. These witnesses heard a single shot followed by a pause, then two shots in rapid succession.

The Connallys' Assessments

Governor Connally told the Warren Commission, "I was turning to look back over my left shoulder into the back seat, but I never got that far in my turn. I got about in the position I am in now facing you, looking a little bit to the left of center, and then I felt like someone had hit me in the back."[1] He elaborated to the House Select Committee on Assassinations (HSCA):

> so I was in the process of, at least I was turning to look over my left shoulder into the back seat to see if I could see him. I never looked, I never made the full turn. About the time I turned back where I was facing more or less straight ahead, the way the car was moving, I was hit. I was knocked over, just doubled over by the force of the bullet. It went in my back and came out my chest about 2 inches below and to the left of my right nipple. The force of the bullet drove my body over almost double and when I looked, immediately I could see I was just drenched with blood.[2]

This sequence of events where the Governor turns to the left just prior to being hit is also reported by Mr. S.M. Holland, who was standing on the triple overpass, in Mark Lane's documentary film, *Rush to Judgment: The Plot to Kill Kennedy*: "The first bullet, the President slumped over and Governor Connally made his turn to the right and then back to the left and that's when the second shot was fired and knocked him down to the floorboard."

Mrs. Nellie Connally supported her husband's description in her testimony to the House Select Committee:

> Mr. Dodd: "So, you are still looking at the President and it is your recollection that you then heard what sounded like a second shot?"
> Mrs. Connally: "Yes."
> Mr. Dodd: "Is that correct?"
> Mrs. Connally: "Yes. What was a second shot."
> Mr. Dodd: "At that point your husband, Governor Connally, slumped over in your direction?"
> Mrs. Connally: "No, he lunged forward and then just kind of collapsed."[3]

What the Governor, his wife, and Mr. Holland aptly describe is Newton's Law of Conservation of Momentum. It says that when an object in motion collides with a stationary one, all momentum will be conserved or, in other words, all momentum will be accountable after the collision. This conservation of momentum results in the deceleration of the bullet, accelerating the torso as the bullet penetrates the body impacting bones, and so forth.

Identifying the Impact

When I learned of these statements concerning the impact of the bullet, it was immediately apparent that such forward motion would pinpoint the time of the impact within one frame of the Zapruder film, so I decided to look for that motion. At frame 224, the time of the Lapel Flap there is no motion that matches the description given by the Governor. So I looked at Frame 236, the shoulder drop, surely if the bullet drove his shoulder down it would have driven him forward; but no. What about frame 238, the puffing of the cheeks? Still no forward motion. Rather than accept that the Governor was not yet wounded, most researchers choose to ignore the statements of the two people most intimate with the event, the wounded man and his wife who was seated next to him at the time of the shooting.

So I continued to let the VCR run in slow motion. During the headshot sequence I thought I saw the governor driven forward. I replayed the headshot sequence time after time at normal speed, in slow motion, and in single-frame step mode, often covering the President with my hand so as to be able to focus completely on the Governor without my eyes being drawn to the headshot.

That was it. The bullet obviously impacted him under the armpit at frame 315 as he attempted to raise himself from his wife's lap. The first evidence of motion is visible at frame 316. He is driven forward and hits the back of the front seat at frame 323. He immediately collapses just as Mrs. Connally had described in frame 326. A second violent motion is noticeable at about frame 338 when run at normal speed. This motion is most likely the impact of the wrist shot that then goes on to cause the thigh injury. Evidence of the Governor's wounding after the headshot was noted by Robert Groden in his book, *The Killing of a President*,[4] as Shot #6.

All indications are that the Governor was the victim of the last two shots of what was at least a four-shot volley aimed at the President's head. The first shot of this volley, at frame 312, was apparently only a tangential hit, gently shoving the President's head forward and possibly denting the windshield frame of the limo. The second shot from the grassy knoll at frame 313 was a solid impact, driving the President's head violently backward. With JFK's head deflected from its targeted location, the third shot sailed past at frame 315 and into the Governor's back shattering his fifth rib, rupturing his right lung and exiting out of his chest. The last shot, fired at about frame 338, impacts the Governor's wrist, shattering the radius bone with the remains coming to rest in his thigh. [*Editor's note:* For an alternative analysis, see David Mantik, Part IV.]

Shots occurring almost simultaneously, such as at frames 312, 313, and 315, would likely not be differentiated, but heard as a single shot and its echoes by witnesses, although some witnesses, including the Governor himself, apparently did hear them as automatic weapons' fire. Whereas, the late shot at frame 338 would certainly be differentiated and heard as a separate shot, thereby matching the reports of the majority of ear-witnesses. Co-ordinating the fire into such volleys is a logical strategy to hide additional shots as echoes.

Having determined that the Governor had been wounded immediately after the headshot to the President, what caused the Lapel Flap, Shoulder Drop, and Puffed Cheeks?

Nellie's Quick Reaction

A close analysis of the Zapruder film will reveal that Nellie Connally was the first to react defensively, by turning and pressing her back against the left side of the car. In frame 190 and the Willis Photo #5,[5] taken at about the same time, Nellie is still facing forward indicating that she had not yet recognized the threat; but in frame 240, she can be seen to be in this position with certainty. Her location as evidenced by her hair, which is essentially all that is visible, appears already fixed as early as frame 225. Considering that she cannot be seen to make a turn after exiting from behind the Stemmons Freeway sign, it is apparent that she had already assumed the position much earlier. Her testimony to the HSCA indicates that she made the turn while hidden from the camera by the Stemmons Freeway sign, "I just heard a disturbing noise and turned to my right from where I thought the noise had come and looked in the back and saw the President clutch his neck with both hands"[6].

While the Secret Service agents appear thoroughly confused, Nellie has analyzed the threat and is galvanized into action to pull her husband from the line of fire and down into her lap. She testified to the Warren Commission, "I just pulled him over into my arms";[7] and to the HSCA,

". . . the only thing I could think of to do was to pull him down out of the line of fire, or whatever was happening to us and I thought if I could get him down, maybe they wouldn't hurt him anymore. So, I pulled him down in my lap." Nellie's left hand can be seen grasping the Governor's left arm to pull him into her lap at frame 273.

The Lapel Flap

Gerald Posner, in his book, *Case Closed*,[8] wrongly described the fact that Governor Connally's lapel flapped up at about frame 224 as evidence of a bullet strike. For such a bullet to penetrate both men, as proposed in the Single Bullet Theory, the right to left trajectory through Connally would have to line up with JFK's neck and the weapon.

At frame 224, Connally is seated erect, relaxed with his torso facing forward. The trajectory of the bullet that entered under his right armpit and exited below his right nipple was measured by Dr. Robert Shaw, Governor Connally's attending physician, at an angle of 27 degrees relative to the forward facing torso.[9] If this trajectory were traced backwards at frame 224, the bullet would have passed several feet to Kennedy's right.

If the lapel flap is not the result of a bullet hit nor the result of wind, as some assume, the only logical cause of the lapel flap is Nellie pulling to the left on the back of her husband's suit coat in her attempt to ". . . pull him down out of the line of fire". Evidence of Mrs. Connally's effort is that the "V" of his lapel is no longer centered, but is moved to the right beginning with frame 223, then causing the lapel flap at frame 224.

The shoulder anchors the lapel at the top while the button anchors it at the bottom. A leftward tug on the back of the coat pulls all slack out of the fabric. As tension continues to increase, the middle of the lapel is able to move. This movement of the middle of the lapel fold causes the fold to flap open.

The Shoulder Drop

Governor Connally's shoulder can be seen to drop sharply at frame 236, while his torso remains essentially stationary. This movement was reported as evidence of a bullet hit by Dr. Cyril Wecht in his testimony to the HSCA.[10] Governor Connally was not hit in the upper arm or the shoulder, either of which could have driven the shoulder down, but instead he was wounded under the armpit. In addition, the trajectory through the body of 25 degrees downward, as measured by Dr. Shaw,[11] would have transferred the majority of its momentum in the forward direction instead of downward, as was noted by the Governor and his wife.

This shoulder motion could only have been the result of a downward pull on his right arm or coat sleeve by his wife in her attempt to extricate him from the line of fire. Since his torso was turned to face the right side of the car at this point in time, his right arm was within Nellie's reach. The fact that his right arm is not visible throughout this event is further indication that it was behind his back. During this time he rotates further around to the right as a result of Nellie pulling on his right arm/coat sleeve. Note that he remains in the same shoulder-down orientation through frame 261, over a second later. If he had been struck by a bullet the shoulder would have rebounded upward after ending its downward travel; instead, it is obviously being pulled down. Additional evidence of the pull on his right coat sleeve is that the collar and lapel of his coat are pulled toward his right shoulder.

The Puffed Cheeks

The puffing of Connally's cheeks, visible at frame 238, is believed by many to be evidence of the compressive effects of a bullet or rib fragments penetrating the lung. At well over 1,000 feet per second, the bullet rips through the chest cavity and the lung, opening them so that no pressure is retained. The puffing of cheeks would require a much slower building of pressure. This puffing of his cheeks may very well be due to abdominal muscular tensioning prior to his lung being ruptured. This is probably the result of being pulled off balance, backward, by his wife. Such abdominal muscular tensioning results in pressure upon the diaphragm. In most cases people hold their breath to add support to abdominal strain, thereby puffing the cheeks. The same condition occurs when exercising the abdominal muscles, such as with sit-ups.

Both attempts of tugging at his coat and arm are consistent with Nellie's final success in getting him into her lap; so too is the puffing of his cheeks as he resisted the backward pull.

Additional evidence that the Governor was not hit between frames 220 and 240, is the fact that he does not exhibit the effects of the impact of a bullet. A high-velocity bullet that destroys five inches of his fifth rib, parts of which practically explode out of his chest, would cause severe pain. It was described to the Warren Commission by Dr. Shaw as ". . . both a shocking and painful wound".[12] The pain would be evident as a grimace of agony on his face. It is *not*! His facial expression is one of being startled and confused. Shortly thereafter, as he is falling into his wife's lap, he can be seen watching the President with interest, an activity that he later denies. This obvious concern for the well-being of another, visible in frame 273, is not the action of a severely wounded man.

Trajectory of the Back Wound

Importantly, while raising himself and turning left, his torso was leaned over toward Nellie from the seat that he originally occupied. This left-leaning angle of the torso, relative to the normal vertical posture, rotates the bullet's apparent trajectory clockwise. With this rotation, the downward angle of the shot gives the erroneous appearance of a more right-to-left trajectory through the body, which of course is exactly what we see with his wounds.

A photo of the limousine taken at Parkland Hospital[13] has evidence of the emergence of this bullet. There is a severe dent in the lower left corner of the chrome panel surrounding the ashtray in the back of the front seat. This final impact before falling to the floor of the car, would be consistent with the trajectory described earlier as well as bullet fragments retrieved from the vehicle.

The Governor Cries Out

According to the Warren Commission Report, "Observing his blood covered chest as he was pulled into his wife's lap, Governor Connally believed himself mortally wounded. He cried out, 'Oh, no, no, no. My God, they are going to kill us all'."[14] It is quite evident on the Zapruder film that he was *not* yet covered with blood when he was pulled into Nellie's lap as is obvious in frame 273; and this sequence of events is not supported by the Connallys' testimony to the HSCA, as noted earlier. But, he does appear to be mouthing these words during this period.

While it makes perfect sense for him to make such an exclamation after hearing the first shot and prior to being wounded himself, it is ludicrous to expect this of a man who had "a sucking wound of the chest". This description of his chest wound and ruptured lung was given to the Warren Commission by Dr. Shaw as, ". . . he had what we call a sucking wound of the chest. This would not allow him to breathe."[15] The "sucking wound of the chest" allows air to be inhaled and exhaled via the wound, rather than through the windpipe or larynx. This inability to breathe would essentially eliminate any significant amount of air across the larynx, precluding his crying out.

Nellie supports the timing issue with her testimony to the Warren Commission: ". . . As the first shot was hit, and I turned to look at the same time, I recall John saying, 'Oh, no, no, no.' Then there was a second shot, and it hit John . . .".[16] She reinforced the timing with her statement to the HSCA: ". . . John had turned to his right also when we heard that first noise and shouted, `no, no, no,' and in the process of turning back around so that he could look back and see the President—I don't think he could see him when he turned to his right—the second shot was fired and hit him."[17] The Governor's statement to the HSCA indicates that he was having trouble keeping his story straight, "When I was hit, or shortly before I was hit—no, I guess it was after I was hit—I said first, just almost in despair, I said, "no, no, no, . . .". [18] This Freudian slip indicates that he actually made the statement before he was wounded, but that did not fit the official story and had to be altered.

The Last Shot

The last shot, apparently a belated final round of the four-shot volley, struck Connally in the wrist and thigh at about frame 338 as he lay across the car. He can be seen to make a violent movement immediately after frame 338, which is evidence of the bullet's impact. Timing for this shot is supported by data developed during the acoustic analysis of the Dallas Police radio tape, as well as data on the camera motion analysis of the Zapruder film by W. K. Hartman, and Frank Scott separately for the HSCA. [19] This bullet's trajectory, if extended back through the approximate location of JFK's head, would most likely originate from the roof of the Dallas County Records Building, where a spent 30.06 cartridge was found in 1975 by an air-conditioner repairman.[20]

Summary

Contrary to popular belief, Governor Connally does not appear to have been wounded until *after* the fatal headshot to the President. Several strange occurrences, such as the lapel flap, the shoulder drop, and the puffed cheeks that have been ascribed to be the result of bullet hits, actually were due to Nellie's continued and eventually successful efforts to pull her husband down into her lap and out of the line of fire. The key to determining the actual timing of the Governor's wounding is the transfer of the bullet's momentum to the torso as it impacts the rib bone. This momentum transfer is visible immediately after the headshot to the President. Both bullets that wounded the Governor were part of a final volley that probably included four shots in a little over one second.

Democracy was Defeated in the Election of 1963

Notes

1. Robert J. Groden and Harrison Edward Livingstone, *High Treason* (New York: Berkley Book, 1990), pp. 272–273.
2. *The Report of the Select Committee on Assassinations*, U.S. House of Representatives; Vol. 1, p. 42.
3. *The Report of the Select Committee on Assassinations*, U.S. House of Representatives; Vol. 1, p. 52.
4. Robert J. Groden, *The Killing of a President* (New York: Penguin Books, 1993) p. 37.
5. Robert J. Groden, *The Killing of a President* (New York: Penguin Books, 1993) p. 24.
6. *The Report of the Select Committee on Assassinations*, U.S. House of Representatives; Vol. I, p. 40.
7. *The Warren Commission Hearings and Exhibits* 4H147.
8. Gerald Posner, *Case Closed*, (New York: Random House, 1993), pp. 329–30.
9. *The Warren Commission Hearings and Exhibits* 4H138.
10. *The Report of the Select Committee on Assassinations*, U.S. House of Representatives; Vol. 1. p. 343.
11. *The Warren Commission Hearings and Exhibits* 4H138.
12. *The Warren Commission Hearings and Exhibits* 4H132.
13. Robert J. Groden, *The Killing of a President* (New York: Penguin Books, 1993), p. 70.
14. *The Warren Commission Report* (1964) p. 50.
15. *The Warren Commission Hearings and Exhibits* 4H139.
16. *The Warren Commission Hearings and Exhibits* 4H147.
17. *The Report of the Select Committee on Assassinations*, U.S. House of Representatives; Vol. I, p. 40.
18. *The Report of the Select Committee on Assassinations*, U.S. House of Representatives; Vol. I.
19. *The Report of the Select Committee on Assassinations*, U.S. House of Representatives; Vol. VI, p. 26.
20. Jim Marrs, *Crossfire: The Plot that Killed Kennedy* (New York: Carrol & Graf Publishers 1989), pp. 308–09.

PHOTOGRAPH FROM RE-ENACTMENT

DISTANCE TO STATION C .... 153.8 FT.

DISTANCE TO RIFLE IN WINDOW .... 190.8 FT.

ANGLE TO RIFLE IN WINDOW .... 20°11'

DISTANCE TO OVERPASS .... 334.0 FT.

ANGLE TO OVERPASS .... +0°26'

FRAME 225

PHOTOGRAPH FROM ZAPRUDER FILM

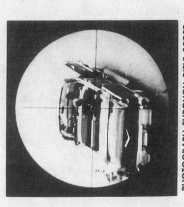

PHOTOGRAPH THROUGH RIFLE SCOPE

Commision Exhibit No. 895

The JFK Assassination Re-enactment:

Questioning the Warren Commission's Evidence

Chuck Marler

On 24 May 1964, in Dealey Plaza, attorneys for the Warren Commission and agents of the FBI and Secret Service conducted a re-enactment of the assassination of President Kennedy. The purpose of this re-enactment was similar to other murder investigations—to obtain precise measurements of the crime scene and determine bullet trajectories. Based upon these findings, they would reconstruct the sequence of events that ultimately became the foundation of evidence in determining if it was possible for the accused suspect, Lee Harvey Oswald, to have committed that crime. Typically, most crime reconstructions are based upon very limited information about the murder. The location of the victim and facts about the body gained from forensic medicine are usually all that is known prior to revisiting the crime scene for further analysis.

Six months prior to this particular re-enactment, however, the Warren Commission had a substantial amount of evidence about the assassination, which included three home movies of the murder, over one hundred eye witnesses accounts, and dozens of photographs of this crime while in progress. The pivotal group of individuals who conducted the re-enactment had previously spent over seven full days in various study sessions analyzing the films and photographs. This group included Arlen Specter, Norman Redlich, and Melvin Eisenberg from the Warren Commission, Thomas Kelley and John Howlett from the Secret Service, and Leo Gauthier, James Malley, and Lyndal Shaneyfelt from the FBI.[1] Armed with this wealth of information, the re-enactment was conducted on 24 May 1964, and later served as source material for the Warren Commission to make several critical determinations: 1) when President Kennedy as well as Governor Connally were hit by bullets; 2) the exact location of the limousine when the occupants were struck; 3) the trajectories from the sixth floor window; 4) the Zapruder frames in which the oak tree obstructed the view of the motorcade from the sixth floor window, and 5) the speed of the limousine as it traveled down Elm Street.

Recent analysis of existing Warren Commission exhibits, along with the discovery of new documents, now establishes a clear and convincing case that the survey measurements made for the Warren Commission by Robert H. West, Dallas County Surveyor, were altered, the 24 May 1964, re-enactment was orchestrated by Arlen Specter to insure his single bullet theory would not be contradicted, and the Zapruder film was altered to conceal footage that would have proved President Kennedy was struck by multiple assassins. Initial evidence of the crime scene and the shooting sequences as established by the Zapruder film produced a different version of the assassination than depicted in the Warren Commission's final report. To understand what occurred , it is necessary to study the evidence and exhibits that had been produced prior to 24 May 1964.

The first survey plat of Dealey Plaza was made by Robert H. West, Dallas County Surveyor, on 26 November 1963, just four days after the assassination. The survey was made for Time-Life, the new owners of the Zapruder film, and was never introduced as a Warren Commission exhibit.[2] The second survey and first government re-enactment was actually conducted by the Secret Service just two weeks after the assassination on 5 December 1963. Utilizing again the services of Robert H. West, the Secret Service took photographs from the sixth floor window of the Texas School Book Depository that tracked the movement of a white Lincoln convertible at various intervals on both Houston and Elm Street. A survey plat of Elm Street along with data from the re-enactment was introduced as Warren Commission Exhibit 585. It is during the re-enactment that Charles Breneman, who assisted Mr. West, was quoted in a 1978 newspaper as saying that he "saw three frames of the Zapruder film which showed large blobs of blood and brain matter flying from Kennedy's head to the *rear* of the car."[3] In the version of the Zapruder film printed in the Warren Commission exhibits, no blobs of brain and blood are seen flying to the rear.

The second government re-enactment in Dealey Plaza was conducted by the Warren Commission on 24 May 1964, approximately six months after the assassination, and once again used the survey expertise of Robert West. A survey plat of Elm Street from this re-enactment was introduced as Commission Exhibit 883. There are, however, significant differences between these two exhibits depicting the crime scene in Dallas. To understand the differences between the two, it is important to remember that when the Secret Service survey was made on 5 December 1963, the Warren Commission was meeting for their first time.[4] As of that date Arlen Specter, the Commission lawyer handling this area of the investigation, had not yet developed the "single bullet theory" necessary for any lone gunman explanation.

A professional survey requires being as exact as is humanly possible. An essential aid in understanding any survey is the explanation of the scale, legends and symbols that are used to produce it. The 5 December 1963 survey (CE–585) is a typical engineering drawing, with a border, the usual title block in the lower right-hand corner, a legend (which explains the symbols used), and a properly signed certification as to the authenticity of the information shown on the drawing.[5] On 30 March 1964, this plat was introduced as Warren Commission Exhibit 585 during the testimony of a Mr. Simmons, who used it in placing targets for rifle tests. Commission Counsel Melvin Eisenberg introduced it with this strange *non-sequitur*: "solely to show the basis which Mr. Simmons was using in his test, and *not for the truth of the measurements* which are shown here."[6] The introduction of the May 1964 survey re-enactment, CE–882, however, received more respect from the Warren Commission lawyers. This survey plat, again made by Dallas Surveyor Robert West, came wrapped and sealed in a container—one which was *never* opened and to date has never been released to the public. It was Commission Counsel Arlen Specter who asked Chairman Earl Warren that the seal not be broken and the plat not be taken out of its container. Mr. Specter instead introduced what was represented as a cardboard reproduction of Mr. West's survey as CE–883. Specter also introduced as CE–884, a tabulation of elevations and angles for selected Zapruder film frames which Specter stated were also contained on the sealed survey map.[7] The 24 May 1964 plat (CE–883), which the Commission relied upon for the truth of the measurements for their re-enactment, is unlike the other survey prepared by Mr. West: it is uncomposed, has no border, no title, no title block, no legend, and no certification.[8] In order to adequately study these exhibits it may be necessary to make enlargements since the plats were reduced in size to less than a half-page photo in Volume 17 of the Commission's hearings. The reason why the only precise measurements of the crime scene are so difficult to identify—and used so sparingly—will soon become obvious.

Yet another difference between these two plats is the location of the three rifle shots. The December 5th survey (CE–585) shows three "X" markings on Elm Street—ones that correspond to President Kennedy's location at Zapruder frames 208, 276, and 358. The three X's represent the locations of the three rifle shots (as verified by lower drawing of the trajectories from the depository building) and is contrary to the Warren Report which concluded one shot missed the limousine and its occupants.[9] The location of the X's also raises questions as to what reference points were used for their location on Elm Street. Certainly a copy of the Zapruder film would also have been available to the Secret Service from its owner, Time-Life. The "X" furthermost west on Elm Street would place the last shot in front of the concrete steps where eyewitness Emmett Hudson stood (calculation based upon reference to pairs of traffic lines on Elm Street and measurement of 294 feet from depository window). This would place the last shot significantly west of the location at Z-frame 313 that was established as the last shot in the May 1964 re-enactment. Two other Commission exhibits also refer to the last rifle shot much further west than Z-frame 313. The location of the "X" on the far left in the December 5th survey is next to an Elm Street "5+00" identification on the survey plat. An examination of Commission Exhibit 875, which refers to the December 1963 re-enactment, states "no picture was taken at 5+00 mark as this was about 4 feet from impact of the third shot."[10] The "5+00" mark is approximately 35 feet west of Kennedy's position at Z-frame 313. Additionally, CE–2111, a memorandum dated 13 February 1964, from Secret Service Agent Sorrels in Dallas, stated "This concrete slab and manhole cover is located on the south side of Elm Street almost *opposite* to where the President's car was located when the last shot that killed President Kennedy was fired."[11] The concrete manhole cover is located over seventy feet from the limousine's position at Z-frame 313. At the bottom of the December 5th survey (CE–585) is a note "Revised 2-7-64" which indicates at least as late as February 1964 that the last shot was still fixed near the concrete steps. It is also interesting to note that in Emmett Hudson's testimony to the Warren Commission he was sure the *second* shot hit Kennedy in the head. After the second shot, a young man standing next to Hudson repeatedly told him "to lay down, they're shooting the President." While Hudson was "close to the ground" he heard a third shot fired when the limousine was "about even with those steps."[12] The Mary Moorman photo shows that Mr. Hudson was still standing when Kennedy was struck in the head at approximately Z-frame 313. James Chaney, the motorcycle officer to the immediate right of the limousine, also stated in a radio interview at Parkland Hospital that the "*second* shot struck Kennedy in the face."[13]

Another significant discrepancy is the number of pairs of traffic lines on Elm Street between the intersection with Houston Street and the triple underpass. The first plat made by West (CE–585) has thirteen pairs of traffic lines, while the May 1964 plat shows twelve. The length of the traffic lines also differ. The lines in the December 1963 survey are all fifteen feet in length with an interval of twenty to twenty-four feet between each pair. The lines in the May 1964 vary in length from fifteen to twenty feet with an interval ranging from fifteen to twenty-six feet (as the May 1964 survey does not provide a scale, one can create his own using the forty feet width of Elm Street). The difference in traffic stripes in the May 1964 survey places the fifth pair of lines further west on Elm Street than the earlier survey. The fifth pair of lines are critical clues since the uncropped photograph taken by Associated Press photographer James Altgens clearly identifies the location of the limousine on Elm Street with its left front tire aligned with the fifth traffic line.[14] As Altgens' photograph was correlated with Zapruder frame 255, the fifth pair of traffic lines are an important crime scene reference. If the location of these lines in the May 1964 survey (CE–883) are in error and placed too far west (downhill) on Elm Street, then all other prior Zapruder frame references would have been affected. This issue is of extreme importance when determining the Zapruder frames in which the oak tree blocked an assassin's view of the motorcade from the sixth floor window.

When one studies the FBI re-enactment of Altgens' photograph in CE–900 the only matching alignments in the photographs is the accurate location of the vehicle's left front tire on the fifth traffic line. In the 24 May 1964, re-enactment photographs: the Secret Service stand-in is further west than Roy Kellerman—who is directly aligned with the edge of the concrete column, the Presidential stand-in is further west than President Kennedy—whose left hand aligns with the edge of the concrete column, and the tree limb blocks out the letter "O" in "Depository"—whereas the "O" is almost fully visible in the re-enactment. Additionally, the vertical alignment of the vehicle's left *rear* tire with landmarks on the depository building demonstrate how far off the re-enactment was from the true location of the limousine in Altgens' photograph. The alignment problem could not be corrected by moving the photographer west (left) without causing the camera's view to switch to one of looking directly into the front of the re-enactment vehicle which already depicts less of its side than the limousine in the Altgens' photo. It is therefore obvious that the re-enactment vehicle is too far west and needs to be backed up approximately seven to eight feet. However, if that move was made, the front left tire would no longer align with the fifth traffic line.

The credibility of the 24 May 1964, re-enactment is rendered further suspect by an examination of the field survey notes retained by Dallas County Surveyor, Robert H. West, which were used to construct the survey plat of Elm Street (introduced to the Warren Commission by Arlen Specter in the sealed container and never opened). Based upon the meticulous work and analysis of assassination researcher Tom Purvis, who has been corresponding with Robert West since 1991, the level of government deceit can now be understood. This is not the first time Mr. West and surveyor, Chester Breneman, have raised questions about the validity of the survey. Both have been quoted as being astounded that the published figures did not match theirs or the figures taken in the 1964 re-enactment.[15] Mr. Purvis, however, has obtained copies of Mr. West's field survey notes and using his Army training in survey combined with close scrutiny of the re-enactment exhibits, has brought new insights to this issue. The survey notes of Robert West that warrant particular study include:

a. Calculations regarding the size and height of the Stemmons freeway sign that blocked Zapruder's view in his film. Request for this information was made on 16 March 1964, by Special Agent John Howlett of the U.S. Secret Service, Dallas office.

b. Calculations of the elevation of the concrete pillar (430.8 feet) on which Mr. Zapruder stood to film the assassination and also the elevations for the concrete steps and wing to the left of Zapruder. Both calculations were made and furnished to the Secret Service two months before the May 1964 re-enactment.

c. Field notes made during the 24 May 1964, re-enactment in which the position of the President's head is spotted on Elm Street coincident with fourteen frames from the Zapruder film. Data from these notes were included in CE–884 as were re-enactment photographs depicting measurements from fixed points, CE–888 through CE–902.

Comparing Mr. West's field notes with CE–884 will prove significant alterations were made. CE–884 is a data block containing Zapruder film frame numbers, elevations, and distances from the re-enactment. It was drawn on the survey plat (CE–883) but apparently was introduced as a separate exhibit due to the difficulty in reading it. When one examines Mr. West's field notes of the fourteen Zapruder frame locations, there are no measurements made for frames 161, 166, and 210 as contained in the data block. However, Mr. West did make measurements for frames 168, 171, and 208, which are not included in CE–884. The distances and elevations he made for these frames have been used for frames 161, 166, and 210 respectively. A closer examination of the lettering of the frame numbers for 161, 166, and 210 in CE–884 indicates numbers that are not consistent with the others. The "1" in 16*1* is not consistent with other "1's"; the "6's" in 166 are not consistent with the shapes of the other "6's", and the "0" in 210 is also inconsistent with other zeros. The fact that Mr. West's data block has been altered with different frame numbers is further corroborated by an enlargement of the original survey plat which indicate that frames 168, 171, and 208 were entered on Elm Street and not the ones that appear in the data block (CE–884). In an interview I conducted with Mr. West, he indicated he was not given the opportunity to look at photographs from the Zapruder film to substantiate President Kennedy's location on Elm Street at designated Zapruder frames. He was merely told that specific locations represented Zapruder frame numbers and to make the necessary measurements. Mr. West told me he was astonished that his May 1964 survey plat was introduced in a sealed container and commented on the altered data block that "whoever changed my numbers didn't even use a Leroy pen (a lettering guide) but did it freehand."[16]

It is difficult to speculate precisely why these exhibits were altered, but is noteworthy that the frames 208-211, not published in the Warren Commission exhibits, are frames these re-enactments focused on. The consequence of the alteration caused the first two frames of the Z film to be positioned further west on Elm street while Z-frame 210 was moved slightly to the east. Using the measurements for the distance the limousine traveled from CE–888 through CE–902, a calculation of speed between frames 168 to 171 indicates the vehicle traveled 3.7 miles per hour but 28.7 miles per hour between frame 207 and 208. Altering Z-frames 208 to 210 would reduce the 28.7 mph to 9.6. However, the speed calculation between the altered numbers on Z-frames 161 to 166 is just 2.2 mph. These calculations demonstrate how erroneous the Warren Commission re-enactment was, as neither the original nor the altered data for Z-frame references are consistent with the speed of the limousine during these sequences.

The alteration of this data block raises further questions as to what other information may have been changed but still undetected today. The third column on CE–884 lists the calculations of the elevation of President Kennedy's head at the specified Zapruder frames. When these figures are juxtaposed with the elevations of the pavement on Elm Street, it yields an average height of forty inches. The top of President Kennedy's head was established by the Secret Service to be 52.8 inches above the Elm Street pavement.[17] Why would the elevations of Kennedy's head in CE–884 be understated by over one foot? Why was the elevation of the structure upon which Mr. Zapruder stood taken along with elevations of the lower steps in March 1964? Why weren't these figures included on the survey plats? What possible evidentiary relevance would the lower steps next to Zapruder have? All of this points towards the obvious question: were these measurements made two months before conducting the re-enactment to help stage a phony one?

Substituting the more accurate difference of 52.8 inches for the distance from Kennedy's head to the street, the corrected elevation at Zapruder frame 222 would be 427.0 feet. Based upon West's survey notes the elevation of the concrete structure that Zapruder stood on was 430.8 feet and the top of the Stemmons freeway sign was 431.42 feet.[18] Using a height of 5'10" for Abraham Zapruder the camera would be held at eye level of 5.25 feet above the elevation of the concrete structure for a total camera elevation of 436.05 feet. At frame 222 the Stemmons sign was approximately 54.5 feet from Zapruder and 55.5 feet from President Kennedy's position. Based upon these measurements and using the corrected 52.8 inches elevation of Kennedy's head from Elm Street, Abraham Zapruder should have been able to film President Kennedy's head (as well as his neck area) above the Stemmons Freeway sign throughout the entire sign obstruction sequence (including Z-frame 222). A close examination of Zapruder's Warren Commission testimony gives indications that he saw more of President Kennedy than is currently visible in the Commission's version of his film. Testifying on July 22, 1964, Mr. Zapruder stated "I heard the first shot and I saw the President lean over and grab himself like this (holding his left chest area)...in other words, he was sitting like this and waving and then after the shot he just went like that." Later as Commission Counsel Liebeler reminds Zapruder that there was a sign that was in the film, Zapruder responds, "Yes, there were signs there also and trees and somehow—I told them I was going to get the whole view and I must have."[19]

Is it possible that the Zapruder film was altered to increase the height of the Stemmons sign to conceal President Kennedy's reactions when struck by the first bullet? The discovery that the Zapruder film was at the CIA's National Photo Interpretation Center (one of the most sophisticated photo labs in the world)[20] may take on additional significance. Did the re-enactment personnel photograph the Zapruder film re-enactments from a lower elevation (concrete steps next to the structure where

Zapruder stood) in order to make the sign block more of the background images? These questions may at first appear as wild and unfounded speculation; however, the re-enactment photographs—allegedly taken from Zapruder's position—do little to give confidence that this did not occur.

The photographs in CE–894 compare the Zapruder frame 222 with the Warren Commission's re-enactment photograph. According to the Secret Service, the Presidential stand-in was 62 inches from the ground (due to a different vehicle being used).[21] The stand-in should have been even more visible above the Stemmons sign based upon the above elevations. Furthermore, in the re-enactment photo there is a considerable amount of space between the concrete wall and the branches of the tree in the background—whereas the Zapruder frame shows that the tree leaves are even with the wall. Is this difference due to a lower camera elevation than Zapruder's or to an absence of wind blowing on the tree limbs during that morning's re-enactment? In another comparison between Zapruder frames 166 and 185 (CE–889 and CE–890), Zapruder has panned his camera left to right to follow the limousine down Elm Street. More of the Stemmons sign is visible in frame 185 and the concrete wall, with the two rows of square openings on the far right, can be seen. In the government's re-enactment of frame 166 and 185 the freeway sign is less visible in 185 and the number of square holes in the concrete wall that are visible has been reduced from seven to five and a half. Additionally, more of the building in the far background at the upper left edge is visible. In frame 185 the photograph also captures more background height. The windows on the building in the background, as well as the freeway signs over the traffic light, are clearly more visible. Is this perspective the result of a lower elevation or the camera being inadvertently tilted up and to the left?

While camera angles may be subject to debate, one of the most obvious observations about the 24 May 1964, re-enactment is that the Presidential limousine was not used. In fact there was not one photographic exhibit from the Warren Commission where the limousine was used. In the 5 December 1963 re-enactment, the Secret Service used a white Lincoln convertible which differed considerably from the dimensions and configuration of the actual vehicle Kennedy was slain in. The photograph in CE–875 shows the vehicle as it clears the oak tree. In this exhibit it would appear that the bullet trajectory going through the Kennedy stand-in would have missed the person directly in front of him—let alone be able to strike him near his *right* armpit area. This photograph was made before Arlen Specter invented the "single bullet theory" explanation. The Secret Service vehicle, dubbed the Queen Mary, was used in all subsequent re-enactments due to its continuous bench style seat that allowed a wide latitude for the Connally stand-in to be positioned. The jump seats in the Presidential limousine were not bench style seats and would make this positioning more difficult. The photograph made of frame 210 in the May 1964 re-enactment shows the Connally stand-in sitting significantly to his left in the "Queen Mary" vehicle to align with a plausible single bullet explanation. Had the Presidential limousine been used, the Connally stand-in would have been balancing his weight on the corner of his right buttock. Arlen Specter's single bullet theory re-enactment was equally insulting. His Connally stand-in is leaning to the right and slumping in a position Connally assumed in Zapruder frame 240 (well after he was hit). The rod Mr. Specter is holding doesn't align with the wound locations and demonstrates a left to right trajectory—even though a trajectory from the Texas School Book Depository would have been right to left. These recreations are so far removed from the truth that they make a mockery out of the entire investigation.

One of the most compelling arguments for alteration of evidence is the recent discovery that at Zapruder frames 302 to 303 and again at frame 316 to 317, the driver of the Presidential limousine, William Greer, has turned his head approximately 100 degrees in one frame or .05 seconds. In attempts to duplicate Mr. Greer's accomplishment, the fastest head turn took four frames or .22 second.[22] The experiment also showed that the farthest the head could turn in one frame after it was already in motion was 47 degrees. The obvious and inescapable conclusion is either that the 54-year-old William Greer was a cyborg with a bionic neck capable of moving his head three times faster than any human being or that frames have been intentionally deleted from the Zapruder film.

The distinct possibility that there was a final shot, one which struck the President *after* Zapruder frame 313, has been once again raised by: studying the precise measurements in the 5 December 1963, survey plat, reexamining the testimony of Emmett Hudson, comparing the reference in CE–875 that the third shot struck at the "5+00" mark (which was west of Z-313), and looking at CE-2111 which stated the limousine was opposite the manhole cover at the final shot (the manhole cover is west of 313). Secret Service Agent Clint Hill also testified he heard the sound of a shot "just about as I reached it (the limousine.)"[23] It is very possible that a double hit to Kennedy's head occurred with the first shot driving him forward and the second shot causing him to fall backward. This sequence would explain why Kennedy's head moves forward at frame 314 and suddenly reverses itself at frame 315. Of course frames 316 to 317 is the suspicious area where the driver makes a 140-degree head-turn in one frame and is the area where the Muchmore film has also been damaged or spliced. Perhaps this is why the three witnesses closest to the area of the double head shot, Emmett Hudson, James Altgens, and Abraham Zapruder, did not testify until 22 July 1964, when the Commission was finalizing the final report.[24] James Altgens' precise location on Elm Street is also a critical issue. Mr. Altgens testified that he was prepared to make a picture at the very instant the President was shot. He had prefocused his camera to 15 feet focal length because he wanted a good close-up. Altgens was certain Kennedy was fifteen feet away from him and had his camera almost up to his eye when the President was struck.[25] As the limousine was in the center lane on Elm Street, a fifteen foot distance placed the last shot directly in front of him. Altgens' position can clearly be seen in the Zapruder frame 349 significantly west of Jean Hill/Mary Moorman and the limousine's position at frame 313. Altgens was standing just east of the concrete steps and his statements support the testimony of Emmett Hudson who said the last shot hit Kennedy "in front of those steps." Hudson's testimony corroborates Altgens' position when he describes a man with a camera across Elm Street and shooting pictures "up toward those steps."[26] A final shot occurring in this area may be why Zapruder frames past frame 334 were not printed in the Warren Commission exhibits.

It is also clear that there were many surveys performed prior to the 24 May 1964, re-enactment. The first survey plat made by Robert West occurred just four days after the assassination on 26 November 1963, for Time-Life—the owners of the Zapruder film (perhaps the Assassination Records Review Board should petition Time-Life to release the survey as an assassination record). The next survey was performed for the Secret Service on 5 December 1963. According to Thomas Kelley, Inspector for Secret Service "we took some photographs of the assassination on 5 December 1963 from the window of the Texas School Book Depository, and from the *street*"[27] Why weren't the photographs made from the street, perhaps from Zapruder's perspective, published in the Warren Commission exhibits in order to be compared with those made on 24 May 1964? Why were the photos made from the depository window the only ones included in CE–875?

Finally, as seen from the evidence presented, the re-enactment on 24 May 1964, is flawed. Vehicles were not aligned with the precise locations established in evidentiary photographs. Survey measurements made by Robert West were altered to conform to other Zapruder film landmarks. Questions also still remain today about the true location of the Stemmons freeway sign. In 1965, the Stemmons sign was removed from Dealey Plaza altogether.[28] The disturbing testimony made by Emmett Hudson on 22 July 1964, that "they have moved some of those signs"[29] gives credence to the argument that any movement of signs could have occurred *after* the measurements of the sign were made on 16 March 1964, and before the May 1964 re-enactment. Mr. Hudson was the groundskeeper for Dealey Plaza and would be very familiar with the physical structures of Dealey Plaza—more so than any other person. He made this statement as a factual observation without attaching any significance to it.

This deception of the American public by the May 1964 re-enactment appears to have been engineered by a small number of individuals. In the sixth floor window of the school depository, manning the master radio control unit for the re-enactment personnel, was none other than Arlen Specter.[30] It is difficult to understand why Specter used the sixth floor window as the control unit for the re-enactment when all photographic evidence to conduct a precise re-enactment was made from the street. It is also apparent that while he was up there, Specter didn't correct the Connally stand-in position to coincide with his own single bullet theory re-enactment as illustrated in CE–903. Arlen Specter, who with a sleight of hand introduced altered evidence (CE–883 and CE–884) and concealed the original survey plat, should be tried for obstruction of justice at the very least. Instead Senator Specter, who was the Senate's top recipient of special interest campaign contributions for 1992 elections[31], had the temerity to announce in November 1994 his unofficial candidacy to become the Republican nominee for President in 1996.

Hopefully, this article provides new research information and raises questions about the assumptions that have been made about the accuracy of the crime scene data used by the Warren Commission. Without all the pieces of the puzzle, it is difficult to state with any degree of certainty precisely how the 35th President of the United States was murdered. But, it is becoming more and more conspicuous that governmental evidence has been obscured, concealed, or altered.

Notes

As the JFK Assassination Records Review Board begins its important work, researchers should not lose sight of the many documents that have already been made public over the years—ones that clearly demonstrate a concealment of the truth regarding the assassination of President Kennedy. We must not allow the release of sealed records to become an endless paper chase that continuously postpones efforts to appoint a special prosecutor. Justice delayed is justice denied. The work of a prosecutor will take many years to complete and can parallel efforts to release all related files.

As a final note, a special note of appreciation is expressed to Mr. Thomas Purvis for providing documents, Warren Commission references, and sharing his analysis and research for this article. Without his contribution, this article would not have been possible.

[1]   *Hearings Before the President's Commission on the Assassination of President John F. Kennedy*, Vol 5, p. 141. (References to this source cited hereafter in format: 5H141).

[2]   Jim Marrs, *Crossfire: The Plot That Killed Kennedy* (Carroll & Graft, 1989) p. 20. Date confirmed with Robert West.

[3]   *Fort Worth Star Telegram*, 14 April 1978

[4]   Jim Marrs, p. 468.

[5]   R.B. Cutler, *Two Flightpaths: Evidence of Conspiracy* (Minuteman Press, 1971), p. 17.

[6]   3H450.

[7]   5H136–137.

[8]   R.B. Cutler, *Two Flightpaths*, p.17.

[9]   Warren Report, p. 117.

[10] 17H871.

[11] 24H540.

[12] 17H560–61.

[13] May 1976, CFTR-Radio, Toronto, Canada, program "Thou Shalt Not Kill". Officer Chaney was never called to testify before the Warren Commission.

[14] A cropped Altgens' photograph with re-enactment appears as CE–900 (18H93).

[15] Robert Groden, *The Killing of a President*, (Penguin Books, 1993), p. 120.

[16] Conversation with Robert H. West, December 1994.

[17] 5H133.

[18] According to West's notes, the street elevation adjacent to the sign was 420.00'. The grass to the bottom of the sign was 5.70' and the height of the sign was four feet. The sign was further elevated another 1.71 feet due to the street curb, slope of sidewalk, and grass area between sidewalk and sign post.

[19] 7H573.

[20] David Lifton, *Best Evidence*, (Carroll & Graf, 1988), p. 556.

[21] 5H133.

[22] "William Greer's Impossible Head Turn," *The Fourth Decade* (November 1994), pp. 42–43.

[23] 18H743.

[24] Hudson (7H558), Altgens (7H515), Zapruder (7H569).

[25] 7H518.

[26] 7H562–563.

[27] 5H134.

[28] Sylvia Meagher, *Accessories After the Fact* (Vintage Books, 1967), p. 33.

[29] 7H562.

[30] 5H144.

[31] Martin L. Gross, *A Call for Revolution* (Ballantine Books, 1993), p. 121.

PHOTOGRAPH FROM NIX FILM

PHOTOGRAPH FROM RE-ENACTMENT

PHOTOGRAPH FROM ZAPRUDER FILM

PHOTOGRAPH FROM RE-ENACTMENT

PHOTOGRAPH THROUGH RIFLE SCOPE

DISTANCE TO STATION C .... 230.8 FT.

DISTANCE TO RIFLE IN WINDOW .... 265.3 FT.

ANGLE TO RIFLE IN WINDOW .... 15°21'

DISTANCE TO OVERPASS .... 260.6 FT.

ANGLE TO OVERPASS .... -1°28'

FRAME 313

PHOTOGRAPH FROM MUCHMORE FILM

PHOTOGRAPH FROM RE-ENACTMENT

Commision Exhibit No. 902

Special Effects in the Zapruder Film:
How the Film of the Century was Edited

David W. Mantik, M.D., Ph.D.

When you have eliminated the impossible, whatever remains,
however improbable, must be the truth.
—Sir Arthur Conan Doyle

On 22 November 1963, I was working toward a Ph.D. at the Biophysics Laboratory at the University of Wisconsin in Madison. Several of my fellow graduate students and I had just finished our lunches and were listening to a noon radio program. Suddenly, a bulletin came through from Dallas, Texas—the President had been shot! Then a few minutes later all of our worst fears were confirmed. Although that event is sculpted into my memory, it is a bit odd that I cannot recall my first viewing of the Zapruder film. Most likely it was the fall of 1975, when I attended a lecture at Los Alamos, New Mexico. By then I had started a new career and was rotating through the University of New Mexico as a medical student. The speaker was the Nobel Prize winning physicist, Luis Alvarez, who presented his personal analysis of the Zapruder film. What I do know is that I did not leave that lecture with a firm belief that JFK's head snap was proof of a conspiracy.

When Oliver Stone's movie appeared in 1991, my interest in the assassination was rekindled. I recalled that, after all those years and many personal moves, I had still retained the preprint (*American Journal of Physics* 1976, 44: 813) from the Alvarez lecture. I now began to review it. Alvarez had concluded that only an external force could produce such a head snap. For this force, he offered a simple explanation from physics— namely, that a jet effect of forward going biological tissue had pushed the

263

head backward. But now, as I read this, and as I read the eyewitness reports, I realized that the head snap was a paradox. So I began to wonder: was Alvarez wrong—or was his idea merely irrelevant? I realized that I had underestimated the seriousness of the problem. It was time to find out who was right.

Now, several years later, I have come to a surprising conclusion—no explanation offered so far is either correct or relevant. I do not believe that a frontal shot, with any reasonable sized rifle or bullet, could produce the observed head snap—too much energy is required. Alvarez's explanation, also, is inadequate and irrelevant. By taking both of these positions, I risk losing any friends that I might have on either side of this issue!

In this essay, I present new information regarding the authenticity of the Zapruder film. I also review old evidence, some well known (but perhaps misunderstood) and some overlooked, but chiefly I attempt to integrate a wide variety and quantity of evidence that bears on this question. It is only recently that this issue has come to the fore. There is an unusual diversity and amount of evidence that points toward alteration—too much, in fact to be ignored:

—there should not be so many witnesses who disagree with the film (none of them agree with it!), but who also agree so consistently with each other;

—there ought not to be witnesses who saw an earlier version of the film that contained scenes not in the present film;

—the film itself should not contain a cornucopia of mysterious and paradoxical features, some of which have come to light only recently.

Finally, I describe my own recent visits to the National Archives where I examined what are described as first generation copies of the Zapruder film and a reenactment film taken with Zapruder's camera. (I have not had an opportunity to see the so-called original film; that opportunity may yet come.)

Some readers may be surprised that none of this evidence rules out alteration, and they should be surprised. Much of it, in fact, points toward alteration. For example, it is striking that two investigators, working independently of one another, have each identified his own (independent) set of strange features on the same frame of the film. Furthermore, for each of these two cases, film alteration is the most sensible explanation—perhaps even the only possible explanation. That surely would not have been expected, but it has happened. Along the way, I also seek to explain some heretofore enigmatic items—ugly ducklings, so to speak. When one explanation for all of these strange puzzles—that extensive film alteration was deliberately carried out—has such enormous explanatory power, and when the quantity of evidence from so many different directions is all so suspicious, then surely this hypothesis deserves a fair hearing. Those who desire to preserve the alleged "authenticity" of the film now are beginning to appear more and more like the Ptolemaic astronomers who added epicycle upon epicycle in their futile attempts to preserve a geocentric paradigm.

The Centrality of the Zapruder Film in the Assassination.

[Editor's note: *Many photographic images are discussed here but few are shown. Serious students should obtain copies of Robert Groden's* The Killing of a President *(1993) and Richard Trask's* Pictures of the Pain *(1994). Black and white reproductions of the individual Zapruder frames from 171 to 334 may be found in* The Hearings of the Warren Commission, *Volume 18. The 35 mm slides are available for public viewing at the College Park facility of the National Archives. Noel Twyman's* Bloody Treason *(forthcoming) will contain 26 color reprints of different frames. Excellent color images were printed in the* Life *magazine issues of 29 November 1963; early December 1963 (Memorial Edition); 2 October 1964; 25 November 1966; and December 1991. For a brief history of the film (and its visit to the CIA), see Mike Pincher and Roy Schaeffer, Part IV.*]

If there had been a trial for Lee Harvey Oswald, or anyone else for that matter, would the Zapruder film have been accepted into evidence by the court? David Wrone ("The Zapruder Film. A Brief History with Comments," 1997), Professor of History at the University of Wisconsin-Stevens Point, has emphasized that there was no chain of possession, nor even an effort to maintain one. If anything, Wrone notes, Warren Commission (WC) staff members Samuel Stern, Wesley Liebeler, and Arlen Specter (now Senator from Pennsylvania) carefully avoided that whole area. No records were obtained from *Life*, no official statement collected regarding the damaged areas at the several splices, no record of who had the film, or where it had journeyed for the several months before it was presented to the WC. (Weisberg had made the same point many years ago; Harold Weisberg, *Whitewash II*, 1966, p. 210.)

Milicent Cranor notes that legal concerns about photographic tampering go back to the 1920s. She also reminds us that, for photographic information to be accepted as evidence in court, the images must be vouched for, and their whereabouts ascertained at all times (*McCormick on Evidence*, 3rd edition, 1984, Section 214). The legal principle is that eyewitness testimony has priority over photographs. This principle was turned upside down by the battalions of lawyers who worked for the House Select Committee on Assassinations (HSCA) and for the WC. For them, against all legal precedent, the assumption was always the reverse: if the witnesses disagreed with the official view, it was assumed that they were in error or even lying. On the other hand, the photographs (and the X-rays, too) were assumed to be immutable monuments to truth. In a real trial, no competent judge would have permitted this illegal approach. In view of the astonishing absence of elementary record keeping for possession of the film, it is likely that no data obtained from the film could have been used in a trial. The paradoxes of the first two reenactments (see below) raise tangible concerns about the validity of the Zapruder film as evidence (timing issues, specifically). An attorney for either side could have emphasized that point in addition to the lack of custody if he (or she) wanted to keep the film out of court.

Furthermore, the WC's marked inattention to details of the Zapruder film was shown all too clearly by staff member Wesley Liebeler's gross ignorance of the most obvious splice in the film at Z-212 (David Lifton, *Best Evidence*, 1980, pp. 24-27). An example of incompetence (some cynics regard this as deliberate deception) is the reversal of the critical frames Z-314 and Z-315, at the moment of the first head shot (Lifton 1980, p. 7)—which was first discovered by a private citizen, Raymond J. Marcus.

It is also somewhat incredible, especially for official investigations of this magnitude, that neither the WC nor the HSCA provided any detailed summaries of the sequence of events in the motorcade (Wrone, in particular, has made this point). Especially for the WC, with its singular lack of interest in the Zapruder film, it would have been expected that such an eyewitness summary of the motorcade events (especially a compilation from multiple witnesses) would have been indispensable to its investigation. At the least, such a summary could have been compared to the Zapruder film to assist in validating the film. Nonetheless, that, too, was not done. So not only is the chain of custody absent, but a coherent compilation of eyewitness accounts is also missing. It is a major task of this essay to complete just such a summary from the eyewitness accounts and then to compare this to the events seen in the film. These two scenarios do not agree at all. Regarding the disinterest in the film shown by the WC, Weisberg notes (*Whitewash II*, 1966, p. 213) that Robert Bahmer, the U.S. Archivist, advised him that "There is no print of the Zapruder film among the records of the Commission that is identified as having been received from *Life* magazine."

Despite these significant points, however, the centrality of the film in understanding the assassination has been assumed by most investigators—

almost without question. The highly respected private investigator and former professor of philosophy, Josiah Thompson (*Six Seconds in Dallas*, 1967, p. 6) stated: "Yet if it is studied with the utmost care and under optimum conditions, it can yield answers to enormous questions. Where did the shots come from and when were they fired?" On the next page he states, "Quite obviously, the Zapruder film contained the nearest thing to the absolute truth about the sequence of events in Dealey Plaza."

Robert Groden (*The Killing of a President*, 1993, p. 19) has also clearly staked out his belief in the authenticity of the film: "The Zapruder film offers the most accurate reflection of the assassination."

And Alvarez (*American Journal of Physics*, 1976, p. 825) added his own endorsement: "That is why I find the photographic record so interesting; it doesn't have the normal human failings." (It is the purpose of this paper to illustrate the enormous irony of this statement.)

In the late 1970s, the HSCA utilized the film extensively—particularly via the work of the Itek Corporation. But no official investigating body has ever raised—let alone explored—questions of authenticity.

Several histories of the film have been written, either exclusively or as part of a larger work. These authors include Philip Melanson, Harrison Livingstone, Noel Twyman, Richard Trask, David Wrone, and Martin Shackelford. Of these, the first two doubt the authenticity of the film, while Twyman, also dubious, explores some of the technical issues in his new book, *Bloody Treason* (1997). Trask (*Pictures of the Pain*, 1994), on the other hand, accepts authenticity almost without comment; even in his very large and well documented work, the word "authenticity" is absent from his index. In a personal conversation (telephone call of 28 July 1997), Wrone also advised me that he believes in authenticity. And Martin Shackelford, a committed student of this case, has also retained a strong vocal commitment to authenticity.

The Availability of the Film.

The film was shown repeatedly during that initial weekend. Zapruder's partner, Erwin Schwartz, has recalled for Twyman that he saw it about 15 times. Dan Rather saw it once and has been vigorously pilloried for describing JFK's head as going rapidly forward (as opposed to rapidly backward—as seen in the extant version). Both of these men describe events in the film that are no longer seen; this is discussed in more detail below. After that weekend and the immediately succeeding days, except for a viewing by the National Photographic and Interpretation Center (Melanson, "Hidden Exposure," *Third Decade*, November 1984), there is no record of another viewing until 27 January 1964 (over two months later), when a second generation copy was shown by FBI Agent Lyndal Shaneyfelt to a small WC audience (Trask 1994, p. 100). In a letter from Secret Service Chief James Rowley (1-27-64) to *Life*'s Washington Bureau chief Henry Suydam, Rowley confirmed that the film had not been shown to anyone outside the Secret Service staff (Martin Shackelford, "A Chronological History of the Zapruder Film," 1995, unpublished). This relatively long hiatus—and the fact that the audiences were different— may have provided a sufficient time interval for film alteration. The original film was shown at a joint meeting with WC staff on 25 February 1964 (5H138); for fear of damage to the film, however, it was not stopped to project individual frames. A copy of the film was subsequently examined in slow motion and also frame by frame (Trask 1994, p. 100). Also see Weisberg (*Whitewash II*, pp. 211-213) for events during this time period.

In early 1969, the film was subpoenaed (and released) from *Time*, Inc., for the Garrison trial. While there, many copies were made and bootleg copies proliferated, especially on college campuses. Even slides of individual frames became available to the public. Public interest in the film accelerated when the backward head snap became widely known. This snap was widely touted by critics of the WC as being obvious evidence of a shot from the front—and therefore evidence of conspiracy.

In early 1975, Groden screened his copy of the film for the Rockefeller Commission (Shackelford, 1975). The film was first shown on public television by Robert Groden on NBC's *Good Night America* with Geraldo Rivera on 6 March 1975. Groden showed his enhanced version, which was a great improvement over previously available copies. A viewing of Groden's version by Congressman Thomas N. Downing (Virginia) and staff in April 1975 helped to trigger the formation of the House Select Committee on Assassinations (HSCA). By concluding that at least two gunman had probably fired in Dealey Plaza, this most recent government investigation contradicted the WC—they rejected the lone gunman theory. By doing so, the HSCA thus turned the JFK assassination into an *officially recognized* conspiracy.

Early Critics of the Film

If not the earliest critic of the film, Harold Weisberg was surely its most vocal, particularly in *Whitewash II* (1966). He cites a particularly curious testimony (p. 180) in which Lyndal Shaneyfelt reports that the FBI reenactment took only 3.5 seconds (between Z-222 and Z-313), as opposed to the expected 5 seconds found in the Zapruder film (*Whitewash II*,

p. 180). This discrepancy was not resolved in Weisberg's discussion, nor has any subsequent investigation put this issue to rest. If the reenactment was accurate, then the limousine's average speed in this interval must have been distinctly greater than the official speed of 11 mph (a time of 3.5 seconds would yield a speed of 15.7 mph, assuming that 11 mph is indeed correct). This issue recurs later when the question of a limousine stop is discussed; if such a stop did occur then the time to transit the required interval during the actual motorcade would be longer—and perhaps consistent with the official time of 5 seconds. Another possibility is that the FBI report for Zapruder's camera speed is incorrect. These issues are all addressed below.

In a manuscript never published but informally circulated (Fred Newcomb and Perry Adams, *Murder from Within*, 1974), questions of authenticity were raised and the authors pointed out several inconsistencies in the film. These included:

1. that Dan Rather reported seeing evidence of a successful shot on Connally's shirt front—a witness is even cited who saw the same event (Bill Newman);
2. that numerous witnesses said that the limousine stopped after shots had been fired;
3. that, between frames Z-280 and Z-300, JFK and Connally virtually disappear; and
4. that, from frame to frame, the limousine displays a variety of irregular movements, including traveling only 10 feet within 21 frames between Z-197 and Z-218 (this is only about one half of the expected distance).

Because they also suggested that William Greer, the driver of the Presidential limousine, had fired the fatal shot, their work was ignored or ridiculed by a large percentage of those (few) readers who did have access to the manuscript. In retrospect, the quality of the images available to them was quite inferior to those widely available today and probably led to an error with respect to Greer. [*Editor's note:* Because the film has been extensively edited, however, this issue appears to be very difficult to resolve.]

Recent Critics of the Film.

Although these writers had raised serious questions, their effort was largely ignored for many years. It was mainly with the publication of Harrison Livingstone's *Killing Kennedy* (1995) that these questions began to be discussed among a wider audience. In his book, the chief contributor to this effort was Daryll Weatherly, a graduate student in mathematics, who offered several original and penetrating observations that are discussed below.

Then in November 1996, several individuals met in Dallas, Texas, under the umbrella of JFK Lancer Productions (headed by Debra Conway) to discuss the film. The chairman for this panel was Dr. James H. Fetzer, McKnight Professor of Philosophy from the University of Minnesota, Duluth. A closed session was held on November 21. This format permitted free and open discussion in a small group setting. Then, in a formal program extending over five hours on November 22, six speakers listed numerous arguments against authenticity of the film. Besides Fetzer, this panel included Jack White (photo analyst), Noel Twyman, Chuck Marler, David Lifton (*Best Evidence*, 1980) and me. In the ensuing several months, particularly by e-mail, discussions raged pro and con as others passionately joined in the arguments over authenticity.

Arguments Favoring Authenticity

The arguments against authenticity may be better understood after first reviewing (and responding to) those arguments that favor authenticity. Most of these have been summarized by the National Archives in "Technical review of the Zapruder film from NARA's courtesy storage holdings," by Charles W. Mayn (21 December 1995). Although this report is available to the public, it has remained little known. Despite discussing several important issues, it left unaddressed several questions that currently occupy students of the film. These arguments are listed first, after which item by item responses (indicated in italics) are offered. Items 1 to 6 are in the NARA report. Items 7 to 10 have been suggested by others.

1. The film has two different segments of identification leader spliced to its head with identifying information handwritten on the leader. This is typical of film that has been processed, with the leader being added later. *This is necessary, but not sufficient evidence. It would have been possible to imitate this.*

2. Intersprocket images are present. This is characteristic of most regular 8 mm cameras. *This is probably a necessary requirement; if intersprocket images can be copied, however, it is not sufficient.*

3. A splice exists at a point known to have been damaged historically. *This does not preclude alteration elsewhere in the film.*

4. Another splice occurs where a tree trunk lies to the right of the sign; this is historically consistent. *These are necessary requirements, but the film could have been altered before—or even after—this damage occurred.*

5. There are no images from a prior generation—i.e., no edge prints (manufacturer's ID symbols), no images of splices, no images of sprocket holes, and no images of prior damage. *This is a strong requirement. It is addressed in great detail below.*

6. The color is consistent with Kodachrome film exposed in daylight as opposed to the color "cast" often seen in duplicate films. *This is also necessary, but not sufficient. Jack White [Editor's note: See Jack White, Part IV.] states, from his extensive experience in still photography, that it is often impossible to distinguish an original from a copy. I put this same question to Bruce Jamieson (telephone conversation, 24 July 1997), who produced the first generation copies of the Zapruder film on 22 November 1963 in Dallas. He said that although out-of-camera Kodachrome is distinctive film, a good copy could be difficult to distinguish—unless compared side by side with the original. But that is a catch-22 in this case—it is the original that is in doubt.*

7. The emulsion side faces away from the viewer. *That would be expected for a camera original—or for every alternate generation after that. Within the camera, the emulsion faces forward (to minimize loss of image). Therefore, in order to view the image correctly, it is necessary to look through the film from the opposite (shiny) side—so that light enters the eye in the same manner that it enters the camera. It would be possible to make a first generation copy with the emulsion side facing away; there are no particular constraints on how this is done. (This observation was offered to me by the author of the NARA report.) This condition is necessary but not sufficient.*

8. There was not enough time for the task. *This argument is the most difficult for me to address since it presupposes an expert's understanding of the time required for specific tasks, such as excision of frames and editing within frames. I have already noted above that there were over two months between the assassination and the first known WC viewing. A lengthy editing period would also seem to be required since the editors could not have known what other films or photographs might later appear and contradict their edited version. In fact, the FBI collected many movie films (e.g., Nix and Muchmore) and photographs in the following weeks. It should also be remembered, however, that films that were collected too late could still have undergone alteration. Finally, viewers of the film from that first weekend report seeing events not present in the current version; so it is not likely that all the film editing was completed during the first night. Having said all of this, however, I am still impressed at some of the images in the 29 November 1963 issue of Life. Shackelford notes that this issue was on the newsstands by the following Tuesday (November 26). This issue included frames with the Stemmons freeway sign, the street lamp (in which Connally begins to vanish off the bottom of the film), several frames from the Z-320s in which JFK is near the bottom edge and a portion of his head is grossly missing, and multiple frames after this in which the limousine moves abruptly upward in the field of view. In light of the discussion below (in which I conclude that the bottom of frames before and after Z-313 have been deliberately cropped), at least some editing within frames must have been completed within the first few days. Whether that is too fast or, instead, is quite feasible, will naturally depend on the facilities and personnel available; but about this, nothing at all seems known at this time. During all of this discussion, however, one important point should not be lost—no intersprocket image was reproduced for the public until 25 No-*

vember 1966 (Life). It is in this region especially that work was required by the editors; this same region is the focus of much discussion below. My best guess is that, unless time permitted, this work was completed in stages, with images first being sucessively prepared for the two early issues of Life, but with all frames not completed until some time before the first WC showing on 25 February 1994.

9. No optical printers existed for copying film to include the intersprocket scenes. (Robert Groden has even recalled an unsuccessful offer of a reward to anyone who could provide such a machine.) *It is known that a copy of the "home movie" portion of the film does include intersprocket images. (I have seen these.) Whether the motorcade sequence would also be copied into the intersprocket area seems to be in some doubt. See the discussion of printers below, especially with respect to contact printers and the issue of visualizing edge prints. Also note comments below by Bruce Jamieson. Optical printers are extremely useful for copying huge numbers of frames and long lengths of film. However, when the length of film to be copied is only slightly over 6 feet long and contains fewer than 500 frames, it may be sufficient to construct a custom copier (perhaps operated manually) so that the intersprocket images could be incorporated into the new version. There would almost certainly not be any technical barrier to assembling such a device. The main challenge, as usual, would be resources and time. [Editor's note: See Pincher and Schaeffer, Part IV, for a possible system for copying the film.]*

10. No film editor inclined to a lone gunman scenario would have left the head snap in. *Although no final answer can be given to this objection from common sense, several responses may be offered. The first was actually noted by WC Assistant Counsel, Wesley Liebeler, who admitted that the WC never paid much attention to the head snap—at least not until the critics seized upon it (KTTV, Los Angeles, February 1967). It was, in addition, shown to the WC and that seemed not to cause any concern. And, as I noted above, I do not recall being convinced by it in 1975 either. A second response is that the film's editors worked only with still photographs; they did not concurrently view their work as a movie film. When they did view their final product (as a movie), they may have recognized some problem areas but were unwilling (or unable, given the time constraints) to embark on another round of alterations. It is likely that removal of the head snap would have been technically feasible. The more pertinent question, though, is: at what cost of time and effort? Editing within a fair number of additional frames (a labor intensive task) would most likely have been required. A complete excision of the head snap would have left JFK leaning forward in his slumped position for an exceptionally long time, including many frames before Z-313 and for many afterwards, too. Such an image may have conflicted too much with eyewitnesses who saw something quite different: some saw JFK moving to an erect posture, while others saw JFK hit while sitting erect. Finally, it should be recalled that this film was never intended for wide viewing—nor did that actually occur until 1975, twelve years later, and then only by private efforts, mainly by Robert Groden. By then, whoever had issued the orders for film alteration had no doubt*

achieved his (or her) purpose—the ballgame was already over. The cover-up did not need to be perfect; it needed only to succeed for a limited time interval—and that was achieved. In addition, an imperfect cover-up does not surprise many critics who see evidence for such human imperfections in other (attempted) cover-ups in this case.

Arguments Against Authenticity.

These arguments are divided into several categories for ease of discussion. They are presented in the following sequence.

1. Disagreements between eyewitnesses and the film.
2. Disagreements between early viewers of the film (November 1963) and what is currently seen.
3. Disagreements between the film and other photographs or movies.
4. Disagreements between the film and the first two reenactments
5. Internal inconsistencies in the film.

1. Disagreements between eyewitnesses and the film.

Did the Limousine Stop? Arguments Pro

In UPI's *Four Days* (1964, p. 17), the author notes: "In the right hand picture [a frame from the Muchmore movie film], the driver slams on the brakes and the police escort pulls up." And Merriman Smith (p. 32) states: "The President's car, possibly as much as 150 to 200 yards ahead, seemed to falter briefly." This book became available in early 1964, only a few months after the assassination. *Newsweek* (2 December 1963, p. 2) wrote: "For a chaotic moment, the motorcade ground to an uncertain halt." And *Time* (29 November 1963, p. 23) asserted: "There was a shocking momentary stillness, a frozen tableau."

Even Trask (*Pictures of the Pain*, 1994, p. 209), who does not raise questions of authenticity, quotes Bobby Hargis, the motorcycle man on the left rear, as saying, "I felt blood hit me in the face, and the Presidential car stopped immediately after that and stayed stopped for about half a second, then took off at a high rate of speed." (6H294; i.e., Volume 6 of the Warren Commission Hearings, p. 294.) How Trask reconciles this statement with the film he does not say. To my knowledge, Hargis is the only witness who states a specific time interval for the limousine stop. Hargis, as a motorcycle officer on the left rear, was positioned perfectly to recognize whether or not such a stop had actually occurred.

Even Gerald Posner, an ardent supporter of the WC and surely a supporter of film authenticity, does his cause no good at all when he writes (*Case Closed*, 1993, p. 24): "Incredibly, Greer, sensing that something was wrong in the back of the car, slowed the vehicle to almost a standstill." It would be interesting to ask Posner to point to this moment in the film.

All of these comments are in obvious conflict with the film. No abrupt slowing of the limousine is seen and it certainly does not stop. Furthermore, new observers of the film almost never comment on such a marked deceleration. In a detailed frame by frame analysis, Alvarez did identify a sudden deceleration from about 12 to 8 mph, centered at about Z-300 and extending over about 0.5 seconds (nine frames); this would begin at about Z-295, only a few frames before the head snap begins. This slowing, however, is subtle and is not usually noticed by viewers of the film.

It is peculiar that this modest, almost imperceptible, deceleration—lasting only one half of a second(!)—should be what prompted several dozen eyewitnesses to describe this as a marked slowing, or even a possible stop. If this event made such an impression in Dealey Plaza, why do observers of the film not respond in similar fashion today? Vince Palamara ("47 Witnesses: Delay on Elm Street," *The Third Decade*, January/March 1992) has since updated his original article to now include at least 48 witnesses who described a limousine stop on Elm Street. (Also see "Questioning the Limousine's Speed on Elm Street," by Chuck Marler, *The Fourth Decade*, May 1994, p. 19.) A partial list of such eyewitnesses follows (where the letter "H" represents one of the 26 volumes of the Warren Commission Hearings and the first number identifies the volume and the second number the page):

a. Marrion Baker: "the car stopped completely, pulled to the left and stopped . . . Several officers said it stopped completely." (3H266) [Motorcycle officer, several cars behind the limousine.]

b. Charles Brehm: "between the first and third shots the President's car only seemed to move some 10 or 12 feet . . . almost came to a halt after the first shot . . . " (22H837) [To the left rear of the limousine, near the curb.]

c. Earle Brown: "when the shots were fired, it [the car] stopped." (6H233) [Police officer on overpass.]

d. James Chaney: "after the first shot rang out, the car stopped completely." (3H221) [Motorcycle officer at right rear of limousine.]

e. J.W. Foster: "immediately after [JFK] was struck . . . the car . . . pulled to the curb." (Commission Document 897, pp. 20-21) [Police officer on overpass.]

f. Bobby Hargis: "The [limo] stopped immediately after that and stayed stopped for about half a second, then took off . . . " (6H294) [Motorcycle officer at left rear of the limousine.]

g. Harry D. Holmes: He noticed the car pull to a halt, and Holmes thought: "They are dodging something being thrown." (Jim Bishop, *The Day Kennedy was Shot*, 1967, p. 176; 7H291) Postal inspector, Post Office, one block away, using binoculars.]

h.   Douglas Jackson: "the car just all but stopped . . . just a moment." (Newcomb and Adams 1974, p. 71) [Motorcycle officer, right rear of limousine.]

i.   Robert MacNeill: "The President's driver slammed on the brakes—after the third shot . . . " (*The Way We Were, 1963. The Year Kennedy was Shot*, 1967, p. 193) [Press car in the motorcade.]

j.   Billy Joe Martin: He saw the limousine stop for "just a moment." (Newcomb and Adams 1974, p. 71) [Motorcycle officer, left rear of the limousine.]

k.   Mary Moorman: She recalls that the car was moving at the time she took her photo and when she heard the shots, and has the impression that the car either stopped or slowed before accelerating. (19H487) [Immediately left of the limousine near the curb.]

l.   Bill Newman: "I believe Kennedy's car came to a full stop after the final shot." (Bill Sloan, *JFK: Breaking the Silence*, 1993, p. 169) [Immediately right of the limousine near the curb.]

m.   Alan Smith: "The car was ten feet from me when a bullet hit the President in the forehead . . . the car went about five feet and stopped." (*Chicago Tribune*, 11/23/63, p. 9; Newcomb and Adams 1974, p. 71) [Unknown location.]

n.   Roy Truly: "I saw the President's car swerve to the left and stop somewheres down in this area." (3H221) [In front of the Texas School Book Depository.]

o.   Major Phil Willis: "The party had come to a temporary halt before proceeding on to the underpass." (7H497) [Across the street from the Texas School Book Depository.]

Notice an extraordinary concordance here: all four motorcycle men who were closest to the limousine recalled a stop! Surely if anyone would recall this event correctly, they would. As is discussed below, the probability for eyewitnesses being wrong on a simple fact like this is surprisingly low—but here we have all four recalling the same event in the same way. In addition, Moorman and Newman were extremely close witnesses, one on each side of the limousine. It is also odd that a list of individuals who said that the motorcade never stopped or slowed has never been assembled. (An essential requirement, of course, would be that they be uninfluenced by subsequent viewing of the film.)

Did the Limousine Stop? Arguments Con

Several arguments against a stopped (or noticeably slowed) limousine have been advanced. An inevitable one is psychological—at moments of high drama, events seem to slow down. This phenomenon certainly occurs; many of us are doubtless familiar with it. Regarding the events in Dealey Plaza, however, it can be replied that many of these eyewitnesses simply did not know what was happening—or even that it was important. Many did not immediately recognize that they were witnessing an assassination—or anything else of historical importance. Some thought that firecrackers were going off (see 50 such witnesses in Newcomb and Adams 1974, p. 86), while others thought they had heard the backfire of a motorcycle (see 19 such witnesses in Newcomb and Adams 1974, p. 86). In either of these cases, strong psychological reasons for perceiving time as slowed down are absent. Despite this, however, a large number do recall a notable change in the limousine speed. To give added support to the accuracy of their memories, the probable reliability of eyewitnesses for recalling such a fact is addressed below.

Another objection to a limousine stop is that those vehicles farther back in the motorcade may have stopped but the Presidential limousine continued without delay, so that reports of stopping were misapplied to the limousine. Indeed, it is likely that followup vehicles did slow, but that cannot be the entire explanation. Many of the closest witnesses (e.g., the motorcycle men, Mary Moorman, the Newmans) would have had no reason to watch any other part of the motorcade, especially during those brief moments when the limousine passed them. But these witnesses, too, recall a dramatic deceleration of the limousine.

Can these Eyewitnesses be Trusted?

It has long been standard practice to impugn the reliability of eyewitnesses in general, but particularly so in the two official investigations of the Kennedy assassination. Whenever conflicts arose between their desired conclusions and the eyewitness reports, both the WC and the HSCA persistently either ignored the eyewitnesses (several in the best locations—Bill Newman, Marie Muchmore, Orville Nix—were not even asked to testify) or it was claimed that they had to be mistaken. Even John Connally was not believed (he originally reported that he saw JFK hit before he felt any shot himself). Both he and his wife always remained thoroughly convinced that these were two separate shots. But to concede this would have been to admit one too many shots—and so his testimony had to be ignored. Seth Kantor, a Scripps-Howard newspaperman, is another example. When he described seeing Jack Ruby at Parkland Hospital, he was ignored by the WC. No reasonable explanation was offered by the WC for why Kantor (who had known Ruby personally) would be mistaken on such a simple observation or why he would have lied. Kantor later wrote a book about his own experiences and always insisted that he really had seen Ruby. Later, the HSCA also agreed with him.

Robert Blakey, the General Counsel for the HSCA, in his conspicuous and self-proclaimed public passion for objective data, seemed almost to run a vendetta against eyewitnesses. Rather than rely on eyewitnesses, he chose instead to emphasize data that he could label as scientific. The chief example of this was the acoustic data on which the HSCA based its conclusion of probable conspiracy. And this, Blakey, in turn, pinned on the Mafia, who were his own special area of interest. A subsequent review, by a panel from the National Academy of Sciences, refuted those acoustic conclusions, thus detonating the main pillar of Blakey's case—his purported passion for scientific data thereby exploding in his face. The acoustic data is still discussed occasionally—it is possible that the issue is not totally settled, but it was not settled by Blakey's staff and experts. (Also see Thomas Canning's comments below on Blakey's modus operandi.)

On another occasion, Blakey's comments showed that he failed to understand even the fundamental basis of the scientific method and the conclusions reached thereby. When interviewed by Bob Beckel about the neutron activation analysis work on the bullet fragments, he said, "The single bullet theory is proven beyond reasonable doubt for anyone who has reasonable technical competence and will study the physical and other evidence" (*Larry King Live*, CNN, 21 May 1992). What Blakey had failed to understand is that scientific truth is never final, but is always subject to further testing. And if incontrovertible new data emerges, then any scientific paradigm can be overthrown, even after centuries of acceptance. The geocentric paradigm has already been noted above as a model for this process. (The authenticity of the Zapruder film is in the same category—it deserves acceptance as authentic so long as emerging new data do not conflict with it at too many points.)

It is useful to recall that both the WC and the HSCA were not only led by attorneys but almost entirely staffed by attorneys. The WC sought only minimal expert opinion. Although the HSCA employed many experts, including scientific and medical consultants, its final conclusions were almost always formulated by attorneys—over whom the experts could exercise no veto power whatsoever. [*Editor's note:* See Ronald F. White, Postscript.]

The expert asked to analyze bullet trajectories for the HSCA, Thomas Canning, stated his frustration to Chief Blakey in a letter of 5 January 1978 (HSCA Agency File #014258): "The compartmentalization which you either fostered or permitted to develop in the technical investigations made it nearly impossible to do good work in reasonable time and at reasonable cost . . . .The most frustrating problem for me was to get quantitative data—and even consistent descriptions—from the forensic pathologists . . . . Much of this rather negative reaction to the hearings themselves stems from my being strongly persuaded to rush through a difficult analysis at the last minute, abandon my regular pursuits for two days, try to boil down forty-five minutes of testimony to thirty, and then listen and watch while two hours of excellent testimony is allowed to dribble out over most of a day."

And so Blakey's attempt to prove a conspiracy, by ignoring the eyewitnesses, failed. By ignoring them, however, he overlooked a small mountain of clues. There is no question but that eyewitnesses are notoriously unreliable for identifying faces of strangers only briefly glimpsed. They also do poorly at recalling the specific details of a complex sequence of events. However, when the degree of complexity is lower, and particularly for observations that are considered important, an altogether different conclusion results.

At the University of Michigan, an experiment with an unexpected result was performed in 1971 (by sheer coincidence, I was Assistant Professor of Physics at Michigan at that time). Elizabeth Loftus summarizes this work in *Eyewitness Testimony* (1996). Her book won the National Media Award for Distinguished Contribution from the American Psychological Foundation. The book jacket says what you would expect it to say—it implies that eyewitness testimony is unreliable. However, Table 3.1 on page 27 tells quite another story. The data cited are from J. Marshall, et al., *Harvard Law Review* 84 (1971): 1620-1643.

A total of 151 observers were shown a two-minute movie in color and sound—with a fairly complex set of actions. The researchers identified about 900 items present in the film that could have been mentioned. The observers were interviewed immediately after the viewing; they were urged to recount, in all possible detail, what they had seen. The researchers then assessed these responses based on accuracy, completeness, and saliency. Accuracy and completeness were determined by what was actually seen in the film. Saliency, however, was determined, not by the researchers, but rather was defined internally—i.e., by the responses of the observers themselves. Specifically, if an item was described by over 50% of the observers, it was considered highly salient.

Marshall, et al. then listed the accuracy and completeness of the responses vs. saliency, as follows:

Saliency	Accuracy	Completeness
0	61	64
1-12	78	81
13-25	81	82
26-50	83	92
51-100	98	98

In view of all that has been said about eyewitness *unreliability,* these data are quite astonishing—if over 50% of the witnesses considered an item to be salient, then they were 98% accurate and 98% complete! Did the HSCA consider this? It is noteworthy that this study was published in 1971, years before the HSCA even came into existence. It is doubtful that Blakey had taken time to search for evidence of this nature on eyewitness reliability.

Therefore, when many dozens of witnesses all recall an event—such as the slowing of the limousine at a critical moment—this Michigan data strongly suggests that they are recalling the event correctly. As a not entirely hypothetical example, if a single witness has only a 2% chance of being wrong (as in the table above), and if 10 witnesses report the same event, what is the probability that they are all wrong? This subatomic number is $(0.02)^{10} = 10^{-17} = 0.00000000000000001$! Actually, these witnesses might even claim a higher level of accuracy than the Michigan film viewers, because the events in the Zapruder film lasted for only a few seconds, while the Michigan film lasted for two minutes. And if many of these witnesses recall *in a consistent manner*—as they do—that the limousine slowed or that JFK's head moved in a particular sequence, then this Michigan experiment stands as a serious warning to all of us that such testimony cannot be dismissed out of hand, as Blakey was only too eager to do.

Did JFK's head move backward abruptly?

Another major disagreement between the film and the eyewitnesses is the backward head snap. This is so dramatic and has been so popular among WC critics that it has been accepted for decades as evidence of a frontal shot. In fact, when Alvarez asked for the best evidence of a conspiracy, the head snap was offered to him. Unfortunately for his view, however, although a weak jet effect may sometimes occur under optimal conditions, there is now much evidence against the jet effect as an adequate explanation for the head snap. [*Editor's note:* See Ronald White, Postscript.]

It should first be noted that the jet effect in the Alvarez experiments resulted from soft nosed bullets. When he used full metal jacketed bullets (like those purportedly fired by Oswald), the jet effect was greatly reduced. John Lattimer's shooting experiments were claimed by him to provide strong evidence for the jet effect. He filled 12 real human skulls with fresh brain tissue and white paint, shot them with 6.5 mm full metal jacketed bullets and filmed the entire sequences. In all 12 cases he claimed that brain tissue exited explosively and the skulls moved toward the shooter every time (*Kennedy and Lincoln,* 1980, p. 251). The only other experiment to use human skulls was reported by the Edgewood Army Arsenal. These results were reported in 1978 (1 HSCA 404). In 10 successive skulls filled with gelatin, all 10 skulls went *forward*, in the direction of the bullet! *None* went backward!

> Also, you will see that as the skull goes forward, some of the material of the skull and the contents were blown out toward us. Consequently, the opposing momentum carries the skull away from us . . . . In fact, all 10 of the skulls that we shot did essentially the same thing . . . . they also lost material toward us, that is, toward its right and therefore rotated toward its left. (1 HSCA 404.)

In this last phrase, "toward us" refers to the viewers who were to the right of the skulls. These results therefore stand in dramatic contrast to Lattimer's. To date, Lattimer is the only individual to claim a useful jet effect with full metal jacketed bullets.

As a personal footnote, I heard Lattimer present his data at a Chicago conference in Spring 1993. To this date, as we shall soon see, his results remain unconfirmed. Several critics of his work have noted that he unnecessarily added a new interacting mass—the ladder upon which he placed his skulls. That the ladder definitely moves—thereby taking up energy and complicating the experiment—is obvious from his photographs (Lattimer, p. 257). Recently, based on two new sets of shooting experiments, Lattimer's apparent results with full metal jacketed bullets have been called into serious question. This work has been done independently by Doug DeSalles, M.D., a physician from Sacramento, California, and by Art Snyder, Ph.D., a physicist at the Stanford University Linear Accelerator Center (SLAC). Like Alvarez, both experimenters used melons. In repeated attempts, their experiments showed either no jet effect at all, or, at most, only a minimal wavering in the backward direction. (With hunting type ammunition, however, a jet effect was seen.)

Milicent Cranor ("The Joker in the Jet Effect," *The Fourth Decade*, January 1996, p. 28) astutely notes that Alvarez overlooked one important interaction. Alvarez (1976, p. 819) wrote: "My analysis involves three interacting masses, the bullet, the jet of brain matter . . . and the remaining part of the head." But there is one more interaction—the one that occurs when the bullet breaks up (into many tiny pieces) on striking the posterior skull. This interaction, however, would have expended a great deal of energy, leaving that much less available for the jet effect. And this interaction was left out of Alvarez's calculations.

To make matters noticeably worse for the jet effect, Snyder also noted that Alvarez's calculations had assumed that the bullet actually stopped within the melon—Alvarez had used the classical model of the ballistic pendulum. That was, of course, far from the case, since the bullets had actually exited at very high speeds from the opposite side of the melons.

And this was especially true for those with full metal jackets. For the jet effect to be successful, a great deal of energy must be deposited within the melon—and the only source for this energy is the bullet. So when the bullet traverses the target nearly unimpeded, very little energy can be left behind, and that, in turn, greatly reduces the jet effect. This observation alone—to say nothing of the actual results of the shooting experiments—casts serious doubt on the jet effect as a relevant explanation for the head snap. It is therefore most likely that the correct explanation for the head snap must be sought elsewhere.

The other traditional explanation for the head snap has been the "neuromuscular reaction." This was first proposed to the HSCA not by any neuroscience specialist, but by a wound ballistics expert based on his viewing old films of goats being shot in the head. To date no official testimony has been obtained from appropriate specialists (the neuroscientists) on this question. At the very least, interspecies differences in neurophysiology would leave this conclusion open at least to some doubt. In addition, the usual reaction to such brain trauma is not the highly directed movement observed in the Zapruder film but rather random muscular activity. Even Alvarez concluded that the highly directional recoil seen in the Zapruder film required the application of an *external* force.

Yet another objection to the decerebrate rigidity invoked by the HSCA is the time of onset; even the HSCA admitted that this would develop only after several *minutes*. I have been unable to find any literature references that even hint that this reaction could occur within milliseconds in human subjects—as is required for the head snap as seen in the film. Furthermore, in a large collaborative study (A.E. Walker, *Cerebral Death*, 1981, p. 33) with over 500 patients who experienced cerebral death, 70% were limp when observed just before death and an additional 10% became limp at about the time of death. At the very least, therefore, based on all of these considerations, the attempt by the HSCA to implicate a neuromuscular reaction is open to serious doubt. Moreover, the minimum requirement has never been met—the appropriate experts have never been officially consulted.

An additional argument against a neuromuscular reaction is that the observed reaction in the film is much too fast to fit with such a reflex. By the analysis of more than one study, within the space of one Zapruder frame interval (55 msec), the head clearly moves backward. Typical human reflex times are 1/4 to 1/2 second (250 to 500 msec). This is an extraordinary discrepancy—a factor of 5 to 10, which, all by itself, makes this scenario quite unlikely.

Alvarez described ejection of 10% of the melon mass. For a 5 kg head (based on my personal measurements and calculations) this corresponds to an ejection of 500 gm of brain and skull. The combined mass of the bone fragments brought to the autopsy plus the Harper bone fragment (found later) would yield about 80 gm (assuming a density of 1.65 gm/cc, a total area of 67 square cm, and a skull thickness of 3/4 cm), thus requiring an additional loss of at least 400 gm of brain tissue. The autopsied brain, however, was a remarkably large 1500 gm, which implies little or no loss of brain tissue. Unless there was a major loss of brain tissue therefore, the jet effect becomes insignificant for this particular case. Alvarez never commented on any of these issues. (The above figure of 1500 grams for the autopsied brain is disputed by many critics, including Robert B. Livingston, M.D., a greatly respected neuroscientist. [*Editor's note:* See his "Statement of 18 November 1993."] I have also performed many point by point optical density measurements of the skull X-rays. These are radically inconsistent with the 1500 gram figure. The above illustration uses this number merely because it is given in the Supplemental Autopsy Report.)

The chief pathologist, James J. Humes described 2/3 of the right cerebrum as missing (*JAMA*, May 27, 1994, Volume 272, p. 2798); this would probably correspond to less than 400 gm. In the above paragraph the estimate of 400 gm was very conservative. It assumed that nearly all of the bone and brain fragments went straight forward. If, instead, these fragments had a significant component of vertical (or even backward) momentum, the required mass of ejected brain tissue would be correspondingly larger, perhaps even much larger. It is possible both to calculate and to measure the speeds of the ejecta from the Alvarez paper; the ejecta speeds are 40–50 ft/sec. The distance traveled by the bone fragments in Lattimer's experiments are consistent with these speeds. With this information it can be shown that the ejected masses required to produce the JFK head recoil speed of 1.6 ft/sec are indeed significant. But there is simply not enough missing brain—even as reported by Humes—for this purpose. Alvarez never did discuss where this tissue for the jet effect was supposed to come from.

What happens to real human heads when they are shot? In 1992, China executed six prisoners. This was videotaped and shown on *ABC Nightly News*. Michael T. Griffith has viewed this; I have condensed his report here. Each prisoner was shot in the back of the head with what appears to be an SKS or type 56 rifle. The bullet energy is similar to the Mannlicher-Carcano; it is also a full metal jacketed bullet. All men were kneeling and leaning forward at angles similar to JFK's before frame Z-313. None of the heads exploded as seen in Z-313. In all cases the heads were thrust forward and all six fell forward, away from the rifle. The chief difference from Z-313 was that the muzzle was only about one foot from the head. Nonetheless, this videotape is compelling evidence against the explanation that Alvarez has advanced.

A final explanation for the head snap was revisited by Jacob Cohen (*Commentary*, June 1992, p. 32), an arch supporter of the lone gunman theory. He posits a shove from Jackie as the primary mechanism. Even this, however, flies in the face of common sense; it would surely be odd for Jackie to force her husband's head back with such almost inhuman speed, particularly if he was already injured—which she surely suspected by then. That she might have done so at a much slower speed, however, is likely; that evidence will be discussed below. If such a backward movement of the head had been assisted by a sudden acceleration of the limousine, then the head snap might be remotely possible. However, the movement of the other limousine occupants makes that unlikely. Their motions at that moment are not consistent with a dramatic acceleration. In any case, the Itek measurements (see below) placed the final nails into this coffin.

The traditional critics' explanation—a frontal shot—was taken to task by Itek as part of its work for the HSCA. A double pendulum model (one mass for the head and a separate mass for the torso) was used. The increase in gravitational energy to an erect posture for an initially forward leaning torso and head is quite significant. I revised some of Itek's biological values, but even after this, I still found their conclusion convincing: no reasonable bullet had enough energy to lift JFK's head and torso against gravity and also to deliver the observed kinetic energy. WC critics are often unhappy with this result, but the calculations are quite convincing. Unfortunately, they are far too long to print here.

The Itek work offered one more astonishing conclusion (Trask 1994, p. 125)—that has been overlooked by everyone. They noted that Jackie moved forward by an amount similar to JFK at Z-312 to Z-313. Even more astonishing is that she moves backward at Z-313 to Z-314 with even greater magnitude than JFK! This is the moment of the famous head snap! Thompson (1967, pp. 90–93) had earlier described JFK's double movement in these frames (like Raymond Marcus and Harold Weisberg before him) and had correctly noted the enormous magnitude of JFK's acceleration and deceleration in rapid succession—a magnitude of several g's. (As is discussed below, automobile decelerations rarely exceed 0.4 g.) He concluded from this that JFK was hit once in each frame, first from the rear at about Z-312 and then from the front at Z-313. But if the rapid changes in JFK must be attributed to two bullets, then the even greater changes in Jackie require an even more creative hypothesis. (Also note that Jackie's movements in the same *direction* as JFK in this brief interval make it virtually impossible for her to push him back at all—if she had done this, she should, of course, have gone in the *opposite* direction.)

In summary, the jet effect really does not apply to this case—nor does the neuromuscular reaction. And a frontal bullet cannot do what is seen in Z-313; too much energy must be expended against gravity. Furthermore, even if any of these might possibly work, an explanation for Jackie's incredible excursions would still be missing. And so, at this surprisingly remote point in history, there is still no explanation for the head snap—an extraordinary state of affairs. It is the purpose of this essay to offer an alternate hypothesis—one that explains not just the head snap but an entire menagerie of curious creatures including a bird. [*Editor's note:* See the "Postscript" to David Mantik, Part I.]

How did JFK's head move after the head shots?

Yet another serious disagreement between the eyewitnesses and the film is the specific path that JFK's head followed in those brief moments after the head shots. This is a new issue, one that has emerged from several independent lines of evidence. As more and more data in favor of film alteration appeared from many sources, I began to realize that it was time to question some deeply rooted impressions. Repeated viewing of the film—with its vivid movements, its brief spray of blood, Jackie's reaction, Clint Hill's rescue attempt, and the final acceleration—all these had irresistibly left a strong impression on me that I had just seen something real. But now it was time to ask a new question: *if the film had been altered, then what really had occurred and how could we know?* In particular, I wondered now, did the film initially show evidence of two successful head shots? As this new door opened for me (two head shots) a surprising sequence of hitherto vaguely puzzling observations slowly began to make sense. I began to realize that the remarkably vivid image of the single head shot had so transfixed my memory that I had forgotten—or simply overlooked—the eyewitness reports that suggested two different head shots. Even those who disagree with the lone gunman theory—and who even believe in two head shots—often speak of "the head shot." This is further evidence of the persistence and power of the visual image for the human brain.

There is a surprisingly wide variety of evidence that favors two successful head shots. For this scenario, the eyewitnesses merely provide the key for unlocking the door. Behind that door, however, lies a small mountain of evidence—much of it indirect, but at the same time remarkably consistent.

What had happened to me, however, was the opposite—I had blundered into this room, only later to discover that the eyewitnesses held the key to the door. It was late one night that I finally began to suspect that there might be a pattern to the eyewitness accounts of the head shot sequence, if only I would look for it. And, as I began to review their statements, I was startled at the concordant pattern that emerged. I was astonished that I had not seen it before and I wondered how I had found consistency in their statements before. It seemed most unlikely that the remarkably consistent pattern that emerged would have occurred at random. Although that initial review postponed my bedtime, it was only in the next several days and weeks that I fully realized how well the eyewitness accounts made other data more comprehensible. But this new scenario was quite inconsistent with the movement of JFK's head as seen in the film. To avoid the confusion that would probably result by presenting the evidence first, I next present my current understanding of what the witnesses saw; the evidence for this interpretation is then presented in the following table.

A Reconstruction of the Two Head Shots.

After an early shot hit JFK in the throat, his head (and torso) slumped forward noticeably with elbows raised, and he stayed forward briefly. While in this position, the limousine began to slow and he was struck by the first head shot (from the rear, the one discovered by the pathologists)—but no head snap followed. He fell forward more—probably into Jackie's lap, as the limousine (probably) continued to brake. Several witnesses describe his head as jerking slightly to the left with this shot; others saw his hair rising up, but there was no bloody spray. Zapruder may have seen him grasp his left chest at the moment of this head shot (7H570). A bloodless bone fragment (probably from the skull vertex) was briefly glimpsed over his right shoulder (by Jackie; also seen in the Moorman photograph), after which it fell into the limousine (where it was later found), but there was no spray of blood. After this, Jackie, now clearly aware that something was wrong, slowly raised JFK's head to an erect position so that she could look into his eyes (this is seen in the film as the head snap). Then the second head shot struck while he was sitting mostly erect—entering from the front at his hairline, superior to the lateral border of his right orbit. He went forward for a second time and fell into Jackie's lap for his final rest. This shot occurred much farther down Elm Street (probably 40 feet farther) and produced a bloody halo that was seen by many witnesses. (Such a downhill site was actually identified on a Newsweek *photograph (22 November 1993, p. 74); their source was listed as the National Archives.) The time interval between these two successful head shots cannot be known with certainty, but multiple lines of evidence (more than eyewitness reports, as we shall see) strongly suggest that it was greater than one second; it may well have been several seconds. At about this time, the limousine had begun to speed up. (It is outside the scope of this essay, but the rising bullet trail on the lateral skull X-ray is entirely consistent with a second head shot while JFK was erect—in fact, only when the head is erect can such a trail occur for a frontal bullet. For any reasonably positioned frontal gunman, a rising trail could never occur for a frontal shot with the head oriented as seen in Z-312. Frames immediately thereafter are not possible either.)*

The evidence for this scenario initially derives from those eyewitnesses closest to the limousine. Included are bystanders on both sides of Elm Street, the motorcyclists, and the Secret Service (SS) agents, mainly those from the first vehicle behind the limousine (nicknamed the Queen Mary). Of about twenty close witnesses who offered an opinion, eight to ten (depending on the criteria being used) describe *another shot* after the first head shot—either by their direct or indirect statements. The other witnesses don't deny this—they simply don't mention it. At least eight witnesses describe exactly what happened to JFK with the second head shot—he fell forward! Some witnesses even recall specific events that occurred between these two head shots—thus buttressing the case for two closely spaced, but readily distinguishable, shots. And no one saw a head snap! In addition, Secret Service (SS) agents in the followup car are consistent in describing JFK's reactions and movements. [*Editor's note:* See Bonar Menninger, *Mortal Error* 1992, Appendix, for their statements.]

These data are assembled in more detail in the following table, based in part on the findings of Milicent Cranor. (Her findings will be published in *Probe* this fall; also see "The Magic Skull," *The Fourth Decade*, July 1995, p. 36.) I believe that I am in agreement with her interpretation; she may, however, interpret some of the data in this table differently from me. Note that many witnesses recall an audible shot after a visible head shot. And none of these witnesses describe a head snap, although all of them were looking at JFK during the critical interval. And the one individual (Altgens) who heard a last shot coincident with a head shot was so far down the street that it could not correspond to Z-313. Instead, his recollection fits extremely well with the first reenactments, which are discussed below.

A Reconstruction of the Two Head Shots

Frame	Comments	Evidence
250	Kellerman leans forward, begins left turn to rear (complete at Z-270), turns forward by Z-285, speaking into car radio by Z-327.	Z-film
276-290	Shots are fired.	A,B

	A shot may have hit Connally (JBC) here (or earlier).	C
295	Limousine begins braking.	D
	Driver (Greer) still looking forward (but preparing to brake).	Z-film
302-304	Greer completes rapid right turn to rear.	Z-film
	Greer brakes while looking back.	E
305-315	Greer looks back for entire interval.	Z-film
	Greer continues to brake.	F
	JBC begins falling forward—at least until Z-334.	G
	Limousine slows to a stop.	H
	Motorcycles begin to overtake limousine.	I
306-313	**First Head Shot.** Strikes right occiput. Time is *approximate*.	J
	JFK's hair flew up.	K
	Skull fragment *without blood* seen by Jackie; also see Moorman photo.	L
	No bloody halo was seen with this shot.	M
	JFK grabs his left chest.	N
312-314	Much time and space are missing. JFK's neuromuscular control is gone—he "slumps" into Jackie's lap as the limousine brakes.	O
	Jackie screams just after this.	P
313-315	The limousine goes five feet after the first head shot and stops.	Q
315-317	Greer turns forward—and begins to lift his foot from the brake.	R
	More time and space are missing.	S
317-321	Moorman photo taken after first head shot; bone fragment seen over JFK's right shoulder. Moorman hears more shots after this.	T
	Secret Service men (including John Ready) enter the street.	U
314-321	JFK's head moves to an erect position as Jackie lifts him upward (slowly) and looks into his face.	V
	More time and space are missing.	
	Several witnesses proceed to describe the second head shot.	
	JFK falls forward—for the second time.	
	No head snap is reported by anyone.	
315-343	Clint Hill begins to run—touches limousine at Z-343.	W
	Clint Hill hears second head shot *after* he touches limousine.	X
c. 321+	**Second Head Shot**. Time and space are missing again. The limousine is actually farther down Elm St. The film's editors have moved the limousine uphill—according to the witnesses it should be closer to Z-358. A bullet strikes the right temple/forehead— the right occiput is blown out. No head snap is seen.	Y
321+	A frontal head shot can only produce the metallic X-ray trail when the head is far back, i.e., within several frames of Z-321.	Z
	A bloody halo (or explosion) is seen.	AA
321+	(Some time after first head shot.) Spectators scatter, fall to the ground, run up the knoll, and then, *after all this*, another shot is heard.	BB

327-337	A new skull defect becomes apparent.	CC
	JFK falls forward. According to the witnesses, this event must occur just after Z-358 (as seen in the current film). As before, time and space have been lost through the editing process.	DD
343+	The limousine finally accelerates.	EE

Evidence

A. First reenactments: See below. Camera jiggles at Z-290 (Stroscio).

B. Kellerman (SS): "I turned around to find out what happened when two additional shots rang out and the President slumped into Mrs. Kennedy's lap . . . .I heard Mrs. Kennedy shout, "What are they doing to you?" I yelled at William Greer to "Step on it, we're hit!" and grabbed the mike from the car radio, called to SA Lawson that we were hit . . . ." He added that he was facing forward during the "flurry" (when he was on the car radio), and that he did not look back again until Jackie was on the trunk. [Kellerman sat next to the limousine driver.]

C. JBC shirt faces Zapruder, Newman, Rather. JBC's movements may have shown a shot.

D. Alvarez speed analysis.

E. Common sense; typical time to brake. Kinney also suggested that Greer took his foot off the accelerator during this time.

F. Common sense—he is still looking back; also, brake light is on in Muchmore film (at least for "Z-311 to Z-319").

G. Z-film; also common sense—brake is still on. This also suggests no limousine acceleration before Z-334, which is confirmed by Clint Hill's testimony below.

H. See above witness table regarding limousine stop—also see Moorman, Muchmore blur analysis in the discussion below.

I. All 3 movie films: Nix, Muchmore, Zapruder.

J. Nix film: Cranor sees a bone fragment seven frames before "Z-313." Brehm: "The President was leaning forward when he stiffened perceptibly; at the same instant . . . a rifle shot sounded . . . the President seemed to stiffen and come to a pause when another shot sounded and the President appeared to be badly hit in the head . . . and then [he] roll[ed] over to his side . . . ." Brehm then heard a third shot. Cranor: JFK's head made a slight "tic" of a movement to the left. Jean Hill: "Just as I yelled, 'Hey,' to him, he started to bring his head up . . . and just as he did the shot rang out . . . ." After the second shot she saw JBC "fall to the floor." With the third shot, "President Kennedy was hit again and . . . further buffeted his body and . . . [she noticed] his hair standing up . . . it just rippled up like this." Moorman: She heard a firecracker sound almost simultaneously with her photograph; then she saw JFK "sort of jump," and slump sideways; then Mrs. Kennedy screamed. Schwartz: JFK's head "kind of twisted" to the left.

K. Brehm: He saw JFK's hair fly up with a head shot and then he heard a third shot. J. Hill: "the hair on the back of his head flew up." Hickey: "The first shot of the second two seemed as if it missed because the hair on the right side of his head flew forward." Kinney: The second shot hit

JBC, the 3rd hit JFK; with this he saw "hair coming up." He hit the siren; Clint Hill began to run.

L. Jackie: "I could see a piece of his skull and I remember it was flesh colored . . . No blood or anything." Also note bone fragment seen in Moorman photograph.

M. Denied by Hill. Not reported by Moorman, or other nearby spectators. Although the Newmans did see blood, they did not describe a halo. They were in the best position for a close look at the right side of JFK's head, where some blood might have been expected.

N. Zapruder: "Well, as the car came in line almost [i.e., Z-313], I heard the first shot and I saw the President lean over and grab himself like this [holding his left chest area]. I heard a 2nd shot [most likely this was the 2nd head shot farther down the street] and saw his head open up . . . ."

O. Many witnesses (or viewers of an early film version) describe "slumping." Especially note Cranor, Finck, Jackie Kennedy, Lattimer.

P. Jean Hill, Mr. and Mrs. Bill Newman; see Mary Moorman above.

Q. Alan Smith: "The car was ten feet from me when a bullet hit the President in the forehead . . . the car went about five feet and stopped."

R. Z-film; also, it is common sense to stop braking when looking forward. Note that as the braking stopped, the limousine could still have coasted downhill slowly.

S. Z-film; Greer's head turn is too fast. For a more realistic turn, see Kellerman's turn between Z-270 and Z-285.

T. See background objects for the site of the photograph.

U. Bill Newman: "A car filled with SS men was just behind the President's car, and when it was right beside us, it paused, and I saw several men with what looked like Thompson machine guns get out of the car." Marrion Baker: "and that was when the SS were trying to get in the car." John Ready (SS): "At this time the SS car seemed to slow and I heard someone from inside this car say: 'He's shot.' I left the followup car in the direction of the President's car but was recalled by ATSIC Emory Roberts as the cars increased their speeds. I got back on the car and seated myself beside Mr. Roberts on the front seat."

V. Z-film: Thompson (1967) graph, p. 91. Note that JFK was most posterior at Z-321. Schwartz: "What she kind of did was push him back upright . . . Kind of pushed him like she was looking at him, saying, 'What's wrong?' And then his head goes like that [probably with the second head shot—he has already described the slight leftward rotation with the first head shot that several witnesses saw] . . . And whew! The whole half of it come off." Ault: "Following the first shot . . . Kennedy appeared to raise up in his seat . . . and after the second shot the President slumped into his seat." Hargis: "I heard the 1st shot . . . the President bent over . . . Connally turned around . . . it looked like the President was bending over to hear what he had to say . . . [when JFK] straightened back up in the car . . . his head exploded." Hickey (SS): "He was slumped forward and to his left, and was straightening up to an almost erect sitting position . . . .[When] he was almost sitting erect I heard two reports . . . [The] last shot . . . made him fall forward and to his left again."

Kinney (SS): "The first shot was fired . . . and it appeared that he had been shot because he slumped to the left . . . Immediately, he sat up again . . . . At this time Clint Hill jumped off and ran to the President's car . . . .At this time the second shot was fired. With this, simultaneously with the President's car, we stepped on the gas. I released the siren at that time." Newman: JFK "went across Jackie's lap, then he went back. He went both ways."

W.   Shaneyfelt testimony, based on Z-film.

X.   Landis (SS): "When I heard the sound [like a high powered rifle] there was no question in my mind what it was. My first glance was at the President . . . .I did not realize that [he] had been shot . . . .I immediately [looked] over my right shoulder . . . I saw nothing . . . .Jack Ready said, 'What was it—a firecracker?' So far two or three seconds [had elapsed]. [After checking the crowd, the limousine tires, and thinking about what to do] I glanced toward the President and he appeared to be fairly upright . . . leaning slightly toward Mrs. Kennedy with his head tilted slightly back. I also remember Clinton Hill attempting to climb onto the . . . President's car. It was at this moment that I heard a second report and it appeared that the President's head split open with a muffled exploding sound." Clint Hill (SS): "The sound came from my right rear and I immediately moved my head in that direction . . . .[As I did so] I saw the President hunch forward and then slump to his left. I jumped from the followup car and ran . . . . I heard a second firecracker noise but it had a different sound—like the sound of shooting a revolver into something hard. I saw the President slump more toward his left." Clint Hill: "This is the first sound that I heard; yes, sir. I jumped from the car . . . [and] ran . . . .Just about as I reached it there was another sound . . . —it seemed to have some kind of echo. I put my right foot . . . on the left rear step, and I had a handgrip . . . when the car lurched forward. I lost my footing and I had to run three or four more steps before I could get back up in the car. Between the time I originally grabbed the handhold and until I was up on the car—the second noise that I heard had removed a portion of the President's head, and he had slumped noticeably to his left."

Y.   Clint Hill: See immediately above. Also note the following exchange. Arlen Specter: "Now what is your best estimate on the time span between the first firecracker type noise you heard and the second shot which you have described?" C. Hill: "Approximately five seconds." Hudson: "and so the first shot rung out and, of course, I didn't realize it was a shot . . . I happened to be looking at him when that bullet hit him—the second shot . . . .it looked like it hit him . . . a little bit behind the ear and a little above the ear [on the right side] . . . this young fellow that was standing there with me . . . he says, 'Lay down, mister, somebody is shooting the President.' . . . he kept repeating, 'Lay down,' so he was already laying down one way on the sidewalk, so I just laid down over on the ground when that third shot rung out . . . ." Hudson: "He was looking directly at JFK and saw his head slump sideways with the first shot. He heard two more shots in rapid succession. He estimated that he was thirty feet from the car when he heard the shots . . . " (FBI

Report, File #DL-89-43). Hudson: "He said that the last shot hit JFK near the steps, just in front of where he was standing. He is also sure the second shot hit JFK in the head. After this second shot he was told to lay down." (FBI Report #DL 100-10461). Hudson: "I don't know if you have ever laid down close to the ground, you know, when you heard the reports coming, but it's a whole lot plainer than it is when you are standing up in the air." (Hudson stood near the top of the stairs.) Rather: JFK "went forward with considerable violence."

Z. Lateral skull X-rays: the trail rises within the skull, from front to back.

AA. Altgens: He saw the second bullet just knock JFK straight down. He saw " . . . flesh, blood, and bones fly from the right side of JFK's head . . . to the left of the limousine." He was also sure that this was the last shot. "At the time JFK got the fatal blow to the back of his head, I was officially fifteen feet from the car—the distance on my camera showed that footage [he was a professional photographer for AP]—a distance for which I had already prefocused." Decker: "I distinctly remember hearing 2 shots. As I heard the first, I looked back over my shoulder and saw what appeared . . . to be a spray of water come out of the rear seat of the President's car." Hargis: "I heard the first shot and I saw the President bent over and Governor Connally turned around . . . When President Kennedy straightened back up in the car . . . his head exploded." Landis (SS): "I heard . . . the report [first audible shot] . . . from behind me, over my right shoulder . . . I heard a second report and . . . I saw pieces of flesh and blood flying through the air and the President slumped out of sight toward Mrs. Kennedy." E. Roberts (SS): [I heard the] "first of three shots fired, at which time I saw the President lean toward Mrs. Kennedy. I do not know if it was the next shot or third shot that hit the President in the head, but I saw what appeared to be a small explosion on the right side of the President's head, saw blood, at which time the President fell further to his left . . . .About this time I saw SA C. Hill trying to get on the . . . car . . . ." After SA Hill got on the rear step . . . it appeared that SA John Ready was about to follow and go for the right rear step; however, I told him not to jump, as we had picked up speed, and I was afraid he could not make it." Mr. Willis: He heard three separate sounds, was sure from his war experience that all three hit their target, and he also saw a red halo. Mrs. Willis: She saw the second shot take off JFK's head and produce a red halo. Zapruder: "I heard the first shot and I saw the President lean over and grab himself like this (holding his left chest area) . . . I heard a second shot and then I saw his head open up . . . ."

BB. Kivett (SS): "As the motorcade was about 1/3 of the way to the underpass . . . I heard a loud noise . . . .It sounded like an extremely large firecracker. As I was looking . . . to my right rear I heard another report . . . .I looked toward the Vice Presidential car, and as I did so, I could see spectators, approximately 25-50, scattering—some were falling to the ground, some were running up a small hill, and some were just standing there stunned—here I heard the third shot." C. Roberts: "Just seconds after that I heard . . . backfire . . . .saw a man sprawled over . . . his daughter . . . I saw a policeman running across the park . . . pulling his pistol . . . I heard a second shot . . . ."

CC. Z-film: Note how the light reflection changes over the skull vertex.

DD. Altgens, Ault, Finck, Kinney, Landis, Rather, and many more.

EE. C. Hill (SS): He had his hand on the handgrip, heard a shot hit, then lost his grip as the limousine accelerated. Shaneyfelt places his first touch at Z-343. Kellerman (SS): "We just literally jumped out of the God-damn road."

Trask (1994), p.71, quotes a Mike Wallace interview with Clint Hill twelve years after the assassination. Hill believed that if he had been 0.5 to 1.0 seconds faster he could have taken the final bullet himself. Since Hill is seen (Shaneyfelt, 15H699—see intersprocket area) first reaching the car at Z-343, even one second earlier would have been only at Z-325, still well after the supposed single head shot at Z-313. Hill had not changed his story—it was still grossly at odds with the film.

Jean Hill has denied seeing a red halo. It is striking that the halo was also not reported by her adjacent friend, Mary Moorman. If the red halo was associated with the second head shot, but not the first one, that would explain their experiences. Both Jean and Mary were probably distracted by gunfire that seemed to them to come from directly across the street. Most likely they stopped tracking JFK at that point and therefore did not observe the halo, which was associated only with the second head shot. That such a spray should be seen only with the second shot is quite understandable. The blood available during the first shot is only the amount pumped through a lacerated blood vessel per frame exposure time. However, for the second shot, the situation would be quite different. In that case, blood could actually accumulate within the intracranial cavity for many, many exposure times; the time interval between shots was probably at least one second and may have been longer. Even in a one second interval, however, the amount of pooled blood available would have been greater by a factor of at least ten—perhaps even much greater—thus making a spray of visible blood quite likely.

James Altgens, an AP photographer far down Elm Street, was strategically located to see the second head shot. He had just finished another photograph (later correlated with Z-255). Since he was busy preparing for his next shot, he did not see the first head shot but saw only the second, which was much closer to him. In his letter to Doug Mizzer (21 November 1994; see Livingstone 1995, p. 135), he writes as follows:

As for my position of being alongside the limo at the time the fatal shot was fired, I believe we are dealing in inches [meaning that was just about right]. Realizing that the limo was constantly moving, with airborne fragments coming my way, I still maintain that those fragments landed at my feet. And, the reflex of JFK's head—back then forward—as claimed in the Zapruder film, I did not see the backward movement. When first told about it I figured that it was an optical illusion . . . .At the time JFK got the fatal blow to the back of his head, I was officially fifteen feet from the car—the scale on my camera showed that footage—a distance for which I had already prefocused.

It is noteworthy that, unlike the witnesses above, he does not hear any more shots after this head shot. That is because it was the *second* head shot. His observation of airborne debris is also consistent with other witnesses who saw this with the second head shot. Finally, his report of being 15 feet away must be taken seriously. Altgens was a professional photographer for AP and it was his business to know distances. If he is right about being only 15 feet from JFK at the time of the second head shot—and he is certainly emphatic about his distance—then this shot must have occurred well after Z-313. In fact, it matches the last shot in the first reenactments very well (see below). This is about 40 feet farther down Elm Street from Z-313. (Altgens' photograph at about Z-255 was one of the most widely circulated; he took this (Livingstone 1995, p. 135) with his 105 mm lens set for infinity, which was 60 feet or beyond.)

These witnesses do not all report the same specific details. They are in different locations so they hear and see different parts of the whole scene. They also pay attention to different aspects of the live scene unfolding before them. This is all quite different from the Michigan experiment, in which all viewers had the same perspective (they all watched the same film). Within those constraints, however, the consistency of all these witnesses with one another is really quite striking. It seems unlikely that, randomly, they would all devise such compatible stories. Most of all, though, their concordant *disagreement* with the WC is quite overwhelming—*none* of them report what the WC concluded.

Was tissue debris visible in the air after the head shots?

Several eyewitnesses reported debris in the air after the head shots. The left motorcycle officer, Bobby Hargis, for example, testified: "It seemed like his head exploded, and I was splattered with blood and brain, and kind of a bloody water" (6H294). The day afterwards he reported, "I thought at first I might have been hit" (*The New York Daily News*, 24 November 1963, p. 100). This has generally been assumed to mean that he thought a bullet had struck him—he knew, after all, that something had hit him.

Vince Palamara (*The Third Alternative*, 1993, handwritten appendix, p. 1) reports that the driver of the follow-up car, Samuel Kinney, said that he saw the right rear of the President's skull blown out by the fatal shot, and that the left windshield of the follow-up car and Kinney's left arm had been splattered by blood and brain matter. James Altgens (see above comments) and SS agent Paul Landis both saw pieces of flesh and blood flying through the air. Mrs. Eva Grant (Jack Ruby's sister) reported that Tom Howard, Ruby's attorney, was trying to sell a photograph that showed half of JFK's skull in the air (14H479).

Mary Moorman's famous Polaroid photograph (Groden 1993, p. 34; Trask 1994, p. 235, p. 247) may show a skull fragment. JFK's right shoulder, especially on the clearest available copies, is topped by an Alpine mountain. This very white object may also appear between JFK and the seatback in Z-323 to Z-338. It also seems to be described by William Manchester (*The Death of a President*, 1967, p. 160): "and one fragment, larger than the rest, rises over Kennedy's falling shoulders and seems to hang there and then drift toward the rear." This was presumably based on Manchester's reported viewing of the film on 75 occasions (John Corry, *The Manchester Affair*, 1967, p. 45). This is also consistent with Jackie's comment that she saw a flesh colored (and bloodless) skull fragment.

Trask reports that the time interval between Z-313 and this Moorman Polaroid is about 0.2 seconds. This interval may also be estimated from elementary physics. Assuming that the vertical distance from the top of JFK's head to his right shoulder in this photograph is about eight inches (it would be more if he were erect), and that the skull fragment traveled no appreciable distance above the skull vertex, the time of flight may be calculated to be a minimum of about 0.20 seconds. It could have been longer— even a good deal longer if the fragment had first ascended. This time interval would correspond to 3.7 frames. Therefore this fragment should be seen at about Z-316, or sometime thereafter in the Zapruder film. It may be visible between JFK and the seatback in Z-323 to Z-338. Charles Brehm told Mark Lane, "That which appeared to be a portion of the President's skull went flying slightly to the rear of the President's car and directly to its left. It did fly over toward the curb to the left and to the rear." (This is cited by Thompson, 1967, p. 99.)

The only suggestion in the film for flying objects are the two forward going streaks seen in Z-313 and, to a lesser degree, in Z-314. For many reasons, however, these are inconsistent with the eyewitness reports of debris in the air. First, the speed of these streaks can be calculated to be extraordinarily high. The distance traveled by the upper streak within the exposure time of an 18.3 fps camera (1/36 sec) is about 7-8 feet. This yields a minimum speed of 135 ft/sec. It could well be higher if the flying object had started its flight any time after the shutter opened. Elementary physics then yields a maximum ascent of 252 feet (neglecting air resistance) and a total flight time of 8 seconds. These are both quite incredible. To make matters even worse, the horizontal displacement for the lower streak would be 424 feet, well beyond any reasonable distance reported by the observers. Interestingly enough, it is also well beyond the distances of 20 to 40 feet that Lattimer reported in his own experiments (Lattimer 1980, p. 251). Furthermore, even if these streaks did represent such tissue, then by conservation of linear momentum JFK's head should go *downward* and backward, not *upward* and backward, as is seen. (See Milicent Cranor's "The Joker in the Jet Effect," *The Fourth Decade*, January 1996, p. 28.) Therefore, based on all of these arguments, whatever these two streaks represent, they cannot represent biological tissue from JFK's head.

How fast was the limousine moving?

Regarding the speed of the Presidential limousine during the assassination, SS agent Samuel Kinney observed that at the time of the first shot, the speed of the motorcade was "3 to 5 miles an hour" (HSCA Document # 180-10078-10493). For comparison, Alvarez described it as 12 mph. But Alvarez is required to assume a camera speed of 18.3 fps. This is called into question below. The reenactment time of 3.5 seconds (*Whitewash II*, p. 180), as discussed above, is also inconsistent with Alvarez's speed.

HSCA Document # 180-10099-10491 is an eight page summary report of an interview with SS agent William Greer, the driver of the limousine. He reports motorcade speeds which ranged from ten to thirty miles an hour, although when he made the turn into Elm Street from Houston his speed had slowed to about three to five miles per hour. "We were almost stopped," Greer said. Note also the comments of Roy Truly (above): he describes the limousine as almost striking an abutment and nearly stopping as a result.

Did all the witnesses hear the same 3 shots?

Although the WC was at great pains to limit the total number of shots to three, they spent little time trying to decide if all the ear witnesses actually heard the same three shots. Milicent Cranor ("The Magician's Tools", *Probe*, November/December, 1995, p. 7) reports the following (also see table below). Independent of what they did or did not see, the majority of witnesses said that the last two shots were close together. The witnesses listed below were more specific about how close together these shots were. Each heard only one shot, followed by a pause, and then a flurry at the time the head exploded. Between the first shot and the flurry they heard no shot. That means that they missed one of the first two shots. (See Carol Hewitt's ground breaking work on rifle silencers in the same reference as above.) I would add that Thompson (1967, pp. 254-

271) has also compiled a long and detailed list of witnesses. This list confirms that many, if not most, witnesses (of those who report) did not hear three equally spaced shots. Any two closely spaced (authentic) shots are incompatible with a single gunman firing a Mannlicher-Carcano. If *only one* of these ear witnesses is correct, the Warren Report is wrong.

One Shot, then a Flurry. In Between: No Shot.

Witness	Statement
C. Ault	"close enough to be from an automatic rifle" (24H534)
J. Bell	"in quick succession" (*The New York Times*, 11/23/63, p. 5)
G. Bennett	"a second shot followed immediately (18H760)
L. Bowers	"Like this: Bang, . . . , bang, bang", as he rapped his knuckles on a table to demonstrate (6H288)
J. Connally	"The thought immediately passed through my mind that there were either two or three people involved . . . or someone was shooting with an automatic rifle . . . because of the rapidity of these two." (4H133-4, 138, 147; 1 HSCA 42, 52-53)
W. Greer	"simultaneously" (2H118)
G. Hickey	"in such rapid succession . . . no time element in between" (18H762)
T. Henderson	"in rapid succession" (22H524)
C. Hill	"The second shot had "an echo . . . double sound." (18H742, 2H138-144)
J. Jarman	"third shot was fired right behind the second" (3H204)
(Mrs.) L. Johnson	"in rapid succession" (Robert MacNeill, *The Way We Were*, 1963. *The Year Kennedy was Shot*, 1967, p. 192)
R. Kellerman	"flurry . . . plane breaking the sound barrier . . . bang, bang" (2H76) [After turning forward at Z-285, he spoke into the car phone by at least Z-327; he heard the *flurry* while he was on the phone; Jim Marrs, *Crossfire*, 1989, p. 12.]
K. O'Donnell	"almost simultaneously" (7H448)
W. Taylor	"In the instant that my left foot touched the ground, I heard two more bangs." (Commission Exhibit 1024, p. 783)
C. Walther	"almost at the same time" (Commission Exhibit 2086)
L. Willis	"two real fast bullets together" (7H498)
M. Woodward	"The second two shots were immediate . . . as if one were the echo of the other . . . ." (Nigel Turner, *The Men Who Killed Kennedy*, 1988)
S. Weitzman	"simultaneous" (7H106)
R. Youngblood	"in rapid succession" (MacNeill 1967, p. 193)

Did JFK raise his hand to his head just before he collapsed?

Thompson (1967), p. 16, claims that, among Manchester's many errors, one is particularly substantial and especially difficult to understand, because Manchester claimed to have memorized every movement (*Look*, 4 April 1967). Manchester (1967, p. 158) states: "Now, in a gesture of infinite grace, he raised his right hand, as though to brush back his tousled chestnut hair. But the motion faltered. The hand fell back limply. He had been reaching for the top of his head. But it wasn't there anymore." Thompson adds, "We know from the Zapruder film that no such gesture ever occurred."

But what are we to think when Jackie says nearly the same thing? In her WC testimony she states: "I could see a piece of his skull and I remember it was flesh colored. I remember thinking he just looked as if he had a slight headache . . . No blood or anything. And then he sort of did this (indicating), put *his hand to his forehead* (emphasis added) and fell in my lap." (5H180). Is it likely that she is making this up—and that it simply happens to coincide so closely with Manchester's account of the film? (This disagreement is reminiscent of a similar one that Milicent Cranor discovered in speaking to Bill Newman. He had tried to tell Garrison that JFK fell downward and leftward as if struck by a baseball bat. But Garrison would not believe him—because it was not in the film.)

When did Zapruder begin filming?

Zapruder told *CBS News* that he began filming as soon as the limousine turned onto Elm Street from Houston Street (*CBS News*, 23 November 1963; see also Commission Document No. 7, p. 12). [*Editor's note:* See Mike Pincher and Roy Schaeffer, Part IV, for the FBI interview with Zapruder.] But the film shows a long gap between the earlier motorcycles and the limousine's first appearance at Z-133. Several questions naturally arise at this point. Why would Zapruder expend valuable film footage on the motorcyclists but not take all possible footage of JFK? He had been extremely frugal in using only 17 frames to film his acquaintances at Dealey Plaza—actually less than one second at 18.3 fps! He had also made a trip home during the day to retrieve his camera for this special occasion. And he had just switched his film to the second side so that he would have the entire track available. Furthermore, he had enough space on the film to catch this event—the motorcade occupies only 6 feet 3 inches of film length, whereas a standard track has at least 25 feet. Even if he had filmed in slow motion (48 fps), he still would have used only about 16 feet (assuming the limousine speed calculated by Alvarez). So it is quite puzzling that he waited so long to begin filming. Or did he really begin filming when the limousine was at the top of Elm Street, just as he said he did?

2. Disagreements between early viewers of the film (November 1963) and what is currently seen.

Erwin Schwartz was Zapruder's business partner and during that weekend he was often at Zapruder's side. He was recently interviewed by Noel Twyman and Richard Bartholomew (*Bloody Treason*). Schwartz recalls viewing the film about 15 times during that initial weekend. He saw tissue debris flying to the rear—an event not seen on the current film. He does not report a head snap, but does recall Jackie lifting JFK's head upward and backward (presumably in order to see his face better). He also describes JFK's head as twisting to the left (possibly with the first head shot), something also suggested by the comments of Mary Moorman and Jean Hill. Experts had also previously noted that such a head rotation could occur with head shots (7 HSCA 171).

Manchester watched the film, perhaps as many as 75 or even a 100 times. He recalls seeing JFK sitting upright, waving, and then slumping. "A fine spray of blood and pieces of skull are thrown into the air in one quick upheaval." (Corry 1967, p. 45.) Also notable here is the absence of a head snap—and JFK's upright posture at the time of the (second) head shot.

Chester Breneman [*Editor's note:* See Jack White, Part IV] wrote a three page personal letter to his nephew on 9 April 1973, describing his experiences. He and Robert West had been the surveyors for the *Life* magazine and Secret Service reenactments of November and December 1963. For this task, he had been provided with enlargements of frames from the Zapruder film—to assist him in determining locations and distances. On page three, he states, "On three frames after a *frontal* (emphasis added) entry shot, we saw blobs leaving the *back* (emphasis added) of the President's head and disappearing on the fourth frame."

An interview with Breneman by Jim Marrs also appeared in the *Fort Worth Star-Telegram* (14 April 1978), in which he made the same point. In fact he made it even more forcefully—he described the blobs of backward flying debris as *large* (emphasis added). What Breneman had seen led him to say, "The only thing I know for sure is that shots came from two different directions." Elementary physics also suggests that such debris should be seen on multiple frames (see below). Breneman added one other curious comment. He reports that one of the *Life* investigators said that his own life (no pun intended) was not worth a plugged nickel and Breneman recalls, "Then he pulled back his shirt and showed me his bullet proof vest. I thought that was a little odd."

The experiments of Alvarez and Lattimer also support this conclusion. Debris remains visible for many frames in each of their films. So why isn't it (easily) visible for multiple frames in the Zapruder film?

Dan Rather (CBS News, 23 November 1963) offered his own description of what is currently not seen in the film: "Governor Connally, whose coat button was open, turned in such a way to extend his right hand out towards the president . . . And as he turned he exposed his entire shirt front and chest because his coat was unbuttoned—at that moment a shot very clearly hit that part of the Governor."

Milicent Cranor has advised me in personal conversations and correspondence that in 1992 she saw an unusual version of the film at the NBC Archives. She studied this repeatedly in slow motion on superior equipment. This is her summary.

> Kennedy was hit in the right temple while Moorman and Jean Hill were visible in the background. JFK's head rotated slightly counterclockwise (i.e., left)—just a tic. A flap of skin or bone swung out on a vertical hinge. The hinge became horizontal and the flap became part of what looked like a giant clam. I never saw the famous "blob" nor did I see clouds of gore. I only saw thin translucent lines intersecting the head that scientists (in fluid dynamics) tell me are most likely condensation lines left in the wake of a bullet. One line suggested the shot came from Zapruder's immediate left. About 1/2 second later JFK went flat across Jackie's lap, not forward but leftward, away from the viewer. JFK then came back up to about where he was before. His head made two nearly imperceptible jerks, a tip to the left, a tip to the right. Then he bucked backward—but there was no head snap. He moved all of a piece, as if given a shove in the sternum.

She then adds: "I recently realized that an early description of the film—by John Lattimer of all people—fits my own impression of this version." Lattimer, in describing Z-313 to Z-320, stated that "the President's body, which had already tilted to his left, with his head hanging downward and forward, moved slightly forward at the moment of impact, but then stiffened and lurched completely over to his left, onto the rear seat of the automobile, from which Mrs. Kennedy then rose and pivoted, to allow him to lie down on the seat" (*Resident and Staff Physician*, May 1972, p. 60). He later changed his story to match the public version of the film (*Kennedy and Lincoln*, 1980, p. 248).

Is it pure chance that Dr. Pierre Finck, one of the autopsy pathologists, actually agrees with Lattimer's first description? In his "Personal notes on the Assassination of President Kennedy" (1 February 1965) written to his superior, Brig. Gen. J. M. Blumberg, he states: "On 16 March 1964 I also had the opportunity to examine COLOR PRINTS, approximately 10 x 20 cm, stamped 'US Secret Service, Washington, DC' on the back and made from the only color film taken at the time of the Assassination of Kennedy . . . .[These] clearly show how Kennedy slumped forward from a sitting position . . . .This sequence of photographs is compatible with a bullet hitting Kennedy in the back and with another bullet hitting him in the head, both from behind." This document was released only in the past several years from the Otis Historical Archives at the National Museum of Health and Medicine, Armed Forces Institute of Pathology. His description is, of course, quite at odds with the current public version of the film, which displays a grossly obvious backward head snap—an event that neither Lattimer nor Finck (nor Cranor) saw in an apparently different version of the film. These seemingly fantastic intimations of multiple versions of the film even surfaced in *Life* magazine (2 October 1964). Frame Z-323 had a caption that described JFK's head "as snapping to one side." Another version of the same date has this picture replaced by Z-313 and a caption saying that JFK's head went "forward," consistent with a shot from the rear. Paul Hoch and Vincent Salandria (Newcomb and Adams, p. 143) together discovered six different versions of *Life* for this same date.

Dan Rather (*The Camera Never Blinks*, 1977, p. 127) of CBS has reported that security at *Life* for the film was extremely poor and that any major executive could order his own version of the film. Is it possible that some of these (possibly) unaltered films have persisted through the years? Did Cranor see one of these?

3. Disagreements between the film and other photographic evidence.

In prior discussions, I have listed the Moorman photograph as possible evidence for a limousine stop, mostly because the foreground motorcycles are blurred while the limousine seems as well defined as the background. That analysis is, however, complicated by issues of proximity and perspective. I shall therefore turn instead to another film taken during the shooting on Elm Street—Marie Muchmore's 8 mm movie film. Thompson's map (p. 253) places her (witness #104) on the grass of Dealey Plaza, just in front of the wall (*Archives*, CD 735, I, p. 8). But Trask disagrees (inside front cover)—he places her on the other side of the wall, closer to Main Street! The grass in front of the wall is easily seen in the Zapruder film, but she is not there. However, her unattached shadow may be there (see discussion below)! Her location is also discussed by Milicent Cranor ("The Magic Skull," *The Fourth Decade*, July 1995, p. 36). Cranor notes one other anomalous feature: even though Muchmore was closer to the book depository than Zapruder, the spastic camera motions in Zapruder's film (that have been attributed to his reaction to Oswald's gunshots) are *not seen* in Muchmore's film at the supposed time of the Z-313 head shot!

Muchmore's view was across Elm Street toward Zapruder; she was noticeably farther away from the limousine than Zapruder at Z-313. Because of her distance, the resolution of her film is not as good as the Zapruder film. Her camera, however, ran at a purported 18.5 frames per second (fps), according to the FBI (Trask 1994, p. 206). This nearly one to one correspondence with the Zapruder camera rate (as also determined by the FBI) should make intercomparison of frames straightforward. Close inspection of the limousine in the Muchmore film shows that the right taillight is on (only the brake would cause this—the blinkers controlled only the front lights) for nine successive frames; these correspond to about Z-311 to Z-319 (Groden 1993, pp. 33 and 37, shows two of these frames; see also the back of the dust cover). Before and after these frames, the taillight is not visible. Therefore the brake was on for at least nine frames (about half a second) or perhaps even longer; that cannot be determined from this film. If the brakes were applied just before the head shots, then the limousine would probably have slowed. If a shot occurred around Z-276 (see first reenactments below), then the braking that begins around Z-295 (per Alvarez) may be a reaction to this shot. The time interval of about 20 frames would be long enough for a braking response to occur—even using the official camera speed of 18.3 fps.

The Muchmore film may provide better evidence of limousine slowing than the Moorman photograph: there are more images, but even more importantly, it does not suffer the drawbacks of proximity and perspective that are evident in the Moorman photograph. By examining the Muchmore frame shortly before Z-313, as printed in Groden (1993, p. 33), the reader may draw his own conclusions. Note the reflected highlights on the rear of the near motorcycle: they are distinctly blurred. So is the image of the tire and the rear fender. For comparison, look at the limousine. On the rear tire, the whitewall trim seems quite well defined—as compared to the motorcycle tire. Also examine the limousine right rear taillight and immediately adjacent fender. Again, this seems better defined than the motorcycle fender. Also compare the clarity of the limousine hand grip (seen against the background grass) to the rim of the motorcycle windshield. All of this is consistent with a very slow limousine speed. Also note that the foreground characters are seen quite clearly, implying that the camera tracking is quite slow at this time. Even the closest female figure on the far right is not blurred due to her proximity to the camera. Since the limousine image is clearer than the motorcycle, we know that the camera is preferentially tracking the limousine. And, since the bystanders are sharply defined, the logical conclusion is that the limousine speed is much closer to the bystanders (zero) than to the motorcycles. I have also viewed all of the adjacent frames in the Muchmore film with a loupe and cannot avoid the same conclusion there (based on the degree of relative blurring)—the limousine is hardly moving. This deceleration appears to begin shortly after Z-300, just as Alvarez said. Simply from qualitative appearances, however, this deceleration appears to be much larger than he suggested, with a final speed much less than his 8 mph. (David Lifton provided me with excellent individual frames from the Muchmore film.) It is also striking that in the Zapruder film, in Z-315 and in Z-317, the pedestrian in the background grass is also seen with great clarity—just as would be expected if the limousine had stopped at that time.

There are other photographic clues to the slowing of the limousine. In both the Zapruder and Nix films (probably in Muchmore, too), the two motorcycles on the left rear begin to overtake the limousine after about Z-305. That would be consistent with limousine slowing. The timing of this event is particularly compelling since the other evidence (especially the eyewitnesses) also suggests that the limousine slowed at precisely this time. The Nix film, however, shows a near uniform speed through Dealey Plaza. Twyman has calculated this to be 9.2 mph after the equivalent of frame Z-300. (This assumes that the film was shot at 18.5 fps (Trask 1994, p. 190), as was reported by the FBI.) It would also be most useful to measure the speed before the frame that corresponds to Z-300, so that a comparison to the Zapruder film can be made. A distinct head snap is also visible in the Nix film.

Supporters of Zapruder film authenticity have argued, quite naturally, that alterations of the Zapruder film are unlikely because appropriate alterations of both the Nix and Muchmore films would also have been required. Although, at first glance this inevitable argument from common sense seems compelling, some reasonable responses can be offered. It should first be noted that the FBI made extensive efforts to capture all possibly relevant photographic evidence. Nix turned his original film over on December 1 (Trask 1994, p. 183). The Muchmore film was sold to UPI and was featured in *Four Days* which was published in early 1964 (Trask 1994, p. 205). The FBI received a copy by about mid-February 1964.

After requesting and receiving a copy of his film from the FBI, "He [Nix] stated that the copy . . . does not appear as clear as his usual pictures." (Trask 1994, p.190). Some years later, Nix's granddaughter, Gayle Nix Jackson, said that the government kept the original film and still refused to make it available to her. She added that her grandfather believed that the government altered the film and the copy returned to him, though she simply doesn't know the truth (Trask 1994, p. 197). In a conversation with Milicent Cranor (May 1993), she said that her grandfather believed that frames had been removed from his film. In a technical report (21 December 1995) on the Nix film at the National Archives, Charles Mayn stated that their copy is not an out-of-camera film. Groden reports (1993, p. 32) that after Nix's film was returned to UPI in 1978 by the HSCA it was never located again.

These films actually may not agree with one another as well as is widely believed. Doug Mizzer (Livingstone 1995, p. 138) has pointed out an apparent discrepancy between the Zapruder and Nix films. Clint Hill testified that he grabbed Jackie and put her back into her seat (2H138-139). In the Nix film, Hill gets both feet onto the limousine and puts one hand on each of Jackie's shoulders. He even seems to be hugging her head and shoulders as he pushes her back into the seat. But the Zapruder film shows that he did not reach her until she was already back in the seat.

Although Shaneyfelt (15H699) testified that Clint Hill did not touch the limousine until Z-343, my review of individual frames of the Muchmore film shows him there by (the equivalent of) Z-332; by (the equivalent of) Z-336 his foot is rising to touch the rear step, an impossible manuever unless he already had a handgrip.

This fall, Milicent Cranor will publish in *Probe* a powerful summary of eyewitness evidence that motorcycleman Chaney passed the limousine while going to report to police chief Curry before the final head shot. In the Nix film, there is no sign of this event. Nor are there any spectators running up the knoll before the final head shot in this film (see *Reconstruction Table*), as several witnesses reported seeing before the final shot was heard. And Emmett Hudson recalled actually being on the *ground* during the last shot (5H560-561), but he is not in this position anywhere in the Nix film. Furthermore, he also described his young companion as being on the ground *before* him. That is not seen either.

I have been struck by how difficult it is to see the acceleration of the limousine after the head shots—in the Nix and Zapruder movie films (Muchmore stops too soon to know). This dramatic acceleration caused Clint Hill to lose his grip after his first contact with the limousine. Its magnitude is typified by Glenn Bennett's (SS) comment: "The President's car immediately kicked into high gear" (18H722-784). This nearly uniform speed, especially for the Nix film, seemed very obvious in the frame by frame, slow speed, and normal speed modes available on the Medio Multimedia's *JFK Assassination: A Visual Investigation* (1995). Twyman has confirmed this visual impression by measuring the limousine speed for frames on the Nix film that correspond to Z-301 to about Z-326. The graph of position versus frame number is a beautiful straight line, consistent with a speed of 9.2 mph (assuming 18 fps). What needs to be done, however, is to continue this graph for the entire film, or at least for the portion that includes the moment of the dramatic limousine acceleration. It will be most interesting to see if that acceleration can be quantitatively corroborated by the Nix film.

Insofar as the Muchmore film is concerned, Groden (1993, p. 37) notes that while UPI had the original film, it "was cut or mutilated at the frame that showed the moment of the head shot." The original copy cannot be located. In a technical report (21 December 1995) on the Muchmore film at the National Archives, Charles Mayn states that their copy is not an out-of-camera film. It is therefore not possible simply to say about either of these films that the original film agrees (or disagrees) with the Zapruder film. The originals are gone.

If the Zapruder film has been edited, then it should also have been possible to alter both the Nix and Muchmore films. It is even likely that less effort would have been required for these two films. The above comments on the Nix film, however, do raise very serious concerns about its authenticity. It should also be recalled that we have only the FBI statement for the film speeds. In any case, if the Zapruder film can be shown to be altered, then these two other films, of necessity, must also have been modified. On the other hand, if the Zapruder film survives all attacks, then the issue is moot. I have therefore, for the most part, decided to focus on the Zapruder film. However, there is much that could still be done with the other two films. For example, no one—to my knowledge—has yet attempted an analysis of streaks in any frames of these films (see below discussion regarding Weatherly's work on the Zapruder film).

Pincher and Schaeffer have developed an ingenious observation into a compelling conclusion. [*Editor's note:* See Mike Pincher and Roy Schaeffer, Part IV.] By comparing the blink pattern on the front of the limousine on Main Street (as seen on the Hughes movie film) to the same pattern on the Zapruder film, a paradox ensues. Since the Hughes camera speed is known, the blinker frequency can be calculated. Then a prediction can be made for the Zapruder film between frames Z-133 and Z-238 when these blinkers are visible: each blinker should be on for about 7 frames. In fact, between Z-133 and Z-181, the blinkers are consistently on for about 9 frames. Between Z-182 and Z-211 the blinkers are hidden behind the sign and after this an irregular (but also inexplicable) pattern is seen. If the blinker speed was truly constant, the only way for more than 7 frames to appear in sequence is for Zapruder's camera to be running faster than the purported 18.3 frames per second (fps). This is powerful and direct evidence that something is wrong with the film—in particular, the camera speed of 18.3 fps is called into serious question. The observed blinker frequency in the Zapruder film is actually more consistent with 24 fps than with 18 fps. However, that speed (24 fps) was not available on Zapruder's camera. Pincher and Schaeffer therefore propose that Zapruder's camera had actually run at 48 fps and that frames were excised so as to bring the nominal speed down to a range of 12 to 24 fps. Although, at first sight this may seem inconceivable, there is a surprising range of otherwise puzzling data that begins to make sense with this new hypothesis. I shall return to this issue later.

4. Disagreements between the film and the first two reenactments.

Independently of one another, Chuck Marler [*Editor's note:* See Chuck Marler, Part IV] and Daryll Weatherly (*The Investigator*, Winter 1994–95, p. 6) completed a superb job of detective work on the first two reenactments. These were done on 26 November and 5 December 1963. Because of the extensive and detailed nature of their work, only a brief summary of their conclusions can appear here. The chief finding is that the second survey (conducted by the SS) showed "X" marks on Elm Street for the three shots (see photographs and diagrams in Weisberg, *Whitewash II*, pp. 243-248; also Livingstone, 1995, photographs 9-16)—these correspond (approximately) to frames 208, 276, and 358 (the frames had not been numbered yet).

This map is accompanied by supporting data (CE 585). It is tantalizing that the first of these shots occurs within the small number of frames supposedly damaged at *Life* magazine (a very unusual event, according to Marler, who has worked extensively with such film); these frames were missing for several years until 1967, when they were printed in *Six Seconds in Dallas*. The other odd feature, of course, is that the limousine and its occupants are almost completely hidden behind the freeway sign at this point! One naturally wonders how a successful shot could have been identified at that point, but that is where these early reenactments consistently place it.

To further compound the mystery of these (supposedly) accidentally damaged frames, it should be duly noted that one of the reenactment frames (from 24 May 1964) was a missing frame, Z-210! Although this frame was not published with the other frames in volume 18 of the Hearings, it was printed (intact) in CE 893 along with the corresponding photograph of the reenactment! The intersprocket image does appear to be absent, however, just as it was later when printed in *Six Seconds in Dallas* (1967).

Some investigators have proposed that the Stemmons sign was deliberately elevated by the editors in order to hide JFK when he was struck by the bullet at this time. (A related issue, that the sign was moved very soon after the assassination, was raised on 16 December 1963 by WC member John J. McCloy (Newcomb and Adams 1974, p. 131): "You see this sign here (pointing to a Z-frame); someone suggested that this sign has now been removed.") At first such an editing change seemed likely to me, but as I analyzed all the pertinent photographs, I became convinced that the superior and far edge of the sign had not been altered. The left portion of the sign was stretched out, however, as the magnification studies showed. This latter conclusion also derived support, in my view, by careful comparison of the relative position of the left post to the reflected highlights on the small tree above and just to the right of the post. The horizontal separation between these two objects actually increases over successive frames; this also was evidence for a composite image. Nonetheless, it seemed most unlikely to me that the sign had been elevated in order to obscure JFK. But that still left a problem: why did the reenactments place a shot where JFK was invisible?

The enigma of how the first reenactments could have identified a shot while JFK was hidden behind the sign was addressed by Livingstone (1995, p. 61-63). Weatherly had discovered an astonishing document (CD 298, p. 11) that described the location of Nix in a wholly impossible manner. In this document, he is placed precisely—with distances specified—where the well known "Babushka Lady" was standing, on the grass on the far side of the limousine! Nix was actually located near the corner of Houston and Main, nearly a block away! The images on this film are even summarized:

> Nix . . . photographed the motorcade as it approached the triple underpass. Nix photographed the left side of the Presidential car with Mrs. Kennedy in the foreground waving when the President's head suddenly snaps to the left and the car picks up speed as a man jumps on the left handhold. The Nix film runs about 8 seconds.

Livingstone adds that this is clearly not the Nix film—that film is only about 6.5 seconds long (Trask 1994, p. 185). The extant Nix film does show a backward head snap, but this film describes only a sharp leftward movement, consistent with the second head shot as I have described it above. As further confirmation that this leftward movement coincides with the second head shot, note that Clint Hill climbs onto the limousine—and the limousine accelerates—only well after the first head shot; therefore, what is being described can only fit with the second head shot.

This supposed film of Nix, of course, is missing. That this film was of some interest to the investigation is confirmed by an interview that was actually conducted with the photographer (Commission Document No. 2, p. 31). By now the question should be obvious: since JFK was obscured in the Zapruder film at the site of the first shot in the first reenactments (Z-208), was the film of the "Babushka Lady" used to identify this first shot?

There is a surprising amount of unexpected additional support for a final shot at about Z-358 (such a shot is, of course, no longer seen on the extant film). It should first be noted that the data table places this shot at 294 feet from the depository window, near the bottom of the steps below Emmett Hudson. This is well beyond the 265 feet cited in the Warren Report for the last shot (frame Z-313). A second WC exhibit (CE 875) actually displays a photograph of Elm Street in which this last shot is identified as being nearly 40 feet past frame Z-313. Finally, there is CE-2111, a SS report which describes the manhole cover as located almost opposite the limousine site at this last shot. This manhole cover is actually 70 feet beyond Z-313—hardly opposite the official last shot at Z-313. Marler also quotes the testimony of Hudson (cited above); Hudson describes the last shot as about even with the steps and he also describes his actions between the two head shots. The statement of James Altgens, a professional photographer (cited above) also supports this whole scenario—he was only 15 feet from JFK, with his camera pre-focused, when the final shot hit. This indubitably places the last shot far after Z-313. (Altgens can be seen in Z-349, far west of Hill and Moorman.) Marler adds the coup de grace by noting that a data table (CE-884) has actually been altered. This is known both from close inspection of the shape of the numbers (the altered digits have a different shape from other digits of the same number) and from comparison to surveyor Robert West's still existing field notes. For further details the reader is strongly encouraged to read Marler's and Weatherly's reports. [*Editor's note:* See Chuck Marler, Part IV.]

If everything were simple and straightforward, none of the above anomalies should exist. Not only do they exist, but all of the available points of disagreement are consistent with one another—a truly astonishing state of affairs. But there is even more. Michael Stroscio, a physicist associated with Duke University, has recently published a short article ("More Physical Insight into the Assassination of President Kennedy," *Physics and Society*, October 1996, p. 7) in which he identifies more camera jiggles than the three conceded by Alvarez. [*Editor's note:* See the Enclosure.] One of these occurs shortly before Z-290 and it is not a small one. Alvarez was aware of this but chose to ignore it based on his speculation that a siren had gone off just before this. (There was—and still is—no evidence for a siren at this time. Regarding the siren, see above comments by Kinney.) The concordance between the large jiggle seen just before Z-290 and the first reenactment is truly intriguing. In case there is any concern about the apparently imperfect match between Z-290 and the second shot in the first reenactments (at Z-276), several items should be kept in mind: (1) there is a time delay for impulses to show up on the jiggle analysis; (2) at the first reenactment, the frames had not yet been numbered—only the approximate site on the street was identified; and (3) if film editing has occurred, then the frames with the jiggles could have been moved by a modest distance, consistent with the natural resolution within the frames. This site on the street could have been misidentified (or even deliberately moved) by virtue of the natural uncertainty of position within the frames. (See comments below from Salamanowicz for the HSCA on this issue.)

To close this section, it might be asked what the shot at Z-276 (or thereabouts) represented—surprisingly enough, the reenactments do not clarify this. Initially, I had thought that it was the first head shot, but that does not fit. The strongest argument against this is the Moorman photograph. The background images in this photograph clearly place this photograph after Z-313. Furthermore, a skull fragment is seen over JFK's right shoulder and the limousine is seen on Elm Street downhill of Z-313. If the shot at Z-276 had been the first head shot, then elementary physics tells us that this skull fragment must have sailed over 150 feet vertically before coming down to its position on the Moorman photograph. If, however, its maximum elevation had been only three feet (it could have been less, of course), then it should have been airborne for only about 8 frames (less than half a second) and it should appear about where it does in the Moorman photograph— assuming a first head shot at Z-313. I had to conclude, therefore, that the shot at Z-276 was not a head shot. Nonetheless, something about it had been obvious—or it would not have been identified as it was. It seems most likely that it was the shot that hit Connally. This moment may have been identified in one of the original films by his movements or perhaps by the appearance of blood on his shirt.

5. Internal inconsistencies in the film.

Many of these issues are summarized by Jack White and also by Pincher and Schaeffer [*Editor's note:* See Part IV for both contributions.] These items include the white object at JFK's right temple, the spray of blood, Greer's head turn, Connally's invisible left turn, apparently superhuman movements by multiple individuals, as well as other items. Not all of these items are discussed here.

The rapid head turns of the limousine driver, William Greer, between about Z-302 and Z-304 and again at Z-315 to Z-317 seem impossibly fast to many observers. I have looked at these frames many times myself, in the slides at the Archives, on high quality copies made from the Lifton movie version, and on 8 mm film rented from the Zapruder attorney. These all appear the same to me and the angular displacement per frame interval does seem unnaturally large, just as reported independently by each of Twyman, Schaeffer, and Marler. I found this rapid turn especially convincing on a CD-ROM titled *JFK Assassination: A Visual Investigation* produced by Medio Multimedia (1995). In this format, it is possible to move quickly between frames (in either direction) so that the rapid turn is readily visible. Experiments with athletic subjects by each of Twyman and Marler have been unable to reproduce this angular speed.

Immediately related to this issue is the lack of motion blurring during these rotations. Given the angular displacement and the approximate exposure time per frame of 1/36 sec (the denominator is 18.3 times 2), blurring must be seen—that is simply unavoidable. Experiments by Twyman and Marler confirm this; Twyman even saw large blurs at 60 fps, for a fit athlete attempting his fastest turn. Rapid movements are seen at other sites such as the movement of Jackie's right arm between Z-327 and Z-328; there is a significant displacement, which seems both too large for the short time interval, as well as too large not to show a blur. Such considerations again raise the question: were frames excised at fairly regular intervals—thus speeding up the action?

That the spray of blood at Z-313 is clearly visible for only one frame initially struck me as incomprehensible, particularly in view of Alvarez's experiments with melons. It also seemed unlikely to me that so many eyewitnesses would distinctly recall such an event if the spray really had lasted for only 1/18 of a second. This was the first objective item to cause me to consider film alteration seriously. These melon frames are printed in the Alvarez article. Melon debris is readily visible in the air, even in these poor quality prints, for at least 5 to 6 frames. Although the camera speed here was faster (24 fps), this is still an enormous discrepancy visa vis the Zapruder film. Even simple physics calculations show that an object starting from rest at 52.8 inches elevation (see Marler for the position of JFK's head above Elm Street) will take 0.52 seconds to reach the pavement. That would correspond to 9 or 10 frames in the Zapruder film. Similar results are seen in Lattimer's experiments with human skulls. No experiment has shown near total disappearance of such a spray within one frame, or even in two or three frames.

Schaeffer has noted a remarkably symmetric plus sign at the center of Elm Street at Z-028. This does not exist at the same site in the frames before or after this. Nor have other such symbols been seen in the film, except for one I describe below at Z-308. It is possible, however, that more of these will be discovered when a thorough search is made, especially since my own discovery was accidental. Schaeffer conjectures that this may have been used as a register mark for aligning the film during copying. (I also saw this plus sign in the best SS copy at the Archives—see below.)

The Soaring Bird

Twyman has recently identified a new and extraordinary feature within the intersprocket area. It is seen in both the WC prints and in the Archives slides. This feature is particularly obvious in some frames, e.g., Z-226. (It even appears on the front cover of *Life* for 25 November 1966.) For convenience in locating it, however, refer to Z-241. First identify the helmet of the far motorcycle man. Then draw an imaginary line straight up to the bottom of the sprocket hole. At almost the bisector of this line is a small dark spot, slightly smaller than the holes in the retaining wall. Running through this dark spot is a line from 8 o'clock to 2 o'clock; the entire image looks vaguely like a soaring bird at an angle, as it catches an updraft. In Z-226 this dark spot is surrounded by a bright halo. And above the halo (just barely discontinuous from it) is an imperfectly rectangular white area that covers the top of the wall and extends slightly over it. This "Soaring Bird" image repeats very frequently (but not always) throughout the WC images and the Archives' 35 mm slides. It is absent in Z-224 and Z-225, then returns in Z-215 to Z-223. It is present in many (but not all) frames before Z-200, often surrounded by a white halo. The halo seems inconstant in shape, sometimes looking more like a square than a circle. The dark spot (hereinafter called "The Black Hole") always seems positioned at the same point with respect to the sprocket hole, as if it had been placed there on purpose.

The Soaring Bird recurs through multiple frames after Z-241, including many frames in the Z-300s and Z-400s. It is also seen during the head shot sequence. The questions raised by this apparition are, to say the least, consequential. Why does this specter (pun intended) occur only intermittently? Why does it occur at the same place below the sprocket hole? Why does the halo change shape? Is a similar image seen in the "home movie" portion? Is it seen in the first 17 frames of the motorcade track? Was The Black Hole used as a register mark for positioning the film? And why does the rectangular shape *above* the soaring bird in Z-226 (also in Z-227 and possibly in Z-225) appear so rarely? And why have all those prior Zapruder film experts not brought this to our attention? Surely, at the very least, if they noted it, they should have sought to explain it. And then there is Shaneyfelt, the FBI agent who numbered the frames (5H139) and who was the FBI's primary expert on the film before the WC. With his first hand knowledge of the film, why did he not relate what he knew about this figure? Finally, anyone who believes in film authenticity will certainly want an explanation for this strange entity.

Twyman adds one more peculiarity. In the slides from the Archives (supposedly made directly from the original film), the intersprocket images suddenly vanish in Z-413 and Z-414; the intersprocket area is simply black. Why is this? Are these intersprocket images truly absent from the "original?" And, if not, why was the intersprocket image excluded from these slides? Are these intersprocket images now on any images at the Archives? Can the "original" 8 mm be checked to see if the intersprocket images are there for these frames?

In the upper one-third (approximately) of the intersprocket area, beginning at about Z-310, a superimposed image appears; this persists through Z-334, the last image printed by the WC. In several frames this is particularly well seen, Z-327 for example. There can be little doubt but that this is the front tire, strut, and fender of a motorcycle on the *right side* of the limousine. This part of a motorcycle on the left side would be blocked from Zapruder's view by the limousine. On several frames, the trunk of the limousine even seems to be visible behind the motorcycle. The reader may judge this similarity for himself by comparing the motorcycle image as seen in the Muchmore film (see the rear dust cover of Groden's book) to the image as seen in the intersprocket area. These images seem identical to me.. This image abruptly vanishes on the first frame after those printed by the WC, as can be seen on the Archives' slides.

Even on photocopies that I made from the WC Hearings, I could see this image—in fact, that was when I first noticed it. It is even more obvious on the slides in the Archives and in the large, high resolution prints made by Twyman. The appearance of this image is odd since it is never seen in the central (projected) image. The second odd feature is that, uncannily, it begins just before the head shot sequence. The third odd feature is that such superimposed images do not occur elsewhere in the film— only here during the head shot sequence! The fourth odd feature—it is really quite striking—is that this superimposed image appears in the same location that The Soaring Bird and The Black Hole appear above. In fact, The Black Hole is usually seen superimposed on the front of the tire, or very close to it. Bruce Jamieson (personal conversation of 24 July 1997) told me that any superimposed image in the intersprocket area would be most unlikely. And he certainly could offer no explanation for the sudden appearance of an image when there had been none before.

Such a superimposed image is also missing from the first track (the "home movie" side). Why such an overlap occurs only during the head shot sequence and nowhere else—unless an artifact of alteration is accepted—is a mystery. Was the faint image of the motorcycle wheel placed here deliberately in order to distract the viewer from its true intention of providing a useful background for inserting The Soaring Bird and Black Hole, so that registration of frames could be keyed to these images during editing?

If this hypothesis is correct—namely, that the motorcycle image has been deliberately superimposed (to assist in frame registration)—then the position of this image might not be entirely consistent from frame to frame. That would be because it was merely placed to assist in registration of frames and not necessarily to appear in a true relationship with other objects in the scene, such as the limousine. So I measured the distance of the top of the fender from the bottom of the sprocket hole and then calculated the fraction of the intersprocket area that this distance occupied. I did this for all frames available to me. I used large color magnifications (about 8 x 11 inches) supplied to me by Noel Twyman. These distances were measured with an EKG caliper; with this precision tool, I have *generously* estimated the measurement error for most frames as about 1%. These results are shown in the following table.

Intersprocket Image: Distance from Fender to Sprocket Hole

Z Frame	Fraction of Frame (%)	Z Frame	Fraction of Frame(%)
312	13.5 ± 0.1	322	(not available)
313	13.5	323	6.3
314	15.2	324	4.4
315	17.9	325	2.2 ± 0.07
316	19.8 ± 0.15	326	5.9
308 (sic)	(+)	327	5.1
318	17.6	328	5.2
319	8.95 ± 0.07	329	9.1 ± 0.07
320	5.15	330	8.5
321	6.7	331	6.7

The effects of measurement error are selectively displayed above. Between Z-312 and Z-318 the limousine position is quite constant with respect to the bottom of the frame. But in this interval the fender moves a huge amount with respect to the sprocket hole. This is easily visible to the eye once it is noticed. It also far outside the measurement error. Furthermore, the frame to frame changes are not monotonic (that would occur if the motorcycle were moving away from or toward the limousine): in particular, notice the position reversal within one frame interval (55 milliseconds) in the sequence from Z-315 through Z-318. After this, the erratic behavior only worsens. None of this would be expected for a real image as initially recorded by the camera. However, for a deliberately superimposed scene, with only slight attention paid to proper placement of the new image, such a random skipping around by the motorcycle would be expected. To make this point even more powerfully, note how precisely the limousine follows the curb from about Z-300 to the last printed frame (Z-334). During this long interval, the driver (Greer) exercises near surveyor's precision—despite gunshots and his turn to the rear, and also despite eyewitness testimony that he swerved to the left and stopped.

One frame is shown out of sequence above: Z-308. It actually appears in the National Archives slide carousel at this point—where it has replaced Z-317. This is an old problem—first pointed out decades ago by Harold Weisberg—and still not corrected. What is curious about this frame, though, is that a plus sign similar to the one that Schaeffer first noted on Z-028 reappears. It is seen just below the sprocket hole, close to where the black hole inevitably is located (when it is present); this frame, however has no soaring bird nor a black hole. These were probably not needed here since the plus sign was available. This plus sign is visible on the 35 mm slide in the Archives and also on the large print that Twyman made.

I also had the unique advantage, for all of this work, of constantly checking my observations against black and white photographic prints made directly from those printed in the WC Hearings (Volume 18). These images are, of course, superior to those printed by the WC. This plus sign was also visible on Z-308 in this set. Shackelford has suggested that these plus symbols are mere random artifacts in the image and are found elsewhere in the film as well. In fact, to date I have not found any others, nor has anyone else to my knowledge. They are quite geometric, not what would be expected from random lines. And if Shackelford knows of any more, he has not publicly identified them.

There is another bizarre event that supports this conclusion of deliberate superposition of images at this point in the film. In the frames that include the right sided motorcycle, it remains within the intersprocket area while background objects progress regularly across the field of view. The lone pedestrian in the background grass provides a guide to this progress. However, between Z-321 and Z-322 there is almost no change in the relative position of this pedestrian and the motorcycle. It is as though the motorcycle has suddenly stopped within one frame interval and then restarted within the next frame interval. This is all, of course, easily understandable if these images are merely the result of careless film editing.

The image of the right motorcycle wheel, strut, and fender implies another conclusion, one of momentous importance. Recall that this image never appears in the central portion of the frame. The arguments above (and the comments by Jamieson) make it quite certain that this apparition did not originally appear in this intersprocket area—it was added later. But if this is true, then where did the image come from? There can be only one possible answer to this question: it must have been present on the original image (in the main portion of the frame). It has merely been edited out of the bottom of the frame—possibly in order to exclude the Newmans (and adjacent spectators) from the bottom of the image. If they had been left in and frames had been irregularly excised (e.g., during a limousine stop), then their positions with respect to the limousine would have revealed non-uniform motion of the limousine. In addition, movement by any of them would have appeared either unnaturally accelerated or simply too erratic.

This deletion of the bottom of the frame has placed JFK, and Connally, too, at nearly the edge of the image. This has often struck viewers as odd, especially since Zapruder was quite confident that he had filmed the entire sequence. In fact, the current images show that he almost missed JFK during the head shot sequence, and Connally appears quite beheaded in some frames. This is most peculiar because Zapruder had no difficulty centering JFK in the frames before or after the head shot sequence. It cannot be argued that he was distracted by the sounds of the head shot, because they had not yet reached him—the supposed jiggles from this are seen in Z-318 and later. And if the gunshots had caused him to lose his tracking, then such errors should be seen after the head shot. In fact, just the opposite is seen. He regains his tracking skills again—just when he should have lost them.

But this almost fatal (presumed) tracking error was so outrageous that I thought it would be interesting to see how other photographers at Dealey Plaza performed that day during the motorcade procession down Elm Street. So I combed carefully through the photographs in the books by Groden (1993) and Trask (1994). Many of these images are present. I measured the location of JFK's head with respect to the center of each frame (I recognize that it is possible that some of these may have been cropped; nonetheless, particularly flagrant tracking errors would not be correctable). Nearly everyone of these showed JFK within 10% of the frame center. Even those rare exceptions where he was more eccentric were nowhere near as inept as Z-313. I performed the same measurements for successive Zapruder frames and graphed these; the worst frames were obviously those near the head shot sequence, as though Zapruder knew the head shots were coming and he wanted to miss them. Furthermore, these frames were grossly worse than the rest. This analysis, therefore, provides indirect support (certainly not proof) for the excision of the bottom of the head shot frames.

Weatherly's Streaking Analysis

Weatherly, in an insightful analysis (Livingstone 1995, pp. 371-381), takes Alvarez's work to its logical conclusion and raises new and curious issues related to image streaking. For example, between Z-193 and Z-194 the camera moves to the left. This is easily determined by simply looking at the right edge of the frame—the image shifts with respect to the frame edge, presumably as a result of uneven camera movement (i.e., poor tracking). As Alvarez noted, such a movement should produce streaking—of the background figures, the sign, and the closer bystanders. But none of this is seen—it is all quite paradoxical. Based on this, Weatherly proposes that this is a composite scene. This is a remarkably simple and powerful argument. It is difficult to avoid this conclusion.

Meanwhile, from Z-194 to Z-195 the motorcade occupants appear unchanged, but both the *background and foreground* are very fuzzy in Z-195—quite different from Z-194. If the limousine is being tracked similarly in these two frames, then why should the clarity of the background (and foreground) be so different between these two frames? Weatherly notes that this phenomenon occurs repeatedly throughout the film—one part of a frame changes a great deal while another part (inexplicably) stays the same. This might be expected if these frames were composites; it is extremely difficult to imagine any other explanation. Another example of contradictory information is Z-212. Here the posts on the Stemmons sign are quite blurred, but the holes in the masonry wall in the background are quite well defined. Since neither of these objects is moving their visual definition should be similar—but it is not.

Between Z-198 and Z-199 the camera obviously moves to the left—note the disappearance of the tree trunk at the right edge. As a result of this, some streaking should be seen in Z-199—unless Zapruder knew how to stop moving when the shutter opened. But no streaking is seen—not even on tiny highlights (observe the background for these). Weatherly again concludes that different parts of the frame indicate two incompatible actions for the camera. In both cases, a composite scene is the simplest explanation. Weatherly adds one more significant point—no frames between Z-166 and Z-216 were published by *Life* in late November, so none of these composite frames had to be completed by then. Also recall that no images published by *Life* contained any intersprocket images until 1966.

Between Z-302 and Z-303 (during Greer's rapid head turn to the rear) the camera moves quite uniformly with the limousine—i.e., it tracks well.

The evidence for this is that the bright reflection in front of the windshield appears in the same place (at the right edge of both frames). In Z-302, Jean Hill and Mary Moorman (standing) are very fuzzy, but in Z-303 they are extremely clear. Even if it is conceded that the camera tracked normally immediately before the shutter opened for Z-303, then stopped when the shutter opened, and then tracked well again when the shutter closed, there must be blurring of the motorcade (since the camera would have had to move abruptly between tracking and not tracking). However, no blurring is seen.

Similar comments apply to Z-308 to Z-311 for Moorman and Hill. And more paradoxes occur in Z-313 to Z-315. In Z-315 (one of the most interesting of all of the frames), the background pedestrian suddenly becomes quite clear whereas in the frame before she is quite blurred. And this occurs despite (supposedly) excellent tracking—note the similarity of the image at the right edge of the frame. Also note the double image of the motorcycle windshield within the intersprocket area, even though the limousine image appears single. This is also the frame immediately before Greer's rapid head turn and the frame in which the head snap begins to accelerate. Weatherly interprets this data to mean that frames have been excised from the head shot sequence, possibly to remove evidence of a frontal head shot. Any reader with a logical bent for objective data is advised, in the strongest terms, to review Weatherly's analysis thoughtfully. It is beautifully simple and the conclusions are inescapable.

The above examples are merely several of many that occur throughout the film. The intersprocket area, especially, is home to many of these odd features, particularly image doubling—sometimes of only part of the intersprocket image. Because of the selective nature of these double images, vibration of the film edge during exposure cannot be accepted as an explanation. Some of the most astonishing peculiarities involve the appearance of JFK and Jackie. In frames Z-316 and Z-317 Jackie has no facial features (even on the slides in the Archives), even though other objects seem well defined. Compare this to Z-312 where her facial features are well defined. In Z-327 to Z-330 a large wedge is missing from the top front of JFK's head (Jackie's upper torso and left shoulder are visible where his head should be). All of these events could easily have occurred in an improperly prepared composite frame.

A particularly obvious and inexplicable event occurs on frame Z-213. (Roy Schaeffer brought this to my attention.) Near the center of the right border are two shadows (at about the level of the tree—ignore the two near the curb), apparently from two bystanders off the edge of the frame. Their length, shape, and direction are all consistent with shadows of other nearby bystanders. (Curiously, one of the shadows does not extend all the way to the right edge.) However, these shadows are absent in the preceding and following frames. In fact, they do not reappear again until Z-217—but here they are in a slightly more superior location (as if both bystanders had moved away from the camera). These shadows are never seen again. And the area in which such bystanders should have stood can clearly be seen in multiple subsequent frames—but no bystanders ever appear. I have noted above that Thompson shows Muchmore in approximately this area on his map. Was one shadow due to Muchmore? If so, how did she and her companion appear and disappear within one frame interval?

Alvarez detected a sudden deceleration from about 12 to 8 mph, centered at about Z-300 and extending over about 0.5 seconds (nine frames); this would begin at about Z-295. From this, Art Snyder (e-mail, 20 December 1996) calculates a deceleration of about 0.37 g. He notes that this rapid slowing should toss things about and adds that most cars do not decelerate more than 0.4 g. He cautions, however, that Alvarez's data are not very accurate and that the slowing could have taken longer than 0.5 seconds. When I examined the frames immediately after this, however, I could see no visible effect on the occupants from such a dramatic deceleration. JFK, in particular, should be observed because he no longer had voluntary muscular control and should have been thrown forward. But over many, many frames before and after this he seems quite immobile.

In reality (as opposed to the film) he should have been—and probably was—tossed forward by the deceleration—recall the many witnesses who reported that he slumped (or fell) forward. Also recall several reports of his falling into Jackie's lap (see Cranor, Lattimer, and Finck above). Did this occur when the limousine braked? If so, then those frames have been removed. And if the limousine stop was real, but no longer visible in the film, then JFK's slumping would also no longer be seen in the film—both events would have disappeared at once. Furthermore, if this falling into Jackie's lap had occurred, then Jackie would, quite naturally, have lifted his head in order to look into his eyes. *With frames excised, this would have looked like the head snap in the current film.* Is there some other explanation for the multitude of witnesses who describe "slumping", especially in the sequence in which it is often described?

The White Spot in the Grass

Between Z-313 and Z-336, there is a white spot in the grass beyond the limousine. At first I thought that this object had been added to the film (to give the illusion of uniform motion) because it was not visible in the *Life* images published on 29 November 1963, because it conveniently appeared for the first time in the head shot frame (Z-313), and because its behavior was so odd. I was later reminded by Jack White that Bothun photo #4 (Trask 1994, p. 156) does show a white object in the grass—at about the right location. Nonetheless, this object, as seen in the Zapruder film still has peculiar features. I have projected slides of these frames and traced the size, shape, and location of this white object. First I centered each frame from left to right based on the far left light atop the limousine roll bar, and from top to bottom by using the curb. The distance of the projector was held constant throughout. On a very long sheet of white paper I traced the white spot from frame to frame, drawing its size and shape as exactly as I could. As a control, I also traced the size and shape of the above noted light on the roll bar.

Next, I measured Zapruder's (supposed) camera tracking errors by measuring (with an EKG caliper) each successive shift of the image at the right edge of the frame. (This is the same principle that was used by Weatherly.) This provided a wealth of data, all of which should be consistent. But it turned out to be far from that. When the image at the right edge of the frame stayed constant or nearly so, it (should have) meant that Zapruder was tracking the limousine very well. Therefore, the width of the light should be at its smallest. Although there was a trend in this direction, there were several occasions in which the width was two, or even three times, larger than the smallest width. This made no sense at all.

On the other hand, when Zapruder's tracking slowed down (the frame image is shifted to the left), then the width of the white spot should be smaller than when he is tracking well (because the camera's relative speed with respect to the white spot is lower). The pattern seen here was even more erratic than above. The width was seemingly unrelated to Zapruder's (supposed) tracking; on many occasions it was two or more times larger than it should have been. And this was far outside the measurement error during tracing. In fact, once I noticed this, I could simply look at the image and perceive immediately—without even measuring—that it was paradoxical.

Similar paradoxes persisted when the width of the white object was compared to the width of the light. In addition, the frame to frame displacement of the white object was particularly egregious as it passed into the intersprocket area. Between Z-334 and Z-335, the displacement was 180% of normal; for Z-335 to Z-336 it was only 50% of normal. (Abnormalities in magnification within the intersprocket area are discussed below.) In view of all of this, therefore, it is most likely that composite frames are being viewed again. The white spot plays a remarkably effective role—it yields a convincing impression that the limousine is moving uniformly, during a period in which virtually all the eyewitnesses tell quite another story. And, as often seen above, the worst editing again occurs within the intersprocket area, which was probably not intended for public viewing.

The analysis above was only for the horizontal direction. But tracking can also be examined in the vertical direction. By measuring the distance from the bottom of the frame to the light on the roll bar (the far left one), Zapruder's (supposed) vertical tracking can be determined. At frame Z-332, the limousine suddenly jumps superiorly by a huge amount—meaning that the camera (supposedly) lurches downward. There is a jogger at the top of the frame with his feet widely spread. The frame jump is about the same distance as the separation between his feet (or more). Such an Olympian downward displacement of the camera cannot avoid producing a severely blurred image of everything in the frame. But nothing like that is seen. Surely this frame is displaying a physical impossibility. This event, in all probability, occurred because of defective film editing. It may also be telling us that the bottom of Z-331 has been edited out and is therefore no longer seen.

Magnification Anomalies.

When I measured the width of an object, or the distinct separation between two stationary objects, from frame to frame, then that interval remained constant—until that interval (or object) crossed the junction between the intersprocket image and the central image. And when that occurred, the measured distance increased progressively, getting larger as the interval progressed into the intersprocket area. An excellent example of this is the measured width between the two posts on the back side of the Stemmons Freeway sign between Z-212 and Z-218. (See Figure 1.) The prints in the WC volumes were used for this purpose. This measured distance increased by over 12%—for only 6 frame intervals. By contrast, between Z-191 and Z-207, before the first post enters the intersprocket area, this interval remained quite constant. I have found this effect repeated in virtually all frames (measurable objects are required, of course) between Z-212 and Z-313. I am continuing to examine other parts of the film.

A simple excuse for this is inevitable—perhaps the camera lens was nonlinear for objects this far off the central axis. Even if this were true, however, it would still be odd for such discontinuous changes to occur so abruptly within the lens—as if the manufacturers had devised the lens to be adequate precisely up to the very edge of the field with no tolerance for error at all and then managed to produce a sudden change at just that point. Besides this oddity, lens aberrations do not typically occur in such a discontinuous fashion.

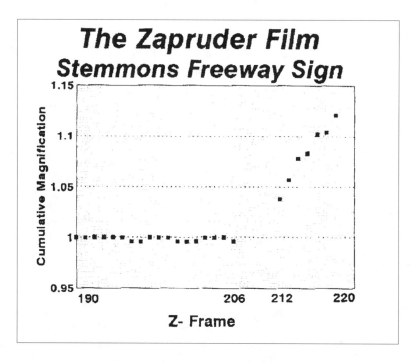

Figure 1. Magnification measurements on the Stemmons Freeway sign

Unfortunately, the problem is even worse than it appears. If this were a simple matter of lens aberration, then such magnification changes should be uniform through the intersprocket area for all of the frames. But that is not the case. For example, examine what happens between frames Z-173 and Z-189, in which multiple bystanders are seen to the left of the freeway sign. For these frames, the interval measured was between the left sign post and the seventh bystander left of the sign. This particular interval was chosen because the total length measured (on an individual frame) is very similar to the separation of the two signposts (as was used above). The magnification change over this 16 frame interval is only 1%. This poses a serious paradox: if lens aberration is the explanation, then why should it be 12% for a short interval (6 frames) but only 1% for a longer interval (16 frames)? At the very least, this is an uncommon optical phenomenon.

I close this section with two bizarre scenes. Recently, Marler rented an 8 mm copy of the Zapruder film. At Z-316 in this version of the film, a solitary pedestrian is seen in the background. In the two frames he has provided, compare her continuous shadow in the first frame (Figure 2.) with her discontinuous shadow which extends well into the intersprocket area (Figure 3.). On this particular frame the shadow is clearly broken into two parts. When I tried to rent this same film, however, I was advised that there were no films with intersprocket images. I am grateful to Marler for making these frames available for publication here.

Several summers ago, while visiting me in the mountains, David Lifton gave me an 8 mm film in a light blue plastic container with a red and white label. In handwritten black ink it was titled: *ZAPRUDER #2 FILM (WITH) "OPTICAL EFFECTS."* Lifton does not recall where he got this. After I determined that the sprocket holes would not fit into my father's old 8 mm (silent) projector (I have all of his many old films and still show them) I put it aside for several years. Then, out of curiosity one day, I began to look at it frame by frame. I was stunned. A large number of frames had either obvious double exposures or some other unnatural feature. For example, when Clint Hill tries to climb onto the back of the limousine, the curb can be seen through his leg! In the "original" Zapruder film, in at least Z-344 through Z-362 (the last frame I examined), there is a self-luminous appearance to Clint Hill's image just above the sprocket hole.

This is grossly obvious and cannot be explained by sunlight—this area, after all, should be in total shade. This odd image in the "original" film reminded me of the luminous appearance of Clint Hill in this most peculiar film from Lifton. Raymond Fielding (*The Technique of Special Effects Cinematography*, 1965/85, p. 177), while discussing traveling mattes (see below), reports that a typical effect seen in such superposition special effects is the 'phantom' phenomenon, in which background detail can be seen *through* an actor. I have since looked at many of these frames (from Lifton's film) under the microscope and have made slides of them through the microscope. The symbols for the date of manufacture of this strange film are two solid triangles—the same symbols that occur on the Zapruder film. According to information provided by Kodak, films with this symbol were manufactured in 1941, 1961, and 1981. Is it possible that this version may play a role in understanding some of the mysteries of the Zapruder film? Why should such frames exist at all? Who made them? And for what purpose? (Special effects are discussed in greater detail below.)

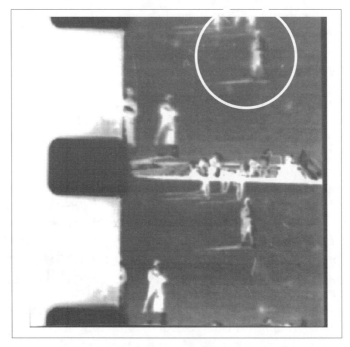

Figure 2. Pedestrian with normal shadow

Figure 3. Pedestrian with broken shadow

Personal Observations at the National Archives.

In order to settle these many issues, a review of the original film at the National Archives would be ideal. I therefore requested the support of the ARRB for this purpose. Although I received a sympathetic reply from the board, further events were already in place. Within a very short time after my letter, the ARRB officially recommended (24 April 1997) that the film be made public property. Although I could still ask the Zapruder family attorney for permission for such a review, the implications against authenticity might not be cheerfully received, particularly since the purchase price could be adversely impacted. I resolved instead, for the moment, to review only the May 1964 reenactment film and, for a second time, to review the FBI and Secret Service copies of the film, all of which are held by the National Archives. I am grateful to the Archives for permission to view these items. My two visits to the Archives took place in October 1996 and in June 1997 (shortly after my letter).

In an attempt to simulate Zapruder's effort on 22 November 1963, a reenactment film was shot on 24 May 1964, through Zapruder's camera. When I looked at this film, I was immediately surprised—it contained no intersprocket images! The intersprocket area is simply black. This was fairly conclusive proof that this film was not the original, but rather a copy. Staff members assured me that this was the only copy in their possession and that they did not know where the original was or if it existed at all. Additional evidence that this is a copy is that the emulsion side faces the viewer. Even more evidence is that images appear to be out of sequence (spliced in) yet no physical splices are visible. There are actually two successive reenactments, i.e., the vehicle is filmed twice as it travels down Elm Street. Lyndal Shaneyfelt, the FBI expert confirmed this in his testimony (5H162). A third sequence was also filmed with Zapruder's camera—at stationary points en route—and I viewed this also.

Despite the fact that this film was a copy, the image color and clarity were very good. To my amateur photographer's eye, I could not easily distinguish it from an original. (Such comparisons, of course, are best made with known originals side by side; I did not have that opportunity.) Unlike the film shot by Zapruder, there are no anomalies such as portions of frames alternately going in and out of focus, and there is minimal blurring due to camera or subject movement. Some of this may be explained by the use of a tripod—which Zapruder had not used.

For this reenactment, Shaneyfelt (5H176) stated that the time interval between the sites corresponding to Z-222 and Z-313 was 3.5 seconds—instead of the 5 seconds assumed by the WC. This latter was based solely (there is no other time clock) on an assumed camera speed of 18.3 fps: for the 91 frame intervals between Z-222 and Z-313 then, this time interval is 91 ÷ 18.3 fps = 4.97 seconds, just as Shaneyfelt said. Using Shaneyfelt's time interval, the speed of the limousine in the reenactment is 11 mph x (5 ÷ 3.5) = 15.7 mph!

As I was very interested in the camera speed, I counted the number of frame intervals between two fairly well defined points: the first corresponded to Z-222 (the tree in the background identifies this site with very good accuracy—certainly within one frame interval) and the second was where the limousine is exactly opposite the camera (where the roll bar is precisely vertical—this corresponds to Z-316). I counted the number of frame intervals several times and got a consistent number: reenactment frame intervals = 81±2.

For the physical interval cited by Shaneyfelt (between the sites of Z-222 and Z-313 in the "original" film) the reenactment film shows 78 frame intervals (naturally three less than the above interval). Since the time interval was stated by Shaneyfelt to be 3.5 seconds, the camera speed is simply 78 ÷ 3.5 = 22.3 fps! This is a serious discrepancy—one to which the WC remained totally oblivious. How could the camera speed have increased from 18.3 fps on 22 November 1963 to 22.3 fps on 24 May 1964? Or was Shaneyfelt grossly in error when he said that the time interval was 3.5 seconds? And, if he was, when else might he also have been grossly mistaken? Was the camera speed really 18.3 fps? For the WC to leave the only quantitative reenactment—the only one shot through the actual camera—in such a state of confusion does nothing to reassure us of their competence unless, of course, it was more than mere incompetence. We have only the FBI's word that Zapruder's camera speed was 18.3 fps. (For the Nix and Muchmore camera speeds of about 18.5 fps, there is also only the word of the FBI, nothing more.) If they were so undeniably incompetent during the reenactment, what assurance can there be that Zapruder's camera speed was correctly measured—or correctly reported? (It is impossible to know at what level this problem lies.) And without reliable data on the camera speed, there is no way of knowing how fast *anything* in the film happens, except by indirect inference. Even the interval between shots cannot be estimated with any precision.

There is one other means of determining the limousine speed. From Cutler's widely used map of Dealey Plaza, the physical distance between Z-222 and Z-313 can be measured as about 77 feet (Robert Cutler, *The*

Umbrella Man, 1975). Using the time of 5 seconds in the Zapruder film, the speed can be quickly calculated to be 15.4 ft/sec or 10.5 mph. This is consistent with the 11 mph stated above. For the reenactment, the speed would be 22 ft/sec. or 15 mph, also in good agreement with the value calculated above.

There are two FBI copies and two SS copies of the film in the Archives. One SS copy has very good color and clarity. In the second one, the color is faded (I have made this observation of an obvious difference in quality on both of my visits; it was not something I had prejudged in any way. My notes still show my sense of surprise at this obvious difference.) The two FBI copies are likewise of inferior quality, with notable loss of color. These observations by themselves bear some discussion. Recall that three copies of the film were made by Bruce Jamieson on 22 November 1963. Since they were all made at the same time on the same film stock, they should still be of similar quality, unless they have been handled or stored differently. Based on this alone, only one of the above copies would seem to qualify as a first generation copy. The ARRB has indicated (letter to Noel Twyman with a copy to me, 11 July 1997) that a third ("*Life* magazine") copy is in private hands, but is in degraded condition. This implies that the Archives considers the poorer quality SS version to be a first generation copy, despite its differences from the better version.

But there is more information on this point. To my great surprise, I immediately noticed that none of these four copies of the motorcade sequence contained any intersprocket images. That area was simply black. Since my long anticipated controls were now missing, I was quite disappointed. Should I have expected to see intersprocket images? In an interview with Bruce Jamieson (who was at the Dallas laboratory on 22 November 1963) by Noel Twyman (*Bloody Treason*), he said that a contact print process was used for copying the film. When I spoke to Jamieson (phone conversation, 24 July 1997) he recalled that for 16 mm film only one intersprocket image was copied. The other side was masked out—so that a sound track could be installed there. He also recalled that their contact printer was custom built and was of very high quality, perhaps even superior to Bell and Howell's version. But if Jamieson's memory is correct—and he did not seem uncertain about this—then the absence of intersprocket images in the first generation copies of the motorcade made by him should not have been a surprise to me.

Life magazine admitted to damaging frames Z-207 to Z-211 during its initial work (*The New York Times*, 30 January 1967, p. 22). Later, however, Time-Life released these missing frames (Thompson 1967, p. 216). These replacement frames contain no intersprocket images. Had intersprocket images been present, they would have provided overwhelming evidence that these images were present on first generation copies. Their absence, however, is consistent with Jamieson's memory. (My own subsequent analysis of these frames proved interesting. Using the analysis of streaks as described above, at least some of these frames appear to be composites, thus suggesting that they also are not from the original film.)

The remainder of these copies at the Archives revealed no more surprises. I did, however, search for—and find—the purported register mark on Z-028 that was discovered by Roy Schaeffer near the center of Elm Street. I did not make a thorough search for other similar marks, as that would have been extremely time consuming and lay well beyond the scope of my goals for those visits.

According to Zapruder (5H571-576), he had shot the first side of the film earlier and had then reversed the film in the camera so that he would be ready to shoot the second side. The first few frames on the second side were taken in Dealey Plaza, before the motorcade arrived; the remainder contains the motorcade sequence. The first side (the "home movie" side), however, is present in the Archives and is full of images. To my delight, the intersprocket areas were all intact— including the adjacent (left) portion of the scene in the main image area. At last, some controls were available.

On this first track, I noted that there were two sets of edge prints (Kodak ID symbols) within the intersprocket area. One set was printed upside down and reversed, so that there could be no question about this conclusion. Furthermore, the phrase, "Processed by Kodak D Nov 63," appeared more than once across this area. So this was evidence that the first generation copies had shown an image in the home movie portion, i.e., this sequence on the first track was obviously a copy (it had two sets of edge prints) and yet it did contain intersprocket images of scenes. Therefore, the first generation copy must have included intersprocket images. Furthermore, the copy that I saw was made shortly after the original—the copying date was explicitly stated to be "Nov 63." (Alternately, the date was stamped during the initial processing on 22 November, but then we would naturally ask why no date appears on the motorcade sequence.) What could still not be determined directly from this, however, was whether the first copy of *the motorcade sequence* (the opposite side of the film) had included the intersprocket area. At this point there is only Jamieson's recollection for this, plus the apparent absence of images in this area on all of the available films.

I also noticed that the quality of the intersprocket scenes (especially near the center of this small area) was similar to that of the projected (central) image. In fact, for the large majority of these frames, the color, clarity, contrast, and shading of the intersprocket image seemed indistinguishable from the adjacent central image. This seemed true over the entire 32-33 feet (including leaders and splices without images) of film, for both indoor and outdoor sequences. This similarity of image in the intersprocket area and the central image of the "home movie" portion is quite different from the motorcade in either the WC prints or in the slides housed in the National Archives—particularly after about Z-235. In both of these latter cases, the intersprocket areas are distinctly darker than the central image. (I am grateful to David Lifton for first bringing this issue to my attention.) On the other hand, I am told by someone who has seen the "original" that the intersprocket area shows *less* color intensity and seems more washed out. It was not clear to me, however, whether this description was meant to apply to frames *after* Z-235.

I looked for anomalies in the intersprocket area (as discussed above for the motorcade sequence) of the "home movie" sequence—these also were not evident: no frame to frame alteration in resolution was seen, no missing portions of images, no blurring due to a hand held camera, no single and double images in the same area, and no overlapping images in the intersprocket area.

The Kodak edge prints within the intersprocket area, as printed in the WC Hearings, contain two solid triangles. According to Noel Twyman, who discussed this with the Zapruder attorney, this identifies the film as produced in 1961 in Toronto. All of the other symbols, both on the reenactment film and on all copies in the Archives, contain the symbol of a solid triangle and a solid circle. Again, according to information from Twyman, these films are thereby dated to 1963. I was subsequently able to confirm these years from an *Eastman Kodak Film Edge Guide*, in which the symbols repeat at 20 year intervals.

To my great surprise there were no symbols that would permit dating the "home movie" portion—none anywhere. If symbols appear on the motorcade track, why would they be absent from the "home movie" portion? I discussed this with Jamieson. To my surprise, he reported that dating symbols should appear only on one track of a 16 mm film.

One other point can be made. In the reply I received from the ARRB, it was explicitly stated that the original of the first track (the "home movie" portion) has not been located nor, apparently, is there any information as to its whereabouts. This is quite significant. If the original were still available, it might be possible to analyze in great detail (by chemical and physical techniques) the composition of the emulsion. This analysis could then be compared to the "original" film now in the National Archives. It seems likely now, though, that this can never happen. Not only is this original "home movie" portion missing, but there is apparently no documentation of any kind as to where it has gone. (This is reminiscent of another critical missing piece of evidence in the case—the brain of JFK.) The following table summarizes this data:

Summary of the Films

Film		Expected	Actual
Reenactment		original version	copy
SS copies	A	first generation	first generation (?)
	B	first generation	later generation
	C	first generation	privately held
Z-"home movie track"		original	later generation
		dark intersprocket images	normal images
		partial image overlap	no overlap
Archives slides:			
Z-413, Z-414		intersprocket image	none
Muchmore		original	copy
Nix		original	copy
"Nix"		somewhere	nowhere
4x5 transparencies			
from *Life*		somewhere	nowhere

In this table, the SS copies A, B, and C, refer to the three that were made by Jamieson on November 22. The better SS copy could be an authentic first generation, if, indeed, the first generation contained no intersprocket images. (A claim that this is truly a first generation copy is, however, no stronger than the claim that the "original" is authentic; and since there is no way to distinguish a first generation from a later one, that ambiguity still persists.) The partial image overlap refers to the intersprocket area. The expected images on the first track are those that would be expected based on what is seen in the motorcade track. The film referred to as "Nix" is the one improperly attributed to Nix (see above discussion), and which was filmed from the position of the "Babushka Lady."

Synthesis

It is time to draw all of these threads together. Although every thread of the tapestry will never be seen, a faint view of the landscape may now be possible. It has proved surprisingly difficult to rule out film alteration. In fact, there are simply too many threads out of place, too many scenes (and whole film copies) missing, and too many peculiar features. Precisely what was done to the original film—which frames were excised and which frames were retained (but altered)—may never be completely clear. What follows is a current best guess, subject to revision based on new evidence. What is proposed, however, does explain a wide array of bizarre features.

Frames were excised, particularly those that showed tissue debris going backward. Backward going debris would have been overwhelming evidence of a frontal shot (or shots) and would have posed too serious a threat to the official story of only posterior shots. But the original edge prints also presented an ominous hazard; if any of these symbols remained in the final version of the altered film, their very presence would have tipped off even a casual viewer that something was wrong—an original cannot contain two sets of edge prints (or even part of a second set). In addition, frames showing the limousine stop were removed.

Whether these latter frames were coincidentally the same as ones as for the airborne debris is impossible to say with certainty—it is conceivable that some of them were. Whether any independent reason demanded removal of frames of a stopped (or slowed) limousine is debatable. The Secret Service, of course, may have wished such action (or lack of action) removed simply because it was potentially embarrassing. And, of course, if the limousine did stop, or slow a great deal, then a block of frames could have been excised during that interval. Portions of these could then have been available for insertions into other scenes, as needed.

A large block of frames was probably excised from the top of Elm Street to the first limousine frame at Z-133. Zapruder's comments are consistent with this interpretation, as discussed above. The goal of this excision may have been to eliminate an embarrassing limousine turn (almost hitting the curb—see Roy Truly's statement above), which ought to have given the "lone, demented gunman" his best possible shot!

Roy Schaeffer has proposed that the original film was shot at 48 fps. [*Editor's note:* See Pincher and Schaeffer, Part IV.] A 25 foot track of film would contain about 2100 frames (7 frames/inch), or about 44 seconds of action at 48 fps. This would have been sufficiently long to film the entire motorcade, long enough even to encompass a limousine stop and an initial speed as low as 3 to 4 mph. Especially if Zapruder knew this about the film and the camera, he may have filmed at 48 fps, hoping later to rerun all the action in slow motion.

There are several direct arguments for 48 fps. It is also possible, now that this issue has come to the fore, that further direct arguments for 48 fps may still be discovered; this is a rather new area of exploration. The major one is the blinker light cycle time. The other significant one is the absence of significant blurring during rapid motions, such as the two Greer head turns and Jackie's hand movement. Alvarez described the hand clapping cycle of Charles Brehm in Z-278 to Z-296 as 3.7 cycles per second (about five frames per cycle). Alvarez found that he could clap comfortably at this rate, but that a rate even 30% higher (i.e., a camera speed of 24 fps) felt unnatural. He therefore concluded that the camera speed was closer to 18 fps than to 48 fps (the only other speed on the camera). If, however, the original film had been shot at 48 fps and two of every three frames had been removed from this part of the film, then Brehm's clapping cycle would appear about as it does in the current film and the clapping analysis would be unable to detect this loss of frames.

There are also powerful indirect arguments for 48 fps—in fact, many of them. A film shot originally at 18 fps would make frame excision quite difficult (perhaps impossible)—without being overtly obvious. Such an abbreviated film, made from an 18 fps original, would yield too much jerkiness—or, if this were corrected (if possible at all) by fabrication of new frames, then an extraordinary effort would be required for many such frames. Furthermore, the 18 fps scenario would still leave unexplained the lack of blurring during rapid movements—where some blurring would be expected (the exposure time would be shorter at the faster camera speeds).

Weatherly discusses (Livingstone 1995, p. 377) the use of double images in cinematography to serve as filler frames. For this purpose, images before and after the required frame are combined in a double exposure. In a movie film, such a filler frame would restore the visual impression of a continuous image. Roy Schaeffer has noted that many of the double images seen in the Zapruder film represent about four inches of separation in real space. Since each frame represents a displacement of about one foot (at 12 mph and 18.3 fps), the four inches would correspond to one-third of a frame interval (in the WC scenario). But if the film had actually been shot at 48 fps, the displacement from frame to frame would be only about four inches. So the question becomes obvious: have these double image frames been deliberately created from original (and sequential) frames shot at 48 fps (which no longer exist)?

Recognizing that Zapruder's camera had only two speeds (18 and 48 fps), the film editors would have recognized that, after frame excision, the film would no longer be realistic at 48 fps. The only other choice (consistent with Zapruder's camera) was 18 fps. As a first step, every other frame could have been excised—at least for much of the film. That would immediately eliminate some undesirable frames and yield a 24 fps film. The work of Pincher and Schaeffer on the emergency blinker rate is compelling evidence that some portions of the film may have been left just like that. The eyewitness accounts of JFK's movements, the airborne debris, and the limousine stop would require excision of more frames.

Art Snyder has explored the removal of frames during a limousine deceleration by means of computer modeling. He had expected to be able to rule out frame excision, but found that this was nearly impossible to rule out at 48 fps. He suggested that an original 48 fps film could be cut down to 12 fps and then filled in with extra frames to return the speed to about 18 fps. The chief reason that this approach could work is the limited resolution within each frame. The uncertainty issue has been explored previously by Paul H. Salamanowicz for the HSCA (HSCA # 180-10102-10425). He concluded that positions from frames Z-151, 173, and 193 could be determined to within 0.5 meters whereas frames Z-272, 313, and 410 were accurate to within 2.0 meters. If the limousine moved at about 1 ft/frame (12 mph, 18.3 fps), then the first uncertainty above would correspond to about 1.5 frames, and the second to about 6 frames. (Snyder believes that these estimates by Salamanowicz may be too high.) It would appear quite likely, however, that there is some room to excise frames during a deceleration

Two head shots have been combined into one. The witnesses saw a bloody spray and tissue debris with the second head shot (near Z-358 in the first reenactments) but apparently no halo and little debris with the first head shot. That such a halo was seen with the second shot, but not with the first one is eminently reasonable. Only after disruption of major intracranial blood vessels and passage of a brief period of time (during which blood could accumulate) would there be enough blood to see a halo.

Another persistent puzzle that may be solved by this proposal of two quite separate (rather than two immediately successive) head shots is the intact appearance of JFK's right occiput in Z-313 and immediately afterwards. Most likely the skull was still intact at that moment. The bloodless bone that Jackie saw with the first head shot was probably from the skull vertex (one of the bone fragments at the autopsy appeared to fit there). Only with the second head shot did the remainder of the skull explode with a halo of blood and with a blowout of the right occipital area. (The X-rays show that this occipital bone was mostly present, but hanging on a kind of vertical hinge at the side of the head. This is astonishingly consistent with Dr. Robert McClelland's observations at Parkland Hospital (6H33) that the occipital bone was fractured in its lateral half and had sprung outward.) In fact, close inspection of the top of JFK's head at frames in the mid Z-330s shows a distinct change in contour at about this time. Suddenly the light reflection at the skull vertex changes shape, thus implying that a skull defect abruptly appeared at this time. This image of a defect extends far posteriorly, possibly into the upper occipital area. (The hinged occipital bone would lie directly inferior to this level. This lower occipital area might well look intact in the film—even though the bone was fractured and somewhat displaced, but not actually missing—just as described by McClelland.) This (presumed) parietal-occipital defect is seen in multiple frames in a consistent manner. (It must be remembered that, even if this conclusion is accepted, it would not necessarily prove that the second head shot occurred precisely where the limousine now appears on Elm Street in Z-330 to Z-335. This is because the image of JFK's head could have been extracted from original frames near Z-358, where the first reenactment and so many of the witnesses place the second head shot, and then simply imported to where it now appears as a composite image. See discussion below for editing within frames.)

The head snap would then inevitably result from frame removal—the backward action would be accelerated, perhaps by a factor of 2 or 3, or even more. In real time, Jackie probably did (slowly) lift JFK's head so that she could look into his face—she needed to know immediately how badly he was hurt and what better way to do this than to look into his eyes? The (inexplicably sudden) forward and backward movements of both JFK and Jackie are probably related to imperfect frame excision—or to poor internal frame editing.

In the Zapruder film, with the possible exception of the final acceleration (that still needs to be examined), the limousine advances quite uniformly between the two last shots of the first reenactments, i.e., Z-276 to Z-358. En bloc removal of frames could not be done here (so as to skip entirely over one of the head shots) without causing the limousine suddenly to leap forward. It seems likely, therefore, that frames were left in so that the limousine would appear to be progressing uniformly. However, JFK's positions in the limousine would then require alteration, at least for some of these frames, in order to eliminate the impression of two clearly separate head shots.

This problem could have been solved by transparency retouching [*Editor's note:* See Jack White, Part IV] ,which was a well developed skill by that time. Jack White notes that he frequently had to rely on this process in his own work and that the results were typically undetectable. Such a process (imprecisely done) could explain the apparent absence of facial features in Jackie in one frame and the inexplicably missing portion of JFK's head in several frames. An alternate possibility is the use of some portions of already excised frames—or a combination of the these two options. (Transparency retouching can also be used in conjunction with the traveling matte process, which is discussed below.)

In addition, portions of some frames may have been repeated over and over—in order to replace necessarily excised frames. This may have been done for JFK (and possibly for Jackie, too) in that long, apparently stationary, sequence preceding Z-313. Other frames where this may have occurred are those that show the bystanders to the left of the Stemmons Freeway sign, where the magnification is unusually invariable over so many frames. The peculiar *absence* of magnification changes (especially when they are so uniformly seen otherwise) for this intersprocket area has already been noted. Regarding these bystanders to the left of the sign, it is extraordinary that Weatherly, via his analysis of streaks and camera motion, *independently* concluded that these bystanders have been inserted as a composite image. With two such independent lines of evidence—both for these particular frames—a conclusion of composite frames becomes very difficult to avoid.

The intersprocket area is the location for many of these queer features. There is a specific reason that it may have posed unique problems. The edge prints are located along the film edge in the intersprocket area. In the WC images these edge prints are *KODACHROME II 1. 1: 37 . . . SAFETY FILM.* Where the three dots appear here in my description there are actually symbols on the film: a solid (white) vertical bar followed by two identical solid (white) triangles. These latter two triangles date the film to 1961.

If every other frame had initially been excised (or any other regular pattern of elimination used) then this entire intersprocket pattern of edge prints would have been disrupted. Loss of a portion of any of these edge prints would have been obvious evidence of tampering—absence of known letters (or even parts of letters) would give the game away. So a decision had to be made: either to leave the intersprocket area out entirely, or to replace it so that it looked like an original. If the first option had been chosen, it might have worked. We have so little intersprocket information today that we might not have known what to expect. When Zapruder's camera was used to shoot the May 1964 reenactment, the sudden appearance of intersprocket images would have been embarrassing—but only if the FBI had shared such information. Nonetheless, the original reenactment film is not now available—there is only a copy with no intersprocket images. It is possible, however, that copies of individual frames of the original Zapruder film had been made by then. Such copies were made for the surveyors within the first week. (At a 25 February 1964 WC meeting, Herbert Orth of *Life* volunteered to make 35 mm slides. Whether such slides existed before that seems unlikely.) If any copies of individual frames included the intersprocket areas, the first option may have been considered too danger-ous. (That the 4 x 4 transparencies were made from the original film is strongly suggested by Thompson 1967, p. 17. He cites the testimony of FBI agent Lyndal Shaneyfelt for this likely conclusion.) In any case, there could still have been concern that any subsequent film shot through Zapruder's camera would show an intersprocket image. If so, a question of authentic-ity would immediately arise—or perhaps even worse, an actual proof of inauthenticity.

It is likely, therefore, that the second option, that of including standard edge prints, had to be chosen. Their first concern then would have been to remove the edge prints from the original film. If these had been left in, the new copy would contain two *sets* of edge prints—and anyone would have concluded that it was a copy. Techniques for removing and for inserting scenes had been available in cinematography for many years. In fact, when I put this question (on how to remove edge prints) to Bruce Jamieson (tele-phone conversation, 24 July 1997), he mentioned—without any hesitation—the traveling matte technique (Fielding 1985, p. 183).

While on a trip to visit Noel Twyman, I had previously purchased five out-of-print books on cinematography (from the period just after 1963) from Wahrenbrock's Book House in San Diego. From these, I learned that matte shots are used to prepare composite photographs by a double expo-sure (analogous to what I had already successfully done with X-ray im-ages): one part of the film is blocked out for the first exposure, then the complementary part is blocked out for the second exposure. What results is a composite and complete image, with parts from both originals, side by side in the same frame. Almost any combination of originals can be used. Fielding prints a wonderful still photograph from the nineteenth century (1965/85, p. 73). He adds that fine composite photographs were being ob-tained by the 1850s, before the Civil War! He also shows a photograph of a scene from *The Great Train Robbery* (1903), in which a locomotive appears through a window (1965/85, p. 74). Such techniques were refined enor-mously over the ensuing decades. A classic use of the traveling matte ap-peared in the movie, *Mary Poppins*, in which a similar process was used, frame by frame, to insert animated figures into live action scenes (Fielding 1965/85, p. 212, shows a studio photograph from this production in which a sodium vapor traveling matte process was used.) It is noteworthy that *Mary Poppins* was produced in 1964, the same year as another well known production—*The Warren Report*.

To prepare a traveling matte (Fielding 1985, p. 183) the image is pro-jected (enlarged) onto a surface where it can be traced. Then the portion that needs to be blocked out is actually painted black. This is done frame by frame for the entire scene, and then a movie film is exposed, frame by frame, of this succession of partially blacked out frames (the matte) onto a high contrast stock film. When this matte film strip is placed directly on top of an original film (label it "A") inside an optical printer (the two films actually touch each other and run through the projector together like Siamese twins), the combined image is exposed onto new film stock ("B"). The new film ("B") will then have a (latent) image only in a selected portion of each frame, with no image appearing in the rest of each frame. (Film "B", however, is not developed at this point.)

A negative of the original matte film (the one that was made from the black painting) is next prepared—so that areas that were black before now become white and vice versa. When this (reversed) matte film is run through the optical printer on top of film "B" (still not developed), a latent image can now be imprinted onto another new film stock ("C") for the area that was blocked off before, thus producing a composite and complete image for each frame on the final version—film "C". Fielding describes the use of an out-of-focus lens to produce a soft matte junction between the two joined images. This is usually desirable for blending closely matched detail and tones—so that the junction line is undetectable. Fielding (1965/85, p. 215) also describes the use of contact printing (as opposed to optical printers) for production of traveling mattes.

The reader is warned that this is a greatly simplified version of an enormously complex undertaking in an area in which I cannot claim a high degree of expertise. Thus, the language used here may be viewed as that of a layman. Please see appropriate references for this purpose. (Another source is Leslie Wheeler, *Principles of Cinematography*, 1953/69, especially Chapter 9.) Such a process could be used, for example, in split frame scenes in which an actor's twin image appears in a scene with him. Or it could be used for superimposing titles and credits over a scene. (See, for example, L. Bernard Happe, *Basic Motion Picture Technology*, 1971, p. 226).

In the Zapruder film, such a process could have been used, first to mask out the edge numbers, and then, in a second step, to copy an image (of a scene) into the masked out area. For this purpose, similar images from nearby frames (those without any overlapping edge prints) could have been superimposed to fill in the area where the original edge prints had been removed. When developed, this new film would show edge prints only from the new film stock (all film stock has such latent edge prints, according to Jamieson). A traveling matte process could also have been used elsewhere in the Zapruder film, particularly to fill in for excised frames—or to paste in images for portions of frames. Such images could have been borrowed from excised frames that no longer appear in the film, or even borrowed from frames that do appear. It is possible that some of the double images that remain (especially in the intersprocket area) are leftovers from such composite shots for which both images were permitted to print through (the reason for permitting this to occur is not clear, unless the intersprocket image was simply deemed to be unimportant).

It should be added that the optics of these printers is quite flexible. Fielding shows a photograph in which the bellows extension lens can be moved to and fro on geared mounts (1965/85, p. 135). On some printers it was even possible to view the entire width of the film (Fielding 1965/85, p. 134), *including the edge numbers*. This view of the edge numbers permitted selection of frames for the aperture. In my conversation with Jamieson, he stated that some printers even used a separate light source in order to reproduce the edge numbers onto the copy film; this was done so that the individual frames could easily be referenced for film production purposes. Fielding adds that such optical printers could also be used to enlarge the film size to 65 mm or to reduce it to 8 mm—the size of Zapruder's film (1965/85, p. 134). Alterations on the Zapruder film were probably not done in 8 mm format. More likely, these alterations were done in a larger format and then later reduced to 8 mm. (See *Bloody Treason*, Exhibit 12-5, for a schematic of possible steps in such a process.)

Is there any evidence that such a process was used in the Zapruder film? To address this, let us first assume (in the current absence of any other information) that the existing edge prints and the original edge prints had the same symbol size, position on the film, and interval between occurrences. The current edge prints are black upper case letters on a white background strip (see an example in Trask 1994, p. 65). If these symbols had been erased via a matte, then what would be left behind? What we would expect is either a uniform white strip or a uniform black strip (depending on how the editors wished to do this) where the symbols had previously appeared. And that is precisely what is seen in Z-194—it is particularly obvious on the black and white prints (donated to me) that were made from the WC originals. Here there is a darkened vertical strip in exactly the same area where the symbols had previously appeared. The width of this dark strip matches the original size of the letters as closely as I can measure it.

To make this even more convincing, a very thin strip of the original white background appears to persist (immediately to the right of the dark strip) just where it was located in the unaltered white background. Other frames that show this effect are Z-195 through Z-200. (Of these, Z-198 is the least definite.) It is possible that additional frames also exhibit this appearance but, in the resolution available to me, these were the ones that seemed most certain. A similar effect occurs on the back of the Stemmons freeway sign at Z-218 through Z-222 (this is also entirely within the intersprocket area). Another inexplicable feature occurs in Z-213 (the first intact intersprocket area after the damaged frames) through Z-218: two broad white strips intersect just above the lower sprocket hole. This effect is precisely confined to the intersprocket area and the intersection produces a right angle (on the inside corner of the intersection) where the sign is extremely dark. All of this only raises further questions: was this device also used to erase edge prints here?

Between these two sites of the film lies the region of the damaged frames: my black and white set includes five frames without intersprocket images: Z-208, 209, 210, 211, and 212. If original edge prints had occurred in these frames, they would simply have vanished along with the damaged frames. The current edge print (*KODACHROME II 1. 1: 37 . . . SAFETY FILM*) occupies 17 frames. If 2 of 3 frames had been excised at this point from the original film, then each current frame would represent 3 original frames—i.e., a total of 15 lost intersprocket images. Besides this, however, 1-2 frames would be missing immediately before Z-208 and the same number would also be missing immediately after Z-212, thus making a total of 17-19 missing frames. It would therefore be possible, by this means, to totally eliminate an entire edge print (since it occupied only 17 frames). Is this why these frames were said to be damaged?

After about Z-222, odd lighting effects appear on the back of the Stemmons Freeway sign in some frames, but the original intent (if any) seems obscure. Then, at about Z-235, another transition occurs—the intersprocket area becomes noticeably darker than the central image (and remains like this at least through Z-412, where my review stopped; Z-413 and 414 contain only black intersprocket areas) and numerous odd features enter the intersprocket scenes. So another question arises: were the original intersprocket images excised after this point in the film, only to be replaced by nearby adjacent scenes? And, if so, why? This device would, of course, have effectively removed any original edge prints—no small accomplishment for the editors. The area removed could then be replaced with nearby (and almost indistinguishable) images that did not contain the troublesome original edge prints.

This could have been done in a simple sequential manner, or, in a less obvious fashion, by alternating intersprocket images from different frames. Whether or not this hypothesis is correct will take some effort to explore—I have not yet done that. If this had been done, however, then the intersprocket images over multiple frames would be too similar (or even identical) to match reality. I note only one small example as an illustration for further study: in the four frames including Z-235 through Z-238, the two motorcycle antennae remain exactly the same distance apart for all frames (and in the same position with respect to the helmets)—even though these antennae are obviously vibrating and changing positions in the frames following this. Is this an example of filling in with the same image?

Artifacts from film alteration may have been left behind: the shadow discontinuity at Z-316 discovered by Marler, the entire 8 mm film loaned to me by Lifton (with so many obvious composite frames), the magnification changes that commonly occur across the intersprocket interface, the double images that are sometimes seen in the intersprocket area (often only in a portion of it), the overlapping image in the top third of the intersprocket area, and the fact that the image is darker in the intersprocket area (especially for frames after about Z-235) than in the central image. (Such intersprocket image darkening is not seen on the "home movie" track and is not apparent in frames before about Z-235 either.) Jamieson was unable to explain why the intersprocket image for the motorcade sequence should appear darker (or different in any way for that matter) from the "home movie" portion; he also could not explain why there was an image overlap in the intersprocket area for the motorcade sequence but not for the "home movie" portion. The plus sign on Z-028 and Z-308, "The Soaring Bird" figure on so many frames, and the irregular white rectangles on Z-226 and Z-227 would all have been invaluable aids in positioning each frame according to the desires of the editors. This is a surprisingly long list of oddities—where none at all should exist. The fact that they can all be explained by the single hypothesis of film alteration is also compelling.

In addition, of course, such editing explains virtually all of the other odd features that have been discussed in this essay. It is ironical that one author (Ernest Walter, *The Technique of the Cutting Room*, 1969, p. 127) uses the "obvious" example of a moving car as an illustration of the traveling matte technique! Frame excision and traveling mattes (for frame alteration) can explain multiple curious features: the absent limousine stop, the altered movement of JFK's head (including the contraction of two head shots into one), the loss of Connally's left turn, the disappearance of obvious blood on Connally's shirt front, the excessively rapid movement of multiple individuals, the disappearance of tissue debris from the limousine trunk and from the air, the register mark at Z-028 and Z-308, and more.

I would like to offer one final observation. When the original film was copied, it would have been critical to overlap the real sprocket holes of the new version with the sprocket hole images from the original. For this purpose, The Black Hole (and perhaps the plus signs) would have been invaluable. So the question naturally arises: is there any residual evidence of an imperfect overlap? Although I do not yet claim that this evidence is definitely incriminating, I do offer the following considerations. Around each current sprocket hole, on almost all frames, is a thin halo—it is like a white reflection of the actual sprocket hole. This effect occurs repeatedly, frame after frame, most often to the right of the sprocket holes. (In Trask 1994, p. 65, this phenomenon can be seen faintly to the right of the upper sprocket hole on even this degraded image.) This halo follows the contours of the current sprocket hole with great precision—it can even be seen at times to round the corner of a hole. A more distinct example of this effect is seen in the reproductions of the Nix frames (18H81-83); here the halo is much larger. In these Nix frames, the intersprocket area is black, so that we can be reasonably certain that these images derive from a later generation copy. Therefore, images of sprocket holes (from previous generations) would not be surprising—that is most likely what the halo represents in the Nix film.

In the Zapruder film, however, this effect need not necessarily derive solely from images of the original film. In fact, on very close inspection, a real and continuous image of the scene seems to appear between the halo and the sprocket hole. If this is correct, any explanation that invokes a cutting artifact (during the removal of film from the sprocket holes) will not work. Such an effect, however, might derive from an intermediate film that contained a traveling matte, especially if it had been transparent (or possibly even black) near the sprocket holes. In that case, the Zapruder halo would be a faint image of one of these sprocket hole edges. (The index of refraction through the edge of the sprocket hole is slightly different from unity—i.e., the edge is often visible even on a transparent film.) What is incontestable, however, is that when *Life* magazine first printed intersprocket images (25 November 1966), these sprocket holes were all blocked out. So instead of being able to see the sprocket holes, every one of them was simply covered over with a black patch that was shaped a sprocket hole. And this black patch was just large enough to cover the halo effect.

It might be argued in reply that this approach was quite innocent since it permitted *Life* to print readily visible frame numbers (white) onto this black area; a reasonable response, however, is that black frame numbers on a white background (the real color of a sprocket hole) would show up just as well—and without all the extra work; it would also be more authentic. I can add that such a halo does not occur in my father's old 8 mm films nor on copies that Roy Schaeffer has sent me that were taken with a camera not too different from Zapruder's. It is not my purpose in this paragraph, however, to draw a final conclusion about these halos. It is enough for now to know that this observation can be evaluated by a simple act—simply filming through the original Zapruder camera (now under the jurisdiction of the National Archives) should tell us whether the original camera yields such images or whether they are other artifacts of film editing.

Summary

A strong case can be made for extensive editing of the Zapruder film. In fact, the conclusion seems inescapable—the film was deliberately altered. No other explanation is in the same league, in terms of explanatory power, for the myriad of anomalous characteristics that are seen everywhere in this case. Many frames were excised, some individual frames were extensively altered, others were changed only enough to fill in for missing frames, and others were left alone. Frames that were excised were simply too embarrassing for the official story or contained troublesome edge prints. What is perhaps most remarkable, though, is that, even in the past several years, to say nothing of the past several months, yet more evidence has accumulated—all of it pointing toward alteration. One can only wonder what still remains to be discovered.

What can be made of the absurd paradoxes of (supposed) camera tracking errors that are totally inconsistent with what actually appears in the relevant frame? When the frame contents shift by enormous amounts, corresponding blurs must be seen. There is no cinematic magic that can avoid such realities. And what can be said about intersprocket magnifications that are grossly different in two frames, particularly when tracking nonsense surfaces in the *same* frames? And now, thanks to Noel Twyman, we have the image of The Soaring Bird and of The Black Hole. These could have provided precisely the kind of reference points for pin registration that would be essential for frame to frame editing.

Why else are these images there? They do recur persistently throughout the film. And when they are absent, where do they go—unless someone has deliberately omitted them? And where exactly did the intersprocket image of the *right* motorcycle come from? And why is it never visible in the central image? Why does the intersprocket image of the motorcycle skip around? Why is the intersprocket image darker after about Z-235? Why do so many odd features occur within the intersprocket area? Why is the intersprocket image missing in frames Z-413 and 414?

And so the questions come, one after another, like automatic rifle fire. How much more evidence is required before reason prevails? At the very least, this proposal of film alteration deserves extensive consideration and serious discussion—even among those who are still inclined to be doubters. For these individuals, there is now much to explain. It is time for them to put on their ten-league boots and begin climbing this small mountain of data.

[Editor's note: *During the final production of this book, we had what appears to have been a close encounter with the CIA. In the course of ordinary events, we have become familiar with a person claiming to have been a high-ranking official of the CIA, who has told us that the Zapruder film was in the hands of the CIA almost immediately and that it was edited under the authority of the National Security Agency, part of which was done prior to the publication of selected frames in* Life. *He has advised us that instructions for this undertaking would have had to emanate from a level of government at least equivalent to that of Lyndon B. Johnson or of J. Edgar Hoover. We are unable to confirm specific details of his claims, which deserve further investigation. He maintains that he was not personally involved in these activities, however, and his reports are not comparable in evidential significance to the scientific findings presented here. But we have found much of what he has to say quite fascinating and, in general, consistent with our discoveries. See Mike Pincher and Roy Schaefer, Part IV.]*

Acknowledgments

It always amazes me to consider how little I would have accomplished by working in isolation. I have tried to credit appropriate individuals in the text. I trust that those who frown where I have forgotten them will understand that no malice was intended. If Lady Fortune smiles there will be a second edition to correct the (certain) undetected errors of the first. I have tried hard to get them out, but, like pulling weeds on my father's farm as a youth, I know that their roots are deep. I alone take credit for these roots.

My deep appreciation goes to our editor, Jim Fetzer, for insisting that this work come to print and for resolutely encouraging me to continue. Robert Livingston, M.D., has been an enormous pillar of support throughout. His passion for truth, forthrightness, courage, and basic humanity are unsurpassed. I am honored to count him a friend.

Milicent Cranor, Roy Schaeffer, and Noel Twyman have been unrelenting conversationalists—always with "good stuff." I also have the greatest admiration for the work of Chuck Marler and Daryll Weatherly, good friends all. And then there is Jack White—photo analyst, friend, but most of all, a very good man.

Special thanks must go to David Lifton, Harrison Livingstone, Philip Melanson, and Harold Weisberg for their initial skepticism of the film; their pioneering efforts inspired me to explore this trail. I hope they will not think that I have strayed too far off their maps.

Though still counted among skeptics of alteration, I must not forget Josiah Thompson or Martin Shackelford. "Tink" has offered a patient listening ear, high quality photographs, encouragement, documents, and a useful historical perspective. Martin could always be counted on to close one gap or another in my knowledge of the film—and he always forced me to try harder. And Robert Groden, also a skeptic, has been patient with my unending questions.

I must also thank the ARRB and the National Archives (particularly Charles Mayn) for their indispensable assistance.

Finally, there are Christopher (11), Meredith (9), and Patricia (??), who are really not very interested in any of this. Maybe some day they will understand. I thank them for permitting me to miss some fun with them on the beaches of Kauai.

It is ironic that I have met all of these individuals through the misguided efforts of JAMA. As so often in life, unintended consequences are the rule— surely *JAMA* did not intend for us to meet. Likewise, I also had not intended to resign from the AMA, but that too happened. I could not in good conscience stand by and do nothing. Perhaps someday (under a different editor) even *JAMA* will recognize, in a matter that is so critical to our national self-knowledge, the grossness of its blunders and will finally assist in putting matters right.

References for Reconstruction Table

Ault, C. 24H534

Altgens, J. 6H517-8

Altgens, J.; Letter to Doug Mizzer, 21 November 1994.; see Livingstone 1995, p. 135

Baker, M. 3H266

Brehm, C. 22H837

Campbell, O. 22H485

Curry, J. 4H173, 315

Decker, W. 19H458

Hargis, B. 6H294

Hickey, G. 18H762

Hill, C. 18H742

Hill, C. 2H138-139, 144

Hill, J. 6H214

Hudson, E. 7H560-561

Kellerman, R. 2H74, 76, 77, 81, 85

Kellerman, R. 18H726

Kennedy, J. 5H180

Kinney, S. 18H731-732

Kinney, S. HSCA Document 180-10078-10493, p. 5

Kivett, J. 18H778

Landis, P. 8H754-755

Moorman, M. 19H487; 22H838; 24H217

Newman, Bill and Gayle; Conversations with Milicent Cranor (September 1993); also see Bill Sloan, *JFK: Breaking the Silence*, 1993, pp. 168-174

Rather, D.; CBS News, 23 November 1963

Ready, J.; Statement of 22 November 1963. Menninger, B., *Mortal Error*, 1992, p. 289

Roberts, C.; MacNeil, R. *The Way We Were*, 1963. *The Year Kennedy was Shot* (1967), pp. 192, 197.

Roberts, E; 8H737

Schwartz, E.; Twyman, N. *Bloody Treason*, forthcoming; interview of 21 November 1994.

Shaneyfelt, L. 15H699

Smith, Alan. (*Chicago Tribune*, 11/23/63, p. 9; Newcomb and Adams 1974, p. 71)

Willis, L. 7H498

Willis, P. 7H497

Zapruder, A. 5H571

[*Editor's note:* The testimony of the Secret Service agents is printed in Menninger, 1992, Appendix A. It may also be found in 18H722-784.]

More Physical Insight into the Assassination of President Kennedy

Michael A. Stroscio

The assassination of President Kennedy has been investigated at length by professionals from diverse fields, but twenty-three years after this tragic event the physics community has published little on this matter. There are isolated, albeit important, exceptions such as the revealing physics analysis published by Luis Alvarez.[1] Herein, the Alvarez analysis is extended and new insights are gained which cast doubt on the one gunman, three-bullet theory which is the cornerstone of the findings of the Warren Commission's report.[2]

Physical Basis for the Analysis

The physical basis for analyzing the assassination of President Kennedy is identical with that proposed by Alvarez.[1] Specifically, it is known that disturbances such as the sound of gunfire or the sound of a siren cause neuromuscular reactions that inevitably produce rapid jerking motions of a hand-held camera. These jerking motions cause blurring of the images recorded in the still frames of a motion picture. On first consideration, this phenomenon may appear to be too ill-defined to be of use in shedding light on the assassination of President Kennedy. However, it is well-known that such neuromuscular reactions are involuntary and that the power spectrum for such jerking motions has a peak near a period of about one-third of a second[1]. The results of this article will verify that the angular acceleration of Abraham Zapruder's camera at the only precisely-known time of a shot at President Kennedy — when President Kennedy was struck in the head — exhibits the expected characteristics.[1] Such angular acceleration episodes provide clues that shed light on the time-history of the shots fired at President Kennedy limousine as it traveled down Elm Street in Dallas, Texas on November 22, 1963.

Analysis of the Zapruder Film

The angular acceleration of A. Zapruder's camera as a function of time may be calculated straightforwardly[1] from the measured streak lengths associated with the blurring of President Kennedy's limousine in the separate frames of the Zapruder film. Since the image on each frame was recorded during the one-thirtieth of a second when the shutter was open, such a streak length in a particular frame is directly proportional to the average angular velocity — averaged over the one-thirtieth of a second exposure time — of Zapruder's camera relative to a fixed point on the limousine. During the periods when Zapruder's tracking was steady, there is minimal blurring of the limousine's image since the relevant relative angular velocity of the camera was small. The angular acceleration is the derivative of the angular velocity, so the constant 18.3 frames per second recording speed of Zapruder's camera and the difference in the streak lengths recorded on successive frames can be used to determine angular acceleration.

In calculating the time-series for the angular acceleration of Zapruder's camera it is convenient to adopt the conventions of Ref. 1. Specifically, units and sign conventions are adopted as follows: streak lengths are assigned values from 0, for no streaking, to 5, for maximal streaking; one unit of time is taken to be the 1/18.3 second between successive frames; the sign of the angular velocity is taken as positive if the pointing axis of the camera is advancing in a clockwise sense relative to the limousine as viewed from above the camera in the camera-limousine system; and the sign assigned the angular velocity is negative for counterclockwise relative motion.

The streak lengths in the individual frames recorded by A. Zapruder on November 22, 1963 are readily visible upon inspection of the still frames of the Zapruder film. Alvarez analyzed only frames 171 to 334 since they were apparently the only frames available to him[3]. If he had had access to frames before 171 he would have quickly come to new insights . As pointed out by Alvarez, selected frames of the Zapruder film exhibit blurred images of the President's limousine that make the limousine appear to have been displaced by as much as a few inches relative to the clear image that would have resulted if the camera had been pointed at the same point on the limousine throughout the one-thirtieth of a second exposure interval. Since the President's limousine was never closer than about seventy feet from Zapruder's camera, a one-inch streak length corresponds to a maximum angular displacement of only about $1/(12*70) = 1/840$ of a radian.

The calculated angular accelerations are shown in Figure 1. The frame numbers are indicated along the vertical lines and points to the left of the time-series line indicate clockwise angular accelerations. The fact that the angular acceleration is a more significant indicator of sudden jerking than the angular velocity was emphasized in Ref. 1, but this physical insight was missing completely in the analyses of the consultants in the 1978 U.S. House of Representatives investigation of the assassination of President Kennedy.[4] These consultants did analyze Zapruder frames before 171 but they based their analyses on the simple magnitude of the streaking of each frame as well as on the fluctuations of the absolute direction of the camera's optical axis. Unfortunately, contributions to these angular displacements and angular velocities come from both gradual fluctuations and rapid changes in the pointing direction of the camera, but it is only the rapid variations that are sensitive indicators of responses to disturbances such as the sounds of gunfire or a siren.

The angular-acceleration time series displayed on the second through sixth vertical lines of Figure 1 is an excellent approximation to that published in Ref. 1. However, the angular-acceleration episode on the first vertical line is completely absent in Ref. 1, because Alvarez used the Zapruder frames published in Ref. 2 which did not include frames before 171. The four angular-acceleration episodes commencing at frames 180, 220, 290 and 313 were explained in Ref. 1 as follows:

- Based on the clear visual evidence, the episode beginning at frame 313 is unambiguously assigned to the shot that struck President Kennedy in the head.
- Since the Warren Commission asserted that there were three shot fired on November 22, 1963 with the first shot missing its target and since President Kennedy was holding his throat on emerging from behind a street sign on Elm Street at the time of frame 224,

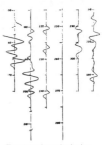

Figure 1. Angular-acceleration time series versus frame number displayed along six vertical lines. Points to the left of the vertical time-series lines denote clockwise angular accelerations as described in the text.

Enclosure. Stroscio's study of the motion of Zapruder's camera while filming the assassination of President John F. Kennedy the angular-acceleration episode commencing at frame 220 was associated with the "magic-bullet" shot that presumably caused seven wounds to President Kennedy and Governor Connally.

• The angular acceleration episode commencing at frame 180 was associated with the bullet that missed its target since it was the only episode known to Alvarez that occurred before frame 220.

• Finally, to explain the angular-acceleration episode that begins at frame 290, it was noted that a siren sounded at about the time of the bullet that struck President Kennedy in the head.

The association of the blast of a siren with the angular-acceleration episode that begins at frame 290 was made by Alvarez[1] but he stated clearly that he was not sure this assignment was correct. Indeed, as correctly pointed out by Alvarez, most eyewitnesses claimed that siren sounded after the fatal wound to President Kennedy's head. These witnesses held that the siren first sounded well after frame 313 and the siren could not be responsible for the angular-acceleration episode that began at frame 290. Alvarez points out[1] that eyewitnesses frequently have flawed memories of stressful events, but it is difficult, indeed, to understand why many witnesses[2] would make the same error. At any rate, these are the interpretations made in Ref. 1 for the four angular acceleration episodes beginning at frames 180, 220, 290 and 313. The interpretation of Ref. 1 appears to be consistent with the Warren Commission's conclusion that there was no conspiracy since a single gunman could have fired the three shots associated with the angular-acceleration episodes commencing at frames 180, 220, and 313.

With these assignments of times for the three sounds of gunfire and one siren blast, it was possible for Alvarez to state that the available scientific evidence supported the findings of the Warren Commission. However, if Alvarez had had access to frames before 171 he would have discovered that there was a fifth angular-acceleration episode that commenced at frame 152, about 1.5 seconds before the time of the "first shot" identified in Ref. 1. The magnitude of this episode is accentuated by the fact that the limousine is farther from the camera at frame 152 than at frames 180 to 334 but there can be no doubt that the angular-acceleration time series beginning at frame 152 represents a sudden jerking motion of Zapruder's camera.[5] It is significant that the time interval is only 1.5 seconds in duration because investigators[4] have agreed consistently that the minimum firing time between shots with the Mannlicher-Carcano rifle found in the sniper's nest on the sixth floor of the Texas Schoolbook Depository was 2.25 seconds.

Discussion and Conclusions

By following Alvarez's prescription of taking the differences between streak lengths to obtain angular accelerations, it is straightforward to construct a time-series of the angular-acceleration of A. Zapruder's camera as he filmed President Kennedy's limousine as it traveled down Elm Street in Dallas, Texas on November 22, 1963. This extended time-series contains a strong angular-acceleration episode which commences during the interval from frame 152 to frame 153, which was not discovered by Alvarez because he analyzed only the frames that were reproduced in the Warren's Commission's report. The most easily drawn conclusion from the extended time series is that the angular-acceleration episode commencing at frame 152 occurs about 1.5 seconds before the time which Ref. 1 denotes as the "first shot". This is a significant conclusion because the angular-acceleration episodes beginning at frames 152 and 180 could not have been caused by shots fired by one person using the Mannlicher-Carcano that was found on the

sixth floor of the Texas Schoolbook Depository[2].

The establishment of this fifth jerking episode of Zapruder's camera makes it extremely difficult to use Alvarez's method to support the Warren Commission's single-gunman, three bullet theory and their conclusion that there was no conspiracy. Critics of the Alvarez analysis may hold that the techniques of Ref. 1 are just not suitable technique for shedding insight in the assassination of President Kennedy. However, in this case it would also be impossible to use this analysis to support the findings of the Warren Commission. This conclusion is especially significant for the physics community since Ref. 1 is the only paper published in the physics literature that attempts to use physical data and laws to understand the assassination of President Kennedy.[6]

References

1. L. Alvarez, Am. J. Phys., 44, 83 (1976).
2. Report of the President's Commission on the Assassination of President John F. Kennedy, Investigation of the Assassination of President John F. Kennedy, with twenty-six volumes on Hearings and Exhibits, U.S. Government Printing Office, 1964; also published by Associated Press, Bantam, Doubleday, McGraw-Hill, and Popular Library, 1964.
3. The Warren Commission's report published only frames 171 to 343; however, today there are many commercially-available videos containing the full Zapruder film including the earlier frames from 150 to 171 which also recorded the motion of President Kennedy's limousine after it had turned on to Elm Street on November 22, 1963.
4. Report of the Select Committee on Assassinations, U.S. House of Representatives, Investigation of the Assassination of President Kennedy, U.S. Government Printing Office, March 1979.
5. It is unfortunate that frames 155 and 156 of the Zapruder film are missing. However, the absence of these frames does not change the conclusion that a rapid jerking motion of Zapruder's camera began at frame 152. In the analysis done for the present article, it was rediscovered that these frames are missing. This rediscovery was made from the fact that in the first existing frame following frame 154, the limousine appears to have traveled three times its normal frame-to-frame distance; in fact, it has been known for many years that frames 155 and 156 have been removed from the Zapruder film. What is unknown is why the frames were removed and who removed them. It is also not known when these frames were removed. What is well-known is that the Zapruder film was kept from the public for many years; for a portion of this time it was retained by those who had paid A. Zapruder for rights to the film. Today, the Zapruder film is copyrighted and those wishing to reproduce, and make general use, of the frames from this famous film are asked to negotiate suitable terms through the Washington, DC law firm represented by James Lorin Silverberg, Esquire.
6. The Report on the Committee on Ballistic Acoustics, National Academy Press, Washington, DC, 1982 as summarized in Science, Volume 218, page 127, 1982 does apply the laws of physics but this Committee, under the chairmanship of Norman F. Ramsey, concluded that suspected sounds on gunfire recorded on the Dallas Police Department's dictaphone recorders could not have been gunfire since the receiving microphones were not turned on in Dealey Plaza, Dallas, Texas during the few seconds when shots were fired at President Kennedy on November 22, 1963. The Committee concluded that these suspected sounds of gunfire were recorded about one minute after shots were fired and that these noises were therefore not due to gunfire. The nature of this study is distinctly different from that of Ref. 1: the National Academy of Sciences study concluded that no relevant physical data existed on the Dallas Police Department's audio recordings.

Michael A. Stroscio is with Duke University, Physics Department, Durham, North Carolina 27708

Enclosure. Stroscio's study of the motion of Zapruder's camera while filming the assassination of President John F. Kennedy

Epilogue

On the basis of the results presented during the Zapruder Film Symposium in Dallas on 22 November 1996, which I organized and moderated, I suggested to the audience in closing that we now have what appears to be "conclusive evidence" that the Zapruder film has been extensively edited using highly sophisticated techniques. This characterization generated a certain degree of controversy in subsequent discussion, especially over e-mail, during which I sought to place these issues within a broader framework.

That framework reflects nuances in the use of the language of *proof* in relation to claims that arise within various contexts, such as those of courts of law, of pure mathematics, and of empirical science. The sense of "proof" appropriate to empirical science, for example, is less stringent than that appropriate to pure mathematics, but more demanding than that appropriate to courts of law. For the purpose of this volume, I have taken my original piece, which was devoted to this issue relative to the Zapruder film, and expanded it to include the medical evidence.

It would be appropriate, at this juncture, I believe, to emphasize the importance of a form of reasoning that occurs in both scientific and non-scientific contexts, which is known as *inference to the best explanation*. This pattern of reasoning involves selecting one member from a set of alternative hypotheses as the alternative providing the best explanation of the available evidence. Hypotheses that explain more of the available evidence are preferable to those that explain less. Those that are preferable when sufficient evidence is available are also acceptable.

Hypotheses that are incompatible with the available evidence are rejected as false. Hypotheses may be false even when they are acceptable, which makes inference of this kind *fallible*, but they remain the most rational among those alternatives under consideration. A difficulty that confronts inference of this kind is ensuring that every alternative that deserves to be considered receives consideration. Even when an hypothesis has been accepted, it may subsequently confront rejection because new alternatives or new evidence have been discovered. (See James H. Fetzer and Robert Almeder, *Glossary of Epistemology/Philosophy of Science* 1993.)

Consequently, even the most strongly entrenched scientific hypotheses remain vulnerable to subsequent rejection, as occurred in the case of the most highly confirmed hypothesis in the history of science of its time—classic Newtonian mechanics—when it was eventually confronted with the new alternative of Einstein's special relativity and the new evidence of Eddington's African expedition. When I described our evidence in support of the hypothesis that the Zapruder film has been extensively edited using highly sophisticated techniques as "conclusive," I was not denying the possibility that new evidence or new alternatives might eventually be discovered.

I was asserting that the authenticity of the Zapruder film is massively inconsistent with the available evidence. That the film has been extensively edited using highly sophisticated techniques explains the evidence better than any alternative hypothesis, such as that the film's anomalies are spontaneous effects, accidental artifacts of incompetent processing, or predictable consequences of features of the camera and conditions of filming. The evidence available appears to be more than sufficient. This does not *guarantee* that it has been faked: if features of the film that justify this finding could be "explained away" on reasonable grounds, the conclusion might have to be withdrawn. But absent new alternatives or new evidence, the matter has been settled.

Some illustrations may be helpful here. Consider the crash of TWA Flight 800, in relation to which three alternative hypotheses have been proposed as possible explanations, namely: (h1) that the explosion was the effect of the plane being hit by a missile; (h2) that the explosion was the effect of a terrorist bomb explosion; and (h3) that the explosion was the effect of some unsuspected design failure. From the point of view of reasoning, this case has been difficult to resolve, not because of a lack of possible explanations but because of an absence of evidence.

What has been available has ranged from eyewitness reports to expert analyses and has appeared in a wide range of publications, from tabloids, such as the *Star* (26 November 1996) in support of (h1) to national magazines, such as *Newsweek* (23 December 1996) in opposition to (h2), and our nation's newspaper of record, *The New York Times* (24 May 1997), in support of (h3). The fact that tabloids support (h1), moreover, does not mean that (h1) must therefore be false any more than that *The New York Times* should support (h3) would guarantee that it is true. (*The Times*, after all, published a fatuous review that heaped praise on the blatant assassination hoax, *Case Closed*.)

If explaining the crash of TWA Flight 800 has proven difficult because of the absence of sufficient evidence, the opposite appears to have been the case in the criminal trial of O.J. Simpson for the murder of Nicole Brown and Ronald Goldman. If we consider our hypothesis (h1) to be that O.J. committed the crime, then possible alternative explanations advanced by the defense included (h2) that it was a drug-related hit, where Faye Resnick, a friend of Nicole's, was the intended victim; and (h3) that the true target was Ronald Goldman, where Nicole was just an innocent bystander.

Insofar as Faye Resnick was a casual user of cocaine who had plenty of money to support her habit, (h2) really will not do; and since almost no one (outside the Mezzaluna Restaurant where he worked) could have known Ron Goldman was returning Juditha Brown's glasses to her daughter, (h3) cannot be taken seriously. The evidence itself—including O.J.'s blood at the scene, in the Bronco, in his home, and so on, the matching gloves, the hair follicles, the Bruno Magli shoe prints, the photographs, etc.—all seemed to provide overwhelming evidence that alternative (h1) had to be accepted.

So what happened? Having spent far more time and effort in the study of this case than I would ever want to admit in print, I have arrived at the conclusion that Simpson was acquitted in part because the jurors did not understand the nature of reasonable doubt. They appear to have believed that, if any part of the prosecution's case was open to doubt, then they could properly disregard it all. Consider, for example, the following exchange between Geraldo Rivera, journalist, and Armanda Cooley, the jury foreman:

> GERALDO RIVERA: How can you explain away O.J.'s blood at the murder scene, found hours befor his blood sample was taken?
> ARMANDA COOLEY: We can't explain it away. I don't think anybody has really tried to explain it away. Me, personally, I have not tried to explain it away at all. That was not one of the issues and that was definitely not the reasonable doubt we based our decision on.
> —Armanda Cooley et al., *Madam Foreman* (1995)

The inferential problem here, of course, is that the presence of the blood of the accused at the scene of the crime ordinarily constitutes sufficient evidence to convict. In the absence of a reasonable alternative explanation, the only reasonable explanation would be that the blood of the accused was at the scene of the crime because the accused was at the scene of the crime, which he committed. If the presence of the blood of the accused cannot be "explained away", then it must be "explained" by hypothesis (h1) implicating the accused in the crime. That explains it. Using inference to the best explanation, Simpson's guilt is apparent.

When it comes to the assassination of JFK, alternative possible explanations include (h1) that he was killed by a lone, demented gunman by the name of Lee Harvey Oswald, (h2) that he was killed by the Mob, (h3) that pro- or anti-Castro Cubans killed him, (h4) that it was the work of the KGB, or (h5) that his death was the result of a *coup d'état* involving the CIA, the Mob, anti-Castro Cubans, and powerful politicans, such as LBJ, Richard Nixon, and J. Edgar Hoover, fully financed by Texas oil men and elements of the military-industrial complex. These views represent no-conspiracy, small-conspiracy, and large-conspiracy perspectives, respectively.

Since even the HSCA inquiry accepted the probable existence of a conspiracy, (h1) does not seem to have much to be said in its favor. It could be amended to maintain that Lee Harvey Oswald and a small band of conspirators—whose identities are destined to remain unknown—were responsible, which some may find nearly as appealing. The problem, which carries over to other small-conspiracy theories, is that the available relevant evidence—concerning X-rays of the President's cranium, diagrams of a brain in the National Archives, the Zapruder film itself, and even the backyard photographs of Oswald—completely undermines their plausibility. We now possess persuasive proof that the most basic evidence in this case has been subject to alteration, fabrication, or modification, which is something small bands of conspirators could not have done.

The importance of falsification as a research methodology in the case of the death of JFK, therefore, cannot be overemphasized. The elimination of (h1), (h2), (h3), and (h4) dictates taking (h5) seriously. We cannot prefer an hypothesis that explains only part of the evidence to an alternantive that explains more. If we want to exercise rationality to avoid naiveté without becoming paranoid, then we cannot fulfill that obligation without following reason where it leads and letting the chips fall where they may. It may be unpleasant to be forced to the conclusion that our country was taken from us on 22 November 1963, more or less as Oliver Stone proposed in *JFK*. But if that is indeed the case, then we had better understand it—or else forfeit our freedom forever!

—*James H. Fetzer, Ph.D.*

Assassination Science and the Language of Proof

James H. Fetzer, Ph.D.

If science is incapable of "irrefutable proofs", "incontrovertable evidence" and the like, then questions inevitably arise concerning the degree of assurance with which anything can be known about anything—but especially about controverial subjects such as the assassination of JFK. This issue has arisen in an acute form at least twice during the course of my research, once relative to the medical evidence in this case and again in relation to the Zapruder film symposium. These questions are decidedly philosophical, since their answers depend upon the definition of "knowledge" and the conditions that have to be satisfied for beliefs to count as "justified", as "warranted", or even as "rational".

According to the standard conception of knowledge, a person knows something, such as that there is a bottle of beer in the refrigerator, for example, if that person believes that there is a bottle of beer in the refrigerator, if that person is justified (or warranted) in that belief, and if that belief is true, which means, in this instance, that there is a bottle of beer in the refrigerator. Two of the three branches of philosophy thus concern what it means for something to exist (or to be true), which is known as *ontology*, and what it takes for someone to know that something exists (or that something is true), known as *epistemology*. The nature of proofs turns out to be a problem in epistemology. The third branch of philosophy, which shall not concern us here, is *axiology*, also known as the theory of value.

The Meaning of "Proof"

Whether or not anyone can prove anything, after all, obviously depends on the language of "proof" and the conditions that "proofs" are expected to fulfill. Most importantly, from the point of view of the theory of knowledge, "proof" turns out to be an ambiguous term, since there are different expectations with regard to what it takes to qualify as a "proof" as a function of context. Let me therefore begin by differentiating between three distinct contexts in which "proofs" may occur but where the conditions they must satisfy are, in general, quite different. These three different senses emerge within the context of law, the context of mathematics, and the context of science, more or less as follows.

Legal Contexts: "Proof" in Courts of Law

The language of proof is ambiguous, meaning that there is more than one meaning attached to "proof" as a function of different contexts. Consider, for example, the use of "proof" in legal contexts and in courts of law. In this sense, proof of crime exists whenever incriminating evidence exists. So O.J.'s blood at the scene, in the Bronco, in his home, and elsewhere, the matching gloves, the hair follicles, the Bruno Magli shoe prints, the photographs, etc., all qualify as "proof" that O.J. committed the crime. In this sense, call it *Proof(1)*, of course, "proofs" may or may not be conclusive, since there may be alternative explanations that are just as reasonable as that O.J. committed the crime. When no alternative explanation is reasonable, given the totality of the evidence, however, then the evidence may qualify as "proof beyond a reasonable doubt".

Abstract Contexts: "Proofs" in Mathematics

A second use of "proof" occurs within the context of pure mathematics and deductive logic, where "proofs" involve deductive demonstrations from premises that are true as a matter of definition or of stipulation. When these premises are axioms of a formal system, the conclusions that follow from them deductively are known as theorems. This is the strongest sense of "proof", which might be referred to as *Proof(2)*. This is a sense that is so strong that "proofs" in this sense are seldom encountered outside of abstract contexts of inquiry. But that is because ordinarily the premises on which reasoning is based reflect the results of observation, measurements, or experimentation, which are not true by definition or by stipulation. A typical use of the term in this sense would be claims to have discovered a proof, say, of the Pythagorean Theorem or of Fermat's Last Theorem.

Empirical Contexts: "Proof" in Science

Alternative uses of the term "proof" sometimes occur within the context of empirical inquiries in senses that are stronger than the legal sense of *Proof(1)* but weaker than the mathematician's sense of *Proof(2)*. However, the mathematician's sense is so strong that empirical scientists tend to avoid the use of this term in order not to convey a stronger sense of certainty than they intend. The premises upon which scientific arguments are based, moreover, typically involve definitions but require empirical evidence that has been derived from observation, measurements, and experiments. The conclusions of these arguments are often but not always inductive and general, drawing conclusions about classes of things and relations between properties in a search for laws, which may be deterministic or indeterministic. The discovery of the existence of new phenomena, such as species that have evolved in short periods of time, however, could still be cited as "proof" such things are possible.

An alternative but more prevalent use of the term in scientific contexts arises when evidence is cited that establishes within a narrow margin of error that some hypothesis or conjecture is *false*. Eddington's expedition to Africa to measure the deflection of rays of light in the vicinity of the Sun's gravitational mass was a crucial experiment in the history of physics, because it provided evidence that (inconclusively) confirmed Einstein's theory of relativity and (conclusively) disconfirmed Newtonian gravitational theory. The phenomenon of light deflection was inconsistent with Newton's theory, but predicted by Einstein's. What is most important about this sense of "proof", which we might refer to as *Proof(3)*, is that it establishes a negative result in falsifying a general hypotheses on the basis of observations and measurements that are subject to replication.

The Medical Evidence

Thus, in response to my first round of letters to the Trustees of the AMA, I received a phone call from John J. Ring, M.D., the Past President of the Board, who wanted to know the degree of "metaphysical certitude" with which these things could be known. I wrote to him to explain that, when a John McLaughlin uses that phrase, no doubt, as a former Jesuit, he has in mind arguments such as Aquinas' five proofs of the existence of God, which are intended to be conclusive arguments from premises that are very difficult, if not impossible, to challenge. Thinking about the assassination from this perspective, I asked myself whether there might be arguments about the assassination that, even if they cannot be as "conclusive" as proofs in mathematics, might nevertheless be strong arguments that are based upon premises that are difficult, but not impossible, to challenge.

The ten proofs that I proposed to Dr. Ring are supported by considerable photographic and documentary evidence. Apart from the autopsy photographs and X-rays, to the best of my knowledge, none of these photographs and documents has ever been challenged with respect to its authenticity. In several cases, they are reprinted between the numbered pages of various books, where the pages on which they appear do not have separate page numbers. In those cases, I have used an alphabetical notation to identify them. When there are sixteen pages of photos between pages 432 and 433, for example, I refer to them as pages 432*a*, 432*b*, and so forth, for convenience of identification.

Proof 1: The Argument from Addition and Subtraction.

According to the official report of the Warren Commission, only three shots were fired at the Presidential motorcade, one of which hit President Kennedy in the neck, one missed and hit a curb near the Triple Underpass, and one hit the President in the head, killing him. If there were more than three shots, then the official report cannot be correct. The following photographs and documents, however, indicate that more than three bullets were recovered. The existence of more than three bullets in this case can be established by a simple process of addition and subtraction, roughly as follows:

#1 and #2 Lifton's *Best Evidence* (1980), p. 234*m*, publishes photographs of two bullet fragments (very substantial fragments that appear to be of two bullets), that were recovered from the limousine. (They were Warren Commission Exhibits 567 and 569.) The total number of possible bullets, given this evidence: **2**

#3 Groden and Livingstone's *High Treason* (1989), p. 146*o*, reprints photographs of damage to the Presidential limousine caused by bullet fragments, including especially a substantial impact in the chrome just above the windshield (as photos in Thompson's *Six Seconds in Dallas* 1967, p. 113, also display).   **3**

#4 Groden and Livingstone's *High Treason* (1989), p. 146*l*, also reprints several photos of an unidentified man picking up a bullet from a grassy area opposite the grassy knoll as a deputy sheriff and police officer look on (an event also reported and discussed in Marrs' *Crossfire* 1989, p. 308*h*, for example).   **4**

Apparent impact of bullet on chrome strip

#5 Groden and Livingstone's *High Treason* (1989), p. 146*m*, moreover, also prints a photograph of James Tague, a bystander who was hit by a fragment from another bullet, which impacted with the curbing adjacent to the Triple Underpass. (This is the bullet that the Warren Commission agreed had missed.)   **5**

#6 Groden and Livingstone's *High Treason* (1989), p. 28*j*, prints a photograph of a receipt for a "missile" that was turned over to two FBI agents at Bethesda, which was probably the same bullet that fell from the President's back as described in Livingstone's *High Treason 2* (1992), pp. 209–210, for example.   **6**

#7 Thompson's *Six Seconds in Dallas* (1967), p. 146, also prints a photograph of a bullet recovered at Parkland Hospital from a stretcher. This is the missile that has come to be known as "the magic bullet" because of the immense damage it has to have caused while remaining intact for the Warren Commission's scenario to be true.   **7**

#8 Thompson's *Six Seconds in Dallas* (1967), p. 147, prints a photograph of some of the fragments that were removed from Connally's body. A comparison of a diagram of the complete set of fragments in comparison with a photograph of bullet **#7** also appears in Livingstone's *High Treason 2* (1989), p. 305. Total: **8**

Although there may be photographs concerning other possible missiles, these should suffice for the purpose of this argument. If each of the photos and fragments were about distinct missiles, then there would have to have been at least eight bullets fired at the President. Since the damage to the limousine (#**3**) and the damage to Connally (#**8**) may perhaps have been caused by and therefore be identical with the first two bullets (#**1** and #**2**), we can conservatively subtract them, leaving a total of at least six bullets fired at the President (#**1**, #**2**, #**4**, #**5**, #**6**, and #**7**). But if this is right, then the offical report is wrong.

Perhaps it ought to be emphasized that the bullet that was turned over to Agents O'Neill and Sibert at Bethesda was not the same bullet discovered at Parkland. These were separate missiles that were discovered at different locations at different times. Apart from the FBI's subsequent denial of *receiving* the missile for which O'Neill and Sibert acknowledged receipt, what has been described here appears difficult to challenge. Even subtracting the lost bullet from Bethesda, at least five bullets were fired at the President. As long as six and five are numbers greater than three, this argument appears very strong.

Indeed, even Humes testified, in agreement with Connally, that the missile that hit Connally was not one of the missiles that hit the President, as Livingstone's *High Treason 2* (1989), pp. 163–164, reports. That testimony on its own supports the conclusion that more than three bullets were fired in Dealey Plaza that morning: the one that hit the President in the back, the one that hit James Tague, the one that hit the President in the head, and the one that hit Connally. This adds up to at least four bullets fired, which contradicts the official report. The argument from addition and subtraction provides strong grounds for believing more than one assassin was involved.

Proof 2: The Argument from the Harper Fragment

The best photographic evidence that the President was killed by bullets fired from above and behind is a photo reprinted in Lifton's *Best Evidence* (1980), p. 586*a*, which displays a small entry wound near the crown of his head. A copy of this photograph was featured in a *NOVA* television special narrated by Walter Cronkite. It was also presented during *Good Morning, America* as an aspect of an interview with Charles Crenshaw following an appearance by George Lundberg on Thursday, 21 May 1992. Charlie Gibson was in a state of disbelief as Crenshaw suggested this photo had been faked. Yet Crenshaw is hardly the first person to arrive at precisely that conclusion.

The evidence that Crenshaw is correct is very strong. It includes a piece of the President's cranium that was discovered the next day at the scene of the assassination by Billy Harper, lying approximately twenty-five feet to the left of the car's path. A photograph of this fragment of occipital bone is reprinted in Menninger's *Mortal Error* (1992), p. 169, showing it to be about 2–1/2 inches wide and 2–1/4 inches high. Moreover, a fragment of roughly this size can be seen flying from the President's head in the movie, *The Two Kennedys*, which includes a second motion picture of the assassination taken from the side opposite the grassy knoll. Although the existence of this film is not widely known, it may be available at your local video store.

A blow-out to the back of the head has been confirmed by eyewitness reports, including that of Joe Hagen, who prepared the body for burial; see Livingstone's *High Treason 2* (1992), pp. 579–581. [*Editor's note*: Gary Aguilar, M.D., has collated over forty eyewitnesses who observed a blow-out of this kind.] It is corroborated by Boswell's sketch of Kennedy's cranium, reprinted as "Photo 27" in Lifton's *Best Evidence* (1980), p. 234*p*. The argument from the Harper fragment thus establishes that at least one photograph widely alleged to support the commission's report is not authentic and that autopsy evidence has been doctored. That this is the case has been widely recognized and discussed; see Groden and Livingstone, *High Treason* (1989), p. 28*a*, for example.

Proof 3: The Argument from the Autopsy X-rays and Photographs

Even apart from the argument from the Harper fragment, there exists ample evidence that X-rays and photographs that are alleged to be of the President's body have been faked or forged. The best study of this material can be found in Livingstone's *High Treason 2* (1992), which reprints more than sixteen pages of X-rays and photographs between pages 432 and 433 that might not be of the same body. For example, some X-rays show a large area of missing bone on the right front of a person's face, including the eye and forehead, while other photographs show the face to be intact. They are not consistent. [*Editor's note*: See Part I and Appendix L.]

The evidence that is brought together in this specific volume seems to be of a kind that physicians can readily assess. The possibility that some of these X-rays and photographs might not be reproductions of those that were made parts of the official autopsy evidence, moreover, could also be resolved by comparing them with those held at the National Archives, to which access has been granted to various investigators over the years. [*Editor's note*: David Mantik, M.D., Ph.D., has verified their correspondence with the originals and has established that at least some of the autopsy X-rays have been fabricated. See his contributions to Part I and to Part II.]

Proof 4: The Argument from U.S. News and World Report

The cover story of *U.S. News and World Report* (17 August 1992), pp. 28–42, was more revealing than its authors' may have intended. As the photograph on pp. 38-39 clearly reveals, the Warren Commission staff reconstructed their assassination scenario using a Cadillac instead of a Lincoln limousine. These automobiles, however, have very different characteristics, including the location of the seats, their relative height from the ground and other properties, as can be seen in photographs and diagrams found in Menninger's *Mortal Error* (1992), pp. 108*b*, 108*f*–108g, and 108*l*, which show both the President's Lincoln and the Secret Service Cadillac.

There is no doubt that the Cadillac was used to reconstruct the crime, as Warren Commission Exhibit 900 clearly displays. [*Editor's note*: See James H. Fetzer, Part I.] What is astonishing to consider is the possibility that everyone in America except the Warren Commission staff should have known that Kennedy was riding in a car of a different make than the one they used to reconstruct the crime. If this was done in ignorance, then the commission staff was incompetent; but if it was done knowingly, then the commission staff was corrupt. Since the difference is a matter of common knowledge, evidence that the Warren Commission staff contributed to covering-up the crime of the century is very strong.

Proof 5: The Argument from JAMA

With some exceptions, the evidence that is cited in Proofs 1 though 4 has been available to serious investigators for some time. One of the first detailed studies of the assassination, Thompson's *Six Seconds in Dallas*, for example, appeared in 1967. Lifton's *Best Evidence* was published in 1980. Groden and Livingstone's *High Treason* and Marrs' *Crossfire* both appeared in 1989. Menninger's *Mortal Error* and Livingstone's *High Treason 2* both appeared in 1992. With the exception of Menninger's book, which suggests that Kennedy was killed by an errant bullet fired by a Secret Service agent riding in the follow-up vehicle, these are standard works on the assassination, most of which are available at bookstores such as Borders, Waldenbooks, and Barnes & Noble.

As though any further evidence were needed of an ongoing effort to coverup the evidence of conspiracy in the assassination of John Kennedy, new articles have appeared in *JAMA* (27 May 1992), pp. 2791–2807; *JAMA* (7 October 1992), pp. 1736–1738 and pp. 1748–1754; and *JAMA* (24/31 March 1993), pp. 1540–1547, which have been subjected to extensive dissection elsewhere in this book. There are many reasons for believing that these articles were produced through the application of improper principles of inference, which yield misleading and unjustifiable conclusions. Without rehearsing considerations advanced in previous chapters, there is ample evidence here of an ongoing "cover-up of the cover-up" by *JAMA* in the assassination of President Kennedy, which appears very difficult to deny. [*Editor's note*: See Part I.]

Proof 6: The Parkland Observations Differ from those at Bethesda

There were striking differences between the observations made by the doctors at Parkland Hospital and those conducting the autopsy in Bethesda:

The Neck

	Parkland	**Bethesda**
Rear Neck Wound:	Not Observed	Entry above shoulder
Throat Wound:	Entry	Exit
Trajectory:	Front-to-Back	Back-to-Front

The Head

	Parkland	**Bethesda**
Rear Entry Wound:	Not Observed	Small hole below large defect
Large Defect:	2–3/4 inches exiting at rear	5–1/8 inches exiting from top right
Trajectory:	Front-to-Back	Back-to-Front

The evidence for these differences is enormous, including, for example, the autopsy report itself. [*Editor's note:* See Appendix (F).] (See also Thompson, *Six Seconds in Dallas*, 1967, Groden and Livingstone, *High Treason*, 1989, and other works). The summary presented here follows Lifton, *Best Evidence* (1980), p. 339, which is supported by extensive, detailed analysis, especially in his Chapters 11 and 13. As a point of logic, it cannot be the case that both sets of observations are correct if they are of the same body at the same time (though, as a point of logic, they could both be mistaken if the large defect, for example, were some size, such as approximately 4–1/4 inches, other than those described). The problem thus arises of accounting for the discrepancies between them.

As Lifton, especially, has emphasized, four possible explanations seem to be available. First, that the Parkland doctors were right and the Bethesda doctors were wrong. Second, that the Bethesda doctors were right and the Parkland doctors were wrong. Third, that both the Parkland and Bethesda doctors were right. Fourth, that both the Parkland and the Bethesda doctors were wrong. The most plausible explanation for doctors being wrong, however, would appear to be that they were either incompetent or were lying. An alternative explanation might be that they were neither incompetent nor lying but that the body had been surgically altered in the meanwhile.

If the body had been changed surgically between its departure from Parkland and the autopsy at Bethesda, then neither set of physicians has to be either incompetent or lying. The Warren Commission, as it happens, took the results of the autopsy to be the "best evidence" and, pursuing the lawyer's propensity to make his case, established (on that basis) the strongest case that could be constructed with the then-available evidence, including the single-bullet theory. The evidence currently available, however, suggests that the physicans were either incompetent or untruthful, or else the body was altered—or all the above! [*Editor's note*: See the Prologue and Part I.]

Proof 7: The Autopsy Report Conflicts with the X-Rays and Photos

Perhaps even more striking than the divergence between the Parkland observations and those of the Bethesda physicians is that the autopsy report and the autopsy X-rays and photographs are inconsistent. [*Editor's note*: See Part I and Appendix L.] This point differs from that made by Proof 3, which affirms an inconsistency between the X-rays and autopsy photos *without regard for the body or the autopsy report*. Evidently, if the X-rays and photos are correct, then the autopsy report is wrong; and if the autopsy report is correct, then the X-rays and photographs are wrong. Lifton, *Best Evidence* (1980), especially p. 506, summarizes them:

	Autopsy Report	**X-Rays and Photos**
Head Entry Wound:	Low on back of head	High on back of head
Head Exit Wound:	Top right-side/back	Top right-side/forward
Evidence of Exit:	None	Present
Occipital Bone:	Missing Fragment	Intact
Trajectory:	Back-to-Front (steeply upward)	Back-to-Front (slanting downward)

The missing occipital bone is partially the fragment that was the subject of Proof 2. While it may be not entirely unreasonable to suppose that the Parkland physicians might have had observations that were in conflict with those of the Bethesda surgeons, it is extremely difficult to reconcile differences between the autopsy report itself and these X-rays and photographs. Those who doubt this is the case might take another look at the X-rays and autopsy photographs that appear in Groden and Livingstone, *High Treason* (1989), p. 210*b*, Livingstone, *High Treason 2* (1992), pp. 432*a*–432*m*, and Lifton, *Best Evidence* (1980), pp. 682*c* and 682*d*, in relation to Humes' diagram and Boswell's sketch, which are found, for example, in *High Treason* (1989), pp. 28*b* and 28*c*.

Proof 8: Chain of Custody was Violated for the Most Important Evidence

Although it may be difficult to believe, the chain of custody which is required for evidence to be legally admissible in a court of law appears to have been violated for the most important evidence in this case, including the autopsy X-rays and photographs (Lifton, *Best Evidence*, pp. 521–524), several bone fragments brought into the autopsy after it had begun, which provided the basis for the alleged wound of entry (Lifton, *Best Evidence*, pp. 614–617), the Zapruder film (Lifton, *Best Evidence*, pp. 555–557), and even the President's body itself (Lifton, *Best Evidence*, Part VI, pp. 567–652). I wish I could deny that this is the case, but the evidence is very persuasive.

This evidence raises the possibility that perhaps those who were conducting the investigation and handling the evidence were not interested in preserving a legal chain of custody; otherwise, presumably, they appear to have been remarkably incompetent. The problem is that the various ways in which the chain of custody was violated in these cases seem to be quite deliberate and not "accidental". (The choice of obviously incompetent physicians to perform this most important autopsy tends to vividly confirm this impression.) Moreover, it is fascinating that Lundberg, who emphasized to me the permissibility of disregarding evidence lacking a legal chain of custody, nevertheless seems oblivious to the problem in relation to *JAMA's* own reports.

Proof 9: JAMA Did Not Ask Key Questions of Humes and Boswell

Moreover, a number of important and unsettling questions were not asked of Humes and Boswell, even though they presumably could easily have been raised. These include the following very important questions:

(i) Why did Humes testify (about the fatal bullet), "Scientifically, sir, it is impossible for it to have been fired from other than behind. Or to have exited from other than behind."? (see Lifton, *Best Evidence*, p. 188)

(ii) Had surgery been performed on the President's body before the autopsy took place as Sibert and O'Neill asserted in their FBI report, namely: that "It was apparent that a tracheostomy had been performed as well as surgery to the head"? (Lifton, *Best Evidence*, especially Chapter 18).

(iii) Had Humes given a bullet that had fallen from the body to Sibert and O'Neill as indicated by a receipt they signed (a copy of which has been reprinted in Groden and Livingstone, *High Treason*, p. 28j, and extensively discussed in Lifton, *Best Evidence*, especially pp. 590–591, 645–651)?

(iv) Could Humes explain why one of his assistants at the autopsy, James Curtis Jenkins, has denied recalling any discussion of "beveling" at all during the autopsy, even though Humes claims that this is the centerpiece of the whole case? (See Lifton, *Best Evidence*, p. 448, pp. 533–534 and pp. 614–619, Livingstone, *High Treason 2*, especially Chapter 11.)

(v) Could Humes explain the 100 mm difference between his autopsy report and that of the panel of four forensic pathologists appointed by Attorney General Clark to review the controversy surounding the location of the entry wound to the head? (Lifton, *Best Evidence*, pp. 427–432)

(vi) Could Humes explain whether there was a "pre-autopsy autopsy" or a post-autopsy reconstruction of the head, as considerable evidence currently suggests? (Lifton, *Best Evidence*, especially Chapters 18 and 30)

(vii) Could Humes account for varied discrepancies between his autopsy report and Boswell's observations, including Boswell's notes of "vomer crushed", "globe rt [right] eye-fracture through floor"; a 10 x 17 cm area marked "missing"; a 10 cm fragment on the left side that appears to have fallen to the floor when Humes "moved the scalp about"; an oblique line, possibly corresponding to one of four symmetrical scalp tears, on the left and one on the right; the notation of falx being "loose" from the sagittal sinus? (Summarized by Lifton, *Best Evidence*, pp. 458–459)

(viii) Could Humes explain what he meant when he testified that "There was a longitudinal laceration of the right hemisphere which was para-sagittal in position" that ran from the tip of the occipital lobe to the tip of the frontal in describing the brain? (Lifton, *Best Evidence*, pp. 190–191) [*Editor's note*: This appears to be one of the crucial questions in this case with respect to possible surgical alteration of the President's head.]

These eight questions are among the most important questions that remain to be answered in order to better understand a number of peculiar aspects of the President's autopsy. Since Lundberg had unique access to the autopsy surgeons, it is very odd that none of them appear to have been raised. If Lundberg was unaware of these questions or their importance, however, then he had not done his homework and was not properly prepared to discuss the autopsy with Humes and Boswell. If Lundberg was aware of the importance of these questions but nevertheless chose not to raise them, then he irresponsibly forfeited an opportunity of enormous potential importance.

Proof 10: The JAMA Editor Surely Ought to Have Known Better

It is difficult to escape the conclusion that Lundberg should have known enough about the assassination to recognize that the report he was about to publish would bring the great weight and immense prestige of the AMA to bear in a biased and partisan fashion on behalf of false or disputed propositions about the medical evidence in this case. The reasons for believing that he had to have extensive familiarity with the controversial character of the evidence stems from common knowledge about the Kennedy assassination. There are excellent reasons to believe that he should have had an understanding of this case sufficient to take more than normal precautions.

One reason for thinking so is that standard works on this subject have received wide-spread publicity. Thompson's *Six Seconds in Dallas*, for example, was the subject of a cover story in the *Saturday Evening Post* (2 December 1967). Lifton's *Best Evidence* has been a national bestseller reviewed in *Time, The Los Angeles Times, The Miami Herald, The Washington Star*, and other papers and magazines. It was even a Book-of-the-Month Club selection. Groden and Livingstone's *High Treason* has been a *New York Times* bestseller. If Lundberg is not familiar with these works, then there would appear to be good reason to question his competence in this matter.

Another reason for thinking that Lundberg should have known the controversial character of the evidence in this case is that the movie, *JFK*, has stimulated a revival of general interest in these questions. A meticulously documented screenplay of the film—Stone and Sklar, *JFK: The Book of the Film* (1992)—has been published that reprints nearly one hundred articles and commentaries, which have appeared in an enormous variety of newspapers and magazines. If Lundberg was not familiar with this public controversy, then that would be another good reason to question his competence. Surely the editor of *JAMA* should have undertaken a task of this kind only if he could handle it properly, yet the AMA is now vulnerable to the charge of having contributed to a cover-up in the assassination of John F. Kennedy.

These are the ten "proofs" that I sent to Dr. Ring in 1992. Each of them provides proof—in the sense appropriate to the law—of the existence of conspiracy or cover-up. Some are even stronger. Today, as a consequence of the important work of David Mantik and Robert B. Livingston, among others, we know much more. In my estimation, the strongest evidence of conspiracy and cover-up results from Mantik's discovery that autopsy X-rays have been fabricated to conceal a massive blow-out to the back of his head and to impose a 6.5 mm metal object, Livingston's determination that diagrams of a brain in the National Archives must be of the brain of someone other than Jack Kennedy, and our more recent finding that the Zapruder film has been extensively edited by means of highly sophisticated techniques, a matter to which I shall now turn.

The Zapruder Film

In discussions of Zapruder film authenticity, it is important to note that, from a logical point of view, the hypothesis that the film is authentic possesses the character of a *general hypothesis* asserting that, in every respect, the Z-film has not been altered, modified, or forged—except perhaps in some obvious respects that are acknowledged by everyone (such as the large splice at frames 207–210 and an earlier splice). This is the position of Robert Groden, Randy Robertson, M.D., Josiah Thompson, Ph.D., and perhaps Joseph Riley, Ph.D., among others. Notice, however, that if it should turn out that we discover the existence of specific features of the film that indicate that it has been altered, modified, or forged—in respects other than those that have been admitted—then the hypothesis that the film is authentic might be falsified, even "conclusively".

Presumably, of course, the conclusive falsification of such an hypothesis should be based upon observations, measurements, or experiments subject to replication by anyone with the appropriate background, training, and technology at their disposal, who would be expected to arrive at the same conclusions on the basis of the same evidence. Thus, scientific objectivity may best be understood as *intersubjective reliability*, in the sense that different students of comparable competence using the same methods and standards of proof examining the same evidence should arrive at (more or less) all and only the same conclusions, accepting as true, rejecting as false, or suspending judgment when the evidence is inadequate, as appropriate.

In the case of the Zapruder Film Symposium, which I organized and moderated, many different arguments were advanced based upon many different features of the film that appear to be inconsistent with its authenticity. For simplicity, let me refer to these features as "anomalies". These are feaures of the film that establish what might be called a *prima facie* case for the film's lack of authenticity as apparent indications of alteration, modification, or forgery. During a workshop held on 21 November 1996, the participants exchanged views about the anomalies they had noticed and the plausibility of various explanations for them. The results that we presented during the Zapruder Film Symposium on 22 November 1996, therefore, had already been subjected to preliminary critical scrutiny by the participants.

To illustrate the inferential situation, therefore, I shall mention four different kinds of evidence that were presented there:

Case 1: White's Compendium of Zapruder-film Anomalies

Jack White has noticed numerous anomalies in the film, including the pink "spray", Greer's head-turn, the missing car-stop, the missing Connally left-turn, the peculiar changes in the visual field, a sequence of frames in which the line of spectators near the Stemmons Freeway Sign are virtually motionless (even though they are seen smiling and waving at that same time in the Muchmore film), and has reported other anomalies noticed by Ray Redmon, Chuck Marler, Milicent Cranor, Richard Bartholomew, David Mantik, Harry Livingstone, Daryll Weatherly, Robert Morningstar, Alan Eaglesham, and no doubt others unnamed.

The observations he has summarized support the following argument:

P1: If these observations of anomalies are well-founded,
then the film has been subjected to alteration.

P2: These observations of anomalies are well-founded.

C1: The film has been subjected to alteration.

Viewing and discussing these anomalies with White and other participants, both premises appear to me to be well-founded. I therefore accept conclusion C1. [*Editor's note*: See Part IV.]

Case 2: Twyman's Studies of the Greer Head Turn

Noel Twyman has conducted extensive studies using highly-conditioned athletes to measure the speed at which a person can turn their head from looking back over their right shoulder to looking straight forward, as Greer appears to do in the film. He has compared the speed of his subjects with that of Greer and has calculated that Greer's turn is approximately twice as fast as his subject's. This may not sound impressive at first, until you consider that a runner who runs a four minute mile would correspondingly have run a two minute mile. His findings thus suggest that at least several frames have been "vertically edited," as it were.

Twyman's studies support the following argument:

> P3: If Twyman's studies of the Greer head turn are well-founded, then at least several frames have been edited from the film, which has been altered at least to that extent.
>
> P4: Twyman's studies of the Greer head turn are well-founded.

> C2: At least several frames have been edited from the film, which has been altered at least to that extent.

The discussion of this subject has been marred by students who have failed to appreciate that the frame labeled "Z-317" by the National Archives appears to be a duplicate of frame Z-308. I believe that Twyman's studies are well-founded and therefore accept conclusion C2. [*Editor's note:* See Noel Twyman, *Bloody Treason* (forthcoming).] .

Case 3: Mantik's Accumulation of Eyewitness Testimony

Mantik has also brought together the reports of at least ten eyewitnesses who reported that the Presidential limousine was brought to a halt in Dealey Plaza after shots had begun to be fired, including Harry D. Holmes, Mary Moorman, James Chaney, Roy Truly, James Simmons, Billy Martin, Douglas Jackson, Earle Brown, B. W. Hargis, and Bill Newman. Since the chance of one witness being in error in this case, given the study he cites, turns out to be 2%, the chance that ten independent witnesses, who report the same thing, should all be mistaken by chance equals .02 to the tenth power—or somewhat less than the chance of picking a needle from a haystack using a pair of tweezers on a single try. These eyewitness reports support the following argument:

P5. If the eyewitness testimony Mantik has accumulated should be accepted in this case, then the Zapruder film has been edited.

P6. The eyewitness testimony Mantik has accumulated should be accepted in this case.

C3. The Zapruder film has been edited

The principles of evidence even require that eyewitness testimony has priority over photographic evidence, which needs eyewitness testimony to be admissible. The reports he has collated are numerous, consistent, and uncontradicted. I therefore also accept C3. [*Editor's note*: See Part IV.]

Case 4: Mantik's Studies of Background Magnification.

Mantik has discovered that background features in the film increase in their degree of magnification monotonically from about the Stemmons Freeway Sign through the head shot at Z-313 in spite of no increase in relation to the limousine. This strongly suggests that features of the foreground have been deleted by "horizontal editing," as it were, to conceal the removal of whole frames, and that background features have been increased in size to compensate in relation to an incomplete visual field, etc.

Mantik's studies support the following argument:

P7: If Mantik's studies of magnification are well-founded, then the Zapruder film has been extensively edited using sophisticated techniques.

P8: Mantik's magnification studies are well-founded.

C4: The Zapruder film has been extensively edited using sophisticated techniques.

This argument, of course, is deductively valid, which means that its conclusion cannot be false if its premises are true. Based upon my familiarity with Mantik's studies and appreciating the quality of his very precise and meticulous research, I am convinced that its premises are true. Consequently, I accept conclusion C4. [*Editor's note*: See Part IV.]

Detailed elaboration of each of these lines of argument—as well as those of many others supporting similar conclusions—may be found elsewhere in this volume. These findings appear to provide conclusive, but not therefore *infallible*, evidence that the film has been subjected to extensive editing using highly sophisticated techniques. Those who resist this conclusion, therefore, are obligated to explain in what ways these studies have gone wrong or run the risk of qualifying as irrational. *Rationality* in this sense involves accepting or rejecting conclusions on the basis of the available relevant evidence. In the case at hand, an hypothesis—namely, that the Zapruder film is authentic—has been decisively falsified on the basis of evidence that is subject to objective replication. In a sense weaker than the mathematician's sense but stronger than the legal sense, it appears to be entirely justified to assert that the case for Zapruder film tampering has been proven.

The Death of JFK

The application of inference to the best explanation proves illuminating in relation to the contents of this book. The assassination of John F. Kennedy, after all, could be explained by a variety of alternative hypotheses, including (h1) that he was killed by a lone, demented gunman named Lee Harvey Oswald, (h2) that the Mob did it, (h3) that pro- or anti-Castro Cubans did it, (h4) that the Soviet KGB did it, or (h5) that his death was the result of a *coup d'état*, involving the CIA, the Mob, anti-Castro Cubans, and powerful politicians, such as LBJ, Richard Nixon, and J. Edgar Hoover, and fully financed by Texas oil men and other elements of the military-industrial complex. [*Editor's note:* See *Newsweek* (22 November 1993), p. 99.]

JFK was controversial on many grounds, including his forceful actions in support of integration, his attempts to reduce the oil depletion allowance, his opposition to monopolistic pricing policies, his negotiation of a Limited Nuclear Test Ban Treaty with the Soviet Union, his failure to support the invasion of Cuba, his resolution "to shatter the CIA into a thousand pieces", his decision to withdraw American forces from Vietnam, his placing covert operations under the supervision of the Pentagon, and his brother Bobby's relentless attack upon organized crime. It looked quite likely that he would drop LBJ as his 1964 running mate and, following his reelection, would retire J. Edgar Hoover as Director of the FBI.

Now consider some of the most important findings reported in this book. David Mantik has discovered that lateral X-rays of the President's cranium have been fabricated to conceal a massive blow-out to the back of his head and that a 6.5 mm object has been superimposed upon the original AP X-ray. Robert Livingston has concluded that diagrams of the brain in the National Archives must be of some brain other than that of John F. Kennedy. A group of experts on various aspects of photographic evidence has found that the Zapruder film has been extensively edited using highly sophisticated techniques. If we accept this evidence on the basis of the studies presented here, then what does it tell us about the assassination?

The impact of this evidence appears to be considerable. The Mob, for example, would not have had the power to reach into Bethesda Naval Hospital to fabricate X-rays of the President's cranium. Neither pro- nor anti-Castro Cubans could have substituted diagrams of someone else's brain for that of John Fitzgerald Kennedy. The KGB could not have have had access to the Zapruder film in order to subject it to extensive editing, even if it had the ability to do so. Neither could any of these things have been done by Lee Harvey Oswald, who was in custody or already dead.

None of these hypotheses is consistent with this new evidence, which means that none of these things appears possible. We now have evidence, not previously available, which cannot be reconciled with the truth of (h1), (h2), (h3), or (h4). At least, it cannot be reconciled with those hypotheses when they are intended to be the truth, the whole truth, and nothing but the truth about the assassination. It remains the case that, even though the Mob, for example, could not have fabricated X-rays, substituted diagrams of a brain, or edited the Zapruder film, it could still have put up guns or money. That would not be especially surprising.

What, then, about (h5)? I have discovered at least fifteen indications of Secret Service complicity in the assassination of John F. Kennedy, from the absence of protective military presence to a lack of coverage of open windows, to motorcycles out of position, to Secret Service agents failing to ride on the Presidential limousine, to the vehicles arranged in an improper sequence, to the utilization of an improper motorcade route, to the driver bringing the vehicle to a halt after bullets began to be fired, to the almost total lack of response by Secret Service agents, to the driver washing out the back seat with a bucket and sponge at Parkland Hospital, to the car being dismantled and rebuilt (on LBJ's orders), to the driver giving false testimony to the Warren Commission, to the windshields being switched, to the autopsy photographs being taken into custody before they were developed, and more (as I explain in my video, *JFK: The Assassination, the Cover-Up and Beyond*).

Those who would like to excuse conduct of the kinds that I have described might argue that these are things that can happen some of the time, where it was just a matter of "bad luck" so many happened in this case. If we assign an improbability of 1 in 10 to their occurrence by chance, however, such that each of them is supposed to be an independent event causally unrelated to the others, then if we take only eight or nine of these events, their improbability of occurring by chance is only 1 in 100,000,000 to 1 in 1,000,000,000, which are stunning numbers considering that hypotheses in science are rejected when their improbability equals or exceeds 1 in 20. The evidence that the Secret Service set him up is therefore overwhelming. And it is difficult to imagine that members of the Secret Service would have participated in the assassination of the President of the United States without direction from higher authority.

This simple statistical argument, which tends to confirm hypothesis (h5), receives support from other directions that also implicate the CIA. Chauncey M. Holt, for example, has reported that he was a counterfeiter who, while working as a contract agent for the CIA, brought fifteen sets of forged Secret Service credentials to Dealey Plaza for use by persons in the immediate vicinity (*KOGO* AM-Radio, San Diego, 22 November 1995). He has told me that he arrived there in the company of Charles Harrelson, father of Woody, who was a notorious hit man for the Mob. Harrelson once said that he killed Kennedy, later retracting it and claiming that he was out of his mind when he said it and the very fact that he said it showed as much. He is serving a life-sentence for the assassination of a federal judge with a high-powered rifle, a very similar crime.

The 'three tramps', identified by Chauncey Holt as Charles Harrelson (the tallest), Chauncey Holt (wearing a hat) and Richard Montoya (the best dressed)

Madeleine Brown, who was LBJ's mistress and by whom he had a son who lived to be forty and only died in 1990, has said that LBJ told her that he was not going to put up with embarrassment from those Kennedy boys after tomorrow. When she subsequently confronted him about rumors that he had been involved, LBJ told her that the CIA and the oil boys had decided that Jack had to be taken out. She has written a book vividly describing these events, the first of which occurred at a social gathering at the home of Clint Murchison on the eve of the assassination, which included J. Edgar Hoover of the FBI, Richard Nixon, John J. McCloy of Chase Manhattan Bank—whom LBJ would later appoint to the Warren Commission—George Brown of Brown and Root (heavy construction), and (later) Lyndon Johnson. When LBJ arrived, they went into a private meeting for about twenty minutes; after they emerged, Lyndon made the remark I described above (Brown, *Texas in the Morning* 1997). Madeleine has told me that she specifically recalls that Richard Nixon was driven to the gathering by Peter O'Donnell, a local Republican leader.

In his autobiography, Richard Nixon describes learning about the death of JFK during a taxi ride in New York City. According to The Minneapolis Star *(23 November 1963), p. 7A, however, reporters caught up with him at Idlewild upon arrival after a flight from Dallas, where he had been on business.*

Moreover, the Zapruder film appears to have been in the hands of the CIA as early as the evening of 22 November 1963. As David Lifton has reported, in 1976, Paul Hoch, using the Freedom of Information Act, obtained a group of documents indicating that the film was already in the hands of the National Photo Interpretation Center run by the CIA Friday

CABELL, Charles Pearre, business cons.; b. Dallas, Tex., Oct. 11, 1903; B.S., U.S. Mil. Acad. 1925; grad. Air Corps Primary Flying Sch., 1931, Advanced Flying Sch., observation course, 1931, Command and Gen. Staff Sch., 1940; Army and Navy Staff Coll., 1943; m. Jacklyn DeHymel, 1934; children—Charles, Catharine, Ben. Commd. 2d lt., F.A., A.U.S., 1925, advanced to general (U.S.A.-F), 1958; served successively as asst. chief operations sect., tng. and opeations div., as chief, photo unit, and as chief, tech. coordination br., Office of Chief of Air Corps, Wash., D.C., 1941-42; mem. advisory council Hdqrs. Army Air Forces, Washington, D.C., 1942-43; assigned 8th Air Force, European Theater of Operations, Oct. 1943, comdr. combat wing, Dec. 1943; dir. of plans, U.S. Strategic Air Forces, Apr.-July 1944; mil. air adviser to U.S. representative on European Adv. Commn., London, May-July 1944; dir. operations and intelligence, Mediterranean Allied Air Forces, July 1944-May 1945; chief strategy and policy div. of air plans, Hdqrs. A.A.F., Washington, 1945; dep. and U.S. air representative on mil. staff com. of UN N.Y., 1946-47; dir. of intelligence, Hdqrs., USAF, Washington, 1948; dir. Joint Staff, Joint Chiefs of Staff, 1951; dep. dir. Central Intelligence, 1953-62; now business cons. Awarded D.S.M., Legion of Merit, Air Medal (Oak-Leaf Cluster), Distinguished Flying Cross, Bronze Star; Distinguished Intelligence medal; Hon. Comdr. Brit. Empire, Officer French Legion of Honor, Croix de Guerre; mem. Order of St. Laurice and Lazarus of Italy. Address: 2506 Ft. Scott Dr., Arlington, Va. 22202.

CABELL, Earle, congressman; b. nr. Dallas, Oct. 27, 1906; s. Ben E. and Sadie (Pearre) C.; student Tex. A. and M. Coll., 1925-26. So. Meth U., 1926; m. Elizabeth Holder, Feb. 22, 1932; children —Elizabeth Lee (Mrs. Pulley), Earle. Salesman, Morning Glory Creameries, Houston, 1926-28; plant supt. Mistletoe Creameries, Amarillo, Tex., 1928-30; owner Cabell's Dairy, Pine Bluff, Ark., 1930-32; with Cabell's, Inc., 1932—successively sec.-treas., exec. v.p., 1932-52, pres., 1952—, chmn. bd., 1961—; chmn. bd. Cabell's Dairies, Dallas; dir., exec. com. Grand Av. State Bank; mayor City of Dallas, 1961-64; mem. 89th U.S. Congress, 5th Dist. Tex. Pres. Dallas Crime Commn., 1954-56; mem. Gov.'s Econ. Adv. Commn., 1954-56; adv. bd. Tex. Indsl. Commn.; active Boy Scouts Am.; sec., mem. exec. com. Tex. Law Enforcement Found. Dir. Jr. Achievement. Served from capt. to lt. col., Tex. State Guard, 1941-46. Mem. Southwestern Law Enforcement Inst. (exec. com.), East Tex., Dallas chambers commerce, Dallas Sales Execs. Club (past pres.), Dairy Products Inst. Tex. (past pres.), Tex. Mfrs. Assn. (past pres.), Dallas Salesmanship Club, Dallas Sales Execs. Clubs: Dallas Country, Dallas Athletic (past dir.), McKinney Lake (past pres.), City, Stump and Storm. Home: 3701 Turtle Creek Blvd., Dallas 75219. Office: 1111 Commerce St., Dallas; also House Office Bldg., Washington.

Cabell biographies from Who's Who, *circa 1965*

night immediately following the assassination, where an original and three copies were struck, the same number that Abraham Zapruder had had made during the afternoon in Dallas [*Editor's note*: See Mike Pincher and Roy Schaeffer, Part IV]. To those who are skeptical that photographic techniques could have been equal to the task at the time, I am fond of pointing out that the film, *Mary Poppins*, with its many special effects, was released in 1964. [*Editor's note*: See David Mantik, Part IV.]

At the operational level, however, I believe that the key connection links the CIA and the Mob to Dallas. The Deputy Director for Operations at the time of the Bay of Pigs invasion was an Air Force Lt. General by the name of Charles Cabell. Cabell had overseen attempts by the CIA in collusion with the Mob—which wanted to regain its casinos and resorts in Havana, where it was running the largest money-laundering operation in the Western hemisphere—to take out Castro. It was Cabell who, in the presence of Dean Rusk, called JFK to plead with him for the close air support he believed the President had promised, but which JFK refused to provide. He would later return to the Pentagon, after being relieved of his position at the CIA by JFK, where he would describe the President as a "traitor".

Charles Cabell was born in Dallas in 1903. His brother Earle was born near Dallas in 1906. In 1961, Earle Cabell became Mayor of the City of Dallas. In his capacity as Mayor, he not only supervised the police department but oversaw ceremonial activities, including parade routes and motorcades. There is no way that the Presidential motorcade could have taken the peculiar and improper route it took through Dealey Plaza—which even contradicted the route published in the morning paper—without the approval of the Mayor. The two combined motive, means, and opportunity. The psychodynamics of the assassination, as I reconstruct the crime, thus appear to have pitted two rich and powerful right-wing politicians against two rich and powerful left-wing politicians.

The crucial consideration was not killing the President but taking over the government undetected. It would be helpful if the conspirators could control the legal apparatus that would process information in this case from the Chief of Police to the District Attorney, perhaps by taking the matter out of the hands of local and state authorities, even though the only offense that had been committed was the murder of someone who happened to be a government official. The evidence would have to be filtered through friendly authorities to insure that the official cover story not be blown. The FBI could select evidence supporting that account and eliminate the rest. If necessary, evidence could be fabricated. This appears to be exactly how it was done. Understanding the cover-up thus provides the crucial link to understanding the conspiracy in the death of JFK.

Evelyn Lincoln

4701 Willard Avenue
Chevy Chase, Maryland 20815
(301) 654-6570

October 7, 1994

Dear Richard:

It was a pleasure to receive your kind letter concerning your desire to obtain my assessment of President Kennedy's administration and assassination to pass along to your students.

I am sending along to you an article which was written by Muriel Pressman for the "Lady's Circle" October 1964, and was recently reprinted in a current issue of that magazine, which will give you an insight into my impression of the man.

As for the assassination is concerned it is my belief that there was a conspiracy because there were those that disliked him and felt the only way to get rid of him was to assassinate him. These five conspirators, in my opinion, were Lyndon B. Johnson, J. Edgar Hoover, the Mafia, the CIA and the Cubans in Florida. The House Intelligence Committee investigation, also, came to the conclusion that there was a conspiracy.

My very best wishes to you and your students.

Sincerely,

Evelyn Lincoln
Evelyn Lincoln

Letter from JFK's Personal Secretary to "Richard" of 7 October 1994

C.I.A. BREAKS LINKS TO AGENTS ABROAD

Crimes of the 100 Outweighed Their Worth as Informers

By TIM WEINER

WASHINGTON, March 2 — Breaking with its past, the Central Intelligence Agency has severed its ties to roughly 100 foreign agents, about half of them in Latin America, whose value as informers was outweighed by their acts of murder, assassination, torture, terrorism and other crimes, Government officials said today.

According to The New York Times *(3 March 1997), the CIA has now severed its connections with 100 foreign agents because "their value as informants was outweighed by their acts of murder, assassination, torture, terrorism, and other crimes", actions the agency has denied for decades that it ever engages in. Considerations of democracy, justice, and morality do not appear to have significantly influenced its decision.*

Postscript

Some general themes that provide a philosophical framework for the contents of this book are found in the Postscript by Ronald White, Ph.D., who discusses the assassination as an historical event. Surveying the literature on the subject, he finds publications ranging from "apologist" works, which are intended to support the lone assassin theory, such as Gerald Posner, *Case Closed: Lee Harvey Oswald and the Assassination of JFK* (1993), to work by "critics", such as Robert Groden and Harrison Livingstone, *High Treason* (1989), which are meant to refute it. As White observes, national sentiment appears to favor the critics when measured by interest in books and attendance at movies.

Even if most Americans do not believe they have been told the truth about the assassination, that opinion could still be false. To assume that an opinion must be true because it is widely held is to commit the fallacy of *popular sentiments*. If truth were merely a matter of majority sentiment (which may be a useful mechanism for rendering decisions for action within democratic societies), then the majority opinion in this case has decided the case remains "open" rather than "closed". If truth is more than a matter of opinion, we need to know what more might be involved.

Recent studies of the assassination, including the articles in *JAMA*, have emphasized the importance of "scientific evidence" and "expert testimony", suggesting that scientific principles of inquiry and methods of procedure could make a difference here. The areas that appear to be most promising

373

for scientific findings, moreover, are the *physical evidence* (especially involving the Zapruder film and the ballistics) and the *medical evidence* (especially involving the autopsy and supporting materials). These resources, of course, would ordinarily be expected to converge on a logically coherent assassination scenario, where evidence of these two kinds should be mutually reinforcing—as in the case of the studies presented in this volume.

At Large ████████████████████████

With Dennis L. Breo

JFK's death—the plain truth from the MDs who did the autopsy

There are two and only two physicians who know exactly what happened—and didn't happen—during their autopsy of President John F. Kennedy on the night of November 22, 1963, at the Naval Medical Center in Bethesda,

Lt Col Pierre Finck, MC, who participated as an expert consultant; Finck, who now lives in Switzerland, declined to come to Florida for the joint interview.) Humes says he is breaking his 29-year silence "because I am tired of

fragments and reconstructed this gaping wound where the bullet exited, we found this same pattern—a small wound where the bullet struck the inside of the skull and a beveled larger wound where it exited. This is *always* the pattern of

---

JAMA's *articles on the assassination appeared in three installments in its issues for 27 May 1992, 7 October 1992, and 24/21 March 1993. The article shown here was the first in the series.*

Problems with the evidence, however, abound. Whether or not Oswald owned a Mannlicher-Carcano, whether or not a rifle of that kind was used in the assassination, whether or not the film has been edited, whether or not the autopsy was properly performed, whether or not the X-rays have been fabricated and the photographs have been faked are only a sampler of problems within this domain. Merely knowing that something counts as "evidence" when its presence or absence or its truth or falsity makes a difference to the truth or falsity of an hypothesis is just not enough. We need to know what properly counts as *evidence* in this particular case.

White attempts to place these issues within a broad philosophical context. Utilizing work by Thomas Kuhn and by Sir Karl Popper, for example, White suggests, in effect, that the official government account of the assassination—three shots fired from above and behind by a lone, demented assassin—may be viewed as a theory that has been falsified (Popper) or as a paradigm laden with anomalies (Kuhn), where its survival has been largely facilitated by institutions like *JAMA*, the national press, and (I would add) the Department of Justice, whose exercise of power defines what is taken to be "knowledge" (Foucault), even when that exercise appears to be abusive. [*Editor's note:* See Part I and Part III.]

Thus, White suggests that the critics tend to be Popperians in their insistence that the lone gunman theory has already been falsified by the available evidence. Their Popperian stance tends to imply their commitment to *realism*, in the sense that they believe there is a truth in this matter, where one account may be closer to the truth than another, however difficult that might be to measure. The apologists, by comparison, tend to be Kuhnians in their willingness to countenance incompatible evidence as "anomalies" that need not overthrow an accepted paradigm, which leads them to the proliferation of *ad hoc* explanations of anomalies rather than to rejection of the theory.

White illustrates the problems with these anomalies in relation to the number and timing sequence of the shots, the amount of material that is or is not missing from the "magic bullet", and the "jet effect", which has been advanced as an alternative explanation of why the President's head seems to move in two different directions—first forward, then backward and to the left, relative to the limousine—on the Zapruder film, which suggests that JFK was hit at least twice in the head: once from behind, propelling his head forward, then again from in front, propelling his head backward, as Josiah Thompson, *Six Seconds in Dallas* (1967), has maintained.

Thus, to take the case of the "head snap", an alternative explanation for the motion of the President's head has been advanced by Luis Alvarez, a Nobel-Prize winning physicist, who appeals to a phenomenon he calls the "jet effect" as a causally relevant factor. According to Alvarez, when the bullet enters the skull, it creates forward momentum, but as it exits the skull, it creates a reaction in the oppose direction brought about by blood and brains blowing out the defect created by the bullet in its exit. Thus, when all the relevant factors that make a causal difference to the effect to be explained are taken into account, the official scenario can be saved.

Although White does not formulate the point in this language, what is at stake here is that every factor whose presence or absence made a difference to the outcome—the *maximal-specificity* condition—has to be taken into account in order to secure an adequate explanation for any event. The problem with the specific explanation that Alvarez has advanced, however, is the existence of the very "jet effect" factor to which his alternative explanation appeals. If the kinds of experiments upon which he depends do not provide the kind of evidence he needs to establish its existence, as White explains, then he has merely offered a pseudo-hypothesis that does not qualify as a genuine alternative to the two-or-more-shot explanation.

In his discussion of the problem of identifying "experts", White notes that Josiah Thompson, for example, was a professor of philosophy at the time of his research, that Charles Crenshaw knew so little about it when his book was published that his words were set in bold type, that Gerald Posner was trained as a lawyer and possesses no apparent qualifications with respect to ballistics, acoustics, or forensic pathology, and that a lack of background knowledge has not inhibited the national press from effusive praise of Posner, even including a summary of his apologist's conclusions in a 22-page tribute in *U.S. News and World Report* (30 August 1993).

We are not therefore unable to sort these matters out. Thompson may not have been a scientist by background and training, for example, but his research is a model of thorough and systematic analysis. Crenshaw simply happened to be on the staff of Parkland Hospital at the time; the accuracy of his observations does not depend on his expertise on the assassination. Reports from Thompson, Crenshaw, Posner and everyone else ought to be appraised by a common set of standards, including the logical coherence of what they have had to say and how well it withstands critical scrutiny.

Unfortunately, we cannot simply assume that what appears in prestigous journals such as *JAMA* must be true. Among the most important and sobering conclusions that emerge from White's study are that we cannot depend upon our government to investigate itself, that we cannot take for granted that even authoritative publications are not abusing their scientific standing, and that we cannot count on the nation's press to be able to assist us in telling the difference between truth and falsehood, even in matters of the greatest significance to our nation's history. Fortunately, research can also be evaluated by the empirical support it receives from repeatable, scientific experimentation. [*Editor's note:* See Part IV.]

The scientific findings presented elsewhere in this volume—which establish that the autopsy X-rays have been fabricated to conceal a massive wound to the the back of the President's head and to include a 6.5 mm object, that diagrams of a brain in the National Archives must be of someone other than John Fitzgerald Kennedy, and that the Zapruder film has been extensively edited using highly sophisticated techniques—indicate the importance of attempts to falsify hypotheses, as Popper, especially, has emphasized. Conjectures that the X-rays are authentic, that the diagrams are of Jack Kennedy's brain, and that the Zapruder film provides a reliable record of the assassination, appear to have been conclusively disproven, dramatically expanding our understanding of the death of JFK.

— *James H. Fetzer, Ph.D.*

Postscript
Apologists and Critics of the Lone Gunman Theory:
Assassination Science and Experts in Post-Modern America

Ronald F. White, Ph.D.

The assassination of John F. Kennedy on 22 November 1963 has proven to be an historical event of enduring public interest. Indeed, the book publishing industry has profitted substantially in meeting this demand. The On-Line Computer Library Center (OCLC) lists 816 book titles on the assassination, and the Assassination Archives and Research Center in Washington D.C. has collected more than 2,000 books on the assassination and other related topics. In light of this immense historiography, at least two schools of thought continue to dominate the literature.

(a) There are the "apologist" works like Gerald Posner's *Case Closed: Lee Harvey Oswald and the Assassination of JFK* (1993) that accept the Warren Commission's "lone gunman theory." The claim here is that Lee Harvey Oswald, firing from the sixth floor of the Texas School Book Depository Building, was the only assassin present at Dealey Plaza.

(b) There is also an alternative genre of works such as Robert J. Groden and Harrison Edward Livingstone's *High Treason: The Assassination of President John F. Kennedy and the New Evidence of Conspiracy* (1989). These authors not only reject the commission's lone gunman theory, but also detect a conspiracy to kill President Kennedy and/or a government cover-up of the evidence.

Public opinion polls suggest that national sentiment favors the critics. In 1992, four books espousing various conspiracy theories made *The New York Times* best-sellers lists (Ambrose, 1992, pp. 23–25), and a film by Oliver Stone titled *JFK* was a box office success that earned $200 million (not including video sales) and received widespread media coverage (Raskin 1992; Rogin 1992; Rosenstone 1992). A recent survey of 1,026 Americans by ICR Research Group of Media, Pennsylvania revealed that only 12% of the American public believe they have been told the whole truth and 71% think Oswald was part of a larger conspiracy.[1]

The hallmark of the most recent works by both apologists and critics has been the priority given to "scientific evidence" and "expert testimony." The assumption seems to be that the testimony of ordinary witnesses is unreliable and that the more objective methodologies of science alone can eventually "confirm" or "disconfirm" the lone gunman theory and thus settle the historical record once and for all.

In exploring the various puzzles raised by the evidence, students of the assassination have cultivated two broad areas of scientific investigation: *physical science* in the study of the 8mm Zapruder film and the ballistics; and *medical science* in the analysis of the autopsy report, X-rays, and autopsy photographs. The "scientific" findings in these areas of research have typically been published in scientific and medical journals, which, in turn, are frequently cited as authoritative in other works.

This essay will address three main themes. *First,* scientific and historical methodologies will be examined based upon two schools of philosophical thought: the "realists" (Hempel and Popper) and the "relativists" (Kuhn, and Foucault). It will be argued that, to a great extent, the debate between the "apologists" and the "critics" over the lone gunman theory can be related to the longstanding philosophical debate between the realists and the relativists. *Second,* the three main scientific puzzle areas associated with the Kennedy assassination will be examined: the timing sequence and number of shots, the "pristine bullet" and the "head snap." It will be shown that the necessary conditions for scientific realism have been undermined both by allegations that the primary evidence has been tampered with, and by the government's policy of restricting access to those materials. *Third,* the ethical implications of the use of prestigious scientific journals in the assassination debate will be explored. It will be argued that these journals often abuse scientific authority and misrepresent the nature of scientific inquiry. By perpetuating the naive view that science can solve the major puzzles of the Kennedy assassination despite the tainted chain of evidence, scientific journals misinform the public, discredit legitimate science, and threaten the survival of scientific discourse in our post-modern world.

Science and History

The relationship between historical and scientific modes of explanation has long been a subject of philosophical debate. During the 1950s, Karl Popper, a noted philosopher of science, was keenly interested in the scientific status of the social sciences, especially history. He described two conflicting schools of thought. His own "pro-naturalistic" perspective espoused the view that the methods of natural science are applicable to the social sciences and that sociological laws are not significantly different from natural laws. The opposing "anti-naturalistic" perspective, or "historicism," held that scientific methodology cannot be applied to the social sciences because sociological laws are fundamentally different from physical laws. Historicists claimed that, while the "laws of nature" capture invariable physical uniformities that remain true over space and time, "sociological laws" can only represent uniformities applicable in specific places (Dallas) and specific times (22 November 1963). In short they "depend on a particular historical situation" (Popper 1957, p. 5). All historical explanations are, therefore, theoretically untestable and hence non-scientific.

Today the historicists would have argued that because the unique set of micro-events that comprised the assassination of President Kennedy cannot be replicated, we cannot directly test the lone gunman theory or any other hypotheses related to that event. The pro-naturalists would insist that this argument fails to take into account the fact that all events are unique in the sense that they occupy a particular place and time. Indeed, this form of ontological uniqueness does not impede the scientific explanation of ordinary physical events, because the natural laws governing the assassination are not limited by place and time (see Fetzer 1975). After all, water boiled at 212 degrees Fahrenheit in Dallas in November 1963 and in Cincinnati in November 1993 because the physical properties involved in both events remain constant. So, although the Kennedy assassination was a unique event, it still remains, nevertheless, amenable to causal explanation to the extent that it is subject to natural laws. For example, historians might employ general statements hypothesizing that political assassinations in general are more common in violent societies where guns are easily purchased, or that as a general rule political assassination is easier to accomplish in democratic societies. One might even explain the government's clandestine investigation of the assassination in terms of a Cold War ideology that contaminated American democratic institutions over the past fifty years.

The pro-naturalists currently hold the edge over the historicists. Philosophers and historians no longer quibble over whether scientific methodology is applicable to historical analysis. Today, the philosophical issue for both science and history is to what extent scientific methodology can yield objective knowledge. Two distinct schools of thought dominate the literature, "realism" as defended by Carl Hempel and Karl Popper, and "relativism" as proposed by Thomas Kuhn and Michel Foucault. Taken together, these perspectives provide a foundation for understanding the philosophical assumptions underlying the apologists and critics of the lone gunman theory of the Kennedy assassination.

The Realist Position

Several key epistemological assumptions underlie the "realist" interpretation of theories. Realism defends the view that science aims at true descriptions of the world, which can provide explanations of the phenomena accessible to experience (Fetzer 1993a, p. 148). This position entails a belief in the independent reality of at least some events and that true statements in science or history correspond to this reality. Realists are inclined to draw sharp dualistic distinctions between knower and what is known, value and fact, theory and fact, and historical fact and fiction (Novick 1988, p.2). In general, the realist's claims are intended as *prescriptive* of the way science ought to be and not necessarily *descriptive* of the way science has been conducted in the past. Finally, realists tend to prefer knowledge based on scientific methodology over other forms of discourse.

Carl Hempel and the Covering Law Model of Scientific and Historical Explanation

Much of the groundwork for realism in historical explanation can be found in Carl Hempel's article, "The Function of General Laws in History" (Hempel 1942). Hempel argued that historians explain [or ought to explain] historical events in the same way that scientists explain natural events. In both disciplines, the aim is the discovery of the general laws governing the events in question. An explanation, then, takes the form of a deductive argument with a set of premises containing at least one general law (explanans) and a conclusion (explanandum), which follows deductively from the explanans. The "covering laws" contained in the explanans are to be stated in the form of universal conditional statements "capable of being confirmed or disconfirmed by suitable empirical findings" (Hempel 1965, p. 231). An hypothesis is "confirmed" or "verified" when it generates accurate predictions and "disconfirmed" or "falsified" when predictions prove false. The more often the theory is verified by experience the more likely it is to be true. An explanation is deemed "adequate," if and only if the argument contained in the explanans is valid and the individual premises are true. A "complete" explanation of an event would include the totality of all the universal laws governing the event. As an explanation approaches completeness, the greater its "explanatory power." Only the most highly confirmed and complete hypotheses can be elevated to the status of theories.

Because his early studies emphasized deductive explanations with universal laws, Hempel was initially criticized for implying that deductive certainty could be attained within both science and history. Arguments that are *deductive* in form, however, are not therefore *certain* in content, especially within empirical science. That was never his position and, most realists, including Hempel, now accept both inductive explanations and probabilistic laws within the covering law framework.

Because historical explanations deal with major human events such as wars, religious revivals, reform movements, and political elections, historians often dissect the larger "macro-events" into component "micro-events." Thus, we find historians studying individual battles in minute detail in order to contribute toward the explanation of a war. While it is often the case that the discovery of the physical laws governing a "micro-event" may become a part of the explanans of the more complex "macro-event," in the end we would also hope to discover political laws accounting for the transition of power within regimes, sociological laws explaining human violence, and psychological laws relating to the mindset of assassins.

While it is impossible to present an absolutely complete explanation of the Kennedy assassination, an explanation will possess greater "explanatory power" if it can satisfactorily account for the most significant micro-events. Some micro-events resist plausible explanation and are treated as "anomalies." The problem then becomes one of assessing the impact that anomalies have upon the status of theories.

Karl Popper and the Falsification Criterion

As a pro-naturalist and a realist, Popper followed Hempel in asserting that the methods of science are applicable to history and the social sciences. But Popper disagreed substantially with Hempel's views on the nature of the scientific method and developed his own distinctive account of the nature of theories, observation, and scientific inquiry.

Theories, according to Popper, are the product of human intuition and imagination and not simply the result of an accumulation of observations as the verificationists proposed. Observations in science are always made in the context of testing theories, therefore theory and observation, the two key components of scientific inquiry, are not logically independent. Popper also recognized that the realist's reliance on the principle of "verification" leads to paradoxical consequences and that David Hume's "problem of induction" sets certain theoretical limits on its usefulness. A universal statement such as "All swans are white", for example, cannot be conclusively verified unless the entire class of present and future swans has been observed to be white, which is impossible. Popper noted that universal statements can, however, be disconfirmed by a single instance of a non-white swan.

The hallmark of scientific theories, then, according to Popper, is not their potential to be verified, but falsified. Based on his principle of falsification, he argued that scientific theories "must be designed in such a way that they do not protect any statement in science against falsification" (Popper 1959, p. 54). Popper therefore saw the history of science as a sequence of "conjectures and refutations." Therefore, he thought the distinguishing characteristic of scientific inquiry is its "susceptibility to revision" (Popper 1959, p. 49). The more falsifiable an hypothesis the more scientific it is, as long as it has not been actually falsified. Some general statements in metaphysics ("God is omnipotent") and some pseudo-scientific statements ("The Id is driven by instinct") can never be refuted by any set of observations and therefore are not amenable to scientific study. Popper's views cast serious doubts on the validity of the verification principle and brought falsification to the forefront (Popper 1959).

From a Popperian perspective, the critics of the lone gunman theory can take one of two standpoints: either the theory is falsifiable and reliable observations (or anomalies) have already refuted it, or, the theory is not falsifiable by any possible observations and therefore it is not a fitting subject for legitimate scientific inquiry. Apologists, in contrast, tend to either dismiss or explain away anomalies that contradict the lone gunman theory or defend a relativist approach to scientific inquiry. Thomas Kuhn and Michel Foucault have been the most influential defenders of this relativist perspective.

The Relativist Position

The relativists say that if there is a such thing as "objective reality" science doesn't have the capacity to penetrate it. Truth, therefore, is not a simple correlation between statement and reality but a communal agreement and therefore science cannot be severed from its distinctly human context. Relativists also deny other sharp realist distinctions between theory and fact, and historical fact and historical fiction. Hence, science is neither objective nor value-neutral and not necessarily worthy of privileged status. Relativists argue that the failure to adequately appraise the history of science, led the realists to neglect the psychological, sociological, and cultural laws that govern the behavior of communities of scientists and historians. This failure has resulted in the realists' highly idealized conception of science.

Thomas Kuhn: Paradigm Formation and the Scientific Community

Thomas Kuhn's classic work *The Structure of Scientific Revolutions*, first published in 1962, has had a profound influence on how historians approach the objectivity question and how they assess the role played by scientific institutions in the production of scientific truth. For good reasons, Kuhn himself did not much care for the term "relativism." He did, however, reject the most important element in the realist agenda, the correspondence theory of truth.

There is, I think, no theory-independent way to reconstruct phrases like 'really there'; the notion of a match between the ontology of a theory and its 'real' counterpart in nature now seems to me illusive in principle (Kuhn 1970, p. 206).

Kuhn's definition of "normal science" stressed the communal nature of the scientific enterprise. Normal science, wrote Kuhn, is defined as "research firmly based upon one or more past scientific achievements, achievements that some particular scientific community acknowledges for a time as supplying the foundation for its further practice" (Kuhn 1970, p. 10). The formation of a scientific community, then, presupposes a shared commitment to a certain set of problems, methodologies, and standards. Kuhn calls this body of shared commitment a "paradigm." "Men whose research is based on shared paradigms," says Kuhn, "are committed to the same rules and standards for scientific practice. That commitment and the apparent consensus it produces are prerequisites for normal science, i.e., for the genesis and continuation of a particular research tradition" (Kuhn 1970, p. 11). Although science can be conducted in the absence of paradigms, the acquisition of paradigms "is a sign of maturity in the development of any given scientific field" (Kuhn 1970, p. 11).

Once a paradigm is accepted by a scientific community, puzzles or anomalies naturally begin to appear. The explanatory power of a paradigm or theory, therefore can be measured by its ability to resolve what the community deems to be, the most important puzzles. So the very existence of a paradigm tends to set the parameters for the kinds of puzzles that come under investigation, the steps by which conclusions may be reached, and even the rules governing the range of acceptable solutions (Kuhn 1970, p. 38). Hence, Kuhn agrees with Popper that no sharp distinction can be made between theory and observation.

The evolution of a paradigm occurs in stages. The early stage of paradigm formation consists in the indiscriminate gathering of information characterized by different theories. Paradigms emerge when one point of view proves to be more successful in solving a few key "puzzles" the community regards as the most acute. When consensus emerges, interschool debate subsides and the paradigm(s) forms the parameters of the community. Kuhn's analysis, therefore, suggests that scientific inquiry is far from immune from disagreement. Indeed there are countless examples where equally competent scientific investigators come up with conflicting hypotheses to explain the same event. Scientific journals function as a vehicle for exposing these disagreements to the scrutiny of other members of the scientific community. The emergence of a scientific community, then, is signaled by the appearance of scientific societies, journals, and standards for training future members. The adjective "Science," therefore, refers to the activities conducted by a community of scientists and "Scientific Truth" is relative to what a particular community accepts as true at any particular time.

If both scientific and historical explanations involve the articulation of general laws, then we might say that the Warren Commission's lone gunman theory was the first paradigm offered to explain the Kennedy assassination. Realist critics of the lone gunman paradigm, armed with their own arsenal of scientific experts, have identified numerous puzzles or anomalies inherent to the lone gunman theory.

One important point of contrast between Popperian realists and Kuhnian relativists centers around the relationship between anomalies and theories. While Popper was inclined to overthrow entire theories when confronted with anomalies, Kuhn recognized that in the course of "normal science" scientists often temporarily isolate theories, especially in the early stages of development, from the falsification process. Imre Lakatos attempted to reconcile this debate over anomalies between the Popperians and the Kuhnians by introducing the concept of a "research programme." Lakatos argued that theories are simply organized structures designed to guide future research. The "hard core" of a theory, which consists of a body of very general hypotheses, may be temporarily protected from the falsification process by a "protective belt" of auxiliary hypotheses, initial conditions, and so forth. Theories or research programmes are therefore assessed based on the satisfaction of two necessary conditions: 1. Theories must possess a degree of logical coherence that enables future investigators to map out a definite program for future research. 2. Theories must at least occasionally lead to the discovery of novel phenomena (Chalmers 1982, pp. 77–87).

The critics of the lone gunman theory insist that the apologists have been overzealous in protecting its "hard core," which possesses neither coherence nor heuristic value. The fundamental philosophical issue for the lone gunman theory, therefore, is how long "temporary immunity" should endure (Fetzer 1993a, p. 137).

While the critics have produced a plethora of alternative hypotheses to explain the assassination, they have yet to settle on a single paradigm. To those unfamiliar with how scientific and historical communities actually go about problem solving, this lack of consensus may seem troubling. But it is a mistake to expect that even competent scientific investigators of the Kennedy assassination will necessarily come to the same conclusions.

Kuhn's analysis of scientific revolutions suggests that honest disagreement among scientific experts investigating the Kennedy assassination ought to be understood as a necessary part of normal science and not merely as a temporary disruption in the inexorable quest for truth. Although there may be some issues upon which most assassination scientists agree, universal consensus alone cannot be taken as the criterion of absolute scientific truth. As Paul Feyerabend observed:

> Unanimity is often the result of a *political* decision: dissenters are suppressed, or remain silent to preserve the reputation of science as a source of trustworthy and almost infallible knowledge. On other occasions unanimity is the result of shared prejudices: positions are taken without detailed examination of the matter under review and are infused with the same authority that proceeds from detailed research . . . Then again unanimity may indicate a decrease of critical consciousness: criticism remains faint as long as only one view is being considered. This is why unanimity that rests on "internal" considerations alone often turns out to be mistaken. (Feyerabend 1978, p. 88)

For Kuhn, disagreement within a scientific community can often be reduced to a differences between individual scientist's perception of the value of the attributes of a given theory. Hence, the apologists for the Warren Commission continue to defend the lone gunman theory because they value its key attributes: not only its relative simplicity, but also its ability to accommodate their own unshakable belief in the integrity of the U.S. government.

Michel Foucault: Power-Knowledge and Science

Like Kuhn, Michel Foucault denies the basic assumptions of realism. His works have focused on the relationship between "power" and "knowledge" and how the interaction of these concepts condition our perception of truth. The epistemological basis for the belief in the privileged status of science, or scientism, is the mistaken notion that scientific truth is discovered in a vacuum-sealed container devoid of the trappings of human folly.

According to Foucault, truth [or knowledge] is inseparable from the strategies, mechanisms, and techniques of exercising power.

> We are subjected to the production of truth through power and we cannot exercise power except through the production of truth. This is the case for every society, but I believe that in ours the relationship between power, right and truth is organized in a highly specific fashion . . . Power never ceases its interrogation, its inquisition, its registration of truth: it institutionalizes, professionalizes and rewards its pursuit. (Foucault 1980 p. 93)

Hence the production of truth cannot be severed from the relations of power contained within a regime; thus the Foucauldian term "power-knowledge." Many philosophers have construed the concept of power as merely a negative force in the history of ideas, as illustrated by the censorship of the heliocentric cosmology during the late Middle Ages by the Roman Catholic Church. Power, however, is not always simply repressive but often productive.

> If power were never anything but repressive, if it never did anything but to say no, do you really think one would be brought to obey it? What makes power hold good, what makes it accepted, is simply the fact that it doesn't only weigh on us as a force that says no, but that it traverses and produces things, it induces pleasure, forms knowledge, produces discourse. It needs to be considered as a productive network which runs through the whole social body, much more than as a negative instance whose function is repression. (Foucault 1980 p. 119)

In his account of the history of the human sciences (especially: psychiatry, medicine, and penology), Foucault argued that the "birth of the human sciences goes hand in hand with the installation of new mechanisms of power" (Foucault 1988, 106). Thus he exploded the modern myth that the rise of "human science" in the late eighteenth century elevated the study of human beings to new standards of objectivity. Surely the historical record in support of scientific objectivity is feeble at best. One need look no further than American science's longstanding tendency to support social and political agendas. For example, nineteenth-century biology's scientific arguments demonstrating the racial inferiority of blacks; or, the early twentieth-century's claims of the genetic unfitness of southern Europeans.[2] Foucault's writings have led many historians and philosophers to explore how this ubiquitous exercise of power influences scientific discourse.

From Foucault's perspective, the history of the Kennedy assassination, therefore, can be seen as a case study of how knowledge was produced by invisible Cold War power structures in the United States; and how scientific experts unwittingly contributed to that warped perception of reality.

Realism, Relativism and the Kennedy Assassination

The rift between the apologists and the critics over the status of the lone gunman theory can be related to the philosophical debate between the realists and the relativists. The critics are Popperian realists in their insistence that observations have already falsified the lone gunman theory. They view the falsification of scientific theories as a revolutionary activity marked by conjectures and refutations. The critics are also realists insofar as they firmly believe there is an ultimate truth to be ascertained and that we are closer to that truth today than we were in 1964.

The apologists, in contrast, are more conservative in their assessment of the timing of scientific revolutions and therefore they are less likely to overthrow the lone gunman theory because of the mere presence of anomalies. Hence, they have been inclined to proliferate *ad hoc* explanations for the anomalies rather than abandon the lone gunman. As relativists, the apologists are quick to point out that scientific theories almost never explain all possible anomalies. After all, "If Newtonian mechanics could not explain the perihelion of Mercury, why should we expect the lone gunman theory to explain every facet of the Kennedy assassination?" Many apologists are also relativists by virtue of their blind reliance on expert testimony, for example, "The Warren Commission studied the Kennedy assassination and arrived at the lone gunman theory, therefore it must be true."

It is evident that neither the realists nor the relativists can provide a satisfactory account of the nature of science nor the Kennedy assassination. In the absence of a vigorous application of the falsification principle, science loses its distinctive character. Therefore, the realists are right in their devotion to falsification. On the other hand, we must also acknowledge that science is a communal activity, which is not immune from mass delusion, and that scientists often protect their theories from anomalies. From Foucault's point of view, it is imperative that we recognize that the same power structures that condition the American public to reject or accept conspiracy hypotheses, are also at work within the scientific community. Hence, we must be wary of proclamations of infallible truth by the scientific community, especially when political issues are at stake. Kuhn, in turn, points us toward the analysis of the social institutions of science such as professional organizations, educational institutions, and scholarly journals; which set the parameters of what is taken as true at any point in history. Finally, we must be aware that not every community of scientific investigators play by the same rules.

The lone gunman theory set parameters for the kinds of scientific questions future assassination investigators would pursue. By conducting experiments and reenactments intended to establish that it was at least physically possible for Oswald alone to have assassinated the president, the Warren Commission set a pattern that would be acritically emulated by subsequent investigators. From a realist perspective, the limits of that line of investigation are obvious when you consider that the best the apologists could ever hope for, would be the conclusion that the lone gunman hypothesis does not violate the laws of nature. On the other hand, the critics could actually disconfirm the lone gunman theory by showing that the theory is inconsistent with observations or that it violates a single law of nature.

The apologists, blinded by their naive faith in the integrity of government, nevertheless continue to support the lone gunman theory despite an accumulation of anomalies. In light of these considerations, it is worthwhile to examine how some of the key puzzles of the Kennedy assassination have been treated by the scientific community.

Science and the Puzzles of the Kennedy Assassination

Scientific evidence and expert testimony have played a major role in both articulating and addressing the various puzzles raised by the lone gunman theory. The FBI established this tradition when it called in physical scientists, ballistics experts, and other forensic technicians in compiling its report on the assassination. This document became the substance of the 1964 *Warren Report*. The tradition of employing experts was later reinforced by consecutive government investigatory commissions, especially the Clark Panel (1969), the House Select Committee on Assassinations (1979), and the Ramsey Panel (1982).

Published in 1967, Josiah Thompson's *Six Seconds in Dallas: A Micro-Study of the Kennedy Assassination*, was one of the early critical works on the assassination repleatwith ballistics, trajectories, and technical medical evidence. It was also the first book to examine the Zapruder film in minute detail and articulate some of the major puzzles that it poses for the lone gunman theory. Since then, investigators of the Kennedy assassination have scrutinized the Zapruder film and the ballistics in conjunction with the laws of physics. Their mistake, however, has been to assume that all of the variables associated with the shooting could be quantified—such as the speed of the film, the forces and trajectories of the bullets, the motion of the vehicle, and the movement of Kennedy's head upon being struck—and that the precise location and number of snipers could be deduced from those premises with the same kind of certainty we would expect from a physicist.

Three major puzzles amenable to investigation by physical science have challenged the lone gunman theory since the 1960s. *First* is the puzzle of the number of shots actually fired, their trajectories, and the timing required for a lone gunman to execute those shots accurately against a moving target. *Second* is the puzzle raised by the bullet found on a stretcher at Parkland Memorial Hospital. Despite its relative "pristine" condition, the lone gunman theory requires that this single bullet caused Kennedy's back and throat wounds, as well as Connally's multiple wounds. *Third* is the retrograde motion of President Kennedy's head evident in the Zapruder film (or "head-snap") which seems physically impossible, if the shot was fired from above and behind, as required by the lone gunman theory.

This essay will show that the "assassination science" inspired by the three main puzzles has been conducted in violation of basic principles of scientific inquiry and outside of its institutional foundations.

The Number, Timing, and Sequence of the Shots

From the earliest stages of the investigation, two key micro-events placed physical limitations on the possible number, timing, and sequence of the shots fired at Dealey Plaza on 22 November 1963: the discovery of the alleged murder weapon and the film taken by Abraham Zapruder.

Based on their examination of the bolt-action, clip-fed, Mannlicher-Carcano rifle, firearms experts for the Warren Commission established that at least 2.3 seconds per shot would be required for Oswald to execute the assassination. The shutter speed of Abraham Zapruder's Bell and Howell movie camera operated at about 18.3 frames per second (*Warren Report* 1964, p. 97). After numbering each individual frame, tracing the movement of the vehicle, and taking into account other factors, the Commission hypothesized that since the view from the sniper's nest would have been obscured by the foliage of an oak tree between frames Z-167 and Z-210, the earliest the president could have been shot was Z-210. Zapruder's view of the motorcade was blocked by a road sign between frames Z-207 and Z-225, but when Kennedy appears from behind the sign he is beginning to react to the throat wound. The commission therefore reasoned that the President was shot in the neck between frames Z-210 and Z-225. Based on Connally's reactions in the Zapruder film, he was apparently struck between Z-236 and Z-238. These observations, however, were puzzling. If Kennedy was struck in the back at Z-225 and Connally at Z-238, that would entail a 13-frame time span or 0.71 seconds. But that would have been impossible since Oswald would have needed at least 2.3 seconds to fire two shots. Even if Kennedy was shot as early as Z-210, that would still be only a 28 frame time span, or 1.53 seconds. Therefore, Oswald apparently could not have shot both Kennedy and Connally. Logically this left the Warren Commission four options: abandon the lone gunman theory, assume that Oswald somehow managed to hit the President while shooting through the tree, lower the 2.3 second estimate of the time required to operate the rifle mechanism, or assume that a single bullet struck both Kennedy and Connally (*Warren Report* 1964, p. 105). The Commission took the fourth option, known as the "single bullet hypothesis," and concluded that three shots were fired within a 4.8 to 7 second time lapse, and that at least one of the three probably missed the target, although they could not determine with certainty which of the three missed (*Warren Report* 1964, p. 117).

The single-bullet hypothesis generated its own puzzles. The most serious problem was that it contradicted Governor Connally's testimony stating that he thought he was shot after Kennedy. Defenders of the hypothesis claim that it simply took longer for the older Connally to react to the wound. But if we postulate a delayed physiological reaction, there is no way of setting empirical limits on the length of time consumed by that delay and therefore mathematical objectivity must give way to mere conjecture. The same holds true with the tree foliage puzzle. Once we entertain the notion that Oswald might have shot through the trees, then we have 44 frames or about 2.4 more seconds to account for. This would provide enough time to get off a shot, but it would be empirically untestable.

Since the Warren Commission elected not to extend the time frame in this way, they concluded that the entire assassination took place between frames Z-210 and Z-313, or a time span of 5.62 seconds, just enough time to get off three shots. Any competent gunman would have had the rifle already cocked for the first shot, in which case the bolt would have been operated only twice and the absolute minimum time expended operating the bolt would have been 4.6 seconds. But if four shots were fired, the rifle would have been cocked three times requiring 6.9 seconds. So, if four shots were fired there must have been more than one gunman at Dealey Plaza. Of course, if the Commission had accepted the possibility that the first shot was fired through the tree at Z-166, then their estimate of 5.62 seconds could be extended by 2.4 seconds to about 8 seconds, more than enough time for a lone gunman to get off even four shots.

Another way of extending the time necessary to fire three shots is to shorten the estimated firing time per shot. Since the publication of *The Warren Report* the time required to operate the rifle has been sharply reduced by consecutive studies. In 1975, eleven volunteers for a CBS documentary demonstrated that Mannlicher-

Carcano rifles could accurately fire three bullets at a moving target in an average of 5.6 seconds with 2/3 of the shots on target. At least one of those volunteers got off the three shots in 4.1 seconds.[3] In 1977, the House Select Committee on Assassination's marksmen precipitously lowered the total required time to 3.3 seconds (Posner 1993, p. 318). But neither of these more recent tests were conducted with the same individual rifle found on the sixth floor of the Texas Book Depository Building. Therefore variation between the operating mechanisms of individual Mannlicher-Carcano rifles may account for the discrepancy between firing times. In summary, the three crucial but unknown variables—the tree, the sign, and the firing mechanism—leave much room for idle speculation in respect to the timing puzzles. These fuzzy parameters also account for much scientific disagreement.

Based on his early examination of the Zapruder film and other evidence, Josiah Thompson set forth his own hypothesis concerning the timing and sequence of the shots.

> Three assassins fired four shots from three different directions. The first and third shots were fired from the Depository—most likely from the sixth floor . . . The second shot, wounding the Governor, was fired from the east side of Dealey Plaza-most likely from a building rooftop. The fourth and final shot was fired from a point near the corner of the stockade fence to the north of Elm Street. (Thompson 1967, p. 137)

Since then, experts have attempted to determine the exact number, timing and sequence of the shots by subjecting the Zapruder film to streak analysis, computer enhancement, and computer reenactments.

In 1976, Luis W. Alvarez, a Nobel Prize winning physicist at the University of California, Berkeley, studied the Zapruder film and noticed a ". . . striking phenomenon in frame 227. All of the innumerable pointlike highlights on the irregular shiny surface of the automobile were stretched out into parallel line segments, along the "8 o'clock–2 o'clock' direction" (Alvarez 1976, p. 815). Alvarez hypothesized that this "streaking" phenomenon which appeared in the form of pulse chains beginning at frames 182, 221, and 313, were caused by Abraham Zapruder's neuromuscular reaction to the sound of the rifle. Taking into account Zapruder's five-frame neuromuscular reaction time, Alvarez concluded that the first shot, which missed, was fired at frame 177; that the second, which struck both Kennedy and Connally occurred at 215.5; and that the third, head shot, took place at frame 307 of the film. Interestingly, Alvarez detected at least two other weaker sets of neurological pulse chains. The existence of a chain between 290 and 298—which Alvarez somewhat tentatively dismissed as Zapruder's reaction to a siren—is especially noteworthy in that it raised the possibility of a fourth shot fired near frame 285.

Alvarez's findings are, of course, limited by the fact that Zapruder's neuromuscular system would not have been able to react to shots fired nearly simultaneously, which would be a distinct possibility if more than one assassin were firing on the motorcade. Moreover, there is the problem of establishing a causal connection between the sound of gunfire and the movement of the camera. He may have subconsciously reacted to some other phenomenon such as a cough, sneeze, or a bump by another person. Hence, Alvarez's analysis of the Zapruder film is necessarily incomplete and therefore cannot establish with certainty how many shots were actually fired at the motorcade.

In the past few years, assassination researchers have had access to computer-enhanced copies of the Zapruder film and computer generated reconstructions of the events at Dealey Plaza. On the basis of these new forms of evidence, and other recent scientific studies, Gerald Posner has argued that the first shot, which missed, occurred between frames 167 and 210, and was executed with a partially obstructed view through the trees. The second shot struck Kennedy and Connally at frames 223–224, as evidenced by the Kennedy's neurological response to that shot known as the "Thorburn Reflex"[4] and by the apparent movement of Connally's coat lapel in frame 224 near the exit wound in his chest (Posner 1993, p. 329). The third shot struck Kennedy in the head at frame 313, as indicated by the appearance of a spray of brain matter and skull fragments (Posner 1980, pp. 322–334, and Appendix A, pp. 478–479).

All scientific speculation based on the study of the Zapruder film must be exercised with extreme caution. Critics claim that there is considerable evidence that the original film was tampered with by the FBI, and later by Time Incorporated after they purchased it. Groden and Livingstone insist that frames 208–211 have been removed. Beginning in 1969, after the Garrison trial, numerous "bootleg" copies of the film of variable quality began to circulate. But even if some versions of the film have been preserved intact, researchers have interpreted the various movements of the President's body apparent on the grainy film very differently. Because investigators are not always in agreement as to what they actually see on the film, expert testimony based on the photographic evidence has been contradictory and indecisive. Indeed not everyone has been able to detect movement in Connally's coat lapel, the alleged gunman in frame Z-413, or even agree exactly when Kennedy's arms begin to raise up in reaction to the throat or back wound.

Another area of physical science that has generated hypotheses concerning the number, timing and sequence of the shots has been acoustics. Researchers had long known of the existence of a six minute dictabelt recording of a Dallas motorcycle policeman's radio transmissions on November 22, 1963. Although the original dictabelt had mysteriously disappeared from the National Archives, critics pressured the House Select Committee on Assassinations to get the tape scientifically analyzed. They had it analyzed by Dr. James Barger, an acoustics expert from the firm Bolt, Beranek and Newman of Cambridge, Massachusetts.

After filtering out the background noise Barger and his associates detected at least six sequences of impulses ten decibels above every other sound that could have been caused by gunfire (HSCA 1974, Vol. 5, Vol. 2, Vol. 8, *Final Report*, p. 68).[5] Barger converted the sounds on the tape into digital waveforms represented on a graph. In August, 1978 experts attempted to reconstruct the waveforms at Dealey Plaza using stationary microphones. They concluded that with an 88% probability, shots #1 and #2 were fired from behind; a 50% probability that shot #3 came from the right near the grassy knoll; and a 75% probability that shot #4 was also from behind. They also determined that shots #1 and #2 were fired too close together to have been fired by Oswald's rifle (HSCA 1979, Vol. 4, p. 5, p. 615; Groden 1990, pp. 261–262). Hence, the lone gunman theory was seemingly disconfirmed by both the timing of the first two shots and by the third shot which exhibited acoustic characteristics of a shot from the grassy knoll.

The House Select Committee on Assassination enlisted the service of acoustic experts Mark Weiss and Ernest Aschkenasy to further study the dictabelt recording. In their concentrated study of waveform #3 they concluded that there was a

95% probability that it was fired from the grassy knoll. Based mostly on the acoustics evidence, the House Select Committee on Assassinations concluded that there probably was a conspiracy involving a second gunman at Dealey Plaza.

But later that year the credibility of those scientific analyses began to deteriorate. Steve Barber, a rock drummer from Ohio, purchased a copy of *Gallery* magazine which contained a recording of the dictabelt evidence. At the point where the four impulses were purportedly fired, he detected (what turned out to be) the voice of Sheriff Decker saying, "Hold everything secure . . ." Based on a timeline provided by another police recording, this indicated that the four sounds on the tape actually occurred minutes after the assassination. The government decided to reexamine the acoustic evidence. The National Academy of Science brought together a group of twelve experts to be headed by Dr. Norman Ramsey. On 14 May 1982 they issued their highly critical 93-page Ramsey Report, which cited numerous methodological flaws in the original acoustic research. The panel found Barger's process of selecting the four crucial impulses to be highly subjective:

> The impulses selected for the BRSW study were not always the largest impulses. Frequently, large impulses were omitted and some impulses close to the noise level were retained. There are far more impulses that do not fall into the BRSW classification of 'probably sounds of gunfire' than do. Since the results of correlation coefficient calculations are highly dependent on the impulse and echo selection process, it is especially critical that the scheme used to distinguish these sounds stand up to close scrutiny, with the process used being spelled out in detail so others can duplicate the analysis. From the published reports, it is impossible to do so. Furthermore, weak spikes on the Dictabelt often are selected to correspond to strong patterns, in the test patterns and vice versa. (CBA 1982, p. 363; Livingstone 1993, p. 363)

Even more serious was the fact that the acoustic researchers were unable to link the sounds recorded on the tape to the events at Dealey Plaza (Posner 1983, p. 240). Moreover, if the tape is a recording of a recording as some critics allege, then until its natural history can be established (including the various tape recorders used), or until the original dictabelt recording is found, acoustic science will not advance our knowledge of the timing of the assassination.

It is important to note that both the "nervous impulse researchers" and the "acoustic impulse researchers" detected physical evidence of at least four shots being fired. However, the matter of how they interpreted that fourth impulse varied significantly. Rather than admit that the fourth nervous impulse constituted evidence of a fourth gunshot, which would have disconfirmed the single gunman theory, Alvarez chose to devise an *ad hoc* hypothesis to explain it. By contrast, Weiss and Aschkenasy readily interpreted their fourth acoustic impulse as a gunshot, even though they might have also employed an alternative hypothesis to explain it. Therefore, the question of whether an "impulse" represents a gunshot, or some other phenomenon, seems to be a matter of interpretation. In neither case will the physical evidence alone justify one interpretation over another. As Kuhn would point out, the level of credence an individual researcher invests in the lone gunman theory will influence his/her perception of what it would take to disconfirm that theory. The obvious lesson here is that the choice between alternative explanations is often influenced by a scientist's values and preconceived notions rather than purely scientific factors.

The Single "Pristine" Bullet Puzzle

The single-bullet hypothesis, first set forth by Arlen Specter, Assistant Counsel for the Warren Commission, holds that one bullet, fired from above and to the rear, entered Kennedy's back and exited the throat, and passed through Connally's chest, wrist, and temporarily lodged in his leg. Given the parameters set by the Warren Commission concerning the number, timing, and sequence of the shots fired, most researchers agree that if the lone gunman theory is true, then the single bullet hypothesis must also be true. Physical science has focused on whether the bullet found at Parkland Memorial Hospital could possibly have caused both Kennedy's and Connally's multiple wounds. Medical science has questioned whether the nature and location of Kennedy's and Connally's wounds are consistent with what one would expect from an assassination executed by a lone assassin firing from above and to the rear of the motorcade.

Physical Science and the Bullet

Ballistics experts have long questioned whether it was physically possible for the jacketed 6.5 mm bullet (CE–399) found on a stretcher at Parkland Memorial Hospital to have inflicted Kennedy's and Connally's multiple wounds and emerge in relatively "pristine" condition. Dr. Alfred G. Olivier, a veterinarian, conducted a variety of tests for the FBI at the Wounds Ballistics Branch of the U.S. Army Chemical Research and Development Laboratories at the Edgewood Arsenal in Maryland. In order to simulate the neck wound, Oliver and others clipped 14 centimeters of goat meat between two goat skins, pinned shirt and jacket over one side of the package, and then fired three 6.5 mm bullets through it (Thompson 1967, p. 52). Based upon this research, the Warren Commission concluded that the holes of entrance would be round, while the exit holes would be "a little more elongated" and "only slightly different from the appearance of the entry hole" (Warren Report 1963, p. 582). However, upon viewing the pictures one could also conclude that exit wounds would be at least twice the size of the entrance wounds. Oliver also fired a bullet from Oswald's rifle into the wrist of a cadaver to determine whether it could cause damage to bone and emerge in relative pristine condition. To the embarrassment of the FBI, the tip of the test bullet (CE–856) was badly deformed. This cast the first serious doubts on the single bullet hypothesis.

In the 1970s, John K. Lattimer, a urologist, conducted experimental firings of Mannlicher-Carcano rifles verifying that 6.5 mm bullets could inflict the bone damage attributed to CE–399 and remain relatively pristine. He even proved that the jacketed bullets could penetrate twenty-five inches of elm wood or forty-seven inches of ponderosa pine without any deformation of the bullet (Lattimer 1980, p. 271). Of course, if Lattimer's findings are valid, it becomes that much more difficult to explain how the head shot bullet could have fragmented enough to leave numerous dustlike bullet particles in the President's brain and obliterate the right hemisphere of his brain.

Another area of concern has been the question of whether the combined weight of the bullet fragments taken from Connally's wrist (CE–842), the fragment which remains in the Governor's left thigh along with several other smaller fragments remaining in his body, might exceed the weight loss of CE–399 (Livingstone 1992, pp. 304–305). The total weight of the pristine bullet is 158.6 grains, compared to the FBI's estimated average weight of 161.2 grains for new 6.5 mm Carcano bullets.

However, Charles G. Wilber says that, according to the 1975 edition of *Gun Digest*, Carcano bullets weigh 156 grains (Wilber 1978, p. 224). By the FBI's weight estimate, the total weight of all the known fragments, cannot exceed 2.6 grains without disconfirming the single bullet hypothesis and by implication the lone gunman theory. According to Josiah Thompson, the larger fragment removed from Connally's wrist weighs 0.5 grains, the smaller one plus the flakes of metal left in the wrist is probably about the same. Therefore one grain total can be accounted for in the wrist. Fragments, however, remain in Connally's wrist and thigh. Based on his best estimates of the weight of these fragments, Thompson concluded that the weight loss of the pristine bullet could account for all of the bullet fragments (Thompson 1967, p. 151).

At the 1991 Dallas Conference on the Assassination of President Kennedy, Audrey Bell, a nurse who had helped treat the President at Parkland, announced that when the physicians removed the bullet fragments from Connally, she put them in a vial. She drew a picture of the size of the vial containing five substantially larger fragments—not three (Livingstone 1992, pp. 304–305). Charles A. Crenshaw, M.D., who was also present confirmed that he ". . . observed Dr. Osborne remove at least five bullet fragments from the governor's arm and hand them to Audrey Bell" (Crenshaw 1992, p. 123).

There are other unknown variables involved in this puzzle, including the well known fact that in 1964 the FBI scraped pieces of the tip of CE–399 to conduct Neutron Activation Analyses (NAA) tests. The weight of these fragments must also be accounted for. Given the slight variation in the estimated weight of individual Mannlicher-Carcano bullets and confusion over the exact size and number of bullet fragments removed from Connally, researchers cannot realistically expect to resolve the bullet weight puzzle. With the recent death of Governor Connally and the family's refusal to allow the other bullet fragments to be removed from his body for analysis, we may never be able to determine their size, weight, or composition.

As early as 1964, the FBI suspected that the some of the puzzles surrounding the single-bullet hypothesis might be resolved if the various bullet-lead specimens linked to the assassination could be subjected to Neutron Activation Analysis. After conducting these tests, the FBI decided that the findings were inconclusive and therefore never published the results. The fact that these analyses were even conducted was not widely known until 1973, when researchers finally gained access to the report under the Freedom of Information Act (Guinn 1974, pp. 485–486).

Vincent Guinn, a chemist at the University of California, Irvine was asked by the House Select Committee on Assassinations to conduct new analyses of the bullet-lead evidence using newer and improved NAA techniques, with Ge(Li) gamma-ray spectrometry.

Guinn observed that, in the context of his earlier measurements on background WCC/MC, "the Dallas samples are in the unusual (through not necessarily unique) concentration ranges of WCC/MC bullet lead: and the specimens show clear-cut evidence for the presence of two and only two, WCC/MC bullets—one of a composition of 815 ppm Sb and 9.3 ppm Ag, the other of a composition of 622 ppm Sb and 8.1 ppm Ag" (Guinn 1974, p. 492). Based on his purely objective scientific investigation Guinn concluded that:

> The nondestructive instrumental neutron activation analysis results have demonstrated that, to a high degree of probability, all of the bullet-lead evidence

specimens are of WCC/MC 6.5-mm brand, that there is evidence for the presence of portions of two-and only two such bullets, and that the Connally stretcher virtually intact bullet indeed caused the fracture wound of Governor Connally's wrist—a previously hotly debated part of the Warren Commission's theory . . . The new results cannot prove the Warren Commission's theory that the stretcher bullet is the one that caused the President's back wound and all of the Governor's wounds, but the results are indeed consistent with this theory. (Guinn 1974, p. 493)

Guinn concluded that CE–399 (the "pristine bullet") and CE–842 (the wrist fragments) are similar in composition and CE–567 (the large fragment found in the limousine), CE–843 (the fragments found in Kennedy's brain), and CE–840 (the small fragments found in the limousine) are similar in composition.

But how convincing are these "scientific" analyses? First of all, it is important to note that out of more than 30 bullet fragments known to be in the President's head and visible on the X-rays, only two were tested. Therefore, it is sheer speculation to infer that all of the dust-like fragments are of the same composition CE–567. There are also several serious flaws relating to how Guinn deduced two and only two bullets from his own data. Actually his analyses seem to support the hypothesis that the composition of individual Mannlicher-Carcano bullets are heterogeneous. After testing four specimen from a single bullet, Guinn's own figures show that the antimony content ranged from 363+39 to 667+5 and that the silver content ranged from 8.3+0.3 to 15.9+0.5 (HSCA 1978, Vol. 2, p. 549, Appendix F.). If the individual bullets are not uniform in composition, it becomes that much more difficult to infer identity and difference between bullets. Moreover, although (CE–842) and (CE–399) are supposed to be similar in composition, CE–842 contained 25% more silver and 850% more copper than CE–399. It also contained 2,400% more sodium and 1,100% more chlorine. And finally, CE–842 contained 8.1 ppm aluminum but CE–399 contained none (HSCA 1978, Vol. 2, p. 538, Appendix B.). Therefore, it is difficult to fathom how Guinn could conclude that the two fragments are similar in composition.

Even if Guinn's findings were valid, they would prove only that CE–399 caused Connally's wounds. In order to confirm the single bullet theory, it would also be necessary to link CE–399 to Kennedy's wounds. Since no bullet fragments were found in Kennedy's back or throat wounds, that variable simply cannot be determined. Perhaps the critical flaw in all the scientific hypotheses involving the bullets is that these analyses presuppose that an inviolate chain of evidence was maintained by the Secret Service and the FBI. According to Anthony Summers, the weights of the fragments examined by Guinn do not correspond to the weights recorded by the Warren Commission (Summers 1989, p. 34; Livingstone 1993, p. 54). Since we also know that at least some of the fragments are missing, a healthy degree of skepticism is surely warranted.

Medical Science and the Wounds

The single bullet hypothesis limits the range of possible locations of the wounds inflicted upon Kennedy and Connally. Therefore, the testimony of the Parkland and Bethesda physicians and the autopsy materials have recently become the subject of intense scrutiny. Unfortunately, the medical testimony and the primary evidence have contributed significantly to the puzzlement of assassination researchers. In fact, the chain of events that unfolded between President Kennedy's arrival at Parkland Memorial Hospital and the subsequent autopsy performed at Bethesda Naval Hospital can only be described as one of the darker episodes in the annals of medical history.

Upon President Kennedy's arrival at Parkland Hospital, the ER team noted two bullet wounds, one to the lower third of his throat and a major head wound. Dr. Malcolm O. Perry immediately performed a tracheostomy on the President by making a small transverse incision through the bullet hole in the throat. The Bethesda autopsy team claimed the incision concealed the bullet wound and consequently they did not know about its existence until the day after the autopsy. [*Editor's note:* See Robert B. Livingston's contributions in Part II.] Therefore, the only authoritative testimony concerning the nature of the throat wound must come from the Parkland medical team. These physicians, originally indicated that it had the characteristics of a frontal entry wound.[6] If this observation were accurate it would constitute a positive disconfirmation of both the single bullet hypothesis and the lone gunman theory. [*Editor's note:* See Appendix C.]

Because the ER team focused exclusively on stabilizing vital signs, they did not turn over the President's body, and therefore did not notice another bullet wound (or wounds) located in the President's upper back. Hence, we have the makings of one the most incredible foul-ups in medical history. The Parkland physicians didn't know of the back wound and the Bethesda autopsy team did not know that the tracheostomy incision concealed a bullet wound.Or, at least, so they have alleged. It is difficult to believe that subsequent controversy over the exact location of the wounds can be attributed solely to an unfortunate communication failure between two groups of physicians.[7]

As David S. Lifton has observed, the circumstances surrounding the transportation of the President's body from Parkland to Bethesda are also puzzling (Lifton 1990 and 1992, Part IV). Lifton concludes that the "best evidence" in this case, President Kennedy's body, may have been surgically altered prior to its arrival at Bethesda. Some of the autopsy photographs,which show a gaping throat wound where Dr. Perry claims to have made a small surgical incision to accommodate a tracheostomy, for example, would certainly be explained by this gruesome hypothesis. At the very least, the discrepancy between them supports the possibility that either the body has been altered, as Lifton believes, or else some of the photographs have been faked.

The autopsy conducted at Bethesda Naval Hospital was riddled by incompetence. The military physicians who performed it (Thornton Boswell, James Humes and Pierre Finck) were hospital pathologists with little, if any, practical experience with autopsies or bullet wounds. In 1967, Cyril H. Wecht, M.D. was one of the first forensic pathologists to point out the numerous flaws in the Bethesda physician's technique and obvious instances where the government's handling of the evidence in the case compromised well-established legal and scientific standards (Wecht 1967). In 1978, Charles G. Wilber, Ph.D. wrote an entire book criticizing the conduct of the autopsy (Wilber 1978).

The conditions under which the autopsy was conducted has also raised suspicion. Dr. Finck in his testimony before the Garrison Hearings indicated that the autopsy room was crowded with high ranking military and civilian personnel, Secret Service agents, and FBI agents (Garrison 1988, p. 290). Given the hierarchical structure of military command, critics have questioned the capacity of the physicians to conduct an independent analysis, a suspicion seemingly confirmed by the military's enforcement of a gag rule applying to all personnel present at the autopsy (Lifton 1992 p. 693).

The location and nature of the back wound is crucial to the single bullet hypothesis. Typically, wounds of entrance are marked by a darkened ring around the wound or an "abrasion collar." In their description of the back wound, the autopsy team noted both an abrasion collar and a 45 to 60 degree downward trajectory and thereby determined that it was an entry wound. When the autopsy report was finally completed the day after the assassination, Boswell's autopsy face sheet and Admiral Burkley's death certificate located the back wound near the third thoracic vertebra. But if the entry wound was, in fact, this low, and if the exit wound was in the lower third of the throat, then the angle of trajectory would seemingly be inconsistent with that of a shot fired from the sixth floor.

The President's clothing also seems to disconfirm the autopsy's findings. According to the FBI's measurements, the bullet hole in the back of President Kennedy's shirt and jacket are located 5–3/8 inches below the top of the collar 1–3/4 inches to the right of the midline (Thompson 1967, p. 48). Apologists have presented two *ad hoc* counter-arguments: first, that the holes are low on the coat and shirt because the clothing was bunched up in the back as the President waved to the crowd, a conjecture that is not supported by the Zapruder film. Secondly, apologists argue that even if the wound were that low, the trajectory would still be possible if the President was leaning forward when he was struck in the back, which is also not evident in the Zapruder film. Even if Kennedy was leaning forward, it would become less likely that the same bullet could have struck Connally in the right shoulder. Critics therefore conclude that at least one of the two wounds was not caused by a bullet originating from behind the motorcade, which falsifies both the single bullet hypothesis and the lone gunman theory.

Consecutive inquiries by the Clark Panel (1968), the Rockefeller Panel (1975) and the House Select Committee on Assassinations (1979), which have been permitted to examine the X-rays and autopsy photos, have placed the entry wound higher—at the sixth and seventh cervical vertebra. To the critics, however, this observation suggests that sometime between 1966 (when Humes and Boswell first saw the autopsy photos) and 1968, the original autopsy materials were replaced by materials more consistent with the Warren Commission's findings (Livingstone 1992, pp. 313–356).

Critics have long dubbed the single bullet hypothesis the "magic bullet theory" because of the extraordinary bullet trajectory it postulates. In August, 1992, a computerized re-creation was produced by Failure Analysis Associates as part of a mock trial for the American Bar Association. It seemed to suggest that it was at least *possible*—given certain assumptions concerning the relative positions and postures of Kennedy and Connally—for one bullet to strike them both as the single bullet hypothesis states.

Gerald Posner's account of the single bullet hypothesis is based almost entirely on the Failure Analysis studies and John K. Lattimer's findings. Posner states that the bullet entered Kennedy's upper back at a speed of about 1,700 to 1,800 feet per second leaving a 6.5 mm entry wound. It then grazed vertebra C-6, which brought on the neurological response known as the Thorburn reflex and then exited the throat. When the bullet exited it began to tumble at 1,500 to 1,600 feet per second, which explained the 1–1/4 inch entry wound in Connally's back. It then shattered Connally's fifth right rib, deflected slightly, and exited just below his right nipple traveling at about 900 feet per second. Still tumbling, the bullet then entered the top of his right wrist backwards, and fractured the radius bone. It then exited at about 400 feet per second barely penetrating the skin of Connally's left thigh (Posner 1993, pp. 478–479).[8]

This entire scenario is contingent upon several dubious assumptions, including whether the elliptical wound in Connally's back was caused by a tumbling bullet. In 1992, Dr. Robert Shaw stated that the wound he saw was a clean round wound of entry and that he cut away the edges, thereby enlarging it from 1.5 cm to 3 cm.. He, therefore, insists that the scar did not reflect the original size and shape of the wound (Livingstone 1993, p. 80).

By now, it should be obvious to assassination researchers that the single-bullet hypothesis cannot be falsified. But not because it is true. The dubious nature of the ballistic and medical evidence in the case, and the contradictory testimony of the Parkland and Bethesda physicians actually render the hypothesis immune from the falsification process. Therefore, despite the best efforts of both apologists and critics, science must stand silent.

The "Head Snap" Puzzle

Thompson and other critics of the Warren Commission have long argued that if the lone gunman fired from the sixth floor window of the Texas Book Depository Building, then the backward movement of Kennedy's head (or his "head snap") upon being struck would violate Newton's second law of motion (Thompson 1967, p. 94). Since the publication of the Zapruder film, defenders of the Warren Commission have been somewhat embarrassed by their inability to provide an explanation for this retrograde movement consistent with the laws of physics.

In 1976, Luis Alvarez published an article in the *American Journal of Physics* attempting to provide this explanation. It was titled "A Physicist Examines the Kennedy Assassination Film." The article was an attempt to utilize the laws of physics in analyzing the Zapruder film and several puzzles that have been raised by that film, especially the "head snap." Alvarez explained the gist of his hypothesis as follows:

> I solved the problem (to my satisfaction, and in a one- dimensional fashion) on the back of an envelope . . . I concluded that the retrograde motion of the President's head, in response to the rifle bullet shot, is consistent with the law of conservation of momentum, if one pays attention to the law of the conservation of energy as well, and includes the momentum of all the material in the problem. The simplest way to see where I differ from the rest of the critics is to note that they treat the problem as though it involved only two interacting masses: the bullet and the head. My analysis involves three interacting masses, the bullet, the jet of brain matter observable in frame 313, and the remaining part of the head. It will turn out that the jet can carry forward more momentum than was brought in by the bullet, and the head recoils backward, as a rocket recoils when its jet fuel is ejected. (Alvarez 1976, p. 819)

Alvarez even designed a series of experiments to confirm his "jet hypothesis" by wrapping melons in 1 inch Scotch "filament tape," in an attempt to emulate the construction of the human skull. He then fired upon them with a 30.06 rifle with 150 grain hand-loaded soft-nosed bullets, which hit the melons with a velocity of about 3,000 ft/sec. Six out of seven of the melons exhibited retrograde motion (Alvarez 1976, p. 821).

It does not take a forensic expert to identify the main reasons why we can grant, at best, only limited value to these melon experiments. First of all, there is the fact that the weapon found in the book depository, a Mannlicher-Carcano rifle, would have fired a much smaller 6.5 mm copper-jacketed bullet weighing 161 grains at a slower muzzle speed of about 2,200 ft/sec. Secondly, there is no evidence provided to suggest that a melon wrapped in tape will react to a projectile in a way comparable to a human head. One would surmise that the density of the human skull would slow down and deform the projectile more than several layers of tape, and therefore increase the forward momentum in comparison to the retrograde motion. Alvarez also neglected to take into account the role that the human scalp might play in the equation. We might also question whether brain matter would react in the same way as melon matter did. Perhaps the most significant lacuna is that Alvarez neglected to specify how much tape was used. Therefore, the experiment is essentially non-repeatable by other investigators.

In 1974 and 1975, John K. Lattimer conducted a series of tests intended to correct some of the more obvious deficiencies of the Alvarez experiments. Firing a Mannlicher-Carcano rifle and the same kind of ammunition found in Dallas, Lattimer conducted experiments using packed melon material wrapped in tape (to emulate the scalp) and placed them into human skulls. He found that the retrograde motion was evident, but not as forceful as the Alvarez experiments revealed (Lattimer 1980, p. 251).[9] It is, however, well known that live bone is extremely elastic and therefore would not react to a high-velocity penetrating bullet the same way as dried-out bone. Therefore the validity of these experiments must be regarded with at least a degree of suspicion.

Lattimer also hypothesized that physiological laws ("neurologic spasm") might also account for the head-snap and the fact that Kennedy's body seemed to be catapulted across the back seat. He observed that when the brain of any large animal, such as a goat, is struck by a high speed military bullet:

> there is a massive downward discharge of neurologic impulses from the injured brain, down the spinal chord to every muscle in the body. The body then stiffens, with the strongest muscles predominating. Since these are the back muscles and the muscles of the back of the neck, the neck arches, the back arches, and the body stiffens into an archlike configuration; the upper limbs react next (Lattimer 1980, p. 255)

Lattimer noted that the House Select Committee confirmed this hypothesis with tests conducted at the Aberdeen Proving Grounds where researchers shot goats in the head and observed their movements (Lattimer 1980, p. 258). Obviously the critics would doubt any conclusions based on an analogy between the shooting of a goat in the head under test conditions and the assassination of the President.

What do the Alvarez and Lattimer experiments prove? At best, one might conclude that the tests indicate that the lone gunman theory does not necessarily violate the laws of nature. This modest conclusion, however, does not rule out the possibility that other alternative hypotheses might also explain the head-snap with equal or superior explanatory power. Indeed, Lattimer himself suggests at least two different covering law models (the physics of the jet and the physiology of neuro-muscle spasm) that might be invoked to explain the motion of Kennedy's head and body as seen in the Zapruder film. Unfortunately, there is no way of discerning which, if either, of these laws actually was in play on 22 November 1963. Moreover, one might propose any number of alternative hypotheses that would be equally consistent with the laws of nature, for example, that the head wound was inflicted by two gunmen firing nearly simultaneously from the above rear and from the grassy knoll.

Finally, one must once again question the integrity of the Zapruder film itself. In 1965, J. Edgar Hoover admitted that the order of frames Z-314 and Z-315 had inadvertently been switched during the publication the Zapruder film in Volume XVIII, pp. 70–71, of *The Warren Report*. The effect of this "mistake" was the illusion of a forward head-snap rather than the more problematic retrograde motion (Thompson 1967, p. 89).

The Location of the Head Wounds Puzzle

Another puzzle that has occupied Kennedy assassination researchers relates to the location of the head wounds. The lone gunman theory entails that one single jacketed Mannlicher-Carcano bullet entered near the back of the President's head, fragmented, and exited leaving a massive head wound to the right parietal region. Researchers have focused on the autopsy report, the X-rays, and autopsy photographs as means of verifying these necessary conditions. The key question asked of the autopsy materials has been whether the head wound(s) were inflicted from above and behind, the left, the front right, or from two or more directions.

In the 1960s, competent forensic pathologists possessed ample techniques for estimating the general direction from which the Kennedy and Connally wounds were inflicted. Bullet wounds of entrance and exit could be distinguished by the presence of an abrasion collar around the wound, and, if bones are broken, by a characteristic "bevelling" of the bone where the diameter of the hole is smaller on the impact side of the wound than on the exit side (*Warren Report* 1964, p. 86). It was also known that some high-velocity bullets tend to fragment, produce a wound passage that rapidly increases in diameter as the bullet passes through the head, and cause shock waves, that bone fragments act as secondary missiles which contribute to the damage, and that jacketed ammunition produces a different type of wound than a hunting-style bullet with an exposed lead nose (Wilber 1978, pp. 218–219). Among forensic pathologists it was a well-confirmed fact that when a high-velocity bullet strikes a living bone in the skull it:

> springs back to a smaller diameter hole once the bullet has passed through. The difference in diameter is said to be a regularly occurring event. It is therefore probable that a hole of entrance measured in live skull has been made by a bullet with a diameter of 0.1 to 1.0 millimeter larger than the hole. (Wilber 1978, p. 218)

If the autopsy physicians were accurate in their location and measurement of the 6x15 mm entry wound to the back of Kennedy's head, then that wound was barely compatible with the hole that would have been made by the 6.5 mm bullet found at Parkland. In short, forensic science cannot establish with certainty whether the entry wound in the back of Kennedy's head was caused by a 6.5 mm or a 7 mm bullet (Wilber 1978, p. 218).

The location of this smaller wound has also been a source of puzzlement. Both the autopsy face sheet marked by Boswell and the official *Warren Report* diagram of the head wound placed the entry wound of the head at least three inches lower than the later findings of the Clark Panel and the House Select Committee on Assassinations. The autopsy team still defends this lower position. Again, critics argue that the migration of the entry wound confirms their hypothesis that the autopsy materials viewed by the recent investigatory groups are, in fact, forgeries.

The autopsy report locates the larger of the two head wounds "chiefly in the parietal bone but extending somewhat into the temporal and occipital regions. In this region there is an actual absence of scalp and bone producing a defect which measures approximately 13 cm. in greatest diameter" (*Warren Report* 1964, p. 540). The X-rays reveal numerous dust-like bullet fragments scattered throughout the right hemisphere of President Kennedy's brain. The two largest fragments (CE–843) were removed by Dr. Humes during the autopsy and handed over to the FBI. [*Editor's note:* See the Postscript to David Mantik, Part I.]

In January 1964, The *Texas State Journal of Medicine* published an article based on interviews with the Parkland physicians. Charles J. Carrico stated that the head wound he saw "had caused avulsion of the occipitoparietal calvarium and shredded brain tissue was present with profuse oozing" ("Three Patients", 1964, p. 540). Malcolm O. Perry described the head wound as: "A large wound of the right posterior cranium . . . exposing severely lacerated brain" ("Three Patients", 1964, p. 62). Charles R. Baxter said that "portions of the right temporal and occipital bones were missing and some of the brain was lying on the table" ("Three Patients", 1964, p. 63). Robert McClelland described the head wound as a "gunshot wound to the side of the head" and William Kemp Clark located it in the occipital region of the skull ("Three Patients"1964 p. 63). Clark also noted that the wound begins "in the right occiput extending into the parietal region. Much of the right posterior skull, at brief examination, appeared gone" ("Three Patients"1964, p. 64). M.T. Jenkins described the head wound as "a great laceration on the right side of the head (temporal and occipital)". [*Editor's note:* See Charles Crenshaw, Part 1, and *The Warren Report*.]

In a book published in 1992, another Parkland physician, Charles A. Crenshaw, gave the following description:

> Then I noticed that the entire right hemisphere of his brain was missing, beginning at his hairline and extending all the way behind his right ear. Pieces of skull that hadn't been blown away were hanging by blood matted hair . . . Part of his brain, the cerebellum, was dangling from the back of his head by a single strand of tissue (Crenshaw 1992, pp. 78–79)

The consensus among the Parkland physicians, therefore, was that the wound extended well into the occipital area in the back of the head. However, in 1972, when Lattimer viewed the autopsy materials, he located the wound more toward the front right of the head:

in the front half of the right side of the top of the head, with a very large segment of the top right half of the skull and scalp missing, from about the top margin of the frontal bone back for a distance of approximately 13 cm (5 inches). The defect extended roughly along the sagittal suture in the midline of the head, and must have taken away most of the right parietal bone. (Lattimer 1972, p. 53)

In 1991, a conference was held in Dallas which brought together some of the Parkland and Bethesda witnesses to discuss the assassination. There was a general consensus among the group that the head wound extended well into the occipital area toward the back of Kennedy's head, an observation that seemed to contradict these recent disclosures. The "best evidence" in the case, Kennedy's brain, was removed and preserved in a formalin solution during the autopsy. However, sometime during 1965–1966, it disappeared from the National Archives (Lifton 1992, p. 508).

Although there is still considerable disagreement over the location of the head wounds, everyone agrees that the wound to the right side of the President's head was massive. The severity of the wound itself is a puzzle. The single bullet theory requires that a jacketed bullet could inflict a series of wounds, including substantial bone damage, without becoming deformed. Yet the lone gunman theory must hold that same kind of bullet fired from the same location could fragment enough to blow out the right side of the President's skull leaving over thirty dust-like particles in the brain. Michael L. Kurtz, therefore, has argued that the massive head wound is more consistent with an exploding bullet similar to the one that killed Martin Luther King. (Kurtz 1982, p. 211)

Researchers continue to question whether the nature and location of Kennedy's and Connally's wounds as revealed by the medical materials are consistent with what one would expect from an assassin firing from above and behind the motorcade. Confirmation or falsification of the lone gunman theory is contingent upon knowledge of the precise location of President Kennedy's various wounds. But despite the earnest efforts of several panels of medical specialists, the key puzzles remain. Controversy will continue at least until the X-rays and autopsy photos can be authenticated. It is not clear, however, how one would go about such a process of authentication. At this point in the investigation, it seems far more likely that science will prove the X-rays to be forgeries.

In January 1972, amidst a growing firestorm of criticism of the autopsy, the Kennedy family was finally persuaded to allow a civilian physician to study the X-rays and autopsy photos. Much to the chagrin of the critics, out of a long list of competent forensic pathologists (which included the critics' first choice, Cyril Wecht) the family chose John K. Lattimer, a urologist. Lattimer's association with the military and longstanding published record in support of the Warren Commission cast a long shadow on his objectivity. When he reported that his observations confirmed the *Warren Report*, the critics dismissed his findings as obviously biased. Moreover, the critics also targeted Lattimer's overall competence. Since the practice of medicine is so highly specialized, physicians tend to recognize professional expertise only in conjunction with one's medical training. The fact that Lattimer's area of medical specialization was in urology led Cyril Wecht, then President of the American Academy of Forensic Sciences, to characterize Lattimer as "unbelievably unqualified." When told of Lattimer's selection Wecht remarked, "I don't know what in the world possessed this fellow Lattimer to have the arrogance, the effrontery, to project himself into this. He's a urologist, a kidney-and-bladder man. By definition this is a guy who never moves above the belly button."[10] Given Lattimer's lack of formal forensic training, the critics simply dismissed his research as incompetent.

It is also puzzling that when Lattimer inspected the X-rays he noted that he could see President Kennedy's adrenal glands. [*Editor's note:* As Gary Aguilar and David Mantik have advised me, Lattimer's language is ambiguous and, when read very carefully, only implies he inspected the *area* of the adrenals; see *Resident and Staff Physician* (May 1972), pp. 57, 59.] However, it was common knowledge that Kennedy suffered from Addison's disease, a condition characterized by an atrophying of the adrenal cortex. On 31 August 1992, Boswell confirmed that serial sections of the perirenal fat pads revealed no evidence of either an adrenal cortex or medulla (Lundberg 1992, p. 1737). Lattimer interpreted the appearance of the adrenal glands in the X-rays he saw as signifying successful treatment of the disease (Lattimer 1980, pp. 220–221). Critics interpreted that same phenomenon as proof that the X-rays were not President Kennedy's (Livingstone 1992, pp. 67–68).

The House Select Committee on Assassinations contracted several forensic dentists to verify the authenticity of the X-rays. Their method consisted of comparing 22 dental X-rays taken prior to the autopsy with the autopsy X-rays (HSCA 1978, Vol. 1, pp. 149–175). But since the government has had possession of both sets of X-rays, some critics suspect that both sets are bogus. In 1988, several witnesses appeared on a KRON-TV documentary produced by David Lifton, Sylvia Chase, and Stanhope Gould. When Jerrol F. Custer, the technician who took the X-rays at Bethesda, was shown copies of the X-rays on file at the National Archives, he insisted that they were not authentic (Livingstone 1992, pp. 349-350)

In summary, it has been argued thus far that the scientific work on the Kennedy assassination has been ill-conceived and poorly designed. The root of the problem is that the primary materials subjected to scientific analysis are simply unreliable. But much bad science can also be attributed to the conditions under which it has been conducted and disseminated. Most of it has been generated under the auspices of governmentally sponsored investigatory panels such as the Warren Commission and the House Select Committee on Assassinations, which have been conducted more like legal proceedings than scientific investigations.[11] This traditional procedure has consisted of contracting groups of scientists to conduct highly technical and esoteric forensic research on the primary evidence. Once completed, the scientists are called in to provide expert testimony before the panels. Because the investigatory panels are composed primarily of lawyers, they rarely understand in sufficient depth what has been presented to them. Nevertheless, it is these unqualified panels who are charged with accepting or rejecting that research.

The government's practice of employing individual scientists is also problematic from a Kuhnian perspective because it desecrates the communal context of scientific inquiry. Individual scientists conducting esoteric research under clandestine conditions can produce little more than idiosyncratic research in violation of the most basic principles of scientific research. Most fatal is the way the parameters of the research have been limited by these committees rather than through the channels of normal science. Unfortunately, the final reports of these investigatory panels are published by the government and made available to journalists and other assassination researchers who mistakenly believe that their findings are based on the authority of "science."

In the course of what Kuhn would call "normal science" most of this type of research would have been weeded out by a vigilant scientific community. However, assassination science currently operates well outside of the Kuhnian framework.

Assassination Experts and Normal Science

It has been argued thus far that in order for science to function as a credible tool for solving the various puzzles associated with the Kennedy assassination it is essential that the research be conducted within certain sociological parameters. In the Kuhnian tradition, "normal science" is a communal activity and scientific expertise is regarded as a function of scientific and scholarly institutions. Hence, to be recognized as an authority or expert in a particular sphere of knowledge one must possess a post-graduate degree (usually a Ph.D. or an M.D.), belong to the appropriate scholarly organizations, and publish and present research to those organizations. While one may object to such a narrow definition of expertise, there are no obvious postmodern alternatives, short of denying the existence of standards of competence altogether. The question that continues to plague assassination research is, "Who are the qualified experts?"

Under normal circumstances professional historians would seem to be the most qualified experts to weigh the evidence in the Kennedy assassination. But for the most part, historians have not considered the Kennedy assassination to be a subject worthy of serious scholarly pursuit. There are several good reasons why. Most obviously, trained historians are extremely reluctant to commit years of study to any topic where the bulk of the primary evidence is either inaccessible to researchers or of dubious authenticity. Doctoral students are especially loath to be affiliated with the longstanding tradition of exploitation, sensationalism, and amateurism generally associated with literature on the Kennedy assassination. An on-line scan of *Dissertation Abstracts* indicates that only about thirteen doctoral projects have been written on the topic.[12]

Over the years the community of assassination researchers have attempted to cultivate their own institutional foundations. Currently, there are two organizations that help serve the research needs of the critics of the Kennedy assassination. The JFK Assassination Information Center, in Dallas, Texas, and the Assassination Archives and Research Center in Washington, D.C. Both are primarily repositories of documents and information and therefore cannot enforce research standards. Several journals devoted to the Kennedy assassination publish articles on a regular basis: *The Third Decade*, *The Investigator*, *Dateline*, and *Probe*. The objectivity and scholarly standards of all four is open for debate.

Most of the books on the assassination of President Kennedy have been enormously popular, even "best sellers." Of course, the more controversial and outrageous the book, the more appealing it is to the public. Because of this inherent profitability, these works have been published almost exclusively by the popular presses, which lack the rigorous standards of peer review that academic presses require. In the absence of traditional Kuhnian standards of professionalism, Kennedy assassination research is rife with authors who have written on technical aspects of the assassination without possessing convincing professional credentials. In 1967, when Josiah Thompson, wrote *Six Seconds in Dallas*, he was an assistant professor of philosophy at Haverford College and the author of a book on Kierkegaard. David Lifton, author of *Best Evidence*, a meticulously detailed examination of the medical evidence, was a graduate student in physics at UCLA when he started his project. He never completed his Ph.D., but he subsequently received an M.S. in Engineering Physics from Cornell. Professional credentials in physics, however, cannot confer Kuhnian expertise in biology, medicine, or history. Charles Crenshaw, M.D., co-author of *JFK: Conspiracy of Silence*, was a resident at Parkland at the time of the assassination. Apparently, he knew so little about it that his own observations are printed in bold type, with the majority of the text written by two well-established critics, Gary Shaw and Jens Hensen. Steve Barber, the rock musician from Ohio whose keen ear detected conversation on the dictabelt recording, has even published his interpretation of the acoustic evidence (Barber 1989).

Because of the lack of institutional mechanisms to enforce standards of competence, research standards, or even professional courtesy, the conduct of the community of critics has been a source of controversy. Harrison Edward Livingstone, who is among its most controversial members, recently characterized this community as follows:

> The facts are that there is fraud and misrepresentation in the critical community: hoaxes, opportunism, territorialism, copyright violations, bootlegging, vendettas, misinformation, serious misdirection by critics of other critics, disruption, suppression of vital evidence for commercial purposes, slandermongering, and interference with other researchers and witnesses . . . the critical community is a madhouse. (Livingstone 1993, p. 369)

Gerald Posner has also been highly critical of the commercialism that has accompanied the growth of the critical movement, especially the annual convention in Dallas (Posner 1993, pp. 469–470). In academic historical circles, profiteering does not often impinge on the integrity of research. History journals rarely pay researchers for the right to publish their essays and the royalties offered by university presses are not likely to entice scholars into early retirement. In the public debate, apologists, in general, have benefitted substantially from the rather shady reputation the critics have cultivated.

The profitability of books on the Kennedy assassination has encouraged the participation of professional journalists. But by Kuhnian standards, journalism does not necessarily possess the institutional foundations necessary for the cultivation of expertise. Journalists do not ordinarily read textbooks in journalism or attend journalism schools. The largest professional organization, the Society of Professional Journalists / Sigma Delta Chi, includes only 17 percent of American journalists (Zelizer 1992, p. 6). Even more serious is the fact that journalism lacks a subject matter upon which expertise can be attributed.

Gerald Posner, a former lawyer and now well-published journalist, has appeared on a wide variety of television specials defending his book *Case Closed* and the lone gunman theory. Much of his analysis is based on his naive acceptance of the dubious scientific evidence discussed earlier in this essay. But to what degree can Posner be regarded as an expert in ballistics, acoustics, or forensic pathology? Since 1986, Posner has also published books on Mengele, Chinese Secret Societies, a novel, and a collection of interviews with the sons and daughters of leaders of the Third Reich.

Journalists are also largely immune from the gauntlet of expert peer review. Often times only the editor stands between the publication of truth or falsehood.

Once published, other journalists often provide quasi-critical analysis in the popular media. Indeed, the reception of *Case Closed* by Gerald Posner's peers, in both the printed and electronic media, has been no less than glowing. In fact, Posner's book made the 30 August 1993 cover of *U.S. News and World Report* and included a 22-page summary of its apologist findings. That journal, however, has had a long history of supporting the Warren Commission. A similar issue was published on 10 October 1966, titled, "Truth About Kennedy Assassination: Questions Raised and Answered."[13] That issue also included an extensive interview with Arlen Specter with the headline: "Truth About the Kennedy Assassination, Told by a Top Official Investigator: "Overwhelming Evidence Oswald was Assassin'."[14]

There is, nevertheless, a lingering perception that the independent-minded journalist, free from the bonds of institutional commitment, can provide the objectivity necessary to conduct research on the Kennedy assassination. But despite our expressed faith in the liberating power of the press, one must remember that the mass media is really a corporate entity, imbued with corporate interests. Michael Parenti has noted this "myth of objectivity:"

> Corporate power permeates the entire social fabric of our society. Along with owning the media, the corporate business class, . . . controls much of the rest of America too, including its financial, educational, medical, cultural, and recreational institutions. Thus, the dominant capitalist interests not only structure the way the media report reality, they structure much of reality itself. The ideological character of the news, then, is partly a reflection of the journalist's 'routine reliance on raw materials which are already ideological.' Opinions that support existing arrangements of economic and political power are more easily treated as facts, while facts that are troublesome to the prevailing distribution of class power are likely to be dismissed as opinionated. And those who censor dissenting views see themselves as protectors of objectivity and keepers of heterodoxy when, in fact, they are the guardians of the ideological community. (Parenti 1986, p. 50)

A major part of the problem is that the government remains the chief source of the news media's most cherished commodity: information. Major newspapers, popular news magazines, and network television therefore must rely on the goodwill of the gatekeepers of the government's "official information" to provide the daily ration of press releases, interviews, news sources, and documents. It can be a career-threatening decision for an individual journalist to be too critical of the government's policies. Despite the American public's well-documented interest in the Kennedy assassination, the mass media has managed to steer clear of the most recent developments in the case.

So the community of assassination researchers is currently dominated by journalists who publish their work in the popular presses and by a handful of scientists and physicians engaged in historical research outside of their area of recognized expertise. It is not at all clear how any single paradigm can ever emerge from such a diverse community operating in the absence of institutionalized standards governing their research. Since the late 1960s, some scientific and medical journals have come forth attempting to fill this institutional void.

Scientific Journals and Assassination Research

In 1966, John K. Lattimer set a minor precedent by publishing his first article on the Kennedy assassination in the *Journal of the American Medical Association*. Since then, his writings have appeared in many other medical journals, such as *Medical Times*, *Forensic Science Gazette*, *Bulletin of the New York Academy of Medicine*, *Surgery, Gynecology and Obstetrics*, and *International Surgery*. Lattimer's articles catapulted him into the forefront of the apologist camp of the scientific debate. His work is often cited as authoritative by philosophically naive journalists, like Gerald Posner, who appear to be unduly impressed by Lattimer's publishing record in scientific journals. The participation of scientific journals in the assassination debate, however, is problematic and raises serious ethical issues.

The main source of ethical concern is that articles published in prestigious scientific journals like the *American Journal of Physics* or *JAMA* carry with them an authority rooted in American society's faith in the integrity of science. To many naive Americans, the assumption is that any article that appears in a scientific journal must conform to lofty scientific standards of objectivity under the scrutiny of competent referees. Those who belong to the professional organizations that publish these journals, therefore, are likely to invest great confidence in the "expert" opinions expressed.

But it is a mistake to assume that every article on the Kennedy assassination published by a scientific journal adheres to lofty standards of research. Most obviously, historical research published in scientific journals must always be treated with a healthy dose of skepticism. Scientists simply are not trained in the basics of historical research and therefore are not likely to be very critical of their sources. For the study of the Kennedy assassination, gullibility can easily poison one's research. To make matters worse, the peer review process in scientific journals becomes distorted when the reviewers, who are themselves non-historians unfamiliar with the details of the assassination, serve as referees. Unlike historians who are trained to carefully scrutinize the authenticity of their primary evidence, scientists and physicians tend to limit their professional critique to issues of methodology. Therefore, science journals are notorious for producing bad history. And because these journals often target a highly specialized segment of the scientific community, assassination articles published in them are less likely to be read by competent historians or knowledgable investigators of the Kennedy assassination.

Professional journals, like popular journals in the mass media, can also hide political agendas behind the guise of objectivity. This problem is illustrated most poignantly in the editor's note introducing Alvarez's article in the *American Journal of Physics*:

> As always, we welcome readers' responses to this article and will select some for publication, according to their appropriateness and the space available. We are interested in comments on procedures which Professor Alvarez uses to reach his conclusions and on the pedagogic uses to which the article can be put. We do not feel that this Journal is an appropriate forum for a discussion of alternative theories of the assassination. (Alvarez 1976, p. 813)

Here the assumption seems to be that the methods of physics can only be used to support hypotheses consistent with the findings of the Warren Commission. Hence, the editorial process itself limits the scope of criticism. In this case, one must question the journalistic ethics of publishing an article in a scientific journal under an editorial policy that *a priori* limits both criticism and exposure to alternative hypotheses.

In May 1992, *JAMA* published the first in a series of interviews with some of the physicians who performed the autopsy (James Humes, Thornton Boswell, and Pierre Finck) and the key Dallas physicians who treated Kennedy in the emergency room (Malcolm Perry, James Carrico, M.T. Jenkins, and Charles Baxter). Based on his interpretation of these interviews, George D. Lundberg, editor of *JAMA* confidently concluded:

> I can state without reservation that John F. Kennedy was struck and killed by two, and only two bullets fired from one high-velocity rifle. The first bullet entered the back at the base of the neck and exited the front of the throat. The abrasion and contusion collar of the skin of the back is diagnostic of a wound of entrance. The second bullet entered the back of the head and exploded the right side of the head, destroying the brain with a surely lethal wound. The inward beveling of the bone at the back of the skull and outward beveling at the front is diagnostic of the direction of the bullet's path. Thus, both bullets struck from behind. No other bullets struck the President. A single rifle fired both. These firsthand accounts of the autopsy and the scientific forensic evidence are indisputable. (Lundberg 1992, p. 1738)

Near the end of the Humes-Boswell interview, Lundberg is quoted as saying: "I am extremely pleased that, finally, we are able to have published in the peer-reviewed literature the actual findings of what took place at the autopsy table on November 22, 1963" (Breo 1992, p. 2803).

Despite Lundberg's unabashed confidence in *JAMA*'s "findings," the interviews are really a prime example of how scientific journals can abuse their scientific stature.[15] First of all, the whole project assumes that interviews with scientists can be categorized as scientific literature. Interviews are by definition *opinion*, and therefore not subject to ordinary standards of peer review. In light of the universal condemnation of the autopsy and the miscommunication between the Parkland and Bethesda physicians, one would be hard-pressed to describe these interviews as "expert opinion."

The articles also contain numerous instances where the authors deviate from standard scholarly editorial practices. There is a disturbing pattern throughout the series implying that science deals with "indisputable facts" and that competent scientific investigators have already solved the puzzles of the assassination. More astute scientists and philosophers in the realist tradition follow Popper in rejecting this positivistic mythology. In Popper's view, science must reject "indisputable facts" as inherently non-scientific. Therefore, even if scientific evidence did support the lone gunman theory, it would not "close the case."

There are also numerous uncomplimentary references to the critics. The *JAMA* articles are rife with terms like "assassination-conspiracy buffs" (Breo 1992, p. 2794), "long parade of conspiracy theories" (Breo 1992, p. 2794), "conspiracy buffs" (Breo 1992 p. 2794), "conspiracy fanciers" (Breo 1992, p. 2803), "the growing industry of conspiracy theories from people who are ignorant of the essential facts and yet purport to know how President Kennedy must have been killed, at least in their minds"(Breo 1992, p.2803), and "defamers of the truth" (Breo 1992, 2807). In contrast, Lundberg refers to those who have supported the Warren Commission as "a series of unbiased experts, forensic scientists, pathologists, and radiologists" (Lundberg 1992, p. 1738).

Humes remarked that there were "300 people at a convention in Dallas, each hawking a different conspiratorial theory about how the President was killed. I think this kind of general idiocy is a tragedy—it almost defies belief—but I guess it is the price we pay for living in a free country. I can only question the motives of those who propound these ridiculous theories for a price and who have turned the President's death into a profit-making industry" (Breo 1992, p. 2795). Robert R. Artwohl's article concludes with the observation that "As the years pass, one thing becomes abundantly clear: for the conspirati, it is conspiracy above all else, including forensic science and common sense" (Artwohl 1992, p. 1543).

Taken together these remarks constitute what logicians call "ad hominem arguments." While these kinds of statements often prove effective as rhetorical devices in convincing an unsuspecting audience of a given point of view (and to a certain extent these statements may even be accurate), they are, nevertheless, classified among the fallacies of relevance and are flatly rejected as arguments worthy of philosophical or scientific merit. Professional journals universally eschew these kinds of arguments for logical reasons and out of professional courtesy.

In summary, the institutional void left by professional historians in the study of the assassination of President Kennedy cannot be filled by either journalists or scientists. Historians will continue their informal boycott of the subject until researchers are granted unlimited access to what is left of the primary evidence and until the mountain of FBI and CIA documentation is completely declassified. But even if all of this material were released to public scrutiny tomorrow, it is not certain that historians would immediately migrate to the National Archives. Given the government's unconscionable handling of this evidence over the last thirty years, competent historians will probably continue to doubt its integrity. Young historians will also think twice about devoting years of serious study to an area that has been long associated with amateurism, sensationalism, and commercialism.

It would be most convenient to attribute the failure of assassination research to the erosion of Kuhnian standards of competence. Unfortunately, the event is really only an instance of a larger historical movement in the United States.

Conclusion

In many ways, the assassination of John F. Kennedy in 1963 marks the beginning of the Post-Modern period in the United States. One of the hallmarks of this era has been the growing distrust of all forms of institutional authority. Government officials, scientists, and religious leaders can no longer claim undisputed privileged status among the myriad forms of human discourse. Indeed experts, by any measure, have become an endangered species. The "babble of tongues" that comprises the historiography on the assassination is only a symptom of this Post-Modern mindset.

Much of this disenchantment can be attributed to politics. Recent disclosures indicating that during the Cold War the United States government conducted covert research on radiation exposure on hundreds of American citizens without their consent is only the latest in a long series of similar travesties. Combined with the illegal bombing of Cambodia and spying on U.S. citizens by the CIA during the Vietnam War, the Watergate break-in, and the Iran-Contra Affair, one must begin to seriously question the integrity of our institutions of government.

There are at least two lessons we should have learned from our sordid experience with the Cold war: *first*, we cannot trust the government to investigate itself; *second*, we cannot depend on the free press to bring to light these transgressions in a timely fashion.

Back in 1963, Harry Howe Ransom published a prophetic analysis of how American democracy had become endangered by the institutions of Cold War government. He warned that elements of the defense establishment, such as the National Security Council, Department of Defense, defense budgets, and the CIA, had already begun to operate behind a wall of secrecy beyond the checks and balances of our democratic political system. Ransom predicted that, in the near future, the paradox of protecting national security while maintaining our democratic ideals would become even more intensified. As a result, the goal of providing "national security" would increasingly be used as an omnipresent excuse for secrecy and the control of the flow of information by the government. As the United States competes against a closed Communist society, the basic problem, Ransom insists, ". . . is not whether the American system can continue to provide both defense and democracy, but whether it can provide either" (Ransom 1963, p. xv).

> At the level of democratic ideals, the problem is the existence of a potential source of invisible government. At the level of representatives of the people-Executive and Legislative—the problem is primarily how to control a dimly seen instrument, so hot that if not handled with great skill it can burn its user instead of its adversary. The problem for the scholar is access to verifiable information for objective analysis. (Ransom 1963, p. 173)

Ransom might have added that the shroud of governmental secrecy also threatens the integrity of the scientific establishment. The Cold War is over but the United States government continues to surreptitiously control the flow of information going into the "assassination sciences" thus fatally compromising the necessary conditions for scientific inquiry. In short, if we cannot trust the Cold War regime of the United States to have maintained an objective chain of evidence, and if the government continues to micro-manage the evidence, the greatest scientific minds in the world will not bring us any closer to the truth. The old saying, "garbage in, garbage out" captures the essence of what happens when science becomes a mere instrument of political chicanery.

The scientific method represents a highly idealized and perhaps naive vision of human inquiry. Because scientists are, by their very nature, idealists, they have always been among the first to be duped by political power. Consequently, the post-modern world nurtures a deeply rooted distrust of "scientific experts" proclaiming the Absolute Truth. If science and other forms of scholarly activity are to survive this post-modern onslaught, it is imperative that individual scientists be mindful of the inherent limits of scientific inquiry.

We may lament the loss of "finality" that has accompanied our growing distrust of authority. Many of us may still seek refuge in the belief that science can fill the void left by our defrocked religious leaders, indicted politicians, and incompetent journalists. However, this is a serious mistake. If philosophers like Kuhn and

Foucault are justified in their suspicion of scientific regimes wielding unlimited social and political power, then we must subject scientific experts to the same level of scrutiny we afford the testimony of ordinary human beings.

Notes

1 "Doubts Remain in Shooting: 7 of 10 Say Killing of JFK a Conspiracy", *The Cincinnati Enquirer* (21 November 1993) p. A7

2 For a discussion of how the American scientific community defended slavery during the nineteenth century, see Stanton (1966), Haller (1975), and Gould (1981). For a critical historical study of how social and cultural prejudices have influenced the scientific measurement of human intelligence during the nineteenth and twentieth centuries, see Gould (1981).

3 See Posner (1993), p. 318, and "The Warren Report," CBS News, Part I (25 June 1967), p. 14.

4 An interesting, if totally irrelevant bit of science has been presented to explain the fact that between Frames 224 and 230 of the Zapruder film Kennedy's arms can be seen to raise up. Lattimer attributes this motion to a neurological response to the bullet grazing the President's spinal column; see Lattimer (1980), pp. 168–169 and pp. 240–246. The problem is determining whether the motion was caused by the Thorburn reflex or by a an involuntary reaction to being shot in the throat. There is no empirical basis for preferring one hypothesis over the other.

5 For a less than satisfactory discussion of the dictabelt issue, see Groden and Livingstone (1990), Chapter 12. The author does a better job on the acoustics in his more recent book, Livingstone (1993), Chapter 12.

6 Perry's comments were widely reported by the main new sources: UPI wire at 3:10 CST and *The New York Times* article 11/23/63, and discussed in Chapter 3 of Lifton (1992). [*Editor's note:* See Appendix C.]

7 [*Editor's note:* The thesis that the Bethesda physicians were aware of the tracheostomy and of the wound to the throat but concealed their possession of that knowledge—now called "the throat-wound ignorance theory"—is an hypothesis for which there exists extensive and convincing evidence. It has been a subject of ongoing investigation, especially by Kathleen Cunningham.]

8 The tumbling bullet hypothesis is detailed in Lattimer (1980), p. 268.

9 Similar tests were conducted by the Warren Commission in order to determine whether Kennedy's head wounds were compatible with what one would expect from the Carcano rifle at 270 feet. Interestingly, the Warren Commission did not report that the targets exhibited retrograde motion. See *Warren Report* (1964), pp. 585–586.

10 Quotation originally taken from an article titled, "'Unbelievably Unqualified' Doctor Called Unfit to Judge JFK Data," in *Chicago Daily News* (January 11, 1972). Cited in Lifton (1992), p. 582.

11 For an early critique of the conduct of the Warren Commission, see Lane (1966). Two recent books by critics examine the work of the House Select Committee on Assassinations: are Fonzi (1993) and Summers (1989).

12 One of this notable few is a doctoral dissertation by Barbie Zelizer that doesn't even propose a conspiracy theory. It explores the narrative reconstruction of the Kennedy assassination by journalists and therefore avoids the forementioned

research quagmire. See Barbie Zelizer, "Covering the Body:" The Kennedy Assassination and the Establishment of Journalistic Authority" (University of Pennsylvania Doctoral Dissertation, 1990).

[13] "Truth About Kennedy Assassination" *U.S. News and World Report* 61 (10 October 1966), pp. 48–63.

[14] "Overwhelming Evidence Oswald was Assassin" *U.S. News and World Report* 61 (10 October 1966), pp. 48–63.

[15] For a detailed and devastating philosophical critique of the *JAMA* articles by James H. Fetzer, a noted philosopher of science, see Fetzer (1993a) and Livingstone (1993), pp. 122–124. [*Editor's note:* See James H. Fetzer, Part I.]

References

Government Documents

Warren Report (1964). *The Official Warren Commission Report on the Assassination of President John F. Kennedy*. Garden City: Doubleday, 1964.

HSCA (1979). *Report of the Select Committee on Assassinations, U.S. House of Representatives*

CBA (1982). *Report of the Committee on Ballistic Acoustics*. Washington D.C.: National Academy Press, 1982).

Books and Journals

Alvarez, Luis (1976), "A Physicist Examines the Kennedy Assassination Film" *American Journal of Physics,* 44 (September 1976), pp. 813–827.

Ambrose, Steven E. (1992), "Writers on the Grassy Knoll: A Reader's Guide." *New York Times Book Review* (2 February 1992) pp. 23–25.

Artwohl, Robert R. (1993), "JFK's Assassination: Conspiracy, Forensic Science, and Common Sense." *JAMA* 269 (24/31 March 1993) pp. 1540–1543.

Barber, Steve (1989), *Double Decker*. Privately published by Robert Cutler, 1989.

Chalmers, A.F. (1976), *What is this thing called Science: An assessment of the nature and status of science and its methods*. St. Lucia: University of Queensland Press, 1976.

Crenshaw, Charles A., with Jens Hensen, and Gary Shaw (1992), *JFK: Conspiracy of Silence*. New York: Penguin Books, 1992.

Fetzer, James H. (1975), "On the Historical Explanation of Unique Events." *Theory and Decision* 6 (1975) pp. 87–97.

———. (1993a) *Philosophy of Science*. New York: Paragon House, 1993.

———. (1993b), "A Piece of My Mind: Lundberg, JFK, and *JAMA*." in Livingstone (1993), Appendix H, pp. 635–641.

Feyerabend, Paul (1978), *Science in a Free Society*. Great Britain: Thetford Press, 1978.

Fonzi, Gaeton (1993), *The Last Investigation*. New York: Thunder's Mouth Press, 1993.

Foucault, Michel (1980) *Power/Knowledge: Selected Interviews and Other Writings, 1977–1984*. ed. Colin Gordon, New York: Pantheon Books, 1980.

———. (1988), *Politics, Philosophy, Culture: Interviews and Other Writings, 1977–1984*. ed. Lawrence D. Kritzman. New York: Routledge, 1988.

Garrison, Jim (1988), *JFK: On The Trail of the Assassins*. New York: Warner Books, 1988.

Gould, Stephen Jay (1981), *The Mismeasure of Man*. New York: W. W. Norton, 1981.

Groden, Robert J. and Harrison Edward Livingstone (1990), *High Treason: The Assassination of President John F. Kennedy and the New Evidence of Conspiracy*. New York: Berkley Books, 1990.

Guinn, Vincent (1979), "JFK Assassination: Bullet Analyses" *Analytical Chemistry* 51 (April, 1979). pp.

Haller, John S. Jr. (1975), *Outcasts from Evolution: Scientific Attitudes of Racial Inferiority, 1859–1900*. New York: McGraw Hill, 1975.

Hempel, Carl G. (1942), "The Function of General Laws in History." *The Journal of Philosophy* 39 (1942) pp. 35–48. (1965)

———. (1965), *Aspects of Scientific Explanation and Other Essays in the Philosophy of Science*. New York: Free Press, 1965.

Kuhn, Thomas (1970), *The Structure of Scientific Revolutions*, Second Edition. Chicago: University of Chicago Press, 1970.

Kurtz, Michael L. (1982), *Crime of the Century: The Assassination From a Historian's Perspective*. Knoxville: University of Tennessee Press, 1982.

Lane, Mark (1966) *Rush To Judgment*. New York: Holt, Rinehart and Winston, 1966.

Lattimer, John K. (1966), "Factors in the Death of President Kennedy." *JAMA*, 198 (October 7, 1966) pp. 327–333.

———. (1972), "Observations based on a Review of the Autopsy Photographs, X-Rays, and Related Materials of the Late President John F. Kennedy." *Resident and Staff Physician* (May 1972), pp. 34-64.

———. (1980), *Kennedy and Lincoln: Medical and Ballistic Comparisons of their Assassinations*. New York: Harcourt, Brace, Jovanovich, 1980.

Lifton, David S. (1990), *Best Evidence: The Research Video*. Santa Monica: Rhino Records.

Lifton, David S. (1992), *Best Evidence: Disguise and Deception in the Assassination of John F. Kennedy*. New York: Penguin Books, 1992.

Livingstone, Harrison Edward (1992), *High Treason 2*. New York: Carroll & Graf, 1992.,

———. (1993) *Killing the Truth*. New York: Carrol & Graf, 1993.

Lundberg, George (1992), "Closing the Case in *JAMA* on the John F. Kennedy Autopsy." *JAMA* 268 (October 7, 1992) pp. 1736–1738.

Novick, Peter (1988), *That Noble Dream: The "Objectivity Question" and the American Historical Profession*. New York: Cambridge University Press, 1988.

Parenti, Michael (1986), *Inventing Reality: The Politics of the Mass Media*. New York: St. Martins Press, 1986.

Popper, Karl R. (1957), *The Poverty of Historicism* London: Ark Paperbacks, 1989.

———. (1959), *The Logic of Scientific Discovery*. New York: Basic Books, 1959.

———. (1965), *Conjectures and Refutations: The Growth of Scientific Knowledge*. New York: Harper & Row, 1965.

Posner, Gerald (1993), *Case Closed: Lee Harvey Oswald and the Assassination of JFK*. New York: Random House, 1993.

Ransom, Harry Howe (1963), *Can Democracy Survive Cold War?* Garden City: Doubleday, 1963.

Raskin, Marcus (1992), "JFK and the Culture of Violence." *American Historical Review* 97 (April, 1992) pp. 487-499.

Rogin, Michael (1992), "JFK: The Movie." *American Historical Review* 97 (April, 1992) pp. 500–505.

Rosenstone, Robert A. (1992), "JFK: Historical Fact/Historical Film." *American Historical Review* 97 (April, 1992) pp. 506–511.

Stanton, William (1966), *The Leopard's Spots: Scientific Attitudes Toward Race in America, 1815-1859*. (Third Edition) Chicago: University of Chicago Press, 1966.

Summers, Anthony, (1989), *Conspiracy*. New York: Paragon House, 1989.

Thompson, Josiah (1967), *Six Seconds in Dallas: A Micro-Study of the Kennedy Assassination*. New York: Bernard Geis, 1967

"Three Patients at Parkland." (1964), *Texas State Journal of Medicine* 60 (1964) pp. 60–74.

Wecht, Cyril H. (1967), "A Critique of President Kennedy's Autopsy" in Thompson (1967), pp 278–284.

Wilber, Charles G. (1978), *Medicolegal Investigation of the President John F. Kennedy Murder*. Springfield: Charles C. Thomas Publishers, 1978.

Zelizer, Barbie (1992), *Covering the Body: The Kennedy Assassination, the Media, and the Shaping of Collective Memory*. Chicago: University of Chicago Press, 1992.

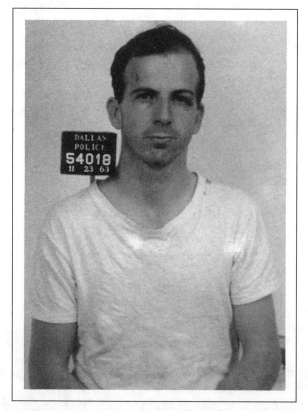

According to The Warren Report, *John Fitzgerald Kennedy, the 35th President of the United States, was assassinated by a lone, demented gunman, Lee Harvey Oswald, pictured here.*

Appendices

(A) Observations of JFK Wounds in Trauma Room 1 by   414
     Charles Crenshaw, M.D.

(B) FBI Report with Summary of Treatment at Parkland by   416
     Kemp Clark, M.D.

(C) Transcript of Parkland Press Conference, 3:16 P.M.,   419
     22 November 1963

(D) Signed State of Texas Certificate of Death for John   428
     Fitzgerald Kennedy

(E) Unsigned State of Texas Certificate of Death for John   429
     Fitzgerald Kennedy

(F) Bethesda Naval Hospital Report of Autopsy on John   430
     Fitzgerald Kennedy

(G) Supplementary Report of Autopsy on John   436
     Fitzgerald Kennedy

(H) Warren Commission Diagrams of JFK Wounds   438

(I) Certificate of Death for JFK prepared by Admiral   439
     George G. Burkley

(J) Partial Transcript of Warren Commission Testimony of   440
     Malcolm Perry, M.D.

(K) House Select Committee on Assassinations JFK Autopsy   441
     Drawings

(L) JFK Autopsy Photographs Corresponding to HSCA JFK   443
     Autopsy Drawings

(M) CIA Dispatch, "Countering Criticism of the Warren   444
     Report", 1 April 1967

(N) CIA Advertisement for Photographers   447

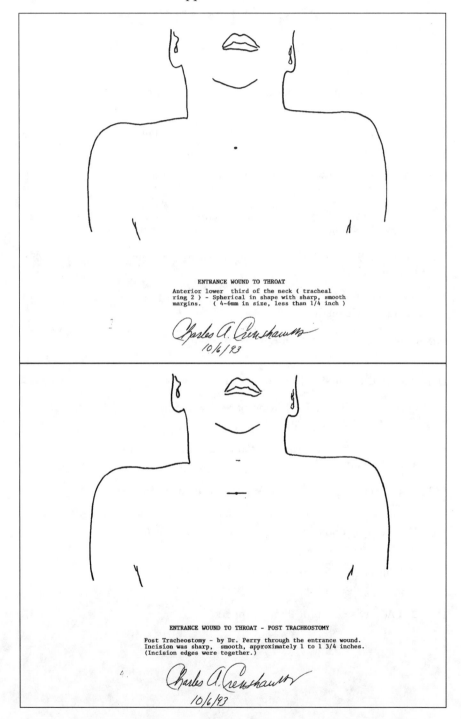

ENTRANCE WOUND TO THROAT

Anterior lower third of the neck (tracheal
ring 2) - Spherical in shape with sharp, smooth
margins. (4-6mm in size, less than 1/4 inch)

Charles A. Crenshaw
10/6/93

ENTRANCE WOUND TO THROAT - POST TRACHEOSTOMY

Post Tracheostomy - by Dr. Perry through the entrance wound.
Incision was sharp, smooth, approximately 1 to 1 3/4 inches.
(Incision edges were together.)

Charles A. Crenshaw
10/6/93

Observations of JFK Wounds in Trauma Room 1 by Charles Crenshaw, M.D.

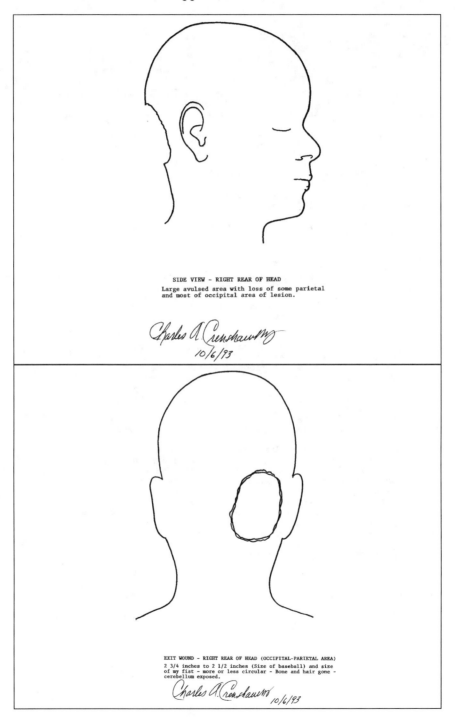

SIDE VIEW - RIGHT REAR OF HEAD
Large avulsed area with loss of some parietal
and most of occipital area of lesion.

EXIT WOUND - RIGHT REAR OF HEAD (OCCIPITAL-PARIETAL AREA)
2 3/4 inches to 2 1/2 inches (Size of baseball) and size
of my fist - more or less circular - Bone and hair gone -
cerebellum exposed.

Observations of JFK Wounds in Trauma Room 1 by Charles Crenshaw, M.D.

J02 (Rev. 3-3-59)   FEDERAL BUREAU OF INVESTIGATION

C - 1

Date ___11-25-63___

          On November 25, 1963, Mr. C. J. PRICE, Administrator, Parkland Memorial Hospital, Dallas, Texas, advised that the Death Certificate and Statements of Medical Treatment relating to President JOHN F. KENNEDY had been taken by GEORGE G. BURKLEY, MD, White House, Washington, D.C., and Secret Service Agents. Mr. PRICE stated, however, that a summary had been prepared by Dr. KEMP CLARK, Director, Service of Neurological Surgery at the request of GEORGE G. BURKLEY, MD, and was transmitted to Dr. BURKLEY by letter dated November 23, 1963.

          Mr. PRICE made available reproduced copies of the summary and letter furnished Dr. BURKLEY.

          The following are the contents of the summary prepared by Dr. KEMP CLARK, verbatim:

                Summary

          "The President arrived at the Emergency Room at 12:43 P.M., the 22nd of November, 1963. He was in the back seat of his limousine. Governor Connally of Texas was also in this car. The first physician to see the President was Dr. James Carrico, a Resident in General Surgery.

          "Dr. Carrico noted the President to have slow, agonal respiratory efforts. He could hear a heartbeat but found no pulse or blood pressure to be present. Two external wounds, one in the lower third of the anterior neck, the other in the occipital region of the skull, were noted. Through the head wound, blood and brain were extruding. Dr. Carrico inserted a cuffed endotracheal tube. While doing so, he noted a ragged wound of the trachea immediately below the larynx.

          "At this time, Dr. Malcolm Perry, Attending Surgeon, Dr. Charles Baxter, Attending Surgeon, and Dr. Ronald Jones, another Resident in General Surgery, arrived. Immediately thereafter, Dr. M.T. Jenkins, Director of the Department of Anesthesia and Doctors Giesecke and Hunt, two other Staff Anesthesiologists, arrived. The endotracheal tube had been connected to a

---

11-25-63   Dallas, Texas   DL 89-43

n _____ at _____ File # _____

y Special Agent SA JAMES W. SWINFORD:L md   Date dictated   11-25-63

FBI Report with Summary of Treatment at Parkland by Kemp Clark, M.D.

2

C

DL 89-43

"Bennett respirator to assist the President's
breathing. An anesthesia machine was substituted for
this by Dr. Jenkins. Only 100% oxygen was administered.

"A cutdown was performed in the right ankle, and
a polyethylene catheter inserted in the vein. An
infusion of lactated Ringer's solution was begun. Blood
was drawn for type and crossmatch, but unmatched
type 'O' RH negative blood was immediately obtained
and begun. Hydrocortisone 300 mgms was added to the intravenous
fluids.

"Dr. Robert McClelland, Attending Surgeon,
arrived to help in the President's care. Doctors Perry,
Baxter, and McClelland began a tracheostomy, as considerable quantities of blood were present from the
President's oral pharynx. At this time, Dr. Paul Peters,
Attending Urological Surgeon, and Dr. Kemp Clark, Director
of Neurological Surgery, arrived. Because of the
lacerated trachea, anterior chest tubes were placed in
both pleural spaces. These were connected to sealed under-
water drainage.

"Neurological examination revealed the President's
pupils to be widely dilated and fixed to light. His
eyes were divergent, being deviated outward; a skew
deviation from the horizontal was present. No deep
tendon reflexes or spontaneous movements were found.

"There was a large wound in the right occipitoparietal region, from which profuse bleeding was
occurring. 1500 cc. of blood were estimated on the
drapes and floor of the Emergency Operating Room. There
was considerable loss of scalp and bone tissue. Both
cerebral and cerebellar tissue were extruding from the
wound.

"Further examination was not possible as cardiac
arrest occurred at this point. Closed chest cardiac
massage was began by Dr. Clark. A pulse palpable in
both the carotid and femoral arteries was obtained. Dr.
Perry relieved on the cardiac massage while a
cardiotachioscope was connected. Dr. Fouad Bashour,
Attending Physician arrived as this was being connected.

FBI Report with Summary of Treatment at Parkland by Kemp Clark, M.D.

<u>3</u>

DL 89-43

"There was electrical silence of the President's heart.

"President Kennedy was pronounced dead at 1300 hours by Dr. Clark.

"
‾‾‾‾‾‾‾‾‾‾‾‾‾‾‾‾‾‾‾‾‾‾‾‾‾
/s/ Kemp Clark, M.D.
Director
Service of Neurological Surgery"

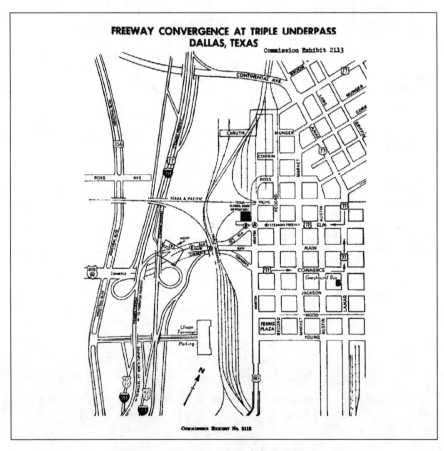

FREEWAY CONVERGENCE AT TRIPLE UNDERPASS
DALLAS, TEXAS

Commission Exhibit 2113

Warren Commission Exhibit CE-2113

This Copy For _ _ _ _ _ _ _ _   B

N E W S   C O N F E R E N C E   TRANS-C→#1

AT THE WHITE HOUSE

WITH WAYNE HAWKS

NOVEMBER 22, 1933

3:16 P.M.   CCT

Friday

Dallas, Texas

MR. HAWKS: Let me have your attention, please.

You wanted to talk to some of the attending physicians. I have two of them here, Dr. Malcolm Perry, an attending surgeon here at the Parkland Memorial Hospital. He will talk to you first, and then Dr. Kemp Clark, the chief neurosurgeon here at the hospital. He will tell you what he knows about it. Dr. Perry.

Q. Were you in attendance when the President died?

Q. Let him tell his story.

DR. MALCOLM PERRY: I was summoned to the Emergency Room shortly after the President was brought in, on an emergency basis, immediately after the President's arrival. Upon reaching his side, I noted that he was in critical condition from a wound of the neck and of the head. Immediate resuscitative measures --

Q. Would you go slower?

DR. PERRY: I noted he was in a critical condition from the wound in the neck and the head.

Q. Could that be done by one shot?

DR. PERRY: I cannot conjecture. I don't know.

Q. A wound of the neck and of the --

DR. PERRY: -- of the head. Immediate resuscitative measures were undertaken, and Dr. Kemp Clark, Professor of Neurosurgery, was summoned, along with several other members of the surgical and medical staff. They arrived immediately, but at this point the President's condition did not allow complete resuscitation.

Q. What do you mean by "complete resuscitation"?

DR. PERRY: He was critically ill and moribund at the time these measures were begun.

Q. Completely ill and what?

DR. PERRY: Moribund.

MORE

Transcript of Parkland Press Conference, 3:16 P.M., 22 November 1963

Page 2 - #1327-C

Q. What does that mean? B - 2

DR. PERRY: Near death.

Q. What was the word you used?

DR. PERRY: Moribund. Dr. Clark arrived thereafter, immediately.

Q. Could you tell us what resuscitative measures were attempted?

DR. PERRY: Assisted respiration.

Q. What is that?

Q. With what?

DR. PERRY: Assisted respiration with oxygen and an anesthesia machine, passage of an endotracheal tube.

Q. Does that mean you stick it in?

DR. PERRY: Yes, place it in his trachea.

Q. Spell it for us, please.

DR. PERRY: E-n-d-o-t-r-a-c-h-e-a-l. A tracheostomy.

Q. They did perform a tracheostomy?

DR. PERRY: Yes.

Q. Would you spell it?

DR. PERRY: T-r-a-c-h-e-o-s-t-o-m-y.

Q. Was there a priest in the room at this time, Doctor?

MR. HAWKS: The doctor is just telling you about the operation.

DR. PERRY: Blood and fluids were also given, and an electrocardiograph monitor was attached to record any heart beat that might be present. At this point, Dr. Clark was also in attendance.

Q. What is his name?

DR. PERRY: Dr. Kemp Clark. And Dr. Charles Baxter.

DR. KEMP CLARK: I was called by Dr. Perry because the President --

Q. You are Dr. Clark?

DR. CLARK: I an Dr. Clark.

MORE

Transcript of Parkland Press Conference, 3:16 P.M., 22 November 1963

B

-- because the President had sustained a brain wound. On my arrival, the resuscitative efforts, the tracheostomy, the administration of chest tubes to relieve any possible --

Q. Could you slow down a little bit, Doctor, please?

DR. CLARK: -- to relieve any possibility of air being in the pleural space, the electrocardiogram had been hooked up, blood and fluids were being administered by Dr. Perry and Dr. Baxter. It was apparent that the President had sustained a lethal wound.

A missile had gone in or out of the back of his head, causing extensive lacerations and loss of brain tissue. Shortly after I arrived, the patient, the President, lost his heart action by the electrocardiogram, his heart then had stopped.

We attempted resuscitative measures of his heart, including closed chest cardiac massage, but to no avail.   ;

Q. That was closed chest?

DR. CLARK: Yes.

Q. Does that mean external, Doctor, closed?

DR. CLARK: Yes, .We were able to obtain palpable pulses by this method, but, again, to no avail.

Q. What is palpable?

MR. HAWKS: What did you ask?

Q. Palpable?

DR. CLARK: Palpable.

Q. Palpable what?

DR. CLARK: Pulses.

Q. Doctor, how many doctors were in attendance at the time of the President's death?

Q. Doctor, can you tell us how long after he arrived on the Emergency table before he expired? In other words, how long was he living while in the hospital?

DR. CLARK: 40 minutes, perhaps.

DR. PERRY: I was far too busy to tell. I didn't even look at the watch.

DR. CLARK: I would guess about 40 minutes.

Q. Doctor, can you describe the course of the wound through the head?

MORE

Transcript of Parkland Press Conference, 3:16 P.M., 22 November 1963

Page 4 - #1327-C

DR. CLARK: We were too busy to be absolutely sure   B - 4
of the track, but the back of his head.

Q. And through the neck?

DR. CLARK: Principally on his right side, towards
the right side.

Q. What was the exact time of death, doctor?

DR. CLARK: That is very difficult to say. We
were very busy, and in answer to someone else's question,
we had a lot of people in attendance. We elected to make
this at 1300.

Q. You elected?

Q. What, sir?

DR. CLARK: We pronounced him at 1300 hours.

Q. Thirteen of?

MR. HAWKS: 1:00 o'clock.

Q. Can you describe his neck wound?

DR. CLARK: I was busy with his head wound. I would
like to ask the people who took care of that part to describe
that to you.

Q. What was the question?

DR. PERRY: The neck wound, as visible on the
patient, revealed a bullet hole almost in the mid line.

Q. What was that?

DR. PERRY: A bullet hole almost in the mid line.

Q. Would you demonstrate?

DR. PERRY: In the lower portion of the neck, in
front.

Q. Can you demonstrate, Doctor, on your own neck?

DR. PERRY: Approximately here (indicating).

Q. Below the Adam's apple?

DR. PERRY: Below the Adam's apple.

Q. Doctor, is it the assumption that it went
through the head?

DR. PERRY: That would be on conjecture on my part.
There are two wounds, as Dr. Clark noted, one of the neck and
one of the head. Whether they are directly related or related
to two bullets, I cannot say.

MORE

Transcript of Parkland Press Conference, 3:16 P.M., 22 November 1963

Page 5 - #1327-C

Q. Where was the entrance wound?   B - 5

DR. PERRY: There was an entrance wound in the neck. As regards the one on the head, I cannot say.

Q. Which way was the bullet coming on the neck wound? At him?

DR. PERRY: It appeared to be coming at him.

Q. And the one behind?

DR. PERRY: The nature of the wound defies the ability to describe whether it went through it from either side. I cannot tell you that. Can you, Dr. Clark?

DR. CLARK: The head wound could have been either the exit wound from the neck or it could have been a tangential wound, as it was simply a large, gaping loss of tissue.

Q. That was the immediate cause of death -- the head wound?

DR. CLARK: I assume so; yes.

Q. There is a rumor that Lyndon Johnson had a heart attack, and I would like to check that out.

DR. CLARK: I have no information.

MR. HAWKS: I don't believe these gentlemen were in attendance with the Vice President.

Q. Where was he when this was going on?

MR. HAWKS: That is not the question you should put to this doctor.

Q. Can you tell us where he is?

MR. HAWKS: I can't now, but Mr. Kilduff will be available later and we will take those details then.

Q. We can't hear you.

MR. HAWKS: They are asking where the Vice President was, but I don't know at the moment. That is not the proper question to put to these gentlemen. They were busy with the President at the time.

Q. Where was Mrs. Kennedy?

MR. HAWKS: I don't know that detail either. As you might suspect, we were all busy around here.

Q. Can't we clear this up just a little more? In your estimation, was there one or two wounds? Just give us something.

DR. PERRY: I don't know. From the injury, it is

MORE

Transcript of Parkland Press Conference, 3:16 P.M., 22 November 1963

Page 5 - KENNEDY

conceivable that it could have been caused by one wound, but there could have been two just as well if the second bullet struck the head in addition to striking the neck, and B - I cannot tell you that due to the nature of the wound. There is no way for me to tell.

Q. Doctor, describe the entrance wound. You think from the front in the throat?

DR. PERRY: The wound appeared to be an entrance wound in the front of the throat; yes, that is correct. The exit wound, I don't know. It could have been the head or there could have been a second wound of the head. There was not time to determine this at the particular instant.

Q. Would the bullet have had to travel up from the neck wound to exit through the back?

DR. PERRY: Unless it was deviated from its course by striking bone or some other object.

Q. Doctor, can you give us your ages, please?

DR. PERRY: I am 34.

Q. You are Doctor who?

DR. PERRY: Perry.

MR. HAWKS: This is Dr. Malcolm Perry, attending surgeon, and this is Dr. Kemp Clark, chief of neurosurgery at this hospital.

Q. How old are you, sir?

DR. CLARK: 38.

Q. Is that C-l-a-r-k?

DR. CLARK: Yes.

Q. Can you tell us whether the autopsy will be performed here or elsewhere?

DR. PERRY: I do not have that information.

MR. HAWKS: I don't know either.

Q. Will there be one?

MR. HAWKS: I don't know that.

Q. Where is the President's body?

MR. HAWKS: I couldn't tell you.

Q. Was the President ever conscious after the bullet struck him?

DR. PERRY: No, not while I was in attendance.

MORE

Transcript of Parkland Press Conference, 3:16 P.M., 22 November 1963

Page 7 - #1327-C

Q. How much blood was used?   B - 7

DR. PERRY: I don't know. There was considerable
bleeding.

Q. How soon did you see him after he got in?

Q. Did you have to send for blood?

DR. PERRY: Blood was sent for and obtained; yes.

Q. Where?

DR. PERRY: From our Blood Bank.

Q. Here in the hospital?

DR. PERRY: Here in the hospital.

Q. How much was used?

DR. PERRY: I can't tell you that.

Q. How much blood?

DR. PERRY: I don't know.

Q. Doctor, were the last rites performed in the
Emergency Room?

DR. PERRY: Yes.

Q. Yes, they were?

MR. HAWKS: Yes, they said they were. Kilduff
told you, too.

Q. Which room was this? What is the room like?

DR. PERRY: Emergency Operating Room No. 1.

Q. How far from the door is that, and which way?

DR. KEMP: Straight in from the Emergency Room
entrance, at the back of the hospital, approximately 40 feet.

Q. Approximately what?

MR. HAWKS: Forty feet from the emergency entrance.

Q. The first floor?

DR. KEMP: The ground floor.

Q. How many doctors and nurses were in attendance
at the time of death?

DR. PERRY: There were at least eight or ten
physicians at that time.

MORE

Transcript of Parkland Press Conference, 3:16 P.M., 22 November 1963

Q. At least eight or ten physicians?

DR. PERRY: Yes.

Q. Did you think him mortally wounded at the time you first examined him, or did you think there was no possibility of saving his life at that point?

DR. PERRY: No, I did not.

DR. CLARK: No, sir.

Q. Did you say there were eight or ten doctors or doctors and nurses?

DR. CLARK: Eight or ten doctors.

Q. Can we get that straight, Doctor? Did you say you did not think there was any possibility of saving his life when you first looked at him?

DR. CLARK: That is what I said; yes.

Q. How long had he been in before you saw him, sir?

DR. CLARK: This I don't know because I was not looking at my watch.

Q. Who was the first doctor who saw him, and how long before he got there?

DR. CLARK: Just a matter of a few seconds.

DR. PERRY: I arrived there shortly after his admission. I can't tell you the exact time because I went immediately and he had just been admitted and I walked in the room. I don't know the exact time. I was in quite a hurry.

Q. Were any members of the family or others in the room besides the doctors, in the Emergency Room?

DR. PERRY: I am afraid I was not aware of that. I was quite too busy to notice.

MR. HAWKS: We will have to get those details from Mac.

Q. Do you have any new details about our plans, what you are going to do?

MR. HAWKS: I can't until I get a reading from you fellows. For instance, you have a new President.

Q. Do we? Was he sworn in?

MR. HAWKS: Well, he went somewhere to get sworn in. I assume he is sworn in at this time, but I wasn't in attendance. Obviously, you are going to have a new President. Let's put it that way.

                    MORE

Transcript of Parkland Press Conference, 3:16 P.M., 22 November 1963

Page 9 - #1327-C

Q. Where is he going to be?

B - 9

MR. HAWKS: That is what I am trying to find out. Mac is with him, trying to get the details, and he will call me or come in here. We will try to find out.

DR. PERRY: Can we go now?

THE PRESS: Thank you, Doctors.

MR. HAWKS: Your plans, what do you want to do?

Q. First, is there anything more about Mrs. Kennedy?

MR. HAWKS: Let's do some "supposing" because we need some planning for your press plane.

Q. How about Mrs. Kennedy? Has she gone back to Washington, or is she going?

MR. HAWKS: That is what Mac is trying to find out now. This takes a lot of doing.

Q. Can we stay here with the new President?

MR. HAWKS: If you want to stay here with the new President, if he stays here. I don't know that he is going to stay here. That is why I want to "suppose" here for a minute.

Q. Let's put it on the basis of what the new President does. If he stays, we stay; and if he goes, we go.

MR. HAWKS: Suppose the body goes back and the new President stays? Do some of you want to stay, or go?

Q. Stay with the new President.

MR. HAWKS: All right, that is what I wanted to find out. You know, there are buses and planes and things like that.

Q. I know I won't be going back in any case. Can I get my luggage back here? How do we get luggage on the press plane off of there?

MR. HAWKS: If we decide to spend the night here, we will get the luggage here. Don't worry about it.

Q. We have luggage in the wire car, but God knows where it is.

Q. Where will the next briefing be, here or where?

MR. HAWKS: Right here, so far as I know. This is where Mac said he could come back to.

END

Transcript of Parkland Press Conference, 3:16 P.M., 22 November 1963

STATE OF TEXAS — CERTIFICATE OF DEATH — STATE FILE NO.

1. PLACE OF DEATH
a. COUNTY: Dallas
b. CITY OR TOWN (if outside city limits, give precinct no.): Dallas
c. LENGTH OF STAY: 2 Hrs.
d. NAME OF HOSPITAL OR INSTITUTION: Parkland Memorial
e. IS PLACE OF DEATH INSIDE CITY LIMITS? YES X NO

2. USUAL RESIDENCE (where deceased lived. If institution, residence before admission)
a. STATE: District of Columbia
b. COUNTY
c. CITY OR TOWN (if outside city limits, give precinct no.): Washington
d. STREET ADDRESS (if rural, give location): 1600 Pennsylvania Avenue
e. IS RESIDENCE INSIDE CITY LIMITS? YES X NO
f. IS RESIDENCE ON A FARM? YES NO X

3. NAME OF DECEASED (Type or print)
(a) First: John
(b) Middle: Fitzgerald
(c) Last: Kennedy
4. DATE OF DEATH: November 22, 1963

5. SEX: Male
6. COLOR OR RACE: White
7. Married X / Never Married / Widowed / Divorced
8. DATE OF BIRTH: May 29, 1917
9. AGE (In years): 46
10. USUAL OCCUPATION: President of the U.S.
10a. KIND OF BUSINESS OR INDUSTRY: United States Govt.
11. BIRTHPLACE (State or foreign country): Brookline, Mass.
12. CITIZEN OF WHAT COUNTRY? U. S. A.

13. FATHER'S NAME: Joseph P. Kennedy
14. MOTHER'S MAIDEN NAME: Rose Fitzgerald

15. WAS DECEASED EVER IN U.S. ARMED FORCES? YES
16. SOCIAL SECURITY NO.: WW II
17. INFORMANT: Evelyn Lincoln

18. CAUSE OF DEATH
PART I. DEATH WAS CAUSED BY:
IMMEDIATE CAUSE (a): Multiple gunshot wounds of the head & neck.
INTERVAL BETWEEN ONSET AND DEATH: Minutes
DUE TO (b):
DUE TO (c):
PART II. OTHER SIGNIFICANT CONDITIONS CONTRIBUTING TO DEATH BUT NOT RELATED TO THE TERMINAL DISEASE CONDITION GIVEN IN PART (a)
19. WAS AUTOPSY PERFORMED? YES X NO

20a. ACCIDENT / SUICIDE / HOMICIDE: XX
20b. DESCRIBE HOW INJURY OCCURRED: Shot by a high powered rifle
20c. TIME OF INJURY: 12:31 Hour / 11 Month / 22 Day / 63 Year
20d. INJURY OCCURRED:
20e. PLACE OF INJURY: 400 Blk Elm St. Dallas, Tex
20f. CITY, TOWN, OR LOCATION: Dallas
COUNTY: Dallas
STATE: Texas

21. I hereby certify that ... November 22, 1963 ... Death occurred at 1.00 P.M. ... Held Inquest
22a. SIGNATURE: (signed) J.P.
22b. ADDRESS: 305 N. 5th St. - Garland, Texas
22c. DATE SIGNED: 12-6-63

23a. BURIAL, CREMATION, REMOVAL: Removal
23b. DATE: 11-22-63
23c. NAME OF CEMETERY OR CREMATORY: Arlington National Cemetery
24. LOCATION (City, town, or county): Washington, D.C.
24. FUNERAL DIRECTOR'S SIGNATURE: O'Neal Inc.
25a. REGISTRAR'S FILE NO.: 6820
25b. DATE REC'D BY LOCAL REGISTRAR: Dec. 11, 1963
BY: Acting Registrar

Signed State of Texas Certificate of Death for John Fitzgerald Kennedy

JUSTICE'S INQUEST DOCKET:

IN THE JUSTICE'S COURT, PRECINCT NO.   INQUEST NO.   110

DALLAS COUNTY, TEXAS

IN THE MATTER OF THE INQUISITION UPON THE BODY OF

John Fitzgerald Kennedy   DECEASED

CERTIFICATE OF DEATH

Dallas	District of Columbia	Austin, Mass.
Dallas	Washington	
Parkland Hospital	1600 Penn Ave. N.W.	
John	Fitzgerald	Kennedy	November 22, 1963
Male	White	May 28, 1917	46
President of the U.S.	U.S. Government	Brookline, Mass.	U.S.A.
Joseph P. Kennedy		Rose Fitzgerald	
026-22-3747		Evelyn Lincoln	

Multiple gunshot wounds
of the head and neck   Minutes

Shot by unknown assassin with
high powered rifle

El "St. W.M. of 400 Elm St. Dallas, Tex.   Dallas   Dallas   Texas
November 22

305 N. 5th St. Garland, Texas 12.0.41

| Removal | Nov. 22, 1963 | Arlington National Cemetery |
| Arlington | Virginia | O'Neal Inc. |

FINDINGS BY THE JUSTICE

I, ... Justice of the Peace, Precinct No. 1,
.... Dallas .... County, Texas, after viewing the dead body of ....
.... John Fitzgerald Kennedy .... and hearing the evidence,
find that ... he came to his death as the result of ... Two gunshot wounds ....
..... (1) Near the center of the body and just above the right shoulder. ....
..... (2) One inch to the right center of the back of the head ....

Witness my hand officially, this the ...4th... day of ... December .... A. D. 1963

....
Justice of the Peace, Precinct No. 1
.... Dallas .... County, Tx

Unsigned State of Texas Certificate of Death for John Fitzgerald Kennedy

Autopsy Report and Supplemental Report

Standard Form 503
Revised August 1954
Promulgated
By Bureau of the Budget
Circular A—32 (Rev.)

CLINICAL RECORD			AUTOPSY PROTOCOL	A63-272 (JJH: ec)	
DATE AND HOUR DIED		A.M.	DATE AND HOUR AUTOPSY PERFORMED	A.M.	CHECK ONE
22 November 1963 1300(CST)		P.M.	22 November 1963 2000(EST)	M.	FULL AUTOPSY / HEAD ONLY / TRUNK O
PROSECTOR (497831)			ASSISTANT (439378)		
CDR J. J. HUMES, MC, USN			CDR "J" THORNTON BOSWELL, MC, USN X		
CLINICAL DIAGNOSES (Including operations)			LCOL PIERRE A. FINCK, MC, USA (04 043 322)		

Ht. - 72½ inches
Wt. - 170 pounds
Eyes - blue
Hair - Reddish brown

PATHOLOGICAL DIAGNOSES

CAUSE OF DEATH: Gunshot wound, head.

APPROVED SIGNATURE

J. J. HUMES, CDR, MC, USN

MILITARY ORGANIZATION (When required)	AGE	SEX	RACE	IDENTIFICATION NO.	AUTOPSY NO.
PRESIDENT, UNITED STATES	46	Male	Cauc.		A63-272
PATIENT'S IDENTIFICATION (For typed or written entries give: Name—last, first, middle; grade; date; hospital or medical facility)				REGISTER NO.	WARD NO.

KENNEDY, JOHN F.
NAVAL MEDICAL SCHOOL.

AUTOPSY PROTOCO
Standard Form 50

Bethesda Naval Hospital Report of Autopsy on John Fitzgerald Kennedy

PATHOLOGICAL EXAMINATION REPORT   A63-272   Page 2

CLINICAL SUMMARY: According to available information the
                                         deceased, President John F. Kennedy,
was riding in an open car in a motorcade during an official visit to Dallas, Texas
on 22 November 1963. The President was sitting in the right rear seat with Mrs.
Kennedy seated on the same seat to his left. Sitting directly in front of the
President was Governor John B. Connolly of Texas and directly in front of Mrs. Kennedy
sat Mrs. Connolly. The vehicle was moving at a slow rate of speed down an incline
into an underpass that leads to a freeway route to the Dallas Trade Mart whenetthe
President was to deliver an address.

                                         Three shots were heard and the President
fell forward bleeding from the head. (Governor Connolly was seriously wounded by the
same gunfire.) According to newspaper reports ("Washington Post" November 23, 1963)
Bob Jackson, a Dallas "Times Herald"Photographer, said he looked around as he heard
the shots and saw a rifle barrel disappearing into a window on an upper floor of the
nearby Texas School Book Depository Building.

                                         Shortly following the wounding of the two
men the car was driven to Parkland Hospital in Dallas. In the emergency room of that
hospital the President was attended by Dr. Malcolm Perry. Telephone communication witl
Dr. Perry on November 23, 1963 develops the following information relative to the observations made by Dr. Perry and procedures performed there prior to death.

                                         Dr. Perry noted the massive wound of the
head and a second much smaller wound of the low anterior neck in approximately the
midline. A tracheostomy was performed by extending the latter wound. At this point
bloody air was noted bubbling from the wound and an injury to the right lateral wall
of the trachea was observed. Incisions were made in the upper anterior chest wall
bilaterally to combat possible subcutaneous emphysema. Intravenous infusions of blood
and saline were begun and oxygen was administered. Despite these measures cardiac
arrest occurred and closed chest cardiac massage failed to re-establish cardiac action.
The President was pronounced dead approximately thirty to forty minutes after receiving
his wounds.

                                         The remains were transported via the
Presidential plane to Washington, D.C. and subsequently to the Naval Medical School,
National Naval Medical Center, Bethesda, Maryland for postmortem examination.

GENERAL DESCRIPTION OF BODY: The body is that of a muscular, well-
                                         developed and well nourished adult Caucasia
male measuring 72½ inches and weighing approximately 170 pounds. There is beginning
rigor mortis, minimal dependent livor mortis of the dorsum, and early algor mortis. The
hair is reddish brown and abundant, the eyes are blue, the right pupil measuring 8 mm.
in diameter, the left 4 mm. There is edema and ecchymosis of the inner canthus region
of the left eyelid measuring approximately 1.5 cm. in greatest diameter. There is edem
and ecchymosis diffusely over the right supra-orbital ridge with abnormal mobility of
the underlying bone. (The remainder of the scalp will be described with the skull.)

Bethesda Naval Hospital Report of Autopsy on John Fitzgerald Kennedy

There is clotted blood on the external ears but otherwise the ears, nares, and mouth are essentially unremarkable. The teeth are in excellent repair and there is some pallor of the oral mucous membrane.

Situated on the upper right posterior thorax just above the upper border of the scapula there is a 7 x 4 millimeter oval wound. This wound is measured to be 14 cm. from the tip of the right acromion process and 14 cm. below the tip of the right mastoid process.

Situated in the low anterior neck at approximately the level of the third and fourth tracheal rings is a 6.5 cm. long transverse wound with widely gaping irregular edges. (The depth and character of these wounds wil be further described below.)

Situated on the anterior chest wall in the nipple line are bilateral 2 cm. long recent transverse surgical incisions into the subcutaneous tissue. The one on the left is situated 11 cm. cephalad to the nipple and the one on the right 8 cm. cephalad to the nipple. There is no hemorrhage or ecchymosis associated with these wounds. A similar clean wound measuring 2 cm. in length is situated on the antero-lateral aspect of the left mid arm. Situated on the antero-lateral aspect of each ankle is a recent 2 cm. transverse incision into the subcutaneous tissue.

There is an old well healed 8 cm. McBurney abdominal incision. Over the lumbar spine in the midline is an old, well healed 15 cm. scar. Situated on the upper antero-lateral aspect of the right thigh is an old, well healed 8 cm. scar.

MISSILE WOUNDS: 1. There is a large irregular defect of the scalp and skull on the right involving chiefly the parietal bone but extending somewhat into the temporal and occipital regions. In this region there is an actual absence of scalp and bone producing a defect which measures approximately 13 cm. in greatest diameter.

From the irregular margins of the above scalp defect tears extend in stellate fashion into the more or less intact scalp as follows:

   a. From the right inferior temporo-parietal margin anterior to the right ear to a point slightly above the tragus.

   b. From the anterior parietal margin anteriorly on the forehead to approximately 4 cm. above the right orbital ridge.

   c. From the left margin of the main defect across the midline antero-laterally for a distance of approximately 8 cm.

   d. From the same starting point as c. 10 cm. postero-laterally.

Situated in the posterior scalp approximately 2.5 cm. laterally to the right and
slightly above the external occipital protuberance is a lacerated wound measuring
15 x 6 mm. In the underlying bone is a corresponding wound through the skull which
exhibits beveling of the margins of the bone when viewed from the inner aspect of
the skull.

Clearly visible in the above described
large skull defect and exuding from it is lacerated brain tissue which on close
inspection proves to represent the major portion of the right cerebral hemisphere.
At this point it is noted that the falx cerebri is extensively lacerated with disruption of the superior saggital sinus.

Upon reflecting the scalp multiple complete
fracture lines are seen to radiate from both the large defect at the vertex and the
smaller wound at the occiput. These vary greatly in length and direction, the longest
measuring approximately 19 cm. These result in the production of numerous fragments
which vary in size from a few millimeters to 10 cm. in greatest diameter.

The complexity of these fractures and the
fragments thus produced tax satisfactory verbal description and are better appreciated
in photographs and roentgenograms which are prepared.

The brain is removed and preserved for
further study following formalin fixation.

Received as separate specimens from Dallas,
Texas are three fragments of skull bone which in aggregate roughly approximate the
dimensions of the large defect described above. At one angle of the largest of these
fragments is a portion of the perimeter of a roughly circular wound presumably of
exit which exhibits beveling of the outer aspect of the bone and is estimated to
measure approximately 2.5 to 3.0 cm. in diameter. Roentgenograms of this fragment
reveal·minute particles of metal in the bone at this margin. Roentgenograms of the
skull reveal multiple minute metallic fragments along a line corresponding with a line
joining the above described small occipital wound and the right supra-orbital ridge.
From the surface of the disrupted right cerebral cortex two small irregularly shaped
fragments of metal are recovered. These measure 7 x 2 mm. and 3 x 1 mm. These are
placed in the custody of Agents Francis X. O'Neill, Jr. and James W. Sibert, of the
Federal Bureau of Investigation, who executed a receipt therefor (attached).

2. The second wound presumably of entry
is that described above in the upper right posterior thorax. Beneath the skin there
is ecchymosis of subcutaneous tissue and musculature. The missile path through the
fascia and musculature cannot be easily probed. The wound presumably of exit was
that described by Dr. Malcolm Perry of Dallas in the low anterior cervical region.
When observed by Dr. Perry the wound measured "a few millimeters in diameter", however it was extended as a tracheostomy incision and thus its character is distorted
at the time of autopsy. However, there is considerable ecchymosis of the strap
muscles of the right side of the neck and of the fascia about the trachea adjacent
to the line of the tracheostomy wound. The third point of reference in connecting

Bethesda Naval Hospital Report of Autopsy on John Fitzgerald Kennedy

these two wounds is in the apex (supra-clavicular portion) of the right pleural cavity. In this region there is contusion of the parietal pleura and of the extreme apical portion of the right upper lobe of the lung. In both instances the diameter of contusion and ecchymosis at the point of maximal involvement measures 5 cm. Both the visceral and parietal pleura are intact overlying these areas of trauma.

INCISIONS: The scalp wounds are extended in the coronal
                                          plane to examine the cranial content and the
customary (Y) shaped incision is used to examine the body cavities.

THORACIC CAVITY: The bony cage is unremarkable. The thoracic
                                          organs are in their normal positions and re-
lationships and there is no increase in free pleural fluid. The above described area
of contusion in the apical portion of the right pleural cavity is noted.

LUNGS: The lungs are of essentially similar ap-
                                          pearance the right weighing 320 Gm., the
left 290 Gm. The lungs are well aerated with smooth glistening pleural surfaces and
gray-pink color. A 5 cm. diameter area of purplish red discoloration and increased
firmness to palpation is situated in the apical portion of the right upper lobe.
This corresponds to the similar area described in the overlying parietal pleura.
Incision in this region reveals recent hemorrhage into pulmonary parenchyma.

HEART: The pericardial cavity is smooth walled
                                          and contains approximately 10 cc. of straw-
colored fluid. The heart is of essentially normal external contour and weighs 350 Gm.
The pulmonary artery is opened in situ and no abnormalities are noted. The cardiac
chambers contain moderate amounts of postmortem clotted blood. There are no gross
abnormalities of the leaflets of any of the cardiac valves. The following are the
circumferences of the cardiac valves: aortic 7.5 cm., pulmonic 7 cm., tricuspid
12 cm., mitral 11 cm. The myocardium is firm and reddish brown. The left ventricular
myocardium averages 1.2 cm. in thickness, the right ventricular myocardium 0.4 cm.
The coronary arteries are dissected and are of normal distribution and smooth walled
and elastic throughout.

ABDOMINAL CAVITY: The abdominal organs are in their normal
                                          positions and relationships and there is
no increase in free peritoneal fluid. The vermiform appendix is surgically absent
and there are a few adhesions joining the region of the cecum to the ventral abdominal wall at the above described old abdominal incisional scar.

SKELETAL SYSTEM: Aside from the above described skull wounds
                                          there are no significant gross skeletal
abnormalities.

PHOTOGRAPHY: Black and white and color photographs
                                          depicting significant findings are exposed
but not developed. These photographs were placed in the custody of Agent Roy H.
Kellerman of the U. S. Secret Service, who executed a receipt therefore (attached).

PATHOLOGICAL EXAMINATION REPORT   A63-272   Page 6

ROENTGENOGRAMS: Roentgenograms are made of the entire body
                                         and of the separately submitted three
fragments of skull bone. These are developed and were placed in the custody of
Agent Roy H. Kellerman of the U. S. Secret Service, who executed a receipt therefor
(attached).

SUMMARY: Based on the above observations it is our
                                         opinion that the deceased died as a result
of two perforating gunshot wounds inflicted by high velocity projectiles fired by a
person or persons unknown. The projectiles were fired from a point behind and somewhat above the level of the deceased. The observations and available information
do not permit a satisfactory estimate as to the sequence of the two wounds.

                                         The fatal missile entered the skull above
and to the right of the external occipital protuberance. A portion of the projectile
traversed the cranial cavity in a posterior-anterior direction (see lateral skull
roentgenograms) depositing minute particles along its path. A portion of the projectile made its exit through the parietal bone on the right carrying with it
portions of cerebrum, skull and scalp. The two wounds of the skull combined with
the force of the missile produced extensive fragmentation of the skull, laceration of
the superior saggital sinus, and of the right cerebral hemisphere.

                                         The other missile entered the right superior
posterior thorax above the scapula and traversed the soft tissues of the supra-scap-
ular and the supra-clavicular portions of the base of the right side of the neck.
This missile produced contusions of the right apical parietal pleura and of the apical
portion of the right upper lobe of the lung. The missile contused the strap muscles
of the right side of the neck, damaged the trachea and made its exit through the
anterior surface of the neck. As far as can be ascertained this missile struck no
bony structures in its path through the body.

                                         In addition, it is our opinion that the
wound of the skull produced such extensive damage to the brain as to preclude the
possibility of the deceased surviving this injury.

                                         A supplementary report will be submitted
following more detailed examination of the brain and of microscopic sections. However,
it is not anticipated that these examinations will materially alter the findings.

J. J. HUMES   "J" THORNTON BOSWELL   PIERRE A. FINCK
CDR, MC, USN (497831)   CDR, MC, USN (489878)   LT COL, MC, USA
                                                                     (04-043-322)

Bethesda Naval Hospital Report of Autopsy on John Fitzgerald Kennedy

Commission Exhibit No. 391

122

11/6/63

SUPPLEMENTARY REPORT OF AUTOPSY NUMBER A63-272
PRESIDENT JOHN F. KENNEDY

PATHOLOGICAL EXAMINATION REPORT   No. A63-272   Page 1

GROSS DESCRIPTION OF BRAIN: Following formalin fixation the brain weighs 1500 gms. The right cerebral hemisphere is found to be markedly disrupted. There is a longitudinal laceration of the right hemisphere which is para-sagittal in position approximately 2.5 cm. to the right of the midline which extends from the tip of the occipital lobe posteriorly to the tip of the frontal lobe anteriorly. The base of the laceration is situated approximately 4.5 cm. below the vertex in the white matter. There is considerable loss of cortical substance above the base of the laceration, particularly in the parietal lobe. The margins of this laceration are at all points jagged and irregular, with additional lacerations extending in varying directions and for varying distances from the main laceration. In addition, there is a laceration of the corpus callosum extending from the genu to the tail. Exposed in this latter laceration are the interiors of the right lateral and third ventricles.

       When viewed from the vertex the left cerebral hemisphere is intact. There is marked engorgement of meningeal blood vessels of the left temporal and frontal regions with considerable associated sub-arachnoid hemorrhage. The gyri and sulci over the left hemisphere are of essentially normal size and distribution. Those on the right are too fragmented and distorted for satisfactory description.

       When viewed from the basilar aspect the disruption of the right cortex is again obvious. There is a longitudinal laceration of the mid-brain through the floor of the third ventricle just behind the optic chiasm and the mammillary bodies. This laceration partially communicates with an oblique 1.5 cm. tear through the left cerebral peduncle. There are irregular superficial lacerations over the basilar aspects of the left temporal and frontal lobes.

       In the interest of preserving the specimen coronal sections are not made. The following sections are taken for microscopic examination:

     a. From the margin of the laceration in the right parietal lobe.

     b. From the margin of the laceration in the corpus callosum.

     c. From the anterior portion of the laceration in the right frontal lobe.

     d. From the contused left fronto-parietal cortex.

     e. From the line of transection of the spinal cord.

     f. From the right cerebellar cortex.

     g. From the superficial laceration of the basilar aspect of the left temporal lobe.

Supplementary Report of Autopsy on John Fitzgerald Kennedy

PATHOLOGICAL EXAMINATION REPORT   No. A63-272   Page 2

During the course of this examination to
seven (7) black and white and six (6) color 4x5 inch negatives are exposed but not developed (the cassettes containing these negatives have been delivered by hand to GEB Rear Admiral George W. Burkley, MC, USN, White House Physician).

MICROSCOPIC EXAMINATION:

BRAIN: Multiple sections from representative areas as noted above are examined. All sections are essentially similar and show extensive disruption of brain tissue with associated hemorrhage. In none of the sections examined are there significant abnormalities other than those directly related to the recent trauma.

HEART: Sections show a moderate amount of subepicardial fat. The coronary arteries, myocardial fibers, and endocardium are unremarkable.

LUNGS: Sections through the grossly described area of contusion in the right upper lobe exhibit disruption of alveolar walls and recent hemorrhage into alveoli. Sections are otherwise essentially unremarkable.

LIVER: Sections show the normal hepatic architecture to be well preserved. The parenchymal cells exhibit markedly granular cytoplasm indicating high glycogen content which is characteristic of the "liver biopsy pattern" of sudden death.

SPLEEN: Sections show no significant abnormalities.

KIDNEYS: Sections show no significant abnormalities aside from dilatation and engorgement of blood vessels of all calibers.

SKIN WOUNDS: Sections through the wounds in the occipital and upper right posterior thoracic regions are essentially similar. In each there is loss of continuity of the epidermis with coagulation necrosis of the tissues at the wound margins. The scalp wound exhibits several small fragments of bone at its margins in the subcutaneous tissue.

FINAL SUMMARY: This supplementary report covers in more detail the extensive degree of cerebral trauma in this case. However neither this portion of the examination nor the microscopic examinations alter the previously submitted report or add significant details to the cause of death.

J. J. HUMES
CDR, MC, USN, 497831

Supplementary Report of Autopsy on John Fitzgerald Kennedy

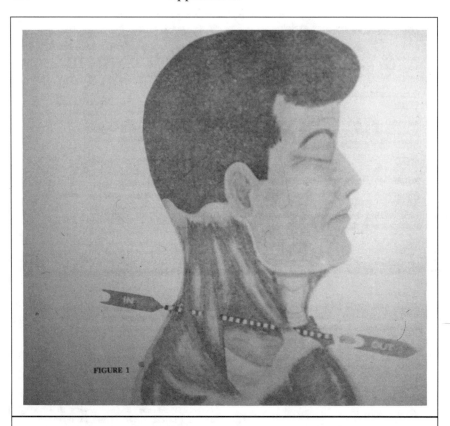

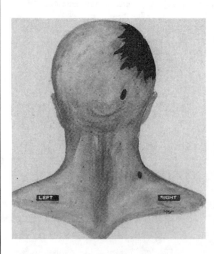

Warren Commission Diagrams of JFK Wounds

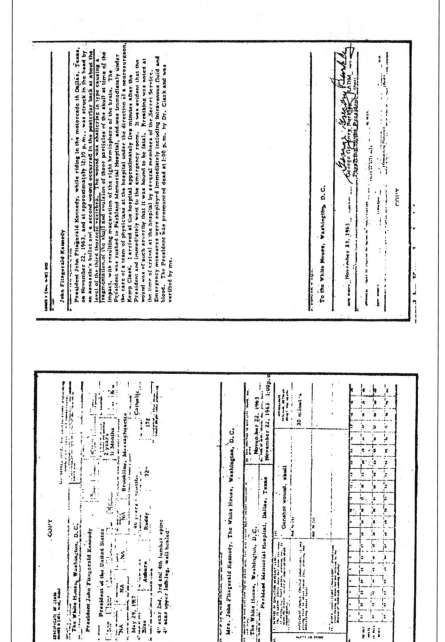

Certificate of Death for JFK prepared by Admiral George G. Burkley

Dr. Perry: "DR HUMES CALLED ME TWICE ON FRIDAY
AFTERNOON, SEPARATED BY ABOUT 30-MINUTE
INTERVALS, AS I RECALL. THE FIRST ONE, I,
SOMEHOW THINK I RECALL THE FIRST ONE MUST HAVE
BEEN AROUND 1500 HOURS, BUT I'M NOT REAL SURE
ABOUT THAT; I'M NOT POSITIVE ABOUT THAT AT ALL,
ACTUALLY."

Mr. Specter: "COULD IT HAVE BEEN SATURDAY MORNING?"

Dr. Perry: "SATURDAY MORNING-WAS IT? IT'S POSSIBLE. I
REMEMBER TALKING WITH HIM TWICE. I WAS THINKING
SHORTLY THEREAFTER."

Mr. Specter: "WELL, THE RECORD WILL SHOW."

Dr. Perry: "OH, SURE, IT WAS SATURDAY MORNING-YES."

Mr. Specter: "WHAT MADE YOU CHANGE YOUR VIEW OF THAT?"

Dr. Perry: "YOU MEAN FRIDAY?"

Mr. Specter: "DID SOME SPECIFIC RECOLLECTION OCCUR TO
YOU WHICH CHANGED YOUR VIEW FROM FRIDAY TO
SATURDAY?"

Dr. Perry: "NO, I WAS TRYING TO PLACE WHERE I WAS AT
THAT TIME-FRIDAY AFTERNOON, AND AT THAT
PARTICULAR TIME, WHEN I PAUSED TO THINK ABOUT
IT, I WAS ACTUALLY UP IN THE OPERATING SUITE AT
THAT TIME, WHEN I THOUGHT THAT HE CALLED
INITIALLY. I SEEM TO REMEMBER IT BEING FRIDAY,
FOR SOME REASON."

Mr. Specter: "WHERE WERE YOU WHEN YOU RECEIVED THOSE
CALLS?"

Dr. Perry: "I WAS IN THE ADMINISTRATOR'S OFFICE HERE
WHEN HE CALLED."

Mr. Specter: "AND WHAT DID HE ASK YOU, IF ANYTHING?"

Dr. Perry: "HE INQUIRED ABOUT, INITALLY, ABOUT THE
REASONS FOR MY DOING A TRACHEOTOMY, AND I
REPLIED, AS I HAVE TO YOU, DURING THIS
PROCEDURE, THAT THERE WAS A WOUND IN THE LOWER
ANTERIOR THIRD OF THE NECK, WHICH WAS EXUDING
BLOOD AND WAS INDICATIVE OF A POSSIBLE TRACHEAL
INJURY UNDERLYING, AND I DID THE TRACHEOTOMY
THROUGH A TRANSVERSE INCISION MADE THROUGH THAT
WOUND, AND I DESCRIBED TO HIM THE LATERAL INJURY
TO THE TRACHEA AND THE COMPLETION OF THE
OPERATION. HE SUBSEQUENTLY CALLED BACK-AT THAT
TIME HE TOLD ME, OF COURSE, THAT HE COULD NOT
TALK TO ME ABOUT ANY OF IT AND ASKED THAT I KEEP
IT IN CONFIDENCE, WHICH I DID, AND HE
SUBSEQUENTLY CALLED BACK AND INQUIRED ABOUT THE
CHEST TUBES, AND WHY THEY WERE PLACED AND I
REPLIED IN PART AS I HAVE HERE. ...HE ASKED ME
AT THAT TIME IF WE HAD MADE ANY WOUNDS IN THE
BACK. I TOLD HIM THAT I HAD NOT EXAMINED THE
BACK NOR HAD I KNOWLEDGE OF ANY WOUNDS TO THE
BACK." (6H16)

Partial Transcript of Warren Commission Testimony of Malcolm Perry, M.D.

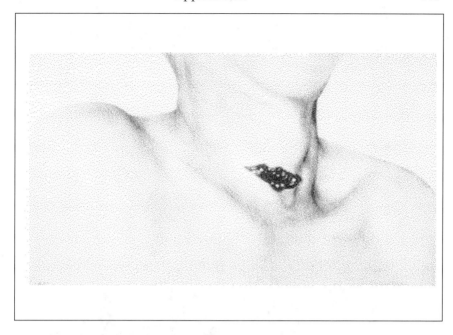

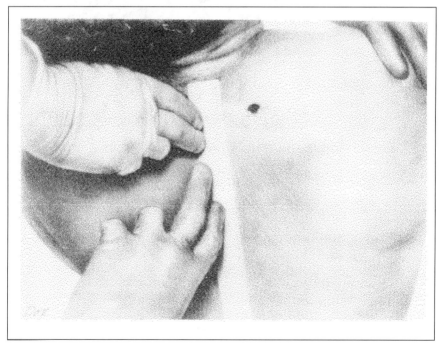

House Select Committee on Assassinations JFK Autopsy Drawings

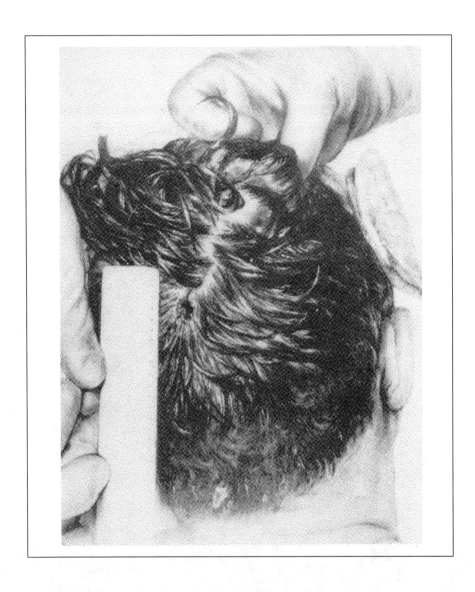

House Select Committee on Assassinations JFK Autopsy Drawings

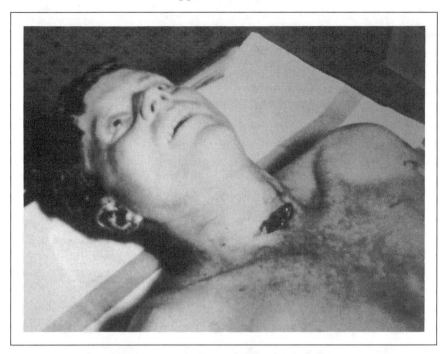

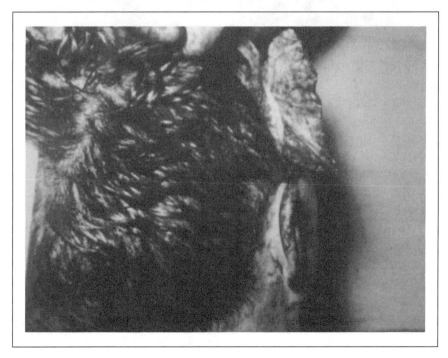

JFK Autopsy Photographs Corresponding to HSCA JFK Autopsy Drawings

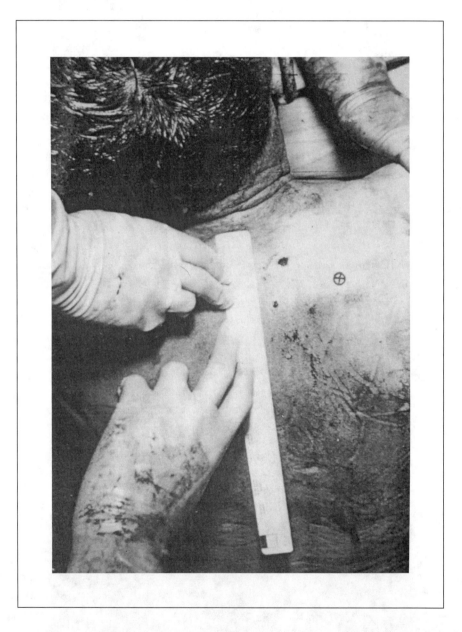

[*Editor's note*: The "circle-x" mark identifies the location of the back wound as specified by the HSCA. See also pages 16, 34, 157-158, 177, 438, and 441.]

JFK Autopsy Photographs Corresponding to HSCA JFK Autopsy Drawings

DISPATCH

CLASSIFICATION	PROCESSING ACTION
	MARKED FOR INDEXING
Chiefs, Certain Stations and Bases	X NO INDEXING REQUIRED
Document Number 1035-960	ONLY QUALIFIED DESK CAN JUDGE INDEXING
for FOIA Review on SEP 1976	MICROFILM

SUBJECT

Countering Criticism of the Warren Report

ACTION REQUIRED · REFERENCES

Oswald for Oswald file 2 class — This was pulled together by in close conjunction with (who the source material), preparation of the themes, and provided general "expertise" on the case. The specific article was written

PSYCH

1. **Our Concern.** From the day of President Kennedy's assassination on, there has been speculation about the responsibility for his murder. Although this was stemmed for a time by the Warren Commission report (which appeared at the end of September 1964), various writers have now had time to scan the Commission's published report and documents for new pretexts for questioning, and there has been a new wave of books and articles criticizing the Commission's findings. In most cases the critics have speculated as to the existence of some kind of conspiracy, and often they have implied that the Commission itself was involved. Presumably as a result of the increasing challenge to the Warren Commission's Report, a public opinion poll recently indicated that 46% of the American public did not think that Oswald acted alone, while more than half of those polled thought that the Commission had left some questions unresolved. Doubtless polls abroad would show similar, or possibly more adverse, results.

2. This trend of opinion is a matter of concern to the U.S. government, including our organization. The members of the Warren Commission were naturally chosen for their integrity, experience, and prominence. They represented both major parties, and they and their staff were deliberately drawn from all sections of the country. Just because of the standing of the Commissioners, efforts to impugn their rectitude and wisdom tend to cast doubt on the whole leadership of American society. Moreover, there seems to be an increasing tendency to hint that President Johnson himself, as the one person who might be said to have benefited, was in some way responsible for the assassination. Innuendo of such seriousness affects not only the individual concerned, but also the whole reputation of the American government. Our organization itself is directly involved: among other facts, we contributed information to the investigation. Conspiracy theories have frequently thrown suspicion on our organization, for example by falsely alleging that Lee Harvey Oswald worked for us. The aim of this dispatch is to provide material for countering and discrediting the claims of the conspiracy theorists, so as to inhibit the circulation of such claims in other countries. Background information is supplied in a classified section and in a number of unclassified attachments.

3. **Action.** We do not recommend that discussion of the assassination question be initiated where it is not already taking place. Where discussion is active, however, addressees are requested:

CS COPY.

DISPATCH SYMBOL AND NUMBER	DATE
	4/1/67
9 attachments h/w	

CLASSIFICATION	HQS FILE NUMBER
1 -	DESTROY WHEN NO LONGER NEEDED
8 - Unclassified	

CIA Dispatch, "Countering Criticism of the Warren Report", 1 April 1967

CONTINUATION OF DISPATCH

a. To discuss the publicity problem with liaison and friendly elite contacts (especially politicians and editors), pointing out that the Warren Commission made as thorough an investigation as humanly possible, that the charges of the critics are without serious foundation, and that further speculative discussion only plays into the hands of the opposition. Point out also that parts of the conspiracy talk appear to be deliberately generated by Communist propagandists. Urge them to use their influence to discourage unfounded and irresponsible speculation.

b. To employ propaganda assets to answer and refute the attacks of the critics. Book reviews and feature articles are particularly appropriate for this purpose. The unclassified attachments to this guidance should provide useful background material for passage to assets. Our play should point out, as applicable, that the critics are (i) wedded to theories adopted before the evidence was in, (ii) politically interested, (iii) financially interested, (iv) hasty and inaccurate in their research, or (v) infatuated with their own theories. In the course of discussions of the whole phenomenon of criticism, a useful strategy may be to single out Epstein's theory for attack, using the attached Fletcher Knebel article and Spectator piece for background. (Although Mark Lane's book is much less convincing than Epstein's and comes off badly where contested by knowledgeable critics, it is also much more difficult to answer as a whole, as one becomes lost in a morass of unrelated details.)

4. In private or media discussion not directed at any particular writer, or in attacking publications which may be yet forthcoming, the following arguments should be useful:

a. No significant new evidence has emerged which the Commission did not consider. The assassination is sometimes compared (e.g., by Joachim Joesten and Bertrand Russell) with the Dreyfus case; however, unlike that case, the attacks on the Warren Commission have produced no new evidence, no new culprits have been convincingly identified, and there is no agreement among the critics. (A better parallel, though an imperfect one, might be with the Reichstag fire of 1933, which some competent historians (Fritz Tobias, A.J.P. Taylor, D.C. Watt) now believe was set by Van der Lubbe on his own initiative, without acting for either Nazis or Communists; the Nazis tried to pin the blame on the Communists, but the latter have been much more successful in convincing the world that the Nazis were to blame.)

b. Critics usually overvalue particular items and ignore others. They tend to place more emphasis on the recollections of individual eyewitnesses (which are less reliable and more divergent -- and hence offer more hand-holds for criticism) and less on ballistic, autopsy, and photographic evidence. A close examination of the Commission's records will usually show that the conflicting eyewitness accounts are quoted out of context, or were discarded by the Commission for good and sufficient reason.

c. Conspiracy on the large scale often suggested would be impossible to conceal in the United States, esp. since informants could expect to receive large royalties, etc. Note that Robert Kennedy, Attorney General at the time and John F. Kennedy's brother, would be the last man to overlook or conceal any conspiracy. And as one reviewer moreover pointed out, Congressman Gerald R. Ford would hardly have held his tongue for the sake of the Democratic administration, and Senator Russell would have had every political interest in exposing any misdeeds on the part of Chief Justice Warren. A conspirator moreover would hardly choose a location for a shooting where so much depended on conditions beyond his control: the route, the speed of the cars, the moving target, the risk that the assassin would be discovered. A group of wealthy conspirators could have arranged much more secure conditions.

d. Critics have often been enticed by a form of intellectual pride: they light on some theory and fall in love with it; they also scoff at the Commission because it did not always answer every question with a flat decision one way or the other. Actually, the make-up of the Commission and its staff was

CIA Dispatch, "Countering Criticism of the Warren Report", 1 April 1967

CONTINUATION OF DISPATCH	CLASSIFICATION	DISPATCH SYMBOL AND NUMBER

c. Oswald would not have been any sensible person's choice for a co-conspirator. He was a "loner," mixed-up, of questionable reliability and an unknown quantity to any professional intelligence service.

f. As to charges that the Commission's report was a rush job, it emerged three months after the deadline originally set. But to the degree that the Commission tried to speed up its reporting, this was largely due to the pressure of irresponsible speculation already appearing, in some cases coming from the same critics who, refusing to admit their errors, are now putting out new criticisms.

g. Such vague accusations as that "more than ten people have died mysteriously" can always be explained in some more natural way: e.g., the individuals concerned have for the most part died of natural causes; the Commission staff questioned 418 witnesses (the FBI interviewed far more people, conducting 25,000 interviews and reinterviews), and in such a large group, a certain number of deaths are to be expected. (When Penn Jones, one of the originators of the "ten mysterious deaths" line, appeared on television, it emerged that two of the deaths on his list were from heart attacks, one from cancer, one was from a head-on collision on a bridge, and one occurred when a driver drifted into a bridge abutment.)

5. Where possible, counter speculation by encouraging reference to the Commission's Report itself. Open-minded foreign readers should still be impressed by the care, thoroughness, objectivity and speed with which the Commission worked. Reviewers of other books might be encouraged to add to their account the idea that, checking back with the Report itself, they found it far superior to the work of its critics.

CIA Dispatch, "Countering Criticism of the Warren Report", 1 April 1967

CIA Advertisement for Photographers

Bobby, Teddy, and Jack, circa 1960. Far-right conservatives not only feared that Jack would be reelected in 1964 but that Bobby would serve two terms after him and Teddy two more, indefinitely perpetuating a Kennedy dynasty.

*A whole new form of government
is going to take over the country . . .*
—Jack Ruby

Index

A

A Call for Revolution 261
a lone demented gunman 412
ABA (American Bar Association) 145, 395
ABC 144
ABC Nightly News 282
abrasion collar 395
acceptance 346
Accessories After the Fact 8, 261
acoustical evidence 389-390
Act of Treason 92
ad hoc arguments 395
ad hoc explanations 375, 385
ad hoc hypotheses 390
ad hominem 92, 407
Adams, Perry 269, 275, 276, 300, 306, 342
adrenal glands 401
affirming the consequent 26
Aguilar, Gary 9, 11, 12, 17, 18, 107, 118,
    122, 138, 141, 144, 151, 158, 174, 178,
    355, 401, 460
Akin, Gene 50
Almeder, Robert 346
Alsop, Joseph 183
Altgens' photograph 143, 217, 253, 261
Altgens' photograph 36
Altgens, James 217, 253, 259, 286, 291,
    292, 292, 294, 307, 342
Altman, Lawrence 63, 69, 77, 144, 178
Alvarez, Luis 120, 139, 263, 264, 267, 274,
    280, 281, 282, 283, 288, 295, 297, 299,
    301, 302, 308, 309, 315, 330, 343-344,
    375, 388, 390, 396, 397, 405, 410
AMA 64, 66, 67, 70, 75, 75, 79, 80, 82, 92,
    149, 361
AMA Board of Trustees 10, 23, 28
Ambrose, Steven 377, 410
American Bar Association (ABA) 145
American Historical Review 411, 412
American Journal of Physics 263, 396, 405,
    410
American Medical Association 9
American Medical News 56
Analytical Chemistry 411
anomalies 380
anti-Castro Cubans 17, 90, 367, 372
AP X-ray scans 129, 130
apologists 373, 377, 379, 385, 395
appeal to authority 88
Appendices 413
Argument from Addition and Subtraction
    352
Argument from JAMA 356-357
Argument from the Autopsy X-rays and
    Photographs 355
Argument from the Harper Fragment 354-
    355
Argument from U.S. News and World
    Report 356
ARRB 5, 122, 204, 205, 259, 260, 323, 325,
    327
Artwohl, Robert 18, 117, 407, 410, 85-92
Aschkenasy, Ernest 389, 390

Aspects of Scientific Explanation 411
assassination buffs xv, 406-407
Assassination Chronicles 19, 461
Assassination Disclosure Materials Act 117
Assassination Records Review Board 5,
    122, 186, 204, 205, 259, 260
Assassination Science xiii
assassination sciences 408
assassination videotape 186, 203, 367
at least six shots 16
Ault, C. 289, 296, 342
authenticity issues 113, passim
autopsy drawings 181, passim
autopsy of JFK xiv, passim
autopsy photographs 51, 52, 53, 54, 55, 57,
    108-111, 181, 394, 434,
autopsy protocol 114
autopsy radiographs 111-113, 120-139,
    153-160, passim
autopsy report 51, 430-435, passim
Autopsy Report Conflicts with the Autopsy
    X-rays and Photos 358-359
autopsy report, supplemental 436-437
autopsy X-rays xiii, 111-113, 120-139, 153-
    160, 399, 401, 435, passim
axiology 349
axioms 350

B

Babcock, Mr. 81
Babushka lady 229, 306, 307, 328
back wound 35, 87, 98-104, 176, 177, 181,
    391, 393, 394, 395, 406, 439, 136-137,
    157-158
back-of-head wound 429, passim
back-of-neck wound 429, passim
backyard photographs 84, 176, 206, 208,
    210
Baden, Michael 106, 111, 137, 138, 139
Bahmer, Robert 266
Baker, Marrion 274, 289, 342
Barber, Steve 390, 403, 410
Barger, James 389, 390
Barrett, Robert 231, 233
Bartholomew, Richard 218, 298, 363
Bartlett, Phyllis 41
Bashour, Dr. 78
Basic Motion Picture Technology 335
Baxter, Charles 40, 41, 42-44, 48, 48, 53,
    54, 57, 69, 78, 81, 399, 406, 416, 417,
    420
Beckel, Bob 277
Belin, David 64, 66, 70, 71
Bell, Audrey 152, 392
Bell, J. 296
Bennett, G. 296
Bennett, Glen 110
Benson, Michael 231
Bernstein, Carl 183, 184
Best Evidence 4, 29, 30, 92, 120, 137, 138,
    168, 180, 209, 231, 261, 266, 352, 354,
    355, 356, 357, 358, 359, 360, 361, 402,
    411, 461

Bethesda Naval Hospital 6
Betzner, Hugh 215, 216
bevelling 398-399
Bishop, Jim 138, 275
Black Hole 310-312, 338, 340
Black, Herbert 46
Blair, Clay 119
Blair, Joan 119
Blakey, Robert 116, 197, 277, 278, 279
blink pattern 330
blink pattern, expected 228, 237
blink pattern, observed 228, 238
blink rate 304-305
blinking light pattern 214
blobs leaving JFK's head 219, 250
Bloody Treason 265, 267, 298, 325, 336, 342, 364
Blumberg, J. M. 94, 99, 300
Boggs, Hale xii
Boston Globe 46, 59, 144
Boswell's diagram 16
Boswell, J. Thornton xiv, 6, 7, 16, 17, 25, 27, 29, 37, 73, 74, 94, 96, 97, 101, 105, 106, 108, 109, 110, 120, 122, 139, 151, 189, 196, 355, 359, 360, 394, 395, 399, 406, 430, 435
Bothun, Richard 318
Bowers, L. 296
brain examination 437
brain missing 400
brain tissue 421
brain weight 436
Brehm, Charles 223, 229, 274, 288, 294, 330, 342
Breneman, Chester 219, 250, 254, 298
Breo, Dennis 6, 7, 8,19, 20, 31, 37, 38, 40, 42, 43, 46, 47, 48, 57, 63, 64, 65, 66, 68, 69, 70, 72, 73, 74, 75, 76, 77, 78, 83, 114, 115, 137, 138, 139, 406-407
broken shadow 320, 322
Bronson, Charles 217, 226
Brown, Charles T. 41
Brown, Earl 364
Brown, Earle 274
Brown, George 369
Brown, Madeleine 368-369
Brown, Nicole 86, 347
Bulletin of the New York Academy of Medicine 405
bullets found 167
Burkley death certificate 439
Burkley, George 16, 17, 99, 110, 176, 395, 416, 439
Burstein, C. L. 138
Bush, George 6

C

Cabell, Charles 90, 370, 371
Cabell, Earle 370, 371
Cahoon, John B. 133
Campbell, O. 292, 342
Can Democracy Survive Cold War? 411
Canning, Thomas 277
Carnes, W. H. 138
Carr, Waggoner 4
Carrico, Charles 399
Carrico, James 42, 43, 44, 48, 48, 53, 54, 57, 59, 78, 406, 416
Carroll & Graf 185
Carroll, Kent 185
Case Closed 140, 144, 145, 147, 176, 179, 180, 232, 243, 247, 274, 347, 373, 377, 403, 404, 411
Case Open 230
Castro, Fidel 371

Cavett, Dick 146
CBS 184, 225, 300
CE-392 43
CE-399 391, 393
CE-585 250, 251, 253
CE-858 252
CE-875 257, 258, 259
CE-882 251
CE-883 251, 251, 253, 254, 260
CE-884 251, 254, 255, 256, 260
CE-888 220
CE-894 257
CE-895 248
CE-900 36, 253, 261, 356
CE-902 262
CE-903 260
CE-2113 418
cerebellar brain tissue 14, 146
cerebellar tissue 161, 163, 164, 169, 173, 175, 182, 417
cerebellum 44, 47, 48, 50, 53, 56, 57, 59, 142, 173, 175, 182
cerebral brain tissue 14, 146
Cerebral Death 139, 281
cerebral tissue 173, 417
cerebrum 59, 106, 173
Chain of Custody was Violated for the Most Important Evidence 359
Chalmers, A. F. 410
Chaney, James 217, 252, 261, 274, 287, 291, 292, 303, 364
Chase, Sylvia 401
chest X-ray 181, 157-158
Chicago Tribune 275, 342
chrome strip indentation 352, 228-29
chrome strip shot 232
CIA xii, 85, 86, 90, 183, 186, 209, 224, 341, 348, 368, 369, 371, 372, 407
CIA and the Media 183, 184
CIA Dispatch 445
Cincinnati Enquirer 409
Clarification 175
Clark Panel 122, 386, 395, 399
Clark, Kemp 14, 15, 50, 56, 61, 78, 96, 110, 142, 146, 148, 150, 152, 163, 399, 416, 417, 418, 419-427, 439
Clark, Ramsey 360
Clinical Summary 431
Clinton, Bill 186, 197, 203
CNN 17, 144, 182
Cohen, Jacob 283
Cold War 408
Colton, Charles C. 1
Commentary 283
community of scientists 382
comparison class 88
computer reconstruction 145-146
conclusive evidence 208, 345
conclusive evidence 365-366
conclusive falsification 362
condensation lines 218
condensation streaks 217
confirmation 380
Conjectures and Refutations 411
Connally left turn 214
Connally turn 215
Connally's back wound 245
Connally's lapel flap 243
Connally's puffed cheeks 244-245
Connally's shoulder drop 243-244
Connally's wounds 396
Connally, John xii, 2, 16, 30, 106, 120, 167, 208, 223, 226, 239, 240-247, 250, 276, 286, 287, 288, 291, 296, 299, 308, 309, 314, 353, 387, 389, 391, 392, 393, 396, 398, 400, 416, 431

Connally, Nellie 223, 240, 242, 244, 245, 246, 431
conspiracy xii, 92, 412, passim
Conspiracy of Silence 5
conspiracy, evidence of 362, passim
conspiracy, officially recognized 268
conspiracy, proofs of 362, passim
contact prints 235
content vs. form 380
Continuing Inquiry 463
Conway, Debra 207, 270
Cooley, Armanda 347
Cooper, John Sherman xii
Corry, John 294, 298
Corson, William 122
Cover-Up 4, 139
cover-up, evidence of 362, passim
cover-up, proofs of 362, passim
covering laws 380
Covering the Body 412
covering-law model 379
cranial X-rays 120-140, 153-160, 286, passim
Cranor, Milicent 217, 218, 274, 280, 286, 288, 289, 295, 296, 297, 299, 300, 301, 303, 317, 341, 342, 363
Crenshaw, Charles 5, 8, 10, 11, 12, 19, 25, 26, 30, 37-60, 61, 62, 64, 66, 68, 69, 70, 71, 72, 74, 75, 76, 77, 79, 80, 81, 82, 91, 101, 138, 197, 354, 376, 392, 399, 403, 410, 460, 461, 462
Crime and Cover-Up 188
Crime of the Century 411
critics 93, 373, 377, 379, 385, 395
Croft, Robert 215
Cronkite, Walter 354, 149-150
Crossfire 4, 92, 213, 247, 261, 352
crucial experiments 351
Cunningham, Kathleen 11, 151, 409, 460
Curry, Jesse 227, 291, 303, 342
Curtis, Don 40
Custer, Jerrol 103, 111, 135, 136, 157, 401
Cutler, R. B. 261
Cutler, Robert 325

D

Dallas death certificate, signed 438
Dallas death certificate, unsigned 439
Dallas Morning News 65, 66, 67, 70, 70, 72, 81, 167
damage to the brain 436
Dateline 402
David, Dennis 101, 103
Davis, David 111, 112
Davis, Joseph 104
Death Certificate, Signed 428, 439
Death Certificate, Unsigned 429
death certificates 16, 99, 152, 176, 189
Death of a President 294
death of JFK xi, 1-22, 366,371, 418, passim
Decker, William ("Bill") 287, 291, 342, 390
deductive certainty 380
Dennis Breo 25
densitometry 447
Department of Justice 18, 185, 186, 187-200, 204, 375
depositions 73-79
DeSalles, Douglas 118, 280
descriptive 379
Deutch, John 186
diagrams of a brain xiii, passim
diagrams of brain 164, 165, passim
diagrams of the brain 197, passim
dictabelt 389, 390
DiEugenio, J. 139

DiMaio, V. G. M. 88
disconfirmation 380
discrediting critics 446
Dissertation Abstracts 402
Dodd, Mr. 240
Double Decker 410
Downing, Thomas N. 268
drawings of back wound 441
drawings of head wounds 442
drawings of neck wound 441
dropping LBJ as his running mate for 1964 366
Dudman, Richard 142, 165, 166, 167, 170, 171, 461
Dulles, Allen xii, 46, 95
Duluth News-Tribune 8, 27, 145
Dziemian, A. J. 137

E

Eaglesham, Alan 219, 363
Eastman Kodak Film Edge Guide 327
Ebersole, John 94, 98, 101, 104, 108, 110, 111, 114, 122, 134, 135, 136, 137, 139, 150, 155
editing, horizontal 209
editing, vertical 209
Einstein, Albert 88
Eisenberg, Melvin 249, 251
emergency blink light pattern 236
emergency light blink pattern 227-228
emulsion removal mark 231
entry wounds 161-162, passim
epistemology 349, 379
Epstein, E. J. 137, 446
eqivocation 89
Evica, George Michael 19, 207
exit wounds 161-162, passim
expert opinion 405, 406, passim
expert testimony 373, 378
experts 376, passim
explaining away 346, 347
exploding bullet 400
eyewitness reliability 210
eyewitness testimony 210, 265
Eyewitness Testimony 210, 278
eyewitnesses 285, 293
Eyzaguirre, C. 139

F

fabricated X-rays xiii, 14, 20, 25, 28, 120-139, 153-160, 181, 197, 355, 365-367, passim
fabricating evidence 86, passim
fabricating X-rays 142
failing to support the invasion of Cuba 366
Failure Analysis Associates 145, 180, 395
fallibility 346
falsification 362, 380, 381
Farewell America 92
FBI 21, 33, 85, 86, 90, 114, 122, 162, 167, 171, 173, 175, 182, 196, 229, 271, 302, 304, 311, 323, 354, 371, 389, 391, 407
FBI autopsy report 96, 98, 99, 121, 122, 130, 131, 132
FBI report 233, 269
Ferrell, Mary 211
Fetzer, James H. xvi, 8, 17, 118, 139, 158, 174, 177, 178, 180, 181, 182, 189, 193-200, 204, 207, 270, 341, 346, 356, 379, 383, 410, 461, 462
Feyerabend, Paul 383, 410
Fidone, S. J. 139
field of view changes 214
Fielding, Raymond 130, 133, 321, 334

Finck, Pierre xiv, 17, 27, 32, 94, 98, 99, 105, 106, 107, 108, 114, 196, 289, 292, 299, 300, 317, 394, 406, 430, 435
First Scene 222
Fisher, R. S. 138
Fisher, Russell 122
flashing lights 217, 219
Fonzi, Gaeton 410
Ford, Gerald xii, 4, 33, 177, 446
Forensic Science Gazette 405
form vs. content 380
Formulating X-ray Techniques 133
Fort Worth Star-Telegram 298
Foster, J. W. 274
Foucault, Michel 374, 378, 379, 381, 384, 409, 410
Four Days 273, 302
Fourth Decade 215, 261, 274, 286, 295, 301
fragments, weight of 391-392
Frame 161 220
Frame 225 248
Frame 313 262
frame excision 329
frame numbers changed 219
Framing of Lee Harvey Oswald 211
Franks, Ronald 8
Freedom of Information Act 11
Freeh, Louis 197

G

Gallery 390
Galloway, Paul 32
Garrision trial 389
Garrison inquiry 19
Garrison trial 268, 394
Garrison, Jim 212, 297, 411, 460
Gauthier, Leo 249
general hypotheses 351
Geraldo 26
Gibson, Charlie 354
Glass, Richard 25, 73, 76, 78
Glossary of Epistemology/Philosophy of Science 346
Goldman, Ron 86, 347
Good Morning America 8, 27, 30, 70, 354
Goodman, Ellen 144
Good Night America 268
Gordon, Colin 410
Gore, Al 197
Gould, Stanhope 401
Gould, Stephen 409, 411
Grant, Eva 294
grassy knoll xii, 169, 175, 389, 390, 398
Greer head turn 213, 217, 223, 230, 289, 309, 316, 330, 363, 258-259
Greer, William 208, 209, 215, 217, 223, 230, 240, 258, 269, 274, 286, 287, 288, 295, 296, 309, 364
Griffith, Michael 282
Groden, Robert 4, 20, 29, 33, 84, 141, 143, 144, 148, 210, 213, 226, 231, 232, 241, 247, 261, 265, 267, 272, 301, 303, 304, 341, 352, 353, 355, 356, 357, 359, 360, 361, 362, 373, 377, 389, 389, 409, 411
Gross, Martin 261
Guinn, Vincent 229, 232, 411, 392-393
Gun Digest 392
Gutierrez, Sherry 207
Gynecology and Obstetrics 405

H

(h1) hit by a missile 346
(h1) O.J. committee the crime 347
(h1) Oswald killed him 348, 366

(h2) he was killed by the Mob 348, 366
(h2) it was a drug-related hit 347
(h2) terrorist bomb explosion 346
(h3) he was killed by pro- or anti-Castro Cubans 348, 366
(h3) Ron Goldman was the target 347
(h3) unsuspected design failure 346
(h4) he was killed by the KGB 348, 366
(h5) he was killed as the result of a coup d'etat 348, 366
Hagen, Joe 355
Hagis, Bobby W. 342
Hall, Joseph 83
Haller, John 409, 411
Hansen, Jens 62
Happe, L. Bernard 335
hard core 383
Hargis, Bobby W. 273, 274, 289, 291, 292, 293, 364
Harper fragment 282
Harper, Billy 354
Harrelson, Charles 368
Harris, Jo Ann 194, 197
Harris, Larry Ray 139, 211
Hartman, W. K. 246
Harvard Law Review 278
Hatfield, S. 139
Hawks, Wayne 419, 421, 423, 426, 427
head shots 209, 258, 284, 285, 285, 331
head snap 263, 264, 279-284, 298, 302, 317, 332, 375, 386, 396, 397, 398
head wounds 5, 15, 30, 38, 42, 44, 47, 48, 48, 50, 52, 53, 56, 57, 61, 65, 87, 94-98, 153-157, 162, 169, 171, 173, 175, 176, 181, 182, 239, 394, 398, 399, 400, 406, 415, 416, 419, 421, 422, 423, 424, 431, 432, 433, 434, 435, 438, 439
head wounds, diagram of 438
Heitman, Wallace 41
Helpern, Milton 107
Hempel, Carl G. 378, 379, 411
Henderson, T. 296
Hensen, Jens 403, 410
Hepler, Ron 207, 208, 460, 461, 462
Hester, Beatrice 222
Hester, Charles 222
Hickey, George, Jr. 289, 296, 342
high powered rifle 428, 429, passim
High Treason 4, 20, 29-30, 33, 92, 141, 232, 247, 352, 353, 355, 356, 357, 359, 360, 361, 373, 377, 411
High Treason 2 30, 35, 92, 138, 141, 152, 168, 188, 353, 354, 355, 356, 359, 360, 411
high velocity bullets 398, passim
high velocity weapon 20, 146, passim
Hill, Clint 110, 258, 284, 287, 288, 289, 290, 291, 292, 296, 303, 304, 307, 321, 342
Hill, Jean 214, 226, 259, 288, 289, 292, 298, 299, 307, 342
Hinchcliffe, Margaret 40
historians 402
historical explanations 380
historicism 378
Hoch, Paul 107, 225, 300, 369
hole in windshield 143-144, 165, 166-167, 168, 170, 171, 173-174
Holland, S. M. 240
Holmes, Harry D. 275, 364
Holt, Chauncey 35, 368
Holt, Patricia 147
Hoover, J. Edgar 41, 90, 341, 348, 366, 369, 372, 398
horizontal editing 209, 209

Houts, M. 138
Howard, Tom 294
Howlett, John 249, 254
HSCA xii, xiv, 2, 4, 18, 59, 73, 100, 101, 102, 103, 104, 106, 107, 108, 109, 111, 112, 113, 114, 119, 122, 133, 137, 138, 156, 157, 158, 181, 185, 193, 195, 196, 199, 229, 240, 246, 266, 267, 268, 276, 277, 278, 280, 281, 283, 308, 348, 372, 386, 388, 389, 390, 392, 395, 399, 401, 410, passim
Hudson, Emmett 252, 258, 259, 260, 290, 303, 307, 342
Hughes film 305
Hughes, Robert 227
Hume, David 381
Humes, James J. xiv, 6, 7, 9, 17, 25, 27, 29, 31, 37, 54, 73, 74, 94, 95, 97, 99, 100, 102, 104, 105, 105, 106, 107, 108, 109, 111, 116, 119, 120, 122, 139, 142, 150, 150, 162, 163, 170, 171, 172, 181, 184, 187, 188, 189, 196, 359-360, 394, 399, 406, 407, 430, 435, 437, 440
Hunt, Jackie 78
hypotheses 345-346
hypothetical question 58

I

improbability of Secret Service mistakes by chance 367-368
In the Shadow of Dallas 151, 188
infallible evidence 365-366
infallible truth 385
inference to the best explanation 210, 345-348
International Surgery 405
intersprocket images 336-337
Intersprocket Measurements 312
intersubjective replicability 362
Inventing Reality 411
Investigator 402
irrationality 366
Itek 283
Itek 267

J

Jackie's arm movement 215
Jackie's face totally blank 219
Jackson, Bob 431
Jackson, Douglas 275, 364
Jackson, Gayle Nix 302
Jacott, William 9, 23, 27, 28, 35, 147
JAMA xiv, xv, 6, 19, 59, 59, 63, 64, 65, 67, 68, 69, 70, 71, 72, 76, 79, 80, 81, 82, 83, 92, 93, 100, 105, 107, 114, 117, 147, 155, 156, 158, 204, 274, 356-357, 359, 376, 405, 406, 410, 411, 460, 463
JAMA Did Not Ask Key Questions of Humes and Boswell 359-360
James, Patricia 118, 138, 158
James, Patricia 341
Jamieson Film Company 224, 233, 328
Jamieson, Bruce 231, 271, 314, 325, 326, 327, 334, 335
Jarman, J. 296
Jaworski, Leon 4
Jefferson, Thomas 93, v
Jenkins, Marion 42, 43-44, 47, 48, 53, 54, 56, 57, 59, 59, 144, 179, 180, 399, 406, 416, 417
jet effect 279–281, 295, 375, 280-284, 396-397
JFK xii, 5, 7, 10, 62, 65, 66, 348, 377, passim

JFK assassination theories 348, 366
JFK Assassination: A Visual Investigation 304, 309
JFK head turn 215
JFK Lancer Conference 207, 219
JFK Lancer Productions 270
JFK, Cuba, and the Garrison Case 139
JFK: Breaking the Silence 275, 342
JFK: Conspiracy of Silence 30, 37, 40, 56, 57, 59, 62, 64, 65, 75, 91, 138, 403, 410, 462
JFK: The Assassination, the Cover-Up, and Beyond 367
JFK: The Book of the Film 361
JFK: The Case for Conspiracy 20, 148, 232
Joesten, Joachim 446
Johns, Zack 181, 461
Johnson, Lyndon B. xi, xii, 6, 22, 33, 38, 41, 42, 62, 68, 69, 90, 183, 341, 348, 366, 368-369, 372, 423, 426
Johnson, Mrs. L. B. 296
Jones, Penn 211, 212, 447, 463
Jones, Ronald 50, 416
Journal of Philosophy 411
Journal of the AMA (JAMA) xiii

K

Kantor, Seth 276
Katzenback, Nicholas DeB. 21, 22
Kellerman head turn 289
Kellerman, Roy 17, 122, 217, 223, 240, 253, 286, 288, 292, 296, 342, 434, 435
Kelley, Thomas 249
Kelly, Jim 122
Kelly, Thomas 259
Kennedy and Lincoln 137, 279, 299, 411
Kennedy, Edward 22, 448
Kennedy, Jacqueline 22, 217, 226, 283, 284, 285, 286, 288, 289, 289, 290, 297, 303, 306, 309, 316-318, 331, 332, 333, 342, 423, 427, 431
Kennedy, John F. xi, xiii, xv, 2, 4, 27, 119, 448, passim
Kennedy, Robert F. xv, 22, 42, 446, 448
Keough, Gary 158
Keough, Leslie 118
Keough, William 118
KGB 17, 367
Kierkegaard, Soren 402
Kilduff, Malcolm 30, 423
Killing Kennedy 218, 269, 330
Killing of a President 311, 314-315
Killing the Truth 141, 147, 151, 411, 461
King, Martin Luther, Jr. xv, 400
Kinney, E. C. 107
Kinney, Samuel 288, 289, 294, 295, 308, 342
Kivett, Jerry 291, 342
Kizzia, Bradley xv, 9, 19, 26, 74, 78, 82, 460, 461, 462
Knobel, Fletcher 446
knowledge, definition of 349
KOGO, San Diego 368
Kritzman, Lawrence 410
KRON 43, 401
KTTV, Los Angeles 272
Kuhn, Thomas 374, 378, 379, 381, 382, 383, 384, 390, 408, 411
Kuhnian expertise 403
Kuhnian perspective 401
Kurtz, Michael 400, 411

L

Lakatos, Imre 383
lampposts change location 216
Landis, Paul 294
Landis, Paul, Jr. 290, 291, 292, 342
Lane, Mark 4, 212, 240, 294, 411, 446
language of proof 345-366
Larry King Live 59, 277
lateral X-ray scans 127, 128, 129
Lattimer, G. 139
Lattimer, J. 139
Lattimer, J. K. 139
Lattimer, John K. 18, 19, 53, 97, 120, 137,
  230, 279, 280, 289, 294, 299, 299, 310,
  317, 391, 395, 397, 399, 400, 400, 401,
  405, 409, 411
Lawson, Winston 288
lawsuit 64-72
leading question 86
legal admissibility 265
Lehmann-Haupt, Christopher 144, 176
Lesar, Jim 158
Lewis, C. S. 118, 139
Lewis, T. 138
Liebeler, Wesley 256, 265, 266, 272
Life 219, 225, 265, 266, 268, 271, 272, 298,
  300, 300, 305, 310, 316, 325, 326, 333,
  339, 341
Lifton, David 4, 29, 30, 96, 103, 118, 120,
  124, 137, 138, 139, 151, 158, 168, 174,
  175, 180, 188, 207, 209, 224, 231, 232,
  261, 266, 270, 320, 321, 327, 338, 341,
  352, 354, 355, 356, 357, 358, 359, 360,
  361, 369, 394, 395, 400, 401, 402, 409,
  409, 411, 461
limousine bench seats 258
limousine jump seats 258
limousine speed 255, 269
limousine stop 213
Lincoln limousine 34, 36, 143, 165, 167,
  168, 170, 171, 227, 250, 356
Lincoln, Evelyn 372
Lipsey, Richard 100
Livingston Curriculum Vitae 190-192
Livingston videotape 189
Livingston, Robert B. xv, 12, 13, 14, 17, 18,
  141, 142, 144, 150, 161-175, 181, 182,
  184, 185, 186, 187, 189, 190-192, 194,
  196, 197, 201, 202, 204, 282, 341, 362,
  366, 394, 460, 463
Livingstone, Harrison 4, 5, 17, 20, 29, 30,
  33, 35, 136-139, 141, 147, 151, 152, 156,
  168, 174, 188, 218, 232, 247, 267, 269,
  303, 305, 306, 315, 341, 352-357, 359,
  360, 361, 363, 373, 377, 389, 391, 395,
  396, 401, 403, 409, 411, 461
Loftus, Elizabeth 210, 278
Look 297
Los Angeles Times 361
loyalists 93
Lundberg, George 6, 7, 9, 11, 12, 18, 22,
  23, 25, 26, 28, 31, 35, 56, 64, 65, 66, 67,
  68, 70, 72, 73, 75, 76, 79, 80, 137, 138,
  139, 147, 354, 359, 361, 406, 407, 411,
  460

M

MacNeill, Robert 275, 296, 342
macro-events 380
Mafia 277 (see Mob)
magic bullet xii, 13, 14, 20, 88, 120, 124,
  141, 179, 181, 214, 239, 353, 375
magnification anomalies 319-321
magnification changes 333

magnification studies 209, 365
Malley, James 249
Manchester Affair 294
Manchester, William 42, 294, 296, 297, 298
Mannlicher-Carcano 3, 20, 87, 104, 114,
  114, 124, 145, 146, 148, 228, 282, 296,
  386, 389, 391, 392, 397, 398, 409, 387-
  388
Mannlicher-Carcano ad 152
Mantik's Accumulation of Eyewitness
  Testimony 364-365
Mantik's Studies of Background Magnifica-
  tion 365
Mantik, Christopher 121, 158, 341
Mantik, David W. xv, xvi, 11, 12, 13, 14, 16,
  17, 18, 19, 20, 25, 104, 137, 138, 141,
  142, 144, 149, 150, 151, 160, 164, 166,
  178, 181, 182, 186, 197, 200, 204, 207,
  209, 214, 218, 242, 284, 355, 362, 363,
  364, 365, 366, 399, 401, 460, 461, 463
Mantik, Meredith 121, 158, 341
Marcus, Raymond 266, 283
Marilyn's arm swing 222
marksman, definition of 147-148
marksmanship, Oswald's 145-146
Marler, Chuck 207, 209, 217, 219, 270,
  274, 305, 307, 309, 310, 320, 338, 341,
  363, 460, 461, 463
Marrs, Jim 4, 213, 219, 247, 261, 298, 352
Marshall, Burke 13, 124, 158
Marshall, J. et al. 278
Martin, Billy Joe 217, 275, 364
Mary Poppins 334, 371
mass media as corporate entity 404
mass of brain 106
maximal-specificity condition 375
Mayn, Charles 270, 303, 304, 341
McCarthy, Roger 180
McClelland, Robert 38, 40, 44, 50, 56, 61,
  69, 77, 78, 81, 167, 331, 332, 417
McCloy, John J. xii, 306, 369
McCormick on Evidence 210, 265, 267
McLaughlin Group 24
McLaughlin, John 24, 351
McNamara, Robert 170, 186, 188, 202
Meagher, Sylvia 7, 261
media contacts 446
medical evidence 374, passim
medical science 378, passim
Medical Times 405
*Medicolegal Investigation of the President
  John F. Kennedy Murder* 138, 412
Medio Multimedia 304, 309
medium velocity weapon 146, 148
medium-to-low velocity weapon 146, 148
Melanson, Philip 209, 225, 231, 267, 268,
  341
Menninger, Bonar 124, 139, 286, 342, 355,
  356, 356
metaphysical certitude 24, 351
Miami Herald 361
micro-events 380
Milam, Wallace 118, 139
Minneapolis Star 369
Miracles 139
misdescribing evidence 86
misdescription of back wound 35
missing car stop 363
missing Connally blood 214
missing Connally left-turn 363
missing Connally movements 218
missing Kennedy movements 218
missing spectators 216, 217
Mizzer, Doug 292, 303, 342
Mob 17, 90, 367, 368, 371, 372
Model, Peter 20, 148, 232

Montoya, Richard 368
Moor, Jeanne 202
Moorman, Mary 214, 226, 229, 252, 259,
    275, 276, 287, 288, 289, 292, 294, 298,
    299, 300, 307, 342, 364
Morgan, R. H. 138
Morningstar, Robert 207, 218, 219, 231,
    363
Mortal Error 124, 139, 286, 342, 355, 356,
    356
Mortiz, A. 138
motion blur 218
motionless spectators 215
motives for killing Kennedy 366
Moulter, Jeff 73
Moyers, Bill 21, 22
Muchmore film 219, 271, 273, 288, 302,
    302, 303, 304, 304, 311
Muchmore film speed 324
Muchmore, Marie 226, 230, 276, 291, 300,
    301, 317
Murchison, Clint 369
Murder From Within 269
mysterious deaths 447
myth of objectivity 404

N

NAA 277
naivete 1, passim
National Photographic Interpretation
    Center 209, 224, 229, 369, 447
national security 408
naturalists 378
neck wound 32, 35, 431, 432, 435, 438, 440
neck wound, diagram of 438
negations of generalizations 208
negotiating Limited Nuclear Test Ban
    Treaty 366
Neurobiology 139
neuromuscular reaction 281, 284
neutron activation analysis 114, 229, 232,
    277, 392
new evidence 187-189, 193-194, 195-197,
    198-199
New Republic 165, 167, 461
New York Daily News 293
New York press conference 135, 141-175,
    178, 182, 185, 186
New York Times 6, 14, 15, 27, 59, 63, 69,
    140, 144, 145, 147, 176, 177, 178, 179,
    180, 183, 184, 186, 326, 347, 361, 372,
    377, 409
New York Times Book Review 410
Newcomb, Fred 269, 275, 276, 300, 306,
    342
Newman, Bill 269, 275, 276, 288, 288, 289,
    289, 291, 297, 314, 342, 364
Newman, Bill and family 214, 218
Newman, Gail 289, 342
Newsweek 35, 172, 174, 185, 273, 347
Nicholas, J. A. 119, 138
Nichols, John 119
Nightline 17, 144
Nix film 271, 288, 302, 303, 304, 339
Nix film speed 324
Nix, Orville 226, 228, 276, 291, 304, 306
Nixon, Richard 348, 366, 369
non-existence claims 208
normal science 382, 402
NOVA 354
Novick, Peter 379, 411
NPIC 209, 224, 225, 229, 369, 447, 267-268

O

O'Donnell, Kenny 296
O'Donnell, Peter 369
O'Neill, Francis 96, 110, 121, 130, 131,
    132, 354
O. J. Simpson trial 347
Observations of JFK Wounds 414-415
Official AP X-ray 123
official information 404
Official lateral X-ray 123
oil boys 366, 369
Olivier, A. G. 87, 137, 391
On the Trail of the Assassins 411
ontology 349, 382
opposing monopolistic pricing policies
    366
optical densitometry 13, 142, 181, 124-
    125, 153-157
optical printers 235
Orth, Herbert 333
Osborne, David 103
Osborne, Dr. 392
Oswald backyard photographs 84, 176,
    206, 208, 210
Oswald photograph 33
Oswald, Lee H. xi, xiv, 2, 3, 4, 7, 17, 20, 21,
    22, 28, 31, 33, 37, 40, 41, 62, 65, 68, 69,
    72, 84, 87, 89, 90, 114, 119, 124, 145,
    148, 176, 179, 185, 206, 208, 211, 221,
    228, 249, 265, 301, 348, 366, 367, 385,
    386, 387, 412, 445, 447
Oswald, Marina 176
Outcasts from Evolution 411

P

Painter, David 158
Paisley, John 122
Palamara, Vincent 274, 294
paradigms 382
paranoia 1
Parenti, Michael 404, 411
Parker, Maynard 172, 175, 185
Parkland Hospital 6, 12
Parkland Observations Differ from those at
    Bethesda 357-358
Parkland press conference 146, 148, 419
peculiar changes in visual field 363
peer review 22, 68, 74, 403, 405, 406
peer-review 32
Perry, Malcolm 12, 15, 28, 38, 42-44, 45,
    46, 48, 54, 56, 57, 59, 61, 78, 86, 99,
    100, 101, 110, 146, 150, 152, 163, 173,
    176, 188, 189, 394, 399, 406, 409, 416,
    417, 419-427, 431, 433, 440
Peters, Paul 41, 50, 78, 417
Petty, C. S. 139
Petty, Charles 95, 120
Petty, Dr. 116
Phillips, Max 225, 234
Philosophy of Science 410
Photo-Lab-Index 231
photograph of back wound 444
photograph of head wounds 443
photograph of magic bullet 179
photograph of throat wound 443
photographic evidence 210, 265
Photographic Whitewash 231
photographs 114
photographs of brain 164
photographs of the brain 197
physical evidence 374
physical science 378
Physics and Society 308, 461

Physiology of the Nervous System 139
Pictures of the Pain 265, 267, 268, 273, 315, 336
Pincher, Mike 209, 214, 265, 272, 297, 304, 305, 309, 331, 371, 460, 461, 463
pink spray 213, 363
placing covert operations under Pentagon supervision 366
planning to retire Director Hoover thereafter 366
Politics, Philosophy, Culture 410
Popper, Karl 374, 376, 378, 379, 380, 382, 406, 411
popular sentiments 210, 373
Portrait of an Assassin 4
Posner, Gerald 140, 144, 145, 146, 147, 148, 176, 177, 179, 180, 232, 243, 247, 274, 373, 376, 377, 388, 389, 395, 396, 403, 404, 405, 409, 411
possible 87
Post Mortem 139
Post-Modernism 407
post-mortem cranial X-ray 160
power 384
power and truth 384
Power/Knowledge 410
pre-mortem cranial X-ray 159
Precision Handloading 148
prescriptive 379
Presidential limousine 34, 36, 143, 167, 168, 170, 171, 227, 356
press conferences 6, 17
Price, C. J. 416
prima facie case 208, 363
Principles of Cinematography 335
pro-Castro Cubans 17, 367
probable 87
Probe 402
problem of induction 381
Proof 1 352
Proof 2 354-355
Proof 3 355
Proof 4 356
Proof 5 356
Proof 6 357-358
Proof 7 358-359
Proof 8 349
Proof 9 359-360
Proof 10 361-361
proof as falsification 351
proof as verification 351
proof beyond a resonable doubt 350
proof in courts of law 345, 350
proof in empirical science 345, 351
proof in pure mathematics 345, 350
proofs of conspiracy 10
proofs of cover-up 10
propaganda assets 446
protective belt 383
proving a negative 208
Purdy, Andy 122
Purvis, Tom 254
puzzles 382

Q

Queen Mary 257-258
question begging 87, 89, 149

R

R. R. Donnelley Graphics Company 225
radiographs 114
Raines, Howell 144, 176
Ramsey Panel 386
Ramsey, Norman 390

Random House 179
Random House ad 140, 144
Rankin, J. Lee xii, 99, 100, 110
Ransom, Harry Howe 408, 411
Raskin, 377
Raskin, Marcus 411
Rather, Dan 216, 225, 267, 269, 288, 290, 292, 299, 300
rationality 1, 366
re-enactment 269
re-enactment film 333
re-enactment, Secret Service 250
re-enactment, *Time-Life* 250
re-enactment, Warren Commission 250
re-enactments 298, 249-258
Ready, John 287, 289, 290, 291, 342
realism 379, 380, 385
realists 378
reality 379, 381
reasonable doubt 347, 350
reasonable inference 26
Redlich, Norman 249
Redmon, Ray 215, 363
reducing oil depletion allowance 366
Regan, Ronald 86
register mark (+) 219, 226
rejection 346
relativism 381, 385
relativists 378
relentlessly attacking organized crime 366
Rennie, Drummond 73
Reno, Janet 18, 185, 186, 197, 187-189
requirement of total evidence 9, 29, 148
research programmes 383
Resident and Staff Physician 299, 401, 411
Resnick, Faye 347
revolutionary science 385
Richardson, Elliott 186, 188, 201
right profile of JFK 159
Riley, Joseph 118, 137, 165, 362
Ring, John J. 10, 23, 351, 352, 362
Rivera, Geraldo 268, 347
Roberts, C. 291
Roberts, Charles 342
Roberts, Emory 289, 291
Robertson, Randy 362
Rockefeller Panel 395
Rogin, 377
Rogin, Michael 412
Rolling Stone 183
Rosen, Alex 41
Rosenstone, Robert 377, 412
Rotoscoping 213
Rowley, James 268
Roy Schaeffer 219
Ruby, Jack 5, 62, 167, 179, 276, 294, 449
Rush to Judgment 4, 212, 411
Rusk, Dean 371
Russell, Bertrand 446
Russell, Richard xii, 446

S

Salamanowicz, Paul 308, 331
Salandria, Vincent 300
Salyer, Ken 38, 40
Saturday Evening Post 225
Scalletar, Rayond 24
Schaeffer, Roy 143, 207, 209, 214, 230, 231, 265, 272, 297, 304, 305, 309, 310, 313, 317, 326, 329, 330, 339, 341, 371, 460, 461, 463
Schwartz, Erwin 267, 288, 289, 298, 342
Science in a Free Society 410
scientific evidence 30, 373, 378
scientific experts 408

scientific objectivity 362
scientific realism 378
scientism 384
Scott, Frank 246
Scott, Peter Dale 168, 174, 188
Seaman, William 111
Second Scene 222
Secret Service 165, 167
Secret Service Cadillac 34, 36, 356, 257-258
Secret Service complicity 143-144, 165, 166-167, 168, 170, 171, 173-174, 209, 227, 367
Secret Service credentials 368
Secret Service dependency upon CIA 225
Secret Service memorandum 234
Secret Service windshield 171, 143-144
selection and elimination 9, 29, 184
settlement 79-83
Shackelford, Martin 207, 267, 268, 271, 313, 341
Shaneyfelt, Lyndal 230, 249, 268, 290, 292, 303, 304, 311, 323, 324, 342
Shanklin, Gordon 41
Shaw, Clay 98
Shaw, Gary 4, 10, 62, 64, 65, 66, 68, 72, 79, 80, 139, 211, 403, 410
Shaw, Robert 243, 245, 396
Shepherd, G. M. 139
Sibert, James 96, 110, 121, 130, 131, 132, 354
Simmons, James 364
Simmons, Mr. 251
Simpson, O. J. 86, 210, 347, 350
Sinatra, Nancy 87
single bullet theory xii, 3, 20, 34, 35, 106, 145, 151, 181, 189, 196, 197, 239, 251, 257, 258, 260, 386, 387, 391, 392, 395, 396, 400
Siple, Donald 156
Sitzman, Marilyn 222
Six Seconds in Dallas 4, 16, 92, 137, 231, 267, 305, 306, 326, 334, 352, 353, 356, 357, 361, 375, 386, 402, 412
6.5 mm bullet 399, passim
6.5 mm bullets 232, 391, 393
6.5 mm metal object xiii, 20, 25, 155, 156, 120-139
60 Minutes 174, 184
Sklar, Zackary 361
Sloan, Bill 275, 342
Smith, Alan 275, 289, 342
Smith, Merriman 273
Smith, R. P. 137
Smith, W. S. 138
Snyder, Art 207, 280, 317
Soaring Bird 310-312, 338, 340
Sorrels, Forrest 41, 224, 231, 252
Spearing, Mary 18, 185, 186, 194, 195, 197, 200
special pleading 87, 88
Specter, Arlen 34, 40, 46, 58, 78, 101, 150, 179, 188, 209, 249, 251, 254, 257, 258, 260, 265, 290, 391, 440
Sprague, Richard 143
St. Louis Post Dispatch 142, 167, 174
Stanton, William 409, 412
Star 347
Stemmons Freeway Sign 209, 215, 259-260, 321
Stern, Samuel 265
Stolley, Richard 225
Stolley, Richard B. 231
Stone, Anthony 32
Stone, Oliver xii, 5, 10, 62, 116, 263, 348, 361, 377

straw man 85, 90, 91
streak analysis 218
Stringer, J. T. 139
Stroscio, Michael 308, 343-344, 461
Structure of Scientific Revolutions 381, 411
Stuart, Mark 70, 73
substituted diagrams 365-367
Sulzberger, Arthur Ochs, Jr. 144, 180
Sulzberger, Arthur Ochs, Sr. 183
Summary of the Films 328
Summary of Treatment by Kemp Clark 416-418
Summer, Anthony 412
sun flare 232, 228-229
supplemental autopsy report 436-437
supporting integration 366
Surgery 405
surgical alteration 394
survey plats 250, 251, 259
Suydam, Henry 268
Swank, Patsy 225
Swinford, James 196, 416
Szabo, John 118, 158
Szabo, Sherry 118

T

Tague, James 2, 16, 353, 354
Task, Richard 283
Taylor, A. J. P. 446
Taylor, W. 296
Technique of Special Effects Cinematography 130, 321, 334
Tenet, George 186
tentorium 170, 173, 163-164
Texas in the Morning 369
Texas State Journal of Medicine 399, 412
That Noble Dream 411
The Camera Never Blinks 300
The Day Kennedy was Shot 138, 275
The Fish is Red 92
The Great Train Robbery 334
The Investigator 305
The JAMA Editor Surely Ought to have Known Better 361-362
The Killing of a President 84, 143, 226, 231, 241, 247, 261, 265, 267
The Last Investigation 410
The Leopard's Spots 412
The Logic of Scientific Discovery 411
The Men Who Killed Kennedy 296
The Mismeasure of Man 411
The Plot to Kill Kennedy 240
The Poverty of Historicism 411
The Technique of the Cutting Room 338
The Two Kennedys 355
The Umbrella Man 325
theorems 350
Third Alternative 294
Third Decade 137, 138, 165, 208, 209, 225, 231, 268, 274, 402, 461
Third Scene 223
Thomas, Evan 185
Thompson, Josiah 4, 16, 137, 209, 231, 267, 283, 289, 294, 295, 296, 300, 317, 341, 352, 353, 356, 357, 361, 362, 375, 376, 386, 392, 395, 398, 402, 412
Thorburn reflex 389, 395, 409
throat shot 285
throat wound 5, 12, 14, 28, 38, 42, 45, 46, 48, 48, 50, 54, 55, 57, 58, 61, 65, 87, 98-104, 157-158, 161, 162, 163, 167, 169, 179-171, 172, 175, 176, 181, 182, 188, 189, 196, 239, 391, 393, 394, 395, 406, 414, 416, 419, 422, 423, 424, 431, 432, 435, 439, 440

throat wound ignorance theory 12, 99,
    150-151, 170-171, 173, 182, 187, 188-
    189, 196, 394, 409, 431, 433, 440
Tilley, Steven 158
Time 273, 361, 389
Time, Inc. 184, 268
Time-Life 326
Tobias, Fritz 446
Torini, Paul 73
tracheostomy 12, 32, 38, 45, 48, 54, 57, 99,
    110, 150, 161, 167, 188, 394, 414, 417,
    420, 421, 431, 433, 440
Trask, Richard 265, 267, 268, 273, 292,
    294, 301, 307
Trauma Room #1 26, 38, 39
traveling matte technique 338, 334-338
triple underpass 169, 175, 353
Truly, Roy 275, 295, 329, 364
truth 379, 381
truth and power 384
Tunheim, John 186, 204, 205
Turner, Nigel 296
TWA 800 346
Two Flightpaths: Evidence of Conspiracy
    261
Twyman's Studies of the Greer Head Turn
    364
Twyman, Noel 207, 217, 231, 265, 267,
    270, 298, 302, 304, 309, 310, 311, 312,
    325, 327, 334, 340, 341, 342, 364

U

U.S. News and World Report 33, 35, 145,
    147, 150, 356, 376, 410
Umberger, G. J. 138
UMD Statesman 180, 181-182, 204, 461
universal generalizations 381
Unnatural Death 137, 139

V

Valenti, Jack 32
van der Lubbe 446
verification 380, 381
vertical editing 209
videotape 186, 189
virtually motionless spectators 363

W

Walker, A. E. 139, 281
Wallace, Mike 292
Walter, Ernest 338
Walther, C. 296
wanting to shatter the CIA into a thousand
    pieces 366
Ward, Theron 152, 189
warranted inference 26
warranted true belief 349
Warren Commission xii, xiv, xv, 22, passim
Warren Report xii, 2, 3, 4, 66, 149, 181,
    passim
Warren, Earl xi, xii, 33, 251, 446
Washington Post 103, 145, 149, 431
Washington Star 361
Watson, Jay 224
Watt, D. C. 446
Weatherly, Daryll 218, 269, 304, 305, 307,
    315, 316, 318, 330, 333, 341, 363
Wecht, Cyril 25, 107, 118, 134, 137, 158,
    243, 394, 400, 412
Weisberg, Harold 20, 138, 139, 230, 231,
    265, 266, 268, 283, 295, 313, 341
Weiss, Mark 389, 390
Weitzman, S. 296

Welsh, David 151
West, Robert 250, 251, 254, 256, 259, 259,
    261, 298, 307
What is this thing called Science? 410
Wheeler, Leslie 335
Where Death Delights 138
white blob 213
white Lincoln limousine 250, 257
white spot 214, 218, 318-319
White's Compendium of Zapruder Film
    Anomalies 363
White, A. 138
White, Jack 207, 208, 270, 271, 298, 318,
    332, 341, 363, 460, 461, 463
White, Ronald 18, 277, 461, 461, 463
Whitewash 20
Whitewash II 230, 265, 266, 268, 269, 295,
    305
Whitewash IV 138
Who's Who in the JFK Assassination 231
Wicker, Tom 176
Widows 122
Wilber, Charles 107, 138, 392, 394, 398,
    399, 412
Will, George 32
Williams, Philip E. 41
Willis, Linda 215, 291, 296, 342
Willis, Phillip 214, 216, 275, 291, 342
Wilson, P. D. 138
windshield substitution 143-144, 171, 367
withdrawing American forces from
    Vietnam 366
Withers, John 148
Woodward, M. 296
World News Tonight 17, 144
wound ballistics 161
wound of entry 172, passim
wound of exit 172-173, passim
wounds of entry 161, passim
wounds of exit 161, passim
Wrone, David 265, 267

X

X-ray, post-mortem cranial 160
X-ray, pre-mortem cranial 159

Y

Youngblood, Rufus 296

Z

Zapruder film xiii, xv, 22, 114, 117, 207-
    344, 369, 386, 388, 396, 398
Zapruder film anomalies 363, passim
Zapruder film authenticity 362, passim
Zapruder film edited 365-367, passim
Zapruder film memorandum 234
Zapruder film processing 224, passim
Zapruder film speed 223, 224, 236, 324,
    226-227, 329-331
Zapruder film tampering 207-344, passim
Zapruder, Abraham xiii, 218, 221, 224,
    225, 233, 254, 256, 257, 259, 289, 291,
    297, 326, 342, 371, 386
Zelizer, Barbie 403, 412, 409-410

Acknowledgments

As the editor of this volume, I must acknowledge an enormous debt to George D. Lundberg, M.D., whose abuse of his position as the Editor-in-Chief of *JAMA* brought about the formation of our research group on the medical evidence and many contributions to this volume. I am extremely grateful to David Mantik, M.D., Ph.D., Gary Aguilar, M.D., and Kathleen Cunningham, L.P.N., with whom I began to collaborate in 1992. My profound admiration for Robert B. Livingston, M.D., goes beyond expression. His contributions, along with those of David Mantik, represent landmarks in understanding the assassination of JFK.

Charles Crenshaw, M.D., and Bradley Kizzia, J.D., have displayed great courage and enormous integrity in pursuing legal remedies against *JAMA*. I consider their success to be admirable, even though I would have preferred to have had these issues explored in open court for the sake of correcting the legal record. As things now stand, the only legal case in the wake of the assassination has been brought by Jim Garrison, for which he deserves our gratitude. At least he sought the truth, which is more than can be said of the Warren Commission, which was a political charade and whose legal significance is open to serious doubt.

I am also grateful to Jack White, Mike Pincher, J.D., Roy Schaeffer, Ron Hepler, and Chuck Marler for their excellent contributions to this volume. As I elsewhere explain, White, Schaeffer, Hepler, Marler, and Mantik participated with me in the Zapruder film workshop held on 21 November 1996, and White, Marler, and Mantik also contributed to the public symposium on the 22nd. Another—and very important—member of that group was David Lifton, whose classic work, *Best Evidence* (1980), was instrumental in inviting the attention of the world to the inconsistent medical evidence in this case. Ronald F. White, Ph.D., contributed a perfect philosophical framework for exploring the issues involved here.

"A Piece of My Mind: Lundberg, JFK, and *JAMA*", previously appeared in *The Third Decade* (March 1993) and, along with "Thinking Critically About JFK's Assassination" (under another title), in Harrison Edward Livingstone's *Killing the Truth* (1993). Both have been revised for publication in this volume. "The Zapruder Film and the Language of Proof," *The Assassination Chronicles* (Winter 1996), has been incorporated into the Epilogue (with revisions). I am grateful to *The New Republic* for permission to reprint Richard Dudman's "Commentary of an Eyewitness" (21 December 1963), to the *UMD Stateman* for permission to reprint Zack Johns' "JFK Cover-Up Exposed by UMD Professor" (27 January 1994), and to the author and the editor for permission to republish Michael Stroscio, "More Physical Insight into the Assassination of President Kennedy", *Physics and Society* (October 1996), pp. 7-8.

—James H. Fetzer, Ph.D.

Each of the authors retains copyright of their contributions as follows:

"The Death of JFK" ©1998 *James H. Fetzer*

"A Piece of My Mind: Lundberg, JFK, and *JAMA*" ©1998 *James H. Fetzer*

"Let's Set the Record Straight: Dr. Charles Crenshaw Replies" ©1998 *Charles Crenshaw*

"On the Trail of the Character Assassins" ©1998 *Bradley Kizzia*

"Thinking Critically About JFK's Assassination" ©1998 *James H. Fetzer*

"The JFK Assassination: Cause for Doubt" ©1998 *David W. Mantik*

"Evidence . . . or Not? The Zapruder Film: Can it be Trusted?" ©1998 *Jack White*

"The Case for Zapruder Film Tampering: The Blink Pattern" ©1998 *Mike Pincher, J.D., and Roy Schaeffer*

"The Wounding of Governor John Connally" ©1998 *Ron Hepler*

"The JFK Assassination Re-enactment: Questioning the Warren Commission's Evidence" ©1998 *Chuck Marler*

"Special Effects in the Zapruder Film: How the Film of the Century was Edited" ©1998 *David W. Mantik*

"Assassination Science and the Language of Proof" ©1998 *James H. Fetzer*

"Apologists and Critics of the Lone Gunman Theory: Assassination Science and Experts in Post-Modern America" ©1998 *Ronald F. White*

Contributors

CHARLES CRENSHAW, M.D., F.A.C.S., of Fort Worth, Texas. Dr. Crenshaw assisted in emergency treatment of President Kennedy at Parkland Hospital and, two days later, of Lee Harvey Oswald. An account of his experiences has been published in *JFK: Conspiracy of Silence*. A former Professor of Clinical Surgery at Southwestern Medical School in Dallas, he is now Chairman Emeritus of the Department of Surgery at John Peter Smith Hospital of Ft. Worth.

JAMES H. FETZER, Ph.D., of Duluth, Minnesota. A graduate of Princeton, Dr. Fetzer received his Ph.D. in the history and philosophy of science from Indiana. A former officer in the Marine Corps, he has published widely on the nature of scientific reasoning and on the theoretical foundations of computer science, artificial intelligence, and cognitive science. He is currently McKnight University Professor at the University of Minnesota and teaches on its Duluth campus.

RON HEPLER of Austin, Texas. A director of engineering in the cable industry, he has interests in aviation and waterskiing as well as in the assassination of John Fitzgerald Kennedy, which he has pursued since 1988.

BRADLEY KIZZIA, J.D., of Dallas, Texas. A graduate of Austin College and of the Southern Methodist University School of Law, Mr. Kizzia has been admitted to practice before all of the U.S. District Courts in Texas, the U.S. Court of Appeals, Fifth Circuit, and the U.S. Supreme Court. He practices law in the State of Texas, where he specializes in general civil litigation.

ROBERT B. LIVINGSTON, M.D., of San Diego, California. Dr. Livingston is a graduate of Stanford who received his M.D. from the Stanford Medical School. A world authority on the human brain, he has held appointments at Stanford, Harvard, Yale, and UCLA, and founded the first ever Department of Neurosciences at UCSD, where he remains Professor Emeritus. Dr. Livingston was the Scientific Director of both the National Institute for Mental Health and the National Instutute for Neurological Diseases and Blindness in both the Eisenhower and Kennedy administrations. During World War II, he supervised the emergency treatment of injured Okinawans and Japanese prisoners of war during the battle of Okinawa.

DAVID W. MANTIK, M.D., Ph.D., of Rancho Mirage, California. Dr. Mantik received his Ph.D. in physics from Wisconsin and his M.D. from Michigan. He is board certified in radiation oncology and is on the staff of the Peter A. Lake, M.D., Center in Rancho Mirage, CA. He has repeatedly visited the National Archives to study the official X-rays and other autopsy materials and, more recently, the Zapruder film. Dr. Mantik resigned from the AMA in protest over the abuse of *JAMA*.

CHUCK MARLER of Riverside, California. A labor relations representative for San Bernardino who has an extensive interest in the Zapruder film, Chuck is also a founding member of Citizens for Truth about the Kennedy Assassination.

MIKE PINCHER, J.D., of Palmdale, California. A graduate of SUNY Albany who has a J.D. from the University of San Fernando Valley College of Law (now LaVerne), Mr. Pincher currently practices as a trial attorney within the Los Angeles area. He has a special interest in the Zapruder film.

ROY SCHAEFFER of Dayton, Ohio. Mr. Schaeffer is a long-time serious student of the Presidential limousine and related aspects of the assassination. He served a six-year apprenticeship in film development sponsored by the federal government from 1963 to 1969.

JACK WHITE of Fort Worth, Texas. A leading expert on photographic aspects of the assassination of JFK, Mr. White produced *The Continuing Inquiry* for the celebrated investigator, Penn Jones, with whom he worked for three years. He served as an adviser on photographic evidence to the House Select Committee on Assassinations during its reinvestigation and to Oliver Stone in producing his motion picture, *JFK*.

RONALD F. WHITE, Ph.D., of Cincinnati, Ohio. Dr. White holds the Ph.D. in history from the University of Kentucky. He has published numerous articles on the history and philosophy of medicine and science and is an associate professor at the College of Mount St. Joseph in Cincinnati.